BIBLICAL PEOPLES AND ETHNICITY

Society of Biblical Literature

Archaeology and Biblical Studies

Andrew G. Vaughn,
Editor

Number 9

BIBLICAL PEOPLES AND ETHNICITY
An Archaeological Study of Egyptians, Canaanites,
Philistines, and Early Israel, 1300–1100 B.C.E.

BIBLICAL PEOPLES AND ETHNICITY

An Archaeological Study of Egyptians, Canaanites, Philistines, and Early Israel, 1300–1100 B.C.E.

by

Ann E. Killebrew

Society of Biblical Literature
Atlanta

BIBLICAL PEOPLES AND ETHNICITY
An Archaeological Study of Egyptians, Canaanites, Philistines, and Early Israel, 1300–1100 B.C.E.

Library of Congress Cataloging-in-Publication Data

Killebrew, Ann E.
Biblical peoples and ethnicity : an archaeological study of Egyptians, Canaanites, Philistines, and early Israel, 1300–1100 B.C.E. / by Ann E. Killebrew.
p. cm. — (Society of Biblical Literature archaeology and biblical studies ; no. 9)
Includes bibliographical references.
ISBN-13: 978-1-58983-097-4 (paper binding : alk. paper)
ISBN-10: 1-58983-097-0 (paper binding : alk. paper)
1. Palestine—Civilization. 2. Egyptians—Palestine—History. 3. Canaanites. 4. Jews—History—To 953 B.C. 5. Philistines. 6. Palestine—Antiquities. 7. Excavations (Archaeology)—Palestine. 8. Bronze age—Palestine. 9. Iron age—Palestine. I. Title. II. Series: Archaeology and biblical studies ; no. 9.
DS112.K476 2005
221.9'3—dc22 2005013286

13 12 11 10 09 5 4 3 2

Printed in the United States of America on acid-free, recycled paper conforming to ANSI/NISO Z39.48-1992 (R1997) and ISO 9706:1994 standards for paper permanence.

To My Parents

Alfred B. and Jeanne M. Killebrew

Contents

ACKNOWLEDGMENTS

The present volume is the result of two decades of research, teaching, and excavation work at numerous sites in Israel. This work was conducted during my years as a full-time resident in Israel and, more recently, at the Pennsylvania State University. I extend my deepest gratitude to my teachers, colleagues, and friends both in Israel and the United States. I am indebted to Trude Dothan, Seymour Gitin, Amihai Mazar, Doug Clark, Michal Artzy, Lawrence Stager, Adam Zertal, and Joseph Greene, who generously granted permission to publish photos and drawings from their excavations and exhibits. Heather Evans drew many of the illustrations. Heather D. Heidrich assisted in the proofreading of the final text and in the compilation of the indices. I am especially grateful to the Institute for the Arts and Humanities and the Research and Graduate Studies Office at the Pennsylvania State University, which provided valued support and generous research funds for the completion of this book. Many of my colleagues, in particular Gary N. Knoppers, Department Head of the Classics and Ancient Mediterranean Studies Department, and Dan Mack, humanities librarian at the Pattee Library, were helpful and supportive during the completion of the manuscript. Bob Buller, Editorial Director of the Society of Biblical Literature, has been a pleasure to work with throughout the entire editorial process. Lastly, special thanks are due to Andrew G. Vaughn and Sandra A. Scham, friends and colleagues, who kindly read through the manuscript, offered much-appreciated comments and critique, and provided continuous encouragement and valuable advice.

Abbreviations

AA	*Archäologischer Anzeiger*
AASOR	Annual of the American Schools of Oriental Research
ÄAT	Ägypten und Altes Testament
AB	Anchor Bible
ABD	*Anchor Bible Dictionary*. Edited by D. N. Freedman. 6 vols. New York: Doubleday, 1992.
ABSA	*Annual of the British School at Athens*
ADAJ	*Annual of the Department of Antiquities of Jordan*
ÄF	Ägyptologische Forschungen
AJA	*American Journal of Archaeology*
AmerAnt	*American Antiquity*
AnatSt	*Anatolian Studies*
ANET	*Ancient Near Eastern Texts Relating to the Old Testament*. Edited by J. B. Pritchard. 3d ed. Princeton: Princeton University Press, 1969.
AOAT	Alter Orient und Altes Testament
AoF	*Altorientalische Forschungen*
AOS	American Oriental Series
ARA	*Annual Review of Anthropology*
ASOR	American Schools of Oriental Research
BA	*Biblical Archaeologist*
BAR	*Biblical Archaeology Review*
BASOR	*Bulletin of the American Schools of Oriental Research*
Ber	*Berytus*
Bib	*Biblica*
BIES	*Bulletin of the Israel Exploration Society* (= *Yediot*)
BMes	Bibliotheca mesopotamica
BO	*Bibliotheca orientalis*
BWANT	Beiträge zur Wissenschaft vom Alten und Neuen Testament
BZAW	Beihefte zur Zeitschrift für die alttestamentliche Wissenschaft
CAH[3]	*The Cambridge Ancient History*. Edited by I. E. S. Edwards et al. 3rd edition. Cambridge: Cambridge University Press, 1970–.
CANE	*Civilizations of the Ancient Near East*. Edited by J. Sasson. 4 vols. New York: Scribner's, 1995.
CBQ	*Catholic Biblical Quarterly*

CHANE	Culture and History of the Ancient Near East
ConBOT	Coniectanea biblica: Old Testament Series
COS	*The Context of Scripture.* Edited by W. W. Hallo and K. L. Younger. 3 vols. Leiden: Brill, 1997–2002.
CTM	*Concordia Theological Monthly*
CurrAnthr	*Current Anthropology*
EJA	*European Journal of Archaeology*
ErIsr	*Eretz-Israel*
FRLANT	Forschungen zur Religion und Literatur des Alten und Neuen Testaments
HSM	Harvard Semitic Monographs
HTR	*Harvard Theological Review*
IEJ	*Israel Exploration Journal*
IJNA	*International Journal of Nautical Archaeology and Underwater Exploration*
IstMitt	*Istanbuler Mitteilungen*
JANESCU	*Journal of the Ancient Near Eastern Society of Columbia University*
JAnthArch	*Journal of Anthropological Archaeology*
JAOS	*Journal of the American Oriental Society*
JARCE	*Journal of the American Research Center in Egypt*
JBL	*Journal of Biblical Literature*
JCS	*Journal of Cuneiform Studies*
JEA	*Journal of Egyptian Archaeology*
JESHO	*Journal of the Economic and Social History of the Orient*
JFA	*Journal of Field Archaology*
JHS	*Journal of Hellenic Studies*
JMA	*Journal of Mediterranean Archaeology*
JNES	*Journal of Near Eastern Studies*
JPOS	*Journal of the Palestine Oriental Society*
JSOT	*Journal for the Study of the Old Testament*
JSOTSup	Journal for the Study of the Old Testament Supplement Series
NEA	*Near Eastern Archaeology*
NEAEHL	*The New Encyclopedia of Archaeological Excavations in the Holy Land.* Edited by E. Stern. 4 vols. Jerusalem: Israel Exploration Society and Carta, 1993.
OBO	Orbis biblicus et orientalis
OEANE	*The Oxford Encyclopedia of Archaeology in the Near East.* Edited by Eric M. Meyers. New York: Oxford University Press, 1997.
OJA	*Oxford Journal of Archaeology*
OLA	Orientalia lovaniensia analecta

OpAth	*Opuscula archaeologica*
Or	*Orientalia* (NS)
OrAnt	*Oriens antiquus*
PEFQS	*Palestine Exploration Fund Quarterly Statement*
PEQ	*Palestine Exploration Quarterly*
PJ	*Palästina-Jahrbuch*
Qad	*Qadmoniot*
RelSRev	*Religious Studies Review*
RHA	*Revue hittite et asianique*
SAOC	Studies in Ancient Oriental Civilizations
SBLABS	Society of Biblical Literature Archaeology and Biblical Studies
SBLDS	Society of Biblical Literature Dissertation Series
SBLSBL	Society of Biblical Literature Studies in Biblical Literature
SHCANE	Studies in the History and Culture of the Ancient Near East
SIMA	Studies in Mediterranean Archaeology
SJOT	*Scandinavian Journal of the Old Testament*
SSN	Studia semitica neerlandica
SWBA	Social World of Biblical Antiquity
TA	*Tel Aviv*
TynBul	*Tyndale Bulletin*
UF	*Ugarit-Forschungen*
VT	*Vetus Testamentum*
VTSup	Supplements to Vetus Testamentum
WHJP	World History of the Jewish People
WorldArch	*World Archaeology*
WVDOG	Wissenschaftliche Veröffentlichungen der deutschen Orientgesellschaft
ZA	*Zeitschrift für Assyriologie*
ZAW	*Zeitschrift für die alttestamentliche Wissenschaft*
ZDPV	*Zeitschrift des deutschen Palästina-Vereins*

List of Illustrations

The following figures were drawn by Heather Evans: 1.2, 1.3, 2.1, 2.11, 2.12. 2.13, 2.14, 2.15, 2.16, 2.17, 2.18, 2.19, 3.13, 3.14, 3.15, 3.16, 3.17, 3.18, 3.19, 3.20, 3.21, 3.22, 3.23, 3.24, 3.25, 3.26, 3.27, 3.28, 3.29, 4.2, 4.10, 4.11, 5.1, 5.13, 5.15, 5.16.

Introduction
Peoples and Ethnicity in the Biblical World: A Conceptual Framework

The final centuries of the second millennium were a period of transformation in the eastern Mediterranean. The transition from the Bronze to Iron Ages witnessed the breakdown of the great Bronze Age power structures of the fourteenth and thirteenth centuries B.C.E. and the creation of a mosaic of local cultures and ethnicities that formed the foundations of the biblical world. The collapse and gradual decline of the Late Bronze Age empires and the ensuing fragmentation of this previously interconnected world-system produced regionally defined peoples who later appeared as the key protagonists and antagonists in the biblical narrative. From the biblical perspective, these groups are depicted as the idol-worshiping Canaanites, the powerful and cruel Egyptian overlords, the uncouth but militarily superior Philistines, and the Yahweh-worshiping Israelites (see figs. 0.1–0.4). The historical books of the Bible, written from the perspective of the last two centuries of the kingdom of Judah and later, define premonarchical Israel as a distinct group comprising twelve tribes united by a single ideology and whose origins are outside Canaan.

The trials and tribulations of early Israel resulting from interactions with the "other" create some of the best-known biblical stories, narratives that have retained their powerful appeal and message even today. These narratives include the accounts of the exodus from Egypt, Joshua's conquest of Canaan, and the numerous interactions, usually hostile, between the Israelites and Philistines. Each of these events pits the Israelites against ethnically defined groups termed Egyptians, Philistines, and Canaanites. The biblical narrative of the emergence of Israel begins with the escape from slavery in Egypt, continues with the conquest of the land, and culminates with the eventual settlement of Canaan by the tribes of Israel in fulfillment of the promise made by Yahweh to Abraham and his descendants. In both ancient and modern times, the events as described in the Hebrew Bible are politically, symbolically, and ideologically charged and inspire strong and, at times, uncompromising attitudes and interpretations.

In the following chapters, I examine these four biblical groups—Egyptians, Canaanites, Philistines, and Israelites—and their appearance in the material culture record within their larger social, economic, cultural, historical, and archaeological contexts. This work synchronically and diachronically engages in an intra- and interdisciplinary dialogue with the related fields of biblical studies, archaeology, ancient Near Eastern studies, Egyptology, and the social and natural sciences, with the aim of crossing artificially constructed scholarly boundaries and integrating fragmented and specialized studies. In its reconstruction of the formation of the biblical world, this book encompasses both longer-term, processual views of the past as well as shorter-term historical and postprocessual contextualized and ideological approaches to the archaeological record.

The primary evidence, including the biblical and extrabiblical texts and the archaeological data, is the starting point of this study of four biblical peoples in their larger eastern Mediterranean framework. Several methodological and theoretical approaches outlined below are employed in the analysis of the data contextualized within its specific historical setting. A detailed typological and technological analysis of thirteenth–twelfth century B.C.E. pottery in Canaan, the most ubiquitous archaeological artifact, serves as a case study in the demarcation of social boundaries corresponding to each of these biblical groups. Although pottery studies in the eastern Mediterranean have usually focused on chronologically oriented linear typologies that are used to date archaeological deposits or strata and to reconstruct interregional economic and trade relations, ceramic analysis can also answer a variety of broader questions concerning cultural processes and ideology. These include questions about the social and political organization of a society, in addition to serving as a means for communicating information regarding a pot's producer, owner, or user that can include group affiliation (see D. E. Arnold 1985; Rice 1987; Sinopoli 1991; Skibo and Feinman 1999). Ceramic technology and technological change in particular can be seen as closely related to political or ideological phenomena in a society (for an overview, see Loney 2000). This combination of typological, stylistic, and technological pottery analyses presented in each chapter is particularly valuable in reconstructing ancient group affiliations.

I conclude that ethnicity in its diverse manifestations can be identified under certain circumstances in the archaeological record. Specifically, during the thirteenth to eleventh centuries B.C.E. it is possible to delineate the social and cultural boundaries of the Egyptians, Canaanites, Philistines, and Israelites. This introduction to ethnicity in the biblical world begins an overview of the history of archaeological and biblical research in its larger intellectual setting, defines several key terms and analytical frameworks employed in this book, and concludes with a presentation of the key themes that are explored in chapters 1–5.

Biblical Archaeology in Its Intellectual Context

Biblical archaeology developed out of a historical approach to the biblical texts with its roots in theology that dominated scholarly interpretation of the Bible for several centuries. For much of the nineteenth and first half of the twentieth centuries, biblical studies and the archaeology of Palestine were closely intertwined, with archaeology of the Holy Land generally playing a supporting role as a handmaiden to biblical studies (see King 1983; Moorey 1991; Killebrew 2003a, 12–22; T. W. Davis 2004). The ultimate goal of these studies was to write a history of biblical Israel and to construct accurate typologies and chronological frameworks related to biblical events, with the optimistic goal of demonstrating the historical accuracy of the biblical narrative. Although various schools of thought vied for dominance, all these views approached the Bible as an essentially historically accurate text, often with theological overtones.

From the mid-twentieth century onward, biblical studies and archaeology splintered into several subdisciplines that were influenced by theoretical developments in the social sciences, comparative literature, linguistics, and the natural sciences.[1] During the 1960s through the mid-1980s, two major schools of thought dominated archaeological practices: a continuation of the traditional culture-historical[2] or "normative" approach that characterized the first half of the twentieth century; and the "New Archaeology," whose scientifically based paradigms challenged what was perceived as the highly subjective nature of culture-historical interpretations of the past. These intellectual trends also impacted biblical archaeology (see Dever 1982; 1985; Killebrew 2003a).

New Archaeology and Later Theoretical Trends

New Archaeology and its later developments, often termed processual archaeology or Middle Range Theory, can be considered as a quantitative and scientifically based approach to interpreting the past. New Archaeology focused on methodologies that were "objective" or measurable and on uncovering universal laws that govern human behavior and material culture deposition in its environmental context. By using scientific approaches to the past that entail a research design and hypothesis testing, the past is knowable and it is possible to formulate paradigms and construct universal systems that reveal the relationship between behavior and material culture as well as between causes and effects. During much of the second half of the twentieth century, positivist notions of an "objective" and scientifically based archaeology began to influence and eventually dominate North American and British archaeological theory and methodology.[3] Within this intellectual tradition, a number of overlapping, theoretical frameworks developed that are usually considered to belong to processual archaeology. These include systemic, adaptive, evolutionary, and functionalist approaches (see M. Johnson 1999; A. Jones 2002).

In the related humanities and social-science disciplines, parallel trends dovetailed with the archaeological theories and methodologies outlined above. In recent decades, increasing numbers of historians and social scientists recognized the limitations of Euro-centric and linear narrative explanations of historical, cultural, and social development. Several analytical frameworks have attempted to integrate various fields in the humanities and social sciences to address the shortcomings of traditional understandings of social and cultural change. Two of these approaches, those of the *Annales* school and of world-systems analysis, reconstruct history and view society chronologically and geographically. Both are based on recognizing the importance and impact of social and cultural interconnections and interregional interaction as major forces in shaping history and society, and both have been applied to archaeological research on a limited basis with various degrees of success.

During the 1980s, archaeology experienced a further fragmentation of its theoretical underpinnings in the form of a reaction against the positivism of processual archaeology. Critics of processual archaeology favored ahistorical as well as historical approaches that included post-structuralist, Marxist, neo-Marxist, contextual, social, agency, and postprocessual approaches (for overviews, see Hodder 1986; 2001; Trigger 1989).

The most successful of these challenges questions the validity of a scientifically based archaeology by proposing that material culture is meaningfully constituted within its specific context, that the individual needs to be understood as part of one's theories of material culture and social change, and that archaeology's closest disciplinary ties are with history. According to this postprocessual approach, causes of social change are complex and involve more than measurable interlocking systems. These processual models are not equipped to take into account belief systems, ideology, symbolism, and the individual in their interpretation of the past, which are based on universal paradigms that see human behavior as a result of predicted responses to adaptive systems. These shortcomings are addressed by postprocessual archaeologists (Hodder 1986, 1–17).

Today, much of the optimism of these early days of faith in science and the ability to construct universal and objective paradigms or to prove hypotheses about human behavior has been replaced by caution and a disillusionment with the applications of some of these approaches to archaeology. There is no doubt that many of processual archaeology's techniques have contributed and continue to contribute methodologically to archaeology as a discipline. This more scientifically based philosophy of archaeology that incorporated analytical techniques borrowed from the hard sciences has instilled a more rigorous and structured approach to archaeological method and data collection. Where it has been less successful is in the integration of material culture and textual evidence. In particular, its application to complex Old World historical societies and highly stratified Near Eastern tells has been more difficult and problematic than its use in analyzing prehistoric cultures and New World archaeology. This is in part due to the vast amount and complexity of historical and material culture data and site formation that characterize historical Near Eastern archaeology, its failure to consider the influence of diffusion in the interconnected world of the ancient Near East, and its inability to address nontangible values such as ideology or symbolic significance. Lastly, processual archaeology is notoriously unable to take into account individual action or any number of unpredictable factors and unique historical or cultural situations that characterize the archaeological record. In the following chapters, I integrate, when appropriate, both processual and postprocessual approaches to the archaeological and textual evidence.

Recent Intellectual Trends in Biblical Studies

Within this larger disciplinary and intellectual setting, biblical archaeology never fully embraced these developments and remained in a culture-historical time warp, focusing on writing a narrative history within the biblical framework by compiling typologies and dealing with chronological questions. Nevertheless, a glance through most textbooks dealing with the archaeology of the lands of the Bible reveals that biblical archaeology has incorporated ad hoc and in a largely unsystematic manner many elements of processual archaeology or other scientifically based methods that project an impression of "objectivity." In archaeological site reports published during the last few decades, elements of "New Archaeology" appear, but mainly as appendices that are seldom integrated into the interpretive body of these works. Processual approaches are more successfully integrated in Old World archaeological surveys and landscape or environmental studies that incorporate scientific and statistical analyses of data and utilize analytical tools such as Geographical Information Systems (GIS).

In a trend that runs parallel to archaeology, biblical studies, influenced by developments in comparative literature and sociology, followed a similar path of theoretical adaptation and fragmentation. From the nineteenth through the first half of the twentieth century, historical-critical approaches (source criticism, form criticism, tradition-historical criticism, and redaction criticism) dominated biblical scholarship. Although there are often overlapping interests, source criticism, form criticism, tradition-historical criticism, and redaction criticism all share a similar philosophical approach to the Bible and are concerned with historical or literary foundations of the text (see J. M. Miller 1999). In recent decades, however, a number of ahistorical methodologies have been used as tools to interpret the Bible. These can be grouped generally under the rubric of "literary approaches" to the text and include, among others, structural criticism, narrative criticism, reader-response criticism, poststructuralist criticism, feminist criticism, and socioeconomic criticism. Other theoretical approaches, such as social-scientific criticism, canonical criticism, rhetorical criticism, and intertextuality, combine historical and ahistorical concerns (see Perdue 1994; McKenzie and Haynes 1999).

In this book I utilize approaches from a variety of the traditions outlined above. In my reconstruction of this formative period, I consider the longer-term history of the region within its specific historical and ideological context and the integrative systems that united these various worlds. This rich repertoire of methods and approaches enhances our archaeological vocabulary and our ability to address complex historical, economic, social, political, and ideological issues that constitute the world of the Egyptians, Canaanites, Philistines, and Israelites.

Theoretical and Analytical Frameworks

Several concepts and terms are integral to all the chapters in this book. Two conceptual approaches to the past, those of the *Annales* school and world-systems analysis, form an integral part of my study of the eastern Mediterranean during the thirteenth and twelfth centuries B.C.E. Fernand Braudel, the *Annales* school's most influential advocate, has defined history as comprising three temporal elements: long-term (e.g., environmental), medium-term (e.g., socioeconomic cycles or "conjuncture"), and short-term (e.g., individual actions/events), with macro-phenomena ultimately determining the course of history.[4] This approach is attractive to many Near Eastern archaeologists because it provides a link between traditional history, with its concern for discrete events or specific context, and the social sciences that are more concerned with processes (see Hodder 1987a and the articles in Hodder 1987b).[5]

A second conceptual approach used in this book, world-systems analysis, is usually aligned with a more systemic processual approach in archaeology but shares features of the *Annales* school. Due in part to its recognition of the role of diffusion in cultural exchange, it has become one of the most promising analytical frameworks for understanding the processes and intersocietal political, cultural, and economic structures of both the past and present. First developed by Immanuel Wallerstein (1974; 1979; 1983), world-systems analysis was originally employed as a fundamental unit of analysis of multicultural networks of economic and social exchange in modern, capitalist societies. Due to the inter- and cross-disciplinary quality of Wallerstein's initial work, which was influenced by the *Annales* school of French historiography, numerous disciplines, including sociology, economics, history, anthropology, and archaeology, have adopted and adapted his sociological approach to social processes and structures.[6] Today, the world-systems perspective is broadly applied in many analyses of intersocietal connections and cultural interactions in the social sciences and humanities (see ch. 1 for a more detailed description).

Three analytical terms (stylistic diversity, social boundaries, and ethnicity) are central to this book. First, *diversity* usually entails the quantification or measurement of variation within a given cultural assemblage (Jones and Leonard 1989, 1–3). It is of particular relevance to highly stratified and economically differentiated societies where diversity in material culture is considered an indicator of social organization and standardization reflects political organization. *Stylistic diversity,* especially as a concept used in Near Eastern archaeology, is often intuitively applied to material culture to mean variation in cultural patterning. Diversity in this context, viewed as a tool for defining the relative similarity or dissimilarity among archaeological assemblages, has played an increasingly important role in stylistic analysis and interpretation of social organization.[7] In this book *diversity* is used in its broader "intuitive" sense to mean difference or variation in the diverse definable ceramic assemblages and material culture of Canaan in the thirteenth–twelfth centuries B.C.E. In these examples, stylistic diversity does not necessarily indicate ethnicity; however, as the case studies discussed later show, there are instances where stylistic diversity is an ethnic marker and can be used to delineate the ethnic boundaries of Egyptians, Philistines, and early Israel.[8]

Second, this study employs the demarcation of *cultural boundaries* and *social boundaries* to define social or ethnic groups. Social boundaries are identified by means of observable synchronic and diachronic variations and distinctive patterning in the archaeological record. Following Miriam T. Stark (1998a, 1), I define social boundaries as based on the relationship of technical choices and variations in style and function discernible in the material culture, considered together with the relevant textual evidence. These patterns can result from a number of causes, such as ethnicity, migration, or economic systems.[9]

A third term used throughout this book, *ethnicity*, is especially important in the study of archaeological cultures, stylistic diversity, and social boundaries. The essence of ethnicity has been explored for the last half-century by anthropologists, sociologists, economists, political scientists, and, more recently, archaeologists working in the Near East.[10] Nevertheless, the term remains elusive and contested, with a multitude of definitions reflecting the diversity and broad spectrum of conditions encompassed by the concept of ethnicity. I begin with a basic definition of ethnicity as "group identity." This definition is general enough to include the variety of human relationships that can lead to ethnic formation within the specific historic context of the biblical world.

The word "ethnicity" is derived from the Greek term *ethnos*.[11] Until the late 1960s, modern anthropological definitions of ethnicity tended to take a structural-functionalist view, which assumed that an ethnic group was a concrete and immutable social factor.[12] Ethnicity was believed to be a category reflecting the social reality of different groups. In the early 1970s, the entire structural-functionalist approach in anthropology was brought into question, and out of this turmoil two new paradigms were developed. One emphasized the permanency and underlying continuity of structural patterns and distinctions within human society (Lévi-Strauss 1967). The second focused on the social processes and changes in life (Turner 1969, 3–25). As a result of this debate, some scholars viewed ethnicity as an essential attribute, a fixed and permanently structured element of human identity (Stack 1986, 1–11; A. D. Smith 1993, 9–25), while others saw ethnicity as a more malleable category that was responsive to changing social settings and circumstances (Rasmussen 1992, 352–65).

Social scientists have attempted to explain the phenomenon of ethnic group solidarity as having either primordial or circumstantial origins.[13] According to the former, genetically based explanation for group membership, one belongs to a particular group because of birth or blood ties; that is, one's parents or ancestors were members of the same group. There is often a historical depth to a group's identity, usually supported by a rhetorical and mythical or religious language that may detail the origin of the group and support social or political structures. These ties based on kinship often are quite conservative, reflected in a great continuity in the group's cultural expression, and can persist for many generations while remaining stable and impervious to change.

A second major approach to ethnicity, termed "circumstantial" or "situational," sees ethnic allegiance as a result of political and economic interests and strategies.[14] From this perspective, self-interest is largely responsible for forming group identity, and material culture or technological boundaries observable in the archaeological record more accurately reflect economic or political, rather than genetic or kinship, ties. Allegiance based on situational ties is generally flexible and more responsive to changing circumstances, particularly in the political, social, or economic environment. If a situation should change so that members of a group feel it is to their advantage to align their "ethnic" identity differently, the boundaries of the group will also change. This flexibility means that the typical behavioral characteristics of an ethnic group cannot be treated as fixed and static indicators of identity.[15]

This study uses a more fluid middle ground that combines the primordial and circumstantial approaches as a more appropriate approach to ethnicity. Although one may question whether ethnicity existed in antiquity, my definition of ethnicity as group identity approaches the concept in its broadest meaning and takes into account the phenomenon of "bounded groups" or social borders (Hegmon 1998, 264–79). This viewpoint interprets ethnicity as resulting from a variety of diverse forces that can bind individuals into a social grouping. Thus, ethnicity is a dynamic and ongoing process of interaction or ethnogenesis (see below, ch. 4) that can take place on many levels between various groups of people.[16] The contact and resulting connection can take place in the political, economic, social, religious, or familial spheres of human activity and is in constant flux. Further, as has been noted, overt ethnicity is most evident under economically difficult circumstances and is often used for political or defensive purposes (Cashmore 1994, 106). These conditions clearly existed at the end of the Late Bronze Age in the eastern Mediterranean and were responsible for the breakdown of Canaanite culture into smaller cultural units and the arrival of new groups that emerge as ethnically defined peoples in the biblical text.[17]

Defining ethnicity based on material culture in modern-day societies has often proven challenging for social scientists. Even greater obstacles are encountered when archaeologists attempt to discern ethnicity and ethnic boundaries based on the very incomplete material record of the past.[18] The relationship between ethnicity and material culture is even more ambiguous and especially problematic for archaeologists (Eriksen 1991, 127–44; Banks 1996). Processual archaeology has generally adopted a pessimistic attitude toward the possibility of "ethnically" defining ancient material culture (Trigger 1977, 22–23; 1995, 277). In recent years, however, there has been a return to recognizing ethnicity as a factor in human behavior, and thus, in certain instances, ethnicity may be manifested in material culture.[19] The challenge for archaeologists is to attempt to define and delineate case studies in the archaeological record in order to begin to construct paradigms for the interpretation of cultural diversity or uniformity. This book argues that the transition between the Late

Bronze II and Iron I periods presents such an opportunity to examine the relationship between material culture, stylistic diversity, and social and ethnic boundaries.

A number of studies regarding the ethnicity of archaeological assemblages or cultures have been published,[20] including several that deal specifically with the problem of ethnicity in Canaan during the thirteenth to eleventh centuries B.C.E.[21] This book differs from these earlier studies by presenting a more complete and integrated picture of this multicultural period of time by not focusing mainly on one group or relying too heavily on one discipline. By examining ethnicity and cultural boundaries via a broader-based and multidisciplinary approach, this study presents a more balanced and integrated view that is neither overly skeptical nor naively optimistic regarding our ability to identity the group boundaries of Egyptians, Canaanites, Israelites, and Philistines in Canaan.[22]

Egyptians, Canaanites, Philistines, and Israelites

In an attempt to define ethnicity and cultural diversity in the biblical world of the thirteenth to twelfth centuries B.C.E., I examine these questions in their chronological and regionally contextualized setting. In the first chapter I summarize the background of the interconnected world of the Late Bronze Age and the events that eventually led to the crisis of the twelfth century B.C.E. Using a world-systems theoretical approach, I evaluate the possible significance of stability and change during the last century of the Late Bronze Age and the early Iron Age. In each subsequent chapter I present a general overview of the written texts and material culture, with an emphasis on pottery, traditionally associated with a specific group within their larger regional and historical context. Other aspects of these peoples are also considered, including modes of social interaction and organization as revealed in the primary and archaeological sources (Wiessner 1989, 56–63; Conkey 1990, 5–17; S. Jones 1997, 124–27). Based on these diachronic and synchronic aspects of thirteenth–twelfth century material culture, in the chapters below I identify culturally sensitive indicators of possible ethnicity or group boundaries of four biblical peoples that can be defined in the functional, technological, dietary, symbolic, cultic, and funerary aspects of their material culture.

Egyptians

The Egyptians play a defining role in any discussion of Canaan during the Late Bronze and early Iron Ages. As one of the region's superpowers, Egypt's imperialistic administrative and economic domination of

Fig. 0.1. Egyptian Scribe

this peripheral region was both exploitative and stabilizing (see ch. 2 for a definition of imperialism and Egypt's impact on Canaan). Egyptian imperialistic policy encouraged direct and indirect Canaanite participation in the international economic system of the period, which led to the development of a relatively homogeneous material culture throughout the region during the fourteenth and thirteenth centuries B.C.E. At a number of settlements, such as Tel Beth-shean, Tell el-Farᶜah (S), Tell es-Saᶜidiyeh, and at several sites in the Gaza Strip and along the coast of northern Sinai, Egyptian presence is evident in the architecture and artifacts and from historical texts of the period. The very "Egyptian" nature of Egyptian-style locally produced ceramics and architecture at these sites attests to the presence of significant numbers of "envoys" at several key sites (e.g., Tel Beth-shean, Deir el-Balah), who were sent by Pharaoh to serve in Canaan as administrators or military personnel, along with Egyptians who provided services for the Egyptian population stationed in Canaanite cities or settlements. This is clearly manifested in the Egyptian-style ceramic assemblages that retained their Egyptian character both typologically and technologically over several centuries. Through the ceramic case study presented in chapter 2, Egyptian ethnic and social boundaries are traced at several Egyptian strongholds spanning the fourteenth to mid-twelfth centuries B.C.E.

Canaanites

Canaan in the thirteenth and early twelfth centuries was defined largely by the imperialistic policies of the Egyptians. During the reigns of Ramesses III and his successors, Canaan experienced cultural fragmentation and population movements that culminated with the colonization of its southern plain by the biblical Philistines and the beginning of the emergence of Israel in its central hill country. Late Bronze Age Canaan was not made up of a single "ethnic" group but consisted of a population whose diversity may be hinted at by the great variety of burial customs and cultic structures (both considered to be culturally sensitive indicators of ethnicity; see ch. 3 regarding the Canaanites and their material culture) that one finds. Although the population of Canaan was of varied origins, it was unified by a common socioeconomic system based on a city-state/hinterland model reflected in most aspects of the material culture as well as in the fourteenth-century Amarna letters and other Egyptian texts. This literature informs us that the city-states in Canaan were administered and controlled economically and politically by Egypt, which provided a relatively stable social environment, and that the extent of direct Egyptian influence on Canaan during the late Nineteenth and Twentieth Dynasties extended to Tel Beth-shean, continuing westward

Fig. 0.2. Canaanite

along the Jezreel Valley. The valley serves as a geographical division separating southern and northern Canaan. This is not only reflected in the historical texts of the period but, in my opinion, is also indicated by subtle but definable differences in the ceramic assemblages north and south of the Jezreel Valley. This imposition of Egyptian political and economic control resulted in a stable economic environment conducive to international trade and a homogeneous material culture that continued to develop slowly in an uninterrupted fashion from the Middle Bronze Age. In this case study, then, ceramic evidence reflects not Canaanite ethnicity but rather the impact of political organization on the standardization of aspects of material culture, most notably the pottery repertoire. Ethnic diversity is hinted at in more culturally sensitive indicators such as the mortuary and cultic practices of the period and in contemporary written texts.

Israelites

The late thirteenth–twelfth century shifts in population and the appearance of numerous villages in the central hill country, a region described by later biblical accounts as the heartland of early Israel, represent the formation of a new social boundary. These small hamlets comprise four-room houses with domestic installations, and their inhabitants produced a ceramic assemblage that developed typologically out of the thirteenth-century B.C.E. repertoire of Canaan. Attempts to identify early Israel in the twelfth- and eleventh-century archaeological record are highly contested. In chapter 4 I propose that we consider the settlement and development of the central hill country region during the twelfth and eleventh centuries B.C.E. as representing a "mixed population" or "multitude" resulting from the upheavals at the end of the Late Bronze and early Iron Ages. These population groups formed the ethnogenesis of what was later to become the people identified as Israel.

These small sites are distinguished by the limited number of ceramic forms and their relative percentages, as well as the agrarian nature of their settlement plans. If our chronological understanding of this period is correct, several phenomena should be stressed regarding the nature and identity of the inhabitants of these small agrarian settlements. The differences between the limited repertoire of ceramic forms at these small hill-country hamlets and sites in the lowlands, often within walking distance from highland sites, are remarkable and do seem to designate a "boundary" that may have resulted from social, economic, or ideological differences with the lowlands and some of the larger settlements in the highlands. Such cultural variation or diversity, situated side by side, cannot be explained as simply different lifestyles.

Fig. 0.3. *Shasu:* "Early Israel"

There seems to be a deliberate isolation and separation of the inhabitants of the large Iron I settlements and the smaller village sites, which are characterized by their size, limited ceramic repertoire, and, to a certain degree, cultic practices, all of which demonstrate Canaanite roots but also ideologically distinguish the highland village settlements from their neighbors. I propose that we are dealing with a mixed population whose ethnogenesis was forged by primordial, circumstantial, and ideological ties and whose origins lie in Canaan.

Philistines

The scenario is quite different with regard to the Philistine sites. The Early Iron I inhabitants of these sites represent colonial and colonizing activities in the region that were accompanied by significant migrations of people from outside of Canaan (see ch. 5 for a definition of colonialism and the impact of the Philistines). The nonlocal origin of the Philistines is reflected in all aspects of their Aegean-inspired material culture, including ceramic typology and technology, foodways, architecture, cultic practices, and city planning.[23] The clear break with the previous ceramic tradition of Late Bronze II settlements at pentapolis cities is sudden and startling, indicating that earlier Canaanite inhabitants were overwhelmed by a new population bringing traditions completely unrelated to any cultural tradition in the immediate or surrounding area.

The most intensely examined aspect of this new material culture is the locally produced Aegean-style pottery assemblage. It differs from the indigenous ceramic tradition in its shape, decorative style, and technological features and shares a remarkable similarity with Aegean-style pottery, especially that of Cyprus. Within several generations these ceramic traditions developed independently and began to acculturate with the pottery repertoire of the surrounding regions. This very distinct material culture, when considered together with the biblical texts, clearly indicates that a new ethnic group, complete with different origin, material culture, religious practices, and, most likely, language settled on the southern coastal plain of Canaan during the twelfth century B.C.E.

In light of this evidence, I suggest that these newcomers arrived as well-organized and relatively prosperous colonizers, representing a large-scale immigration that quickly settled at several sites on the southern coastal plain.[24] My interpretation differs from the majority of previous research in the view that the Philistines do not originate in the west Aegean or Crete. Rather, I see their roots lie in an Aegeanized eastern Aegean and northern Levant, most likely Cyprus, with close ties to coastal Anatolia. Their ability rapidly to construct urban centers (complete with fortifications) at sites such as Tel Miqne-Ekron, and to overshadow the

Fig. 0.4. Captive Philistine Chief

very modest Late Bronze Age settlement at the site indicates that they were not destitute refugees who arrived along the southern coastal plain due to lack of choice. The arrival of the Philistines represents a deliberate act by prosperous colonizers who were well acquainted with the southern Levantine coast.

The transformation that occurred at the end of the Late Bronze Age irrevocably changed the entire ancient Mediterranean world. This period of transition is a fitting case study in cultural diversity and the material manifestations of ethnicity that in some cases correspond to well-defined material culture boundaries. It represents different aspects of culturally or ethnically identified populations resulting from socioeconomic and cultural phenomena—imperialism, ethnogenesis, and colonization—of the tumultuous final centuries of the second millennium B.C.E. This book proposes that economic, political, societal, and ideological developments during the thirteenth–twelfth centuries B.C.E. created an environment ripe for the creation of identifiable group boundaries of Egyptians, Canaanites, early Israelites, and Philistines—key players in the later formation of the world of the Hebrew Bible.

Notes to Introduction

1. See Dever 1997, who convincingly argues that the history of scholarly interpretation of both biblical archaeology and the Bible shares a similar and parallel intellectual development.

2. I define culture-history as the mapping of cultures and cultural influences as a tool in reconstructing the past with the aim of "humanizing" material culture or reading material culture as a document.

3. See, e.g., Binford 1962; 1965; for an especially entertaining and well-known article that satirizes the two approaches, see Flannery 1982.

4. For an overview of the *Annales* school and its development, see Braudel 1972; 1980 (esp. p. 48); Knapp 1993, 7–20.

5. An increasing number of Near Eastern historians and archaeologists have appropriated elements of the *Annales* approach to the past. Mario Liverani's (1973; 1987) insightful historical reconstructions of the ancient Near East are heavily influenced by the *Annales* tradition. Among archaeologists working in the Levant, A. Bernard Knapp (1992a; 1992c; 1993) has been the most passionate proponent of this school of thought, and his work reflects an *Annales* approach in his analysis of Bronze Age society in the Levant. Other Near Eastern scholars and archaeologists whose work shows varying degrees of the influence of Braudel include Lamberg-Karlovsky 1985, Michalowski 1985; Coote and Whitelam 1987; for a brief overview, see Knapp 1993, 3–6. Brinkman 1984 and Bunimovitz 1994b in particular have attempted to combine Braudel's *la longue durée* with the impact of short-term, "episodic" events in their reconstruction of Bronze Age society.

6. For several recent surveys of its application to archaeological research, see T. D. Hall 2000b; Kardulias 1999b.

7. For a discussion of these trends, see Conkey 1989, 118–29; Cowgill 1989, 131–49; Jones and Leonard 1989. In the broader context of diversity, stylistic analysis has been used

to define spatial and temporal distributions (Whallon 1968, 223–24), to locate social units and to monitor changes (Deetz 1965), to measure social interaction and social exchange (Plog 1978, 143–82), as an indicator of social boundaries (Wobst 1977, 317–42), and as a means of communication (Binford 1965, 204–10). For studies dealing specifically with ceramic patterning or ceramic variation, see Dickens and Chapman 1978, 390–98; Dickens 1980, 34–46; Plog 1980; Pollock 1983; Costin and Hagstrum 1995. Ceramic diversity has played an important role in the study of pottery production; see Rice 1989, 110–13; 1991. For a recent review of the various approaches to stylistic analysis, see David and Kramer 2001, 170–73.

8. Depending on the specific context, increased contact between peoples can function as a factor that encourages homogeneity. Conversely, it can encourage the development of material culture distinctiveness or stylistic diversity corresponding to the degree of negative reciprocity between groups (for a discussion, see Hodder 1979; 1986, 2–3). In this latter situation, the more competition between groups the more marked the material culture boundaries between them. Both scenarios are evidence in the material culture record of Canaan during the thirteenth and twelfth centuries B.C.E.

9. Successful attempts to reconstruct social boundaries are based on analyses of technical choices and stylistic studies of material culture (see Green and Perlman 1985; Stark 1998a). In these studies, a close relationship was discernible between boundaries defined by material culture, historical texts, geographic units, social, political, or economic systems, and/or ethnicity (for a discussion of cultural boundaries based on numismatic evidence, see also Kimes, Haselgrove, and Hodder 1982, 113–31). However, there is not always a direct link between cultural boundaries and ethnicity, since many different factors in addition to ethnicity can come into play to account for different patterning of material culture (for examples when differences in material culture are a result of internal social organization or socioeconomic class, see Hodder 1981, 67–95; 1985, 141–59; Bronitsky, Marks, and Burleson 1985, 325–40; for a general discussion of these issues, see Stark 1998a, 1–11). All these different aspects of human and societal behavior must be taken into account on a case-by-case basis when interpreting stylistic diversity and its significance in the archaeological record (Dietler and Herbich 1998, 232–63). For a recent review of the most relevant studies examining ceramics and social boundaries, see Stark 2003, 211–13. In this book, technical styles and systems as well as stylistic and functional variation in material culture are considered both individually and collectively.

10. See, e.g., Kamp and Yoffee 1980, 85–104; London 1989a, 37–55; Dever 1993a, 22*–33*; Redmount 1995a, 181–90; 1995b, 61–89; Sparks 1998. Bruce MacKay and I presented several aspects of this discussion on ethnicity at the 1994 ASOR meetings in Chicago (Killebrew and MacKay 1994).

11. Classical writers used *ethnos* to describe large amorphous groups of beings, either animal or human (Chapman, McDonald, and Tonkin 1989, 12). For a history of the etymology of ethnicity, see Sollors 1996, 2–12.

12. Nagata 1979, 185; Buchignani 1982, 1. According to R. Cohen, the goal of research during the period was "to understand assumedly homogeneous socio-cultural units as entities, the relations of their parts to one another and to the whole, and the relation of the whole and its parts to their physical and socio-cultural environments" (1978, 381). For an overview of approaches to ethnicity, see Banks 1996, 1–48; Sollors 1996.

13. "Primordial" is a term coined by Shils 1957, 130–45; see also Stack 1986, 1–11. For a discussion of the role of the primordial in the shaping of ethnicity, see Nagata 1979, 188–98, who describes this bond that holds people together as "a corpus of basic, elemental, and irreducible loyalties, with a power of their own, whenever the nature of the external social environment" (Nagata 1979, 188). C. Geertz suggests that commonalities in the speech and customs of a particular ethnic group are due not simply to common interest, necessity, or obligation between group members but to the inexplicable and irreducible coerciveness of

their common or actual imagined, ties of blood (1973, 255–310). See also Novack, 1972; Greeley 1974; Isaacs 1975, 29–52; A. D. Smith 1981; Connor 1984, 342–59. Regarding a biological (genetic) approach to primordial ethnicity, see Van den Berghe 1978, 401–11; M. Chapman 1993; for a refutation of the biological approach, see Reynolds 1980, 305–15.

14. See, e.g., Barth 1969, 7–38; Weber 1978. Regarding the social circumstances, or structural conditions, responsible for ethnic solidarity, see Horowitz 1975, 111–40; Yancey, Ericksen, and Juliani 1976, 391–402; Rothschild 1981; Yinger 1981, 249–64; Nagel and Olzak 1982, 127–43; Hechter 1986, 13–24; 1987. A related concept, situational ethnicity, is a rational selection of ethnic identity based on political, economic, or social goals; see A. Cohen 1974a, ix–xxiv; 1974b; Hechter 1974, 1151–78; Parkin 1974, 119–57; D. Bell 1975, 141–74; Patterson 1975, 305–59; Young 1976; Halsey 1978, 124–28; Okamura 1981, 452–65.

15. For a cogent discussion of these two approaches, which he terms "primordial" and "instrumentalist," see Bentley 1987, esp. pages 24–27.

16. For pioneering efforts in this direction, see Doornbos 1972, 263–83; Vincent 1974, 375–79; McKay 1982, 395–420; Jones and Hill-Burnett 1982, 214–46; for a combination of both approaches, see Scott 1990, 147–71.

17. However, E. S. Sherratt cautions: "While the grouping of people under ethnic denominations was an important component of the Egyptian and Hittite diplomatic and military rhetoric, we should not be misled by this into mistaking these for what in the context of the modern concept of the nation state, we would call 'nationalities'" (1998, 307).

18. For a general discussion, see the papers in Stark 1998b; S. Jones 1997. Regarding the development, maintenance, and visible manifestation of ethnic boundaries in historical archaeology, see, e.g., McGuire 1982, 159–78.

19. See Haaland 1977, 1–31; Hodder 1979, 446–54; Kimes, Haselgrove, and Hodder 1982, 113–31. It has been suggested that ethnicity is involved in the "organization of behavior," and in this case it is sometimes possible that under certain conditions, such as economic or political stress, ethnic boundaries are established and more clearly visible in the material culture than in other circumstances (Hodder 1979, 446–54; S. Jones 1997, 124–25).

20. For several classic studies of ethnicity and the archaeological record, see Wiessner 1983, 253–76 (Sackett 1985, 154–59, offers a response regarding the difficulties in interpreting ethnicity in the archaeological record); Brumfiel 1994, 89–102; Pollard 1994, 79–88. Most recently, see J. M. Hall 1995, 6–17; 2002; N. Spencer 1995, 28–42, who examine ethnicity and cultural boundaries in early Iron Age Greece. For the region of the Near East, see Kamp and Yoffee's classic 1980 discussion of ethnicity in the Near East and Redmount's articles defining ethnicity based on the archaeological evidence from Tell el-Maskhuta in the Egyptian Delta (1995a; 1995b).

21. See, e.g., London 1989a, 37–55; Bunimovitz 1990, 210–22; Dever 1993a, 22*–33*; 1995a, 200–13; Bunimovitz and Yassur-Landau 1996, 88–101; Edelman 1996, 42–47; Finkelstein 1997, 216–37; for an overview of the problem, see Small 1997, 271–88; Sparks 1998, 1–22.

22. Several key studies have specifically addressed the issue of ethnicity at the end of the Late Bronze II–Iron I periods. Dever (1993a, 22*–33*) optimistically concludes that it is possible to recognize a group he refers to as "Proto-Israelite," Canaanites, and Philistines based on archaeological historical and biblical evidence. For a critique of Dever's conclusions, see Finkelstein 1997, 221–23; see also London 1989a, 37–55; Edelman 1996, 42–47; and Skjeggesald 1992, 159–86, who question attempts to define "Israelites" ethnically based on the material culture and biblical accounts. For a discussion of the difficulty of using faunal remains to determine ethnicity, see Hesse 1986, 17–28; Hesse and Wapnish 1997, 238–70. Most recently, in an insightful article Bloch-Smith (2003) has addressed the issue of ethnogenesis in her search for the essence of ethnic identity, a concept that I further explore in chapter 5. Bloch-Smith builds upon Emberling's 1997 article definition of ethnic bonds as

based on the "collective memory of a former unity" and upon J. Hall's classic 1997 work, where he explores the powerful bond of the "putative myth of shared descent and kingship." These issues are explored further in ch. 4.

23. No Iron I cemetery has been discovered or excavated at any of the five main pentapolis cities on the southern coastal plan. Thus, Sea Peoples or Philistine burial customs at these major centers are presently unknown.

24. Similar views have been expressed by numerous other scholars; see, e.g., T. Dothan 1995a, 41–59; Stager 1995, 332–48; Barako 2000, 513–30; regarding their later acculturation, see Stone 1995, 7–32; Iacovou 1998, 332–44. Regarding migration in the archaeological record, see Childe 1950; Adams 1968, 194–215; Adams, Van Gerven, and Levy 1978, 483–532; Gmelch 1980, 135–59; Kearney 1986, 331–61; Collett 1987, 105–16; Anthony 1990, 895–914; 1992; 1997. These issues are discussed in detail in ch. 5.

1
The Age of Internationalism: The Eastern Mediterranean during the Thirteenth Century B.C.E. and the "Crisis"

Essential to any study dealing with the formative period of the biblical world is its broader eastern Mediterranean historical and cultural context. The final centuries of the Late Bronze Age, spanning roughly 1400–1200 B.C.E., have often been characterized as an "age of internationalism." But as the thirteenth century drew to a close, this interconnected world of the eastern Mediterranean witnessed irreversible changes and crises that led to the collapse or gradual decline of imperial aspirations and the "old order" that had prevailed throughout much of the second millennium B.C.E.

Prior to this crisis, the cultures of this region formed part of a "global economy," a concept first explored by Immanuel Wallerstein (1974) in his study of the emergence of capitalist world domination. Although the Old World Late Bronze Age economic and political structures differed vastly from the modern capitalistic system, both are characterized by well-developed commercial and political contacts coinciding with the rise of empires and regional imperialism. This interlocking system of economic, political, and cultural relations between center, periphery, semiperiphery, and external areas was reflected in both the textual and archaeological evidence. In addition to the exchange of objects and peoples, there was doubtless large-scale cross-fertilization of knowledge, technology, concepts, ideologies, political systems, and cultural styles and practices. The impact, both positive and negative, of these economic, political, and cultural contacts throughout the eastern Mediterranean during the final centuries of the Bronze Age cannot be underestimated. Due to the overwhelming influence this "world economy" had on the development of identities, ideologies, cultures, and the shorter-term history of the region, this chapter utilizes a "world-systems approach" in order to grapple with the complex interconnected world of the eastern Mediterranean during the Late Bronze Age and its subsequent gradual disintegration. The ensuing fragmentation resulted in the rise of new power centers and political systems, the assertion of indigenous cultures, and, in some cases, the movements of people.

Egypt and Cyprus played an especially influential role in Canaan during this period. Egypt was the major political force in Canaan during the Late Bronze Age, so the later appearance of regionally defined material cultures in Canaan and the ethnogenesis of Israel can be understood only within the framework of the political and economic decline of Egyptian influence in Canaan during the Twentieth Dynasty of New Kingdom Egypt and its subsequent demise (see ch. 2). To the northwest of Canaan, thirteenth-century B.C.E. Cyprus was a major participant in the international trading network, serving as the link or interface between the Levant and the Aegean (see table 1 for comparative chronological terms). Later twelfth-century B.C.E. developments on Cyprus, coastal Anatolia, and in the Dodecanese were a result of the decline of the mainland Mycenaean palace system in the western Aegean and the collapse of the Hittite Empire. The ensuing prosperity experienced in this region, especially on Cyprus during this period (Late Cypriot IIIA), had a direct influence and impact on the appearance of the biblical Philistines and their urban culture along the southern coastal plain of Canaan (see ch. 5). However, perhaps the most fascinating enigma of this period is the cause for the collapse of the world-system that connected the eastern Mediterranean and for the socioeconomic transformation that marked the end of the Bronze Age. This restructuring of the second-millennium Bronze Age world created a multicultural mosaic of cultures and ideologies that resulted in the rise and development of the first-millennium biblical world.

DATE (B.C.E.)	EGYPT	CANAAN	GREECE	CYPRUS
1400				
	18th Dynasty	Late Bronze IIA	Late Helladic IIIA	Late Cypriot IIB
1300				
	19th Dynasty	Late Bronze IIB	Late Helladic IIIB	Late Cypriot IIC
1200				
	20th Dynasty	Iron I	Late Helladic IIIC	Late Cypriot IIIA
1100				

Table 1: Comparative Table of Chronological Terms in the Eastern Mediterranean (ca. 1300–1100 B.C.E.)

World-Systems Approach

The world-systems perspective is a framework for understanding long-term social change based on an analysis of the integrated system of interconnecting economic relations that exist between societies. It is an outgrowth of systems theory, which became a predominant tool of analysis in the social sciences during the late 1960s and 1970s. Systems theory classifies cultural systems into various subsystems with the aim of understanding and tracing societal change over time.[1] As developed by Immanuel Wallerstein (1974; 1979; 1998, 103–6), world-systems analysis combines both systems theory and Marxist elements into a more integrated approach that is in part a statement against evolutionary-based theories of societal and economic development. In his early writings, Wallerstein argued for three basic types of world systems—world economies, world empires, and mini-systems—three systems that in recent years have also been adapted to precapitalist societies.[2] Although Wallerstein initially questioned the applicability of a world-systems approach to precapitalist societies, it has proved to be a useful heuristic tool for analyzing the archaeological record.[3]

Several concepts are crucial to understanding world-systems theory. The terms *core* and *periphery* are well known from the fields of history and geography. In this approach, the economy of peripheral areas (periphery) is closely connected to the exploitative policies of the economic core. Two additional components are often included in world-systems analyses: the semiperiphery (which serves a mediating role between core and periphery) and the external zone (or areas external to the system). The basic premise of this approach is that the inequitable distribution of wealth is a result of center (or core) exploitation of periphery regions as mediated by semiperiphery areas. One of the strengths of world-systems analysis is its recognition of marginal peoples in historical development; in contrast, most theories dealing with long-term, large-scale societal change tend to exclude such groups (Chase-Dunn and Hall 1993, esp. 851–52; T. D. Hall 2000a).[4] The difficulty in applying center-periphery concepts to the archaeological record is that it is not always easy, in the absence of a historical context, to distinguish among core, semiperiphery, or periphery in the material culture (see Champion 1989, 1–9).

The role of the semiperiphery is an especially relevant concept for interpreting economic interconnections in the late second-millennium eastern Mediterranean region. The semiperiphery serves as a buffer zone to protect the core from periphery pressures and often plays a key role in economic interactions between various regions (see Chase-Dunn 1988; Dietler 1989; M. J. Allen 1997, 41–43). In addition, the interaction between center, periphery, and semiperiphery is dynamic, and roles can shift over time, with semiperipheral regions becoming core areas or serving a less pivotal role as a marginalized periphery. The semiperiphery, often located at a crossroads between core regions or core and periphery, can combine both core and peripheral forms of organization and often fulfills the role of "middleman" in their transactions. As a result, the more dynamic semiperiphery is likely to generate new institutional forms, to serve as a fertile ground for social, organizational, and technological innovation, or to establish new centers of resource control at the first signs of weakness on the part of the core powers (see Chase-Dunn 1988, 31; M. J. Allen 1997, 42). The regions that are referred to in succeeding chapters as areas of interface fulfill the role of the semiperiphery and serve as the intermediary between core and periphery areas or between various centers or periphery zones.[5]

During the thirteenth century B.C.E., Egypt, Hittite Hatti, Assyria, and most likely areas of mainland Greece can be defined as "core" areas. Peripheral regions would include portions of the Levant (excluding the major city-states) and the marginal zones of Egypt, Anatolia, and the Aegean. Cyprus, several key cities along the Levantine and Anatolian coasts (most notably Ugarit), and probably other regions of "interface" that experienced various degrees of center control and influence (or what can be termed a "contested periphery") functioned as "middlemen" in the lively international trade network that thrived during the thirteenth century.

Empires, Palace Systems, and City-States

The political and cultural constellation in the eastern Mediterranean region and the Near East during the age of internationalism included the Hittite, Babylonian, Assyrian, and Egyptian Empires. These centers of power reshaped the region throughout most of the second half of the second millennium. Mainland Greece[6] and Cyprus[7] also played an influential role in international affairs. Membership in this elite "club" is reflected in the fourteenth- to thirteenth-century correspondence from archives and inscriptions discovered in Anatolia, Syria, and Egypt. In this diplomatic interchange, rulers of equal status are addressed as "brothers," while vassal subordinates are referred to as "sons." The resulting political system in the ancient Near East during the Late Bronze Age thus combined a double level of political rule with a hierarchical system of large regional units based on a higher level of "great kings" (or "centers") and a lower level of "lesser kings" (or "peripheries/semiperipheries"), who were bound by treaties to rulers of empires (see Cline 1994).[8]

Politically and economically, one of the most noteworthy features of the Late Bronze Age was the appearance of centralized administration in large palace complexes. Throughout the eastern Mediterranean region, the palace served as the administrative center and seat of the local ruler in an urban settlement. In the case of the "small kings," the palaces' control extended to the respective surrounding hinterland. The same centralized system on a larger imperial scale was used by the great kings of the Egyptian, Hittite, and Assyrian Empires to administer their areas of influence, with the smaller urban centers serving as the hinterland to the major centers. Economically, monopolistic production and intensive interregional trade characterized the palace system.[9] The closely interrelated political and economic structure of the eastern Mediterranean region during the thirteenth century was reflected in mass-produced and standardized pottery and the exchange of prestige objects, the former being especially observable in the homogeneous ceramic repertoire of Canaan.[10]

In the Syro-Palestinian region, the double level of political rule was particularly evident because of the numerous small, semiautonomous city-states, each with local dynasties.[11] Greater Canaan was divided between the two major core powers of the region following the Battle at Kadesh on the Orontes River (1285 B.C.E.). Hittite authority extended over parts of northern Levant (Syria), while the Egyptians viewed southern Levant (Palestine) as part of their sphere of influence. Based on Egyptian and Hittite texts, it is evident that the administrative style of the two major powers differed. The Egyptian vassal states had well-defined obligations, while the pharaoh had few. The goal of the Egyptians was the extraction of tribute, control over the major routes crossing Canaan, and the prevention of rebellion. On the other hand, Hittite treaties with vassal states reflected a more mutually beneficial relationship, with clearly defined Hittite obligations to its vassal states (Knapp 1988b, 187; Klengel 1992, 112).

Hittite diplomatic correspondence refers to a region called Ahhiyawa, which many scholars believe was located on mainland Greece.[12] If, in fact, this identification is correct, Mycenaean Greece during this time may have had a great king who is referred to as a "brother" in Hittite texts. The archaeological and Linear B textual evidence, however, does not seem to support the claim of one major center that united Greece under a single charismatic political and divine leader, and currently there is no agreement regarding the socioeconomic and political structure of Mycenaean Greece.[13] Archaeological excavations at several major palace centers such as Mycenae, Argos, Midea, Tiryns, and Pylos seem to support the view of many competing but equal centers.

The Mycenaean Bronze Age palace site at Pylos is a case in point. The results of excavations at Pylos and systematic surveys in the surrounding region of Messenia provide invaluable evidence regarding the evolution of administrative authority in Late Bronze Age Greece. Already an important center in the Early Mycenaean period, Pylos increased and expanded its power during the fourteenth century, apparently at the expense of its neighboring rivals. Much of its wealth resulted from the production of the perfumed oil that played a key role in Pylos' economy (Shelmerdine 1985). Survey data and the Linear B texts[14] found at the site indicate that increased centralization occurred during the thirteenth century B.C.E., which is also demonstrated by additions made to the central palace (see fig. 1.1; Davis, Alcock, Bennet, Lolos, and Shelmerdine 1997; J. L. Davis 1998; Shelmerdine 1998). Nevertheless, this increased centralization in the palace may also have represented attempts to protect the center and its resources during a time of greater economic and political constraints—perhaps even foreshadowing events that resulted in the transformation and decline of the Mycenaean palace system at the end of the thirteenth and early twelfth centuries B.C.E. (Shelmerdine 1999; 2001).

Crete and other areas in the Aegean during the fourteenth and thirteenth centuries B.C.E. were not part of an empire, nor were they united under one great king.[15] Crete's social and economic structure can be characterized as comprising autonomous polities. Its main interest in the Levant and Egypt was apparently economic, as demonstrated by the abundant imported Aegean objects found in the east. Both the textual and the archaeological evidence suggest that the political and economic structure of mainland Greece and its periphery (the Aegean Islands, and eastern Aegean coastal regions) differed from the empire-oriented Near East.[16] Mirroring political developments on the mainland, the second half of the thirteenth century on Crete was a period of upheaval. Gradually, many of the Late Minoan sites were abandoned or destroyed, followed by the establishment of what has been termed in the literature as "refuge sites." More than a hundred settlements have been identified in defensible or remote locations; however, these sites are diverse and do not represent a single settlement pattern (Kanta 1980; 2001; Whitley 1991; Nowicki 2000; 2001; Haggis 2001). As suggested by Anna Lucia D'Agata (2003), these newly established or reoccupied settlements may represent "colonies" of various groups, some foreign in origin, but most a result of the resettlement of local populations.[17]

With the dissolution of the great power centers that commenced in the thirteenth century B.C.E., the concentration of political and economic power in the palaces transformed their physical collapse into a general disaster for several of the larger regional powers. On the other hand, the decline or collapse of these "superpowers" liberated many of those areas that had been under their control and, presumably, exploitation. The breakdown of international lines of communication between the empires was replaced by more local contacts, which resulted in the fragmentation

Fig. 1.1. Schematic Plan of the Palace at Pylos

of Canaan into smaller regionally defined units (Liverani 1987, 66, 69). This is reflected in the development of regional Iron I cultures and the gradual emergence of early Israel.

Contested Semiperipheries: Cyprus, Coastal Anatolia, and the Dodecanese at the End of the Late Bronze Age

Several regions, including Cyprus, coastal Anatolia, and the Dodecanese, served as secondary power centers that were apparently contested territories under the suzerainty of the various core powers. Cyprus, the link connecting the Aegean and the Levant, played an especially key role in the international relations of the eastern Mediterranean during the age of internationalism. Cypriot imports are ubiquitous at all Late Bronze II sites in Canaan and elsewhere in the Levant, Egypt, Anatolia, and the Aegean, and the Cypriots and their agents apparently conducted these mercantile activities in the shadow of the Hittite Empire. Cyprus during the fourteenth–thirteenth centuries is characterized by numerous regional centers, including several that served as major copper-producing areas. The combination of rich copper resources and an ideal position as the connecting link between the Aegean and the Levant in the international trade network enabled Cyprus to play a leading economic role in Late Bronze II culture throughout the eastern Mediterranean.[18] Based on Hittite texts and the identification of Cyprus with Alashiya, Cyprus seems to have been under Hittite influence at times. However, there is little archaeological evidence on Cyprus that would indicate a close vassal relationship with the Hittites in central Anatolia. In reality, Cyprus may well have been neutral in the power struggle between Egypt and Hatti. This relatively independent status of Cyprus may also be hinted at in the Amarna letters, in which the ruler of Alashiya uses the term "brother" to address the Egyptian pharaoh, indicating equal status (Knapp 1988a, 150). Freed of imperial constraints following the crisis that struck the major power centers at the close of the Late Bronze Age, Cyprus and several of these secondary semiperiphery powers flourished.

Strategically located, Cyprus should be seen as a regional "clearing house" or entrepôt connecting the eastern Mediterranean coastline and the Aegean.[19] Close relations existed between Mycenaean Greece and Cyprus, as evidenced by the significant quantities of Aegean material culture appearing on Cyprus during the Late Cypriot II period.[20] In addition to Cyprus's convenient location bridging the Levant and the Aegean worlds and its role as a "middleman" in the exchange between the east and west, Cypriot dominance was no doubt also due to successful exploitation of its copper resources (Knapp 1985a, 249–50; 1986, 70–72; 1996, 20–22; Keswani 1993, 78).

The situation on Cyprus at the close of the thirteenth century is no longer as clear-cut as previously believed. The early excavations at Enkomi, Hala Sultan Tekke, Sinda, and Kition seemed to present a straightforward picture of massive destructions of these Cypriot centers at the end of the thirteenth century B.C.E. Originally these destructions were attributed to external invasions of "Achaeans" or "Sea Peoples."[21] However, reevaluation of these sites and the more recently excavated sites of Pyla-*Kokkinokremos* (Karageorghis and Demas 1984) and Maa-*Palaeokastro*[22] has revealed a more complex situation at the end of the Late Cypriot IIC (ca. 1300–1200 B.C.E.) and the following the Late Cypriot IIIA (ca. 1200–1150/1100 B.C.E.). Today the picture at the end of Late Cypriot II is not uniform throughout the island: some Cypriot sites were abandoned, some were continuously inhabited, and others were rebuilt. In addition, recent excavations and reexamination of earlier excavations have revealed that several of the "hallmarks" of Late Cypriot IIIA culture (Mycenaean IIIC:1b pottery, ashlar masonry, etc.), which were interpreted as representing the arrival of a new group of people referred to as Achaean Mycenaean colonists,[23] appear already in the Late Cypriot IIC.[24] It has now also become clear that many of the local Late Cypriot IIC wares (e.g., white slipped, white shaved, base ring) continue in smaller quantities into the Late Cypriot IIIA (Kling 1989a).[25]

New interpretations have arisen in light of the revised picture on Cyprus at the close of the Late Cypriot IIC period. Vassos Karageorghis (1992b; 1994) suggests that, with the decline of Mycenaean centers in the Peloponnese, refugees from the mainland began to arrive on Cyprus and settle in preexisting Late Cypriot IIC towns, creating a continuous trickle of Mycenaean "refugees" that lasted perhaps for a century. Archaeologically, this is best reflected in the appearance of locally produced Mycenaean ceramic styles on Cyprus already in the Late Cypriot IIC, continuing in larger quantities during the Late Cypriot IIIA period. In contrast, E. Susan Sherratt (1991, 191–95; 1992), stressing that one should not equate locally produced Aegean style pottery with the large-scale arrival of groups with an Aegean origin, sees the phenomenon of Mycenaean IIIC:1b pottery as a local adaptation of Mycenaean-style pottery (for a detailed discussion of Mycenaean IIIC:1b pottery, see ch. 5 below).

James Muhly (1985, 42–43; 1989, 310; 1992) posits that, because a centralized palace system so characteristic of the Aegean and several regions of the Near East never developed on Cyprus, the island did not experience a total collapse at the end of the Late Cypriot II period.[26] In fact, the peak of Cypriot economic influence occurred during the Late Cypriot IIC–Late Cypriot IIIA periods, with major expansion evident in three areas: (1) urban development, especially in the south; (2) industrial expansion in copper production; and (3) continued commercial ties with the eastern Aegean and the Levant.[27] The urban settlements of Cyprus during the Late Cypriot IIIA and its material culture, especially the ceramic repertoire from eastern Cyprus, is quite similar to that of early Philistine settlement along the southern coast of Canaan and several sites in Cilicia, indicating the close connection between these regions.[28]

To the east of Cyprus, thirteenth-century B.C.E. Cilicia was part of the Hittite Empire. Limited archaeological excavations in Cilicia reveal a break with the Late Bronze Age Hittite-influenced material culture following the demise and destruction of the Hittite capital, Hattuša (see Jean 2003). Five sites—Kilise Tepe (Hansen and Postgate 1999), Soli Höyük (Yağci 2003), Mersin (Yumuktepe) (Jean 2003, 83–84), Tarsus (Gözlü Kule) (Goldman 1963), and Kinet Höyük (Gates forthcoming)—are key to understanding the transition between the Late Bronze and Iron Ages. At several sites (Kilise Tepe, Soli Höyük, and Tarsus), the appearance of locally produced Mycenaean IIIC pottery similar to assemblages found on Cyprus during the twelfth century indicates a close relationship to Cyprus following the collapse of the Hittite Empire. Due to the limited work thus far conducted in the region, early Iron Age Cilicia remains largely unknown.

Tarsus is one of the most extensively excavated Bronze and Iron Age sites in Cilicia. Unfortunately, the excavated area was disturbed, with few architectural remains. The resulting ceramic assemblage from the late thirteenth- and early twelfth-century levels is mixed due to the confused stratigraphy, as shown in the final reports.[29] Following the destruction of Late Bronze Age Tarsus, the majority of utilitarian Cilician monochrome wares continued to appear alongside a new element: locally produced Mycenaean IIIC:1b ceramics similar to those known from Cyprus. The style may have been introduced from Cyprus, perhaps indicating closer links with the island and continued trade relations with northwest Syria during the twelfth century B.C.E. (Goldman 1963, 93–95; Yakar 1993, 17–18).

Further to the northwest, insufficient excavations and poorly published results have hampered attempts to reconstruct events in the Dodecanese during the thirteenth–twelfth centuries B.C.E. However, the available evidence seems to indicate that the islands of the Dodecanese, especially Rhodes and Kos, were important centers during the Late Helladic IIIB and IIIC periods. The key site in the Dodecanese is Ialysos, on the island of Rhodes, where an extremely rich cemetery dating to the Late Helladic IIIC period was excavated (Maiuri 1923–24; Jacopi 1930–31). In addition to the large assemblage of Mycenaean IIIC pottery, gold and silver ornaments and objects of steatite, agate, amethyst, carnelian, ivory, and faience, as well as bronze objects such as mirrors, knives, and an axehead found in these tombs, attest to the great prosperity of Ialysos during the Late Helladic IIIC period. A second, more recently excavated cemetery at Pylona, near Lindos on Rhodes, also included imported Mycenaean IIIA, local and imported Mycenaean IIIB pottery, and locally produced Mycenaean IIIC ceramic assemblages (Karantzali 2001; for a discussion of Mycenaean IIIC pottery and its significance to the Philistines, see ch. 5). Based on a very incomplete archaeological picture, Mario Benzi (1988, 261–62) suggests that Ialysos experienced a radical growth in population during the twelfth century B.C.E., based on the large increase in the number of tombs. He further suggests that the rest of the island was largely depopulated or abandoned, resulting in the "nucleation" of sites similar to that observed in other regions, such as the Peloponnese and Crete. On both the islands of Rhodes (Ialysos) and Kos (Meropis) there are no signs of destruction during the course of the thirteenth century B.C.E. (Late Helladic IIIB), such as occurred in the Argolid and elsewhere on the mainland. The rich finds in the twelfth-century Late Helladic IIIC cemeteries indicate that the Dodecanese were continuously occupied throughout the Late Helladic IIIC period and experienced a time of prosperity during these centuries.[30]

The close trade connections between the Aegean, coastal Anatolia, Cyprus, and Canaan are clearly indicated by recent excavations at several key sites and the discovery of Late Bronze Age shipwrecks at Cape Gelidonya (Bass 1963; 967; 1973) and Ulu Burun (Bass 1986; 1987; Pulak 1988; Bass, Pulak, Collon, and Weinstein 1989) on the southwestern coast of Anatolia. Further to the northwest, recent excavations at Miletos (tentatively identified as Millawata or Millawanda of the Hittite texts) and the chamber tombs at Musgebi are key to understanding the influence of Mycenaean-inspired culture in the east[31] and, specifically, Mycenaean IIIC:1b wares in the eastern Mediterranean region.

Lastly, the most recent excavations during the past fifteen years at Troy, located at the northern edge of the western coast of Anatolia, have strengthened the identification of Hisarlik with Wilusa of Hittite texts and legendary Troy. Manfred Korfmann's discovery of a lower city in addition to the previously excavated citadel confirms Troy's position as a major regional capital that held a significant position in the trade networks of the Late Bronze Age.[32] Provenience studies of Mycenaean IIIB pottery have also revealed that already in the thirteenth century B.C.E. Mycenaean-style pottery was being locally produced at Troy, strongly suggesting a gradual "Mycenaeanization" of the eastern Aegean during the final century of the Late Bronze Age (Mountjoy 1997; Mommsen, Hertel, and Mountjoy 2001), similar to the results of recent excavation at other sites along coastal Anatolia. With the destruction of Late Bronze Age Troy VIIa, the site was immediately reoccupied (Troy VIIb) with no break in occupation, indicating a continuation of the Late Bronze Age with only a few changes. A cultural break is evident only in the second phase of Troy VIIb, marked by the appearance of new construction techniques and handmade pottery (Becks 2003). However, interconnections between the Levant and the eastern Aegean continued into the late thirteenth and early twelfth centuries B.C.E., after the cessation of imports from the western Aegean, as demonstrated by the evidence of imported grey Trojan ware in Cyprus and at several sites in Canaan (S. H. Allen 1991; 1994; Killebrew 1996b, pl. 8:1).

Canaan during the Thirteenth Century B.C.E.

Canaan, the object of intense scholarly research for the last century and the focus of this book, was not one of the major powers of this region (see ch. 3). The southern Levant served as a periphery region under Egyptian imperial control. Yet, though not a significant center of power, Canaan played a crucial role as a cultural and commercial crossroads of this region during the Late Bronze II period. Two major international road systems—the coastal route and the King's Highway—and numerous smaller offshoots traversed Canaan, connecting Egypt and Arabia with Syria and Mesopotamia and ultimately the Aegean world via the Mediterranean coast. In contrast to the Middle Bronze II period, when Canaan reached its cultural and economic zenith, Late Bronze Age Canaan witnessed a gradual deterioration in prosperity and cultural expression. This decline in Canaan's economic fortunes is generally attributed to the effects of Egyptian suzerainty over this region during the Late Bronze II period, which continued well into the twelfth century B.C.E.[33]

The unifying forces influencing Canaan's material culture during the fourteenth through the early twelfth centuries were Egyptian political and economic control[34] and the complex system of international trade in the eastern Mediterranean region.[35] The slow decline of Canaanite material culture from the end of the Middle Bronze through the Late Bronze I periods is reflected in the fewer number and smaller size of settlements, increasing gradually in number during the Late Bronze II.[36] Noteworthy is the paucity of settlements in the central hill country, in contrast to the concentration of settlements in the coastal plains and along important communication routes.[37]

The texts, especially the Amarna letters and the Egyptian military annals, present a less uniform and unified sociopolitical picture, testifying to a low degree of integration and central organization, each city being ruled by its own "king." The political situation seems to be volatile, with Canaanite rulers frequently requesting Egyptian intervention to settle disputes between the various urban centers.[38] This type of political structure is often referred to as a "city-state system."[39]

The administration of Canaan, as reflected in the Amarna and Ugaritic texts, was based on a convergence of interests held by the king and the class of high functionaries (*maryannu,* scribes and administrative personnel, merchants, etc.) and depended on the exploitation of village communities (Heltzer 1976). The next rank consisted of artisans under palace control. On the lowest level were the farmers, referred to as *hupsu* or *sabe name,* who were engaged in agricultural production. Outside the urban Canaanite society proper were the *ʿapîru,* independent renegades apparently inhabiting the rural areas of Canaan.[40] The widening gap between the socioeconomic classes may be reflected in the material culture by the gradual debasement of functional domestic material culture, in contrast to the imported luxury goods and conspicuous consumption in the royal palaces (Liverani 1987, 69; but see McGovern 1987, who describes a different scenario for Transjordan).

By the late thirteenth and early twelfth centuries B.C.E., the Aegean and eastern Mediterranean regions were undergoing rapid change. The Hittite Empire was destroyed,[41] the centralized palace system of the Mycenaean world was in the process of disintegration, and the Twentieth Dynasty in Egypt witnessed a period of economic and political deterioration. Canaan entered a period of transition. A number of Canaanite centers were either destroyed or in decline. Several large urban centers associated with the Philistines, one of the groups of Sea Peoples appearing on Ramesses III's reliefs at Medinet Habu, were constructed at sites such as Tel Miqne-Ekron and Ashdod. Additionally, small villages began to appear in increasingly larger numbers in the previously underpopulated hill country and Negev region. *Crisis* is often the descriptive term used to characterize this transitional period of time.

Crisis at the End of the Bronze Age: Causes and Repercussions

The reasons for the decline or collapse of ancient civilizations have been pondered for centuries. The ancient Greeks compared civilizations to organisms that experienced cycles of birth, development, and death. In the twentieth century, two world historians, Oswald Spengler (1926–28) and Arnold J. Toynbee (1933–54) also traced predictable cycles in the growth and destruction of civilizations (for a discussion of this approach to collapse, see Yoffee 1988, 2–8). During the 1970s and 1980s, scholars devoted increasing intellectual resources to questions regarding the collapse of complex societies (see Sabloff and Lamberg-Karlovsky

1974; Tainter 1988; Yoffee and Cowgill 1988). Many of these studies viewed the end of complex societies through a processual prism of systems collapse[42] that later developed into "catastrophe theory," a mathematical calculation of system overload that results in collapse (Renfrew 1978; 1979a). Regarding the actual cause of the "crisis" at the end of the Late Bronze Age, suggestions include destruction by outside forces (hostile migrating groups or raiders); climatic, environmental or natural disasters (e.g., earthquakes, plagues, or drought); technological innovations (metallurgical or military in nature); internal collapse, including social evolutionary theories (e.g., sociobiological, systems collapse, or catastrophe theory); and anthropological or sociological theories dealing with states of inequality and the resulting political struggle especially between center and periphery (at times culminating in violent internal social revolution).

Invading groups of migratory peoples or raiders remains a popular theory that scholars both past and present use to explain the destruction of the Late Bronze Age centers. Various groups of peoples have been proposed as the culprits responsible for the destruction of eastern Mediterranean empires: Sea Peoples from the north, west, or east;[43] Phrygians from the northwest;[44] Kaska nomads from northeast Anatolia; or Dorians from the north.[45] Gaston Maspero first explored the migration theory in his popular two-volume masterpiece, *Histoire ancienne des peoples de l'orient classique* (published in English as *The Struggle of the Nations* [1896]). R. A. Stewart Macalister (1914, 22) and Eduard Meyer (1928) developed this theory further. Maspero (1896) explained the initial migration of Sea Peoples as the result of two earlier migrations: Illyrians from northern Europe displacing various groups, including the Dorians and Phrygians, with the Dorians moving into the Greek mainland and the Phrygians migrating from the Balkans to Asia Minor. This triggered a third migration of Sea Peoples from western Anatolia and set off a chain reaction resulting in hordes of Sea Peoples engaging in an unsuccessful attempt to invade Egypt, followed by the settlement of the *Peleset* along the southern coast of Canaan.[46]

According to Bennet Bronson (1988, 213), outside raiders can play several possible roles in the collapse of a state: (1) they may arrive on the scene as scavengers after the state has been destroyed; (2) they may attack only after the state is in an already weakened condition; (3) they may repeatedly harass and attack an enemy until it becomes weakened, thus playing a critical but not exclusive part in its downfall; and (4) they may be the primary cause of an enemy's downfall without other factors playing a major role.

Natural disasters, such as severe seismic activity, have been proposed as the cause of the destruction of major sites under Hittite control and of many palaces on mainland Greece. Recently this theory has experienced a revival as a result of new evidence of an "earthquake storm" that hit the eastern Mediterranean between approximately 1225 and 1175 B.C.E. (Stiros and Jones 1996; Nur and Cline 2000; 2001). Claude F. A. Schaeffer initially suggested that the Sea Peoples were responsible for the destruction of Ugarit, a key site located on the Syrian coast;[47] later, however, he attributed all the destructions in Syria and Anatolia to seismic activities.[48] Based on his excavations at Troy, Carl Blegen hypothesized that a powerful earthquake destroyed Troy Level VIh.[49]

The destruction of Mycenae on mainland Greece is attributed to an earthquake by Spyros Iakovidis, one of Mycenae's numerous excavators, and Elizabeth French.[50] Klaus Kilian (1980, 193; 1990, 74–75; 1996), one of the excavators of Tiryns, has developed the earthquake theory further to include the destruction of all citadels in the Peloponnese at the end of the Late Helladic IIIB period as a result of a massive earthquake that rocked this region. Paul Åström (1985, 6–7; 1987, 7–10; Åström and Demakopoulou 1996) has also posited an earthquake as the cause of the destruction of the citadel at Midea.[51] Finally, the destruction of the Late Bronze Age settlement at Tell el-ʿUmeiri in the central Transjordanian highlands is also attributed to seismic activity sometime at the end of the thirteenth century B.C.E. (Herr 1998, 254).

Climatic change, often resulting in an extended drought, has also been cited as the cause of this catastrophe. First developed in detail by Rhys Carpenter (1966), this theory suggests that the major Mycenaean centers fell victim to a prolonged drought. It is supported in part by the lack of archaeological evidence for a migration into Greece at the end of the Late Helladic IIIB period.[52] Robert Drews (1993, 81) argues against this theory based on the Linear B economic lists from Pylos and Knossos that show no indication of a shortage of food (Palmer 1989) and on the discovery of large quantities of carbonized foodstuffs in the palace at the time of their destruction (Erard-Cerceau 1988, 185).

Other scholars have proposed drought as the catalyst that set into motion local populations, raiders, or migrating nations who destroyed cities and palaces, either as a result of a systems collapse or from internal or external attack.[53] Textual evidence from Ugarit, Hatti, and Aphek has been used as proof for a famine in Anatolia during this crucial period,[54] but not all the evidence points to a period of dry and hot weather during the end of the thirteenth and early twelfth centuries B.C.E.[55]

Technological innovations have been suggested as the catalyst for the collapse of the Hittite Empire. In one scenario, Phrygians were sent southward by an Illyrian expansion, and these Phrygian invaders were able to conquer western Anatolia because of their superior iron weapons (Drews 1993, 73). V. Gordon Childe (1942, 175–79) suggested a variation of this theory, proposing that the working of iron, a metal mentioned in the Hattuša tablets, developed in Asia Minor during the thirteenth century B.C.E. Ironworking remained a technological secret until peoples under Hittite rule began to produce the metal and, with iron weapons, were able to overthrow Hittite sovereignty. Following their victory over the Hittites, these peoples took to the sea with their new technology and attacked other Late Bronze Age cities in the eastern Mediterranean. However, the archaeological evidence, indicating that iron appears only sporadically at numerous different locations, has discredited this view.[56]

Similarly, Robert Drews (1993, 97) has emphasized a technological change in military tactics as the main cause for changes at the end of the thirteenth century B.C.E. According to this theory, the main military component of the Late Bronze city-state armies was the chariot corps and bow. By the beginning of the twelfth century, the number of chariots became irrelevant due to a new kind of infantry armed with javelins and long swords, as depicted in the Medinet Habu reliefs. The use of the javelin and long sword, combined with guerrilla tactics characteristic of barbarian peoples, proved to be quite effective against traditional chariot attack.[57]

Systems collapse, one of several evolutionary and environmentally oriented processual models, is an oft-cited cause for the collapse of the Late Bronze Age states. A systems collapse occurs when failure in one of the closely interrelated social subsystems of a complex society affects other social and economic institutions, resulting in a domino-like breakdown of the entire system, including patterns of production and established trade networks.[58] Destruction of cities is seen as a result of the internal system's collapse rather than as the cause of the "crisis."

The specific factors that can trigger a systems collapse include drought, plague, reduction in arable land, increase in nomadism, the revolt of peasants, the defection of mercenaries, an increase in social problems, overpopulation or depopulation, or a combination of several culprits mentioned above.[59] The disruption of maritime trade by pirates, marauders, or raiders could interrupt the trade in essential materials such as copper or tin and thus trigger an overall breakdown.[60] The final blow could have been dealt by either an earthquake or by migratory peoples. Thus, according to this theory the destruction of Late Bronze Age cities was a result of the internal system's collapse rather than the source of the "crisis."[61]

The cyclical rise and collapse of urban cultures, a model closely associated with the *Annales* school of thought, appears in some of the more recent literature as the major factor responsible for the crisis that characterizes the end of the Late Bronze Age. Israel Finkelstein (1995b) adapts this theory to explain the changes that occurred during the late thirteenth century in Canaan that eventually resulted in the emergence of ancient Israel. According to Finkelstein, one must combine a concept of a longer-term regional history together with a short-term local history. He traces the cyclical rise and collapse of culture beginning with demise of the Early Bronze Age urban cultures during the final centuries of the third millennium. Following a nonurban interlude, often referred to as the Intermediate Bronze period, Canaan was reurbanized in the Middle Bronze Age, representing one of the cyclical changes from an urban society to a nonurban, rural-pastoral society back to an urban society. He bases this concept of cyclical rise and collapse of urban cultures in Canaan during the third and second millennia on the evidence from archaeological surveys in Israel and the West Bank during the past thirty years. Although he notes that the final collapse of the Late Bronze Age world was connected to broader events in the eastern Mediterranean, Finkelstein also recognizes that local economic and social factors played a key role.[62] However, as will be explored below, no one theoretical model outlined above fully takes into consideration the host of complex forces that transformed the thirteenth and twelfth centuries B.C.E.

The End of the Late Bronze Age: An Interregional Perspective of Transformation

Although it may never be possible fully to reconstruct the factors that led to the transformation of the Late Bronze Age world during the final decades of the thirteenth century, in recent years it has become increasingly clear that the demise of the international world and empires of the Late Bronze Age was a long process that included gradual decline, destruction, abandonment, and/or continuity. Egyptian influence is evident in Canaan through much of the twelfth century; however, by the middle of the century, Egyptian prestige was battered and in decline. Rather than refer to this period of time as a "catastrophe," "crisis," or "collapse"[63]—common terms used to describe the end of the Late Bronze Age—it is preferable to see it as representing a transformation that affected the various regions of the Late Bronze Age world quite differently. There were both "winners" and "losers," depending on one's perspective, with several of the semiperipheral areas (e.g., Cyprus and several Levantine coastal areas) clearly benefiting from the collapse of core or "elite" control over international trade and prestige items. The so-called "crisis" or "collapse" was far more complex than simply the end of a cultural tradition. The multifarious transformations of the multiple thirteenth-century B.C.E. Late Bronze Age core and periphery regions occurred on both macro (global) and micro (local) levels within numerous intersecting and overlapping historical, social, economic, and cultural contexts. Its causes lie in changes that occurred at the intersecting interfaces of contact between the three regions that doubtless impacted the economic structures and political relations between the core areas of power and their related peripheries and margins.

As outlined above, numerous contemporary Egyptian, Hittite, Ugaritic, and Linear B texts provide the basis for our reconstruction of Late Bronze Age society. These texts reveal an economy based on complex political and economic relations and an interconnected constellation of empires, regional or local power centers, together with their peripheries and marginal areas, during the centuries leading up to the transformations of the twelfth century.[64] The international character of this interrelated world linked by economic ties is reflected in the exchange of material culture objects. This is especially evident in the ubiquitous pottery found throughout the region, one of the most valuable sources of information for reconstructing the interdependent economic system that typified the global world of the Late Bronze Age. During the past decades, numerous scientific analytical techniques have provided essential information regarding the provenience of these objects and our reconstruction of the "material culture trail" of economic interdependence.[65]

By combining the material cultural trail with other key data, we are able to create a picture of the ancient world in all its interconnectedness. Thus, figure 1.2 reconstructs suggested Late Bronze Age mercantile sea routes, based on Mediterranean Sea currents and material culture evidence,[66] while figure 1.3 outlines the spheres of political and economic influence during the Late Bronze II, based on the material culture evidence. Three major core areas are illustrated—mainland Greece (with its center in the Argolid), Anatolia (with its center in the Hittite heartland of central Anatolia), and Egypt—together with their spheres of political and/or cultural influence over the periphery regions. This is what has been termed "a triple segmentation of interlocking cycles articulated by major emporia located at their intersections" (Sherratt and Sherratt 1998, 338) and what I refer to as the region of interface between the three core centers. Cyprus, as outlined above, provided the link and interface between trade activities in the Aegean basin and along the Levantine coast and was a major player in maritime trade activities in both the Aegean and eastern Mediterranean.

Employing a world-systems approach to economic interconnections in the second millennium B.C.E., Andrew and E. Susan Sherratt (1991; 1998; E. S. Sherratt 1998; 2001) have reconstructed the development of regional trade interactions. These interconnections and changes over the second millennium provide insights into the mechanism of these relations and the reasons for the sociopolitical and economic transformations of the so-called crisis. During much of the Late Bronze Age, trade along maritime

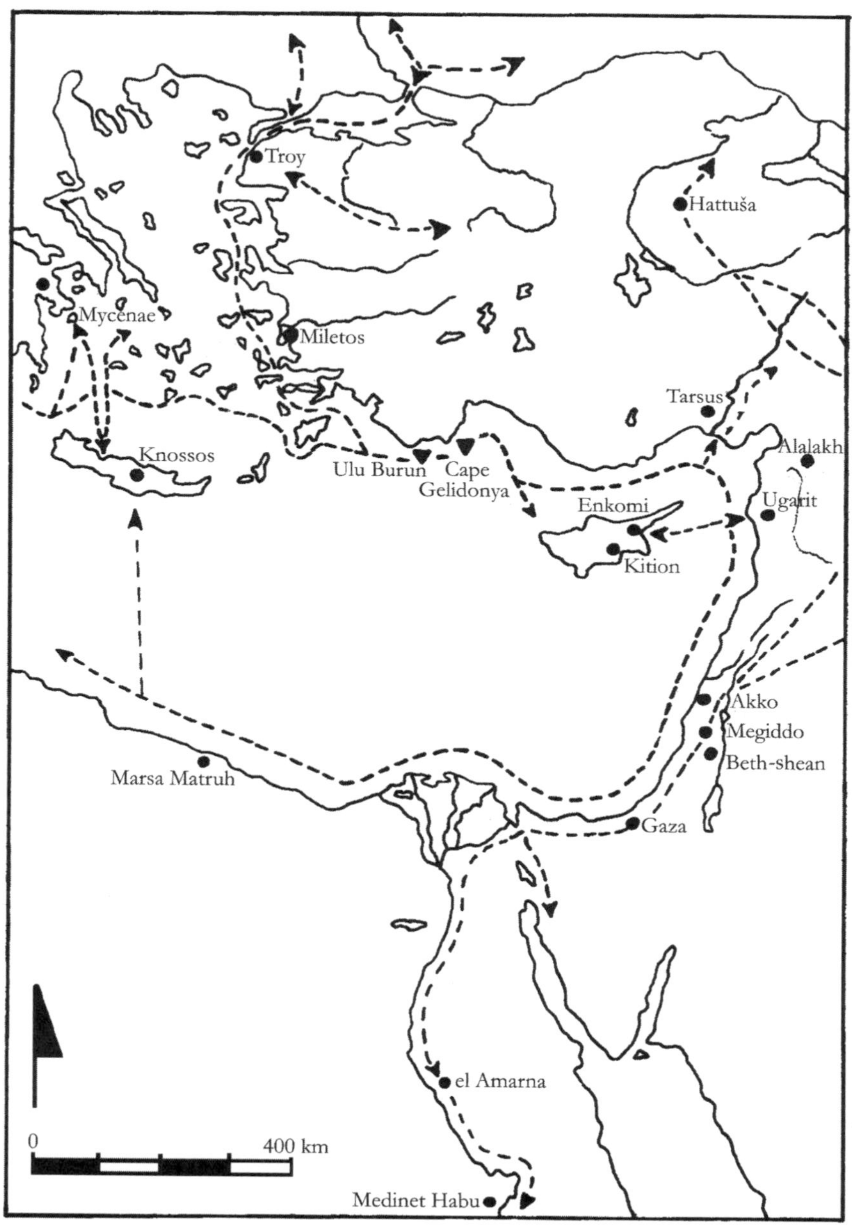

Fig. 1.2. Suggested Trade Routes during the Late Bronze Age

transport routes took place in stages, or "relays," and travel from region to region could take many weeks or even months. It is probable that the local or indigenous populations, especially coastal or nomadic communities, could link producers and consumers by serving as middlemen, bridging both the distance and the cultural gap along the segmented routes (Sherratt and Sherratt 1998, 338). Over time, a two-tiered level of trade control developed: an elite (imperial or royal) group of rulers maintained a monopoly over interregional exchanges of prestige gifts and valuable commodities such as copper; and a parallel unofficial and nonelite trade, a sort of black market, developed in low-value objects such as pottery.

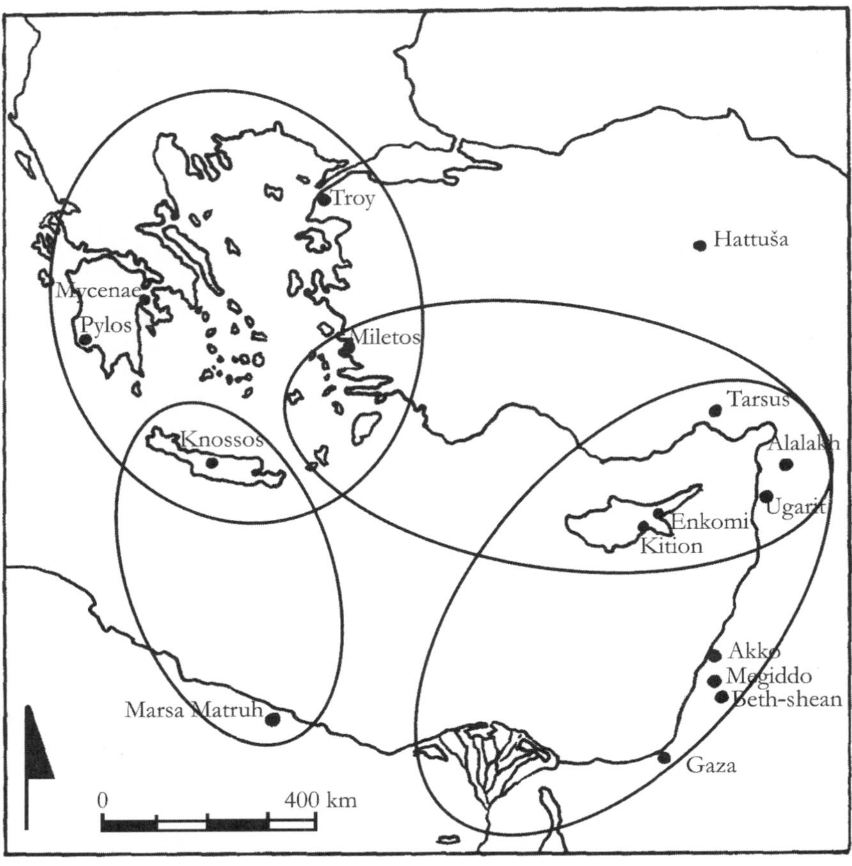

Fig. 1.3. Spheres of Influence and Interface during the Late Bronze II Period

During the fourteenth and part of the thirteenth centuries, Mycenaean Greece's influence clearly included the entire Aegean basin, the western coast of Anatolia, and Cyprus. Over the course of the thirteenth century, as a result of intensified interaction between the west Aegean with coastal Anatolia, the Dodecanese, and Cyprus, Mycenaean influence and culture slowly permeated port cities and regions in the eastern Aegean and Cyprus. In the final decades of the thirteenth century, Mycenaean-style material culture began to be produced and imitated locally at numerous sites. The Hittite sphere of interest included its western and southeastern coasts, Cyprus, and the northern Levant, overlapping in the west with Mycenaean Greece's cultural and economic reach. Hittite control over its western regions was tenuous at best, with both the textual and the material culture evidence indicating that this interface between Greece and Anatolia was a contested region. Further to the south, Canaan belonged to the Egyptian orb of immediate influence. Throughout the thirteenth century, the interface between east, west, and south was coastal Anatolia, the Dodecanese, and Cyprus.

Cyprus's key role in maritime trade transport as the link between east, west, and south slowly increased over the course of the thirteenth century, as demonstrated by the wealth and size of Cypriot city-states and by the ubiquity of Cypriot products, including locally produced Aegean-style material culture. By the end of the thirteenth century, Cypriot dominance, coinciding with the weakening of the Hittite empire (Singer 2000), led to a restructuring of the royal monopolization of trade that had characterized the Late Bronze II period. This is best illustrated by mounting evidence for the breakdown in elite-regulated trade of bronze (an especially valued commodity) and the increased circulation of scrap metal at the end of the thirteenth and the early part of the twelfth centuries.[67] The implications of this gradual transformation and decline of palace monopolies throughout the Aegean and eastern Mediterranean and the impact on the biblical world are explored in detail in chapters 2–5 below.

What is clear from both the textual and archaeological evidence is the marked decline in mercantile links between the western Aegean and the east (including the eastern Aegean, Levant, and Egypt). This is best demonstrated by the gradual breakdown of the centralized production of Mycenaean pottery replaced by a small number of workshops located on mainland Greece. This led to the gradual diffusion of workshops in the eastern Aegean and Cyprus that produced Mycenaean IIIB pottery during the final decades of the thirteenth century. In spite of the fact that direct or indirect connections between the west Aegean Mycenaean world and the Levant were severed at the close of the Late Bronze Age, trade contacts did persist (albeit on a somewhat reduced scale) between coastal Anatolia, the Dodecanese, Cyprus, and the Levant during the late thirteenth and early twelfth centuries (see Killebrew 1998a; E. S. Sherratt 1998, 304–5). Thus, after the cessation of Mycenaean imports from the western Aegean, trade continued between the eastern Aegean, Cyprus, and the Levant but on a notably smaller scale and probably no longer under royal patronage. The crisis did not result in the collapse of maritime trade in the eastern Mediterranean but rather a restructuring of economic control in core-periphery relations. During the twelfth century, these former Bronze Age centers fragmented into many smaller segments, several periphery regions were transformed into small-scale "cores," and hinterlands were "balkanized."[68] As the power base moved from older centers and established authorities, some sites underwent widespread destruction, unrest, and movement of populations. In contrast, many settlements along the Levantine coast and Cyprus (and perhaps other less-excavated regions of coastal Anatolia) experienced great prosperity and expansion. In the marginal regions of the Late Bronze world, these transformations, particularly Egypt's changing role in Canaan, resulted in the rise of the new ideologies and ethnic identities that characterized the first-millennium biblical world.

Notes to Chapter 1

1. For an overview and postprocessual critique of this approach that points out the failure of systems theory to address the importance of ideology and symbolism on the human past, see Hodder 1986, 25–31.

2. A world economy exists when several states and periphery regions interact with one another. If one state dominates the others, the system is transformed into a world empire. A group of interacting, nonstate groups constitute a mini-system (see T. D. Hall 2000a, 4).

3. For one of the first attempts to expand world-systems approach to precapitalist societies, see Schneider 1977. More recently, see Chase-Dunn and Hall 1991; M. J. Allen 1997; Kardulias 1999b; Denemark, Friedman, Gills, and Modelski 2000; T. D. Hall 2000b).

4. Although the applicability of world-systems analysis to the long-term historical and archaeological reconstruction of past cultures, societal change, and interregional connections is obvious, its full potential for archaeological analysis has not been fully exploited, especially in biblical archaeology. Several recent volumes (Peregrine and Feinman 1996; Kardulias 1999b; Denemark, Friedman, Gills, and Modelski 2000; T. D. Hall 2000b) include essays dealing specifically with a world-systems analysis of the archaeological record. Frank (1999) and Peregrine (1996; 2000) discuss general applications of world-systems analysis to archaeology. A number of articles deal with specific regions or archaeological processes in the Americas (Kowalewski 1996; McGuire 1996; Schortman and Urban 1996; R. T. Alexander 1999; Feinman 1999; Kuznar 1999), Mesopotamia (M. J. Allen 1992; Stein 1999; Ekholm-Friedman 2000), Egypt (Warburton 2000), Europe and the Mediterranean (A. Sherratt 1993; 2000), and the Bronze and Iron Age Aegean (Kardulias 1999a; I. Morris 1999).

5. Regarding the eastern Mediterranean region, Andrew and E. Susan Sherratt have produced some of the most relevant and significant studies regarding systemic relations during the thirteenth and twelfth centuries in the Levant. See, e.g., A. Sherratt 1994; 2000; E. S. Sherratt 1994; 1998; 2000; 2003; Sherratt and Sherratt 1991; 1998.

6. Mainland Greece, particularly the region of the Argolid, is often identified with Ahhiyawa in the Hittite texts based on the equation Ahhiyawa = Achaians; see n. 12 below for a detailed discussion.

7. Cyprus or Enkomi is usually identified with Alashiya in the Hittite texts (see Gütterbock 1967, 73–81; Holmes 1971, 426–29; Muhly 1972, 201–19; Georghiou 1979, 84–100; Karageorghis 1982, 66–68; Artzy, Perlman, and Asaro 1976, 171–82; Knapp 1985a; 1990c, cols. 795–800; however, Catling (1975, 201–4) casts serious doubts on the identification with Cyprus). Bass (1967, 78) and Merrillees (1992, 89–90; 1995, 17–22) prefer to place Alashiya along either the coast of north Syria or Cilicia. But most significant are recent petrographic provenience studies of several of the el-Amarna and Ugaritic clay documents dispatched from Alashiya. These analyses indicate that the origin of the clay used in the manufacture of these tablets is Cyprus, in the region of Alassa *Paliotaverna/Pano Manadilaris* or Kalavassos-*Ayios Dhimitrios* (Goren, Bunimovitz, Finkelstein, and Na'aman 2003, 233–55). Regarding the identification of *keftiu*, see Strange 1980, who suggests that Cyprus should be identified as *keftiu* rather than Crete in Egyptian texts (see also Vandersleyen 2003, who proposes an Asian location for *keftiu*).

8. For a discussion of these political structure and Late Bronze Age diplomacy, see Tadmor 1979, 1–14; Zaccagnini 1987, 57–65; Postgate 1992; and, more recently, Cohen and Westbrook 2000c, especially Cohen and Westbrook 2000a; 2000b; A. James 2000; Liverani 2000; Ragionieri 2000; Zaccagnini 2000.

9. For a discussion regarding the economic system during the second millennium and the relationship between core, periphery, and margin in the eastern Mediterranean, see A. Sherratt 1994, 335–45.

10. Excluding the Egyptian strongholds, see Knapp 1993, esp. pp. 81–84 regarding the possible affects of Egyptian control over local pottery production.

11. See Liverani 1987, 66–67. The designation *Canaan*, as used in contemporary ancient Mesopotamian and Egyptian texts and later biblical accounts, refers to a geographical place or region that roughly corresponds to the modern regions of Lebanon, Israel, West Bank, Gaza Strip, Jordan, and southern Syria. Here the term *Canaanites* will be used to refer to peoples living in the region of Canaan regardless of ethnic association or social class. See Nibbi 1989, 7–23; Schmitz 1992, 82–83; Hess 1989, 209–16; 1993, 127; Lemche 1993, 76–89; Na'aman 1994a, 397–418; for a summary of the biblical and linguistic evidence regarding the boundaries of Canaan and the multiethnic origins of the Canaanites, see Rainey 1996, 1–16; 2003, 169–72.

12. See, e.g., Andrews 1955, 1–19; Garstang and Gurney 1959, 81; Yakar 1976, 117–28; 1993, 7; Gütterbock 1983, 133–38; 1984, 114–22; 1986, 33–44; Mellink 1983, 138–41; Singer 1983b, 205–17; Bryce 1989, 297–311; Niemeier 1998; Mountjoy 1998; see also Gurney 1952, 55–56, who suggests Crete as ancient Ahhiyawa. However, scholars have also placed Ahhiyawa in the east Aegean or eastern Mediterranean, regions that demonstrated strong ties with Mycenaean Greece. These regions include the western coast of Anatolia and/or Rhodes (Furumark 1965, 109; Crossland 1971, 848 [Rhodes]; Macqueen 1968, 169–85; Houwink ten Cate 1973, 141–58; Zangger 1994; 1995; Gates 1995, 296; Mee 1998, 142–43; Karantzali 2001, 79–80 [Rhodes]), Cyprus (Schaeffer 1952, 1–10, 350–70), or along the southern coast of Anatolia (Wainwright 1939, 148–53; Košak 1980, 35–48; 1981, 12*–16*; Ünal 1989, 283–87) or Thrace (Mellaart 1968, 202; 1986, 79; 1993). For a discussion of relations between Achaeans and the Hittites, see Ünal 1991. For a detailed discussion of Ahhiyawa and its various identifications, see Niemeier 1998, esp. fig. 3.

13. Renfrew (1975, 12–22; 1979b, 115) and Schallin (1993, 173–87) argue that Mycenaean society should be seen as a consolidation of numerous small independent chiefdoms, or "early state modules" (but see P. M. Thomas 1995, 156–57, who is critical of this view). For recent treatments of the Mycenaean palace system, see Galaty and Parkinson 1999 and S. Morris 2003 (who interprets the Late Bronze Age Aegean as comprising a set of autonomous palatial polities whose main connection to the east was via luxury goods).

14. One of the most important sources of information regarding Late Helladic IIIB Greece is the Linear B texts. These texts speak of a *wanax*, or local ruler of a city, who supervised economic, military, and religious aspects of the palace (see Kilian 1988b, 291–302). A. and S. Sherratt (1991, 351–85) suggest that the structure of the Mycenaean palace economy resembled the Near East but functioned on a smaller scale (see also Heltzer 1988 who sees a similarity in the social and economic structures of these societies). See Rehak 1995 for a discussion of the role of the ruler in Bronze Age Greece.

15. For a recent detailed discussion of the changes that occurred in the Aegean and eastern Mediterranean at the end of the thirteenth and twelfth centuries B.C.E., see Karageorghis and Morris 2001.

16. Several interpretations regarding the nature of mainland Mycenaean influence in the Aegean have been suggested: (1) Mycenaeans as political overlords and colonists in the Aegean (see Desborough 1964, 219; for a discussion of this theory and additional bibliography, see Schallin 1993, 177–83); (2) Mycenaeans as the major economic power in the Aegean, controlling trade activities and establishing emporia (Furumark 1950; French 1986, 278; Mee 1988, 301–5; for a discussion of this approach, see Schallin 1993,177–83); and (3) Mycenaeans as a force who influenced local religious customs and aspects of material culture through "social interaction" (for a summary, see Schallin 1993, 172–77). For a recent summary of the archaeological evidence for the palatial Bronze Age in southern and central Greece and its significance, see Shelmerdine 1997, reprinted in 2001; for a general overview of mainland Greece and its "Mycenaean periphery," see Deger-Jalkotzy 1998.

17. See also Haggis 2001, 54, who proposes that these settlements represent the "assertion of local identity."

18. Regarding the significance of bronze on Cyprus at the end of the Late Bronze Age, see Muhly 1996; Pickles and Peltenburg 1998; E. S. Sherratt 2000.

19. See, e.g., Knapp 1983; Harding 1984, 230, 234–35, 256; Cline 1994, 60–63. For a recent reevaluation of the archaeological evidence, in particular with regard to the Mycenaean ceramic evidence, see van Wijngaarden 2002, 275–77.

20. Due to the persistent appearance of imported Mycenaean wares, scholars such as Karageorghis (1982, 78; 1992b, 137) have proposed that small numbers of Mycenaean Greeks already inhabited Cyprus in the fourteenth–thirteenth centuries, perhaps at *emporia* in the harbor towns of eastern and southern Cyprus. But see Holloway 1981, 55; Harding 1984, 234–35; and Schallin 1993, 189, who dispute this view and suggest that traded goods reached various centers, such as Cyprus, in the Mediterranean and from there were traded onward. For a comprehensive survey of the Mycenaean pottery on Cyprus, see van Wijngaarden 2002, 125–202.

21. See Sjöqvist 1940, 207–9, who claims that these "Achaeans" were of west Anatolian origin; see also Desborough 1964, 196–205; Dikaios 1969–71, 488, 523, 529; Åström 1972, 775–81; Karageorghis 1982, 82–83; 1984b; for the two-wave theory of Sea Peoples and Achaeans, see Karageorghis 1990a. For a discussion regarding the role of the Sea Peoples in Cyprus, see Muhly 1984.

22. At Maa-*Palaeokastro* the excavators (Karageorghis and Demas 1988, 265) suggest that there was either a joint enterprise between Cypriots and Mycenaeans or that the settlement of Mycenaeans was sanctioned by the Cypriots, who may have had strong military and mercantile inducements to accept them. Karageorghis (1992a, 83) proposes that the Mycenaeans, having lost control of the copper-supply centers of western Anatolia, might have sought new sources and that Cyprus may have been the obvious choice.

23. The origins of the concept of an "Achaean colonization" of Cyprus at the end of the thirteenth/early twelfth centuries B.C.E. can be traced to later Greek foundation legends. For a discussion of the problematic nature of attempts to correlate Homeric sources with the archaeological evidence, see Gjerstad 1944; Finley 1956; 1957; Blegen 1962; Snodgrass 1974; Luce 1975; Janko 1981; Easton 1985; M. Wood 1985; Mellink 1986; E. S.

Sherratt 1990; Crielaard 1995. Regarding the transmission of Greek foundation myths in earlier periods, and how they were used to mediate contact with the "other" and conceptualize group identity ("ethnicity") in the archaic and classical periods, see Malkin 1998. Most recently, see Burgess 2001, who argues that "essential elements of what became the myth of the Trojan War, began in the Bronze Age and developed as Greek tribes undertook a series of migrations in the Post-Mycenaean period" (Burgess 2001, 2; for the significance of the reference to Cypria, one of the poems in the Trojan War cycle, see 2001, 252 n. 117).

There are two major schools of thought regarding the origins of possible Achaean Mycenaean colonists on Cyprus: mainland Greece (e.g., Desborough 1964, 204; Karageorghis 1982, 86; Catling 1973; 1975, 207–9) or Anatolia (e.g. Furumark 1965, 110 [Greece via Cilicia]; Schachermeyr 1982, 92–93, 128). For a recent discussion of the archaeological evidence, see Karageorghis 2002, 71–113.

24. See Hult 1983; Negbi 1986; Kling 1987; Cook 1988; E. S. Sherratt 1991; Karageorghis 1987; 1990b, 17, 20. See also the recent excavations at Alassa: Hadjisavvas 1986; 1989; 1991; 1994 for a discussion of the transition from the Late Cypriot IIC to IIIA "without intruders."

25. Also see B. Fischer 2003 regarding the lack of clear indications of foreign settlers in the architectural elements of Late Cypriot IIIA sanctuaries. She suggests, rather, that the more monumental features of these sanctuaries represent a blending of local, Levantine, and Aegean features.

26. But see Peltenburg 1986, 168–71; Knapp 1990a, 114; 1990b, 76; and Zaccagnini 1990, 496–98, who propose that the political structure of Late Cypriot Cyprus was a palatial system similar to that in the Levant and perhaps the Aegean. Regarding the urbanization process, see Keswani 1996. In Knapp's (1997, 48) publication of Late Cypriot society based on the study of settlement, survey, and landscape, he proposes a fourfold settlement hierarchical system comprised of primary (urban) centers, secondary (town) centers, tertiary sanctuary sites, and peripheral agricultural and mining villages. He concludes (1997, 68–69) that, following the widespread crisis in the eastern Mediterranean, demand for copper dropped, which destabilized the interlinked hierarchical settlement system. The initial result was a strengthening of centralized authority at a few key centers (see E. S. Sherratt 1992, 326–28) or the development of a lively system of coastal raiding and thriving maritime trade (Knapp 1997, 69).

27. For a detailed analysis of the mixed archaeological record regarding transition between the thirteenth and twelfth centuries B.C.E. on Cyprus, see Iacovou forthcoming; but see V. Karageorghis's (2002, 71–113) most recent treatment of this transitional period, which continues to supports a clear-cut transition from LCIIC to LCIIIA marked by the arrival of Mycenaean Greek colonists to Cyprus.

28. See Karageorghis 1984a and Stieglitz 1972–75 and 1977 regarding several examples that illustrate similarities between Cypriot Late Cypriot IIIA and Philistine material culture.

29. See Goldman 1956, 206; French 1975, 55. According to Goldman 1956, 203–9, the end of the Late Bronze II was characterized by poverty and a decline in the material culture. The ceramic assemblage includes red and brown burnished wares, some of which are quite different from the classic Hittite repertoire. Large quantities of Cypriot pottery found at the site seem to have been both locally produced and imported (Yakar 1993, 14–15). The Late Bronze settlement was destroyed at the end of the thirteenth century B.C.E.

30. Desborough 1964, 154–56; Benzi 1988, 262; C. F. Macdonald 1986; 1988, 262; however, see Mee 1982, 89–90, who suggests without supporting evidence that Ialysos was destroyed at the end of the Late Helladic IIIB period.

31. See Weickert 1957; 1959–60; Desborough 1964, 161–63; Gödecken 1988, 307; Niemeier 1998.

32. See Latacz 2001 for a summary and Easton, Hawkins, Sherratt, and Sherratt 2002 for a critique and analysis of Korfmann's excavations at Troy and recent bibliography.

33. Most scholars in the past have adopted this viewpoint; see, e.g., Albright 1960, 101; de Vaux 1978, 120; Kenyon 1979, 199–200; Knapp 1987, 1–30. However, more recently, see Bienkowski 1989, 59–63, who claims that Canaanite sites under Egyptian control experienced prosperity, and Liebowitz 1987, 3–24, who asserts that the Late Bronze II period represents a highpoint in cultural and material development.

34. For a general discussion, see Ahituv 1978, 93–105; Kemp 1978, 7–75; Naʾaman 1981, 172–85; Weinstein 1981, 1–28; 1992, 142–50; Redford 1990; Bunimovitz 1993, 444, 448–49.

35. For recent surveys of trade relations in the eastern Mediterranean region, see Knapp 1985b, 1–11; Bass 1991, 69–82; Sherratt and Sherratt 1991, 351–86; Cline 1994; Karageorghis 1996, 61–70. Regarding the archaeological evidence for organic products traded during the Late Bronze II period, see Knapp 1991, 21–68; Haldane 1992, 348–60; Negbi and Negbi 1993, 320–29.

36. For a general overview of settlement patterns during the Late Bronze Age, see Gonen 1984, 61–73; regarding specific examples, see, e.g., Tel Miqne-Ekron (Gittlin 1992, 50–53; Killebrew 1996b, 26–27), Tel Batash, and Gezer (A. Mazar 1989, 65–66). Settlement patterns are discussed in detail in chs. 3–5.

37. See Gonen 1984 for a summary; more recently, Finkelstein 1994a, 173–75. Regarding the "shifting frontiers" of this period, see Bunimovitz 1994b. This theory states that, during the time of the breakdown of centralized control (e.g., LB I–IIA), the frontier "slid" down into the lowlands. During times of stronger centralized control (e.g., LB IIB), the pastoralists were pushed back into the hill country (see Finkelstein 1991, 54–55, for a critique of this theory). Naʾaman (1994b, 233) has suggested that the gradual increase in the number of small settlements during the Late Bronze IIA–B periods should be attributed in part to the integration of nomadic elements into the Canaanite city-state system. See chs. 3 and 4 below.

38. Regarding the importance of the Amarna letters in reconstructing the Canaanite sociopolitical background and Egyptian-Canaanite relations, see Albright 1975a; Liverani 1983; Moran 1995; see also ch. 2 below.

39. S. Bunimovitz (1993, 445) has characterized Canaan during this period as comprising a cluster of semiautonomous city-states in the coastal plain and lowland regions, while the central hill country seems to have been more integrated with larger territorial polities.

40. Census lists from Alalakh mention an armed thief, two charioteers, two beggars, and a priest of Ishtar as members of an *ʿapîru* band (Redford 1992b, 195).

41. Boğazköy, Alaca Höyük, Alishar, and Masat Höyük all were destroyed by a massive conflagration at the end of the thirteenth–early twelfth centuries B.C.E. For a summary of these destruction layers, see Bittel 1983; regarding Boğazköy, Hoffner 1992. See Singer 1987, 2000, regarding the end of the Hittite Empire.

42. See Peregrine 1999 for a theoretical discussion of other examples of the collapse of prestige-based systems.

43. See Akurgal 1983, 70–72; T. Dothan 1982, 289–96; Åström 1985; G. A. Lehmann 1985, 39–49; Yon 1992a, 117.

44. Although this theory is still accepted by many historians, the idea of a Phrygian migration from Europe to Asia Minor at the end of the Bronze Age has been generally abandoned by Anatolian archaeologists. There is no evidence of any newcomers after the destruction of Hittite sites. It is less clear in western Anatolia, where it is difficult to prove, based on the discovery of a few sherds of "barbarian ware" found at Troy VIIb2 and a Gordion, that a Phrygian invasion from the Balkans was responsible for the catastrophe in western Anatolia. At most, the sherds may indicate that immigrants from Europe squatted in the ruins of Troy following the catastrophe (Sams 1992, 58).

45. Based on ancient Greek sources, a number of scholars in the past have associated the destruction and abandonment of many Mycenaean settlements in the Peloponnese at the transition from Late Helladic IIIB to IIIC with an early twelfth-century B.C.E. Dorian

invasion originating from the central Balkans (e.g., Skeat 1932; Desborough 1972; van Soesbergen 1981; Eder 1990 regarding a Dorian invasion; see also Ålin 1977, who proposes that Mycenaean centers were destroyed by external human agents). However, as early as the mid-1970s many scholars questioned a Dorian invasion, suggesting other reasons for the decline of Mycenaean states in the Peloponnese (see Tritsch 1973, who questions great movements of peoples or Dorian invasions at this time and suggests instead that there were small groups of "sackers of cities"; see, e.g., Chadwick 1976, who proposed revolt by the lower classes; see also Snodgrass 1971). Iron I innovations that were once attributed to these Dorian invaders from the Balkans—geometric pottery, cremation burials, and iron working—have been redated to well after 1200 and do not originate from the Balkans. Several artifacts associated with the end of the Bronze Age have been attributed to external invading groups, including handmade burnished ("barbarian") ware, which appears early in the twelfth century B.C.E. (Rutter 1975; French and Rutter 1977; Catling and Catling 1981; Deger-Jalkotzy 1983, 161–68; Bankoff and Winter 1984; Bankoff, Meyer, and Stefanovich 1996; Harding 1984, 216–27; Bloedow 1985; Genz 1997; "barbarian ware" has also been found at Lefkandi, Asia Minor, and Cyprus: Todd 1991, 548; at Tiryns it appears as early as the LH IIIB period: Podzuweit 1982, 69; regarding an indigenous development for "barbarian ware," see Walberg 1976; Sandars 1985, 191–92; Snodgrass 1983; for a summary of various theories, see Small 1990; regarding barbarian ware found in Cyprus, see Karageorghis 1986). Other artifacts that in the past have often been associated with a Dorian invasion include violin-bow fibulae (Desborough 1964, 54–58, proposes that they were a result of trade and later imitated), the Naue Type II sword (Catling 1961, 121, who claims that because these were found in "Greek" tombs during the LH IIIC period these swords in fact arrived in Greece via mercenaries who joined the service of Helladic kingdoms or communities; Drews 1993, 63–65; see Coulson 1990, 14–16, who explains these similarities as a result of trade or parallel development). Wells (1992) suggests that there does seem to be movements of small groups from the Balkans into Greece; however, it is unlikely that these "northerners" were responsible for the Mediterranean palace destructions.

46. See Drews 1993, 48–61, for a detailed discussion of this theory and Silberman 1998 for a discussion of the "migration theory" as reflecting nineteenth-century Victorian period social perceptions of colonial migration and expansion. In addition to the Medinet Habu relief, recent textual evidence provides a strong case for the weakening of Hittite power and hostile attacks from the outside. The Sudburg hieroglyphic inscription of Suppiluliuma II mentions his conquest of southwestern Anatolian provinces, including Lukka, Masa, Ikuna, and Tarhuntassa (Neve 1989; Hawkins 1990; 1994; Hoffner 1992). The 1986 discovery of a bronze tablet at Boğazköy documents a treaty between the Hittite king Tudhaliya IV and his cousin, Jurunta, the king of a Hittite subkingdom at Tahuntassa in southern Anatolia. This may indicate already a weakening of the position of the great Hittite king in Hattuša (Hawkins 1994).

47. Archaeological excavations at Ugarit have uncovered a catastrophic destruction dated to the early twelfth century B.C.E., during which the ancient city was pillaged and abandoned. It has been suggested that this conflagration of Ugarit is related to the destruction of Hattuša, the Hittite capital. With its destruction, the political and social structures vanished, and there was no longer a settlement at this spot (Yon 1992a, 111; 1992b). However, several of Ugarit's satellite cities, such as Ras Ibn Hani and Ras Bassit, continued to be occupied, albeit on a reduced scale (Caubet 1992).

Especially noteworthy are several letters from Ugarit that refer to enemies who had previously attacked Ammurapi, king of Ugarit, and tell how to prepare for an expected attack. The king of Ugarit writes of the destruction of several settlements while his troops are occupied in Hatti and Lukka land. All these texts convey an urgent sense of impending disaster in Ugarit (Astour 1965a; Klengel 1974; 1992, 149–51; Tadmor 1979, 6–7; Yakar 1993, 4–5).

48. See Schaeffer 1968, 753–68; Klengel 1992, 151, who supports this view; however, G. A. Lehmann (1970, 40) and Yon, Caubet, and Mallet (1982, 170) reject Schaeffer's earthquake theory at Ugarit. See also Bittel 1983, 26, who does not accept an earthquake as responsible for the destruction of Hattuša.

49. See Blegen, Caskey, and Rawson 1953, 330–32. This view was later accepted by most scholars (e.g., Podzuweit 1982, 82), but Easton (1985) finds little physical evidence for an earthquake.

50. See Iakovidis 1977, 134, 140; French 1996; 1998, 4. See also Maroukian, Gaki-Papanastassiou, and Papanastassiou 1996. However, note that Taylour (1981, 10; 1983) does not mention the possibility of an earthquake as the cause of the major destruction at Mycenae.

51. For a recent publication dealing with evidence throughout the eastern Mediterranean, see Stiros and Jones 1996.

52. For proponents of the idea that droughts resulted in the collapse of complex states, see B. Bell 1971, who attributes the "dark ages" in the ancient Near East to droughts due to climatic changes; see also Bryson, Lamb, and Donley 1974, 46; Stiebing 1980; and Neumann and Parpola 1987; but see Dickinson 1974, 228–29, and H. E. Wright 1968, 125, who disagree with this interpretation.

53. See Strobel 1976, 173–74; Weiss 1982, 172–98; Shrimpton 1987, 142; Gorny 1989; Na᾽aman 1994b, 243–44; see also Schaeffer 1968, 760–62, who suggests that a drought preceded the earthquakes responsible for the ultimate destruction of these centers.

54. Key evidence regarding the final days of Ugarit and Hattuša is revealed in the so-called "letters from the oven," tablets found in the Late Bronze Age palace of Ugarit. These texts were initially interpreted as having been placed in a baking oven immediately preceding the destruction and abandonment of the city; however, this has been refuted (e.g., Singer 1999, 705). In any case, these letters most likely do date to the final years of Ugarit and reflect a state of emergency in the Hittite kingdom (for a selection of the vast literature written on Ugaritic texts, the "letters from the oven," and its significance for Canaan, see Astour 1965a; 1970; 1972; 1981; Linder 1981; Freu 1988; Pardee and Bordreuil 1992). The desperate state of affairs described in the tablets includes pleas for the transport of much-needed grain, perhaps indicating serious food shortages and famine in Hatti (for a summary of sources related to possible famine, see Wainwright 1959; 1960; Klengel 1974; for the possible implications regarding the end of the Hittite Empire, see Singer 1985a, 122–23).

An additional letter documenting the transport of grain to Hatti from Canaan via Ugarit was discovered at Aphek, the only letter from Ugarit found outside the kingdom. This important text, dealing with a transaction of wheat between Jaffa and Ugarit, provides additional clues to a possible state of famine in Anatolia during the final years of the Hittite Empire (Owen 1981; Singer 1983a). However, see Drews 1993, 81–83, who argues against such an interpretation.

55. See, e.g., Stiebing 1989, 183–84, who cites evidence for such an occurrence; but see Liverani 1968, who refers to evidence for a colder and wetter climate.

56. See G. E. Wright 1939, 458–63; Snodgrass 1964; 1982; 1989; Waldbaum 1978; regarding the appearance of iron, see Wertime and Muhly 1980; Muhly, Maddin, Stech, and Özgen 1985; Åström, Maddin, Muhly, and Stech 1986; E. S. Sherratt 1994; 2003, 40–44.

57. Regarding the techniques of destruction, see D. H. Gordon 1953; but see Liverani 1994 for a critical review of Drews's theory.

58. See Flannery 1972 for a discussion of this evolutionary model of collapse; Renfrew 1978; 1979a, 1979c; 1984 for his development of a mathematical approach to internal collapse referred to as a "catastrophe theory"; Butzer 1980 regarding the "metastable equilibriums" as a tool for interpreting social change and collapse; and Yoffee 1988, 8–11, for a discussion of these theories.

59. See Betancourt 1976, 42–44; Chadwick 1976; Sandars 1985, 197–202; Knapp 1986, 99; Strange 1987, 1–19; Liverani 1987, 69; 1988, 629–30; Portugali 1994.

60. See, e.g., Zaccagnini 1990. The pirates or raiders theory has traditionally been assigned a secondary role in the collapse of Late Bronze II palace system as the outcome of a socioeconomic breakdown, usually combined with the other causes mentioned above. Pirates and raiders often appear in many of the suggested scenarios (see Sandars 1964, 258–62; 1985, 186–89; Knapp 1986, 98–99; Merrillees 1992, 90–91; in combination with migrating peoples, see Ormerod 1967, 86–88; Casson 1959, 31–36). R. Drews (1993, 93–96) adds a new twist to the raiders theory, combining it with the technological innovation theory. According to him, raiders were responsible for the "catastrophe," as he refers to it, but the reason the raiders suddenly enjoyed such success against the eastern kingdoms was due to an innovation in warfare that utilized infantry brandishing swords and javelins, combined with guerilla tactics.

61. However, the theory of systems collapse also has its flaws. For example, tablets dating to the final days of Ugarit and Pylos indicate that it was business as usual when the disaster struck, showing no signs of a systems collapse (Drews 1993, 89–90; Yon 1992a, 114: Ugarit was "frozen by its destruction, in a state reflection a rich and prosperous society, not a decadent and impoverished one").

62. Finkelstein 1995b, 354; see also Bunimovitz 1989; 1994b; 1995. Although Finkelstein does not explicitly state it, the theoretical underpinnings of his approach lay in Annales and systems perspectives on long-term historical cycles. See also Gills and Frank 1992; Frank and Gills 1993; and especially Frank's 1993 analysis of Bronze Age Near Eastern world-systems economic cycles and his critique of this overly simplistic approach to cyclical historical reconstructions in the ancient Near East (405–29).

63. See, e.g., Cowgill 1988, 256, who points out that real "collapse" is a rare occurrence in antiquity. Rather, several parallel phenomena can result, including the political fragmentation of a system into numerous smaller autonomous units or, in contrast, the breakdown of society without political fragmentation. Alternatively, it is possible that large states can fragment without resulting in severe social disruption (see also Yoffee 1988, 14–15).

64. For a comprehensive discussion of complex societies and various approaches to reconstruct past societies and reasons for cultural change, see Paynter 1989.

65. See, e.g., R. E. Jones 1986. Several corpora present extensive lists of Mycenaean, Cypriot, and Canaanite objects of trade found throughout the Aegean and eastern Mediterranean. These include detailed catalogues and synthetic studies of the implications of the evidence of finds. Early studies of the exchange of products, objects, styles, and concepts include Kantor's classic 1947 study. Several studies compile the distribution of Late Helladic IIIB–C Mycenaean pottery throughout the eastern Mediterranean (e.g., Hankey 1967; Leonard 1994). Cline's 1994 catalogue presents a detailed list of imports between the Aegean and the Near East (see also Cline 1995). The imports reached their greatest numbers in the thirteenth century B.C.E., with a rapid decrease in quantities by the early twelfth century B.C.E.

66. For a discussion of the various views regarding possible Late Bronze Age trade routes in the eastern Mediterranean, see Cline 1994, 91–94; Artzy 1997. One of the more significant discoveries during the past few decades is of a Late Bronze II trading center on Bates Island at Marsa Matruh (for a presentation and analysis of the evidence, see D. White 2002a, esp. 35–84; 2002b).

67. See Sherratt and Sherratt 1998, 339–41; Knapp 2000; for an opposing view, see Gale 2001. See also Karageorghis and Kassianidou 1999 and especially E. S. Sherratt 2003, 40–44, for a summary and recent bibliographic references.

68. As pointed out by Sherratt and Sherratt 1998, 337: "the language of 'core' and 'periphery' may suggest an active role for the former and a passive one for the latter; yet the relation between them was creative and dialectical. If cores create peripheries, peripheries also create cores: this conception is radically different from simplistic diffusionism."

2
Egypt in Canaan: Empire and Imperialism in the Late Bronze Age

As a major center of power in the eastern Mediterranean, New Kingdom Egypt's influential role in international affairs during the final centuries of the Bronze Age is undisputed. What remains contested is the nature and impact of Egypt's domination over the peripheral region of Canaan. Numerous New Kingdom texts attest to ongoing Egyptian economic interests in the region and describe military campaigns to curb uprisings and suppress rebellious Canaanite rulers. In spite of the wealth of textual evidence, the significance of Egyptian-style artifacts found in the southern Levant remains a topic of lively debate and speculation. To explain these artifacts, scholars have turned to theories ranging from colonialism to direct or indirect imperialistic activities to elite emulation.

As presented in this chapter, both the textual and archaeological records provide indisputable evidence of an Egyptian imperialistic policy in Canaan. Locally produced Egyptian-style domestic and utilitarian pottery, a largely neglected area of research, is highlighted below. The ceramics, considered with other elements of the material culture, including Egyptian architectural traditions at specific sites, indicate Egyptian presence probably in the form of officials and/or military personnel in Canaan rather than less-direct elite emulation of foreign wares. The clearly demarcated social and cultural boundaries evidenced at documented Egyptian strongholds in Canaan during the thirteenth and twelfth centuries B.C.E. present an ideal material culture case study of the manifestation of imperialism in the archaeological record (see fig. 2.1).

The relative homogeneity of Canaanite culture, which was clearly on the periphery of the Egyptian center, was a result of Egyptian imperialistic policy in Canaan and the region's role during the age of internationalism. The decline and ultimate breakdown of Egyptian imperial policy in the southern Levant left a power vacuum in the region that resulted in the cultural fragmentation, the successful migration and colonization of the southern coastal plain of Canaan by the Philistines, and the emergence of Israel.

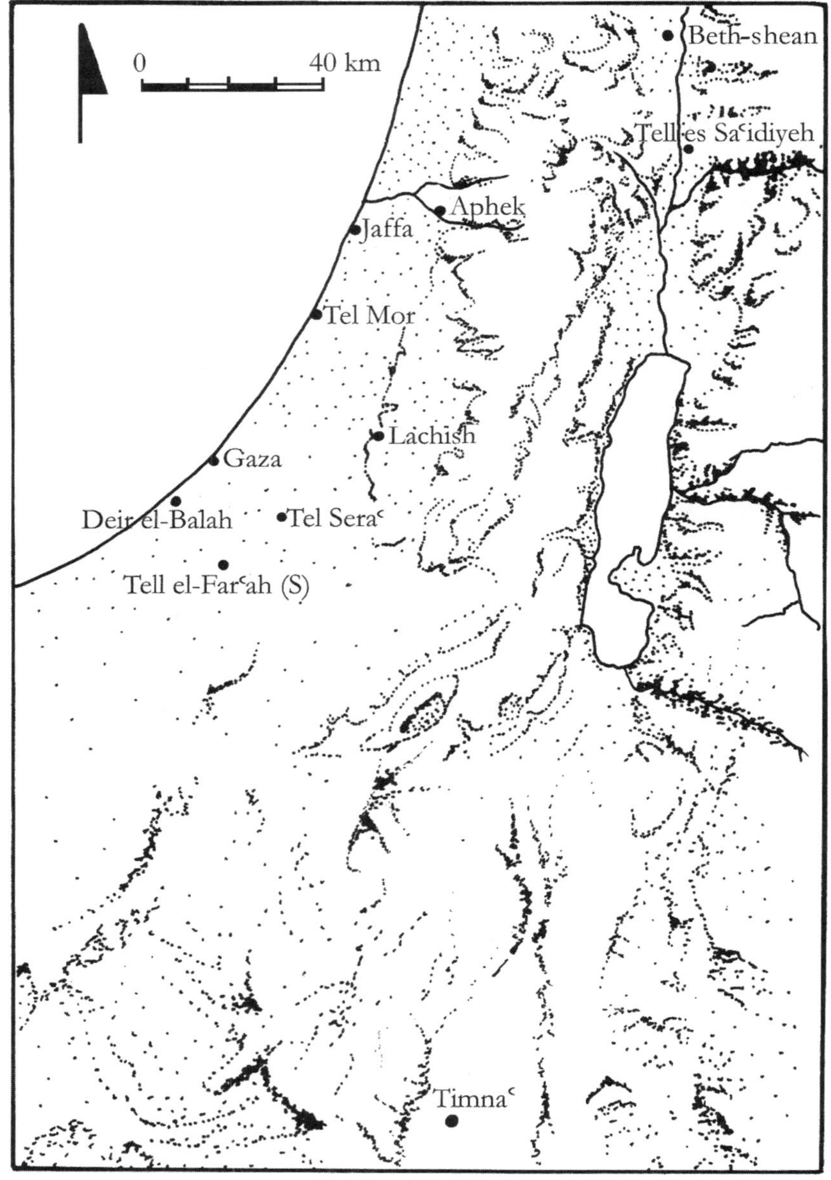

Fig. 2.1. Map of Major Sites with Egyptian-Style Material Culture

Colonialism, Imperialism, and Elite Emulation: A Definition of Terms

The concepts *colonialism* and *imperialism* remain poorly understood in the scholarly literature. No definition suits all perspectives, and one risks the dangers of reductionism, oversimplification, or the imposition of modern notions of these terms on the past. The definitions proposed here provide a general framework for discussing the fluid and complex series of economic, political, and ideological interrelationships between Egypt and Canaan during the Nineteenth and Twentieth Dynasties. Attempts to apply modern terminology and conceptual frameworks to the past are further complicated by the fact that no word existed for "imperialism" or "empire" in the ancient Egyptian vocabulary (Kemp 1978, 7).

Although a vast body of literature exists regarding colonialism and imperialism in its modern context, far less attention has been given to these phenomena in premodern periods of history.[1] My point of departure is Ronald J. Horvath's 1972 article entitled "A Definition of Colonialism."[2] Horvath defines colonialism as "that form of intergroup domination in which settlers in significant number migrate permanently to the colony from the colonizing power" (1972, 50; for a detailed discussion of colonialism, see ch. 5 below). Imperialism, on the other hand, is a result of intergroup domination in which few, if any, permanent settlers from the imperial homeland migrate to the peripheral colony. Horvath further subdivides imperialism into two categories: (1) administrative imperialism, a form of intergroup domination in which formal (direct) controls over the affairs of the colony exist through a resident imperial administrative apparatus; and (2) informal imperialism, a type of intergroup domination in which formal administrative controls are absent and power is channeled through a local elite. Horvath considers this latter type of imperialism synonymous with neocolonialism, semicolonialism, and economic imperialism—what is referred to below as "elite emulation."

Carolyn Higginbotham (1996; 1998; 2000, 6–7) challenges the view that Egyptian policy in western Asia represents imperialism, or what she terms "direct rule." While recognizing that Egyptians were stationed at sites such as Beth-shean, Deir el-Balah, Gaza, and Jaffa (Higginbotham 1996, 164), she rules out Egyptian imperialism as she defines it as a major political force in Canaan. Rather, she proposes that Egyptian intervention was less direct and that the physical remains of Egyptian-style material culture in Canaan can be best characterized as *elite emulation*. The theory of elite emulation, closely related to studies of core-periphery interaction,[3] argues that the peripheries of prestigious cultures sometimes derive a legitimating function from the core cultures. Similar in concept to Horvath's "informal imperialism," elite emulation can be characterized as the adaptation and adoption of elements of the "great civilization" by local elites and their communities. Symbolically this "iconography of power" transfers some of the prestige of the core region to local rulers in the periphery.[4] According to Higginbotham (2000, 8–9), local elites in Canaan depended on an external polity, Egypt, for their access to power. In this scenario, local princes, impressed by Egypt's military and political power and Egypt's role as a center of civilization, emulated Egyptian culture as a means of enhancing their stature.[5]

Higginbotham (2000, 10–12) defines the material manifestations of direct rule (which she also refers to as "imperialism") as comprising Egyptian-style architecture that is indistinguishable from that in the Nile Valley; Egyptian-style artifacts for domestic as well as prestige goods; Egyptian-style objects that appear in domestic as well as funerary and ritual contexts; and an uneven distribution of Egyptian-style material at sites. The closest parallel for the direct-rule model is the Egyptian expansion into Nubia, which is evidenced by the construction of a series of Egyptian-style fortresses and temples at selected locations.[6]

Elite emulation is a second type of core domination over a periphery, one characterized by the lack of Egyptian settlements, modified Egyptian-style architecture, artifacts with combined or hybrid Egyptian and Canaanite features, Egyptian-style artifacts mainly as prestige goods or imported transport vessels and found mostly in funerary and ritual contexts, and a decline in the number of Egyptian-style objects as distance from Egypt increases (Higginbotham 2000, 14–16). In Higginbotham's opinion, the textual and material culture evidence from Canaan points to elite emulation. However based on Higginbotham's (2000) archaeological presentation and the summary below, criteria for elite emulation such as hybrid Egyptian and Canaanite features do not appear in Late Bronze II assemblages. Also lacking is a correlation between the number of Egyptian-style objects at sites in Canaan and their distance from Egypt (see also Hasel 1998, 109).

Although both models (direct rule and elite emulation) are instructive, the data presented in this study show that neither model accurately reflects the nature of Egyptian-Canaanite relations. There are also difficulties in comparing evidence from Canaan with that from Nubia. The latter was a marginal region during the New Kingdom, and Egypt's intentions and goals with respect to Nubia differed from those in Canaan. Egyptian activity in Nubia was not as imperialistic in nature as it was in Canaan, and it more closely fits the pattern of colonization (or direct rule), as manifested by the establishment of Egyptian settlements there. Urbanized Canaan presented a very different challenge to Egypt and, unlike Nubia, was integrated into the world-system of the fourteenth and thirteenth centuries B.C.E. Although I am in general agreement with Higginbotham's summary of the textual and archaeological evidence, I contest her definition of imperialism, which she confuses with direct rule, and her understanding of the physical manifestation of elite emulation in the material-culture record. Egyptian domination of Canaan was neither by direct rule nor by elite emulation, as the evidence discussed below demonstrates. Following Horvath's definition and based on the textual and archaeological evidence, particularly the ceramic repertoire, one should define the Egyptian presence in Canaan throughout much of the New Kingdom period as "formal" or "administrative" imperialism.

The View from Egypt: The Textual Evidence

New Kingdom Egypt has produced a considerable body of textual evidence and reliefs devoted to the Egyptian conquest and subjugation of western Asia.[7] During the Eighteenth Dynasty at least two dozen campaigns to this region are recorded (for a discussion of Egypt's foreign policy, see Redford 1992b, 140–77; Hoffmeier 2004; Morris 2005, 41–56, 142–77, 276–93). These Egyptian texts provide valuable information regarding Egypt's military activities and, less directly, administrative activities in Canaan. The single most important source for understanding the socioeconomic and political structure of Canaan is the Eighteenth Dynasty Amarna letters. Of the 382 known tablets, over forty record correspondence between Egypt and powers of equal status (Babylonia, Assyria, Mitanni, Arzawa, Alashiya, and Hatti). The rest of the tablets in the archive are letters between Egypt and her vassals in Canaan. These documents provide invaluable insights on relations between Egypt and Canaan during the mid-fourteenth century B.C.E.[8]

Continued military campaigns in western Asia characterize Egypt during the Nineteenth and Twentieth Dynasties. In the early thirteenth century, for example, Seti I conducted several major military campaigns to the southern Levant. These are celebrated on the walls of the Great Hypostyle Hall at Karnak and the victory stelae recovered most notably from Beth-shean[9] as well as on several poorly preserved stelae from Tell es-Shihab, Tell Nebi Mend, and Tyre and toponym lists (see Kitchen 1975, 6–32; Hasel 1998, 150; Higginbotham 2000, 19–28). Seti I, according to the textual evidence, focused at least two of his campaigns on Palestine (Spalinger 1979; Broadhurst 1989; Murnane 1990; see Hasel 1998, 119–24; Morris 2005, 402–47).

Seti I's son, the prolific Ramesses II, actively campaigned in western Asia, especially in Syria. He conducted at least six military campaigns in the Levant, including his most famous battle against the Hittites at Kadesh and campaigns to Phoenicia, northern Galilee, and Syria, one of which was celebrated on the Beth-shean Year 18 stela.[10] Other texts dated to the reign of Ramesses II that provide important information about the administration of Canaan include the Battle of Kadesh accounts (Kitchen 1979, 102–24; Goedicke 1985a; 1985b; Broadhurst 1992; Spalinger 2003); the Aphek letter (Owen 1981); a relief from the forecourt of the Luxor temple (Porter and Moss 1960, 2:308); several stelae, statues, and inscribed objects that mention various Egyptian officials and royal envoys (see Higginbotham 2000, 39–41, for a summary); and additional information found in the royal correspondence between Egypt and Hatti (Higginbotham 2000, 41–44; for a recent summary, see Morris 2005, 447–75). Several inscribed architectural elements from Jaffa (Kaplan 1972, 79, fig. 8) and other inscribed objects in Canaan provide tangible evidence for Egyptian activities at these sites (see Higginbotham 2000, 44–46, for a summary).

From Merneptah's reign, the concluding hymnic-poetic unit of the Israel Stela refers to possible military activities in Canaan between years 2 and 5 of his reign (see below, ch. 4). Based on the text of the stela alone, however, scholars are divided as to whether Merneptah actually campaigned in Canaan, with the majority accepting the historicity of the account.[11] In any event, any benefits from Merneptah's punitive campaign to quell the rebellious elements in the southern Levant were short-lived. One text, Papyrus Anastasi III, provides insight on the duel system of administration comprising both the local princes and Egyptian officials in Canaan under Merneptah (Higginbotham 2000, 48–50).

After Merneptah's death, his successors, Seti II and Tewosret, were preoccupied with internal matters and were thus unable to contain the mounting instability on Egypt's Asiatic frontier. There is no evidence of military campaigns in Canaan during their reigns. An additional text from the reign of Seti II, the Michaelides 85 ostracon, which is a copy of a letter from the scribe of a garrison reporting to his commander, suggests that a system of circuit officials existed in Canaan during the closing years of the Nineteenth Dynasty (Bakir 1970, 41–42; Higginbotham 2000, 50–52; for a detailed discussion, see Morris 2005, 475–504).

Nearly a decade later, Ramesses III ascended to the throne. At this time, the early twelfth century, the Egyptian pharaoh faced a deteriorating situation in the eastern Mediterranean region. Egypt stood alone as the major imperial power in the region, and Ramesses III's most famous military encounters involved the Sea Peoples. Those of the eighth year of his reign appear on the walls of his mortuary temple at Medinet Habu (Kitchen 1983, 37–43; see below, ch. 5),[12] while the report of a second battle, a campaign against Libya in the fifth year of his reign, also includes a section mentioning the Sea Peoples. Papyrus Harris I, recorded after Ramesses III's death, documents the aftermath of his encounter with the Sea Peoples (Breasted 1927, 87–92; Edgerton and Wilson 1936, 35) and also offers our clearest description of an Egyptian temple in Canaan during the Ramesside period (Higginbotham 2000, 56–59; for a detailed analysis, see Morris 2005, 690–710).

Several perspectives regarding the nature of Egyptian domination in Canaan have emerged. Wolfgang Helck, Barry Kemp, and Donald Redford all rely heavily on the evidence of the Amarna letters but do not always agree regarding their interpretation. Helck (1971, 246–55) reconstructs a tripartite division of the New Kingdom empire in the Levant consisting of three provinces—Amurru, Upe, and Canaan—each with an Egyptian overseer and often with stationed garrison troops, all of whom reported directly to the Egyptian king (see also Kitchen 1969, 81; Moran 1992, xxvi n. 70). Kemp (1978, 45–48) reaches similar conclusions. Like Helck, Kemp concludes that three provinces (Amurru, Upe, and Canaan) were under varying degrees of Egyptian hegemony, each area with one city where an Egyptian representative resided. Although the hieroglyphic sources reveal little about imperial organization, considerable detail emerges from the Amarna letters. Egyptian-appointed commissioners guaranteed a smooth flow of tribute and loyalty, and there is evidence for small garrisons stationed at some places. Egyptian officials assessed tribute, which may imply a limited Egyptian bureaucracy in place in Canaan.

Donald Redford (1984, 4; 1992b, 201) proposes that Canaan was divided into four provinces with headquarters at Gaza, Megiddo/Beth-shean, Kumidi, and Ullaza/Sumur. According to Redford, however, these were not provinces in the conventional sense of the word. The customary Egyptian system of administration did not rely on long-term, resident administrators but rather on circuit officials, each of whom who made the rounds in a frontier zone or conquered territory (Redford 1990, 35).[13]

In summary, Nineteenth Dynasty textual and iconographic records indicate that Seti I, Ramesses II, and probably Merneptah all campaigned in the southern Levant and mention sites, geographical territories, and socioethnic groups in Canaan. As pointed out by Michael Hasel (1998, 118–93), however, there is little evidence, textual or iconographic, for wholesale conflagrations of Canaanite cities. In fact, the physical impact of Egyptian military activity on sites is less pronounced than is often indicated in the scholarly secondary literature. According to the textual and iconographic sources, the Egyptians apparently were not responsible for the wide-scale destructions occurring in the southern Levant during the Late Bronze/Early Iron Age transition. Rather, Hasel (1998, 92) suggests that Egyptian military action was carried out to reestablish *maat* ("truth, justice, order"), which could be ensured only by Egyptian dominance and imperialism over the region based on economic, political, and ideological concerns.

The View from Canaan: The Archaeological Evidence

A century of excavations in Palestine and Israel complements the corpus of Egyptian texts representing the Canaanite perspective on Egyptian domination.[14] The archaeological evidence can be divided into two categories: Egyptian-style architecture and Egyptian-style artifacts. In the discussion that follows, the latter group is further subdivided to focus on burial practices, inscriptional evidence, and Egyptian-style pottery appearing in Canaan.[15]

Egyptian-Style Architecture

In this brief overview, I follow Higginbotham's (2000, 263–301) treatment of Egyptian-style architecture in Late Bronze Age Canaan. She divides Egyptian-style architecture in Canaan into four main types: center-hall houses, three room houses, administrative buildings, and temples. Her typology, which forms the beginning point of my brief overview of Egyptian architecture below, takes into account both the architectural plan and well-known construction techniques that characterize Egyptian architecture in Egypt, such as mudbrick foundations and sand-filled foundation trenches (see also A. J. Spencer 1979, 120).

Center-hall houses are square structures consisting of a central room surrounded on three or four sides by smaller chambers. These buildings are often referred to as "residencies" in the archaeological literature.[16] They are most similar in plan to the elite-class houses excavated at Tell el-Amarna, which is the primary source for information about New Kingdom domestic architecture in Egypt (Ricke 1932, 21–23; Borchardt and Ricke 1980). A number of large mudbrick structures excavated in Canaan can be defined as center-hall houses. They include Building 1500 at Tel Beth-shean, the Area AA "residency" at Tell es-Saʿidiyeh, Building YR at Tell el-Farʿah (S), and Building 906 at Tel Seraʿ.

The University of Pennsylvania first excavated Building 1500 (see fig. 2.2), assigned to Level VI at Beth-shean (F. W. James 1966, 8–11), and Amihai Mazar (1993, 217–18; 1994a, 80; 2003a) recently reexamined this structure. An almost square building (ca. 23 x 22 m), it was constructed of mudbrick walls on stone foundations. The main room was also almost square, measuring 8.8 x 8.2 m, and featured two massive stone column bases in the Egyptian tradition (fig. 2.3). The central hall was surrounded by rooms on all four sides, similar in plan to New Kingdom houses in Egypt. The building's stone thresholds were T-shaped, a typical Egyptian architectural element. Several of the doorjambs were decorated with hieroglyphic dedicatory inscriptions, and one of the lintels bore the incised figure of Ramesses-weser-khepesh, apparently the military com-

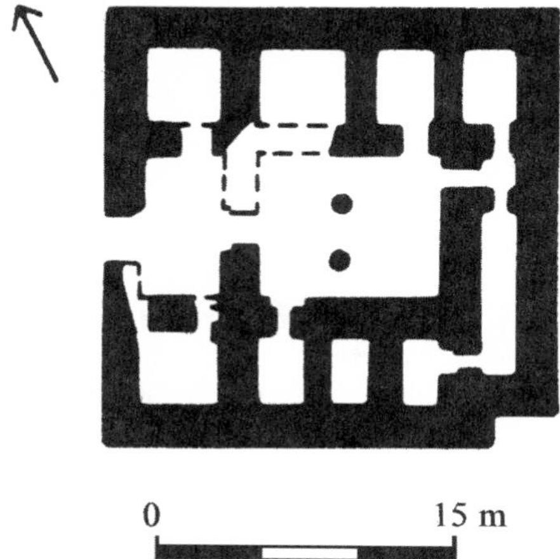

Fig. 2.2. Center-Hall House (Building 1500) at Beth-shean

Fig. 2.3. Interior of Building 1500 at Beth-shean

mander of the Egyptian center at Beth-shean during the reign of Ramesses III (Ward 1966, 161–79).

In Area AA (Stratum XII) of Tell es-Saᶜidiyeh, a building belonging to the center-hall style of house has been dated to the twelfth century B.C.E. (Tubb 1988a, 41). This monumental building utilized Egyptian construction techniques, including deep mudbrick foundations (Tubb 1990, 26; 1998, 82–84), and is similar in plan to structures excavated at Tell el-Farᶜah (S) and Tel Seraᶜ. It demonstrates the use of the typically Egyptian construction methods that characterize these buildings: deep brick foundations rather than the usual shallow stone ones; and brick dimensions that correspond to those found in New Kingdom buildings in the Delta.

One of the first buildings identified as an "Egyptian Residency of a governor" in Canaan (Petrie 1930, 17) was Building YR at Tell el-Farᶜah (S) (fig. 2.4). From the finds associated with this building it is possible to identify the function of some of the rooms, including a bedchamber, bathing room, and wine store (Macdonald, Starkey, and Harding 1932, 27–30, pl. LXIX). Several of its construction techniques, most notably the deep foundations, 1.5 to 2 m in depth and filled with a layer of sand, are typical of Egyptian building practices.

Building 906 at Tel Seraᶜ, a Stratum IX structure measuring approximately 22 by 22 m (fig. 2.5), dates to the twelfth century B.C.E. The plan consists of a pillared main living room (4 x 9 m) enclosed on all sides by auxiliary chambers, including a rectangular entry hall and staircase in the northeast corner (Oren 1984, 39, fig. 2). Egyptian building techniques are clearly evident in the mudbrick foundations that were laid in foundation trenches lined with sand and kurkar.[17]

The three-room house consists of a square main room in the front of the house and two small chambers at the back (Ricke 1932, 13–15; Higginbotham 2000, 281–82). This is the simplest and most basic house plan at Amarna. Thus far excavations have revealed only one site in Canaan, Beth-shean, with three-room houses during the LB IIB–Iron IA period Palestine (James and McGovern 1993, 27).

Administrative buildings have been referred to in scholarly literature as palaces, forts, *migdol*s,[18] or governor's residencies. These structures share several features. First, they are square in size, with small symmetrically arranged chambers, often with a staircase, and most include buttresses or corner towers (Higginbotham 2000, 284–90). It is not entirely clear, however, whether these administrative buildings are of Egyptian derivation. Their Egyptian-style features include buttresses, corner towers, a square plan, and construction techniques such as brick foundations and sand-filled foundations. On the other hand, there are no close parallels to these structures in New Kingdom Egypt or Nubia. As has been pointed out by

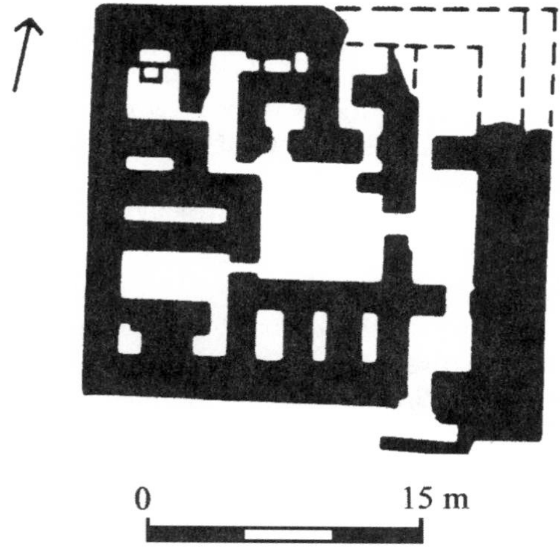

Fig. 2.4. Center-Hall House at Tell el-Farʿah (S)

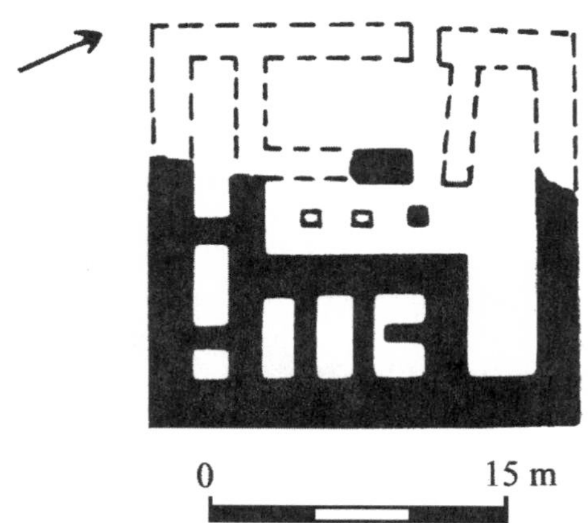

Fig. 2.5. Center-Hall House at Tel Seraʿ

Oren (1987) and Oren and Shershevsky (1989, 15–18), these buildings differ markedly from New Kingdom forts in the Nile Valley and north Sinai. Fortresses in Egypt, Nubia, and North Sinai were monumental, while the administrative buildings in Canaan are more modest in size, with dimensions similar to the center-hall houses (regarding fortresses in Sinai, see, e.g., the recent excavations at Tell Heboua [Abd el-Maksoud 1998] and Tell el-Borg [Hoffmeier and Abd el-Maksoud 2003]). Because of the relative thinness of the walls and buttresses, Oren and Shershevsky (1989, 18) reject the notion that this category of building served primarily a military function. Rather, they propose that these structures functioned as centers for the collection of taxes, as storehouses for trade goods, or as police stations. Administrative buildings in Canaan include the Late Level VII structure (published as a fortress) at Tel Beth-shean, Building 1104 at Aphek, the Strata VIII–VII square building (identified as a citadel) at Tel Mor, and the Stratum VII structure (referred to as a fortress) at Deir el-Balah.

At Tel Beth-shean, the recent Hebrew University expedition partially excavated a structure situated directly below Building 1500. This earlier building, assigned to Late Level VII or Level VII, exhibited several Egyptian construction techniques, including mudbrick foundations and mudbrick floors. The outer walls of the building follow the plan of Building 1500 and measure roughly 20 x 20 m. Its interior plan, however, differs substantially from that of the Level VI center-hall house, and this lower building is nearly identical to the "fortress" excavated at Deir el-Balah (see below; A. Mazar 1994a, 79–80; 2003a).

At Aphek, excavations exposed a monumental building variously referred to as Building 1104, Palace VI, or the Governor's Residence (fig. 2.6). The plan of this square structure, which is assigned to Stratum X12, consists of an entrance hall with a double doorway, a staircase adjoining the entrance hall to the west, two small chambers on the east side of the building, and two long, narrow storerooms on the west side (Kochavi 1990). A structure similar in plan is the administrative building at Tel Mor, where a square Late Bronze IIB "citadel," assigned to Strata VIII–VII, was uncovered (fig. 2.7). This administrative structure measured approximately 23 x 23 m and was reinforced by a series of external buttresses (M. Dothan 1960, 124).

At Deir el-Balah, a square-shaped "fortress" was excavated under the direction of Trude Dothan (1985a; 1985b; 1987; 1998a). Assigned to Stratum VII, this building (fig. 2.8) was partially constructed atop an earlier administrative complex (Stratum IX) that also exhibited Egyptianizing elements. Measuring roughly 20 x 20 m, this square-shaped administrative structure from Stratum VII contains fourteen rooms, with a tower at each of the four corners. Only the foundations of the building, measuring at least 1 m deep, are preserved. Its identifiable Egyptianizing features

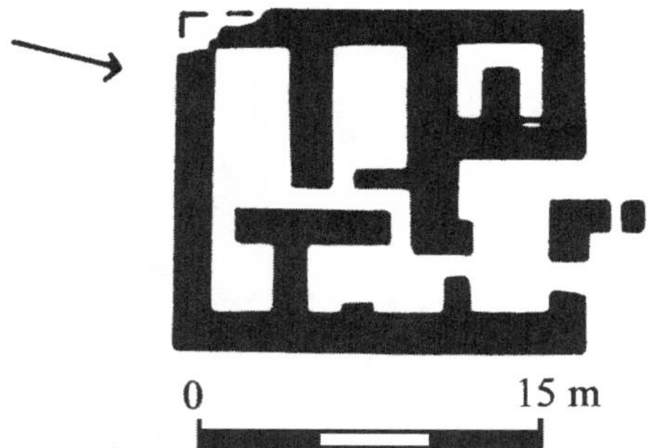

Fig. 2.6. Administrative Building at Aphek

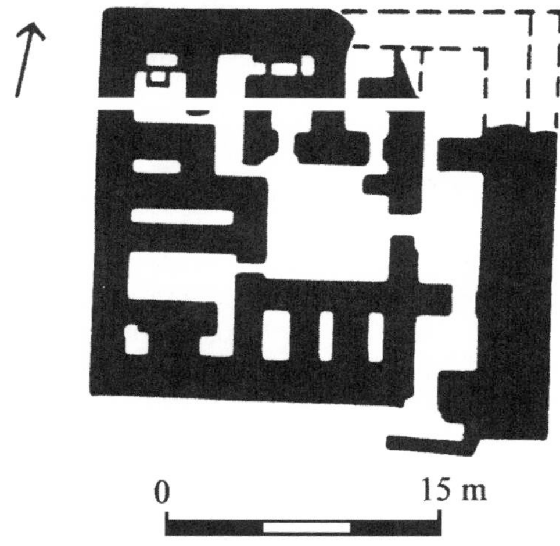

Fig. 2.7. Administrative Building at Tel Mor

include the deposit of sand along the base of the foundation walls and a foundation deposit comprised of two bowls and a lamp (T. Dothan 1981, 127). The dating of this building to the Nineteenth Dynasty is based primarily on a comparison of it with depictions of similar structures on reliefs at Karnak commemorating Seti I's campaign to Western Asia (T. Dothan 1985b, 40).[19] However, this structure should be redated to the Twentieth Dynasty in light of its parallels with other Twentieth Dynasty structures in Canaan and its stratigraphic situation at the site.

Temples in Canaan that incorporate Egyptianizing features form Higginbotham's fourth category of structures showing the influence of Egypt in Canaan (see Helck 1971, 444–45; Giveon 1978a, 122–27; Weinstein

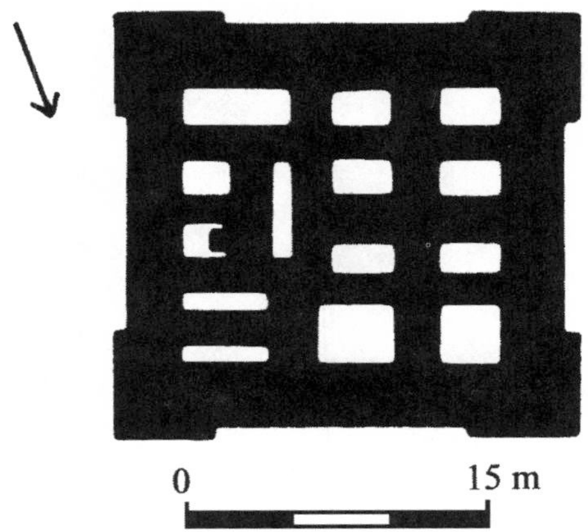

Fig. 2.8. Administrative Building at Deir el-Balah

1981, 19–20; Uehlinger 1988; Wimmer 1990; 1998). Two main types of cultic architecture with Egyptian antecedents have been proposed for the region: Hathor temples (Timnaᶜ) and temples with raised holy of holies (Beth-shean and Lachish; see Higginbotham 2000, 118–19).[20] As James Weinstein (1981, 19) and Stephan Wimmer (1990, 1098) observe, however, the only temple in Canaan proper in which an Egyptian deity was worshiped was that at Timnaᶜ. According to the excavator, the earliest phase of this temple was built by Seti I, with later phases of its use continuing through the reign of Ramesses V (Rothenberg 1988, 276–78). But it has been noted that the single object bearing the name of Seti I may actually date to the reign of Ramesses II or later, thus casting doubt on the attribution of the temple's construction to Seti I (Schulman 1988, 145; Wimmer 1990, 1069).

Several other temples that have often been cited in the literature as displaying Egyptian features are strongly influenced by Canaanite traditions (Wimmer 1990). These include the Strata VI and V temples at Beth-shean (Rowe 1930; 1940; Wimmer 1990, 1077–80) and the Fosse Temple at Lachish (Phases II and III: Tufnell, Inge, and Harding 1940; Wimmer 1990, 1070–71; see also Clamer 1980; Giveon 1983 regarding the Egyptian-style artifacts; see Weinstein 1981, 19–20, and Hasel 1998, 100, for a summary).

Egyptian-Style Artifacts

The material culture of Late Bronze Age Canaan includes a rich repertoire of Egyptian-style objects, some imported and others locally produced. These include ivory objects with Egyptian motifs (Liebowitz 1987; 1989; Hasel 1998, 105–6); inscribed doorjambs and lintels (Weinstein 1981, 19; Hasel 1998, 106–7); stelae, statues, and plaques (Weinstein 1981, 20; Hasel 1998, 107); pendants and amulets (McGovern 1985; C. Herrmann 1994; Hasel 1998, 112); scarab seals (Hasel 1998, 112–13); pottery; anthropoid coffins (see below); and hieratic inscriptions on Egyptian-style bowls (see below).

Three categories of Egyptian-style artifacts are culturally sensitive indicators of social boundaries. Clearly belonging to this category are burial customs, represented by the appearance of Egyptian-style anthropoid coffins at select sites in Canaan where Egyptian presence is documented and, especially significant, hieratic inscriptions written on utilitarian Egyptian-style bowls and a few hieroglyphic texts inscribed on stone found in Canaan. No less significant are the Egyptian-style ceramic assemblages that appear at select sites in Canaan. Most of this pottery was domestic in function and was manufactured locally using Egyptian-style technology. When considered in its larger historical and material culture context, it can be used to delineate the social boundaries of Egyptian imperialistic ambitions in the region.

Burial Customs

Corresponding to the distribution of Egyptian-style buildings and locally produced pottery is the appearance of burials in Egyptian-style anthropoid clay coffins (Gonen 1992, 28; Hasel 1998, 110–11). These coffins, similar to others found in Egypt, are approximately 2 m long with a cut-out modeled lid depicting human features (Bloch-Smith 1992b, 135). The largest number of anthropoid burial coffins has been recovered at the Deir el-Balah Late Bronze Age cemetery, located to the southwest of the town (fig. 2.9). Although only part of the cemetery has been excavated, over fifty anthropoid coffins (the majority illicitly excavated) are known from private collections and excavations, most dating to the thirteenth century B.C.E. (T. Dothan 1972; 1973; 1979; 1985a; 1985b; Beit-Arieh 1985). The coffins are often found in groups of three or more, with simple graves interspersed between the clusters of coffins. A rich assemblage of burial gifts is deposited both inside and outside of these coffins. Storage jars, found near the heads of deceased individuals, mark the burial. The majority of scarabs found in association with these burials date to the reign of Ramesses II (T. Dothan 1973, 138).

Excavations have also recovered anthropoid coffins from other sites in Canaan: two coffins at Tell el-Farʿah (S) (Tombs 552, 562, and 935; Petrie 1930, 6–8, pls. 19–24); over fifty fragments of anthropoid coffins excavated in the Northern Cemetery at Beth-shean (Levels VII–VI; T. Dothan 1982, 268–76; Oren 1973, 129–50); and two coffins from Lachish

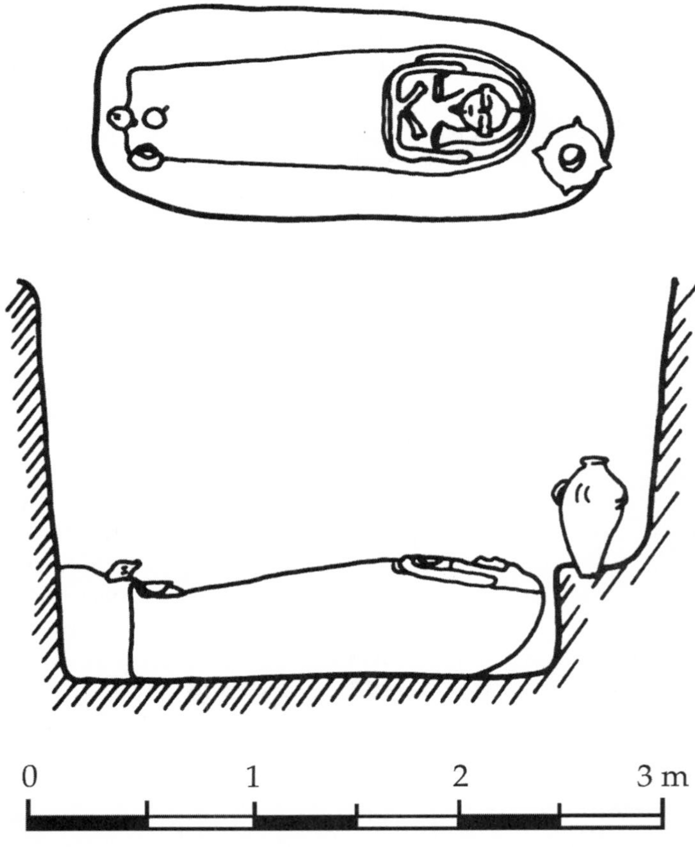

Fig. 2.9. Plan and Section of an Anthropoid Coffin from Deir el-Balah

(Tomb 570; Tufnell 1953, 219; pl. 126). Anthropoid coffins are clearly an Egyptian burial custom and are similar to pottery coffins found in New Kingdom Egypt[21] (Oren 1973, 142–46; for Egypt, see Steindorff 1937, 72; Leclant 1971, 227–28).

Egyptian Inscriptions

Two types of Egyptian inscriptions have been recovered in Canaan: hieratic inscriptions written in cursive script with ink on Egyptian-style bowls; and hieroglyphic inscriptions carved into stone.

Hieratic inscriptions are the more numerous of the two and are apparently related to the economic administration of the region. All these inscriptions, dating broadly to the Ramesside period, have been recovered from sites in Canaan with Egyptian ties: Lachish (Tufnell 1958, 132–33, pls. 44, 47; Gilula 1976, 107; Goldwasser 1982; 1991b, 248–51; Sweeney 2004), Tel Seraʿ (Goldwasser 1984, 77–81), Tel Haror (Goldwasser 1991a), Tell el-Farʿah (S) (Goldwasser and Wimmer 1999, 40), and Deir el-Balah (Goldwasser and Wimmer 1999, 41).

The inscriptions on two sherds recovered from Tell el Farʿah (S) belong to a well-known category of hieratic inscriptions, indicating that this site was one of several centers where taxes, in the form of grain, were collected, most likely during the reign of Ramesses III (Goldwasser and Wimmer 1999, 39–42).[22] The Tel Seraʿ inscriptions, also dating to Ramesses III, were related to grain offerings presented as votives in temples (Goldwasser 1984). Although the Lachish ostraca were not found *in situ,* one of the sherds contains the word for "scribe." Orly Goldwasser (1991b) suggests that this may indicate that Egyptian or Egyptian-trained scribes resided at the site. Taken as a whole, these hieratic inscriptions attest to continued pharaonic sovereignty over the region and seem to be related to tax collection. Their appearance on bowls may further indicate that they also had a votive or cultic function (Goldwasser 1984, 84–85; Wimmer 1990, 1090; Hasel 1998, 113–14; Higginbotham 2000, 59–63).

In addition to these hieratic inscriptions, several hieroglyphic inscriptions carved into stone have also been found in Canaan. Most notable are the three Beth-shean stelae (see pp. 55–56 above) and the inscribed architectural fragments found in association with Building 1500 (Level VI) in Beth-shean. The lintel from this structure bears the name of Ramesses-Weser-khepesh, an Egyptian army officer, royal scribe, and steward (Ward 1966, 161–63, 167, figs. 92:1, 93:1).

A Typology of Egyptian-Style Pottery in Canaan

Egyptian and Egyptian-style pottery in Canaan has been one of the most neglected topics of research into Egyptian-Canaanite relations during the fourteenth to twelfth centuries B.C.E.[23] To remedy this situation, the following discussion outlines the main features of Egyptian-style pottery, both local and imported. Egyptian-style vessels appearing in Canaan will be grouped according to three functional categories, based primarily on vessel proportion and morphology: (I) kitchen wares, which include table and cooking wares; (II) containers, which are subdivided into handleless domestic containers and handled storage containers; and (III) varia, comprising vessels used for household production or industrial purposes. As demonstrated below, locally produced Egyptian-style pottery in Canaan is remarkable for its close adherence to Egyptian morphological and technological features. Almost without exception these vessels lack any discernible Canaanite influence over a period of more than a century, leading to the conclusion that Egyptian potters working at Egyptian strongholds in Canaan were responsible for this locally produced Egyptian-style pottery (fig. 2.10).

Category I—Kitchen Wares: Bowls. Bowls are one of the most ubiquitous Egyptian forms in Canaan. All the Egyptian-style bowls (EG 1–6; see fig. 2.11) have either a shallow or semihemispherical vessel profile with a flat or rounded base. The large number of shallow bowls and the flat base of many of the bowls are especially indicative of the Egyptian-style assemblage. The one exception is Bowl EG 7 (fig. 2.12), which is most likely a cooking vessel (see below).

Bowl EG 1, which is characterized by its shallow depth, straight sides, simple rim, and flat base, is divided into two primary subgroups: EG 1a, which has a simple rim;[24] and EG 1b, with an everted to flaring rim.[25] Bowl EG 2 is similar to EG 1, except for its deeper, semihemispherical shape and different vessel proportions.[26] Shallow Bowl EG 3 is characterized by a round profile with a flaring rim, sometimes forming a carination below the rim, and a rounded base.[27] This bowl is common in Egypt from the Middle Kingdom through the New Kingdom period and appears in Egyptian reliefs depicting offerings.[28] Bowl EG 4 is small to medium in size, with a rounded base and a simple rim.[29] This utilitarian bowl is depicted in wall reliefs from New Kingdom tombs illustrating banquet and offering scenes, where it is shown as containing liquid either for drinking or libation. It also appears in a relief decoration on an ivory inlay from Tell el-Farʿah (S) portraying a seated man (the Egyptian governor?) holding this bowl type while an attendant pours a liquid into it.[30] Bowl EG 5a includes medium-sized bowls with a rounded to straight-sided vessel profile, a simple to slightly incurved rim, and a flat base. A variant of this bowl has a strainer attached to the interior (EG 5b; fig. 2.11).[31] Bowl EG 6 is a large shallow bowl characterized by its thickened rim, coarse ware, and rope pattern decoration on and/or below the rim.[32]

Category I—Kitchen Wares: Cooking Wares. Bowl EG 7 (fig. 2.12) is rare in Canaan.[33] It consists of a deep restricted bowl with a gentle

Fig. 2.10. Assemblage of Egyptian-Style Pottery from Beth-shean

carination less than halfway from the rim. The straight neck is narrower than the widest part of the bowl at the carination. The base seems to be slightly flattened. A red slip was applied to the exterior from the rim to carination. In Egypt, this form is usually classified in publications of New Kingdom pottery as a "bowl," but with the comment that it was used as a cooking pot.[34]

Category I—Kitchen Wares: Juglets. Wide-mouthed juglets EG 8 (fig. 2.12) are distinguished by their unusual shape, wide aperture, and burnished white-slipped exterior. They are often termed "mugs" in the Egyptian literature.[35] Juglet EG 8 belongs to a group of white-slipped and burnished vessels manufactured in Egypt, classified by Holthoer as JU 2 (1977, 92–93). They are well known in Egypt during the Eighteenth to Twentieth Dynasties.[36]

Category II—Handleless Containers: Jars. These containers are divided into handleless domestic jars (EG 9–12; see fig. 2.12) and handleless storage containers (EG 13–15; see figs. 2.13–15). Handleless jars include a large group of portable domestic jars comprising ovoid jars

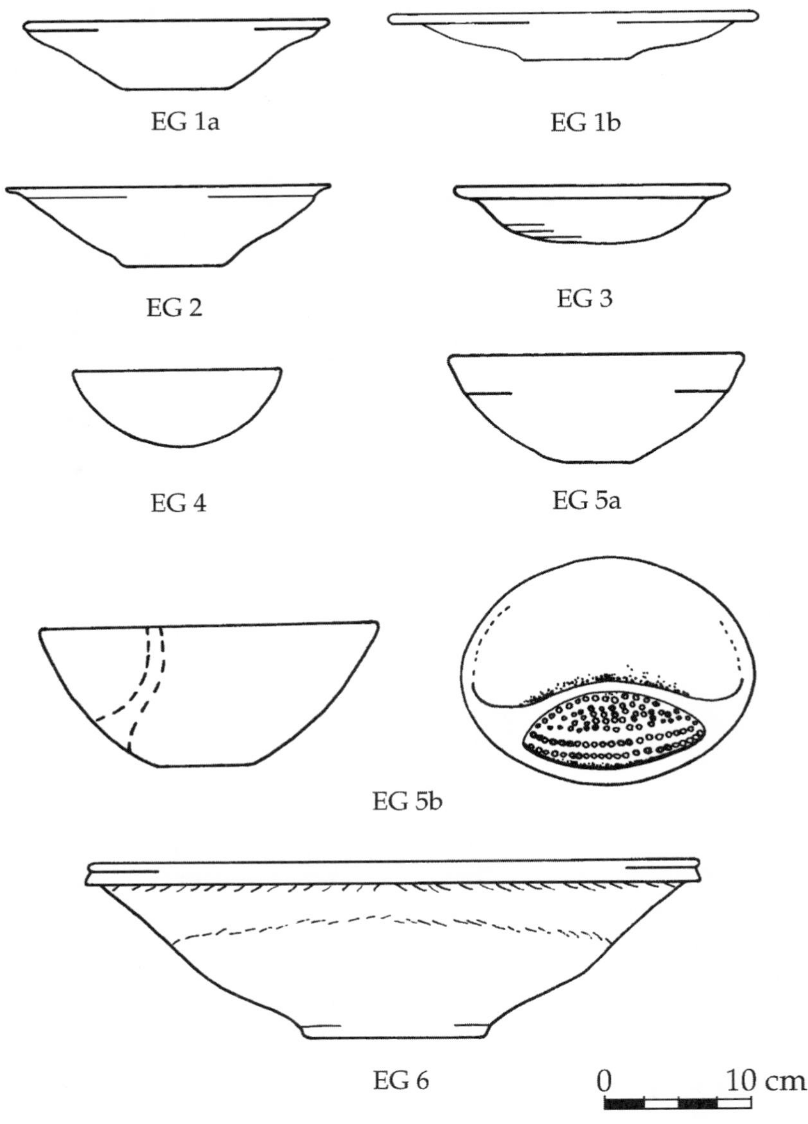

Fig. 2.11. Egyptian-Style Pottery Forms EG 1–6

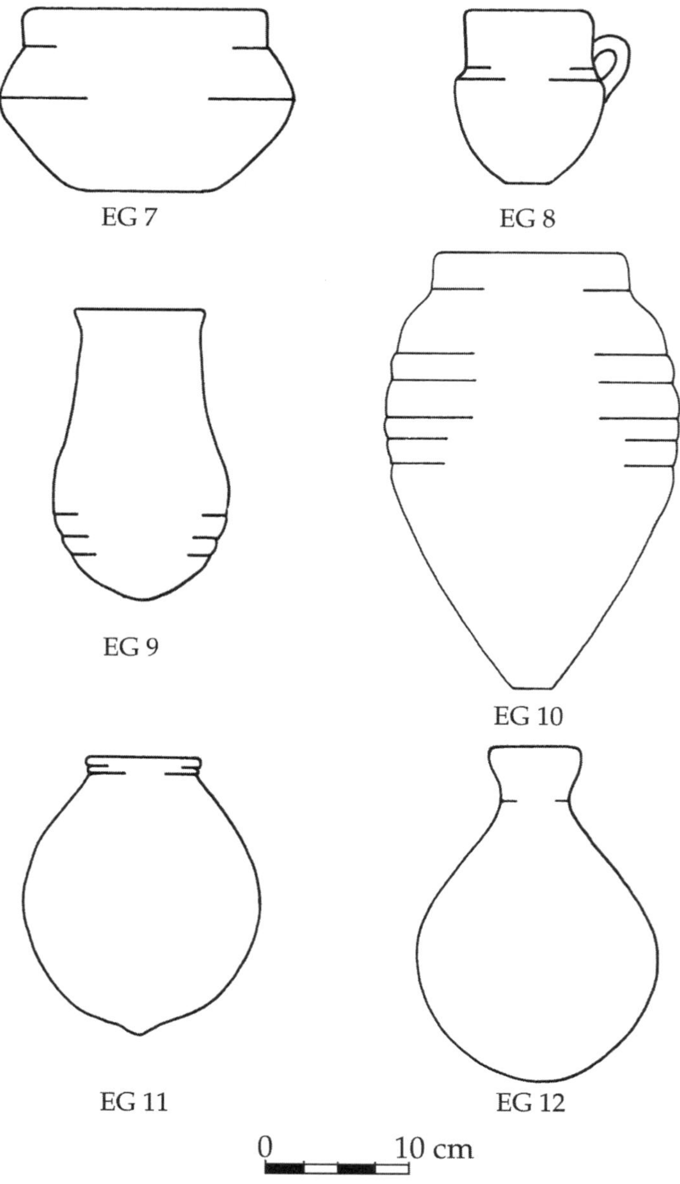

Fig. 2.12. Egyptian-Style Pottery Forms EG 7–12

(EG 9), funnel-necked jars (EG 10), globular jars (EG 11), and broad bottles (EG 12). All these shapes belong to the basic Egyptian pottery repertoire of handleless jars and probably served several purposes, including storage and consumption of everyday commodities.

Ovoid jars EG 9 (fig. 2.12) are characterized by an elongated ovoid-shaped body profile. It is one of the most common vessels with a restricted neck in the ancient Egyptian repertoire, spanning the entire period of ancient Egypt until its disappearance in the Late Period. As a result, ovoid jars exhibit wide variation in shape, size, decoration, and quality. During the Late Bronze II–Iron I periods, the widest part of this vessel is generally near the base. Included in the assemblage are medium-sized decorated or undecorated jars, with either an "ordinary"[37] or "wide"[38] neck (Holthoer 1977, 156–63).

Necked jars EG 10 (fig. 2.12) are a general category of closed handleless Egyptian forms with well-defined necks (Holthoer 1977, 148). In Canaan, most of them belong to the funnel-necked class of jars that includes both tall (EG 10a) and short (EG 10b) forms. Tall funnel-necked jars are rare in Canaan[39] and did not become popular in Egypt until the later Eighteenth through the Twentieth Dynasties.[40] The short funnel-necked jar (EG 10b) is characterized by a short, broad neck, an unmodeled rim, a well-defined transition to the neck, and a rounded to pointed base. This variant of the funnel-necked jar is quite similar in contour, neck shape, and general appearance to beer bottles (EG 19) but lacks the fingerprints and perforated bases so typical of the beer-bottle family. This type is also very rare in Canaan.[41] In Egypt and Nubia, short funnel-necked jars appear in Eighteenth and Nineteenth Dynasty contexts.[42]

Globular jar EG 11 (fig. 2.12) seldom appears in Canaan, and then only at sites with clear Egyptian ties.[43] Form EG 11 includes small globular jars with a slightly elongated body shape, often decorated with painted bands, and medium-sized vessels with either a globular or slightly carinated body shape.[44] It should be noted that in Canaan the smaller globular jar is more numerous than the larger version and the medium-sized globular jar appears only occasionally.[45] In contrast, medium-sized globular jars are widespread at New Kingdom sites.[46]

Globular jars EG 12 (fig. 2.12) are also rare in Canaan (Killebrew 1999a, ill. II:83:7, 8). This shape, though not identical in profile, appears occasionally in Egypt.[47] Rostislav Holthoer (1977, 132) termed similar vessels found in Nubia as Family BR (Broad Bottles).

Category II—Large Handleless Storage Containers. This group includes three subtypes: large ovoid jars (EG 13), hybrid vessels (EG 14), and short-necked bag-shaped vessels (EG 15). As pointed out by R. Holthoer (1977, 80), these vessels are very similar in shape to present-day vessels in Egypt called zirs that serve as water containers.[48]

Ovoid jar EG 13 (fig. 2.13; over 50 cm high) probably served as a storage jar. This larger version of EG 9 (fig. 2.12; under 50 cm high) is uncommon in New Kingdom contexts[49] and even rarer in Canaan.[50]

Hybrid Egyptian-Canaanite vessels EG 14 (fig. 2.14) are extremely unusual in Canaan. Several hybrid storage jars were discovered during excavations in the settlement and cemetery at Deir el-Balah (Beit Arieh 1985, fig. 6:7; Killebrew 1999a, ill. III:22:3, 4). Their unifying features are their lack of handles, general Egyptian-style body shape, and Canaanite-

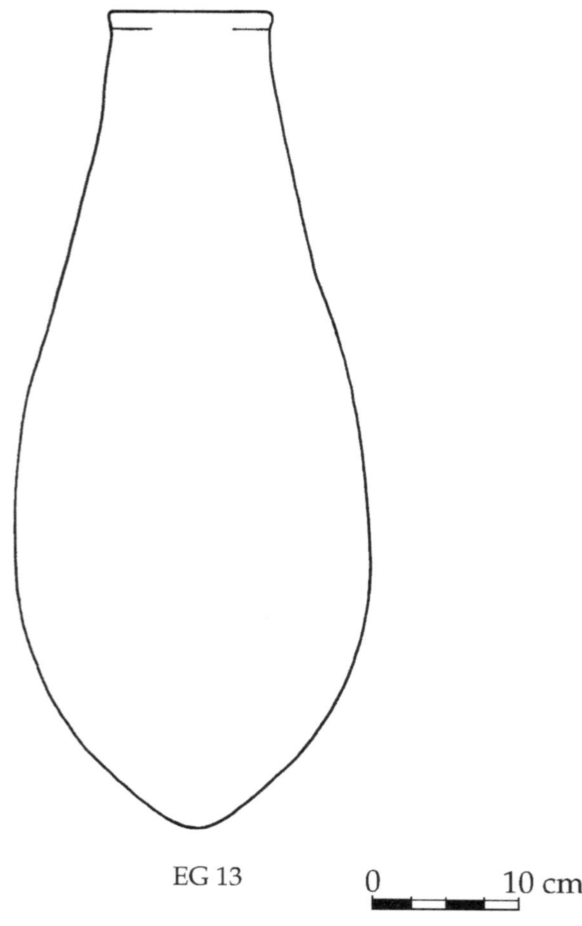

Fig. 2.13. Egyptian-Style Pottery Form EG 13

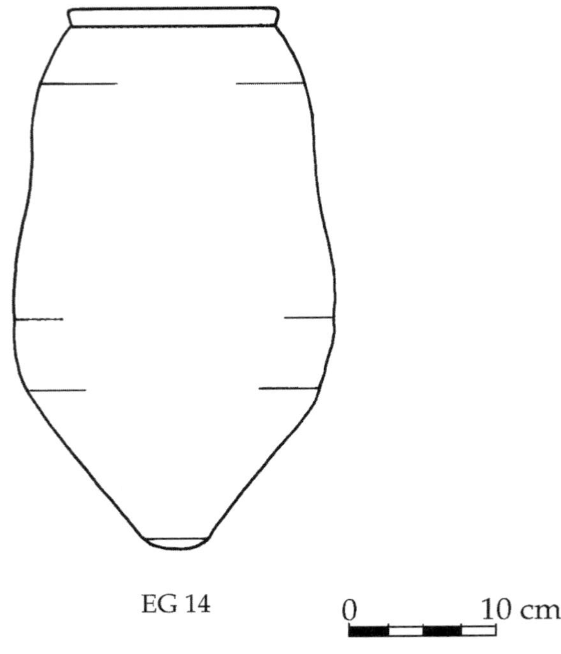

Fig. 2.14. Egyptian-Style Pottery Form EG 14

style base, creating a "hybrid" storage container. These vessels are similar morphologically to larger krater-pithoi.

Bag-shaped hole mouth storage jars EG 15 (fig. 2.15) are large handleless jars, varying in shape from a globular to an elongated bag-shaped profile. In Canaan, they are often decorated or covered with a red slip.[51] These jars are especially numerous in Nineteenth and Twentieth Dynasty contexts.[52]

Category II—Large Handled Storage Containers: Two-handled jars belong to this third group of large containers: a longer, slender jar covered with a white burnished slip (EG 16) and a squatter and more globular white-burnished handled jar (EG 17).

Tall-Necked Storage Jars EG 16 (fig. 2.16) include vessels of large and very large size that have a tall-neck and white-burnished slip characteristic of Egyptian pottery. Storage jar EG 16 is defined by its long slender shape, tall neck, and white slip. There are few published examples of EG 16 from Canaan. Several fragmentary pieces and one complete example of EG 16 jars were recovered from the settlement and cemetery at Deir el-Balah (Dothan 1979, 10–12, ills. 14, 16) and

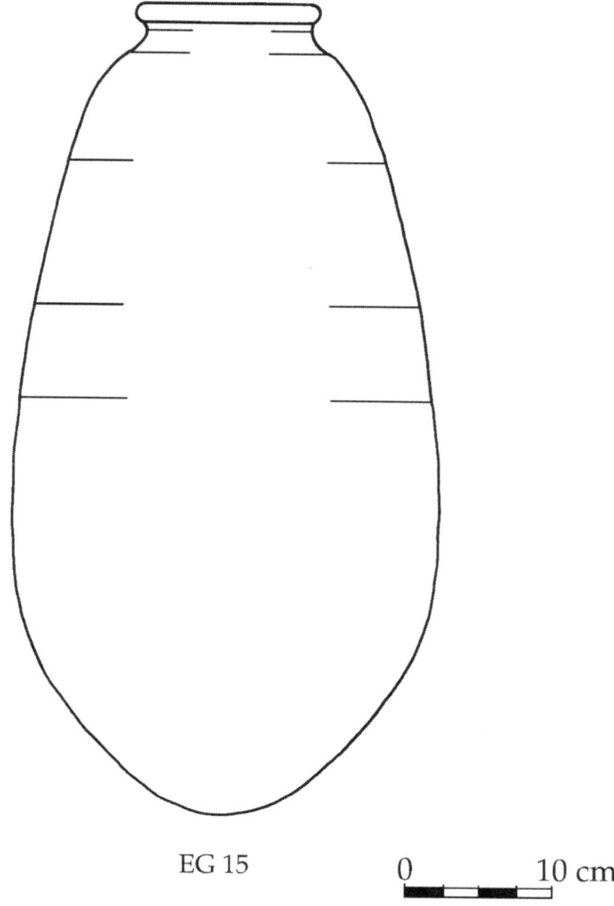

Fig. 2.15. Egyptian-Style Pottery Form EG 15

from a Late Bronze II tomb at Beth-shemesh (Grant 1929, pl. 173:2). Form EG 16 storage jars are well-known in Egyptian New Kingdom contexts.[53] Jars of this shape also appear in smaller sizes.[54] Based on provenience studies, storage jars EG 16 found in Canaan are of Egyptian origin (see below, p. 79). Form EG 16 handled storage jars are depicted in numerous New Kingdom wall paintings.[55] These handled storage jars seem to be an Egyptian imitation and adaptation of the two-handled Canaanite storage jars that were used commercially throughout the Mediterranean during the Late Bronze Age (Grace 1956, 86; Dothan 1979, 10; see pp. 123–25 below).

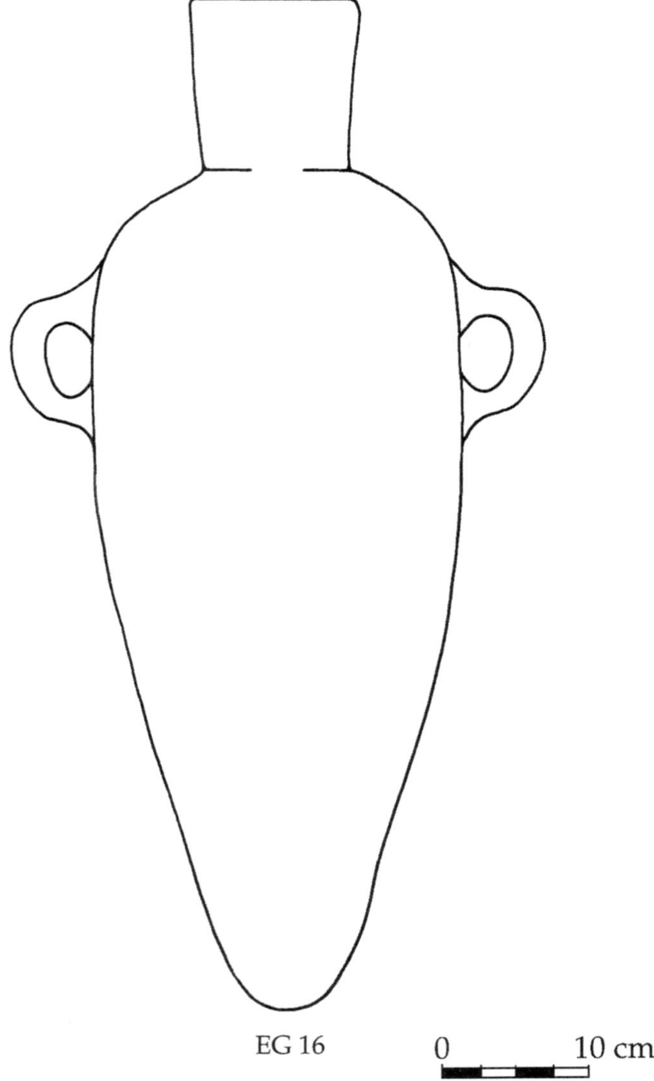

Fig. 2.16. Egyptian-Style Pottery Form EG 16

Tall-Necked Storage Jar EG 17 (fig. 2.17) is a handled storage jar characterized by its more squat globular- to oval-shaped body, very tall convex neck, and white slip. Several complete examples were recovered from Levels VII and VI at Tel Beth-shean (Killebrew 1999a, ill. II:71:4). An

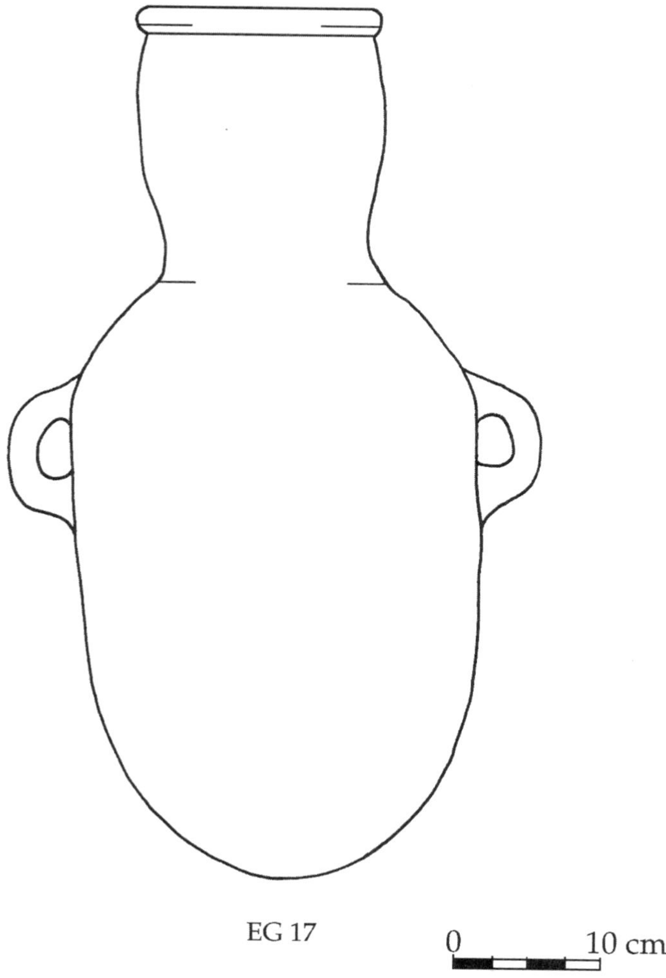

Fig. 2.17. Egyptian-Style Pottery Form EG 17

Egyptian-style jar of this type, though typologically later in style, is known from Tell Qasile (Mazar 1985b, 56; photo 56 and see nn. 90 and 91). It is a well-known shape in Egypt and Nubia, reaching its height of popularity during the Twentieth Dynasty.[56]

Category III—Varia: This category of production and industrial vessels includes two families—spinning bowls (EG 18) and beer bottles (EG 19)—associated with the manufacture of household products.

Spinning bowls EG 18 (fig. 2.18) have one to four handles attached to the interior base and walls of the vessel that are used for spinning thread or yarn. They first appear in Egypt during the Middle Kingdom and continue well into the Late New Kingdom. The spinning bowl is attested in Canaan during the Late Bronze II period and increases in quantity during the Iron Age I period.[57]

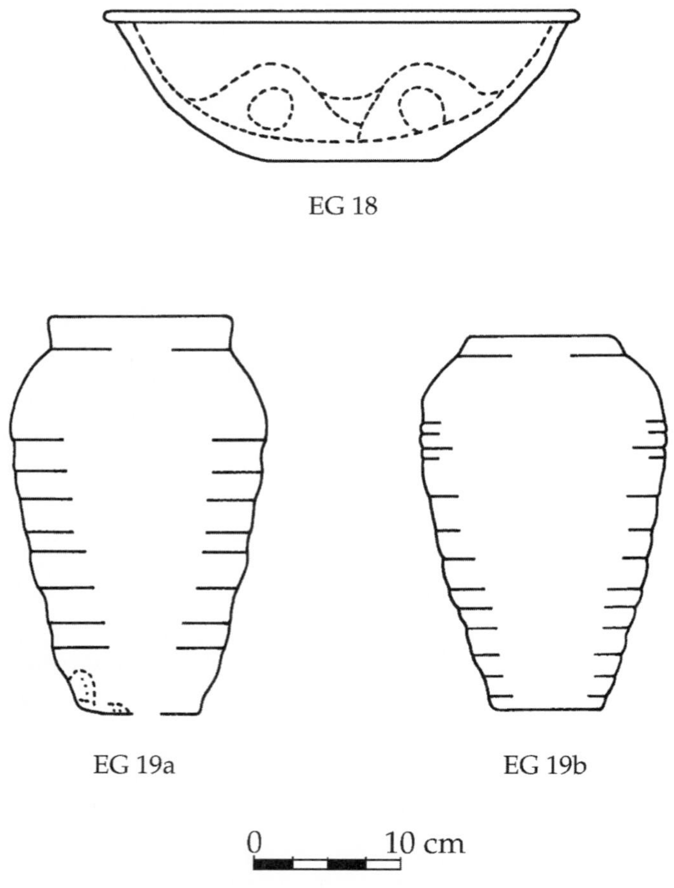

Fig.2.18. Egyptian-Style Pottery Forms EG 18–19

The "beer bottle" EG 19 is a piriform- to oval-shaped handleless bottle with a flat base.[58] It is a crudely made vessel, often with a hole pierced through the base before firing and always with fingerprints marking the lower side walls.[59] Based on Egyptian and Nubian examples, Holthoer (1977, 86–88) defined four subtypes of this vessel: cylindrical (BB 1), transitional (BB 2), simple (BB 3), and ordinary (BB 4). The ordinary subtype (BB 4) is the most common in Egypt and at sites in Canaan with Egyptian influence.[60] The transitional subtype (BB 2), which Holthoer considered to be a kind of catch-all of irregular forms, encompasses vessels that closely resemble a number of beer bottles from Deir el-Balah and Beth-shean.[61]

Egyptian-Style Pottery Technology

Technical choices involved in material culture production are a further indication of social boundaries, and this is particularly evident in the production of Egyptian-style pottery in Canaan. Though a number of excellent technological studies have been conducted on Egyptian pottery in Egypt, there are few published analyses of techniques used to produce Egyptian-style pottery found in Late Bronze Age Canaan.[62] Based on these studies, it is clear that most utilitarian Egyptian-style pottery found in Canaan was locally made and that potters producing these vessels employed techniques typical of pottery manufactured in Egypt. The fact that these techniques differ from those of Canaanite potters leads to the conclusion that Egyptian potters were responsible for the production of this well-defined ceramic assemblage. Studies of this assemblage have focused on two main aspects of production: (1) analyses of pottery wares in order to determine clay provenience; and (2) attempts to reconstruct formation techniques (for a detailed description, see Killebrew 1999a, 187–257; 2004).

Provenience Analyses. Two analytical techniques, Neutron Activation Analysis[63] and petrographic thin sections,[64] have been used in many provenience and ware studies. Extensive sampling of pottery from Deir el-Balah[65] and Beth-shean[66] has indicated conclusively that the majority of Egyptian-style vessels were locally produced, using local clays. Only a small percentage of Egyptian-style vessels, mainly the white burnished slip wares (juglet EG 8 and storage jar EG 16) and a few miscellaneous vessels, were imported from Egypt.

Formation Techniques. One of the few published studies of formation techniques used in the production of Egyptian-style pottery in Canaan is Glanzman and Fleming's 1993 xeroradiographic analysis[67] of Late Bronze II pottery from Beth-shean. Their analysis included Egyptian-style bowls, Canaanite-style kraters, storage jars, ring stands, flasks, lamps, and cup and saucers from Beth-shean. Glanzman and Fleming

(1993, 94–102) analyzed Egyptian-style open everted rim bowls alongside similar bowls from Aniba and determined that in both cases the bowls were made in an upright, off-the-hump mode, either wheel-thrown or tournette-formed on a clay hump. This observation is confirmed by New Kingdom depictions of potters forming vessels on a wheel by using the off-the hump mode (Killebrew 1982, 60–101). The Beth-shean and Aniba bowl bases had been nonuniformly trimmed, continuing partly up the side of the lower wall. The fabric was heavily tempered with straw, allowing a more even drying of the vessel. Though limited in scope, their study indicates that Egyptian pottery formation techniques were used to produce the local Egyptian-style pottery from Beth-shean. Similar features are observable on the Egyptian-style pottery from Deir el-Balah.

Potters' Workshops. A potters' workshop associated with the local production of Egyptian-style and Canaanite pottery was excavated in the settlement at Deir el-Balah. It comprised a complex of rooms where there was evidence of pottery production, including four kilns, moulds, a pit and room with large quantities of raw materials such as ochre and levigated clay and tools such as grinding vessels. The workshop comprised an area of roughly 70 m^2 (Killebrew 1999a, 55–59). Most noteworthy were the four kilns excavated in association with the workshop. One small and simple mudbrick kiln (1312) and three larger, partially subterranean mudbrick kilns (512, 540, and 1313) all date to the Late Bronze II period and, based on the excavated evidence, were used in the firing of both Egyptian-style and Canaanite pottery that was produced side by side in this workshop (Killebrew 1996a). There is also evidence that these kilns were used to fire the lids of anthropoid coffins produced at Deir el-Balah.

The production of Egyptian-style utilitarian pottery in local workshops in Canaan by potters from Egypt lends further support to Egyptian imperial intentions in Canaan. If local Canaanite potters were imitating Egyptian forms, one would expect to observe a hybridization of both the shapes and technological features of Egyptian-style pottery produced in Canaan. At sites such as Tel Beth-shean and Deir el-Balah, where Egyptian-style pottery was produced over a period of more than a century, this assemblage is remarkable for its adherence to both traditional Egyptian shapes and technology. Thus I conclude that at Egyptian centers such as Tel Beth-shean and Deir el-Balah (and most likely other centers where I have not personally examined the pottery), potters from Egypt produced these vessels. The fact that these assemblages remained faithful to Egyptian potting traditions over time and did not develop regional variations (as can be observed in Aegean-style pottery in the eastern Mediterranean during the twelfth and eleventh centuries B.C.E. discussed in ch. 5), reinforces the conclusion that Egypt sent potters to serve in Canaan along with its administrative and military personnel.

The View from Egypt and Canaan: Conclusions

Based on the evidence presented above, I conclude that Egyptian interaction with Canaan was one of a core imperial power to its developed periphery (see ch. 1 for a discussion of these terms). Less certain are the motivating factors behind the Egyptian domination and imperialism in the region.[68] What is clear from the primary evidence is that Egyptian influence and interest fluctuated over the course of the New Kingdom.[69] Egyptian written texts and especially the archaeological evidence in Canaan testify to an increasing Egyptian interest in Canaan during the Nineteenth and Twentieth Dynasties.[70] Through the reign of Ramesses III, Egyptian presence can be defined as a limited military occupation and direct administration, or as "formal" imperialism as defined by Horvath (see above, p. 53). It was characterized by the stationing of military troops at garrison cities and administrative Egyptian personnel at several "governor's residencies" in Canaan.

Intensified Egyptian attention to Canaan during the thirteenth and first half of the twelfth centuries may have been aimed at blocking rebellious tribal elements in the hill country and desert fringes as well as at reinforcing and expanding tax collection in the fertile areas of the southern coastal plain and Shephelah. This change in Egyptian administrative policy, from one mainly of absentee economic and political expansion during the Eighteenth Dynasty to one of exploitation coinciding with a clear Egyptian presence, manifested itself by the increased stationing of Egyptian personnel at several sites in Canaan, especially in the south.[71]

During the thirteenth century B.C.E., Egypt experienced a period of prosperity and stability under Ramesses II. Despite the probable loss of territory in Syria to Hatti after the battle of Kadesh, Egypt's control over Canaan solidified, with clear signs of Egyptian presence at a number of sites in Canaan.[72] The initial stage of Egyptian expansion and control inside Canaan proper, resulting in a *pax Aegyptiaca,* is visible at the Egyptian government center at Gaza (Phythian-Adams 1923; Katzenstein 1982; Oren 1987) and its hinterland (Giveon 1975), Deir el-Balah (T. Dothan 1985a; 1985b), Tell el-Farʿah (S) (Oren 1984), Tel Mor (M. Dothan 1989; 1993b), Aphek (Kochavi 1990, XII), Beth-shean (James and McGovern 1993; A. Mazar 1994a, 75; 1997a), Tell es-Saʿidiyeh (Pritchard 1980; Tubb 1988a, 40–46, fig. 15; Tubb, Dorrell, and Cobbing 1996, 24–30), Tel Seraʿ, probably Jaffa (Kaplan and Ritter-Kaplan 1993, 656–57) and Ashdod, and possibly Lachish. Egyptian influence is hinted at on a more limited scale in the archaeological record from Gezer (Singer 1986–87; Bunimovitz 1988–89), Tell el-Hesi (Oren 1985), and Megiddo.[73]

Egyptian military activities in Canaan appear to have been renewed under Merneptah, and Egypt may have succeeded in establishing control over additional regions.[74] The most significant text relating to Canaan during the reign of Merneptah is the Hymn of Victory (or Israel) Stela dating to the fifth year of his reign[75] and commemorating his victory over Libya and the surrender of Ashkelon, Gezer, and Yenoʿam. Most notable is the appearance of the word "Israel" (as a people) for the first time in an extrabiblical source (for a discussion of the term "Israel" in Merneptah's victory stela, see pp. 154–55 below). If the reattribution of the Ramesses II Karnak relief to Merneptah is correct, this would add additional weight to the argument that Merneptah further tightened Egyptian control over Canaan.[76]

The final years of the Nineteenth Dynasty were a period of chaos and succession crises. Sethnakhte, the founder of the Twentieth Dynasty, claims to have driven out the usurpers, and he was succeeded by the last great ruler of New Kingdom Egypt: Ramesses III (Grimal 1992, 260–71). Ramesses III's reign ushered in the final flourish of Egyptian rule.[77] This second king of the Twentieth Dynasty and the last noteworthy Egyptian pharaoh of the New Kingdom was faced with increasing difficulties on several fronts, repelling three attacks in the Delta in his first eleven years. These challenges included Libyan invasions of Egypt during Ramesses III's fifth and eleventh years and an attack by "Peoples of the Sea" during his eighth year, as recounted in reliefs and inscriptions on his mortuary temple at Medinet Habu and in Papyrus Harris I. According to these inscriptions, Ramesses III was victorious, decisively defeating this coalition and later settling these people in his strongholds (see below, ch. 5).

Two levels of Egyptian intervention in Canaan are reflected in the archaeological remains: one primarily administrative, the other both administrative and military. Sites where Egyptian presence is pronounced, as evidenced by a large percentage of Egyptian-style material culture (architecture, pottery, burial customs, etc.), include Beth-shean,[78] Tell es-Saʿidiyeh (Pritchard 1980; Tubb, Dorrell, and Cobbing 1996), Tel Mor (M. Dothan 1989; 1993b), Tell el-Farʿah (S) (Oren 1984; 1987), Tel Seraʿ (Oren 1985; 1993), and Deir el-Balah (T. Dothan 1987; 1998a) in southern Canaan, as well as numerous additional sites in Gaza and north Sinai. These remains probably reflect a significant number of Egyptians stationed at these sites, serving administrative as well as military functions. These Egyptians would also have included support staff such as craftsmen. A second type of site, exemplified by Megiddo, Gezer, and Lachish, has a limited number of Egyptian artifacts that are generally of a public nature. These remains most likely indicate a small number of Egyptian staff, if any, at these sites. The Egyptians probably served a purely administrative function, most likely tax collection.

The archaeological evidence suggests that the occurrence of Nineteenth and early Twentieth Dynasty Egyptian-style material culture in

Late Bronze Age Canaan is not due to any significant emulation of Egyptians by local subordinates. Rather, we can now speak of a clear Egyptian presence at strategically located sites in Canaan. The role of Egypt was not to colonize Canaan but rather to administer the collection of tribute and to impose minimal security arrangements and a semblance of order on the fractious and quarrelsome Canaanite rulers. The goal was to promote and oversee Egyptian imperial interests and to guarantee the loyalty of the local Canaanite elite. The material culture evidence from Late Bronze Age Canaan, considered together with the Egyptian historical texts, provides an excellent case study and model for identifying the political activities of a dominant regional and imperialistic power in the archaeological record.

Based on the evidence, two theories have arisen regarding the end of Egyptian influence in Canaan—both of them attributable to the advent of the Sea Peoples in the Levant. One proposes that, while Ramesses III restored and strengthened the Egyptian presence in Canaan, he also contributed to the eventual weakening of that presence by allowing a Sea Peoples presence along the southern coastal plain.[79] The second claims that Egyptian control in Canaan was weakened due to the Sea Peoples' incursions during the time of Ramesses III.[80] What is indisputable is that the material evidence for Egyptian presence in Canaan declines at the end of Ramesses III's reign.[81] James Weinstein (1992) posits that this outcome developed over two stages, beginning with the destruction of Egyptian military and administrative centers in Canaan by the Sea Peoples. During the second phase, from the time of Ramesses VI, the Egyptians withdrew from the copper mines at Timnaᶜ and the turquoise mines at Serabit el-Khadim, completing their retreat from Canaan. This view can be supported by the latest Egyptian objects found in Canaan that date to the reign of Ramesses VI, most notably the pedestal of the statue of Ramesses VI from Megiddo (Weinstein 1981, 23).

With Egypt's retreat from Canaan, their control over the major trade and military routes weakened, delivering a death blow to Egyptian influence in the region. The Egyptians left a gaping political vacuum behind them in Canaan that resulted in a return to a fragmented social and cultural landscape. The collapse of a central imperial authority permitted the construction of powerful Philistine urban centers, encouraged the further decline of the Canaanite city-states, and facilitated the eventual emergence of Israel.

Notes to Chapter 2

1. One of the earliest treatments of colonialism and imperialism in the premodern world is a volume of collected essays entitled *Imperialism in the Ancient World* (Garnsey and Whittaker 1978). See also Frandsen 1979; Adams 1984; Dyson 1985; Rowlands, Larsen, and Kristiansen 1987; Champion 1989; Algaze 1993; and Lyons and Papadopoulos 2002a.

2. See Bartel 1989, 173–74, for a similar attempt to define and classify, in a six-cell matrix format, colonial and noncolonial policies with three strategies (eradication-resettlement, acculturation, and equilibrium). Based on his approach, six types of empires can result. Each variation requires different behaviors on the part of the core dominant power and different responses on the part of the dominated group.

3. Regarding core-periphery interaction and the types of relationships that can develop between centers of civilization and peripheral areas, see Bartel 1985; 1989; Champion 1989; 1990; Millett 1990; Rowlands, Larsen, and Kristiansen 1987; Whitehouse and Wilkins 1989; Winter 1977. Higginbotham (2000, 6) applies theoretical and methodological insights from these studies to the problem of the Egyptianization of Palestine.

4. According to Higginbotham (2000, 8), this core-periphery model does not presume a particular pattern of military or economic domination. Rather, it stresses the sociological and ideological dimensions of imperialism from the perspectives of both the center and its periphery, with both parties deriving legitimization from their participation in the imperial system. For an example of elite emulation in the archaeological record, see Millett 1990 regarding the Romanization of Britain.

5. See Bryan 1996 regarding the role of twelfth-century B.C.E. Palestinian ivories in Canaan that in her opinion served as an iconography of power for the local elites. For the most recent treatment of New Kingdom Egyptian imperialism, see Morris 2005, who also challenges Higginbotham's theory of elite emulation. This comprehensive publication appeared only after this book was in press.

6. These sites in Nubia are in essence transplanted Egyptian settlements, and the artifacts, including pottery, are identical to those produced in Egypt. See, e.g., Adams 1977, 183, 218–39; 1984; Kemp 1978, 33–35; Higginbotham 2000, 11–14, table 1; Morkot 2001. For a recent and more nuanced view of imperialism and ethnicity, see S. T. Smith 2003.

7. See Weinstein 1981; Murnane 1992; Ward 1992a, 403–5; for a summary of inscriptions relevant to Canaan during the Ramesside period, see Higginbotham 2000, 17–73. Regarding the role of ideology behind Egyptian activities in western Asia, see, e.g., Frankfort 1948, 7–9; Kemp 1978, 8–11; Hasel 1998, 118–93.

8. See, e.g., Several 1972; Moran 1992; 1995; Giles 1997; Cohen and Westbrook 2000b; Liverani 2001. The relevance of the Amarna evidence for the Nineteenth and Twentieth Dynasties has been challenged on grounds that the Ramesside goals in western Asia differed significantly from those of the Eighteenth Dynasty pharaohs. Most scholars see the introduction of a new expansionist program only during the Nineteenth and Twentieth Dynasties (Singer 1988a; Morris 2005, 1–21). The archaeological evidence supports this view.

9. Kitchen 1975, 11–12, 15–16. For a discussion of these stelae, see, e.g., F. W. James 1966, 34–37, 153; Spalinger 1979; Higginbotham 2000, 22–24.

10. Kitchen 1979; for a summary, see Hasel 1998, 171–78; Higginbotham 2000, 28–34. Regarding the Beth-shean Year 18 stela dating to the reign of Ramesses II, see Kitchen 1979, 150–51; F. W. James 1966, 34–37, 153; James and McGovern 1993, 236. But see Higginbotham 2000, 33, who questions the historicity of the stela by pointing out that the "absence of any historical account argues against the theory that the Beth Shean stela was commissioned on the occasion of a pharaonic campaign."

11. Fritz (1981), Redford (1986, 197–200; 1992a), and Higginbotham (2000, 46–47) claim that Merneptah did not campaign to Canaan but may have conducted a minor punitive action against specific sites. The majority of scholars (supported, e.g., by Kitchen 1982; 2003; Yurco 1986; 1990; 1991; Singer 1988a; Ahlström 1991; Hoffmeier 1997) accept Merneptah's campaign to southern Canaan as a historical event. Additional evidence for this campaign can be found on the Amada Stela, which refers to Merneptah as "Plunderer of Gezer," and by the redating of the Cour de la Cachette relief at Karnak to Merneptah. For further discussion and bibliography, see Hasel 1998, 179–88; 2003.

12. See Breasted 1927, 403; Edgerton and Wilson 1936, pl. 46. Many questions have been raised regarding the reliability of this inscription (see, e.g., Tadmor 1979, 7; Gütterbock 1992, 55; Yakar 1993, 6). However, Cifola (1988; 1991) has analyzed it and concludes that its vagueness and departure from typical Egyptian conventions indicates (1) a lack of knowledge of the enemy ("Sea Peoples") and (2) an unconventional mode of warfare for the Egyptians in that the various Sea Peoples engaged in numerous raids on Egyptian-held lands rather than an organized battlefield attack. In Cifola's opinion, this confirms the historicity of the inscription. Most scholars agree with the attribution to Ramesses III, but Lesko 1992 attributes this relief to Merneptah. See most recently O'Connor 2000; Redford 2000; see also ch. 5 below for further discussion of this text.

13. Naʾaman (1981, 183) posits that Syria-Palestine was divided into two administrative units: Palestine and northern Palestine/southern Syria. The material culture evidence suggests that a cultural boundary passed through the Jezreel Valley, with Beth-shean and Megiddo marking the northern extent of the southern district.

14. One especially noteworthy feature of Canaan during the Late Bronze Age is the lack of fortifications at its urban centers. Although this absence remains a mystery, in all likelihood it is closely connected to Egyptian policy in Canaan.

15. Hasel (1998, 92–117) and Higginbotham (2000, 74–128, 145–301) have surveyed most classes of artifacts found in Canaan that can be considered "Egyptian-style" or imported from Egypt. These include weapons, ivories, doorjambs, lintels, stelae, statues, plaques, anthropoid coffins, pottery, alabaster, pendants, amulets, scarab seals, and inscriptions.

16. A key study of this architectural type is provided by Oren (1984), who examines structures from seven sites: Tel Seraʿ, Tell Jemmeh, Tell el-Hesi, Tell el-Farʿah (S), Tel Masos, Beth-shean, and Aphek. He concludes that all structures except for the building at Aphek (see below, administrative structures) should be classified as "governor's residencies" on the basis of their plan and method of construction. These reflect strong Egyptian influences that can be differentiated from other Syrian-influenced royal palaces known during the Middle and Late Bronze ages at Hazor, Shechem, and Megiddo (e.g., Harif 1979; Fritz 1983b; Oren 1992). Other scholars have since suggested that an additional residency was excavated at Gezer (see, e.g., Singer 1986–87; 1994, 288; but see Maeir 1988–89, who proposes that the residency dates to an earlier time period, while Bunimovitz 1988–89 proposes an entirely different location for the "governor's residency"). During the 1990 season of excavations at Gezer, W. G. Dever reexamined this structure. Although confirming a Late Bronze Age date for the building, he was unable to determine if Macalister's "Canaanite Castle" was an Egyptian-style administrative complex (Dever 1993b, 38–40). Due to the paucity of evidence and lack of adequate documentation, I have not included this building in Higginbotham's center-hall house group and focus only on those structures where sufficient archaeological evidence exists for this classification.

17. See Yannai 2002 for a reanalysis of this building and its dating to the Nineteenth and Twentieth Dynasties.

18. Gardiner (1920) was the first to point out that the earliest use of the term *migdol* to describe and depict forts along the "Ways of Horus" occurred during the reign of Seti I. See Hasel 1998, 96, and more recently Hoffmeier and Abd el-Maksoud 2003, 195–97.

19. Due to the poorly preserved state of this structure, where only the foundations remain, it is difficult to date this administrative building/fortress. I prefer to date the building to the Ramesside period and conclude that it continued in use at least through the reign of Ramesses III. Based on the archaeological evidence, a number of smaller fortifications began to appear along the "Ways of Horus" during the thirteenth century B.C.E. This view is supported by T. Dothan (1987; 1998a), Oren (1980; 1987), Oren and Shershevsky (1989), Kempinski (1992, 138–43), and Gal (1993), who also suggest that these depictions represent an Egyptian fortification system constructed along the "Ways of Horus." According to Oren and Shershevsky (1989), these depictions are fortress hieroglyphs that point to a fortified structure. T. Dothan (1985a; 1987) has suggested a closer similarity between the reliefs and the actual archaeological remains. However, all agree that such sites did exist along the "Ways of Horus" and served as police or customs stations that protected merchants and military traffic (Oren and Shershevsky 1989) or as garrisons and outposts (T. Dothan 1985b; Oren 1987). For a detailed discussion of forts along the "Ways of Horus," see Hasel 1998, 98–99, and and Cavillier 2001. See Hoffmeier and el-Maksoud 2003 regarding the recent excavations at Tell el-Borg and the discovery of a new military site on the "Ways of Horus."

20. I do not include the Sinai region in my discussion of Egyptian-style temples or architecture in Canaan because Sinai does not lie within the boundaries of Canaan.

21. In some of the literature, anthropoid coffins dating to the late thirteenth–early twelfth centuries B.C.E. were associated with the Philistines or Sea Peoples (Albright 1975b, 509; T. Dothan 1982, 252–88). The connection with the Philistines, based on the assumption that Ramesses III had settled Philistines as garrison troops in Palestine, was strengthened by the appearance of what was interpreted as a depiction of a "feathered" headdress on the lid from Beth-shean similar to that depicted on the reliefs at Medinet Habu (T. Dothan 1982, 268–76). Oren (1973, 146–50), disagreeing with the Philistine connection, suggested that the Beth-shean coffins contained the remains of *Denyen,* another group associated with the Sea Peoples. Today most scholars interpret these clay coffins as a purely Egyptian-style burial custom closely associated with Egyptian activities in Canaan (see, e.g., Bloch-Smith 1992b, 135; Gonen 1992, 29; Stager 1995, 342). Neutron Activation Analysis confirms that the coffins from Deir el-Balah were locally produced from the same clay quarries used to manufacture Egyptian-style pottery (Perlman, Asaro, and Dothan 1973, 149).

22. In addition to the ostraca, two scarabs from Tell el-Farʿah (S) are administrative seals of a temple estate of Ramesses III (Uehlinger 1988, 13–15), indicating Egyptian imperial interests at the site.

23. See Killebrew 2004 for a detailed typological and technological discussion of Egyptian-style pottery in Canaan. The first major publication to attempt a serious typology of Egyptian pottery is G. Nagel's 1938 publication of unrestricted open New Kingdom pottery vessels from Deir el-Medineh. In this volume he integrates Egyptian depictions with a typological discussion of these vessels. Unfortunately, he did not complete the classification of closed shapes. A second significant contribution is Holthoer's 1977 comprehensive study of New Kingdom ceramics from the Scandinavian Joint Expedition to Sudanese Nubia (see also Holthoer 1977, 2–4, for a survey of the history of the study of Egyptian pottery). Less helpful is Kelley's 1976 catalogue, which presents a corpus of ancient Egyptian pottery but lacks a descriptive text. See also D. Arnold 1981, an edited volume comprising specific studies on ancient Egyptian pottery, and Arnold and Bourriau 1993, a publication that deals mainly with the technical and technological aspects of Egyptian pottery. More recently, see Aston's 1996 and 1999 comprehensive tomes, which provide a detailed description of Twentieth Dynasty Egyptian pottery in Egypt.

24. Canaan: Deir el-Balah: Killebrew 1999a, ill. II:38:7, 14, 16; Beth-shean (Levels VII–VI): FitzGerald 1930, pl. XLI:2; XLIV:4; James and McGovern 1993, figs. 48:11; 53:10; Killebrew 1999a, ill. 78:6–7; Tel Seraʿ (Stratum IX): Oren 1985, fig. 4:1, 2; pl. 33:1; Lachish

(Fosse Temple III and Stratum VI) Tufnell, Inge, and Harding 1940, pl. XXXVI:25; Aharoni 1975, pl. 39:3; Ashdod (Strata XV–XVI): M. Dothan 1971, fig. 1:1; Dothan and Porath 1993, 45, e.g., fig. 11:3, 5; Tell es-Saᶜidiyeh (Tomb 105): Pritchard 1980, fig. 9:2; Megiddo (Strata IX–VIIB): Loud 1948, pl. 65:18.

Egypt and Nubia: Form EG 1a is present throughout the New Kingdom period in Egypt and the Sudan: Holthoer 1977, Type CU2: 116–117; pl. 25, and see his citations of Eighteenth and Nineteenth Dynasty parallels; see also Dunham and Janssen 1960, fig. 11:28–1–573g. In most Egyptian assemblages, this shape is classified together with our Bowl EG 1b. See Holthoer 1977, 116, where he notes the similarity between his Types CU2 (= our EG 1a) and PL3 (= our EG 1b). This bowl type is also common at the later New Kingdom Nineteenth Dynasty site of Deir el-Medineh: Nagel 1938, pl. IX, Type XIX: e.g., 1165.54 and pl. X, Type XIV: e.g., 356.108.

25. Canaan: Deir el-Balah: Killebrew 1999a, ills. II:38:12, 13, 15, 17; II:42:8; Beit-Arieh 1985, fig. 5:9. Beth-shean (Levels VIII, VII, Late Level VII): James and McGovern 1993, figs. 48:11, 12; 49:1–11, 15.53; Killebrew 1999a, ill. II:57:6, 8; Lachish (Fosse Temple III and Stratum VI): Tufnell, Inge, and Harding 1940, pl. XL: 90; Aharoni 1975, pl. 39:3; Megiddo (Strata VIII–VIIA): Loud 1948, pls. 61:11; 65:19; 69:3; Tell es-Saᶜidiyeh (Tomb 103): Pritchard 1980, fig. 6:1–4; Tomb 104: fig. 7:1; Miqne-Ekron (Stratum VII): Gunneweg, Dothan, Perlman, and Gitin 1986, fig. 3:8; note its possible nonlocal provenience.

Egypt and Nubia: Engelbach 1915, pl. XXXIV:2f, 2g, 2j, 2k; Peet and Woolley 1923, Type XLVII: esp. VII/156, VII/1003; Nagel 1938, pl. XV: Type XXII; see especially nos. 1165.58 and 359.219; Holthoer 1977, 124–26, pl. 27; Rose 1986, figs. 7:2: 54013, 56835; 7.3: 56280.

26. Canaan: Beth-shean (Levels VIII–VI): FitzGerald 1930, pl. XLI:1, 2; James 1966, figs. 31:19; 49:12; James and McGovern 1993, figs. 16:1; 31:2; 49:13; 50:4; 51:2; Killebrew 1999a, ills. II:57:6–8; II:78:8, 9; Tell el-Farᶜah (S): T. Dothan 1982, 266, fig. 8:1; Lachish (Stratum VI): Yannai 1996, pl. 18:12, 13; tomb south of Ashdod: Gophna and Meron 1970, fig. 2:3; Megiddo (Tomb 912D and Stratum VIIB): Guy 1938, pl. 36:2; Loud 1948, pl. 65:20.

Egypt and Nubia: Peet and Woolley 1923, pl. XILVII:VII/10003H; Nagel 1938, Type XXII: pl. XV: e.g., 356.66, 359.277, 1164.69; Holthoer 1977, fig. 27, see esp. 400/10:19; 100/18:24; Rose 1986, 104; fig. 7:2:51560; 1995, fig. 3.4:25.

27. Canaan: Beth-shean (Levels VII and VI): FitzGerald 1930, pl. XLI:3; James 1966, fig. 19:5; Oren 1973, figs. 43:15, 48a:2; James and McGovern 1993, figs. 8:9; 50:6; 51:6; Deir el-Balah: Killebrew 1999a, ills. II:37:2; 38:10, 11; Tell es-Saᶜidiyeh (Tombs 109, 137): Pritchard 1980, figs. 13:2; fig. 38:4; Aphek (Stratum X12): Beck and Kochavi 1985, fig. 2:1, 2.

Egypt and Nubia: Griffith 1890, pl. XV:2; MacIver and Woolley 1911, Type SXXIII: pl. 47; Peet and Woolley 1923, pl. XLVII:V/2; V/85; V/103, V/1005; V/261; Engelbach 1923, pl. XLII:2b; Steindorff 1937, Type 8b:3; Nagel 1938, Types X, XI; see esp. pl. VIII:358.182; 357.37; 1176.3; K.2.149; Holthoer 1977, Type PL 1.

28. Nagel 1938, fig. 148.

29. Canaan: Deir el-Balah: Beit-Arieh 1985, fig. 5:4, 7; Killebrew 1999a, ills. II:38:3, 4, 9; II:42:3; II:48:1; Beth-shean: James and McGovern 1993, figs. 12:8, 12, 13; 39:1. Some bowls have a red painted rim on the exterior or both interior and exterior. Deir el-Balah: Beit-Arieh 1985, fig. 5:1; Killebrew 1999a, ills. II:37:1; II:38:1, 2; Tel Seraᶜ (Stratum IX): Oren 1985, fig. 4:5; Aphek (Stratum X12): Beck and Kochavi 1985, fig. 2:3; Tell es-Saᶜidiyeh (Tomb 109): Pritchard 1980, fig. 13:3–5.

Egypt and Nubia: Peet and Woolley 1923, pl. XLVI, esp. IV/138, IV/201, IV/1002; Engelbach 1923, pl. LXII:12B; Petrie and Brunton 1924, pl. LX:38; Steindorff 1937, pl. 69. Type 6a:2–4; Nagel 1938, pl. III: Type IV; Holthoer 1977, 115–16, pl. 25; Rose 1984, fig. 10:1: Group 5; 1986, fig. 7.2: 54058. This basic bowl form continues into the late New Kingdom and Third Intermediate Period; see Aston 1996, figs. 187:d, e, j, k; 206:i, m.

30. Petrie 1930, 19, pl. LV; Holthoer 1977, 115.

31. Canaan: Deir el-Balah: Beit Arieh 1985, fig. 5:2, 5, 6; Killebrew 1999a, Ills. II:38:5–7; II:49:2; Beth-shean (Levels VII and VI): James and McGovern 1993, figs. 8:2; 12:9; 15:14, 15; 48:1–9; Killebrew 1999a, Ills. II:69:2; II:70:1; II:78:1, 4, 5, 8; Gezer (Stratum XIV): Dever, Lance, and Wright 1970, pl. 28:19; Ashdod (Strata XV–XIV): Dothan and Freedman 1967, fig. 22:2, 3; Dothan and Porath 1993, fig. 11:6, 8, 12; tomb south of Ashdod: Gophna and Meron 1970, fig. 2:2, 3; Lachish (Stratum VI): Aharoni 1975, pl. 39:7; Tel Seraʿ (Stratum IX): Oren 1985, fig. 4:2; Tel Mor (Stratum 6): M. Dothan 1960, figs. 4:9; 5:2; Jaffa: Kaplan 1960, pl. 13:22 bowl in center. Tell es Saʿidiyeh (Tombs 5, 104): Pritchard 1980, figs. 7:1; 8:1; 9:3–5. It is rare at sites in northern Canaan: Megiddo (Stratum VIII): Loud 1948, pl. 61:9 and Hazor: Yadin, Aharoni, Amiran, Dothan, Dunayevsky, and Perrot 1960, PL. XCLIII:4.

Egypt and Nubia: Peet and Woolley 1923, pl. XLVII: VI/160; VI/1002; VI/221; Nagel 1938, Type III, pl. II, especially K.S.50.a.b; Type XIV: pl. X:D.M.22.59; D.M.22.67; D.M.22.73; 1164.43; 1922.85, K.S.61; Type XVIII: pl. XIII: e.g., 359.206, 1172.4.57; Holthoer 1977 118, pls. 26; 28; Rose 1984, fig. 10.1: Group 5; 1986, fig. 7.2: 56453; 1987, 134, fig. 10.2: 63524.

32. Canaan: Deir el-Balah: Beit-Arieh 1985, fig. 5:13; Killebrew 1999a, e.g. ill. II:39:1; Beth Shean (Levels VII and VI): Yadin and Geva 1986, fig. 35:1; James and McGovern 1993, fig. 8:11, 13; Killebrew 1999a, ill. II:69:5, 6; Lachish: Tufnell, Inge, and Harding 1940, pl. XXXVIII:55, 56.

Egypt and Nubia: Engelbach 1915, pl. XXXIV:5P; Wainwright and Whittemore 1920, pls. XXIII:13; XXIV:25; Peet and Woolley 1923, pl. XLVII:IX/242; Nagel 1938, pl. VI: Type IX: K.2.145; Dunham and Janssen 1960, fig. 12:28–1–240; Holthoer 1977, 100; see also Rose 1984, fig. 10:1: Group 11; 1987, 134, fig. 10:2:60413. It continues well into the Twentieth Dynasty in Egypt; see Aston 1996, fig 189a.

33. Canaan: Beth-shean (Level VII): Killebrew 1999a, ill. II:70:3. In shape, bowl EG 7 bears some similarity to a bowl with a red slip assigned to Bowl Type 11 at Tell Qasile (Stratum XII): Mazar 1985a, 2. Note that other examples assigned to Bowl Type 11 from Strata XI and X do not, in my opinion, belong to the same type that appears in Stratum XII.

34. Egypt and Nubia: Peet and Woolley 1923, 137; Type XIV, no. 1006; Petrie and Brunton 1924, Type 12R: pl. LXIV:12R; Nagel 1938, 165–66; pl. VI:1922.80; Rose 1984, fig. 10.1.8; 1987, 133; fig. 10.4.63243; Aston 1996, 61, fig. 179: sixth and seventh drawings from the top; fig. 190:o, p.

35. Canaan: Beth-shean (Level VII and Tomb 227): Killebrew 1999a, ill. II:71:1; Oren 1973, fig. 46:19; pl. 74:11. Note that these vessels occasionally are not slipped. Oren 1973, fig. 48c:26 (Tomb 221A+B of mixed LBII/IAI date); Deir el-Balah: T. Dothan 1979 13, ills. 24; 29; Beit-Arieh 1985, 50, fig. 6:1; Tell el-ʿAjjul (Strata XVIII, XIX): Petrie 1933, pl. XLIV:34C, E; 1934, pls. XI:67; XLIX:34E; Tel Seraʿ (Stratum IX): Oren 1985, fig. 7:4a; pl. 34:3; Megiddo (Stratum VIIA): Loud 1948, pl. 67:15 (Jug Type 404); Tell es-Sa'ideyeh (Tomb 102): Pritchard 1980, Cup Type 29: fig. 5:1.

36. Egypt and Nubia: MacIver and Woolley 1911, pl. 47:SXXXIX; Peet and Woolley 1923, pl. LI:XLII/1009, 1009B; Brunton and Engelbach 1927, pl. XXIX:46h; Steindorff 1937, pl. 81 Form 36a; Thomas 1981, pl. 9:181; Rose 1984, fig. 10.1: Type 25. For Twentieth Dynasty contexts, see Griffith 1890, pl. XV:10; Aston 1996, 65; fig. 202:c-e:Group 44 mugs.

37. Ordinary-necked jars from Canaan: Tell el-ʿAjjul: Petrie 1932, pl. XXIX:31H3; 1933, pl. XXXII:31H8; 1934, pl. XLVIII:31K19; Tell el-Farʿah (S): Starkey and Harding 1932, pl. LXXXVIII:75N1, N4; Lachish (Fosse Temple I): Tufnell, Inge, and Harding 1940, pl. LIV:A&B:335; Tel Mor: M. Dothan 1960, pl. 9:1; Megiddo (Tomb 26, Stratum VIII): Guy 1938, pl. 57:9; Loud 1948, pl. 60:7; Hazor (Stratum XV): Garfinkel and Greenberg 1997, fig. III:16:15; Beth-shean (Stratum IX): A. Mazar 1997c, fig. 4; Deir el-Balah: Killebrew 1999a, ill. III:21:3–4.

Egypt and Nubia: Petrie 1905, pl. XXXVI; 1906, pls. XII:34, 100, 406, etc; XIVA:79, XXXIXC:52; 1907, pls. XXV:8; XXVI:63; MacIver and Woolley 1911, pl. 46: Type SXV; Peet and Woolley 1923, pl. XLIX:XXIV/16; XXV/88; Kelley 1976, pls. 38.2.8, 40.1.6, 47.7:36D, 36H,

50.1:17, 18; Petrie and Brunton 1924, pl. LXII: 92, 93; Brunton 1930, pl. XXVIII:107; Steindorff 1937, pl. 76: Type 22; Aston 1996, esp. p. 63, Group 27, fig. 1951-d. For full bibliographic references, see Holthoer 1977, 156, pls. 35–38.

38. Wide-necked jars from Canaan: Beth-shean (Levels VII and VI): FitzGerald 1930, pl. XLII:30; James and McGovern 1993, figs. 10:6; 13:14; A. Mazar 1997c, fig. 6. Tel Mor: M. Dothan 1960, fig. 11:6; Tell el-Farʿah (S): Starkey and Harding 1932, pl. LXXXVIII:75N3; Tell el-ʿAjjul: Petrie 1932, PL. XLII:31K3.

Egypt and Nubia: Petrie 1906, pl. X, e.g., 55, 65, 67, 74; 1907, pls. XXV:13–14; XXVI: 67; 1909, pl. XLI, e.g., 681; MacIver and Woolley 1911, pl. 46: Type SXVI; Engelbach 1915, pl. XXXV:20h; Brunton and Engelbach 1927, pl. XXI: 38; Steindorff 1937, pl. 72: Type 11a; Nagel 1938, fig. 110:54; Kelley 1976, pls. 47.5.20K, 22D; 47.13.20D. See Holthoer 1977, 162–63, for a detailed discussion.

39. Canaan: Beth-shean (Levels VII and VI): A. Mazar 1997c, fig. 6; Killebrew 1999a, ill. III:21:6; Deir el-Balah: Killebrew 1999a, ill. III:21:7; Tell el-Farʿah (S): Starkey and Harding 1932, pls. XLIX:924; LXXXVIII:75O; Tel Seraʿ (Stratum IX): Oren 1985, fig. 7:2; Tell es-Saʿidiyeh: Pritchard 1980, Jar Type 57: fig. 21:1; Jar Type 58: figs. 5:2; 23:3, 4; 27:1.

40. Egypt and Nubia: Petrie 1906, pl. XXIXC, e.g., 60, 62, 63, 65, 67; Petrie, Wainwright, and MacKay 1912, pl. XIX:101; Engelbach 1915, pls. XXXVI:41d, 42f; XXXVII:42h; Wainwright and Whittemore 1920, pl. XXIII:1, 5, 8, 9; Peet and Woolley 1923, pls. L:XXV/202 and pl. LIV:LXXVIII/236; Petrie and Brunton 1924, pl. LXI: 84; Brunton and Engelbach 1927, pl. XXIV:14–15; XXVI:9; Steindorff 1937, pl. 72: Type 12; Nagel 1938, fig. 63:10; Thomas 1981, pl. 8:186; Rose 1984, fig. 10.1: Type 17; Aston 1996, fig. 194b–e.

41. Canaan: Deir el-Balah: Beit-Arieh 1985, fig. 6:6; Tel Mor: M. Dothan 1960, pl. 11:4 is a similar but more squat version of this type of funnel-necked jar dated to the Iron I.

42. Egypt and Nubia: Peet and Woolley 1923, pl. L:XXVIII/194, is an example of a funnel-necked jar with a flat base. See also pl. XLIX:XXVIII/1017; Brunton and Engelbach 1927, pl.36:37T; Petrie, Wainwright, and MacKay 1912, pl. XVIII:71; Steindorff 1937, pl. 178: Type 27; Rose, 1987, fig. 10.3.64036; and Holthoer 1977, 148–50 for a detailed discussion of this type.

43. Canaan: Deir el-Balah: unpublished; Tell el-ʿAjjul: Petrie 1933, pl. XXVI:16, shows an example with an outward flaring rim; 1934, pl. LII:41V; Tell es-Sa'ideyeh: Pritchard 1980: small version: fig. 18:1, Type 60; large version: fig. 9:8, Type 56.

44. Holthoer 1977, 150–55, pls. 34, 35, distinguishes between two main types: ordinary and wide-mouthed. His ordinary group encompasses the vessels included in our Form EG 11 known at Deir el-Balah.

45. Tell el-Farʿah (S) Cemetery 900: Duncan 1930, Type 41.

46. Petrie, Wainwright, and MacKay 1912, pl. LII:21; Wainwright and Whittemore 1920, pl. XXIV:43; Peet and Woolley 1923, pl. XLVIII:XIX/120; XX/1048; XXI/1049; Engelbach 1923, pl. XLIV:36N, 36P; Brunton and Engelbach 1927, pl. XXXI:21; Rose 1987, fig. 10.3:62026.

47. See, e.g., Petrie, Wainwright, and MacKay 1912, pl. XVIII:66, 68; Brunton and Engelbach 1927, pl. XXXIX: Type 80, esp. 80E; Thomas 1981, pls. 8:183; 10:189.

48. Unlike the handled storage jars (see below), handleless storage containers are rarely depicted in Egyptian wall paintings. For an example of Form EG 13 – Ovoid-Shaped Jar – see the depiction in the 18th Dynasty Tomb of Baka at Qurneh (Petrie 1909, pl. XXXIV) that shows this jar with a handled commercial storage jar. Holthoer (1977, 80) suggests that due to the schematic representations of pottery vessels in Egyptian wall paintings, the vessels included in this category of storage jars could be confused with smaller ovoid jars which are often depicted.

49. Peet and Woolley 1923, pl. L:XXV/205; XXV/247; Petrie and Brunton 1924, pl. LXIV:24f2; Steindorff 1937, Type 28; Nagel 1938, fig. 62:2 (Tomb 1165). See Holthoer 1977, 82, pl. 17: ST 3, esp. 185/643:3 and the references there.

50. Canaan: Deir el-Balah: Killebrew 1999a, ill. III:22:1, 2; Megiddo: Loud 1948, pl. 60:7, Jar Type 108.

51. Canaan: Beth-shean (Levels VII and VI): Killebrew 1999a, ill. III:22:6; Tell el-ʿAjjul: Petrie 1933, pl. XXXIX:6963; Megiddo (Tomb 26, Stratum VIIB): Shipton 1939, Stratum VII typology chart – nos. 24–26; Guy 1938, pl. 57:10; Tomb 26; Loud 1948, pl. 65:3; Tell es-Saʿidiyeh (T. 110): Pritchard 1980, Type 63; fig. 15:5.

52. Egypt and Nubia: Brunton 1930, pl. XXVII:7; Nagel 1938, fig. 110:37; Holthoer 1977, 80–82, pl. 16 ST 2; Aston 1996, 64; fig. 198, Group 36.

53. Egypt and Nubia: Peet and Woolley 1923, pl. LI: XLII/1015; Hope 1978, fig. 1a; Rose 1984, fig. 10:1: Type 21; Thomas 1981, pl. 7:195, 196. For additional examples of Form EG 16, see also Nagel 1938, 15; Tombs 359 (figs. 8:1–4; 9:6–8; 10:11–12; 11:16–18; 12:21–23; 13:16–30); 1159 (fig. 50:8); 1164 (fig. 56:1–5); 1165 (fig. 64:12), and the workmen's village (fig. 109:1–2). Most of these vessels are somewhat longer and more slender than our example. Some of the jars at Deir el-Medineh are described as having a "yellow slip."

54. E.g., Engelbach 1915, pl. XXXVII:46C. For an example of a similar small storage jar from Aphek in Canaan, see Beck and Kochavi 1985, fig. 2:5.

55. Petrie 1909, pl. XXXVI; N. Davies 1943, pls. XLV, XLVIII, XLIX, L; 1923, pl. XXX. In addition to wine, they also contained certain resins, oils, and honey (Holthoer 1977, 97) as well as meat and various spices (Grace 1956, 86, 98–99). For a summary of the evidence regarding the contents of storage jars, see Hope 1978, 24–25.

56. MacIver and Woolley 1911, pl. 45:S11; Engelbach 1915, pl. XXXVII:46O; 1923, pl. XLIV:460; Brunton and Engelbach 1927, Type 46O: see, e.g., pls. XXIX:23 (46O), XXXI:36 (46O); XXXVIII:46O. See also Aston 1996, 66; Group 49; fig. 204a.

57. For a general discussion of spinning bowls, see T. Dothan 1963, 97–112; Aston 1996, fig. 191: Group 15:d. Bowls with a single interior handle are known in Canaan at Tell Jerishe (T. Dothan 1963, 100; fig. 1:10; 11) and in Egypt at Kahun, where the vessel is made of stone (Petrie 1890, 58; pl. XIII:58). Spinning bowls with three interior handles, of stone and pottery, are represented only at Deir el-Medineh (Nagel 1938, 185; figs. 153; 154; pl. XI: Type XVI:1922.M.7; 1922.M.8). See also Aston 1996, fig. 191: Group 15f. A vessel with four interior handles, two rows of two handles, was discovered at Beth-shean in an early Iron Age context (James 1963, fig. 50:2). See also James 1963, figs. 53:23; 55:2; 56:17; Yadin and Geva 1986, fig. 35:2; James and McGovern 1993, fig. 27:10; Killebrew 1999a, ill. III:24:1–3; and Loud 1948, pl. 70:3. Flat-based spinning bowls of similar contour and proportions are also known in Egypt from Tell el-Amarna (Peet and Woolley 1923, pl. XLVIII: Type XIII/20, 79, 188; Rose 1984, fig. 10:1, Type 26) and Deir el-Medineh (Nagel 1938, pl. XI:1922.M.7).

58. The appearance of this type of vessel in Egyptian tombs (EG 19) together with a second type of ceramic form termed "flowerpots" led Holthoer (1977, 86) to suggest that these two kinds of vessels were symbolic of the beer and bread mentioned in popular New Kingdom votive formulae. Thus, Holthoer proposed the term "beer bottle" to refer to the restricted vessels discussed here. See Holthoer 1977, 86–88, for references to beer bottles in Egypt. For a discussion of brewing techniques and their importance in ancient Egypt, see Lucas 1962, 16–23; Miller 1990; Samuel 1994, 1–11; Merrington 1994, 10. Note that bread and beer-making are usually associated with each other.

59. One of the characteristic features of beer bottles is the finger impressions marking the lower side walls. Holthoer (1977, 86) has suggested that these impressions might have been intended to facilitate the handling of the vessel during use. However, this trait may well be the result of a carelessness of fabrication, representing the removal of the vessel from the turning wheel when the potter grasped the base with his fingers. Since the vessel was apparently thrown entirely base down, such fingerprints may well be a technical feature associated with the removal of a vessel from the wheel.

60. Deir el-Balah: Killebrew 1999a, ill. III:24:5–7; Beth-shean (Levels VII and VI): FitzGerald 1930, pl. XLII:11; XLV:7; James 1966, figs. 30:7; 31:9; 49:6; 51:6; 54:1; James and

McGovern 1993, fig. 10:7; Killebrew 1999a, ill. III:24:8; Tell es-Saʿidiyeh: Pritchard 1980, 7–8, fig. 7:5; Type 53. Pritchard suggests that this bottle, found in the cemetery, served a funerary function possibly related to ritual librations for the dead or as a reminder of the rites of beer-making associated with the Egyptian mortuary cult; Tell el-Farʿah (S): Starkey and Harding 1932. pl. LXXXVIII:94; Ashdod: M. Dothan 1971, fig. 81:14.

61. Deir el-Balah: Killebrew 1999a, ill. III:24:9; Beth-shean: Yadin and Geva 1986, fig. 35:3; Killebrew 1999a, ill. III:24:10. This beer-bottle type is one of the most popular in the workmen's village at Tell el-Amarna: Rose 1984, fig. 10.1:15. Simple and cylindrical beer bottles are rare in Canaan; see, e.g., Deir ʿAlla: Franken and Kalsbeek 1969, 107–8, fig. 62:29, pl. XV:fig. 62 no. 29 (beer bottle with solid base). Franken suggests that this vessel was used for "sugar production."

62. Regarding technological studies of Egyptian pottery, see, e.g., Bourriau 1985, 29–42; Bourriau and Nicholson 1992, 29–109; Arnold and Bourriau 1993.

63. This method involves the measurement of chemical elements through the bombardment of the sample's atomic nuclei with neutrons in a nuclear reactor, which transforms the constituent elements of the sample into unstable radioactive isotopes. Analysis of the gamma-ray spectrum emitted from the radioactive isotopes enables the determination of trace elements and their amounts. See, e.g., Peacock 1970, 378; Perlman and Asaro 1971, 182. Though there are numerous drawbacks and potential problems with this technique, NAA has successfully been used in a number of case studies to identify and confirm the provenience of pottery; see Aspinall 1985, 11–12.

64. This technique entails the affixing of a small fragment of pottery to a glass microscope slide that is then ground with a diamond lap or abrasive powder until it is 0.03 mm thick. Under the polarizing microscope, minerals in the pottery sample are transparent and can be identified. Generally it is possible to determine whether the mineralogical composition of the pottery sample matches or differs from the local clay beds and geology of a region in question. See, e.g., Peacock 1970, 375. The relatively inexpensive cost and quick results of petrography have enhanced the attractiveness of this method over more expensive and complex chemical analyses, such as NAA. For best results, however, one should ideally combine thin-section analysis with a chemical analysis. For a recent discussion, see Vaughan 1995, 115–17.

65. Based on NAA analyses, the majority of the Egyptian-style and Canaanite vessels and all the clay coffins were locally produced, while a small number of vessels, mainly the white-burnished slip wares (Egyptian-style storage containers [EG 16] and mugs [EG 8]) were imported from Egypt. See, e.g., Perlman, Asaro, and Dothan 1973, 147–51; Goldberg, Gould, Killebrew, and Yellin 1986, 341–51; Yellin, Dothan, and Gould 1986, 68–73; 1990, 257–61. Similar results were reached via petrographic analysis; for a detailed description and petrographic discussion of the Deir el-Balah wares and local clay sources, see Goldberg, Gould, Killebrew, and Yellin 1986, 341–51; Killebrew 1999a, 207–10; 2004.

66. Regarding NAA analyses, see McGovern, Harbottle, Huntoon, and Wnuk 1993, 88–92. For recent petrographic studies, see Cohen-Weinberger 1998; Killebrew 1999a, 211–15; 2004.

67. Similar to an X-ray, this technique has been successfully employed to examine the structure of a ceramic artifact and can often discern manufacturing techniques such as hand versus wheel formation, direction of wheel rotation, technique of joins, repairs, and later additions to ancient pottery. See, e.g., Alexander and Johnston 1982, 148–49; Glanzman and Fleming 1986, 588–95.

68. The incentives for Egyptian intervention in Canaan might include: (1) the promotion of economic interests (Naʾaman 1981); (2) the attainment of geographic control and access to neighboring areas (Ahituv 1978); (3) the exploitation of Canaan's resources (Albright 1975a; Gonen 1984; Singer 1988a), (4) the development of Canaan's resources (Naʾaman 1981;

Liebowitz 1987); or (5) the affirmation of Egyptian imperialistic or colonialist aims and ideology in the region. It has also been suggested that Egyptian intervention in Canaan was more indirect, resulting in Canaanite emulation of Egyptian culture viewed within a model of core-periphery interaction (Higginbotham 1996; 1998; 2000).

69. James Weinstein's 1981 and 1992 articles systematically catalogue the architectural and inscriptional evidence from Canaan. His conclusion is that these monuments, taken together with the numerous small finds of Egyptian type, indicate a shift in pharaonic policy toward the region beginning in the Nineteenth Dynasty (see also Morris 2005). Weinstein and most archaeologists working on the topic in Israel base their opinion on the dramatic increase in Egyptian objects found in Palestine during the thirteenth and twelfth centuries B.C.E. Weinstein (1981, 17) concludes that, with the Ramesside era, Egyptian policy shifted from economic and political domination to military occupation. For the most recent discussion of Egyptian foreign policies during the Eighteenth Dynasty, which is outside the scope of this book, see Hoffmeier 2004. See also Oren 1984; Singer 1988–89; Dever 1992c, 101; Knapp 1992b, 94; Tubb 1998, 82–83.

70. Weinstein 1981; Goldwasser 1984; Oren 1984; 1985; Ussishkin 1985; Singer 1988a; 1988–89; 1994; Murname 1992; Redford 1992b, 192–240.

71. See Weinstein 1981, 17; Singer 1994, 284; but see Redford (1985; 1990), who claims that Egyptian control did not include annexation or large numbers of Egyptians stationed in Canaan. For a general discussion regarding political domination and definitions of different sources of power, see Earle 1994, esp. 951–57.

72. For a summary of the evidence, see Weinstein 1981, 17–22. Regarding Egyptian military outposts and their depictions along the "Ways of Horus" in the Karnak relief, see n. 19 above for a discussion and references.

73. Singer 1988a; 1988–89. Regarding Egyptian influence in the Jezreel Valley, see Na'aman 1988.

74. Singer 1994, 289. Others, however, claim that this period represented a time of weak Egyptian control; see Faulkner 1975, 232–35; Kitchen 1982, 215ff.; and Goren, Oren, and Feinstein 1995, 104.

75. For a convenient translation of the text, see Wilson 1969b, 377.

76. Yurco 1978, 70; 1986; 1990; Stager 1985b; but see Redford 1986, who rejects this redating.

77. Only a small number of Egyptian artifacts with the names of pharaohs at the close of the Nineteenth Dynasty and the early Twentieth Dynasty, between the reigns of Merneptah and Ramesses III, have been uncovered in Canaan (see, e.g., Goldwasser 1980). Cartouches with the name of Seti II were incised on a storage jar and found inside Building YR at Tell el-Far'ah (S) (Wood 1991, 51–52). A scarab of Seti II was found in Stratum III at Tel Masos (Giveon and Kempinski 1983, 102–4). Most notable is the discovery of the cartouche of Tewosret in the destruction level at the end of the Late Bronze Age settlement at Tell Deir 'Alla (Yoyotte 1962; Franken 1964, 420–21) and a scarab of Tewosret from Akko (M. Dothan 1989, 63–64).

78. F. W. James 1966; Oren 1973; James and McGovern 1993; A. Mazar 1994a; 1997a.

79. Weinstein 1981, 17–22; T. Dothan 1982, 3; Oren 1984; A. Mazar 1985a; Ussishkin 1985; Singer 1985b; 1992a; 1994, 290–94; Negbi 1991; Bunimovitz 1993. Regarding a proposed Sea Peoples presence in Transjordan, see Tubb 1988b.

80. Bietak 1985; 1993; B. G. Wood 1991. See also Stager (1995, 340–44), who traces the beginning of Egyptian decline to Ramesses III, his "stage 1."

81. But see Lesko 1992 who disputes this interpretation.

3
CANAAN AND CANAANITES: AN ETHNIC MOSAIC

The Canaanites are best known from the biblical accounts that portray them as the hostile indigenous inhabitants of Canaan who formed the major obstacle to Israel's attempts to claim their "promised land." The Bible is careful to distinguish between the idol-worshiping Canaanites and the Yahweh-worshiping Israelites, whose origins, according to the biblical tradition, lie outside of Canaan. Unfortunately, we have few insights into how the inhabitants of the southern Levant viewed themselves. Ironically, the "inventors" of the alphabet have left us few second-millennium texts or inscriptions. Until now, no large archives of contemporary documents have been uncovered in Late Bronze Age Canaan.[1]

As a periphery region under Egyptian imperialistic dominance during the Late Bronze and Early Iron Ages, Canaan and its inhabitants are presented to us through the viewpoint of others—mainly via New Kingdom Egyptian, Ugaritic, and Hittite texts or later biblical traditions. The primary body of evidence originating from Canaan is the archaeological record that provides our most valuable source of information regarding the Canaanites. In this chapter, I define Canaan and its inhabitants, the Canaanites, within its larger fourteenth–twelfth century B.C.E. eastern Mediterranean setting. In its role as a semiperipheral or peripheral region in the international Late Bronze Age milieu, I explore Canaan's cultural and social boundaries based on its excavated material culture remains. Its transformation and subsequent cultural fragmentation are traced following the "crisis" and breakdown of the major empires at the end of the Late Bronze and Early Iron Ages. Changes experienced by the entire eastern Mediterranean region during this period particularly effected Canaan and its position as a periphery region under Egyptian imperial domination, created the cultural climate that led to the colonization of its coast by Philistines and other Sea Peoples groups, and facilitated the ethnogenesis of early Israel.

Canaan and Canaanites: A Definition

Today scholarship is divided regarding the concept of a Late Bronze Age Canaanite entity or whether there is a definable region called Canaan. This question has been brought to the forefront with the blurring of the distinction between "Canaanite" and "Israelite" during the past few decades in both archaeological and biblical circles (see ch. 4 below). Some European scholars, particularly those who identify with so-called "minimalist" views, tend to be skeptical of the existence of a specific group that can be called "Canaanites" (see, e.g., Lemche 1991a; 1996; 1998a; Grabbe 1994; for a general discussion, see M. S. Smith 2001, 197).[2] American, Israeli, and more traditional European academic traditions prefer to see "Canaanite" as both a language classification and a definable cultural entity (see Aharoni 1967, 61–70; Rainey 1996; Naʾaman 1994a; 1999; Fleming 1994; Pardee 1997; Hess 1998), with scholarship drawing the boundaries of Canaan as corresponding roughly to the area of the Egyptian "province" in western Asia (de Vaux 1978, 127–28; Naʾaman 1994a, 408).

In this book I use the term *Canaan* as a geopolitical entity that corresponds approximately to the modern states of Israel, West Bank/Gaza Strip, Jordan, Lebanon, and southern Syria. The Middle and Late Bronze Age inhabitants of the region, the Canaanites, were the ancestors of later Iron Age population groups, including the coastal Phoenicians, the Israelites located in the highland regions and the Transjordanian Ammonites and Moabites.[3] One can identify, archaeologically speaking a second-millennium material culture in this region that shares many features in common and forms a "social boundary." Thus I prefer to use the term *Canaanite* to describe this culture and the peoples who produced it and spoke a Canaanite language. However, I am not implying here that *Canaan* or *Canaanite* indicates an ethnic entity. Based on the archaeological evidence, considered in light of the appearance of the terms *Canaan* and *Canaanite* in several second-millennium texts, I use *Canaan* to refer generally to the southern Levant and *Canaanites* with reference to the multiethnic people living in this region during the second millennium.

Textual Evidence

The term *Canaan* appears in Hebrew, Ugaritic, Phoenician/Punic, Akkadian cuneiform, and Egyptian texts.[4] These texts refer to the existence of a place called "Canaan" or a person referred to as a "Canaanite." Several of the most important documents related to this discussion include texts from Mari, Alalakh, Egypt, and Ugarit as well as the later biblical traditions.

Mari

The earliest certain reference to "Canaan(ite)" occurs in a letter written by an Yasmaḫ-Adad, a king of Mari during the eighteenth century B.C.E. (Dossin 1973). The text mentions "thieves and Canaanites" and indicates that its author was "contemplating taking hostile action against unspecified opponents" (Sasson 1984, 90).

Egypt

Another early reference to Canaanites appears on a stela found at Memphis dating to the reign of Amenhotep. The list of booty from his first campaign includes a reference to 640 *Ki-na-ᶜ-nu* ("Canaanites"; see Rainey 1973). Canaan is also mentioned numerous times in the fourteenth century B.C.E. Amarna archives, which contain correspondence between the Egyptian pharaoh and rulers from various regions in the eastern Mediterranean and ancient Near East. These include EA 30 (Moran 1992, 100), which is correspondence from the king of Mitanni addressed to the "kings of the land of Canaan"; EA 8 (Moran 1992, 16) and EA 9 (Moran 1992, 18–19), correspondence from the king of Babylon; EA 162 (Moran 1992, 250–51 n. 10), from the Egyptian pharaoh; EA 36 (Rainey 1996, 7–8; but see Moran 1992, 110), from the king of Alashiya; and EA 109, 110, 131, 137, 148, and 151, letters originating in Byblos, Beirut, and Tyre (for a discussion of the evidence, see Rainey 1996, 6–9). A careful reading of these letters does indicate that there was a region in the southern Levant that was referred to during the Late Bronze Age as Canaan. Lastly, Canaan is also described as "plundered" on the Merneptah Stela (see ch. 4 below).

Alalakh

Several inscriptions recovered from Stratum IV at Alalakh mention the name Canaan in the context of "man of Canaan" or "son of Canaan."[5] The best-known inscription appears on the statue of Idrimi, king of Alalakh, found at the site in 1939 (*ANET*, 557–58). Following a popular revolt in his kingdom, Idrimi was forced to go into exile. Taking with him his mother's relatives, he fled to the "land of Canaan," where he stayed until he was able to launch an attack by ship and reclaim his kingdom (S. Smith 1949, pls. 9–10; Greenstein and Marcus 1976, 64, 67, 73–78; see also Rainey 1996, 3–4).

Ugarit

Two texts from Ugarit also mention Canaan. RS 11.840 = KTU 4.96 is an administrative document that lists "Yaᶜilu, a Canaanite" among the merchants (Rainey 1963). A second document dealing with a judicial decision is RS 20.182A+B (Rainey 1964; Nougayrol 1968, 110–13). This text clearly distinguishes between the "sons of Canaan" and the "sons of Ugarit" and has been used to support the position that Ugarit was not part of Canaan.

Biblical Evidence

As the main antagonists to early Israel's claim to the promised land, Canaanites and Canaan are mentioned some 160 times in the Bible. Most of these references appear in the Pentateuch and in the books of Joshua and Judges and deal primarily with genealogical relationships, the covenant, the exodus, and the conquest. Canaan, grouped with Egypt and the African nations, first appears as the name of one of Noah's grandsons, whose father Ham was cursed after "looking upon" a drunk and naked Noah (Gen 9:18–23). Later God promised the land of Canaan to Abraham (12:1–7) and then instructed Moses to lead the enslaved Israelites into the land of the Canaanites, Amorites, Perizzites, Hivites, and Jebusites (Exod 3:8, 17; for an overview of Canaan in biblical scholarship, see Lemche 1991a, 13–24). The historicity of these biblical passages regarding Canaan and the Canaanites has become more problematic as the archaeological and textual evidence increasingly supports the suggestion that early Israel consisted largely of indigenous Canaanites originating from Cis- and Transjordan (see ch. 4 below).

The borders of Canaan are described in several biblical passages, including Num 34:1–12 and verses on Israel's future inheritance in Ezek 47:13–20; 48:1–7, 23–29. The southern boundary is described in Josh 15:2–4, while 19:24–31 outlines the northern border. The table of nations (Gen 10:19) also indicates a more restricted Canaan (Hackett 1997, 409).

Taken together, second-millennium references to Canaan describe a region south of Alalakh and Ugarit, corresponding roughly to what is sometimes referred to as Syria-Palestine. In these texts Canaanites are distinguished from other groups and often appear as merchants or connected with military activities. Although the biblical texts mentioning Canaan and the Canaanites were edited centuries after the Late Bronze Age, one cannot fail to notice that there is a correspondence between the general contours of Canaan as indicated in second-millennium texts and the boundaries of Canaan in the biblical accounts.

The Archaeological Evidence

In light of the scarcity of textual evidence from Canaan proper, the abundant archaeological data assumes an important role in our interpretations of the Canaanites. This section reviews the archaeological evidence for Late Bronze Age Canaan beginning with a summary of the settlement patterns based on the archaeological and survey data. I then examine the architectural layout of several key urban centers that characterize the the city-state systems in Canaan, including palaces, temples, and burials. A detailed discussion of the ceramic repertoire forms the focus of this discussion of Canaanite cultural and social boundaries.

Settlement Patterns in Canaan during the Second Millennium

Numerous archaeological surveys conducted during the last four decades have contributed tremendously to our knowledge of the sociocultural landscape of Middle and Late Bronze Age Levantine society. This survey data has particularly shaped our understanding of the transformations that marked the early Iron Age in the region (for a detailed discussion, see ch. 4 below). Methodologically, the *Annales* school, especially Fernand Braudel's concept of "long-term history," has played an influential role in the interpretation of survey data and general settlement patterns during the second millennium.[6] This period of time is marked by two well-documented shifts in the settlement pattern of Canaan. The first few centuries of the second millennium B.C.E. were characterized by the gradual development of large urban centers during the Middle Bronze Age (Broshi and Gophna 1986; Gophna and Portugali 1988; Ilan 1995, 301–3). During the sixteenth century, coinciding with the transition from the Middle to the Late Bronze Ages, there was a noteworthy decline in settlement size and urban population. Then, over the course of the Late Bronze Age, the number of settlements gradually increased, reaching its peak during the thirteenth century (Gonen 1984; Bunimovitz 1995, 320–24), with most of the sites located in the coastal plain and fertile valleys (fig. 3.1). At the end of the Late Bronze Age and in the early Iron Age, once again a dramatic shift in settlement patterns is marked by several phenomena: (1) the significant growth in the numbers of small villages in previously marginal areas such as the hill-country region; (2) continued occupation at several Late Bronze Age urban centers in the lowlands; and (3) the appearance of urban coastal centers, especially along the southern coastal plan, associated with the Philistines and other Sea Peoples (see chs. 4 and 5 for discussion and detailed bibliography).

One should note two other features of second-millennium settlement patterns and their associated cultural and social boundaries. In spite of the reduction in size and number of urban centers during the transition from the Middle and Late Bronze Ages, the material culture is marked by continuity. In contrast, the transformation at the end of the thirteenth through the twelfth centuries is characterized not only by a dramatic shift

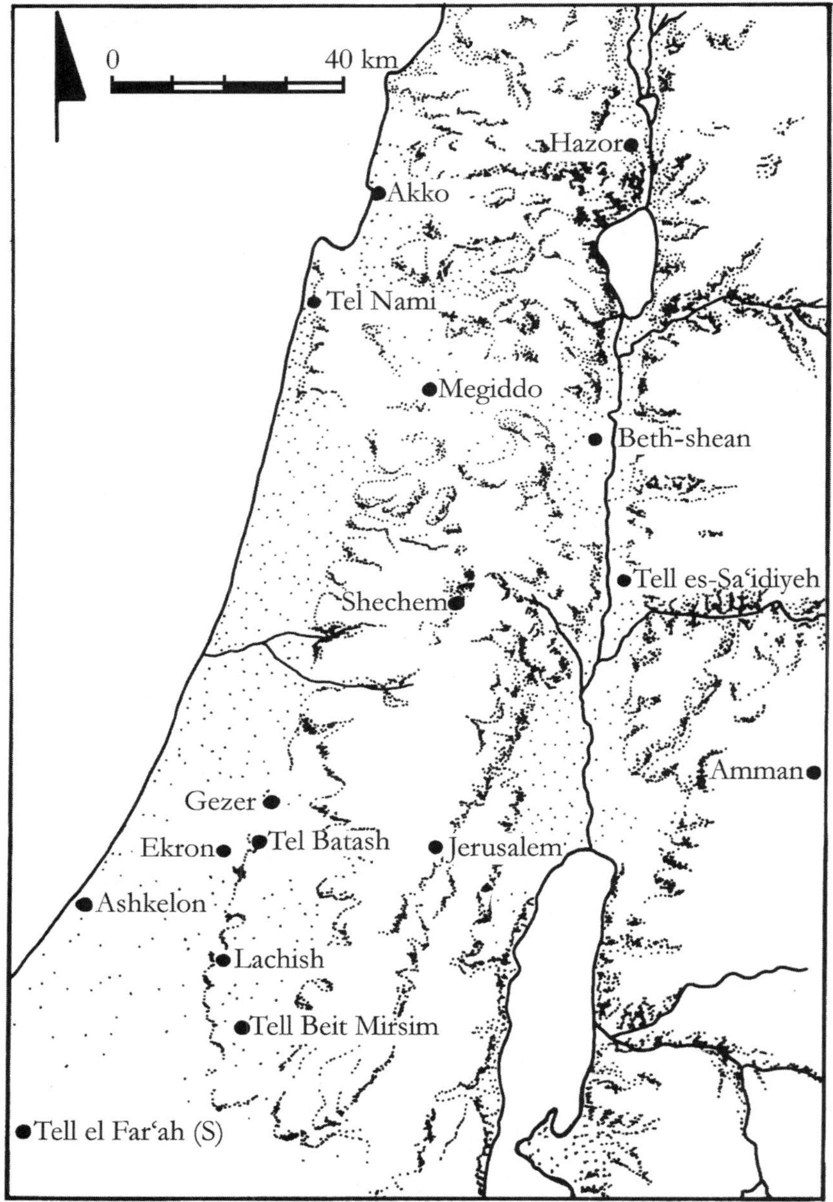

Fig. 3.1. Map of Selected Late Bronze Age Canaanite Sites

in settlement patterns but by the appearance of regionally defined material cultures that created new social boundaries (what Bunimovtiz 1995, 320, terms Palestine's "social landscape"). Thus, though there seems to be general decline and deterioration in the material welfare of Canaan during the mid-second millennium, there is also a great deal of continuity throughout the Middle and Late Bronze Ages, as evidenced in the material culture and general territorial divisions. What does appear to have changed is the numbers of seminomads and marginalized individuals living outside of Late Bronze Age Canaanite settled society.[7]

In recent years, archaeological evidence has been used increasingly to reconstruct Canaan's internal political-territorial divisions, questions first addressed by Albrecht Alt (1939; 1967). In his early pioneering work, which was based mainly on his analysis of New Kingdom Egyptian texts, especially the Amarna letters, Alt identified two different, coexisting political-territorial formations in Late Bronze Age Palestine, both of which were under Egyptian influence: a network of city-states in the plains and valleys, and larger territorial kingdoms in the mountainous regions (see ch. 2 above).[8] Subsequent scholarly work on Late Bronze Age Canaan builds on Alt's historical and topographical contributions. These include Wolfgang Helck's (1971) monumental work on the relations between Egypt and western Asia during the second millennium B.C.E., where he traces the network of Canaanite kingdoms and Egyptian government centers in Late Bronze Age Canaan. Other attempts to delineate the territorial boundaries of Canaanite city-states during the Late Bronze Age have traditionally focused on the textual[9] or archaeological evidence (Bunimovitz 1989; 1995; Finkelstein 1996e).

Basing his work on Alt's conclusions, Nadav Naʾaman (1986; 1988; 1992; 1997) has attempted further to refine the boundaries of Late Bronze city-states. In his initial work, Naʾaman based his reconstruction on the textual evidence, including the Amarna letters and other New Kingdom Egyptian sources as well as the biblical sources, such as the list of Canaanite kings in Josh 12 and the system of tribal boundaries (Naʾaman 1986, 465, 469). He thus proposed that Late Bronze Canaan was divided between thirty-two Canaanite city-states. Israel Finkelstein (1996e) challenged Naʾaman's division,[10] contending that Naʾaman's entities did not control a large enough territorial and demographic hinterland. He also took issue with Naʾaman's dating of the biblical material on the tribal territories to the period of the united monarchy, stating that this is much too early, according to most recent studies.[11]

In his 1997 response to Finkelstein's critique, Naʾaman admits that it is necessary to apply theoretical models and to take into account the region's geographical features and archaeological data (i.e., settlement size and distribution, demography), as well as the long-range perspectives. However, as he notes, the development of territorial-political systems involves many factors, and the written sources should be considered as primary data. Thus, Naʾaman slightly revises the overall number of city-states in Palestine to at least twenty-five, probably more.

Shlomo Bunimovitz (1989; 1994a; 1995) was the first to integrate both the archaeological data and historical documents in his analysis of Canaan's sociopolitical territorial divisions. Bunimovitz follows Naʾaman's basic ideas but incorporates several sociopolitical and geographic methods, including the early-state module and rank-size index.[12] Addressing the evidence from archaeological surveys, Bunimovitz (1994a) suggests that declining populations resulted in a deficit in manpower that provided one of the main motives for several city-states' attempts at territorial expansion (e.g., EA 250). He further argues that this manpower deficit may explain why there was almost no construction of fortifications during the Late Bronze Age and why there is a relative poverty of important Canaanite centers during the Late Bronze II, as indicated in the archaeological evidence.

Regarding the larger second-millennium picture, Naʾaman (1986, 483) argues for territorial continuity from the city-state system of the Middle Bronze to that of the Late Bronze, while Bunimovitz (1989) raises doubts regarding the concept of political and territorial continuity in the Middle Bronze/Late Bronze transition. On this point, I tend to support Naʾaman's view of continuity between the political and territorial systems of the two periods, with two important differences. I would recognize a major demographic crisis in the Middle Bronze to Late Bronze transition accompanied by the decline and transformation of the second-millennium city-state system and the rise of a new order. However, the key factor in understanding the city-state system in Late Bronze Age Canaan remains the Egyptian domination and influence over the region, which provided a framework for the functioning of these city-states within the larger world system (see chs. 1 and 2 above).

Architectural Features of Canaanite Sites

Town Planning

Although no Late Bronze Age town or city has been excavated in its entirety, one can make several general statements regarding their layout and town planning. I follow Jacob Baumgarten's (1992, 145) classification of Late Bronze Age settlements based on excavation and survey data and settlement size. These include: (1) large villages/small towns (ca. 3.5–12 acres);[13] (2) medium-sized towns (12–25 acres);[14] (3) large cities (25–60 acres);[15] and (4) megalopolises (over 60 acres in size), which includes only Late Bronze Age Hazor, the largest tell in the modern State of Israel, whose upper and lower cities cover 200 acres.[16] The surrounding satellite settlements and villages within each city-state's political-territorial boundaries generally range in size from less than .25 acre to 2.5 acres in size. Very few Late Bronze Age villages have been excavated. However, the small fourteenth- and thirteenth-century settlements at sites such as Tel Miqne-Ekron (Gittlin 1992) and Batash (Kelm and Mazar 1995, 39–90; A. Mazar 1997c, 58–72, 252–54) may well be large villages that were satellite sites of larger Late Bronze towns such as Gezer.[17]

First and foremost, the town or city was the focal point of administrative, political, economic, and religious power for the city-state and its hinterland.[18] One of the most extensively excavated ancient mounds is Megiddo. Stratum VIIB represents the thirteenth-century B.C.E. city (fig. 3.2). It includes the city gate and palace (Area AA) in the northwest sector of the site, temple 2048 (Area BB) on the eastern side of the tell, and what may be a second palace or large patrician courtyard house (Area DD), uncovered on the northern edge of the mound, to the east of the gate. All the Late Bronze Age structures excavated at Megiddo are public buildings or appear to be related to public activities or the housing of officials connected with the administration of the city.

One of the most problematic aspects of Late Bronze Age towns and cities relates to the question of fortifications. Thus far there is no evidence for the construction of fortification systems encircling the city perimeter during the Late Bronze Age. This has led to two different interpretations, that settlements were unfortified (A. Mazar 1989; Gonen 1992, 218) or that the Middle Bronze Age fortifications remained in use during the Late Bronze Age (see Kempinski 1992, 136–37).[19] Although there is no evidence for construction of city fortifications, there are indications that the palaces were protected. The most notable example of this is the city gate associated with the palace at Megiddo (figs. 3.2–3). Most structures excavated at sites classified as medium-sized towns and cities are public structures: temples, palaces, administrative buildings, and residencies (for a detailed discussion of these structures, see pp. 58–64 above and 101–8 below).

Palaces

Large residential complexes are notoriously difficult to define, being referred to as palaces, patrician houses, or governors' residencies. I classify as *palaces* very large, multiroom facilities that clearly served multiple purposes, most likely were the residences of local rulers, and often continued an uninterrupted architectural tradition that originated in the Middle Bronze Age. Large residences with central courtyards that are more modest in size are termed *patrician houses* (see the discussion of domestic architecture below). Finally, structures

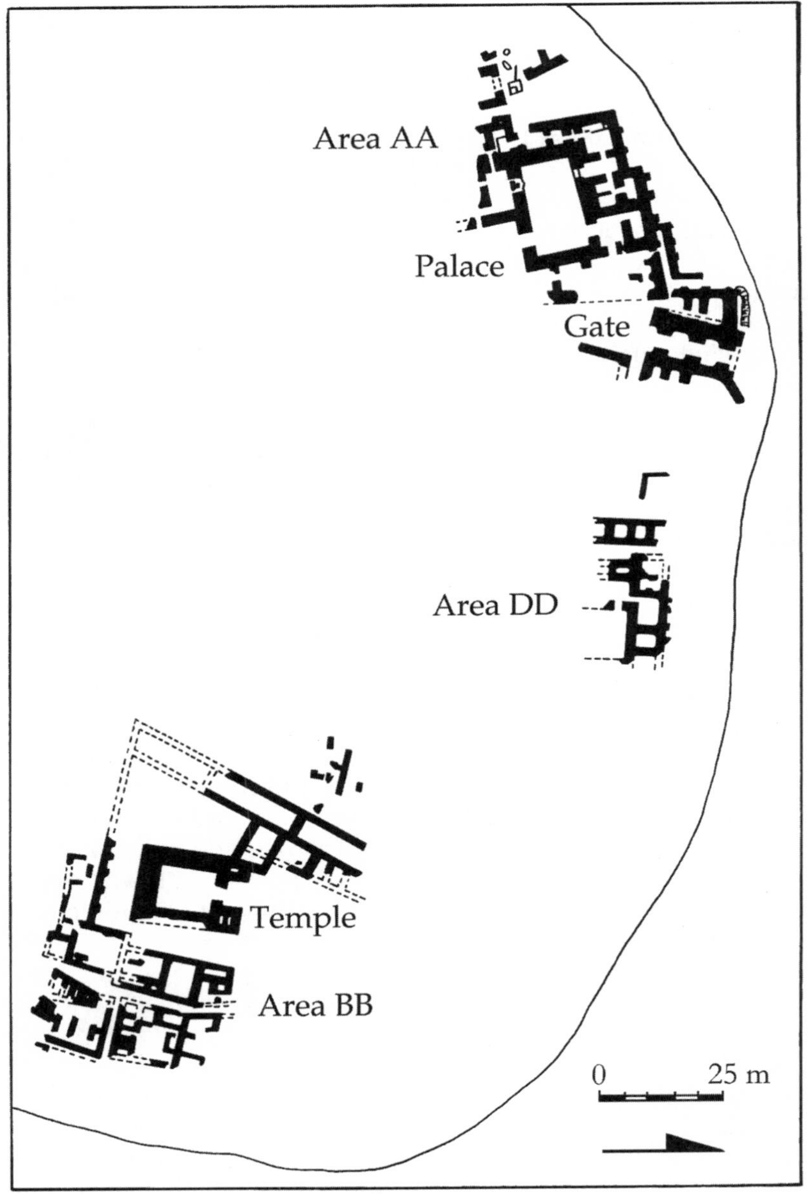

Fig.3.2. Schematic Plan of Megiddo Stratum VIIB

Fig. 3.3. The Late Bronze Age Gate at Megiddo

with Egyptian features are classified as either *center-hall houses* or *administrative buildings* (see ch. 2).

Common to all these structures is a central room or courtyard surrounded by a series of rooms or complexes, similar in plan to domestic structures but far grander in scale. The palace and accompanying gate in Area AA at Megiddo are one of the few extensively excavated Late Bronze Age palace complexes in the southern Levant (figs. 3.2–3; see also the recently excavated palace at Hazor). The Megiddo palace, first erected in Stratum VIII, covered an area of roughly 1,500 m^2. The central courtyard measured approximately 19 x 10 m, and four doorways appeared in its massive walls (ca. 2.5–4 m wide). Three of the doorways led to smaller interior rooms of the palace, while the southeastern doorway, apparently the main entrance to the palace, connected the large courtyard to an internal courtyard with a shell pavement and a basin with two openings in its southern wall leading to additional rooms of the palace (see Loud 1948, fig. 382; Oren 1992, 106–7).

The largest Late Bronze Age palace thus far excavated in the Levant is the monumental palace at Ugarit (Schaeffer et al. 1962, 1462, fig. 21; for the core section of the palace, see fig. 3.4). Although Ugarit is not part of Canaan proper, its palace, which consists of several interconnected courtyard structures, shares several general features (i.e., a large courtyard surrounded by smaller rooms) with smaller palaces in Canaan, particularly those in northern Canaan. It also provides useful comparative evidence and insights into the plan and function of Late Bronze Age palaces.

At its greatest extent, Ugarit's palace covered approximately 7,000 m^2; thus far over one hundred rooms arranged around ten inner courtyards have been excavated (see Margueron 1995; 2000; Yon 1998). The palace comprises several units that include elaborate entranceways with a pair of columns between stone piers (perhaps a precursor to the Iron Age *bit hilani* palace plan that is well known in Syria). A similar monumental structure was uncovered at Alalakh, whose composite plan includes ceremonial, residential, and storage units (see Oren 1992, 114). The recently excavated but as yet unpublished palace at Hazor also shares similarities with these two huge northern Levant complexes. The

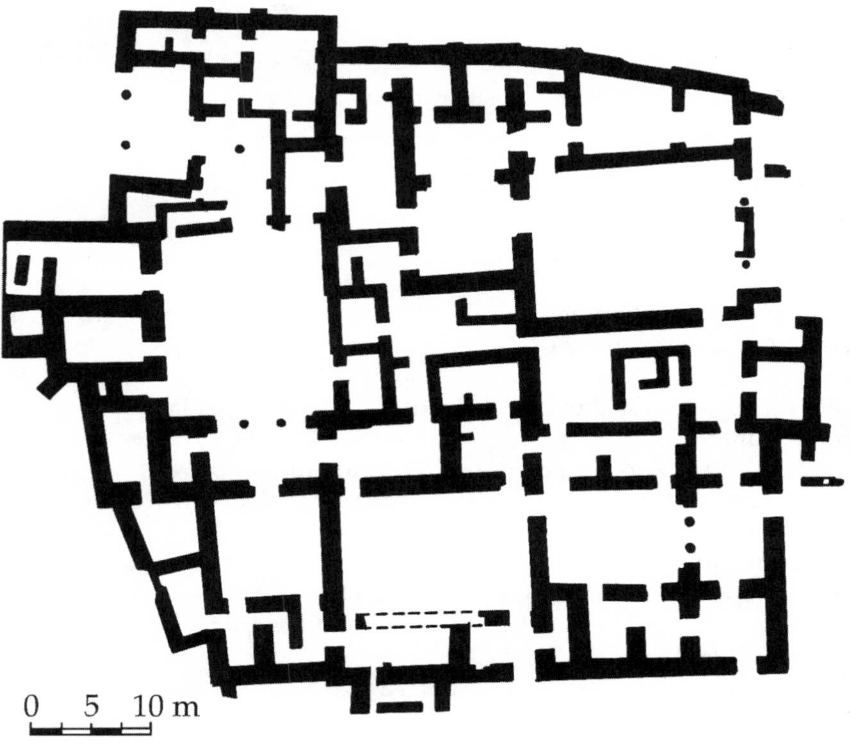

Fig. 3.4. Schematic Plan of Late Bronze Age Palace at Ugarit

palace at Megiddo, though similar in concept, is much more modest in size. It should be noted that the typical Canaanite palace differed from Egyptian-style central-hall structures and administrative buildings in Canaan (see ch. 2) in size and general plan, though they may have served similar functions.

Temples

Diversity in plan and size characterizes the large number of Late Bronze Age temples and cult sites that have been excavated in Canaan. In this section I follow Amihai Mazar's (1992b) classification of Late Bronze Age temple architecture, with a focus on structures that date to the fourteenth through early twelfth centuries B.C.E. (see also G. R. H. Wright 1971; 1985, 215–54; Ottosson 1980; Nakhai 2001, 119–60). Mazar's temple groups include (1) monumental symmetrical temples (e.g., Shechem, Megiddo, Hazor [Area H]); (2) temples with raised holy of holies (e.g., Beth-shean [Strata VII and VI], Lachish); (3) temples with irregular plans (e.g., Lachish [Fosse Temple], Tel Mevorakh, and Beth-shean [Stratum IX]); (4) small temples with a direct access (e.g., Hazor [Area C]); and (5) square temples (e.g., Amman, Hazor [Area F]). The great variety of temple and cultic structures, usually located in urban environments, attests to the rich and diverse cultic heritage of Canaan and its polytheistic ideology, as reflected in the Ugaritic texts dealing with mythology and cultic practices.

Monumental symmetrical temples originated in the Middle Bronze Age (Shechem, Hazor [Area H], Megiddo) but remained in use in the Late Bronze Age (A. Mazar 1992b, 170–73). The Area H monumental temple at Hazor, first constructed in the Middle Bronze Age, underwent several renovations. During the Late Bronze II, the temple included three main elements (fig. 3.5a): a porch, a middle area, and an inner room with a niche in its back wall that was termed a "holy of holies" by Yigael Yadin (1972, 83–95), its excavator. The temple's close ties with Syria and the northern Levant are clear both in the architecture and in many of the artifacts found there (Nakhai 2001, 127–29). Its closest architecture parallels are to the Late Bronze Age temple at Alalakh (fig. 3.5b; Woolley 1955, 71–90; Yadin 1972, 86–87; A. Mazar 1992b, 172). At Megiddo, a large single-room structure (Temple 2048) with massive walls measuring around 4 m wide was uncovered in the "sacred area" (figs. 3.2 and 3.5c; Area BB; Loud 1948, 104–5). The University of Chicago excavators of Megiddo dated the earliest phase of the temple to Stratum VIII. Later reevaluations of the evidence propose that the temple was originally erected in the Middle Bronze Age (e.g., Epstein 1965). The entrance to this temple was via an entrance porch flanked on either side by two square towers (fig. 3.5c). This temple closely resembles the "*migdal* temple" from Shechem (see G. E. Wright 1965, fig. 41).

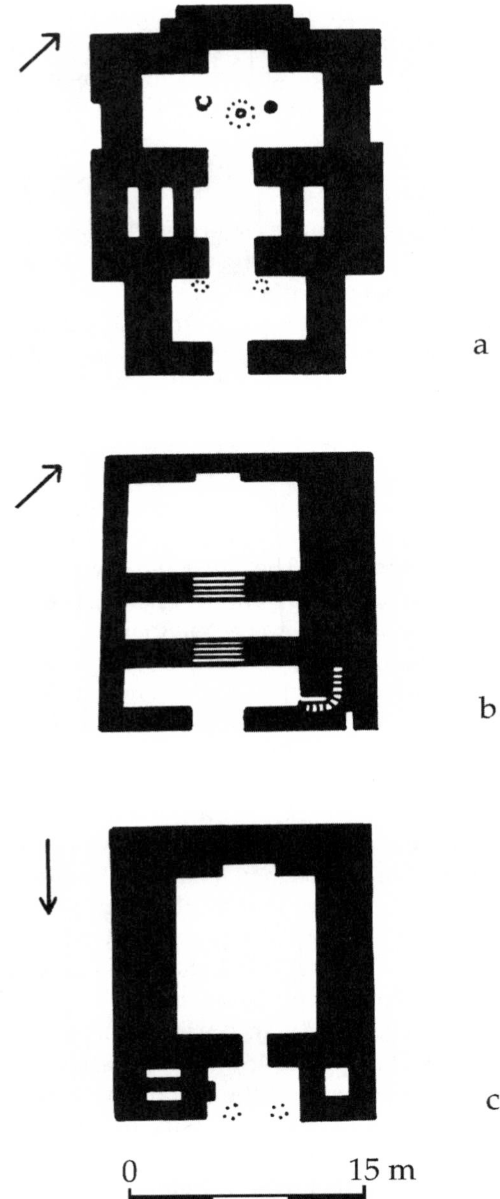

Fig. 3.5. Late Bronze Age Symmetrical Temples from Hazor, Alalakh, and Megiddo

Temples with raised holy of holies are defined, not surprisingly, by an elevated holy of holies located in a niche that was reached by a staircase (A. Mazar 1992b, 173–77). The best examples of this type include the Strata VII–VI temple at Beth-shean and the Stratum VI "summit" temple excavated on the acropolis of Lachish (Ussishkin 1978, 10–25). The Stratum VI temple at Beth-shean (fig. 3.6a) is entered via a forecourt through an entrance flanked by two columns. Proceeding through the porch, one turns left via a bent-axis entrance to enter the cella. The main hall was a broad room with benches along the walls. Opposite the entrance were steps leading to the holy of holies (FitzGerald 1930, 14–20; James 1966, 14–17). Several scholars have suggested that the Strata VII–VI temples at Beth-shean are Egyptian in inspiration and use (e.g., Nakhai 2001, 138), but Stephan Wimmer (1990) has argued convincingly against this attribution, considering the Beth-shean temples to be a reflection of a primarily Canaanite tradition (see also pp. 63–64 above).

Temples with irregular plans characteristically lack symmetry and clear architectural planning (A. Mazar 1992b, 177–80). Most notable in this group are the Lachish Fosse Temples that share many features with this group. Constructed in the moat of the Middle Bronze fortifications, the best preserved of the Fosse Temples was Temple III (fig. 3.6b; Tufnell, Inge, and Harding 1940, 36–43). This temple was entered through a small room north of the cella. Several tiers of benches lined the main room, which was entered through a doorway in the northwest corner of the north wall. A raised platform, set into the south wall, comprised the holy of holies. Two small back rooms probably served as storage areas for cultic objects.

Small temples with direct access include the Area C temple at Hazor (fig. 3.6c; A. Mazar 1992b, 182). This tiny, bench-lined cult room, located in a domestic quarter in the lower city at Hazor, consists of a square-shaped room measuring 4.5 x 5.8 m. The distinguishing feature of this room is the raised niche in the center of the western wall, opposite the entrance where eleven stelae were found in association with the niche (Yadin et al. 1958, pl. 181; 1960, pls. 207, 219; Yadin 1972, 67–69). Its location and small size may indicate that it served as a local or domestic cultic room rather than as a public shrine.

Square temples are an enigmatic group, and questions have been raised as to whether these structures were indeed temples (see A. Mazar 1992b, 182–83). The best candidate for this category is the square building excavated at the Amman airport site (fig. 3.6d; see G. R. H. Wright 1966; Hennessy 1966, 155–62; but see Herr 1983, 25–30, who suggests it was a crematorium).

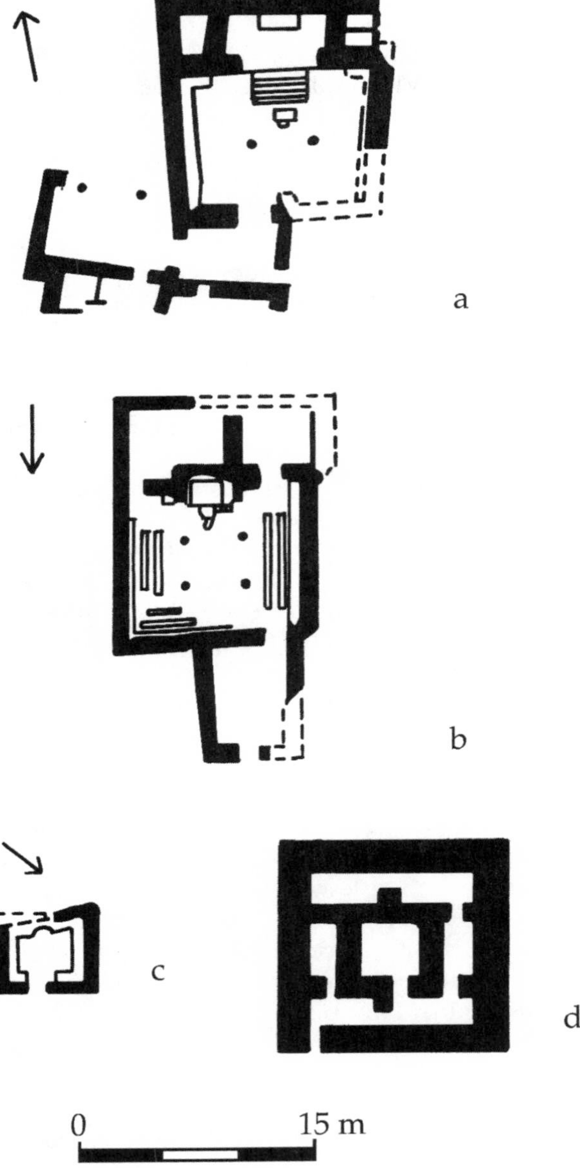

Fig. 3.6. Late Bronze Age Temples from Beth-shean, Lachish, Hazor, and Amman Airport

Domestic Structures

Numerous Late Bronze Age domestic structures have been excavated in Canaan, but due to their poor preservation or inadequate publication, the topic remains obscure (for a discussion of Late Bronze Age houses and domestic activity areas, see Daviau 1993, 219–436; Holladay 1997b). Many of the houses belong to the "courtyard house," that is, a structure with a central hall surrounded by smaller rooms, similar in concept to the larger and more monumental palaces discussed above. Already in the Late Bronze Age a pillared structure interpreted as a domestic house makes its appearance in Stratum VII at Tel Batash (fig. 3.7; A. Mazar 1997c, 58–66, 252–54). The plan of Building 315 consists of two rows of pillars that supported a ceiling. Comparable structures include dwellings from Tel Harasim (Givon 1993, figs. 6–8) and Lachish (Ussishkin 1983, 113, fig. 8). As suggested by A. Mazar (1997c, 253), Building 315 at Batash and other pillared structures seem to be precursors to the Iron I four-room house, hinting that the origins of this ubiquitous Iron Age domestic plan lie in Canaan (see ch. 4 below).

Fig. 3.7. Pillared Late Bronze Age House at Tel Batash

Burials

Burials are another aspect of the material culture that provides clues to the ethnic diversity of the Canaanite population. The Late Bronze Age in particular is known for its great variety of mortuary customs. These include burial caves for multiple interments, pit burials for individual interments, intramural burials, and foreign burials (see Gonen 1992 for an in-depth discussion). Cave burials with multiple interments (fig. 3.8) were an indigenous custom that was the prevalent mortuary practice during the Early and Middle Bronze Ages (Gonen 1992, 41–69). Simple pit burials (fig. 3.9a) and manmade cist tombs with a dromos (fig. 3.9b) are also common burial practices in Canaan with antecedents in the Middle Bronze and Late Bronze I periods. However, during the Late Bronze II their frequency, regional distribution, and relationship to cave burials underwent a change, and they spread along the coastal plain. Pit burials were associated with urban burial customs and reached their greatest distribution during the thirteenth century B.C.E. (Gonen 1992, 35, 70–97). Intramural burials, particularly of infants and children, were also an indigenous practice (Gonen 1992, 98–123, fig. 16). However, intramural burials with adults also appeared during the Late Bronze Age (Killebrew 1996b, 142–43; pl. 16; Phase 11B). These three main types account for most of the burials known from Canaan.

Foreign burial practices included bench burials (fig. 3.10), anthropoid burial coffins (fig. 2.9), loculi burial caves (fig. 3.11), bilobate burial caves, open pits, structural chambers, larnax burials, and jar burials (fig. 3.12; Gonen 1992, 124–47). These nonindigenous funerary practices reflect Aegean, Cypriot, Anatolian, and Egyptian influences, and their numbers increase in frequency during the course of the fifteenth to the early twelfth centuries B.C.E. With the exception of the anthropoid coffin burials that are closely associated with sites where Egyptian presence is well documented (see pp. 65–67 above), the other funerary customs most likely represent the arrival of small numbers of foreigners who, in most cases, probably assimilated into the indigenous population.

Pottery Associated with Canaanite Sites

Typology of Canaanite-Style Pottery and Associated Assemblages

Since Ruth Amiran's (1969) landmark *Ancient Pottery of the Holy Land,* no comprehensive study of Late Bronze Age pottery has appeared.[20] In this analysis of social boundaries in the fourteenth to early twelfth centuries B.C.E. Canaan, I briefly summarize the results of my study and reanalysis of locally produced Late Bronze II pottery. The following discussion outlines the main typological and technological features of Canaanite pottery, focusing on the major forms and types predominating

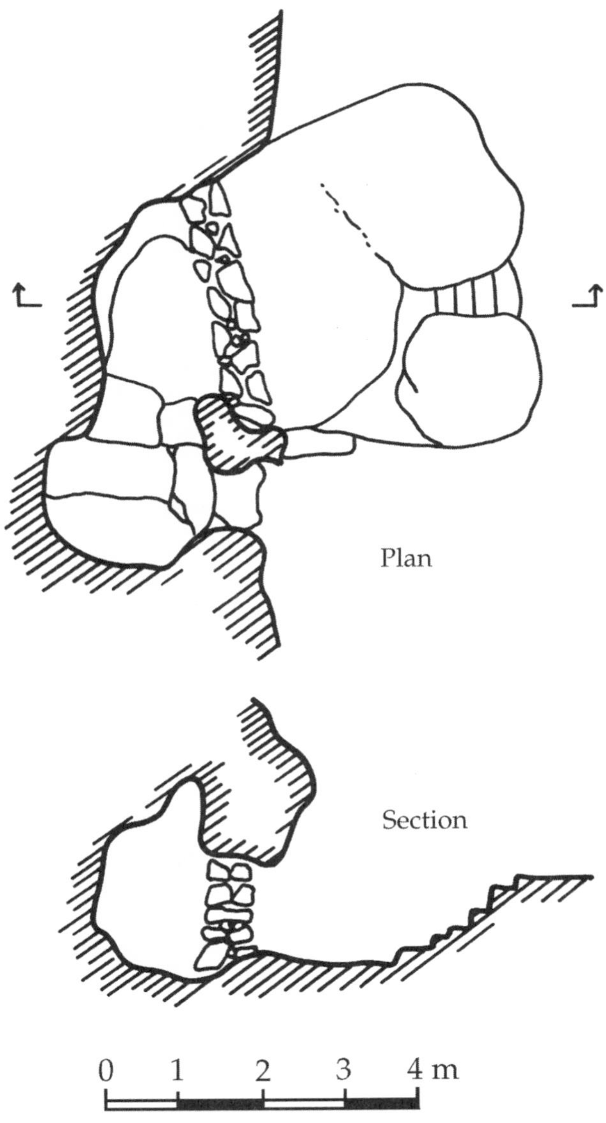

Fig. 3.8. Late Bronze Age Cave Burial at Megiddo

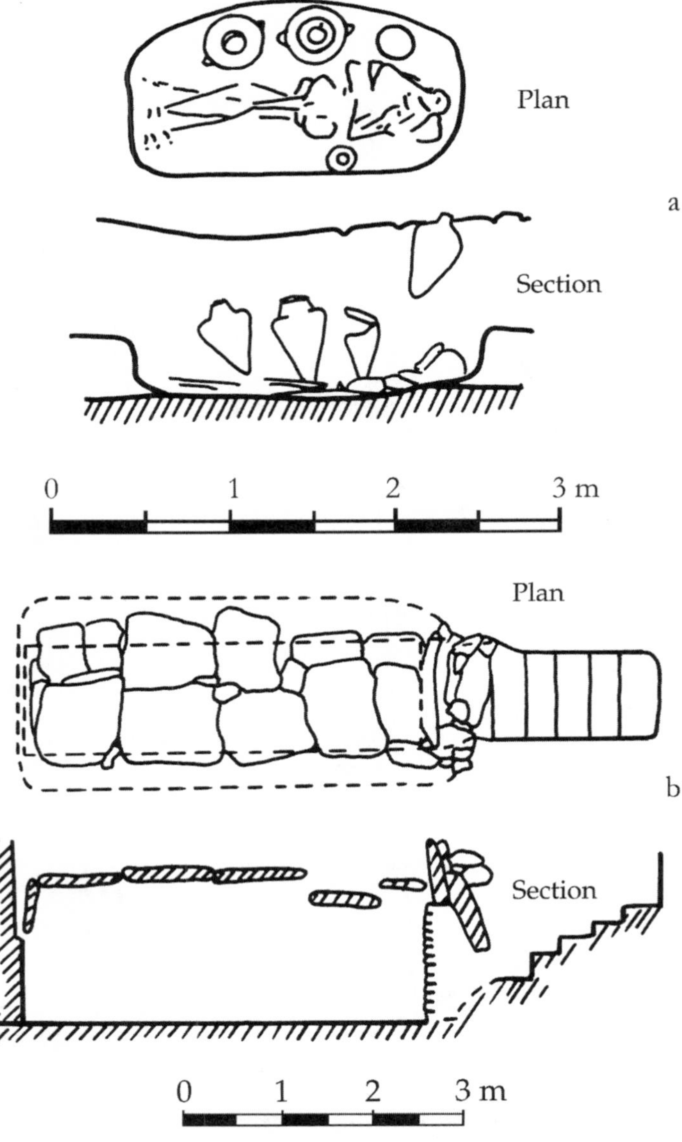

Fig. 3.9. Late Bronze Age Burials: Pit Burial and Cist Tomb with Dromos

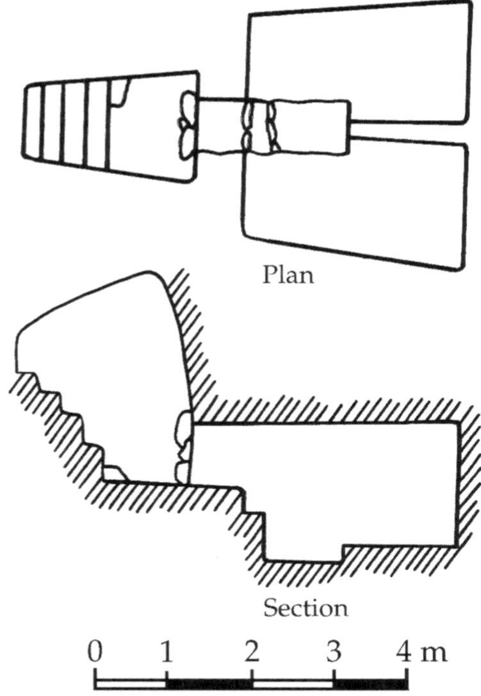

Fig. 3.10. Late Bronze Age Rock-Cut Bench Burial

in Late Bronze Age pottery assemblages. Looking primarily at vessel proportion and morphology, I group Canaanite-style vessels according to three basic functional categories: (1) kitchen wares, including table wares and cooking wares; (2) containers, which are subdivided into handled storage containers and specialty containers; and (3) varia. The Late Bronze Age pottery assemblage is primarily a direct continuation of earlier Middle Bronze Age local pottery traditions, whose roots go back to the third millennium.

Category I—Kitchen Wares: Bowls. Four major bowl forms (CA 1–4; fig. 3.13), either shallow or semihemispherical, characterize the Canaanite assemblage during the thirteenth century. Noteworthy is the absence of hemispherical bowls until the very close of the Late Bronze II period. These latter bowls are one of the few diagnostic features of early Iron I (twelfth century) assemblages. Bowl forms CA 5–8 (fig. 3.13) make their debut at the end of the Late Bronze Age and early Iron I periods.

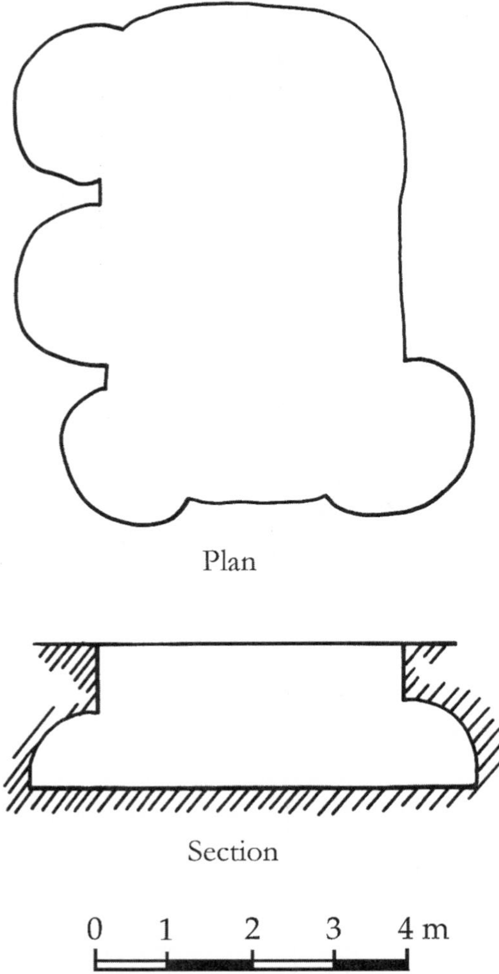

Fig. 3.11. Late Bronze Age Rock-Cut Loculi Burial Cave

Bowl CA 1 includes a number of variants, all united by their shallow to semihemispherical vessel proportions and inward folded rim, usually with a ring or disc base. This bowl type has a long history in Canaan, its prototype appearing as platter bowls already in the Middle Bronze Age (Amiran 1969, 125). Bowl CA 1 is ubiquitous throughout Canaan.[21] Bowl CA 2 is a rounded, semihemispherical bowl with a simple rim. It appears throughout Canaan during the Late Bronze Age and continues to evolve

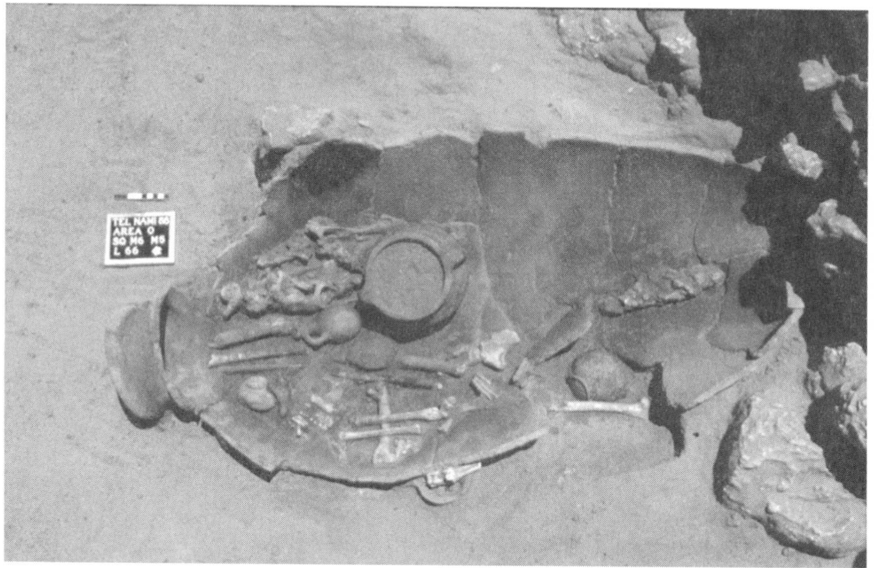

Fig. 3.12. Storage-Jar Burial from Tel Nami

during the Iron I period.[22] Bowl CA 3 ranges in size from medium to large. These bowls usually have a ring or flat to disc base, rounded profile, and a modeled everted to flared rim. This bowl type is most popular in southern Canaan and at sites with an Egyptian presence.[23] Bowl CA 4, with its carinated vessel profile, slightly everted simple rim, and ring or disc base, appears throughout Canaan but is especially popular in the north.[24] This bowl type developed out of Middle Bronze carinated bowls (Amiran 1969, 125–29). Bowl CA 4 seems to disappear at the end of the thirteenth century, to be replaced with Bowl CA 7.

Late Canaanite bowl forms include Bowls CA 5–8. They make their initial appearance during the transition from the Late Bronze to early Iron Ages (late thirteenth/early twelfth centuries B.C.E.). Two shallow bowls, one carinated (CA 5)[25] and one with an incurving rim (CA 6),[26] are two of the few bowl types that appear at Giloh and are known from hill-country sites (see ch. 4 below). The latter probably developed out of Bowl CA 2. Bowl CA 7, with a "cyma" profile (Albright 1932, 64, 66), evolved out of carinated Bowl CA 4. This bowl is common throughout Canaan at the end of the Late Bronze II and early Iron Ages but is seldom found at central hill-country sites.[27] Some of these bowls are decorated with typical Canaanite motifs such as the palm-tree pattern on the interior of the bowl. Hemispherical bowls (CA 8) enter the Canaanite assemblage for

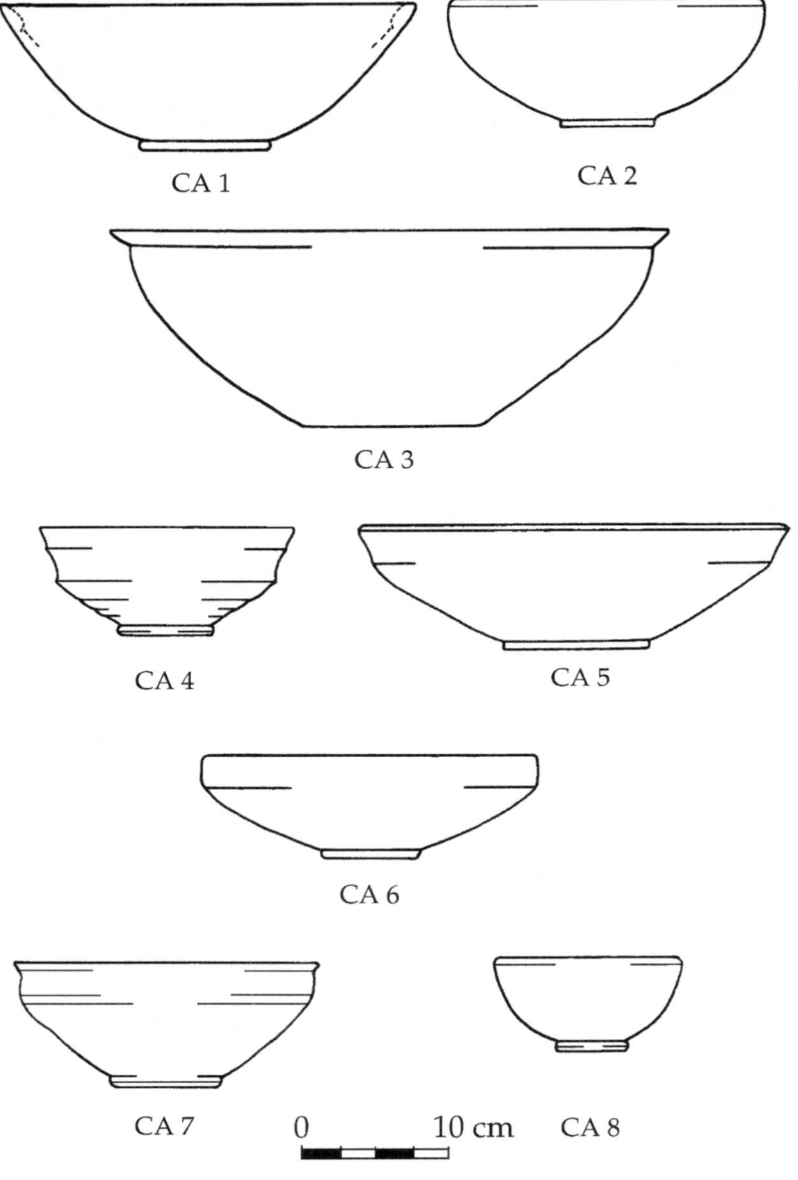

Fig. 3.13. Canaanite Pottery Forms CA 1–8

the first time at the close of the Late Bronze II, becoming one of the more popular forms in the Iron I period.[28]

Category I—Kitchen Wares: Kraters. Three major krater forms, CA 9, 10, and 11, are common during the Late Bronze Age. These large bowls, usually interpreted as serving vessels, include several variations of the krater bowl with a rounded body and various rim profiles (CA 9;

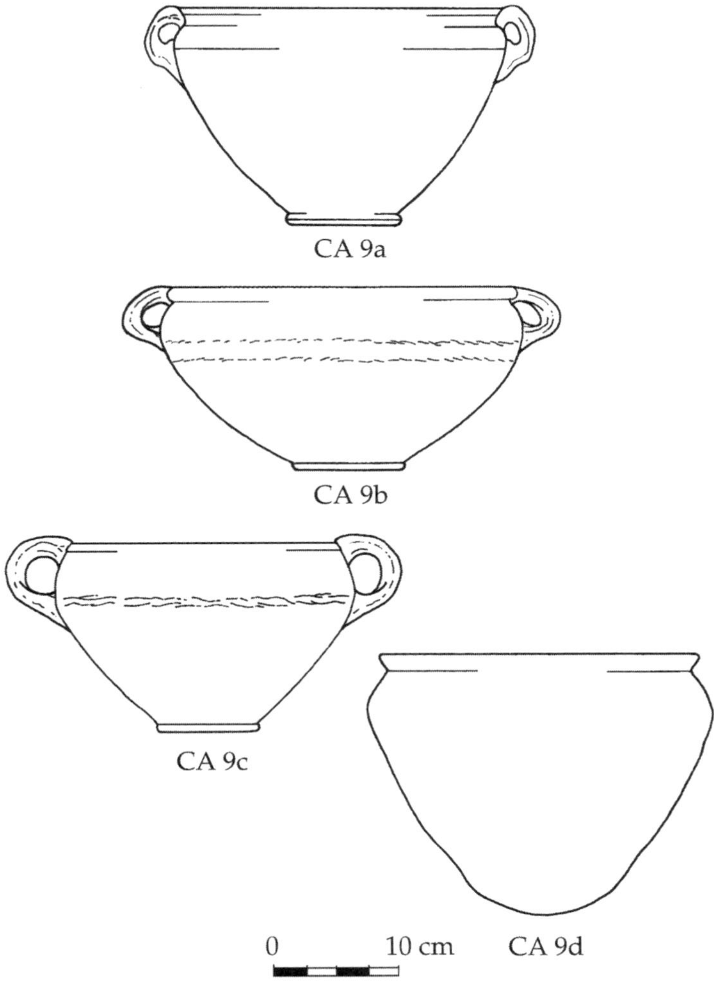

Fig. 3.14. Canaanite Pottery Forms CA 9a–d

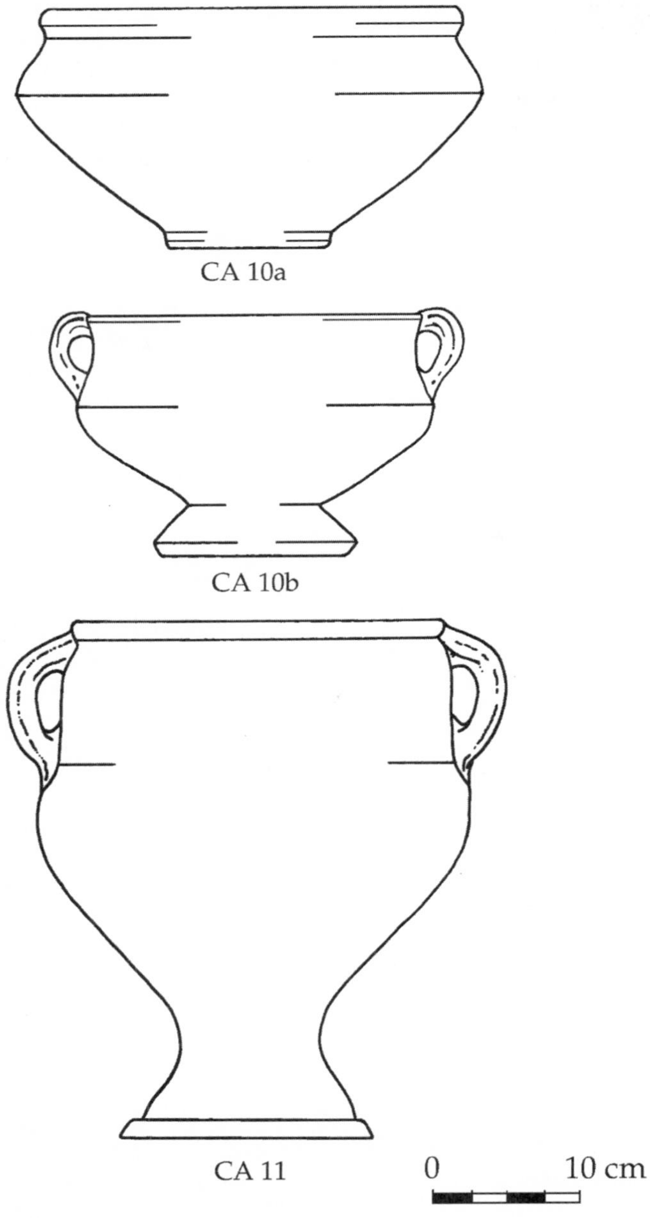

Fig. 3.15. Canaanite Pottery Forms CA 10–11

fig. 3.14),[29] carinated kraters (CA 10; fig. 3.15),[30] some on a raised base, and some with bulging neck and pedestal base (CA 11; fig. 3.15).[31]

Category I—Kitchen Wares: Goblets. Two basic shapes on pedestal bases are classified as goblets. The first type, CA 12 (fig. 3.16), is a deep, narrow, carinated bowl on a pedestal base.[32] It should be noted that the stylistic origins are not clear, since this form appears in both Canaan and Egypt (Killebrew 1999a, 94–95). The second goblet, CA 13 (fig. 3.16), differs significantly from Goblet CA 12, with its restricted form resembling a bottle or handleless jug resting on a pedestal base.[33] Both vessels probably served primarily a ceremonial function.

Category I—Kitchen Wares: Chalices. The chalice category (CA 14; fig. 3.16) comprises shallow open bowls that are attached to a high pedestal base. The rim profiles of CA 14 vary and include simple, inverted, flattened and thickened, or flaring rims.[34]

Category I—Kitchen Wares: Juglets. The main juglet form in Late Bronze II Canaan is CA 15 (fig. 3.16), the dipper juglet. The piriform shaped juglet, CA 15a, is a classic Late Bronze shape.[35] Its later development into the bag-shaped juglet, CA 15b,[36] and rounded juglet, CA 15c,[37] occurs at the close of the Late Bronze II period.

Category I—Kitchen Wares: Jugs. Jugs are single-handled vessels, probably related to the transference of commodities to the areas for food preparation or consumption. Two major types of jugs appear in Canaan during the Late Bronze Age: Jug CA 16 (fig. 3.17) is a high-necked jug with a globular, oval, or bag-shaped body, with either a rounded (CA 16a) or flat (CA 16b) base.[38] Jug CA 17 (fig. 3.17) is characterized by its short neck, carinated biconical shape, and handle on the shoulder.[39]

Category I—Kitchen Wares: Cooking Wares. Typologically, Late Bronze Age handleless cooking pots continue the general open shape and everted rim profile of Middle Bronze IIB–C restricted cooking bowls, except that the vessel proportions vary and the shape becomes increasingly carinated. During the Late Bronze II, the most common form has a folded-over everted rim with a triangular-shaped flange (Killebrew 1999b, 84–93). Cooking pots in this tradition are designated as CA 18 (fig. 3.18), with five subtypes based on their rim profile: CA 18a,[40] 18b,[41] 18c,[42] 18d,[43] and 18e with handles (e.g., Giloh: A. Mazar 1990b, 89, fig. 7:1, 2). Two additional forms of cooking pots also appear in Canaan. Form CA 19 (fig. 3.18) is a later development of the Late Bronze Age cooking pot. CA 19a has a folded-over rim with a straight or slightly inverted stance and a triangular profile.[44] CA 19b has a similar body profile, though the triangular-shaped rim is inturned.[45] Cooking pots CA 20a[46] (fig. 3.18) and 20b[47] continue the general body profile of the Late Bronze Age cooking bowls; however, the upright to inverted rim is usually thickened at the top and pinched midway down, forming a ridge at the base of the rim.

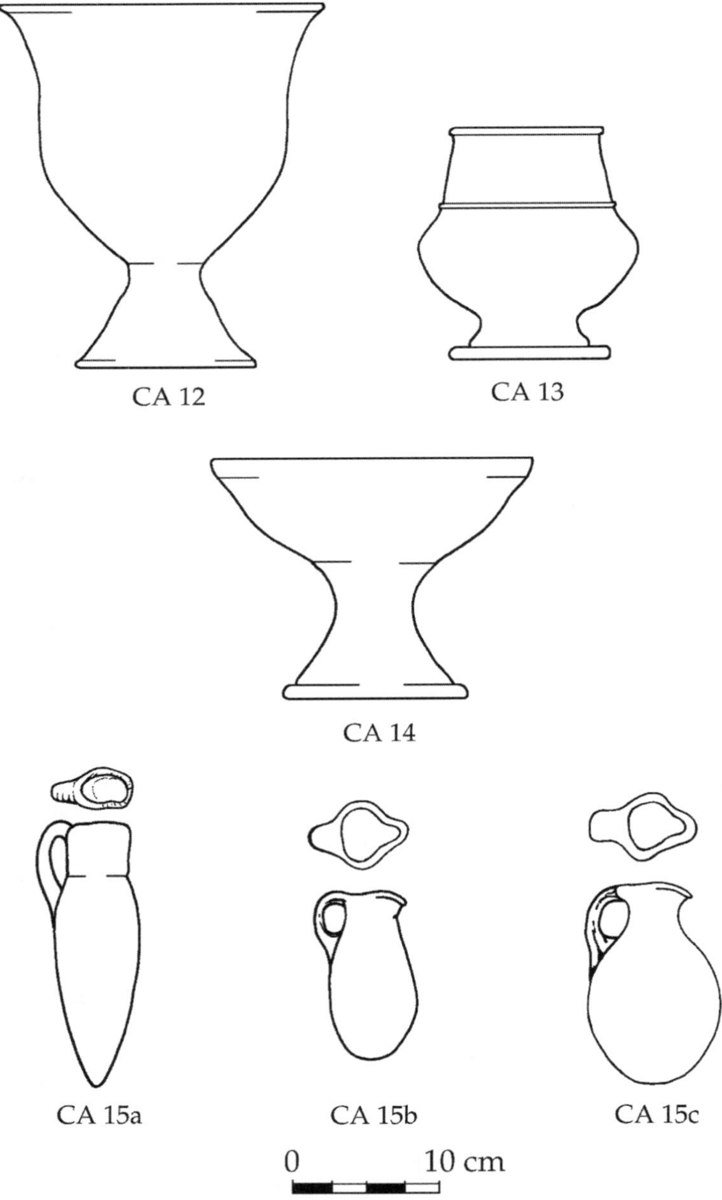

Fig. 3.16. Canaanite Pottery Forms CA 12–15

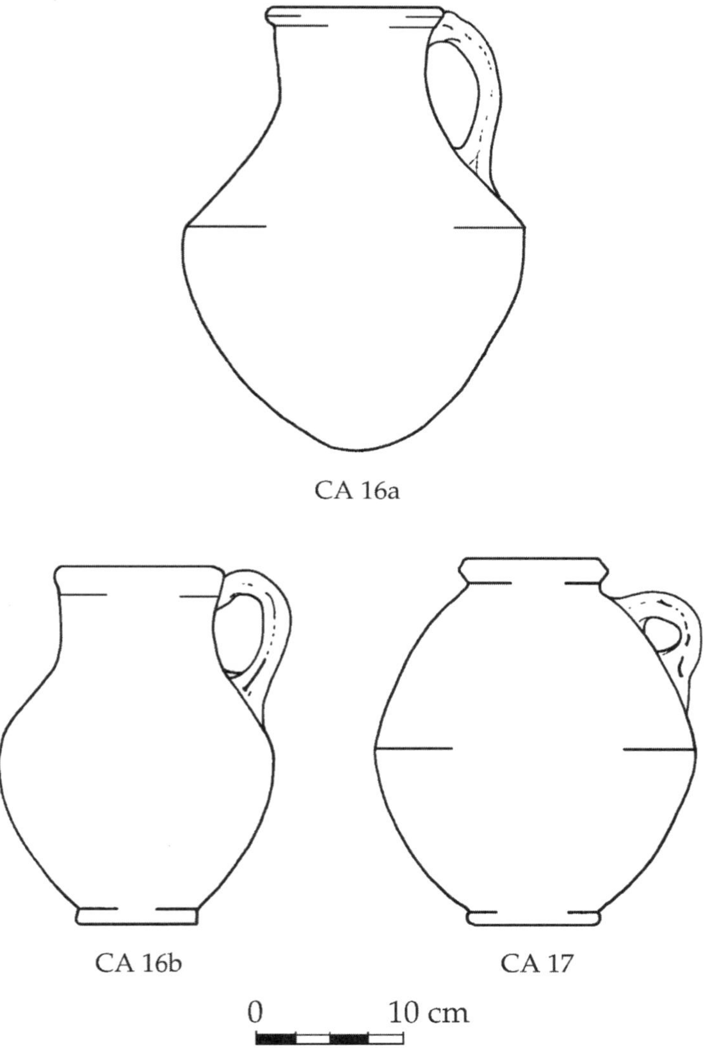

Fig. 3.17. Canaanite Pottery Forms CA 16–17

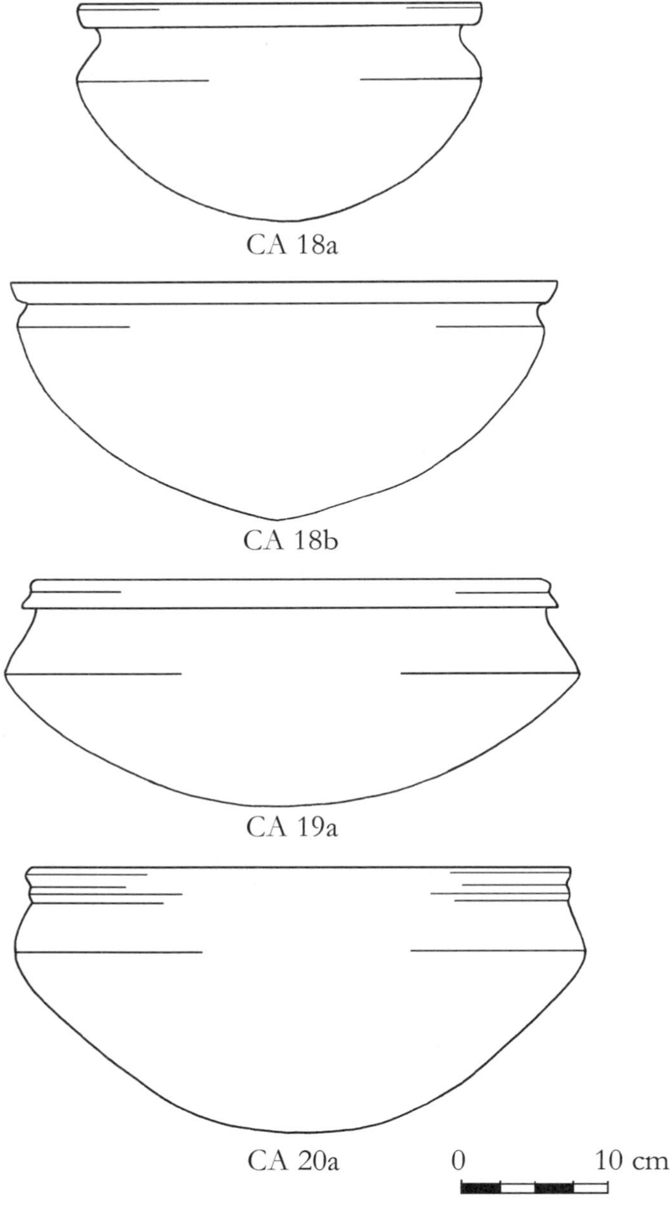

Fig. 3.18. Canaanite Pottery Forms CA 18–20

Category II—Containers: Handled Storage Jars. Handled storage jars are defined as measuring 50 cm or greater in height, with two or four handles. Their main function was to store or transport commodities. I divide handled storage jars into four major groups. The first is composed of piriform-shaped handled commercial storage jars (CA 21a; fig. 3.19),[48] including four-handled jars (CA 21b; fig. 3.20) especially characteristic of the early twelfth century,[49] and storage jars with a carinated shoulder (CA

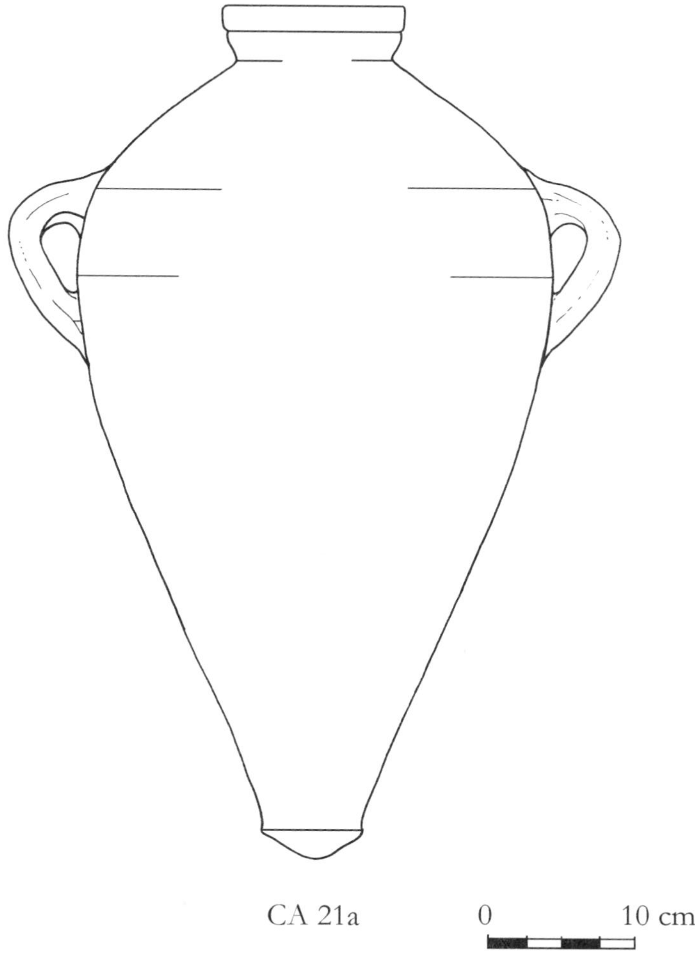

Fig. 3.19. Canaanite Pottery Form CA 21a

22; fig. 3.21).[50] These jars are popularly referred to as "Canaanite" storage jars.[51] A second group of handled jars are oval- to globular-shaped storage jars (CA 23a,[52] CA 23b,[53] and CA 24;[54] figs. 3.22–23). The last two groups include very large jars classified as pithoi (CA 25a[55] and CA 25b[56]; see pp. 177–81 below; figs. 4.10–11) and krater-pithoi (CA 26;[57] fig. 3.24).

Category II—Containers: Handleless Pithoi. Large pithoi CA 27 (fig. 3.25) are characteristic of northern Canaan during the Late Bronze Age. These pithoi do not appear in the south (i.e., south of the Galilee), which lacks a tradition of pithoi until the appearance of the collared pithos CA 25a–25b (see pp. 177–81 below).[58]

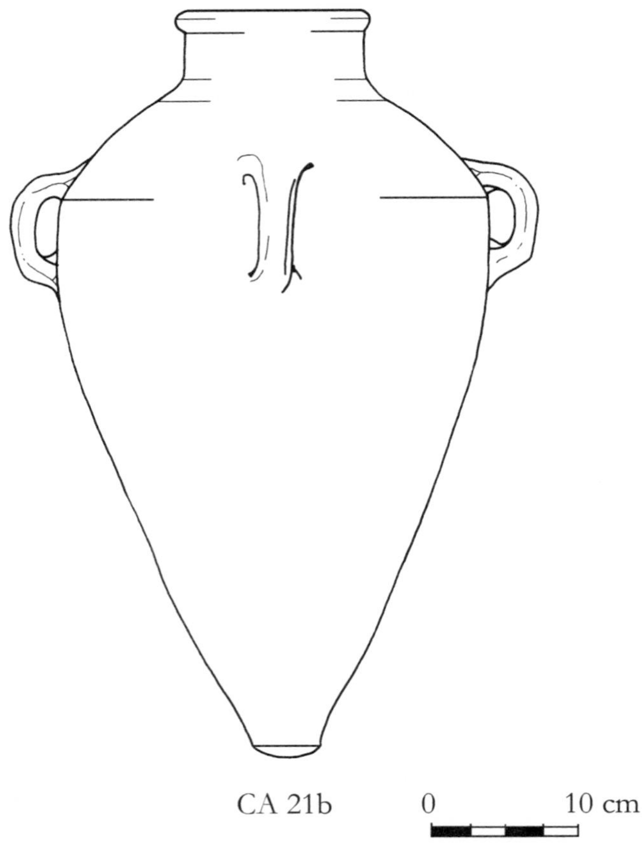

Fig. 3.20. Canaanite Pottery Form CA 21b

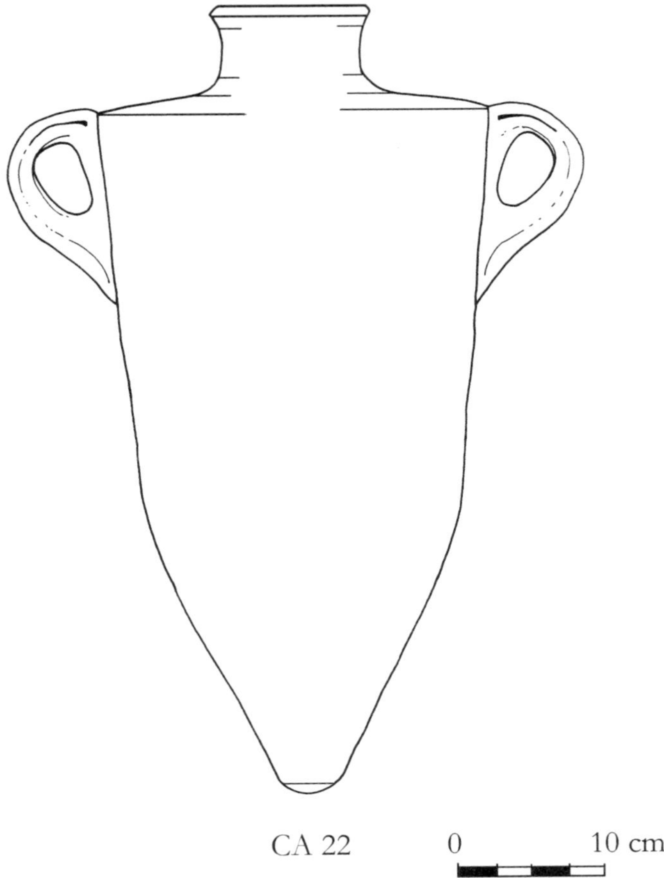

Fig. 3.21. Canaanite Pottery Form CA 22

Category II—Containers: Specialty Containers. This class of ceramics is characterized by its specialized function as a container of, most likely, precious contents such as ointments, oils, or perfumes. These vessels are often found in association with burials or cultic activities. They include flasks (CA 28–30), amphoriskoi (CA 31–32), pyxides (CA 33–34), and imitation imported vessels (CA 35–36).

Flasks are restricted vessels with a narrow neck inserted into a globular or lentoid body. Either one or two handles extend from the neck to the vessel's shoulder. Two major types of flasks can be defined: a baseless

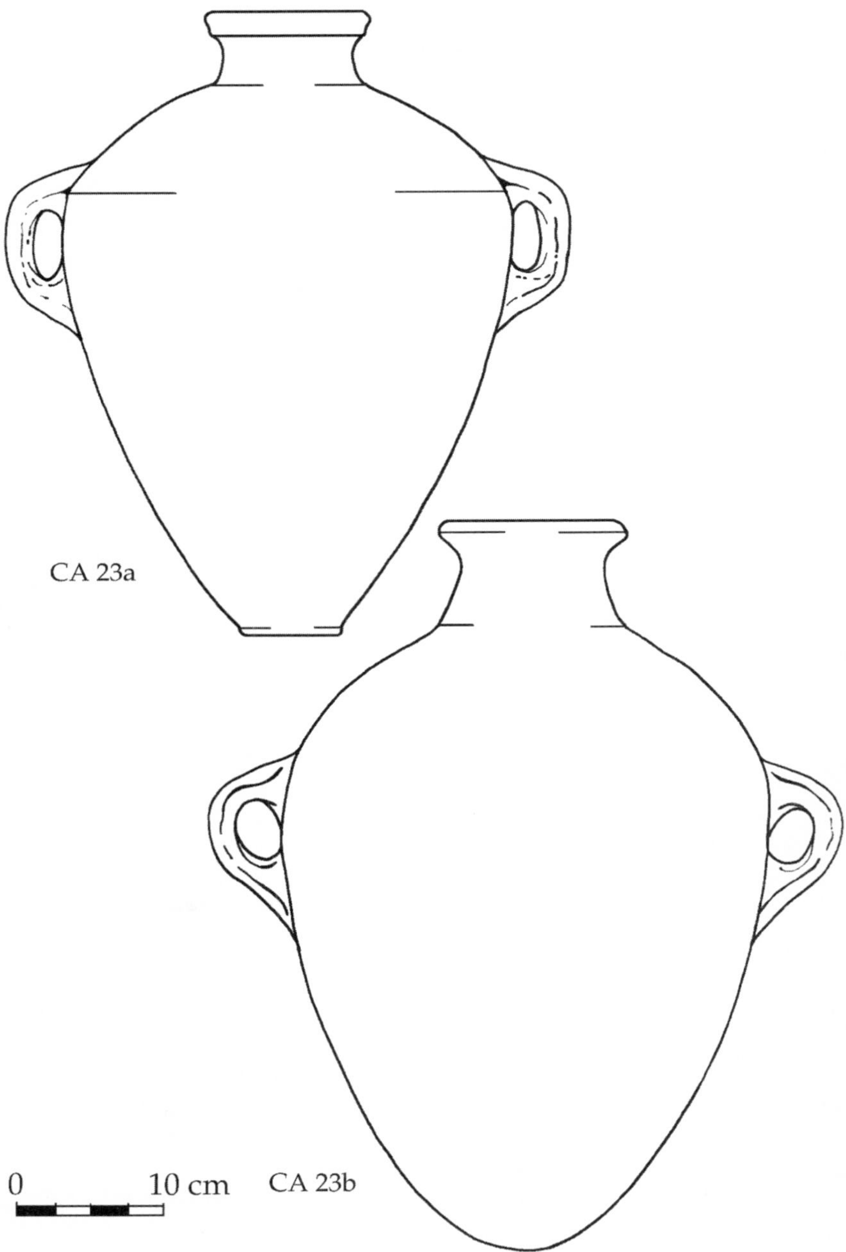

Fig. 3.22. Canaanite Pottery Form CA 23

flask with a lentoid body, appearing in the local ceramic assemblages of Canaan, Cyprus, Mycenaean Greece, and Egypt,[59] and a globular flask with a base, present in the Mycenaean ceramic repertoire.[60] Only the lentoid flask, nicknamed the "pilgrim" flask, was produced locally in Canaan.[61] Flask CA 28 (fig. 3.26) is a lentoid-shaped flask with two handles.[62] Form CA 29 (fig. 3.27) is a lentoid-shaped flask with one handle.[63] Flask CA 30 (fig. 3.27), dating to the Iron I period, developed out of CA 28 but is more globular in shape.[64]

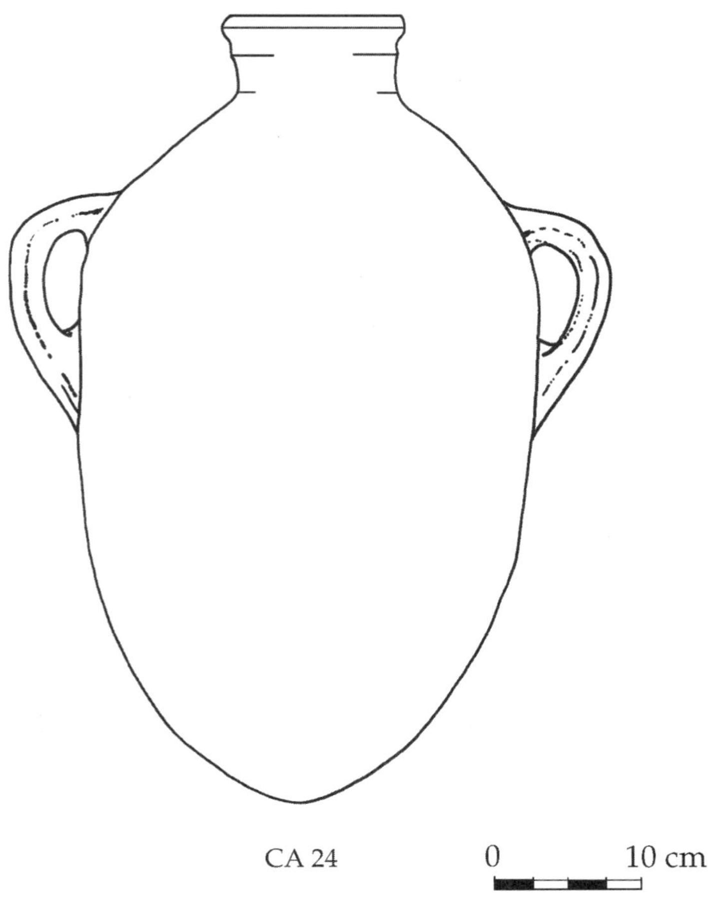

Fig. 3.23. Canaanite Pottery Form CA 24

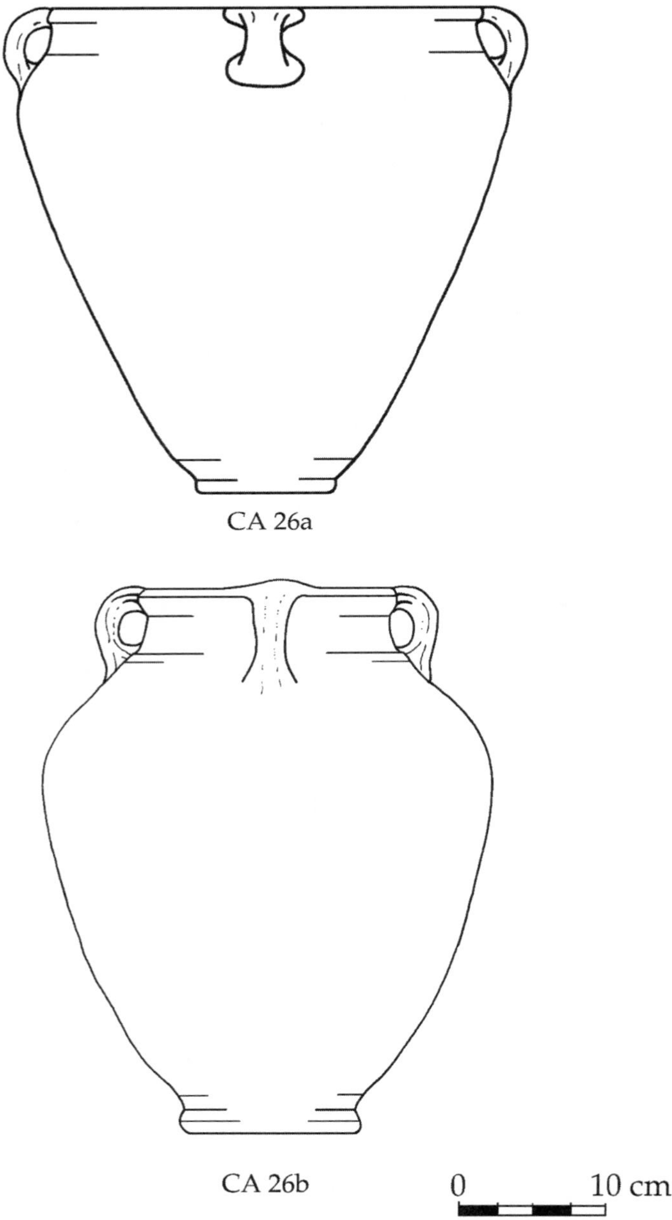

Fig. 3.24. Canaanite Pottery Form CA 26

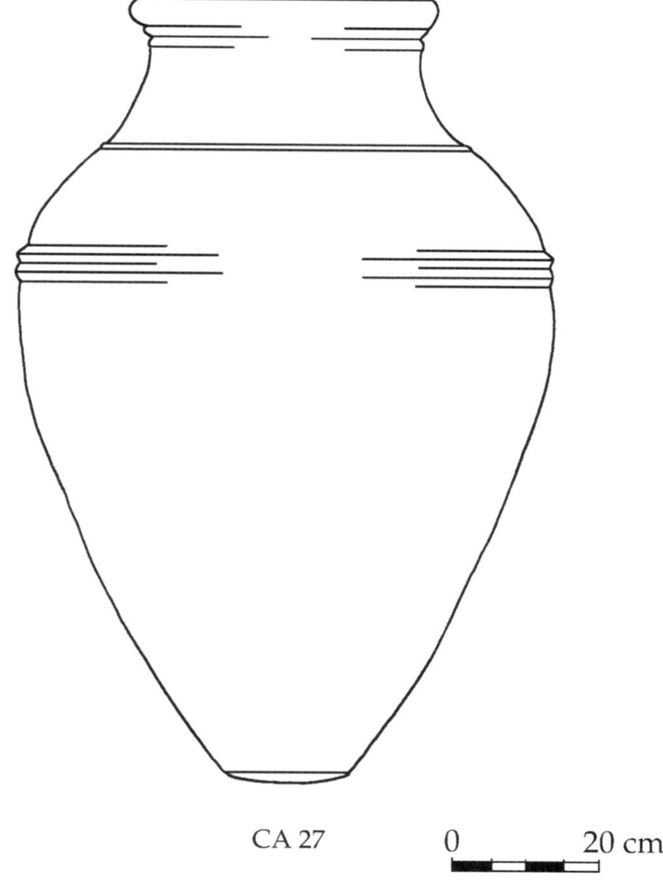

Fig. 3.25. Canaanite Pottery Form CA 27

The amphoriskos (fig. 3.27) resembles a miniature Canaanite jar in its morphological features, such as profile, pair of handles, and button base. Due to its context (found mainly in tombs), its small size, and occasional appearance in precious materials, I classify the amphoriskos as a specialty container. This vessel type begins to appear at the end of the Late Bronze II, increasing in popularity during the Iron I period. I divide amphoriskoi into two main categories: (1) CA 31, which is piriform in shape with two handles and a button base;[65] and (2) CA 32, which is ovoid in shape with two handles and a round to slightly pointed base.[66]

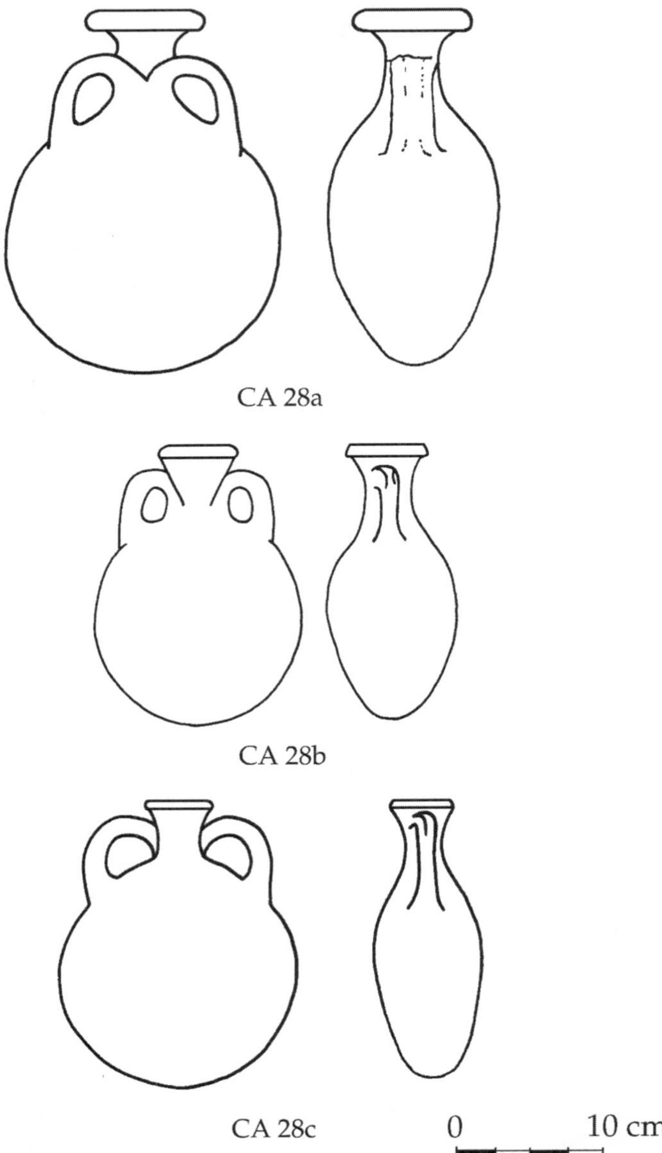

Fig. 3.26. Canaanite Pottery Form CA 28

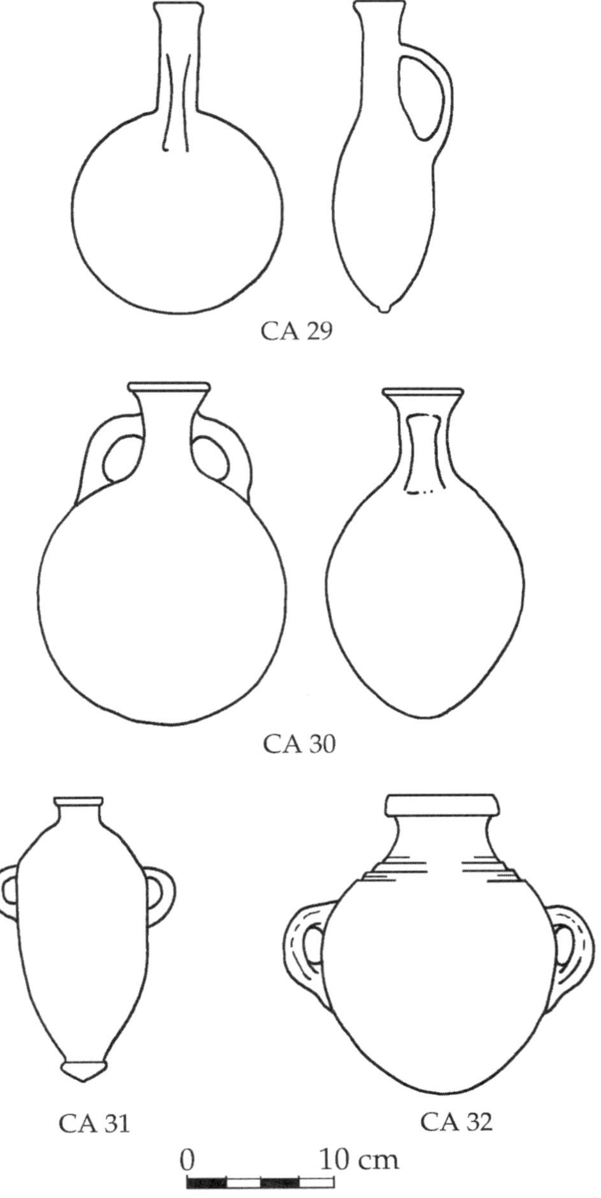

Fig. 3.27. Canaanite Pottery Forms CA 29–32

The pyxis is a small, carinated to rounded squat container with two horizontal loop handles placed just above the shoulder, whose shape originated in the Mycenaean world. This Aegean form is locally imitated in the Late Bronze II period. The pyxis, however, becomes popular only during the Iron I period.[67] Two main types of pyxides can be defined. Form CA 33 (fig. 3.28) is a squat, box-shaped pyxis with a carinated to rounded shoulder, short neck, and a round to slightly flattened base.[68] Pyxis CA 34 (fig. 3.28) is a globular pyxis with a tall neck and raised disc or ring base.[69]

Imitation Cypriot (CA 35; fig. 3.28) and Mycenaean (CA 36; fig. 3.28) vessels also form part of the local Canaanite repertoire. Locally produced imitation Base Ring II jugs (CA 35) are characterized by their use of local clays, difference in production techniques (with clearly visible wheel marks), use of red or dark painted decoration as opposed to white painted decoration used on Cypriot Base Ring II vessels, painted motifs in a Canaanite tradition, and use of a loop handle attached to the exterior of the vessel (as opposed to the strap handle).[70] Numerous locally produced imitation Mycenaean vessels (CA 36) are known throughout Canaan.[71]

Category III—Varia: Lamps. Two types of vessels are designated as lamps. Form CA 37 (fig. 3.28), saucer lamps, are commonly recovered from domestic, cultic, and funerary contexts.[72] CA 38 (fig. 3.28), the cup and saucer, has often been classified as a lamp, though its use is more closely associated with cult, and it is often interpreted as an incense bowl.[73]

In addition to the exceptionally rich repertoire of shapes in the Canaanite pottery assemblage, the Late Bronze Age is characterized by significant amounts of imported Cypriot (fig. 3.29a–d) and Mycenaean (fig. 3.29e–f) vessels. Increasing numbers of imported Aegean-style vessels originating in Cyprus or the coastal Levant are attested at the end of the Late Bronze Age (fig. 3.30). The rich Canaanite pottery repertoire of vessels is in stark contrast with the following Iron I hill-country assemblage, which is characterized by its much-reduced number of shapes, most of which are utilitarian in function.

Decorative Motifs. Although the majority of the pottery was undecorated, occasionally vessels were adorned with bichrome (red and black) painted designs, most commonly simple bands, triglyph-metope friezes, or geometric designs (fig. 3.31a, b, d). Other common motifs appearing mainly on table wares (e.g., jugs [especially biconical jugs], jars, kraters, and goblets) include the ibex and palm-tree motifs (fig. 3.31c, e, f). Painted concentric circles or other geometric designs appeared on flasks, chalices, and bowls, and occasionally a palm-tree motif adorned the interior of late thirteenth/early twelfth-century B.C.E. bowls (fig. 3.31g). Several storage jars were decorated with a triglyph-metope frieze consisting of an ibex or antithetic ibexes and a stylized palm-tree motif or geometric designs.

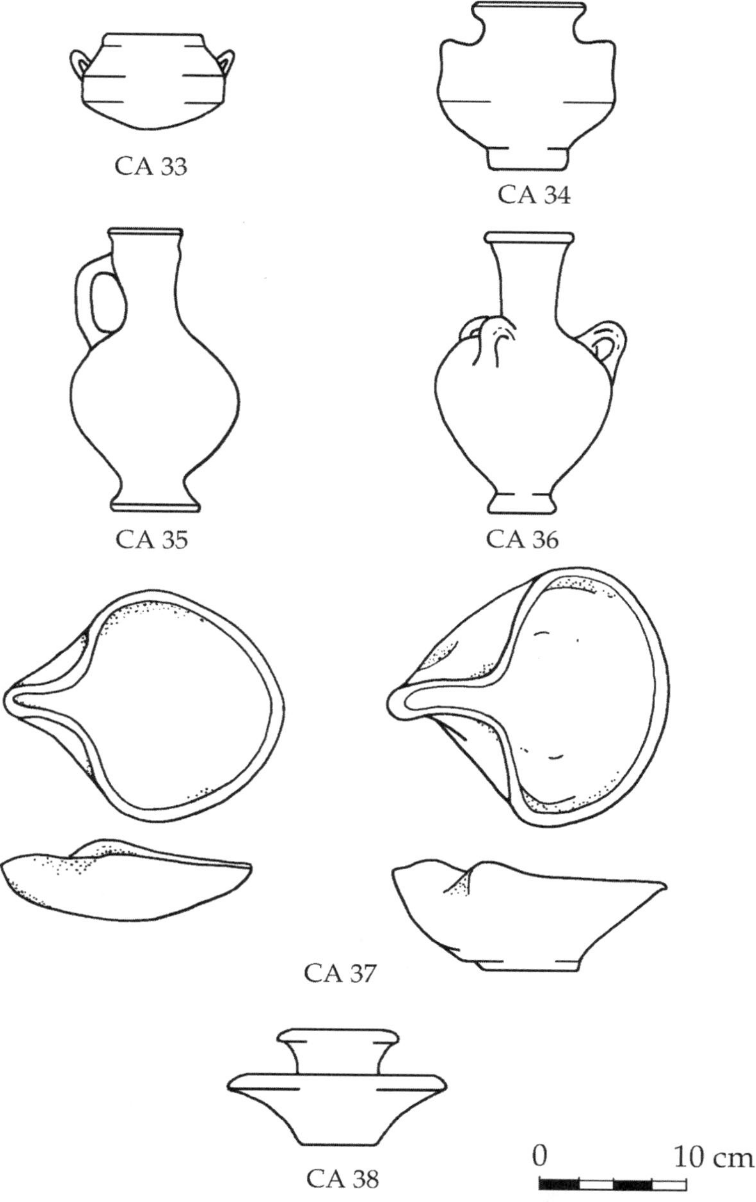

Fig. 3.28. Canaanite Pottery Forms CA 33–38

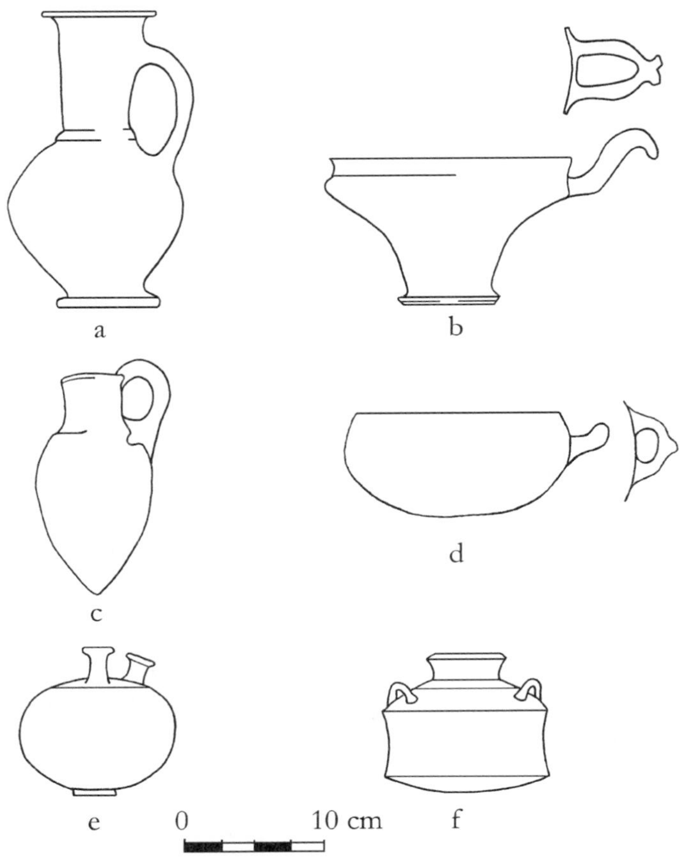

Fig. 3.29. Selection of Imported Cypriot and Mycenaean Vessels in Canaan

Fig. 3.30. Aegean-Style Stirrup Jars from Tel Nami

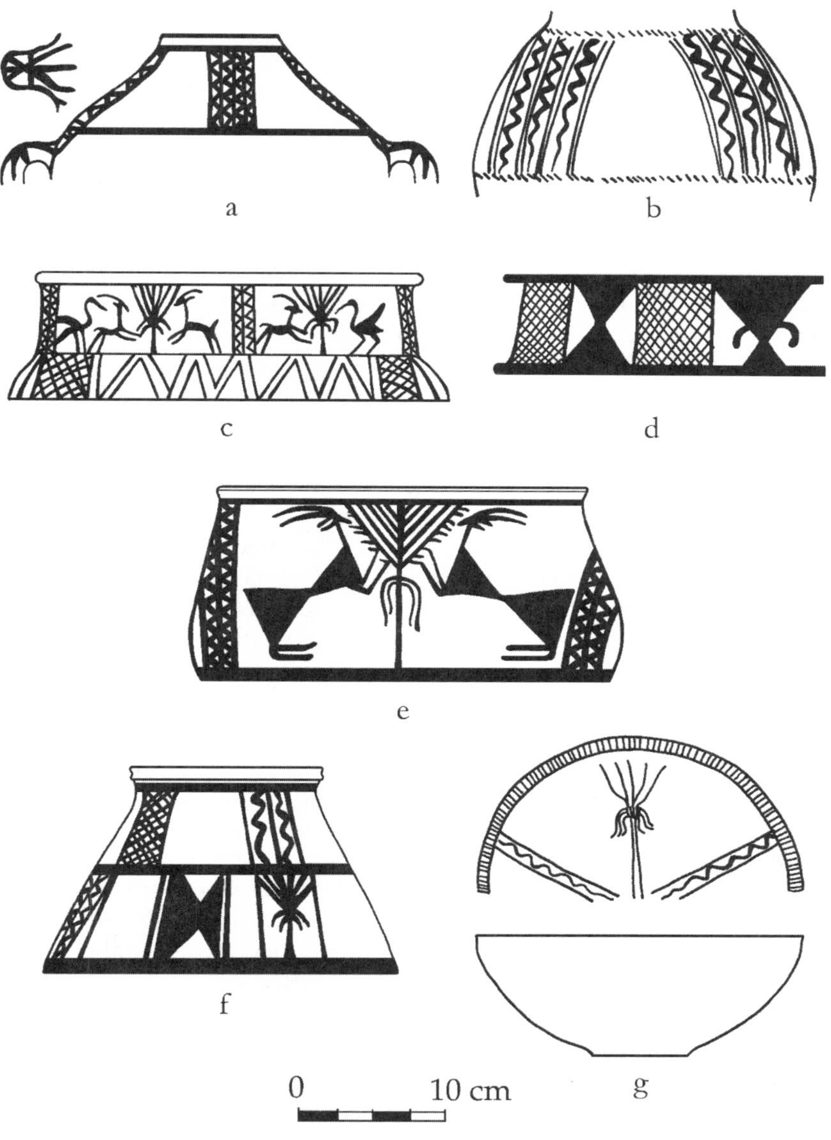

Fig. 3.31. Canaanite Pottery Motifs

These decorated Canaanite storage jars appear mainly in the south. On jars, the main decoration zone is usually located on the area between the two handles or the shoulder of the vessel, often framed by simple painted bands on the neck and belly and linear painted designs on the handle (fig. 3.31a; see Amiran 1969, 125–69, for a discussion and examples).

Canaanite Pottery Technology

This section summarizes several general patterns and trends that can be observed in the Canaanite pottery repertoire, including the relationship between the environment and locally produced ceramics, vessel shape and function, and the technology used to produce them. Both typological and technological aspects of Late Bronze Age Canaanite pottery demonstrate general homogeneity throughout Canaan and continuity with earlier Middle Bronze Age ceramic assemblages.

Of all the vessels petrographically examined, bowls, kraters, jugs, and most of the other Canaanite-style vessels have been shown to have been produced from local clays, with little preparation of the clay and demonstrating little variety (see Killebrew 1999a, 245–46). The clays used in the production of Late Bronze Age cooking vessels, however, are clearly distinguishable from other vessels by their distinctive tempers, which a potter added to the local clays. These special tempers, usually a form of calcite, were added in order to reduce the effects of thermal stress on the cooking pot that results from repeated heating and cooling.[74] It is probably due to these considerations that cooking-pot wares demonstrate greater conformity than the wares of other vessel types, seldom deviating from the standard clay recipe used by a specific potter or workshop.

At the Late Bronze II levels at Deir el-Balah, Tel Miqne-Ekron, and Tel Beth-shean, potters used the same clay to produce the Canaanite-style cooking pots that was used to manufacture other locally produced vessels (Killebrew 1999a, 250). In Canaanite-style cooking pots from Deir el-Balah and Tel Miqne-Ekron, the vast majority of cooking pots were formed out of a paste containing relatively large amounts of shell and smaller amounts of limestone intentionally added to the local clay. This well-known temper was added to cooking-pot wares, especially at sites in the coastal plain and Shephelah, to strengthen them and to reduce the damage due to thermal shock.[75] In the central hill country, Late Bronze Age cooking pots traditionally included large quantities of crushed calcite temper, which is the locally available calcite and represents a ceramic tradition that goes back to the Chalcolithic and Early Bronze Ages (Goren 1987; Porat 1989, 45). The only cooking vessel that did not use a calcite temper is the Iron I Aegean-style cooking jug (see below, ch. 5).

Late Bronze Age storage jars demonstrate the greatest variety of wares. This was undoubtedly due to the movement of these containers in local or long-distance trade (see Killebrew 1999a, 251–52). Petrographic analysis of storage jars from Deir el-Balah and Tel Miqne-Ekron revealed that quartz was the most prevalent temper in these wares, probably resulting from its availability and perhaps due to the properties of sandy quartz temper, which strengthens and increases the hardness of the fabric of the matrix and its ability better to resist stress. Based on a visual inspection of the "Canaanite" storage jar, it is possible to conclude with some certainty that the body was formed on the wheel and that the base was later added by hand (Killebrew 1999a, 252).

Late Bronze Age Modes of Pottery Production.[76] The results from the typological and technological studies and the archaeological evidence from excavated potters' workshops indicate that most of the major Canaanite and Egyptian centers had their own means of pottery production (Killebrew 1996a; 1999a, 187–257; see also ch. 2 above regarding the Egyptian potters' craft in Canaan). In my view, the relative homogeneity of thirteenth-century B.C.E. ceramic assemblages was a result of the long-term cultural and political interrelations in the region that characterized Canaan through the Middle and Late Bronze Ages (Killebrew 1999a, 255). Thus, each major center probably was the main supplier of its own consumers' needs as well as of those in the peripheral areas corresponding to the territorial limits or spheres of influence of each center.[77] Based on the excavations of several Late Bronze Age potters' workshops (Killebrew 1996a) and the technological study of these assemblages (Killebrew 1999a, 187–257), the Canaanite and Egyptian assemblages were probably produced on a professional workshop-level industry.

Two trends discernible in the technological evidence may shed light on the modes of production. At Deir el-Balah and Tel Miqne-Ekron, the Late Bronze Age assemblages demonstrate a great deal of homogeneity in the wares, with the exception of cooking pots. This is especially noticeable with regard to the Egyptian-style and Canaanite vessels produced at Deir el-Balah that were manufactured using the same clay source. This would indicate that one main workshop produced most of the vessels—both Egyptian-style and Canaanite—which may have implications regarding the potters. This has been referred to as an "individual workshop industry" (see, e.g., Peacock 1982, 31; Nicholson and Patterson 1992, 44).

At Tel Beth-shean, the evidence suggests that different clay sources were used for different vessel types, most notably Egyptian-style and Canaanite vessels (Killebrew 1999a, 206–15). Thus, it is possible that more than one local workshop manufactured different types of vessels. This type of workshop industry has been classified as a "nucleated workshop" (Peacock 1982, 9, 42–43; Nicholson and Patterson 1992, 44). Based on this evidence, I tentatively suggest that this may indicate that two groups of potters, one producing Egyptian-style pottery and the other Canaanite pottery, worked in separate workshops at Beth-shean.[78]

Conclusions

Late Bronze Age Canaan was not made up of a single ethnic group but consisted of a diverse population, as implied by the great variety of burial customs and cultic structures—both considered to be culturally sensitive indicators of ethnicity. Although the population of Canaan was probably of varied origins, it was unified by a common socioeconomic system based on a city-state/hinterland, or core/periphery, model that is reflected in most aspects of Late Bronze Age Canaanite material culture and in the Egyptian texts, especially the fourteenth-century B.C.E. Amarna letters. This literature indicates that the periphery city-states in Canaan were administered and influenced economically and politically by an imperial Egypt, which provided a relatively stable social environment. Clear political and material culture boundaries of Egyptian presence are discernible at sites as far north as the Jezreel Valley. This valley seems to mark an internal border that separates southern Canaan from northern Canaan, the latter being more closely affiliated with cultural developments in Syria and northward. This cultural border is reflected not only in the historical texts of the period but also in the ceramic assemblages north and south of the Jezreel Valley, where regional differences do appear.

The imposition of Egyptian imperialism provided a relatively stable economic environment that was conducive to elite control over international trade in Late Bronze Age Canaan and to the development of a largely homogeneous material culture, especially evident in the pottery assemblages. Thus, in this scenario, the different ethnicities and cultural affinities of the inhabitants of Canaan that are hinted at in their mortuary and cultic practices are not easily discernible in most aspects of Canaanite material culture. Nowhere is this demonstrated more clearly than in the ceramic assemblages of the Late Bronze Age, whose relative homogeneity was a result of centralized ceramic production in workshops as well as the impact of core-periphery relations between Egypt and Canaan. The subsequent withdrawal of Egyptian troops and administrative personnel during the second half of the twelfth century B.C.E. created a political and economic vacuum ripe for the ethnogenesis of new ethnic identities and ideologies. Among the groups that eventually emerged from the ruins of the Late Bronze Age world were the Israelites.

Notes to Chapter 3

1. The major exception is the Ugaritic texts, which are written in a dialect similar in many aspects to Canaanite dialects (see Tropper 1994; Pardee 1997) and have traditionally been considered an extremely useful primary source in understanding Canaanite culture, especially religion (see Gibson 1977; Coogan 1978; Day 1994). However, in most recent scholarship there is a consensus that Ugarit, though part of the larger West Semitic Late Bronze Age world that is closely related to Canaanite culture and cult, was not part of Canaan proper (for a summary, see Rainey 1963; 1964; Grabbe 1994; M. Smith 2001, 195–97).

2. N. P. Lemche in his 1991 book on the Canaanites claims that there is no evidence that Canaan was ever used as the name of a specific state or area with fixed and definable borders. Based on Amarna letter EA 151:49–67 and several other Late Bronze Age texts, Lemche (1991a, 39) proposes that the term Canaan was used in an imprecise manner in second-millennium Near Eastern texts and questions whether the inhabitants had a clear idea of the actual size of this Canaan, even suggesting that they did not know exactly where Canaan was situated. He therefore concludes that the textual evidence indicates an "imprecise and ambiguous Egyptian use of the geographical name Canaan and the likewise imprecise understanding of Canaan displayed by the inhabitants of Western Asia themselves" (50). Carrying the argument further, he suggests (52) that the term "Canaanite" simply referred to a person who did not belong to the scribe's own society or state and Canaan was considered to be a country different from the scribe's (but see Naʾaman 1994a; 1999, 31; Rainey 1996; and Hess 1998, who convincingly refute Lemche's suggestions; see also the response in Lemche 1996; 1998a).

3. Etymologically, there seem to be two possibilities for the word Canaan: it derives either from a Semitic word (*k-n-ʿ*) meaning to "be subdued" or from a non-Semitic (Hurrian) word (*kinaḫḫu*) meaning "blue cloth" or to the same word in Akkadian meaning "red purple," connected to the purple dye manufactured on the Canaanite coast. The latter two suggestions are now largely discounted, and it may be that the word Canaan derived from a personal name (for a general discussion, see Astour 1965b; Hackett 1997, 408–9; Schoville 1998, 158–59; Tubb 1998, 15).

4. See Hackett 1997, 408, for a discussion of this term: *knʿn* (Hebrew, Ugaritic, and Phoenician/Punic), *ki-na-aḫ-nu(m)* (Akkadian texts from Mari, Byblos, and Tyre), *ki-in-a-nim* (Akkadian text from Alalakh), *māt ki-na-ḫi* (Akkadian texts from Assyria and Ugarit), *māt ki-in-na-aḫ-ḫi* (Akkadian texts from Egypt, Mitanni, Boğazköy/Hattusa, and Babylon) and *k-3–n-ʿ-n-3* or *k-i-n-ʿ-nw* (Egyptian hieroglyphs). For discussions of these texts, see Aharoni 1967, 366; de Vaux 1968; Naʾaman 1994a; 1999, Rainey 1963; 1964; 1996; Hess 1998.

5. Canaan as a city occurs in AT 48, a sales contract. Baʿlaya, who is involved in this exchange, is described in the text as: "Baʿlaya, a hunter, a citizen of Canaan" (AT 48:4–5; Wiseman 1953, 46 pl. 13). The term also appears in AT 181 as a means of identifying one of a list of armed *ʿapîru* warriors. Line 9 reads "Sharniya, a citizen of Canaan" (AT 181:9; Wiseman 1953, 71; 1954, 11). AT 188, a third Alalakh text where the name "Canaan" occurs, lists armed individuals, often including a patronym or place of origin with names. AT 154 is an additional occurrence of the name "Canaan" (AT 154:24; for a summary, see Rainey 1996, 3–4; Naʾaman 1999).

6. For a definition and discussion of "la longue durée" and the *Annales* school, see, e.g., Knapp 1989a; 1989b; 1992a; 1992b; 1992c; Bunimovitz 1994b: 179–81; 1995; and pp. 6–7 above.

7. Several scholars have proposed that, with the destruction or decline of many urban centers at the end of the Middle Bronze Age during the sixteenth century B.C.E., large-scale nomadization of population groups resulted throughout Canaan (see, e.g., Naʾaman 1994b, 232). But even during times of increasing numbers of seminomadic peoples, it is important to recognize the economic interdependency of urban and nomadic populations and that

these two elements have coexisted side by side throughout history (see Rowton 1973a; 1973b; 1974). Some have suggested that the gradual growth in the number of settlements during the Late Bronze Age may be attributed partly to the integration of some nomadic elements into local urban culture. Thus, the numbers of pastoral or seminomadic peoples fluctuated throughout the second half of the second millennium (see Bunimovitz 1989).

8. Due to the dramatic changes that occurred in the central hill country during the thirteenth and twelfth centuries B.C.E. and attempts to relate this archaeological phenomenon to the emergence of Israel, this region has been of special interest to biblical scholars and archaeologists. Today there is basic agreement that the political entities of the central hill country in the second millennium B.C.E. ruled over larger territories and more complex social systems than the city-states of the lowlands (e.g., Alt 1967; Naʾaman 1982, 216). Several scholars (e.g., Finkelstein 1995b) have borrowed M. B. Rowton's (1973a; 1973b; 1974; 1976; 1977) "dimorphic chiefdoms" and "enclosed nomadism" as a possible model that may explain the sociopolitical structure of the hill country during the second millennium. According to Rowton, a dimorphic chiefdom is a political system based on a government center in a tribal territory whose population is composed of both sedentary and nomadic groups (see Finkelstein 1995b, 361, for a discussion).

9. See, e.g., Campbell 1976; Ross 1967; Rainey 1968; Kallai and Tadmor 1969; Helck 1971; Naʾaman 1975; 1986; 1992; 1997.

10. In his 1996a critique, Finkelstein suggests revised boundaries for the Canaanite city-state system. According to his reconstruction, Canaan comprised no more than thirteen to seventeen relatively large kingdoms that effectively controlled all the areas—inhabited and uninhabited—included in their territories. Finkelstein contends that the texts (the Amarna tablets and other Egyptian sources) do not provide us with a complete set of data on Late Bronze polity and that both branches of archaeology—excavations and results of surveys—need to play key role in our interpretation of the sociopolitical structure of Late Bronze Age Canaan. Finkelstein's analysis considers the Amarna archive and other Egyptian sources, archaeological evidence for Egyptian centers and their expanded numbers during the thirteenth and early twelfth centuries, the biblical sources, and survey evidence. The fourteen to seventeen proposed Canaanite city-states can be divided into three categories: (1) the entities of the highlands—Jerusalem, Shechem, and Hazor—that are characterized by large territories of ca. 2,500 KM^2; (2) medium-sized settlements such as Lachish, Gezer, Gath-padalla, and Rehob that include ca. 1,000 km^2; and (3) city-states that controlled a relatively small territory of ca. 600 km^2, such as Ashkelon, Gath, Megiddo, and Akko.

11. N. Naʾaman initially assumed that the description of the tribal boundaries dates to the time of the united monarchy and that it reflects premonarchic realities. In light of Finkelstein's 1996a critique, Naʾaman (1997, 601) has since modified his view and suggests that the list of Canaanite kingdoms should be composed mainly on the basis of the Amarna letters.

12. Bunimovitz (1989; 1993; 1995, 320–24) employs the early-state module and rank-size settlement distribution in his analysis of second-millennium settlement patterns to determine the sociopolitical organization through an analysis of the level of integration within its general settlement system. However, caution is advised, since rank size is mainly of descriptive value, rather than explanatory. For a discussion of rank-size distribution, see G. A. Johnson 1977; 1980; 1981; Kowalewski 1982; Paynter 1983. For a more recent analysis, see Savage and Falconer 2003.

13. These include Tel Seraʿ, Tell Beit Mirsim, Tel Batash, Beth-shemesh, Tell Balata, and Tell Abu Hawam.

14. These include Tell el-Farʿah (S), Khirbet Rabûd, Taanach, and Megiddo.

15. These include Tell el-ʿAjjul, Gezer, and Ashdod.

16. Another site that can be considered a "megalopolis" is Ugarit. The Late Bronze Age city is nearly 60 acres in size. Although Ugarit is not considered to be part of Canaan proper,

it shares many similarities with Canaanite culture. With approximately 25 percent of the latest Late Bronze Age levels of the tell revealed, it is one of the most extensively excavated sites in the Levant. The palace and numerous public structures comprise a significant part of the city. It is not possible to determine the exact percentage of the city that was occupied by private dwellings, but it is certain that domestic structures occupied the largest percentage of the city. What is evident is the lack of any master or organized urban plan (see Yon 1992c for a discussion of the evidence).

17. Although Baumgarten (1992, 147) suggests that the basic town plan comprised dwellings that "formed a ring adjoining the fortifications on the outside and a circular/peripheral street on the inside," with a peripheral street that ran from the city gate around the central mass of buildings or settlement nucleus, and back to the gate, I do not see clear archaeological evidence for this at medium-sized towns and cities in Canaan. This may be the case at Batash, where limited excavations have indicated that the character of this large village/small town (ca. 6 acres in size) is primarily domestic, consisting of an unfortified ring of houses (Mazar 1997c, 58–72, 252–54).

18. Contra Baumgarten (1992, 147), who claims that the city was "first and foremost a place of residence." With the exception of the megalopolises such as Hazor, there is little evidence for significant domestic quarters within the city itself. I suggest that the domestic structures (which are few in number) that have been excavated on tells are the residences of staff and officials directly related to the administration and running of the city. The vast majority of Canaan's Late Bronze Age inhabitants probably resided in the smaller settlements and villages that formed the satellites associated with each major town or city.

19. One of the most contested proposals regarding the fortification of a Late Bronze Age city is the suggestion that Gezer's outer wall served as the fortifications for the Late Bronze II settlement. See, e.g., Dever 1991, 284–86, and Finkelstein's 1994b rebuttal of Dever's evidence. See also A. Mazar 1997c, 252, for a discussion of the debate.

20. A multivolume and multiauthor updated version of Amiran's pottery typology is in preparation (edited by S. Gitin).

21. Hazor (Strata 1a and XIII): Yadin et al. 1961, pls. 279:15; 162:1–3; Megiddo (Strata X–IX): Loud 1948, pl. 45:3; Aphek (Stratum X12): Beck and Kochavi 1985, fig. 3:3–4; Bethel: Kelso 1968, pl. 52:20; Batash (Stratum VII): Kelm and Mazar 1995, fig. 4:28 (upper lefthand corner of plate); Gezer (Stratum XV): Dever et al. 1974, pls. 23:8; 24:24, 26, 27; 26:13, 14, 23; Tel Miqne-Ekron (Strata IX–VIII): Killebrew 1999a, ills. II:4:2, 3, 4, 8, 9, 10, 11; II:9:4; Tel Harasim (Stratum V): Givon 1991, fig. 1:3; Lachish (Levels VIII–VI): Tufnell, Inge, and Harding 1940, pl. XXXVIII:43; Tufnell 1958, 181–82; Ashdod (Strata XVIII–XVI): Dothan and Porath 1993, figs. 7:1; 8:6; 9:10. These bowls are uncommon at sites with an Egyptian presence, such as Deir el-Balah and Beth-shean.

22. Hazor: Yadin et al. 1958, pl. 87:2, 3; Yadin et al. 1960, pl. 124:2, 7; Yadin et al. 1961, pls. 162:7–18, 21; 179:3–12; Garfinkel and Greenberg 1997, figs. III.15:4–7, 15, 18; Megiddo (Tomb 3; Strata VIII–VII): Guy 1938, pl. 37:9; Loud 1948, pls. 61:14; 71:17; Beth-shean (Level VII): James and McGovern 1993, fig. 8:3; 12:5, 7, 11; Bethel: Kelso 1968, pl. 52:8; Gezer (Stratum XIV): Dever et al. 1970, pl. 28:22; Lachish (Stratum VI): Tufnell 1958, Class H bowls: 594, 595, 596, 597, 600, 601; Yannai 1996, pl. 18:1–6; Ashdod (Stratum XV): Dothan and Porath 1993, fig. 10:3. For its later continuation into the Iron I, see, e.g., Qasile (Stratum XII): A. Mazar 1985b, 33, fig. 11:3, 4. It is uncommon at Deir el-Balah.

23. Beth-shean (Level VII): James 1966, fig. 31:19; Tell es-Saʿidiyeh (Tomb 118): Pritchard 1980, fig. 23:1, 2; Lachish: Tufnell 1958: Class J bowls: 182, pl. 71:611, 617; Yannai 1996, pl. 18:9; Deir el-Balah: Killebrew 1999a, ills. II:38:19–24; II:42:13–16.

24. Hazor: Yadin et al. 1958, pl. XCI:11–16; Yadin et al. 1961, pls. CLXII:22–27; CCLXXIX:16–25; Garfinkel and Greenberg 1997, fig. III.15:30–36; Megiddo (Strata VIII–VII; Tomb 3): Loud 1948, pls. 61:8; 65:15; Guy 1938, pls. 37:10, 11; 43:20, 21; Bethel: Kelso 1968, pl.

53:3; Tel Miqne-Ekron: Killebrew 1999a, ill. II:6:1, 4; Lachish: Tufnell 1958; see, e.g., pl. 68:504.

25. One example of a shallow, thick-walled carinated bowl originates from Giloh (A. Mazar 1981, fig. 6:1). This form is known from Iron I contexts at Tell Beit Mirsim (Greenberg 1987, 65, fig. 6:14), ʿAfula (M. Dothan 1955, fig. 13:1, 11), Megiddo (Loud 1948, pl. 74:3), and Tell Qasile (A. Mazar 1985c, 43, fig. 12:11, 13). However, these bowls are decorated, while the Giloh example is undecorated. A similar bowl profile is known from Late Bronze IIB levels at Bethel and may be the forerunner of Bowl CA 5.

26. Baqʿah Valley: McGovern 1986, fig. 49:3; Tell el-ʿUmeiri: Herr et al. 1991, 241, figs. 4.7:24, 27; 8.6:9; Megiddo (Strata VIIB–VIA): Loud 1948, pls. 65:9; 71:19; Bethel: Kelso 1968, pl. 60:1–2; Giloh: A. Mazar 1981, fig. 6:4; 1990b, fig. 6:1; Gezer (Stratum XIII): Dever et al. 1970, pl. 28:5; Tell Qasile (Stratum XII): A. Mazar 1985c, fig. 11:1; Lachish (Stratum VI): Ussishkin 1983, fig. 16:1; Ashdod (Stratum XIIIb): Dothan and Porath 1993, 56, fig. 16:2, pl. 37:8; Tell Esdar (Stratum I): Kochavi 1969, fig. 12:5. A similar bowl and larger versions of this type are especially predominant in the hill country of Manasseh, leading Zertal (1988a, 295, pls. 21:1, 21; 22:15; 26:4) to term this bowl the "Manasseh bowl." The larger and thicker version of this general form is especially prevalent at Mount Ebal (Zertal 1986–87, 125–26; and see his comment that the Canaanite prototypes of this bowl are smaller, measuring ca. 10–15 cm in diameter, similar to the Giloh example). It also appears in significant quantities at other sites bordering the hill country and Jezreel Valley, such as Taanach (Rast 1978, 12, figs. 1:13–14; 3:6–8; 8:1; 13:1–3; 17:2–3; 25:7–8).

27. Hazor (Stratum XII): Yadin et al. 1961, pls. CLXIV:11–18; CLXX:1–6; CCI:1, 3, 7; CCIII:3; Megiddo (Strata VIIA–VI): Loud 1948, pls. 74:6; 78:4, 5; 84:19; ʿAfula (Stratum IIIA): M. Dothan 1955, fig. 13:7, 8; ʿIzbet Ṣarṭah: Finkelstein 1986, 48–52, Type 3; Gezer (Strata XIII–XI): Dever et al. 1970, pls. 26:12, 19; 27:8; 28:10; Dever et al. 1974, pls. 28:1, 11–13; 29:28; Dever 1986, 78 n. 125, pls. 19:14; 22:1, 2; 24:5–7; 30:4–6; 32:4, 9, 10, 12; 33:20; 34:6, 7; 35:18; 36:1, 2; 38:8, 9; Tell Beit Mirsim: Albright 1932, figs. 29:13; 30:19, 34, 36; Greenberg 1987, 65, fig. 6:15–21; Tell ʿEitun: Edelstein and Aurant 1992, fig. 11:7, 13, 16; Lachish (Stratum VI): Ussishkin 1983, figs. 15:11–12; 16:8; Yannai 1996, pl. 18:18–20, 26–28; Beth-shean: Yadin and Geva 1986, fig. 22:13–15; Tel Seraʿ: Oren 1985, fig. 4:12; Beer-sheba (Stratum IX): Herzog 1984, fig. 17:1; Tel Masos (Strata III–II): Fritz and Kempinski 1983, pls. 131:6; 133:20; 134:10, 13; 134:10, 13; 135:15; Ashdod (Strata XII–XI): Dothan and Porath 1993, fig. 33:9, 11; Dothan and Freedman 1967, fig. 27:1–8; M. Dothan 1971: figs. 2:3; 74:4–5; Tell Qasile (Strata XII–XI): A. Mazar 1985c, 39–41, Type BL 8. It is noteworthy that these bowls appear in the latest Late Bronze levels at Tel Miqne-Ekron (the uppermost levels of Stratum VIII) but are largely absent from the early Iron I levels (Stratum VII), where the bell-shaped Myc. IIIC:1b bowl apparently replaces Bowl CA 7 (Killebrew 1999a, 87).

28. This bowl type premieres at the end of the Late Bronze and early Iron I periods. It appears mainly at sites in southern Canaan. See, e.g., Tell Qasile: A. Mazar 1985c, 33–36 (one of the forms he assigns to Bowl Type 1); Tell ʿEitun: T. Dothan 1982, ch. 2, pl. 8, upper photo, right side; Gezer (Stratum XIII): Dever et al. 1970, pls. 26:10; 27:24; Dever 1986, pl. 23:21; Beth-shemesh (Strata IV–III): Grant and Wright 1938, pls. LVIII:13, 14; LXII:19, 22; Tel Miqne-Ekron (Stratum VII): Killebrew 1998b, fig. 6:1, 15–17; Lachish (Strata VII–VI): Bunimovitz and Zimhoni 1990, fig. 1:3, 11–13, 18, 20; Tell el-Farʿah (S) (Tomb 562): T. Dothan 1982, ch. 5, fig. 8:4; Ashkelon: Phythian-Adams 1923, pl. II:19.

29. This krater includes a number of variations. Krater CA 9a is characterized by a rounded body with a neckless, incurved, and thickened rim (Deir el-Balah: Killebrew 1999a, ill. III:3:1–2; Hazor: Yadin et al. 1960, pl. CXXIV:9; Tel Aphek: Beck and Kochavi 1985, fig. 3:6; Beth-shemesh: Grant and Wright 1938, pl. LVI:11; Megiddo: Guy 1938, pl. 73:1; Loud 1948, pls. 69:12; 84:22). Krater CA 9b is slightly more squat in proportions with two handles (Deir el-Balah: Killebrew 1999a, ill. III:3:3; Tel Miqne-Ekron: Killebrew 1999a, ill. III:3:4; Tel Seraʿ: Oren 1985, fig. 5:1; Hazor: Yadin et al. 1958, pls. LXXXIX:2; XC:8; Megiddo: Guy 1938,

pl. 71:8–14; Loud 1948, pls. 61:23; 66:1; 69:11; 78:14; 84:20; Beth-shean: Yadin and Geva 1986, 56, fig. 23:3–5; James and McGovern 1993, fig. 43:4). Krater CA 9c, with or without handles, is deeper with a wider opening with everted rim and is a continuation of Middle Bronze Age kraters (Deir el-Balah: Killebrew 1999a, ill. III:3:5; Beth-shean: Killebrew 1999a, ill. III:3:6; Hazor: Yadin et al. 1958, pl. CXXXVII:3, 4; Gezer: Dever 1986, 56–58, pls. 9:6; 14:15; Megiddo: Guy 1938, pl. 69:6). Krater CA 9d is even deeper in depth and has a rounded base. It is known only from Beth-shean (James and McGovern 1993, fig. 21:2).

30. Krater CA 10 is characterized by its carination. In CA 10a the carination is located approximately one-third of the distance down from the rim and rests on a low base (Beth-shean: James 1966, fig. 55:4; Killebrew 1999a, ill. III:4:1, 2; Tel Miqne-Ekron: Killebrew 1999a, ill. III.4:3–6; Deir ʿAlla: Franken 1992, fig. 5–3:7; Megiddo: Loud 1948: pl. 66:3, 4; Lachish: Tufnell, Inge, and Harding 1940, pl. XLVIIIB: nos. 243, 250; Tel Harasim: Givon 1992, fig. 15:14). Krater CA 10b rests on a low pedestaled base (Beth-shean: Killebrew 1999a, ill. III:4:2; Megiddo: Loud 1948, pls. 69:16; 70:1; Tell Abu Hawam: Balensi 1980, pl. 9:1:8).

31. Beth-shean (Level VI): Yadin and Geva 1986, fig. 24.

32. Late Bronze Age: Deir el-Balah: Killebrew 1999a, ill. III:3:5; Beth-shean (Stratum VII): James and McGovern 1993, fig. 41:4; Lachish: Tufnell, Inge, and Harding 1940: Fosse Temple I: pl. XLVII:220, 221, 222, 223; Fosse Temple II: pl. XLVII:224, 225; Tel Mor (Stratum XII): M. Dothan 1973, fig. 4:3, which displays both Canaanite and Egyptian traits; Megiddo: Loud 1948, pl. 55:13; Shiloh: Finkelstein, Bunimovitz, and Lederman 1993, fig. 6:35:1, 4; Tel Mevorakh (Stratum XI temple): Guz-Zilberstein 1984, 15, fig. 7:2. Iron I: see A. Mazar 1986a for a discussion of the dating of these goblets.

33. For a recent discussion of CA 13 goblets that appear during the Late Bronze II, increasing in popularity during the Iron I, see A. Mazar 1985b, 49–51.

34. Chalice CA 14a: Beth-shean (Level VII): James and McGovern 1993, fig. 20:3; Tel Dothan: Cooley and Pratico 1994, 160–61, figs. 21:1, 2; 26:1–6; 30:1–6; 33:3–5; 35:7. The excavators date this tomb to the thirteenth century, but I prefer to date the entire tomb assemblage to the late thirteenth–early twelfth century. Tell Qasile: A. Mazar 1985b, 48 and nn. 60–62 for parallels to this general chalice type. Chalice CA 14b: Giloh: A. Mazar 1990b, fig. 6:2; Tell Qasile: A. Mazar 1985b, 48–49, esp. nn. 63–66 for detailed comparative material. For an additional discussion of this type, see Finkelstein 1986, 40–41 (Type 10). Type 14b appears at the end of the Late Bronze Age, becoming increasingly popular in the Iron I period.

35. Deir el-Balah: T. Dothan 1979, 13; Killebrew 1999a, ill. III:5:7–8; Hazor: Yadin et al. 1958, 120, pls. CVIII:10, 11; CXXXIV: 2, 3; Yadin et al. 1961, pl. CCLXXXI:4–8; Yadin et al. 1989, 270. Megiddo (Strata VIII–VII): Loud 1948, pl. 58:6; pl. 63:4; Tell Abu Hawam: Balensi 1980, 353; pl. 14:4–6; Lachish: Tufnell 1958, 194; Class B juglets, pl. 78:784–786; Deir ʿAlla: Franken 1992, figs. 4–15:23; 1–20:13–4–24:12; Tell es-Saʿidiyeh: Pritchard 1980, Dipper Type 32, T. 119: fig. 24:3; T. 123: fig. 27.3; T. 129: fig. 31:2; T. 130: fig. 32:1; Tel Seraʿ: Oren 1985, fig. 4:10.

36. Beth-shean (Levels VII–VI): James and McGovern 1993, fig. 9:12; 13:9; 17:6; 22:5; 31:5; Killebrew 1999a, ill. III:5:9; Beth-shean Valley: Gal 1979, fig. 3:8; tombs near Rehob: Tsori 1975, fig. 5:2; Megiddo (Strata VIIB–VIA): Loud 1948, pl. 75:15; Tell es-Saʿidiyeh: Pritchard 1980: Dipper Type 31, T. 101: fig. 3:5; Deir ʿAlla (Phase E): Franken 1992, fig. 4–15:24; Tell ʿEitun: Edelstein and Aurant 1992, fig. 10:14; Tell Qasile (Strata XI–IX): A. Mazar 1985b, 70 nn. 157–59.

37. Beth-shean (Level VI): Killebrew 1999a, ill. III:5:10; Megiddo (Strata VII–VIA): Loud 1948, pls. 75:14; 81:12; Deir ʿAlla (Phase E): Franken 1992, fig. 4–9:26; Ashdod (Stratum XII): Dothan and Porath 1993, fig. 32:7; Tell ʿEitun: Edelstein and Aurant 1992, fig. 10:13.

38. Jug CA 16a: Deir el-Balah: Killebrew 1999a, ill. II:48:4; Tel Miqne-Ekron: Killebrew 1998b, figs. 1:7; 3:10; Beth-shean (Level VII): Killebrew 1999a, ill. 74:6; Megiddo (Stratum VIII): Loud 1948, pl. 59:4; Lachish: Tufnell 1958, pl. 76:711–715; Persian Gardens cemetery:

Ben-Arieh and Edelstein 1977, 17, fig. 9:9. Jug CA 16b: Beth-shean (Level VI): James 1966, fig. 56:5; Yadin and Geva 1986, 61–64: Type 2; Beth-shean Valley: Gal 1979, fig. 3:7; Megiddo (Strata VII–VI): Guy 1938, pl. 72:12; Loud 1948, pls. 71:1, 2; 73:1; 75:5; Deir ʿAlla: Franken 1992, fig. 5–8:28, 29; Tel Dothan: Cooley and Pratico 1994, fig. 35:7.

39. Deir el-Balah: Killebrew 1999a, ill. III:7; Beth-shean (Levels VII–VI): Killebrew 1999a, ill. II:74:4; James 1966, fig. 56:5; Yadin and Geva 1986, fig. 26:4; tomb near Rehob: Tsori 1975, fig. 5:1, 3; Tell es-Saʿidiyeh: Pritchard 1980, Jug Type 77: T. 108: fig. 11.2; Deir ʿAlla (Phase E): Franken 1992, figs. 4–11; 5–6:21, 22; 5–14:18–20; Tel Dothan: Cooley and Pratico 1994, figs. 20:4, 7; 25:1, 2, 5, 6; 29:1, 2; 32:8, 9; 33:1.

40. It is common throughout Canaan during the Late Bronze II (see Killebrew 1999a, 103–4 for a discussion). In the Iron I, it appears at many twelfth-century sites in the central hill country, such as Giloh (A. Mazar 1981, fig. 7: 5, 11; 1990b, fig. 6:11); sites in the land of Manasseh survey (Zertal 1991, 39 [cooking pot A]); Shiloh (Stratum V: Finkelstein, Bunimovitz, and Lederman 1993, 156, e.g., fig. 6.47:2, 4); Tell el-Fûl (Sinclair 1960, fig. 21:6); and Tell Beit Mirsim (Greenberg 1987, figs. 4:6; 5:18).

41. Deir el-Balah: Killebrew 1999a, ill. III:7:5; Tel Miqne-Ekron (Stratum IX): Killebrew 1996b, pls. 4:14, 15; 5:6; Ashdod (Stratum XIV): Dothan and Porath 1993, fig. 12:10; Tel Seraʿ (Stratum IX): Oren 1985, fig. 5:4; Tel Harasim (Stratum V): Givon 1991, fig. 4:7; 1992, fig. 15:2; Tell Beit Mirsim: Greenberg 1987, figs. 7:11, 13, 14; 10:2, 12; Gezer: Dever 1986, pl. 33:2; Khirbet Rabud: Kochavi 1974, figs. 4:13; 5:6; Giloh: A. Mazar 1990b, fig. 6:10.

42. This cooking-pot type is known mainly from sites in the central hill country: Giloh: A. Mazar 1981, fig. 7: 1–3; 1990b, fig. 6: 5, 7; Mount Ebal: Zertal 1986–87, fig. 14:6; Tell el-Fûl: Sinclair 1960, pl. 21:16, 18; Emek Rephaʿim (Jerusalem): Edelstein and Milevski 1994, fig. 12:1–2, 6.

43. Deir el-Balah: Killebrew 1999a, ill. III:7:11; Ashdod (Stratum XIV): M. Dothan 1971, fig. 81:9; Dothan and Porath 1993, fig. 9:11; Tel Ẓippor (Stratum III): Biran and Negbi 1966, fig. 7:7; Lachish: Tufnell, Inge, and Harding 1940, 369; Tel Harasim (Stratum V): Givon 1991, fig. 4:8; Tell Beit Mirsim: Greenberg 1987, fig. 8:21; Giloh: A. Mazar 1981, fig. 7:6).

44. Cooking pot CA 19a appears at Iron I Age sites throughout Canaan: Beth-shean (Level VI): Yadin and Geva 1986, fig. 25:1; Tell el-Fûl: Sinclair 1960, pl. 21:7–10; Tell Qasile: A. Mazar 1985b, 52 nn. 70–72; Tel Batash: Kelm and Mazar 1995, fig. 5.12; land of Manasseh: Zertal 1991, cooking pot Type B; 39; Gezer (Stratum XI): Dever 1986, pl. 39:7; Deir ʿAlla: Franken and Kalsbeek 1969, 120, Iron Age cooking pot Type 1; Megiddo (Stratum VI): Loud 1948, pl. 85:16; Tel Dan (Stratum V): Biran 1994a, figs. 98:7; 104:9–12; ʿIzbet Ṣarṭah: Finkelstein 1986, Type 12: 65; fig. 6:12.

45. Giloh: A. Mazar 1981, fig. 7:15; Mount Ebal: Zertal 1986–87, fig. 17:6 (Zertal's cooking pot Type C; Zertal 1991, 39); Tell Qasile: A. Mazar 1985b, 52–53 and nn. 73–77 (Mazar's Type 1b); Gezer (Stratum XI): Dever 1986, pl. 39:6; Tel Dan (Stratum VI): Biran 1994, fig. 93:5; Tell el-Fûl: Sinclair 1960, pl. 21:1, 3.

46. Cooking pot CA 20a is a Jordan Valley type; see, e.g., Beth-shean (Levels VII–VI): Killebrew 1999a, ill. III:8:8–9; Yadin and Geva 1986, fig. 25:3; Deir ʿAlla (Phase E): Franken 1992, fig. 5–9:6, 10; Iron I: Franken and Kalsbeek 1969, 119, fig. 26.

47. Cooking pot CA 20b is a Jordan Valley type; see, e.g., Beth-shean (Level VI): Yadin and Geva 1986, fig. 25:2; Deir ʿAlla: Franken and Kalsbeek 1969, 124, fig. 28.

48. The two-handled "Canaanite" storage jar appears throughout Canaan as well as Egypt, Nubia, Greece, Cyprus, and Crete (for parallels outside of Canaan, see Killebrew 1999a, 111 nn. 221–24). For parallels in Canaan, see Lachish: Tufnell 1958, 224; pl. 87:1021; Gezer: Dever et al. 1974, pl. 23:3; Aphek: Beck and Kochavi 1985, figs. 2:4; 5:2–3; Megiddo: Guy 1938, pl. 56:10; Tell Abu Hawam: Anati 1959, fig. 7:4, 6; Akko, Persian Gardens: Ben-Arieh and Edelstein 1977, fig. 10:5; Hazor: Yadin et al. 1960, pl. CXXI:1. These jars are also common at Deir el-Balah, Tel Miqne-Ekron, and Giloh but are rare at Beth-shean (see Killebrew 1999a, 110–12, for a discussion of the evidence).

49. The four-handled "Canaanite" storage jar is especially characteristic of the early twelfth century B.C.E., but it appeared already during the late thirteenth century, mainly in southern Canaan (see, e.g., Beck and Kochavi 1985, 34 [where they note that our CA 24b is attributed to Level VI at Lachish]; B. G. Wood 1985, 402–7 [for a summary of the published and unpublished evidence]). See also Deir el-Balah: T. Dothan 1979, ills. 22, 81, 89, 124, 130; Killebrew 1999a, ill. III:10:1; Lachish: Tufnell 1958, pl. 87: 1020; Aharoni 1975, pl. 49:12; Gezer: Dever 1986, pls. 26:3, 27:1, 2; 30:3l ; Tell el-Farʿah (S): Petrie 1930, pl. XIX, Tomb 552, no. 43 P5; Starkey and Harding 1932, pls. LXXXVI:43 P6; ʿIzbet Ṣarṭah: Finkelstein 1986, 76–77, Type 20: fig. 7:20; Ashdod: M. Dothan 1971, pls. 82:9; 83:1–3; Tell ʿEitun: Edelstein and Glass 1973, fig. 1; Edelstein and Aurant 1992, fig. 10:1; Tell Qasile (Stratum XI): A. Mazar 1985b, fig. 26:14. One example, imported from Canaan, is published from Maa-Palaeokastro on Cyprus: Karageorghis and Demas 1988, pls. LXXXI:545; CXCIV:545.

50. This two-handled storage jar has a tapered body with a carinated or angular shoulder. The jar, which has been referred to by Raban (1980, 6*) as the commercial jar "par excellence," is the commercial jar most commonly found in the eastern Mediterranean. See, e.g., Egypt: Peet and Woolley 1923, pl. LII: Type XLIII/260; Grace 1956; Rose 1984, 135, 137, Group 20; Bourriau 1990; Malkata: Hope 1978, fig. 1:c; Ugarit: Schaeffer 1949, pl. XXX:1; Cyprus, Cilicia, and Greece: Raban 1980, 6*, where he refers to it as Type III, "angular storage jar"; Crete: Watrous 1992, 161, fig. 71, Reg. No. 946, "northern fabric"; see also the Ulu Burun shipwreck: Bass 1986: 277–79, where large numbers of these storage jars and their contents were recovered. Neutron Activation Analyses indicate that these jars were made in two major regions: southern Canaan and the northern coastal plain between Akko and Ugarit, probably near Tyre and Sidon (Raban 1980, 6*). Form CA 22 is found at most Late Bronze II sites from the fourteenth–thirteenth centuries B.C.E., particularly at settlements close to the coast (for references, see Killebrew 1999a, 113–14).

51. For general discussions of the Canaanite storage jar, see Grace 1956; Amiran 1969, 140–42; Parr 1973; Zemer 1977, 4–7; Raban 1980, 5*; Bourriau 1990; Leonard 1999. These jars appear throughout Canaan and the eastern Mediterranean, including Egypt (for recent summaries, see Bourriau 1990; Bourriau, Smith, and Serpico 2001; note the appearance of significant numbers of commercial Canaanite jars at Marsa Matruh [Bates Island; see Hulin 1989, 124–25] and at Buhen [Serpico 1999]), Cyprus (for a recent survey of Canaanite jars from Cyprus, see Åström 1991; for a detailed study of Canaanite jars from Maa-Palaeokastro, see Hadjicosti 1988; from Hala Sultan Tekke, see Fischer 1991; regarding provenience studies of these Canaanite storage jars from Maa-Palaeokastro, see Jones and Vaughn 1988), the Aegean (Grace 1956; Åkerström 1975; Raban 1980, 5*–6*; Kilian 1988a, 127, fig. 4; see Cline 1995, 95–97, regarding Canaanite-style jars at Mycenae), and the coast of Anatolia (Raban 1980, 5*).

52. This squat storage jar with a flat base is more common at northern sites during the Late Bronze II period. See, e.g., Megiddo (LB I): Guy 1938, pl. 51:7 (Tomb 1145B); (LB II): pl. 57:11 (Tomb 26); (Stratum VIII): Loud 1948: pl. 60:2, 4.

53. Storage Jar CA 23b is similar in profile to CA 23a but has a rounded base. This form is prevalent at sites in northern Canaan beginning in the Late Bronze II, continuing into the Iron I. See, e.g., Beth-shean (Levels VIII–VI): James and McGovern 1993, fig. 18:3; Killebrew 1999a, ill. II:72:1; Yadin and Geva 1986, fig. 31:1; Megiddo: Guy 1938, pls. 65:9; 67:7; (Strata XI–VIII): Loud 1948: pl. 60:1; Tel Dan: Biran 1989, fig. 4.10; Hazor (Stratum XII): Yadin et al. 1961, pl. CLXIX:1, 2; Mount Ebal: Zertal 1986–87, fig. 14:9; Shiloh (Stratum V): Finkelstein, Bunimovitz, and Lederman 1993, figs. 6.48:3, 5; 6.61:5, 7.

54. Storage Jar CA 24 is the Iron I development of Storage Jar CA 23. It is especially common in the Jezreel Valley and northern Canaan at sites such as Beth-shean (Level VI): James 1966, figs. 51:15; 54:6–8; Yadin and Geva 1986, 70–71; Megiddo: Guy 1938, pls. 69:4; 70:4; 72:1; Loud 1948, pls. 64:2; 73:6, 7; 76:3; 82:9; ʿAfula (Strata IIIA–B): M. Dothan 1955, figs. 11:1–5, 18–22; 16:1; 19:1, 3, 4; Tel Qiri (Stratum VIII): Ben-Tor and Portugali 1987, figs. 17:6;

32:1; Tel Sasa: Stepansky, Segal, and Carmi 1996, 66, fig. 6:4; Keisan (Levels 9a–c): Briend and Humbert 1980, pls. 58:1, 6, 8; 69:2, 2a; Tel Dan: Biran 1994a, 127, fig. 87:6.

55. Collared Pithos CA 25a is characterized by its tall neck measuring ca. 10 cm or greater in height. This pithos appears at the end of the Late Bronze Age and continues into the early Iron IA (see pp. 177–81 below for a detailed discussion). Its rim is reminiscent of rims on Pithos CA 26 (see n. 57 below). CA 25a appears in noteworthy quantities at the fortified early Iron I site of Tell el-ʿUmeiri (Herr et al. 1991, figs. 5:5, 6, 7, 10; 6:1, 2, 3, 6, 7; Herr 1997, 237–38; see, e.g., figs. 4:14; 4:19:5–8; 4:20:1–3, 5–7), Tel Sasa (Stepansky, Segal, and Carmi 1996, fig. 7:2), and Beth-shean (Killebrew 1999a, ill. III:13).

56. Collared Pithos CA 25b has a shorter neck, usually measuring ca. 5–7.5 cm (see pp. 177–81 below for a detailed discussion). This variation is especially popular in the central hill country (e.g., Mount Ebal: Zertal 1986–87, e.g., figs 12:1; 13:1; 16:8, 13; Shiloh: Finkelstein, Bunimovitz, and Lederman 1993, figs. 6.48:1, 2, 4; 6.49:3, 4; 6.5.51:1, 4, 6; ʿAi: Callaway 1980, figs. 150:17–28; 154; Bethel: Kelso 1968, pls. 56; 57:1–5; Tell en-Naṣbeh: Wampler 1947, pls. 1:2, 3–11; 2:12–22; Tell el-Fûl: Albright 1924, pl. XXVIII:17–24; Sinclair 1960, pl. 20:10–18; Jerusalem: Steiner 1994, figs. 4–6; Edelstein and Milevski 1994, 19–20, fig. 121–2; Beth-zur: Funk 1968, fig. 7), though it does appear occasionally in the Galilee, Jordan Valley, and the northern coastal plain throughout the Iron I period (see ch. 4, pp. 177–81).

57. Krater-pithoi CA 26 is a family of containers that includes very large kraters, measuring at least 50 cm high. At the end of the Late Bronze II and continuing into the Iron Age, oversized kraters are far more common in the north than in the south. Variations of these large kraters, often with multiple handles, also appear during the Iron I period in Samaria and at Tel Dan, sites often associated with the emergence of Israel. This krater-pithos is a slightly restricted to restricted, deep krater, usually with multiple handles. CA 27 is known from Beth-shean (Levels VII–VI): James and McGovern 1993, 72, fig. 20:4, 5; James 1966, figs. 49:2; 57:17; Yadin and Geva 1986, 81, fig. 33:3, 4; Deir ʿAlla: Franken 1992, fig. 4–21; Hazor: Yadin et al. 1960, pl. CXLI:23; Yadin et al. 1961, pls. CLXIV:23; CCLXXX:12; Tel Dan (Iron I loci): Biran 1994, ill. 103:8. The well-known Khirbet Raddana krater (Callaway and Cooley 1971, fig. 7) also belongs to CA 27.

58. See, e.g., Yadin et al. 1960, pl. CXLV:3–5; 1961: pl. CCXCVIII:8, 9. Pithoi similar in shape and rim profile to those at Hazor are also known from Tell es-Salihiyeh near Damascus (von der Osten 1956, pl. 35:84).

59. For a description of the two-handled Mycenaean version, see Furumark 1941b, 32, 67, 102, 103, 616 (Form 47). A single-handled lentoid shaped flask appears in Cypriot, Mycenaean, and Canaanite assemblages.

60. See Furumark 1941b, 32, 33, 67, 82, 92, 93, 99, 101, 102, 616 (Forms 48 and 49).

61. Regarding imported Mycenaean lentoid flasks in Canaan, see most recently Leonard 1994, 81–83.

62. Flask CA 28a, 28b, 28c, and 28d are flasks with two handles. Forms CA 28a, 28b, and 28d are locally produced, while CA 28c is manufactured outside of Canaan. Locally produced CA 28 appears at most Late Bronze Age IIA–B sites in Canaan and occasionally in New Kingdom Egypt. See Killebrew 1999a, 126–29, for a detailed description.

63. Flask CA 29 is a locally produced imitation of imported Base Ring and Red Lustrous Ware Cypriot flasks. They are found throughout Canaan, especially in tomb contexts. See, e.g., Deir el-Balah: T. Dothan 1979, 39, 56; ills. 85, 92, 129, 135; Beth-shean: Oren 1973, 114, figs. 47b:19; 48b:14; 75:3; Gibeon: Pritchard 1963, fig. 12:69; Lachish: Tufnell 1958, 211, pl. 82:908.

64. Flask CA 30 is similar to Flask CA 28, though the body is more globular in profile and has a slightly elongated neck. Flask CA 30 differs from the typical Iron I flask in its body proportions (e.g., its larger body and shorter neck). It should be considered a "transitional type," bridging Flask CA 28 and the typical Iron I flasks. This form dates to

transitional Late Bronze/Iron I or Iron I contexts. It is best known in the north and Jordan Valley. See, e.g., Beth-shean (Stratum VI): James 1966, fig. 53:21; Yadin and Geva 1986, 70, fig. 27:13; Deir ʿAlla (Phase E): Franken 1992, fig. 3–7.11; Megiddo (Strata VIIB–VIA): Loud 1948, pls. 67:2; 80:5; 86:7; Kefar Yehoshua: Druks 1966, fig. 4:1–2; Tell Keisan: Briend and Humbert 1980, pl. 76; Hazor (Stratum XII): Yadin et al. 1961, pl. CLXVI:13; Tel Dan (transitional Late Bronze/Iron I and Iron I): Biran 1994, ills. 87:5; 93:4.

65. Amphoriskos CA 31 appears mainly in southern Canaan: Tel Miqne-Ekron (Stratum IX): Killebrew 1998b, fig. 1:9; Lachish: Tufnell 1958, pl. 85:977; Tell el-Farʿah (S): Starkey and Harding 1932, pl. LXXXVII: Type 55W6; Duncan 1930, Types 55W6 and 55W8; Tel Seraʿ: Oren 1985, fig. 7:5; Tell Jemmeh: Duncan 1930, Type 55W5; a tomb between Ashdod and Ashkelon: Gophna and Meron 1970, fig. 2:7; Zakariya: Bliss and Macalister 1902, pl. 43:1, 4; Duncan 1930, Type 55W7.

66. Amphoriskos CA 32 appears in southern Canaan and the Jezreel and Beth-shean Valleys at the end of the Late Bronze and Iron I periods. See, e.g., Beth-shean (Level VI): Yadin and Geva 1986, fig. 27:11; Megiddo (Stratum VI): Loud 1948, pl. 84:4; Lachish: Tufnell 1958, pl. 85:971, 975, 976, 979; Tell el-Farʿah (S): Starkey and Harding 1932, pls. LXXXVII: Type 55W3.

67. For a discussion of pyxides, see Pritchard 1963, 14; T. Dothan 1982, 130–31; A. Mazar 1985b, 77–78.

68. Pyxis CA 33 is a local imitation of imported Mycenaean pyxides. Small numbers of this local imitation are known throughout Canaan during the Late Bronze II and continue into the Iron I period. See Killebrew 1999a, 133–34, for a detailed discussion of CA 33.

69. Pyxis CA 34 appears mainly during the Iron I period at sites throughout Canaan. It should be noted that CA 34 is less prevalent than CA 33. See A. Mazar 1985b, 77 (Type PX 2), for a detailed discussion of this type.

70. Although Tufnell (1958, 210–11) suggests that local imitations of Cypriot imports became significant only after the cessation of imports, the evidence does not support this claim. Imitations and imported Base Ring II vessels appear side by side at numerous sites throughout Canaan (see Prag 1985, 162; Dajani 1964, pl. XXXVIII: nos. 8 and 9 [Cypriot imports] and 10 and 11 [local imitations of Cypriot imports]). Local imitation Base Ring II jugs are widespread throughout Canaan, especially during the thirteenth century B.C.E. (see Killebrew 1999a, 134–35, for a detailed discussion).

71. Imitation Mycenaean vessels, Form CA 36, are less common than imitation Cypriot containers. Imitation piriform vessels are known from Deir el-Balah: T. Dothan 1979, 39, ills. 84; 91; Killebrew 1999a, ill. III:18:6; Beth-shean (Level VII): James and McGovern 1993, fig. 9:15; Tell Jemmeh: Duncan 1930, pl. 55V2; Gibeon: Pritchard 1963, fig. 12:76; and Lachish: Tufnell 1958, 216, pl. 82:940–944.

72. The saucer lamp is the typical lamp of the Middle–Late Bronze Ages in Canaan. It has a shallow, slightly rounded bowl with a pinched spout. During the Middle Bronze through Late Bronze I periods, the spout is slightly pinched and becomes increasingly pinched during the Late Bronze IIA–B. As Amiran (1969, 190) notes, there is little if any distinction between Late Bronze IIA and Late Bronze IIB lamps. They appear at all Late Bronze II sites in Canaan and continue into the Iron I period. For detailed lamp typologies, see Tufnell 1958, 185–87; Killebrew 1999a, 136–38.

73. Form CA 38, the cup and saucer, first appears in the Early Bronze Age and continues through the Iron II period (Amiran 1969, 303). The cup and saucer has usually been identified as a lamp and is often found in cultic contexts; however, Aston (1996, 61, fig. 191:a, b) refers to this form in Egypt as an incense bowl. This suggestion seems quite probable in light of their context, often appearing in relatively large numbers in cultic sites such as the Area F temple at Hazor (Yadin et al. 1960, 155; pl. CXLVI:8–13), Fosse Temples II and III at Lachish (Tufnell, Inge, and Harding 1940, pl. XLIV:179–183; see also Bunimovitz and Zimhoni 1990, fig. 1:17), and the Deir ʿAlla sanctuary (Franken 1992, figs. 3–7.4; 4–15.29;

4–20.16). They are also attested in Nineteenth and Twentieth Dynasty contexts in Egypt. See Killebrew 1999a, 139–40, for a detailed discussion.

74. For a description of the effects of heating and cooling on ceramic cooking pots, see Amberg and Hartsook 1946; Kingery 1955; Bronitsky and Hamer 1986; for a discussion of the thermal properties of clay, see Rice 1987, 367–68. See Woods 1986 for an alternative view regarding thermal stress. See also Braun 1983 for a discussion of the physical properties of cooking pots.

75. For a detailed discussion of the use of shell as temper in clays and the effects this temper has on different aspects of pottery manufacture, see Feathers 1989; Matson 1989. For a petrographic description of the cooking-pot ware from Tel Miqne-Ekron, see Killebrew 1999a, 203; 1999b, 96–98; for a description of Canaanite cooking-pot wares from Lachish that are remarkably similar to those from Tel Miqne-Ekron, see Magrill and Middleton 1997, 69.

76. Several models based primarily on the ethnographic record have been proposed to describe the organization of pottery production (see, e.g., Balfet 1965, 162–63; van der Leeuw 1976; 1984; Peacock 1981; 1982; Redman and Myers 1981, 289–90; Rice 1981; Tosi 1984, 23–24; Santley, Arnold, and Pool 1989; Costin 1991), its distribution, and its demand (see Pool 1992, 280–83). These models consider technological features such as formation techniques and the variability of both raw materials and products, as well as ecological, economic, and social criteria such as frequency and seasonality of production; number of workers; their age, sex, and status; degree of labor division; kind and extent of the investment in special space or tools; and proximity of consuming groups (Rice 1987, 183–84). Van der Leeuw (1976, 394–98, 402–3) suggests the following division of pottery production into different states of pottery economy: domestic production (including household production and household industries) and professional production (workshop industries, village industries, large-scale industries, and individual industries).

77. This is contra B. G. Wood 1990b, who concludes that the widespread homogeneity of Canaanite pottery during the Late Bronze II period was a result of a small number of large-scale production centers, perhaps staffed with itinerant potters who traveled from workshop to workshop. I do not see such widespread diffusion of vessels that were produced at a small number of workshops or by a relatively small number of potters.

78. P. McGovern (1989) reached similar conclusions regarding the potters' craft at Beth-shean. However, he suggests that the potters were Canaanites trained in Egyptian techniques of production, while I favor the idea that the potters were probably Egyptian due to the close similarity between pottery produced in Egypt and that manufactured in Canaan at Beth-shean.

4
EARLY ISRAEL: A "MIXED MULTITUDE"

Recent research on the emergence of Israel points unequivocally to the conclusion that biblical Israel's roots lie in the final century of Late Bronze Age Canaan. As outlined in chapters 1–3, the disintegration of the Bronze Age empires during the thirteenth and twelfth centuries B.C.E. triggered wide-scale cultural, political, and social fragmentation in the Levant, resulting in the assertion of local identities and the establishment of new social boundaries. Although this is widely recognized, during the past fifty years questions regarding the origins and emergence of biblical Israel have been one of the most contentious issues facing biblical scholars and archaeologists. These discussions have culminated in the question of whether ancient Israel even existed.[1] In recent years it does seem that the pendulum is swinging back toward a more contextualized and integrated approach to the biblical texts. Postmortems proclaiming that historical approaches to the Bible have reached a dead-end or that it is not possible (or desirable) to write a history of ancient Israel are premature.[2]

Unlike many recent discussions, which focus on Israelite ethnicity and identity, I adopt a more nuanced approach. That is, I propose that the emergence of ancient Israel should be interpreted as a process of ethnogenesis, or a gradual emergence of a group identity from a "mixed multitude" of peoples whose origins are largely indigenous and can only be understood in the wider eastern Mediterranean context.[3] Following Herwig Wolfram's (1990, 30–31) definition, the process of ethnogenesis that forms the core ideology of a group often comprises three characteristic features: (1) a story or stories of a primordial deed, which can include the crossing of a sea or river, an impressive victory against all odds over an enemy, or combinations of similar "miraculous" stories (e.g., the exodus); (2) a group that undergoes a religious experience or change in cult as a result of the primordial deed (e.g., reception of the Ten Commandments and worship of Yahweh); and (3) the existence of an ancestral enemy or enemies that cement group cohesion (e.g., most notably the Canaanites and Philistines).[4] These basic elements form the key themes in the biblical narrative about the emergence of early Israel.

In what follows, I explore the ethnogenesis of biblical Israel through a multiperspective historical approach that takes into consideration culture-historical elements, longer-term processual aspects, and post-processual concerns, including ideology and agency. I also trace the changing social, cultural, and political boundaries evidenced in the material culture record, based on the textual and archaeological evidence directly or indirectly related to the thirteenth–eleventh centuries B.C.E., with a focus on developments in the highland regions of Canaan within their larger regional context. While acknowledging the complex and often ambiguous nature of the textual evidence and material manifestations of ethnic identity, my response to the question of whether or not a history of ancient Israel can be written is a qualified yes (see, e.g., Grabbe 1997 for various responses).

This chapter opens with a review and critique of the primary textual and archaeological evidence, followed by a survey in which various theories regarding the interpretation of this evidence are reviewed and reassessed. Lastly, based on the primary textual and archaeological evidence, I delineate the social boundaries of a mixed multitude whose core groups resided in the central highlands of Cisjordan (i.e., the western bank of the Jordan River) and Transjordan. Over time these disparate groups were united by the worship of Yahweh, a powerful ideology that formed the core of early Israelite ethnogenesis and distinguished them from their Canaanite origins.

The Textual Evidence

The Biblical Tradition

The biblical narrative of the emergence of Israel as a nation begins in the biblical book of Exodus with the story of Moses and the subsequent escape from Egypt and the exodus, continues in the book of Joshua with the conquest of the land under the leadership of Joshua, and culminates in the book of Judges with the settlement of the Israelite tribes. It is beyond the scope and purpose of this chapter to include a detailed critical analysis of these texts. Commentary is confined to general observations regarding the narrative texts that purport to be "historical" and are traditionally related to the emergence of Israel.

The Exodus

According to the Bible, the emergence of ancient Israel was preceded by a long period of enslavement in Egypt that was ended by a large-scale exodus from Egypt and followed by forty years of wandering in the wilderness. The biblical narrative presents the desert experience as a transformative period that created the foundations for Israelite identity and religious ideology. Due to the miraculous nature of the exodus saga, this narrative has sometimes been termed a "folktale."[5] Folktale or not, this powerful narrative of a journey from slavery to freedom is, undoubtedly, the single most important and unifying theme in Israel's history—both past and present.

For the post-Enlightenment historian, the exodus and the supernatural events associated with the escape from Egypt have proven to be one of the most challenging chapters in Israel's past.[6] This event, as well as others that defy modern sensibilities and concepts of historicity, have given rise to critical methods of textual analyses whose goal is to untangle the various layers of composition so that a history of ancient Israel may be written.[7] Based on the application of several approaches employed in traditional biblical criticism (source and form criticism), many historically oriented biblical scholars consider two poetic texts, the Song of the Sea (Exod 15) and the Song of Deborah (Judg 5), as among the earliest texts, with their origins possibly dating to the thirteenth–twelfth centuries B.C.E.[8]

From the Egyptian perspective, there is universal agreement that there is no direct reference to the exodus in the Egyptian sources. Moreover, attempts to assign a specific date to this tale have been plagued with difficulties. Suggestions to place this event in a particular century—sixteenth, fifteenth, and thirteenth–twelfth centuries B.C.E.—have proven inconclusive due to various inconsistencies between the biblical account and the historical and archaeological data.[9] Thus, rather than attempt to identify a particular moment in history, I will seek to describe something of greater significance: the cultural setting of the exodus story. In short, numerous aspects of the account accurately reflect the archaeological and historical context in Canaan and Egypt during the Late Bronze and early Iron Ages.

One of the major themes of the exodus story is the bondage of *bene Israel* in Egypt. Significantly, the presence of foreign slaves is well documented in Egyptian New Kingdom texts.[10] According to the Egyptian evidence, slaves fulfilled a multitude of roles in Egyptian society, from menial tasks to key service roles in the royal household to serving as members of the priesthood (Redford 1992b, 221–27; Hendel 2001, 604–8; Redmount 2001, 72–76). Asiatic slaves included prisoners of war, uprooted peasants, exiled Canaanites, human tribute, or Canaanites sold into bondage by local slave merchants. The escape of slaves was also a common event, as recounted in the Papyrus Anastasi V, which dates to the end of the Nineteenth Dynasty (see Malamat 1997, 20–21 nn. 11–12). Thus, the theme of Egyptian tyranny and enslavement and the accounts of runaway slaves returning to their homeland must have resonated throughout Canaan and other regions under Egyptian imperial control (Malamat 1997, 19–21; Hendel 2001, 620–22).

While the primary theme of the exodus story—bondage in Egypt and escape to freedom—fits the general milieu of Late Bronze Age Canaan, numerous particulars of the story indicate a historical multilayering and complex redaction of this account of Israelite redemption. Details that hint at the complexity of this process include the mention of Pithom and Rameses, cities that some have identified with the sites of Tell el-Maskhuta or Tell el-Retabeh and Tell ed-Dabᶜa, respectively. However, excavations have revealed that none of these sites was inhabited during most of the New Kingdom period.[11] Much has also been made of the Egyptian origin of several of the names of key characters in the exodus narrative, including Moses, Phinehas, and Hophni. However, the chronological context of these names is debated.[12] The detail-laden account of the forty years of desert wandering is also fraught with historical and archaeological inconsistencies and does not appear to reflect one historical context but rather a layering of numerous historical events over time (for a summary, see Dever 2003, 18–21).

In light of the lack of evidence in the Egyptian texts and the archaeological remains of an exodus of this magnitude, it is not surprising that scholars have suggested that the exodus does not represent a specific historical moment but rather numerous "exoduses" of runaway Asiatic slaves that were "telescoped" into a single event.[13] It is difficult if not impossible, and probably unwise, to attempt to pin this saga to a particular historical event. Rather, we should see it is as reflecting a powerful collective memory of the Egyptian occupation of Canaan and the enslavement of its population, which reached its greatest impact during the thirteenth and twelfth centuries B.C.E. (Weinstein 1981, 17–22; Singer 1994, 284–94).

The Israelite "Conquest" and Settlement of Canaan

The biblical text recounts that, after four decades of wandering in the wilderness, the Israelites journeyed through Transjordan in anticipation of entering the land promised to the patriarch Abraham, the nation's progenitor (Gen 13).[14] Deuteronomy, the last of the five books of Moses (also referred to as the Pentateuch or Torah), ends with the death of Moses at Mount Nebo, but the following book of Joshua continues the saga with the conquest of Canaan, initiated with the spectacular destruction of Jericho by the Israelite tribes united under the leadership of Joshua. Almost without exception, scholars agree that the account in Joshua holds little historical value vis-à-vis early Israel and most likely reflects much later historical times.[15] Additionally, as has been pointed out by modern scholarly research during the past two centuries, Joshua and the following book, Judges, present two differing and at times contradictory accounts of the settlement of the tribes of Israel.[16]

Joshua and Judges belong to what most scholars refer to as the Deuteronomistic History (DH), which includes the books of Deuteronomy (law), Joshua, Judges, 1 and 2 Samuel, and 1 and 2 Kings (for a general overview, see Knoppers 2000). The Deuteronomistic account presents a coherent narrative spanning the conquest of the promised land to the end of the monarchy. The first scholar to theorize the existence of a Deuteronomist Historian was Martin Noth, who proposed in 1943 that these books were the work of a single author who composed this account during the exilic period (Noth 1981). According to this view, the Deuteronomistic Historian based his account on oral histories and authentic archival source materials that spanned several centuries in date. Since Noth's original work, several revisions of his theory have been proposed, most notably the "Harvard"[17] and the "Göttingen"[18] schools, which suggest more than one author and additional layers of redaction.[19] In spite of these diverse opinions, most historically oriented research acknowledges that several hundred years separated the composition of the account and the time that the events are purported to have occurred.

Joshua 1–12 describes a successful campaign against the Canaanites by a united Israel. Joshua's military conquest begins in the center of the country, continues with a campaign to the south, and concludes in the north, culminating in the conflagration of Hazor, the "head of all those kingdoms." With the notable exception of Hazor, this account finds little historical or archaeological support.[20] Both the internal biblical contradictions and these external discrepancies between the conquest account and the archaeological evidence reflect the passage of time between Israel's protohistorical period and the actual composition of the texts (Naʾaman 1994b, 222–27; Stager 2001, 97–102; Dever 2003, 39–50). Consensus exists that, whatever its "sources" (either oral and/or written), the conquest account as narrated in the book of Joshua is historically problematic and should be treated with caution.

The book of Judges presents an alternative account of early Israel's history and the settlement of the tribes. Here Israelite settlement is depicted as gradual, fragmented, and fraught with difficulties (see Soggin 1993, 177–93; Hackett 2001). Contrary to the claim in Josh 11:16–23 that Canaan had been conquered and the land allocated to the twelve tribes, according to Judges the Canaanites were still a group to be reckoned with. Consequently, there were periodic violent encounters between coalitions of various Israelite tribes and the indigenous populations. Scholars traditionally have given more credence to the Judges account,[21] in part because critical analyses of the book point to a more complex stratigraphic layering of the textual source materials, some of which are believed to date to the premonarchical period (see Gooding 1982). Especially relevant to our discussion is the Song of Deborah (Judg 5), whose original composition is often assigned to the twelfth–eleventh centuries B.C.E. and which has been described as a "self-portrait" of premonarchic Israel.[22] What both Joshua and Judges do share in common is the insistence that the Israelites were outsiders, a nonindigenous group that was distinct from the Canaanites.

The Egyptian Sources

The Israel Stela

The starting point for any discussion of the ethnogenesis of ancient Israel is the late thirteenth-century B.C.E. victory stela of Merneptah, which dates to his fifth year and documents his campaign in Canaan (regarding the historicity of Merneptah's campaign, see p. 56 above). The complete inscription, which actually appears on two stelae (Petrie 1897, pls. xiii–xiv; Lichtheim 1976, 73), is often referred to in the singular as the Israel Stela. It is our only late second millennium B.C.E. written source that mentions an entity named "Israel."

The first question regarding the significance of this inscription for the origins of Israel has to do with the reading of the word *ysry3r/l*. The different readings of this term include Israel, Jezreel (Margalith 1990), or a word with no relationship to the name Israel at all (Nibbi 1989, 38–44, 73–75). However, the majority of Egyptologists agree that *ysry3r/l* should be translated "Israel."[23] A second question often raised is whether there is a connection between *ysry3r/l* and biblical Israel. Mainstream scholarship accepts the connection between Merneptah's Israel and a biblical Israel, concluding that the Israel Stela is a key chronological marker relevant to the emergence of biblical Israel.[24]

A third question relates to the translation of the Egyptian phrase used to describe Merneptah's actions against Israel: *ysry3r/l fkt bn prt.f* ("Israel is laid waste; his seed is not"). Michael G. Hasel (2003) interprets this text as depicting the destruction of Israel's subsistence sources, a practice common in second and first millennia B.C.E. military campaigns, and indicating that Israel had a sedentary nature at the end of the thirteenth century. However, Anson Rainey (2001) challenges this interpretation. He believes the phrase refers to the destruction of Israel's progeny or offspring, a translation that he uses to support his claim that Merneptah's Israel was pastoral in nature and closely related to the *Shasu,* an Egyptian term that appears only in Egyptian New Kingdom texts and designates a group of people and a region that apparently originated in Transjordan (see Ward 1992b; Hasel 1998, 217–36).

A fourth matter of debate is the location of the region inhabited by Merneptah's Israel. Based on the structure of the hymnic-poetic unit and the order of the inscription's toponyms, most scholars place Israel as residing generally in the highlands, either in Cisjordan (as the majority propose)[25] or Transjordan.[26] Although the identification of Yenoʿam, one of the sites mentioned in the account of Merneptah's actual or fictitious campaign against Israel, remains uncertain, there does seem to be strong circumstantial evidence to locate Israel in the central hill country.

The Karnak Reliefs

Four battle scenes incised on the western outer wall of Karnak's "Cour de la Cachette" (Wreszinski 1935, taf. 58, 58a) are a lesser-known Egyptian source that some consider to be an depiction of "early Israel." These four reliefs depict the conquest of three fortified city-states: Ashkelon is specifically mentioned, but the names of the other two cities are not indicated. Against the traditional attribution of the reliefs to Ramesses II, Frank J. Yurco (1986; 1990; 1997) assigns the battle scenes to Merneptah. Based on a comparison with the campaign described in Merneptah's Stela, he suggests that the two unnamed sites are Gezer and Yenoʿam. The fourth badly damaged scene depicts a battle in a hilly environment that lacks any indication of a fortified city and is directed against a foe that is portrayed as Canaanite. Yurco suggests that these Canaanites should be identified with the same Israel mentioned in the Israel Stela (fig. 4.1).[27] If this attribution to Merneptah is correct, we have a second possible reference to "Israel," one in which the people are represented as "Canaanites" (Stager 1985b; Yurco 1990; 1997). Although this is an attractive suggestion, not all Egyptologists accept Yurco's attribution of these battle scenes to Merneptah (see, e.g., Redford 1986; 1992b, 275 n. 85; 2000, 4).

Archaeological Evidence

The archaeological evidence, though fragmentary, contributes to our understanding of the longer-term history of processual changes over time as well as the shorter-term historically specific context of the thirteenth and eleventh centuries B.C.E. (Bunimovitz 1995; Finkelstein 1995b). Of special relevance to this discussion are the excavations and surveys conducted during the past thirty years in the central hill country of Israel and the Transjordanian highlands. Surveys and preliminary attempts to analyze the results within the framework of the broader field of landscape archaeology[28] have transformed our understanding of the textual evidence related to Israel's emergence. This evidence shows that a notable

Fig. 4.1. *Shasu:* "Early Israel"

shift in settlement patterns throughout much of Canaan occurred during the course of the late thirteenth through the eleventh centuries. These far-reaching structural changes corresponded to the region-wide fragmentation and dislocation of peoples that characterized the collapse of the Late Bronze Age world of empires and international connections in the eastern Mediterranean. Following centuries of declining sedentary populations, increasing social and economic polarization, and deteriorating conditions in Late Bronze Age city-states and in the countryside, dozens of small hamlets and villages appeared over the course of two centuries in the highlands, especially in the central hill country between Shechem and Jerusalem. The archaeological record seldom documents such large-scale change and regional diversity as that demonstrated during the transition from the Late Bronze to Iron Ages. The resulting settlement and material culture patterns created new cultural and social boundaries that defined Iron Age Canaan.

Three standard works summarize the archaeology of Iron I highland sites traditionally associated with the emergence of ancient Israel. Israel Finkelstein's comprehensive *The Archaeology of the Israelite Settlement* (1988)[29] remains a landmark study. Israel Finkelstein and Nadav Na'aman's edited volume, *From Nomadism to Monarchy: Archaeological and Historical Aspects of Early Israel* (1994b), is an essential study for anyone dealing with the Iron I period. The most recent addition and timely update to the archaeology of the emergence of Israel is William G. Dever's semipopular *Who Were the Early Israelites and Where Did They Come From?* (2003).

Many of the characteristic features of the archaeology of the central hill country have been previously discussed in depth in numerous publications during the past three decades.[30] These newly established twelfth–eleventh century villages are characterized by modest numbers of domestic structures, usually a version of the three- or four-room pillared house; few, if any, public structures or fortifications; a proliferation of silos; the appearance of cisterns and agricultural terraces; absence of pig bones; paucity of burials; and, most notably, a very limited repertoire of utilitarian ceramic containers that continue the tradition of Late Bronze Age pottery shapes. The major results of surveys and excavations in both Cisjordan and Transjordan are presented below followed by a summary of the main features of highland material culture, with a focus on the pottery types associated with the heartland of the central hill country and a case study of the "collar rim" pithos as an indicator of social boundaries.

Regional Surveys and Excavation Results from Representative Iron I Sites

The combination of archaeological surveys and excavations in Israel and Jordan during the past thirty years has produced invaluable data that has shaped our current understanding of the Iron I period and its implications for Israel's protohistory. The published results, albeit incomplete, of these surveys and limited excavated sites are reviewed here.[31] The most dramatic changes in the archaeological record are evidenced in the highland regions (the central hill country and Transjordanian plateau). Although archaeological exploration is far from complete, the Transjordanian evidence regarding the thirteenth–eleventh centuries B.C.E. transition generally parallels developments in the central hill country of western Palestine and is marked by a noteworthy increase and shift in settlement patterns. These well-documented changes are the best indicators of the creation of new social boundaries that can be examined in light of the primary evidence from both a processual long-term historical perspective as well from a shorter-term specific historical and ideological context. Of secondary, and mainly comparative, significance are the neighboring Galilee and Beer-sheba Valley regions, where the archaeological record is mixed, presenting a picture of continuity and gradual change. The following discussion focuses on one aspect of the settlement archaeology—site distribution—in tandem with evidence from select excavated Iron I type sites in order to explore the process of transformation that occurred during the transition from the Late Bronze to Iron Ages in the highland regions of Canaan (see fig. 4.2).[32]

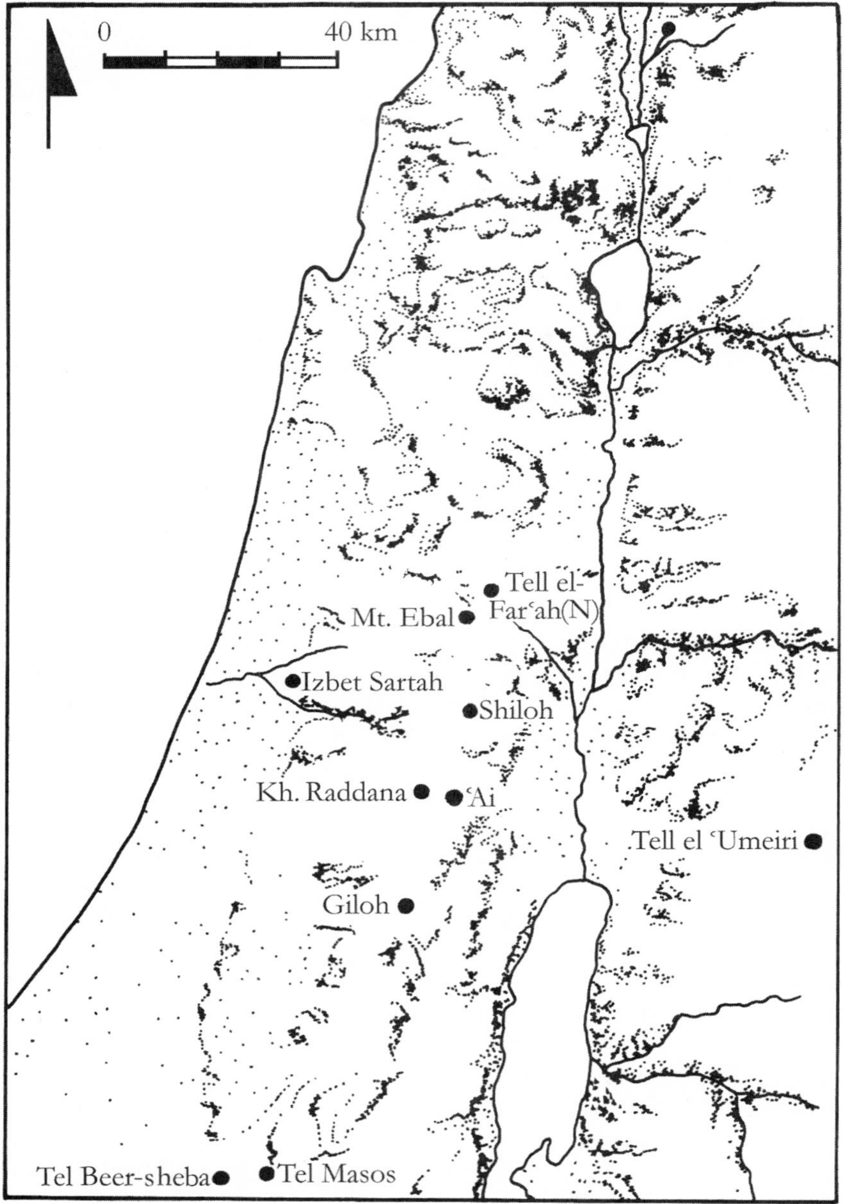

Fig. 4.2. Map of Selected Iron I Sites Associated with Early Israel

Central Hill Country

The central hill country, bordered by the Jezreel Valley on the north and the Beer-sheba Valley on the south, is essential to the biblical narrative of the emergence of Israel. Following traditional biblical geographical designations, the central hill country comprises two major geographical units: Samaria and Judea. Samaria was more hospitable for habitation due to its fertile valleys, so it is not surprising that it was the more densely settled region during the Iron I period (for a gazetteer of Iron I sites in Samaria, see R. Miller 2003). The southern region was less hospitable to permanent habitation and, based on recent surveys, was more sparsely occupied by sedentary populations until the Iron II.[33] Based on the biblical tribal allocations, this region is further divided into four traditional geographic subunits: northern Samaria (Manasseh), southern Samaria (Ephraim), the plateau between Ramallah and Jerusalem (Benjamin), and the Judean hills (Judah), regions that usually form the modern research boundaries of most archaeological surveys in the central hill country.[34]

Samaria. Northern Samaria is often referred to by its biblical tribal designation: Manasseh. Adam Zertal's (1992; 1994; 1996; 1998; 2001; Zertal and Mirkam 2000; see also Campbell 1991) ongoing survey of Manasseh has continued for well over two decades and is the most extensive and detailed of all surveys conducted in the hill country. Zertal (1998) documents several variables that differentiate the twelfth- and eleventh-century settlement patterns from those of the Late Bronze Age. These changes are evident in the settlement patterns, the small site size, the architectural layout and structures, the general lack of settlement continuity from the Late Bronze into the Iron I, the limited pottery inventory that characterizes the Iron I, a change in diet, metallurgical finds, new cult practices and cultic places, an increase in sedentary population, and a break with previous cultural tradition.[35] Few excavated sites date to the initial phase of settlement in the early twelfth century B.C.E., with the majority attributed to the later twelfth and eleventh centuries. Key excavated and published sites dating to the first half of the Iron I period include Mount Ebal (Zertal 1986–87) and the Bull Site (A. Mazar 1982a).[36]

The late thirteenth and twelfth century B.C.E. site on Mount Ebal, popularly known as the location of the much-disputed "Joshua's Altar" (Josh 8:30–35; Zertal 1985; Machlin 1990), is one of the most extensively excavated early Iron I settlements in northern Samaria (Zertal 1986–87; 1994, 61–65). During excavations from 1982 to 1989, Zertal distinguished two strata: one dating to the second half of the thirteenth century (Stratum II), and one to the first half of the twelfth century (Stratum I). The site was subsequently abandoned. The principal Stratum I archaeological remains include a large, rectangular structure constructed of unhewn stones that measures 9.5 x 7.1 m and is 3 m high (figs. 4.3–4.4). Its interior structure was filled with layers of fieldstones, earth, and ash deposits. The ashes contained burnt bones of bull, sheep, goats, and fallow deer (Kolska-Horwitz 1986–87). An inclined perpendicular wall is interpreted as a ramp leading to the top of the rectangular structure. Numerous other installations are contemporary with the use of the rectangular structure. Inner and outer enclosure walls encompass the site, with an entrance located in the southeast. Initially several scholars expressed skepticism regarding Zertal's interpretation of structure as an early Iron I open-air altar site associated with the emergence of Israel.[37] However, the consensus today tends to support the cultic interpretation of this early Iron I site, if not the biblical one (see Mazar 1990a, 348–50; Coogan 1987; 1990; Zevit 2001, 196–201).

Southern Samaria, or its tribal equivalent Ephraim, includes the region between Shechem and Ramallah (Finkelstein 1988, 121–204; Finkelstein and Lederman 1997).[38] According to these surveys, Middle Bronze Age settlements are well represented in southern Samaria, paralleling settlement patterns in Manasseh. The territory of Ephraim witnesses a marked decline in permanent settlements during the Late Bronze Age, followed by a notable increase in small hamlets in the late thirteenth/twelfth and eleventh centuries B.C.E. These newly established Iron I villages are usually located in close proximity to stable water sources. Bethel is one of the few Late Bronze Age sites that, following its destruction at the end of the thirteenth century, was reoccupied during the Iron I.[39] Key type-sites in southern Samaria include Shiloh (Finkelstein 1988, 205–34; Finkelstein and Magen 1993),[40] Khirbet Raddana (Callaway and Cooley 1971; Cooley 1975; Lederman 1999), Bethel (Kelso 1968), and ʿAi (Marquet-Krause 1949, 22–24; Callaway 1965; 1969; 1976).[41]

Khirbet Raddana, a small archetypical Iron I village, is one of the most extensively excavated hamlets located in the heartland of the central hill country. Joseph Callaway conducted excavations at the small agricultural site from 1969 to 1974 (Callaway and Cooley 1971; Cooley 1975; Lederman 1999). Sections of seven different houses were uncovered in areas R, S, and T, revealing an irregular village plan protected by a defensive wall (fig. 4.5). A similar irregular settlement plan was uncovered at neighboring ʿAi (fig. 4.6). All the domestic structures belong to the three-room pillar house type (Lederman 1999, 49). One three-room house in Site S was completely excavated (fig. 4.7). Based on the excavations, Lederman (1999) suggests that Khirbet Raddana should be considered a typical Iron I agricultural village that comprised four to six extended families or self-sufficient households.[42]

Fig. 4.3. Monumental Structure at Mount Ebal

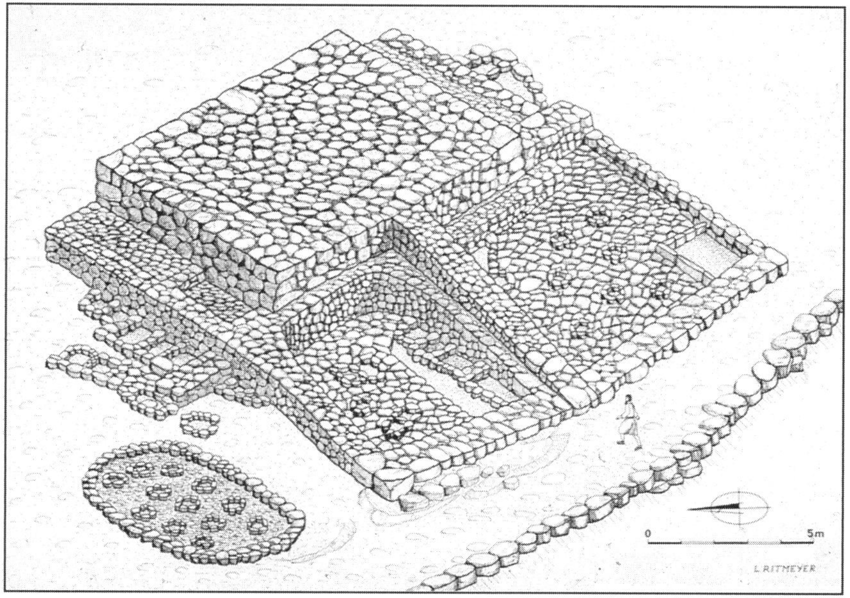

Fig. 4.4. Reconstruction of the Altar at Mount Ebal

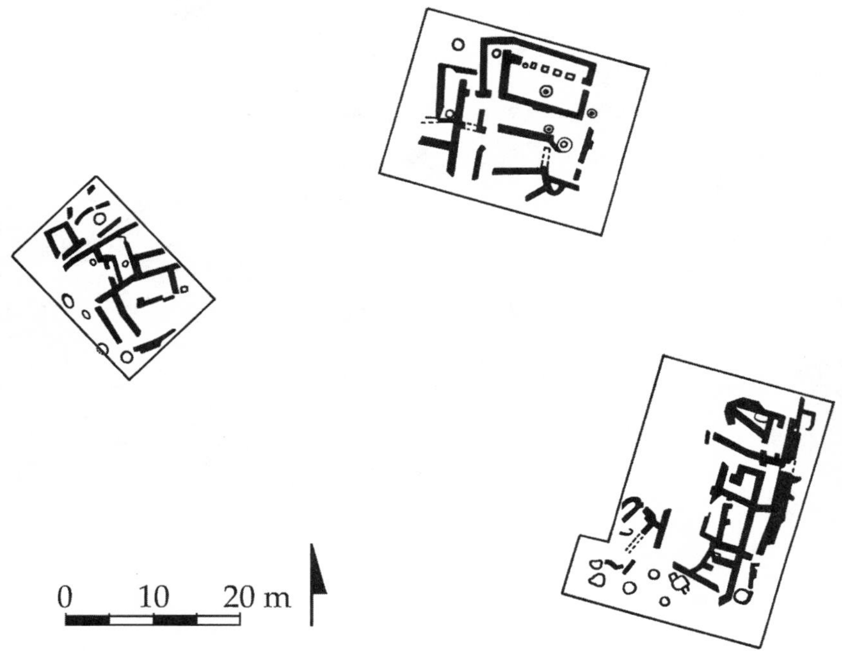

Fig. 4.5. Plan of Excavated Areas at Khirbet Raddana

The central plateau between Ramallah and Jerusalem corresponds to the biblical tribal boundaries of Benjamin. Although this region was less densely settled than Samaria during the second half of the second millennium B.C.E., settlements in Benjamin increased in number and size during the course of the Iron Age, especially in the east and desert fringe (see Yeivin 1971; Kallai 1972; Finkelstein 1988, 56–65; Finkelstein and Magen 1993).[43] Published excavations of Iron Age sites include Tell el-Fûl (Albright 1924; Sinclair 1960; N. Lapp 1978), Tell en-Naṣbeh (McCown 1947; Wampler 1947), Khirbet ed-Dawara (Finkelstein 1990b), and Gibeon (Pritchard 1962; 1964).[44]

Judea. The Judean hill country is bordered by Jerusalem on the north and the Beer-sheba–Arad Valley on the south. According to Avi Ofer's archaeological survey (1993; 1994; 2001), the Judean highlands also witnessed a decrease in settled occupation during the Late Bronze Age. Six surveyed sites date to the Late Bronze Age. The number of identified Iron I sites increases to seventeen or eighteen and constitute a built-up area of roughly 30–45 acres.[45] Khirbet Rabud (Debir) is remarkable for its stratigraphic sequence that spans the Late Bronze and Iron Ages (Kochavi

Fig. 4.6. Plan of Iron I Village at ʿAi

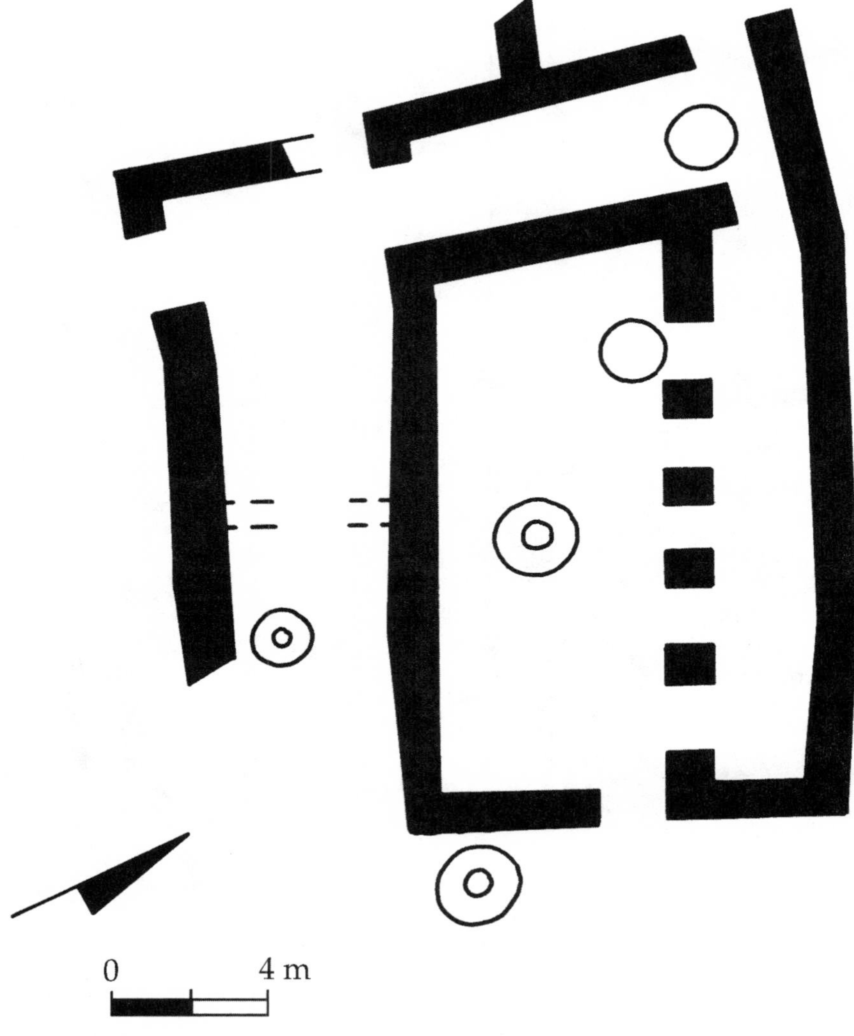

Fig. 4.7. Plan of Three-Room House at Khirbet Raddana

1974). The archaeological evidence for Jerusalem during the Late Bronze Age is especially ambiguous, and the same data has been used both to support (Cahill 2003, 27–33) or dispute (Steiner 2001, 24–41; 2003, 348–57) the existence of a fourteenth–thirteenth century settlement. Published surveys of the Jerusalem area have revealed approximately thirty small Iron I settlements, mainly to the north and west of the City of David (Kloner 2001; Lehmann 2003; forthcoming). Jerusalem's modest size and the paucity of settlements in Judah until the eighth century B.C.E. highlights the relative insignificance of the southern central hill country vis-à-vis Samaria, or the northern central hill country.

Giloh, one of the few excavated early Iron I villages in the Jerusalem area, is considered a type-site associated with the emergence of ancient Israel. Overlooking Emek Rephaim, this site is situated in the modern neighborhood of Giloh, a suburb south of Jerusalem. This short-lived and poorly preserved enclosed Iron I site settlement included an outer defensive wall system, at least one inner enclosure where a pillared domestic building was discovered, and an Iron I tower outside the defensive walls (A. Mazar 1981; 1990b; 1994b). Suggestions regarding the function of this site include a herdsman's hamlet, a farmstead, or a stronghold of a wealthy land or flock owner (A. Mazar 1994b, 83); a Canaanite site (Ahlström 1984b); or an open-air cultic site (Zevit 2001, 197–98 n. 122, suggesting that the "tower" is an altar platform).[46] Due to similarities between Giloh's ceramic assemblage and the limited repertoire of pottery characteristic of Iron I central hill villages, Amihai Mazar (1994b, 88) concludes that Giloh should be accepted as an early Israelite highland site.[47]

Transjordanian Plateau

The Transjordanian highlands, bordered to the west by the Jordan Valley and to the east by the Syrian-Arabian desert, are traditionally subdivided into several smaller geographical regions that correspond to their biblical designations: Gilead, Ammon, Moab, and Edom. Archaeological exploration in Transjordan has been less intensive and systematic than work conducted during the last twenty-five years in Israel. As a result, our understanding of this region is incomplete and somewhat fragmentary. What has been becoming increasingly evident is Transjordan's close material-culture connections with the central hill country during the twelfth and eleventh centuries B.C.E. Considered together with the Transjordan's place in the conquest narrative of Canaan, this plateau plays a key role in understanding the emergence of Israel (for a comprehensive study of this region during the Late Bronze and Early Iron Ages, see van der Steen 2002).

Nelson Glueck (1934; 1935; 1939) conducted the first systematic surveys in Transjordan from 1932 to 1947. He investigated hundreds of sites and concluded that there is little evidence for settled occupation during most of the Middle and Late Bronze Ages. Glueck (1971, 153) proposed that noteworthy changes in settlement patterns coincided with the emergence of the kingdoms of Ammon, Moab, and Edom at end of the Late Bronze Age. The resulting dramatic increase in new Iron Age settlements was the result of waves of migrations and invasions of "semi-Bedouins."[48] Subsequent research has modified Glueck's pioneering work, revealing a more complex picture of settlement patterns during the second millennium, disputing much of his interpretation of settlement patterns during the second millennium.[49] Current archaeological results indicate some continuity between the Late Bronze and Iron Ages in Gilead, with increased settlement at the end of the Late Bronze and Iron I periods in Ammon, the appearance of new sites during the Iron I in Moab, and significant settlement emerging in Edom only during the Iron II (Herr and Najjar 2001, 323).

Northern Transjordan: Gilead and Ammon. Survey and excavation work in the region north of the Dead Sea indicates that the region was settled during the Middle and Late Bronze Ages. Siegfried Mittmann's survey of some three hundred sites in the region bordered by the Yarmuk and Jabbok Rivers notes a significant increase in settlements from fifteen Late Bronze Age sites to seventy-three Iron I settlements.[50] In the central Transjordanian plateau, surveys reveal that Ammon during the sixteenth to the mid-thirteenth centuries B.C.E. had only a few settlements. The end of the Late Bronze Age was marked by an increase in settlements, rising from less than a handful to at least fifteen, while in the mid-twelfth to eleventh centuries the number of settlements jumped to nearly seventy. These included both farmsteads (.25–1.25 acres in size) to medium-sized settlements (1.5–25 acres) that can be classified as cities, towns, villages, or hilltop forts (Younker 2003).[51]

The existence of larger settlements at the end of the Late Bronze Age and early Iron I periods is one feature distinguishing the northern Transjordanian settlement pattern from that in Samaria, where few larger settlements are documented during the twelfth century. Tell el-ʿUmeiri, south of Amman, is a type-site belonging to the larger fortified towns documented in Transjordan. Three uninterrupted phases (13–11) of occupation spanning the fourteenth to mid-twelfth centuries B.C.E. are present in Field B (D. Clark 1989; 1991; 1997; 2000; 2002; Herr 1998, 253–57). Phase 13 spans the fourteenth and thirteenth centuries B.C.E. At the end of the Late Bronze Age (Phase 12), inhabitants repaired the rampart fortifications originally dating to the Middle Bronze Age. Phase 11, built over the Late Bronze Age remains, was an impressive town dating to the early Iron I.[52] A fortification system comprising a perimeter wall, rampart, retaining wall at the base of the rampart, and the reuse of the Middle Bronze moat is the earliest documented casemate wall and distinguishes Tell el-ʿUmeiri from the more modest unfortified village settlements in Cisjordan. At least two domestic pillared structures have been excavated

Fig. 4.8. Four-Room House at Tell el-ʿUmeiri

within the fortifications (fig. 4.8). Dozens of collared rim jars, some belonging to the earlier tall-necked type (see below, fig. 4.10), were recovered from these four-room houses. Following the massive destruction of Phase 11, architectural remains dating to the eleventh century assigned to Phase 10 were excavated (Herr personal communication, updating Herr 2002, 16–17).

Moab. Recent reassessments of Glueck's survey data from Moab by James Sauer (1986), Robert Boling (1988), and J. Andrew Dearman (1992) suggest modifications to Glueck's conclusions proposing that there is less of an occupational gap in Moab during the Middle and Late Bronze Ages. The most extensive and detailed fieldwork in Moab is J. Maxwell Miller's Kerak Plateau archaeological survey (J. Miller 1989; 1991; 1992; see also Mattingly 1992; for a critique of this survey, see Finkelstein 1996d). As documented by Miller (1989, 11; 1991, 19–20), there was a less dramatic increase in settlements during the Iron I period compared to the archaeological evidence in the northern half of Transjordan and in the northern central hill country. He also argues that there is insufficient evidence to conclude that there was a strong, region-wide system of fortified sites in the early Iron Age forming an early Moabite state, one of the cornerstones of Glueck's interpretation of the entire Transjordanian highlands.[53] Rather, as documented at Khirbet el-Mudayna el-ʿAliya, dated to the second half of the eleventh century B.C.E. (Routledge 2000), fortified sites developed gradually during the course of the Iron I, increasing in number in the eleventh century.

Edom. Edom lacks evidence for permanent settlements during most of the second millennium B.C.E.. Initially Glueck (1935, 125) argued for a sudden appearance of dense settlement in the Iron I period (see also Sauer 1986, 10). However recent reevaluations of the evidence based on the excavated sites of Buseirah, Tawilan, Umm el-Biyara, and Ghrareh, together with the results of the Wadi el-Hasa survey, indicate a more complex picture (MacDonald et al. 1988; 1992; Bienkowski 1992c). In spite of the confusion surrounding the dating of Edom's Iron Age pottery, most reanalyses of the evidence conclude that Edom was sparsely settled in the Iron I. In both Edom and Judah, large-scale settlement and state formation began only in the last centuries of the Iron II period.[54]

Comparison of the Central Highland Regions

According to the available archaeological evidence, settlement patterns in Jordan paralleled those in western Palestine (see Finkelstein 1996d for a preliminary comparison and critique of the evidence). The northern Transjordanian highlands were settled in the Middle Bronze Age but experienced a decrease in occupation during the Late Bronze Age, while the region south of the Wadi az-Zarqaʿ was comparatively empty during most of the second millennium B.C.E. Settlement increased in Gilead and Ammon toward the end of the Late Bronze Age, in the Karak region during the Iron Age I, and farther south during the second half of the Iron II. There are a number of sites on the Transjordanian plateau, especially in the north and central areas (e.g., Abila, Amman, the Baqʿah Valley, Umm al Dananir, and el-ʿUmeiri), where continuity from the Late Bronze Age to Iron I suggests a peaceful transition. The emerging settlement pattern indicates that occupation spread gradually in a southward direction through the course of the Iron Age (Herr and Najjar 2001, 323–28).[55]

The ongoing excavations at Tell el-ʿUmeiri have irrevocably changed our understanding of the transition from the Late Bronze to Iron Ages in the central Transjordanian highlands. Based on the utilitarian nature of the ceramic assemblage and its comparisons with Mount Ebal, Giloh, and other sites surveyed in Samaria, the excavators classify el-ʿUmeiri as a hill-country site closely connected to early Iron I developments in the northern central hill country. As noted by the excavators, the settlement at Tell el-ʿUmeiri reflects the regional intensification pattern prevalent in northern and central Transjordan (Herr 1998; 2002).

Although paralleling the demographic developments in the central hill country of Cisjordan, the transition from the Late Bronze to Iron I Ages in the Transjordan highlands reveals elements of both continuity and change with a larger sedentary population. Lacking is a systematic analysis and detailed comparison of the archaeological record of the central hill country in Cisjordan and the Transjordanian highlands—the two heartlands of early Israelite settlement, according to the biblical account. What have been noted are the close material-culture ties between the northern central hill country (especially the region of Manasseh) and the central Transjordan (especially the region of Reuben; see Herr 1998, 258–60). This corroborates the biblical traditions indicating close kinship relationships between several tribes inhabiting the highland regions of western and eastern Palestine.[56]

Galilee and the Beer-sheba Valley

Two peripheral regions, the Galilee and Negev, are also associated with Israelite traditions. These areas are less significant to the initial phases of Israelite ethnogenesis and the early settlement process. The archaeological evidence from these regions is more ambiguous, reflecting greater continuity with the preceding Late Bronze Age and/or a more gradual transformation during the Iron I period.

Galilee. The Galilee is traditionally divided into two subregions defined by geographical features: the Upper and Lower Galilee. High mountains, bordered by the Litani River to the north and the Beth HaKarem Valley in the south, characterize the Upper Galilee. The Jezreel Valley borders the Lower Galilee in the south. Surveys and excavations in the Upper Galilee demonstrate a large degree of cultural continuity during the Late Bronze and Iron I Ages. Recent fieldwork and reevaluation of the evidence reveal fourteen Late Bronze Age sites. Settlements numbered seventy-one during the Iron I period and then declined to thirty-six during the Iron II. Most noteworthy is the observation that the distribution of Iron I sites indicates continuity of Late Bronze Age regionalism (see Aharoni 1957b; Frankel et al. 2001, 104–7; Lehmann 2001, 74–75, 83–87; Nakhai 2003a). The material culture of the Upper Galilee differs from that of the central hill country and continues indigenous connections of the Canaanite and later Phoenician world, so it should be considered part of the Phoenician hinterland (Frankel 1994, 25–34). This is most evident in the pottery assemblages. The archaeological evidence stands in contrast to the biblical narrative, which indicates the common origins of the Galilean and central hill-country tribes. With the possible exceptions of Hazor and Dan, there is little archaeological evidence in the Galilee for any of the events described in the conquest narratives.[57]

Based on his survey of the Lower Galilee, Zvi Gal (1994) documents shifts in settlement patterns at the end of the Late Bronze Age and concludes that major changes occurred in the region during the twelfth century B.C.E. The appearance of new settlements was concentrated mainly in the southern geographical unit in the Nazareth region and around the Beth Netofah valley. These villages prospered well into the Iron I, perhaps due to residual Egyptian control of the valleys during much of the twelfth century (Nakhai 2003a). However, recent excavations at Tell el-Wawiyat (Nakhai 1997; 2003a) and Tel ʿEin Ẓippori (Dessel 1999) reveal a more complex picture of the combination of continuity and diversity during the thirteenth and twelfth centuries in the Lower Galilee. The Lower Galilee's role as a transitional zone between the Upper Galilee and the central hill-country regions is best epitomized by the appearance of both the collared pithos, a type typical of the central hill country, and the Galilean pithos, a northern ceramic form (Jorgensen 1999, 35).

Beer-sheba Valley. Following a gap in settlement throughout much of the Late Bronze Age, the archaeological evidence indicates that the Beer-sheba valley was sparsely resettled during the Iron I period. Excavations document that Tel Masos, the largest site in the region, was established in the late thirteenth and early twelfth century B.C.E. The eleventh century witnessed a gradual increase in the number of settlements, including Tell Esdar, Tel Arad, and Beer-sheba. Settlements become significant in number only in the tenth century and later (for a summary, see Finkelstein 1988, 37–48; Herzog 1994; Bloch-Smith and Nakhai 1999, 103–5).

Tel Masos serves as a type-site for Iron I settlement in the Beer-sheba Valley (Fritz and Kempinski 1983). The initial phase included a fort and several three- and four-room houses forming what the excavators interpreted as a belt of houses enclosing the site. The site reached its apex during the eleventh century B.C.E. and included pillared structures that resemble storage rooms. As the principal site in the region, it formed the nucleus of the settlement process and probably served as a center for trade and distribution. Nearby Beer-sheba was first settled in the mid-twelfth century. Pits characterize this initial settlement, prompting the excavators to conclude that the inhabitants lived in tents.

Due to the heterogeneous character of the material culture, there are various views about the Iron I ethnic component of the Beer-sheba Valley. These include associating these new settlements with the Israelites (Aharoni 1976) or regarding them as a result of a symbiotic relationship between Israelites and indigenous Canaanites (Fritz 1980). Others prefer to identify these settlers as Amalekites, suggesting that Tel Masos served as their center (see Finkelstein 1984; Naʾaman 1987; Herzog 1983; Eitam 1988), or as Canaanites (see Ahlström 1984a; Edelman 1988).[58]

The settlement processes in the Galilee and Beer-sheba Valley regions should be considered as case studies for the gradual transformation and crystallization of a new ethnic identity in areas peripheral to the heartland of Israelite ethnogenesis and their later integration into a larger Israelite ethnos.

Conclusions

Changes that occurred during the early Iron I period are most clearly delineated in the central highland regions on both sides of the Jordan River, first appearing in the northern regions and gradually spreading to the southern and marginal regions. Such dramatic changes in settlement patterns are usually attributed to the forced settlement of nomadic populations, due either to climatic changes (Cribb 1991, 61–67), socioeconomic and/or political factors (Finkelstein 1994a; McGovern 1986, 335–42; Worschech 1990), population increases,[59] or a combination of some or all of the above. Although one cannot totally discount any of these factors, the impact of Late Bronze Age Egyptian imperial rule on traditional tribal and kinship relationships has been underestimated. The increasing settled population in the central hill country during the Iron I, which reached its peak only during the eleventh century B.C.E., corresponded to Egyptian retreat from Jordan Valley administrative and military strongholds such as Beth-shean and Saᶜidiyeh sometime during the second half of the twelfth century B.C.E. The weakening of Egyptian influence and the coinciding deterioration of Late Bronze Age urban centers gradually removed restrictions and control over indigenous populations and permitted the increase of population movements and contacts between Cisjordan and Transjordan. Egyptian imperialistic activities in the Jordan Valley and efforts to impose order on the diverse and fractious Canaanite population should be seen as a short-term interruption of long-term (millennia-long) traditional tribal or clan relations and contacts between highland regions of both sides of the Jordan River.

Characteristic Features of Iron I Highland Material Culture

Architecture

Settlement Planning. Most Iron I central highland sites are characterized by their lack of monumental public architecture, small size (1–5 acres), pillared three- or four-room domestic structures, and various installations, including silos and cisterns.[60] A perimeter wall often surrounds these hamlets, and agricultural terrace walls are also common. Israel Finkelstein (1988, 237–54), Zeev Herzog (1992, 231–38; 1997, 195–99), Volkmar Fritz (1995), and Gloria London (2003) have suggested several different planning principles and basic architectural plans for Iron I village sites in Israel.

Finkelstein's (1988, 237–50) work on the topic was greatly influenced by his notion that the settlers of the hill-country sites were originally nomads who underwent a sedentarization process at the end of the thirteenth and early twelfth centuries B.C.E. He proposed that the sites that he interpreted as having an elliptical plan (e.g., ʿIzbet Ṣarṭah [Stratum III], Beer-sheba [Stratum VII], Tell Esdar [Stratum III], and sites in the Negev highlands) originated in the nomadic encampment and represented the transition from the tent to fixed architecture.[61] His second phase of development of Iron I site layout includes settlements characterized by a belt of three- or four-room houses forming the perimeter of the site (e.g., ʿIzbet Ṣarṭah, Khirbet ed Dawara, and several Negev highland sites; Finkelstein 1988, 250–54). One of the difficulties in any attempt to classify the settlement plans of these villages is the fragmentary nature of Iron I sites in the central hill country. Because of limited excavations, the accuracy of these schematic reconstructions is open to question.

Herzog (1992, 231) classifies Iron I settlements into seven general types, only one of which is designated as an Israelite settlement plan. Herzog's Israelite settlement layout comprises an irregularly planned site filled with dwellings and lacking a central court (Herzog 1992, 233–37; see, e.g., Khirbet Raddana and ʿAi, figs. 4.5 and 4.6). Sites typified by dwellings encircling a central court (equaling Finkelstein's elliptical plan) are considered to be Canaanite in origin and not related to a nomadic prototype.

Fritz (1995, 69–71) defines three main Iron I settlement plans. Influenced by both Finkelstein's and Herzog's classification, he first associates the ring-shaped village with early Israelite settlements.[62] The second main plan Fritz identifies is the "agglomerated village," similar to Herzog's Israelite settlement village. This form of settlement is characterized by its indiscriminate construction comprising individual buildings or complexes with several houses each and an irregular plan. The agglomerated village is best exemplified in the central hill country at Khirbet Raddana (fig. 4.6) and ʿAi (fig. 4.7).[63] Fritz's third type of settlement is the farmstead, which includes single structures surrounded by a wall, the latter most likely serving as an enclosure for domestic animals. Giloh is the best example of this type of site. According to Fritz, what all these sites share in common are basic plans that reflect the needs of agriculturally based communities.

Building on her earlier notions of the impact of lifestyles on ceramic assemblages, London (1989a; 2003, 79–81) proposes that four types of sites typify Late Bronze/Iron I hill-country sites. Her division is based on the site's function, location, material-culture assemblage, and population size. Tell el-ʿUmeiri serves as the example for her first, larger, settlement type: permanent settlements where the full range of daily activities occurred. London designates a second settlement type as "workstations," that is, seasonal or temporary homes of agriculturalists. The limited ceramic assemblage at such sites reflects the basic functions that took place at these sites. Her third type of site includes burials and cemeteries. Although there is an ongoing debate regarding the identification of Iron I highland cemeteries (Kletter 2002; see below), London identifies some of the multiple burials in the cemeteries at Dothan, Taanach, Shechem, and Gibeon as cemeteries serving the inhabitants of the workstations. The fourth site category pertains to sacred space, including pilgrimage sites and shrines. London's classification is original, but one can challenge her conclusions regarding the seasonal or temporary habitation of the hundreds of hamlets she designates as workstations and her premise that there is a clear-cut division in pottery assemblages based on the functional use of sites.

The variety of interpretations of settlement layout, function, and classification is a result of the fragmentary, incomplete, and ambiguous nature of the archaeological evidence as well as attempts to relate or disassociate these remains from the biblical account of the Israelite settlement. Several conclusions can be drawn regarding settlement typology. Most of the evidence in the central hill country thus far points to a proliferation of small hamlets with irregular plans and enclosure walls. There are few larger settlements that can be considered contemporary with these hundreds of villages and that could have served as home bases for the inhabitants of these hamlets. Limited archaeological excavations and surveys indicate a similar picture in the Transjordan highlands, with the addition of larger fortified settlements already in the twelfth century. What is clear are the close cultural ties between these regions.

The Three- and Four-Room Pillared House. The hallmark of Iron I highland settlements is the four-room pillared house. Its characteristic features include a rectilinear plan that is divided into three, four, or sometimes more spaces. The archetypical four-room house comprises one or two rows of stone pillars that separated a larger central space from one or two parallel side rooms (figs. 4.6–4.8). A rectangular room runs perpendicular to the parallel rooms. The entrance led from an exterior courtyard or street into the larger central space.[64]

Recent publications on the four-room house have focused on three issues: its origins, house reconstructions, and the functional use of space. Undoubtedly due to its early association with the emergence of Israel, the origins of this ubiquitous Iron Age house have often been associated the basic plan of the nomadic tent and the process of sedentarization (see Fritz 1977; Kempinski 1978, 36; Finkelstein 1988, 254–59; Netzer 1992,

193). Yigal Shiloh (1973) considered this Iron Age house to be an Israelite invention, while G. Ernest Wright (1978, 154) attributed the architectural origin of northern examples of the four-room house to the Phoenicians. Straddling the fence, Kenneth Schaar (1991, 91) claims that the four-room house is a hybrid plan reflecting components from both sedentary and nonsedentary traditions. Others have convincingly argued that its roots go back to Late Bronze Age Canaanite architecture.[65]

Attempts to reconstruct the four-room house are numerous. These include traditional presentations of plans and sections (Netzer 1992, 196–97) or artistic renditions (Holladay 1997a, 341; King and Stager 2001, ills. 10, 15), museum exhibits (Museum Eretz-Israel, Tel Aviv; Harvard Semitic Museum, Boston [fig. 4.9]), on-site restorations (Tell Qasile, Tel Aviv: A. Mazar 1999), and experimental reconstructions (Tell el-ᶜUmeiri: D. Clark 2003). Excavated examples of the four-room house indicate that it can be a single story with an open courtyard (e.g., Tell Qasile) or a two-storied structure (for discussion, see Netzer 1992, 196–98; Holladay 1997a, 339–40). The central space has been reconstructed as being roofed over (Bloch-Smith and Nakhai 1999, 113; King and Stager 2001, ills. 10, 15 [fig. 4.9]) or with the ground floor roofed over with an open central space on the second floor (Netzer 1992, figs. 6, 7).

Fig. 4.9. Four-Room House Reconstruction at the Semitic Museum

The plan and suggested reconstructions of the four-room house are closely connected to its functional use. Most interpretations are rooted in traditional agro-pastoral daily life activities. Holladay's (1997a, 339) detailed discussion of functional use assumes that the majority of these houses were two-storied structures, based on their massive pillars, the occasional appearance of stairs that led to a second floor, and the lack of evidence of living quarters. Based on the archaeological evidence and ethnographic analogy, he suggests that the first floor was devoted to the economic domain, including stalls for donkeys and other livestock. The remaining ground-floor spaces served as storage rooms, and the large central room was used as a workspace. According to Holladay's reconstruction, the second floor served as the family's living quarters, with kitchen facilities in the central space.[66] He suggests that there may have been a third floor in some cases.

In a return to Shiloh's original suggestion and in agreement with Holladay's (1997a, 337) conclusions that the four-room house is essentially an "Israelite house," Shlomo Bunimovitz and Avraham Faust (2003a, b) explore the possible impact of Israelite ideology and cognitive doctrines on the fully developed form of the four-room house.[67] In their view, the four-room house can be considered an ethnic marker by the end of the Iron I and through time enhanced Israelite ethnic coherence associated with early Israel. Specifically, they propose that the plan of the four-room house facilitated separation between purity and impurity.[68] Additionally, the nonhierarchical plan corresponds to the egalitarian social fabric of early Israel, conveying a "canonical message essential for the structuring of Israelite society" (Bunimovitz and Faust 2003a, 418). In an equally original interpretation, Gloria London (2003, 76) theorizes that the hundreds of Iron I four-room houses in the central highlands served as storage facilities, workstations, or depots for tools, produce, and the small groups of people who worked in the surrounding agricultural lands.

As is evident from the various interpretations outline above, the origins, form, and use of the four-room house remains obscure. Most likely a variety of influences (practical or "ideological"), architectural possibilities, and functions led to this utilitarian plan. It can be concluded that the general plan of the pillared Iron Age house suits the basic division of space into traditional functional uses observable in all premodern societies: courtyard, storage space (possibly including stabling of animals), and multipurpose living room(s) that are adaptable in various ways suitable to agro-pastoral lifestyles, ethnicities, and functional uses of space that were adapted to the specific needs of the individual family.

Silos, Cisterns, and Terrace Walls. Several architectural features usually associated with agricultural activities are present at many Iron I highland hamlets.[69] These include silos, cisterns, and hillside terracing systems. Stone-lined silos used for storage are common features of villages such as Khirbet Raddana and ʿAi. Plaster-lined water cisterns, necessary for year-round habitation of these sites, are also architectural features connected with the agrarian lifestyle of these villages. Neither of these installations is unique to these villages, nor were they invented in the Iron I period (for a recent summary, see Dever 2003, 115–17). Terraces connected to hillside agriculture activities are a third feature of many of these villages. Although it has been commonly claimed that terrace walls were an Iron I (and presumably Israelite) invention (see Dever 1998, 227; 2003, 113–15), others (Stager 1985a, 5; Finkelstein 1988, 309; Gibson 2001) have demonstrated that agricultural terracing systems predate the twelfth century B.C.E.[70] In light of the evidence, these installations and technologies are most likely indigenous and appear, at least sporadically, prior to the twelfth century.

Diet: Animal Bones

Sheep and goats, typical of traditional small-scale stockbreeding, comprise from 45 to 80 percent of the faunal assemblage from these sites. Evidence for cattle, oxen, and donkeys is also present, animal species that appear at most sites in the ancient Levant. One species, the pig, is notably absent. Much has been made of the scarcity of pig bones at highland sites. Since small quantities of pig bones do appear in Late Bronze Age assemblages, some archaeologists have interpreted this to indicate that the ethnic identity of the highland inhabitants was distinct from Late Bronze Age indigenous peoples (see Finkelstein 1997, 227–30). Brian Hesse and Paula Wapnish (1997) advise caution, however, since the lack of pig bones at Iron I highland settlements could be a result of other factors that have little to do with ethnicity.

Burial Customs

Often considered a culturally sensitive marker of group identity and ideology, the burial customs associated with the hundreds of small hill-country hamlets and settlements are a key element of the highland material-culture repertoire. At present, Iron I hill-country funerary practices remain largely unknown, though two interpretations of the limited available evidence have emerged. Elizabeth Bloch-Smith (1992a, 1992b; see also Spronk 1986) advocates continuity in burial practices from the Late Bronze through Iron I periods. Raz Kletter (2002) reaches the opposite conclusion, presenting credible evidence that, in contrast to other regions in Iron I Canaan, the central hill country is characterized by a paucity of burials associated with the hundreds of small highland villages.[71] If Kletter is correct, the dearth of burials that can be clearly dated to the twelfth and eleventh centuries

B.C.E. is noteworthy and may indicate a break from the burial customs of the preceding period.

Pottery Assemblage

Iron I highland pottery, the featured component of this study of social boundaries, is remarkable for its continuity with Late Bronze Age ceramic traditions and, simultaneously, for its distinctive limited repertoire of shapes that characterize the central highland settlements. Large pithoi (CA 25; figs. 4.10–4.11), popularly termed collared-rim jars (or collared jars), storage jars (CA 21a; fig. 3.19) that continue the tradition of the Canaanite jar, and cooking pots (CA 18a–e and 19a–b [fig. 3.18]) dominate Iron I highland assemblages. In significantly smaller quantities, bowls (CA 5 and 6 [fig. 3.13]), kraters (similar to CA 10 [fig. 3.15] but often characterized by the addition of multiple handles), chalices (CA 14b [fig. 3.16]), and jugs (similar to CA 16b [fig. 3.17]) complete the main elements of this assemblage of utilitarian vessels (for a detailed description of these vessels and comparative material, see pp. 113–36 above).[72] Most noteworthy is the paucity or nonexistence of many other types of vessel forms, such as flasks (CA 30 [fig. 3.27]), pyxides (CA 34 [fig. 3.28]), many bowl types (CA 1, 2, 3, 4, 7, 8 [fig. 3.13]), juglets (CA 15 [fig. 3.16]), jugs (CA 17 [fig. 3.17]), and painted decoration at Iron I hill-country agricultural villages.[73]

The Collared Pithos: A Case Study. The collared pithos and its relationship to the emergence of Israel have been the topic of countless studies (figs. 4.10–4.11; for a recent detailed discussion, see Killebrew 2001). Hans Kjaer (1930) first identified this specific ceramic type, describing it as a storage jar whose rim was folded over with a ridge in low relief at the base of the neck. This ridge is the defining characteristic feature that later inspired the term "collared storage jar" or pithos. Once considered a type fossil of early Israelite sites, its appearance at the end of the Late Bronze Age is now well documented.[74] Although rare in late thirteenth-century contexts, the collared pithos increased in popularity during the Iron I and continued to be a favorite container into the early Iron II periods.[75] Noteworthy is the distribution of this vessel type. Pithos CA 25 is found in large quantities in the central hill country,[76] in moderate quantities in the Transjordan,[77] in smaller quantities in the Galilee[78] and Jezreel Valleys,[79] and in minute quantities on the coastal plain and Shephelah.[80] Although it is impossible and undesirable to attribute an "ethnic" identity to the users of these jars, the numbers and percentage of these jars in the overall assemblage of a site, their provenience, and function are significant and indicate a social boundary.

One of the main characteristic features of pithos CA 25 is the wide variety of rim and body profiles. Several attempts have been made to

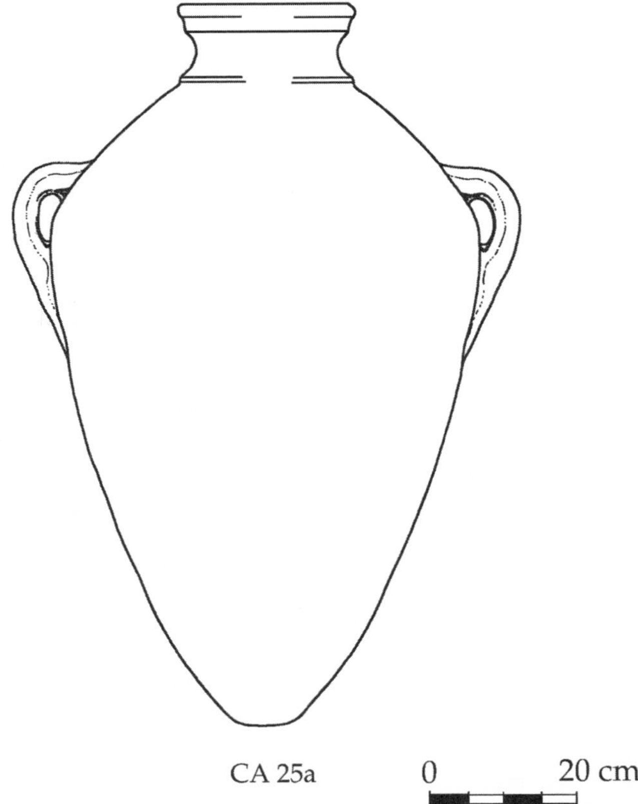

Fig. 4.10. Canaanite Pottery Form 25a

trace a typological and chronological development.[81] Rather than interpreting this feature as a chronologically meaningful indicator, I would suggest that the numerous rim variations are most likely a result of different potters and/or workshops.[82] More significant are the proportions of the rim and neck, which seem to be the key typological feature with chronological relevance. This study divides collared pithoi into two main categories, CA 25a (fig. 4.10) and CA 25b (fig. 4.11), based on morphological features of the entire rim and neck. These two types share basic features, including a piriform-shaped body profile and a raised "collar" at the base of the vessel. Their distinguishing attribute is the length of the neck measured from the collar to the top of the rim. Collared pithos CA 25a has a neck measuring roughly 10 cm or greater in height,[83] while the neck of pithos CA 25b is shorter, usually measuring 5–7.5 cm. [84]

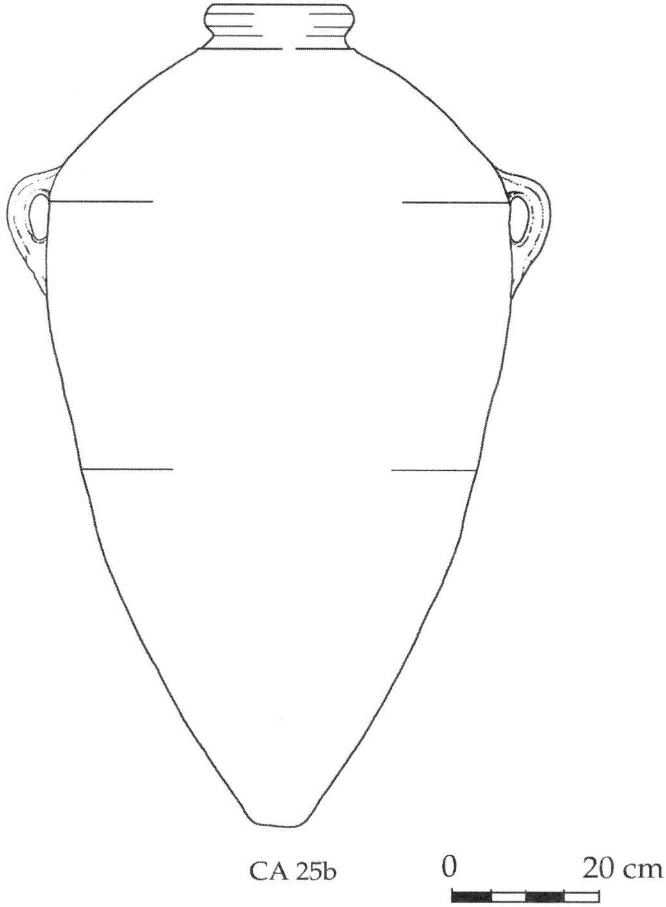

Fig. 4.11. Canaanite Pottery Form 25b

The function of these jars has also been debated. It is noteworthy that the earliest appearance of the collared pithos is at sites along thirteenth-century Egyptian controlled trade routes such as Tel Nami, Beth-shean, and Tell es-Saᶜidiyeh (Artzy 1994, 137–38, presents evidence that these were used as transport jars). At an increasing number of sites, such as Sahab (Ibrahim 1978, 122–23), Tel Nami (Artzy 1994, 127–28; 1995, 25–26), Tel Zeror (Ohata 1970, pl. 56), and Tell es-Saᶜidiyeh (Tubb 1995, 142–43), these jars were used as burial containers. However, in the central highland regions where the collared pithos comprises a significant percentage of the assemblage, it is usually suggested that this large, handled vessel served as a container for basic liquids and dry goods. Adam Zertal (1988b) has suggested that their popularity in the region of Manasseh was due to their use as water containers. Israel Finkelstein (1988, 282–83), however, argues that, based on the appearance of collared jars in regions with abundant water, they were used as storage containers for various other types of liquids in addition to water, including olive oil and wine (see also Ibrahim 1978, 122, for ethnographic comparisons). At Tell el-ʿUmeiri, flotation of the contents of collared pithoi produced remains of lentils, chick peas, wheat, barley, and spices, leading the excavators to suggest that these jars were used as container for dry goods (Herr et al. 1991, 159).

Several publications have examined the provenience of these large jars. At lowland sites, where these jars make up a smaller percentage of the overall assemblage, it has been observed that the pithoi were produced in different locations. It seems that many of these containers were not locally manufactured but rather transported overland from neighboring areas where specialized workshops may have existed (Cohen-Weinberger and Wolff 2001, 639–57). The transport of such large containers, either empty or full, would have been viable only with the domestication of the camel at the end of the Late Bronze Age and its use as a beast of burden connected with the caravan trade.[85] Similar studies of pithoi from other sites outside the heartland of the central hill country have produced similar results.[86]

In contrast, petrographic studies of collared pithoi in highland sites such as Giloh (for a detailed ware description, see Killebrew 2001, 384–87) and Khirbet Raddana (Lederman 1999, 74–77) have indicated that the large numbers of pithoi were locally produced. Although additional provenience studies of collared pithoi will be necessary to determine the origins of the countless pithoi found at other small highland village sites in Cisjordan and the Transjordanian plateau, preliminary results do indicate different functions, contexts, and modes of production (Killebrew 2001; Raban 2001). These features appear to indicate a social boundary delineating and distinguishing isolated and small, central hill-country agrarian communities from the larger settlements in the lowland sites of the northern coastal plains and valley regions of Canaan.

A mixed picture thus emerges regarding possible modes of production of collared pithoi at various Iron I sites. No workshops or kilns relating to the manufacture of pithoi have been excavated to date. Due to the quality and level of difficulty involved in the production of the collared pithos, a professional potters' craft is indicated. The diversity of wares and origins of the collared pithoi signify that there was not a central workshop; rather, individual professional potters or several workshops were involved in their production. At sites such as Giloh and Khirbet

Raddana, where all the pithoi were produced in the general vicinity but exhibit a large degree of variation in their wares, the evidence best suits a mode of production by itinerant potters who traveled from village to village in the region (Killebrew 2001).[87] The relatively small number of highly skilled independent potters producing these pithoi, perhaps both in workshops and as itinerant potters, may in part explain several basic common elements, such as their standard size and generally similar morphological features (Raban 2001). At the same time, the itinerant mode of production may be reflected in the diversity of such details as rim profiles and choice of materials within an assemblage produced in the same region.

The pithoi from Giloh and other central highland sites are a case in point. The production of collared pithoi by itinerant potters could explain some of the remarkable similarities in detail between some highland Iron I assemblages, such as those from Tell el-ʿUmeiri in Transjordan and from sites in the central hill country of Cisjordan. The appearance of similar incisions on rims or handles from sites in Transjordan and small hamlets in the hill country of Cisjordan may also indicate specific, perhaps itinerant, potters or workshops.[88] The possible ties between these two regions implied by shared elements of the pottery assemblages mentioned above is also hinted at in the biblical description of the close relationship between the Transjordanian tribe of Reuben and several tribes in Cisjordan (Cross 1998).

Synthesis

Based on the textual and archaeological evidence outlined above, most approaches to the emergence of Israel fall into one of four general theories—conquest, peaceful infiltration, social revolution, or pastoral Canaanite theories[89]—schools of thought that not only mirror periods of increased archaeological fieldwork but also reflect research and political trends over the past eighty years (see Moorey 1991). These theories often reveal not only scholarly opinion and the fashion of the times but also deeply held personal beliefs. The first two approaches, the conquest and peaceful infiltration theories, postulate an external origin for the Israelites. However, numerous aspects of Iron I hill-country material culture that continue Late Bronze Age traditions, such as the ceramic repertoire and elements of cult, tend to cast doubts on a purely external source. More recent schools of thought, recognizing a closer relationship with indigenous traditions, propose an internal, or Canaanite, origin.

The Four Schools of Thought

The *unified military conquest theory*, first developed by William F. Albright, accepts the biblical account as described in the book of Joshua as historically accurate (Albright 1935, 11–18; 1937, 22–26; 1939, 11–23). Following in the footsteps of Albright, Yigael Yadin (1979; 1982; 1985, 22–24) strongly advocated this theory, based largely on evidence from his excavations at Hazor that revealed a massive conflagration of the Late Bronze II city (regarding the renewed excavations, see Ben-Tor 1998; 2002; Ben-Ami 2001). Additional support for this approach has been based on analogies with nomadic tribes that succeeded in destroying urban societies, an interpretation that has been largely discredited (see Isserlin 1983).[90] Few scholars today accept the book of Joshua at face value, making this theory the most problematic, both archaeologically and textually, of all the viewpoints presented here.[91]

The *peaceful infiltration theory* proposes that the origins of Israel lie in the migration of transhumant pastoral groups paralleling narratives that appear in the book of Judges. This school of thought was first proposed by Albrecht Alt and later elaborated by Martin Noth, Yohanan Aharoni, Moshe Kochavi, Adam Zertal, and Anson Rainey.[92] This approach combines the biblical account in Judges with toponymy, second-millennium Near Eastern texts, ethnographic analogy to seminomadic Bedouin lifestyles, and archaeological discoveries based on surveys and excavations.[93] According to this theory, nonindigenous seminomads originating from the desert regions wintered in the Transjordanian desert and summered in the highlands outside the control of Egypt in areas not populated by permanent settlements.[94] During this process, they formed peaceful relations with the inhabitants of Late Bronze villages and cities. Eventually they began to settle down, building villages in the sparsely populated hill country, and gradually began to expand into the more fertile regions, occasionally resulting in violent confrontations with the lowland peoples.

It has been tempting to identify these pastoralists with various groups mentioned in Near Eastern texts. Alt, Noth, and Aharoni argued that the early Hebrews belonged to an ethnically defined *ʿapîru* of Near Eastern texts.[95] Raphael Giveon (1971), Manfred Weippert (1974), Anson Rainey (1991; 1995b), and Shmuel Ahituv (1998) have identified them with the *Shasu* mentioned in Egyptian texts (Hasel 1998, 217–39; 2003, 28–32, 36). Archaeologically, the close cultural contacts between the Cisjordanian central hill country with regions in Transjordan (especially the territory of Reuben in Moab) may be reflected in biblical traditions that indicate a close connection of several Israelite tribes in western Palestine with those on the eastern side of the Jordan River (van der Steen 1996; Herr 1998; Killebrew 2001, esp. 391).

The *social revolution theory* proposes that the origins of Israel can be traced to a conflict between the Canaanite elite ruling class and the dissatisfied peasant class. This sociocultural and anthropological approach sees an indigenous origin for Israel.[96] George Mendenhall (1962; 1973; 1976) first developed this theory in 1962, claiming that Israel originated from the "exodus" of discontented native peasant groups from lowland city-states into the highlands. He identified the ancient Hebrews as *ʿapîru,* a sociopolitical group in Late Bronze Age Near Eastern texts. He further suggests that they were unified by a common religious ideology or "covenant." Norman K. Gottwald elaborated upon and modified this approach, utilizing Marxist theory in order to explain the phenomenon described by Mendenhall as a peasant revolt. He took this theory a step further and suggested that the emergence of Israel was a result of a violent class struggle between the rural peasantry and the urban elite upper classes of Canaanite society.[97] These "drop-outs" and deserters from Canaanite society then reorganized in the unpopulated hill country and marginal areas of Canaan.[98] A variant of this school of thought sees an internal rural-nomadic hill-country origin for ancient Israel (see de Geus 1976, 164–81; Coote and Whitelam 1987, 117–38). What distinguishes this theory is that it is not based on the primary textual or archaeological sources. Rather, it relies on a modern sociological approach to Late Bronze Age society.

The *pastoral Canaanite theory* developed by Israel Finkelstein (see 1990a; 1991; 1992b; 1994a; 1995b; 1998b) examines the emergence of ancient Israel from a long-term historical perspective. Although this approach is often presented as a variation of the peaceful infiltration theory, it deserves special attention because it does not depend upon any biblical evidence but relies almost entirely on archaeological evidence. Based largely on survey results, Finkelstein stresses the indigenous origins of the hill-country villagers over the external source of the seminomadic "peaceful infiltrators".

Finkelstein characterizes the settlement patterns as cyclic "demographic processes that characterized the hill country in the third–second millennia BCE." This was a result of a "long process that started with the destruction of the urban culture of the Bronze Age and the uprooting of large population groups in vast areas, and the subsequent settlement of various pastoral and uprooted groups and individuals in the highlands of Canaan" (Finkelstein and Naʾaman 1994a, 15). Thus, in his view the Early Iron Age inhabitants of villages in the hill country should be seen largely as the descendants of those Canaanites who had reverted to pastoralism toward the end of the Middle Bronze Age and for several hundred years led a nomadic way of life on the fringes of the land.[99] This nomadic population, resulting from the crisis at the end of the Middle Bronze Age, returned to sedentary life at the end of the Late Bronze Age due to the dissolution of the Canaanite city-state system and the ensuing breakdown of the symbiotic relationship between the nomadic pastoralists and the settled population.[100] Contra to this theory, ethnographic studies indicate that there is seldom such a clear-cut division between pastoral and agricultural activities; rather, the same individuals in rural society were usually involved in both endeavors.[101]

As should be evident, one can offer archaeological support for each of these theories. However, no single theory satisfactorily takes into account *all* the evidence currently available to us. What has become increasingly clear over the past decade is that none of the four major schools of thought satisfactorily explains the complex processes and events that led to the emergence of Israel. These different theories, developed over the past century, are in fact all elements, in varying degrees of relevance and accuracy, of the "mixed multitude" that led to the formation of the world of ancient Israel.

The Mixed Multitude Theory

The *mixed multitude theory* interprets the biblical and archaeological evidence as reflecting a heterogeneous, multifaceted, and complex process of Israelite ethnogenesis (Killebrew, forthcoming b).[102] Prior approaches to early Israel tended to interpret ethnic formation as a linear and evolutionary development.[103] However, recent ethnographic, anthropological, and sociological research suggests that ethnicity is a complex process rooted in diverse antecedent groups that converge and diverge over time.[104] The binding component of group formation and identity usually includes an empowering narrative of shared experiences, woven into an epic account of primordial deeds, miracles, and genealogies.[105] In the case of Israel's prehistory, its enduring epic narrative, the Bible, recounts the journey from slavery to salvation in a land promised to them by the Israelite God, Yahweh. The central theme of Israel's ethnogenesis is the saga of their unique relationship as the chosen people of Yahweh. The worship of Israel's God formed the core ideology of ancient Israel and Judah and is still an essential component of Jewish identity.

Ancient Israel's mixed multitude is defined here as a collection of loosely organized and largely indigenous, tribal, and kin-based groups whose porous borders permitted penetration by smaller numbers from external groups.[106] Although it is impossible to reconstruct with certainty the protohistory of Israel's origins, it most likely comprised diverse elements of Late Bronze Age society, namely, the rural Canaanite population, displaced peasants and pastoralists, and lawless *ʿapîru* and *Shasu*. Fugitive or runaway Semitic slaves from New Kingdom Egypt may have joined this mixed multitude. Nonindigenous groups mentioned in the biblical narrative, including Midianites, Kenites, and Amalekites (the latter perhaps connected with the control of camel caravan trade routes between

Arabia to Canaan), may also have formed an essential element.[107] Egypt's decline and eventual retreat from Canaan undoubtedly was one of the major contributing factors in Canaan's return to a more fragmented kinship-based tribal society and Israel's subsequent ethnogenesis.

Attempts to locate Israel's ethnogenesis in the small Iron I villages in the hill-country and marginal regions ultimately go back to the biblical narrative as recounted in the books of Joshua and Judges. Corroborating evidence is found in the archaeological record that documents noteworthy changes in twelfth- and eleventh-century B.C.E. settlement patterns and in the distinct material culture that characterizes the central highland regions on both sides of the Jordan. As summarized above, elements of continuity and discontinuity as well as stability and change distinguish the archaeological record of the Iron I highlands. These distinctive features include settlement patterns, demography, architecture, economy, social structure, political organization, burial practices, and aspects of cult that distinguish it from both the Late Bronze Age and Iron I lowlands material culture. The differences between the limited repertoire of ceramic forms and their modes of production at these small hill-country hamlets with sites in the lowlands are especially noteworthy and do seem to demarcate a "boundary." This border may have been a result of social, economic, or ideological differences with the lowland sites.

Using the rich variety of available sources, including the archaeological evidence from Canaan during the Iron I, a cautious and critical reading of the biblical texts, and the appearance of the word "Israel" as a people in the Israel (Merneptah) Stela, it is possible to begin to demarcate the shifting social boundaries that characterized twelfth- and eleventh-century material culture. When considered in its larger eastern Mediterranean context, the process of Israelite ethnogenesis is by no means unique. Similar processes of breakdown, fragmentation, and transformation were occurring simultaneously throughout much of the region.[108] The impact of the disintegration of the Hittite and Mycenaean spheres of influence appeared in the form of a new group of peoples who settled the southern coast of Canaan and entered biblical history: the infamous Philistines.

Notes to Chapter 4

1. See especially Davies 1992; Thompson 1997; 1999; 2000; Lemche 1998b; and the essays in Grabbe 1997.

2. Regarding historical approaches to the biblical texts, see the essays in Long 1999. For the most recent treatments from an archaeological perspective, see Dever 2001; A. Mazar 2003b.

3. I use the term "mixed multitude" to describe the character of early Israel (see Killebrew forthcoming b). The term originates from Exod 12:38, which refers to the Israelites as a mixed multitude. Its use is not meant to make a statement regarding the

historicity of the account of the exodus from Egypt. Similar approaches to the emergence of Israel are mentioned briefly or indirectly referred to in several earlier studies on this topic. See, e.g., Stager 1985b, 61*, who defines ancient Israel during the period of the judges as a loose confederation of tribes "comprised of diverse segments, ranging from pastoralists to village farmers to seamen. But the active core of this confederation was based in the central highlands."; Finkelstein and Naʾaman 1994a, 13–15, who state that there were groups from other origins as well; Schloen 1993, who suggests some "extra-Palestinian" elements as well as the possibility of pastoralists. Based on the biblical texts, Bright (1981, 134) also stresses the complexity of early Israel's origins, pointing out that they were by no means all descendants of Jacob but rather included in their midst a "mixed multitude" or "rabble."

4. But see Bowlus's 1995 critique of Wolfram's 1990 work on the application of ethnogenesis in the formation of Bavarian origins. Bowlus's objections to ethnogenesis and its application to the formation of a medieval Bavarian ethnic group bear an uncanny resemblance to debates surrounding the origins of Israel as regards its indigenous versus external origins.

5. E.g., Malamat 1997, 15–16. Hendel (2001, 601–2) aptly points out that a folk tradition does not rule out the relevance of a critical historiography of these narratives. He proposes that historical elements can be recovered from collective memories of a culture that tend to be a mixture "of 'authentic' historical details, folklore motifs, ethnic self-fashioning, ideological claims, and narrative imagination. They are communicated orally and in written texts and circulate in a wide discursive network" (see also Assmann 1997 and his concept of a mnemohistory, or the past as remembered).

6. Countless books and articles have been written regarding the historicity of the exodus. For several of the more recent treatments, see Stiebing 1989; Halpern 1992a; 1993; 2003; Redford 1992b, 408–22; 1997; Hoffmeier 1997; Frerichs and Lesko 1997; Kitchen 1998; Millard 2000; Hendel 2001; for a summary of the evidence and bibliography, see Dever 2003, 7–21. For an alternative view that the exodus is made up of literary elements with little if any historical value, see Lemche 1998b, 44–61; see also Van Seters 1994, 127, who states that "we are no longer dealing with ancient traditions but with an exilic composition throughout."

7. For a general overview of the various sources that make up the accounts relating to the exodus, see Halpern 1992a. For a popular summary describing when and how the Bible was written, see Friedman 1997.

8. See, e.g., Cross and Freedman 1955; Robertson 1972; Cross 1973, 112–44; Gottwald 1979, 507–15. However, Van Seters 1994, 147–48, dates the Song of the Sea to the postexilic period.

9. See, e.g., Redmount 2001, 77–79, for discussion; but also see Kitchen 1998, who places the exodus firmly in the thirteenth century B.C.E.

10. For a recent summary, see Hendel 2001, 605–8; see also Redford 1990, 37–39; 1992b, 221–27; Loprieno 1997, 200–212.

11. For a summary, see Redford 1963; 1987; Malamat 1997, 17–18; Dever 2003, 13–15; but see Yurco 1997, 44–45.

12. For a discussion of the name Moses and its chronological implications, see Redford 1963, 401–19; 1987, 137–61; 1992b, 417–19.

13. See Naʾaman 1994b, 245; Malamat 1983, 307; 1997, 16; Hendel 2001, 608; but see Kitchen 1998, who supports a thirteenth-century date for the exodus.

14. Regarding the problematic nature of the historicity (or rather lack thereof) of the patriarchal narratives, see Thompson 1974; 2000, 12–15; Van Seters 1975; Dever 1977; Millard 1992 and the bibliography there.

15. Most scholars today accept that the majority of the conquest stories in the book of Joshua are devoid of historical reality; see Miller 1977, 87–93; Van Seters 1983, 322–37;

Schoors 1985, 77–92; Naʾaman 1994b, 218–30, 249–50. But see Kitchen 1998, who supports the historicity of the account in Joshua.

16. The Hebrew Bible does contain traditions portraying the rise of Israel in terms of a military conquest (Josh 1–12; Num 21:21–31; 32:39–42), but other texts describe a more peaceful and gradual settlement of the Israelites in Canaan and Transjordan (Judg 1–16; Num 32:1–38) and indicate that the Israelites even co-existed with the Canaanites (Judg 1:1–2). The accounts in Joshua and Judges stress the nonindigenous origins of the Israelites (see Whitelam 1989). Although the debate still rages regarding the use of the Bible as a historical source (for an excellent collection of essays addressing this topic, see Long 1999; regarding the attempt to write a history of Israel in light of the biblical and archaeological evidence, see Dever 2001; 2003), I accept that there are elements of historicity in the biblical account of the emergence of Israel, which may or may not be recoverable. On the other hand, I also recognize the important contributions of more critical or skeptical analyses of the biblical text as represented by Frick 1985; Coote and Whitelam 1987; Whitelam 1991; Davies 1992; Thompson 2000, who have highlighted many of the difficulties in reconstructing a history based on the biblical account. For a highly critical review of this "minimalist" approach to Israelite historiography, see Rainey 1995a; Dever 2001, esp. 23–52.

17. Best represented by Frank Cross's (1973, 274–89) work and that of his students (Halpern 1988; Nelson 1981; Knoppers 1993–94), proposes that the DH underwent two redactions: a preexilic and an exilic redaction. Cross argued for a seventh-century date for the preexilic redactor, dating him to the period of Josiah. However, others have suggested an earlier date for the first redactor; see, e.g., A. D. H. Mayes (1981, 133–38), who dates the earlier phase to the time of Hezekiah, and Ronald Clements (1983, 209–20), who proposes dating it to the time of Zedekiah. See Knoppers and McConville 2000, whose edited volume includes a collection of articles representing these various views.

18. This school of thought claims that the DH underwent three redactions, each by a redactor with a different perspective—a history writer (DtrG), a prophetic redactor (DtrP), and a nomistic redactor (DtrN; see Smend 1981, 110–25; Dietrich 1987; Würthwein 1994)—or suggests additional textual layers (see Smend 1971; 2000; Spieckermann 1982).

19. Knoppers 2000, 1–7; Person 2002, 2–7. For an alternative view, see Van Seters 1983. Regarding a comprehensive discussion of the various theories, see Schniedewind 1996; Knoppers and McConville 2000.

20. For a summary of the archaeological evidence, see Finkelstein 1988, 295–302; Stager 2001, 98–99; Dever 2003, 37–50.

21. As aptly pointed out by Sandra Scham (2002), the very implausibility of these "hero" stories indicates that at least some of these tales are based in legend or tradition. She further suggests that the narratives in Judges can be used effectively as ethnographic analogies for interpreting Iron Age material culture. In general terms, the plots of narratives in Judges include the Taming of the Wild (Ephraim), the "Optimization" of the Natural World (Manasseh), and the Existence of Nature for Human Exploitation (Benjamin and Judah) and reflect values of early "agro-pastoralist" villages in Palestine. Regardless of when these accounts were written, the book of Judges expresses symbolically an early phase of development of later Iron Age cultures, what I would refer to as elements of the ethnogenesis of biblical Israel.

22. For an early premonarchic date, see Albright 1968, 13; Robertson 1972, 31–34; Boling 1975, 98–100; Cross and Freedman 1975, 5; Halpern 1983a, 32, 117; 1983b; Stager 1988; 1989; 2001, 92–93; Schloen 1993; Yurco 1997, 45; Sparks 1998, 109–24. But see Ahlström 1986, 80–81; Axelsson 1987, 52; Garbini 1988, 32; Redford 1992b, 412 n. 89; Diebner 1995, 106–30, who propose later dates and a different context for the composition of Judg 5.

23. See Breasted 1927, 257–58, 264; Kitchen 1966a; 1966b; Wilson 1969b; Lichtheim 1976; Hornung 1983; Yurco 1986; 1990; Murnane 1992; Hasel 1994, 47; 1998, 194; Hoffmeier 1997, 30; 2000; for discussion, see Sparks 1998, 95–97.

24. For a discussion of the evidence, see, e.g., Stager 1985b; Coote 1990; Dever 1992a, 26–56; 2003, 201–8; Ahlström 1993; Hasel 1998, 194–204. But see Thompson 1997, 173–74, who questions this association.

25. E.g., von Beckerath 1951, 67; de Vaux 1978; Ahlström and Edelman 1985; Ahlström 1986; 1991; 1993; Lemche 1998b, 37–38; 1992; Yurco 1986; 1990; Dever 1995a; Sparks 1998, 105–9; Hasel 1998, 203; most recently, Dever 2003, 201–8. Other interpretations include Israel as a nomadic entity before its later settlement in the hill country (see, e.g., Bimson 1991), a "metaphorical" parent "of three towns destroyed by the Egyptian army" (Thompson 1999, 79), while a small minority sees Israel as residing in Egypt (Nibbi 1989; Rendsburg 1992, 518).

26. See, e.g., Naʾaman 1994b, 248; Herr 1998, 260, who places the location of Israel within the tribal territory of Reuben.

27. Bimson 1991, 23 and n. 1, but see Rainey 1991, 56–60, 93; 1992; 2001, 68–74, who objects to Yurco's identification of Scene 4 with Israel and prefers to interpret Scenes 5–8 as depicting *Shasu*/Israel.

28. For a recent discussion of landscape archaeology within a Mediterranean context, see Alcock and Cherry 2004 and bibliography there. For preliminary attempts to analyze the extensive survey data from the Israel and Jordan within its broader landscape, see most recently e.g. Lehmann 2003.

29. Israel Finkelstein (1988) describes in detail the archaeological evidence from most excavated sites and the results of several regional surveys; however, it should be mentioned that Finkelstein has since modified the conclusions presented in his 1988 book (see, e.g., Finkelstein 1990a; 1991; 1994a; 1995b).

30. For a thorough discussion of the main features of highland settlements during the Iron I period, see Finkelstein 1988, esp. 235–92. See also A. Mazar 1990a, 328–52, and, most recently, Dever 2003, 101–28.

31. The most detailed summary is I. Finkelstein's overview of surveys and excavations in the highlands and Beer-sheba and Jordan Valleys (1988, 34–117). See also Kochavi 1985; Stager 2001, 100–101, table 3.2; van der Steen 1996; Bloch-Smith and Nakhai 1999, 78–92, 101–14; and Dever 2003, 201–17. Regarding recent synthetic treatments of the settlement data from specific highland regions, see Kamlah 2000; Zwingenberger 2001; and R. Miller 2003.

32. During the past forty years, archaeological surveys in the region have produced an abundance of data, though thus far there have been few analytical studies within the larger framework of landscape or settlement archaeology. The few studies that have been published tend to focus on economic aspects. One exception to this approach that illustrates the potential uses of the largely unexamined survey data is G. Lehmann's (forthcoming) attempt to reconstruct the social fabric and connections of the Iron I inhabitants. He suggests that Iron I territorial differentiations reflect societal interactions related to endogamic and exogamic marriage practices (see also Knoppers 2001, who discusses the practice of marriage outside the clan). Lehmann interprets the appearance of the archetypal Iron I village as comprising a *bet-ʾab*. Each settlement includes four to six dwellings or households. According to Lehmann, the resulting marriage alliances between clusters of villages undoubtedly played a significant role in the later development of more complex social structures and state formation that characterized the Iron IIB–C periods in the Land of Israel.

33. Based on the biblical tradition, the central highlands were occupied by two different alignments of people: the house of Joseph (Ephraim, Manasseh, and possibly Benjamin) in the north occupying the former territory of Shechem (Josh 16:1, 17–18; Judg 1:22, 35); and Judah and associated tribes in the south occupying the territory of Jerusalem (for the relations between the Late Bronze territorial division and the allotments of the Israelite tribes, see Alt 1967; Naʾaman 1986; Finkelstein 1995b, 361).

34. There is some confusion in the literature regarding the divisions and definitions of the various geographical regions. I prefer Miller and Hayes's (1986, 43–46), Finkelstein's (1995b, 353–54), and Finkelstein and Lederman's (1997, 3) straightforward delineation that defines the central hill country as including the highland region between the Jezreel and the Beer-sheba Valleys. See also Dever 2003, 206, who defines the central hill country as corresponding to the region north of Jerusalem (equaling Samaria as noted above), and Aharoni 1967, 24–29, who includes Galilee, Mount Ephraim, the Judean hill country, and the Negev highlands as belonging to his "central mountain" range.

35. Based on the Manasseh survey, Zertal (1991; 1994, 66–68; 1998) suggests that during the second half of the thirteenth century, outside groups arrived from Transjordan via the Wadi Farʿah and Wadi Malih valleys. In the earliest stages the new population co-existed with Late Bronze Age "Canaanites," the former distinguished from the indigenous population by several distinctive features, including new settlement patterns, architecture, and different exploitation of water, soil, and topography (see also Zertal 1988b). Finkelstein (1988, 90) challenges Zertal's thirteenth-century date for the beginning of the settlement process in Manasseh as well as his view that the new settlers penetrated the country from the outside steppe (see also Finkelstein 1990a; 1991; 1994a; 1995b).

36. I have not included Tell Balata, Dothan, and Tell el-Farʿah (N) in this list. Contrary to previous preliminary accounts, the recently published stratigraphic and architectural final report from Tell Balata (Shechem) documents an occupational gap at the end of the "terminal" Late Bronze Age (ca. 1150 B.C.E.) through the early Iron II (ca. 975 B.C.E.), demonstrating a break in continuity during the Iron I Age (Campbell 2002; G. R. H. Wright 2002). Based on the published material from Stratum 4 at Tell el-Farʿah (N), I would date this stratum to the eleventh century B.C.E. (see Chambon 1984 regarding the Iron Age at Tell el-Farʿah [N]). Dothan remains largely unpublished, except for a preliminary publication of several of the tombs (see Cooley and Pratico 1994). There are two possible scenarios: either there is a period of coexistence and overlap between the final Late Bronze occupation of these tell sites and the appearance of numerous small villages, or these hamlets were settled following the abandonment of the major Late Bronze tell settlements. Due to incomplete or inadequate publication of the evidence from these sites, it is not possible at this time to determine the chronological relationship between the terminal Late Bronze Age settlements and the smaller hamlets that were established sometime during the twelfth century B.C.E.

37. See Kempinski (1986; 1993) and Dever (1992a, 32–34), who suggest that the rectangular structure should be identified as a watchtower or foundation for another structure. See also Finkelstein (1995b, 359), who accepts its cultic identification but proposes it should be dated to the Middle Bronze Age on the basis of the pottery, a suggestion that is refutable by examining the published pottery (Zertal 1986–87).

38. Finkelstein divides this region into six geographical regions: (eastern) desert fringe, northern central range, southern central range, northern slopes, southern slopes, and (western) foothills (Finkelstein and Lederman 1997, fig. 1.2). Although Finkelstein and his team's final analysis of the data remains unpublished, Finkelstein (1988, 121–204) has published summaries based on the database (Finkelstein and Lederman 1997). For a recent reevaluation of the survey data from the central hill country, see Zwingenberger 2001.

39. Based on an examination of the archaeological data in light of the ecological and economic background of the region, Israelite settlement was initially concentrated on the desert fringe, the northern central range, and the southern central range. In these units subsistence was based on field crops and, in part, on animal husbandry. Finkelstein (1988, 202–3) concludes that most of the settlers came from a pastoral background, but see Callaway 1976, 29; Lederman 1999, 145–54, who dispute a pastoral or seminomadic origin for the hill-country inhabitants.

40. Excavation results from Shiloh support the biblical traditions that this site most likely served as a regional Iron I cultic center associated with the emergence of early Israel (see Finkelstein, Bunimovitz, and Lederman 1993, 385–89).

41. I do not include ʿIzbet Ṣarṭah in this list because it is not located in the central hill country proper but rather on the western edge of the foothills, adjoining the coastal plain. I prefer to see ʿIzbet Ṣarṭah as belonging to the cultural sphere of the coastal plain.

42. Lederman (1999) proposes that the roots of Khirbet Raddana's inhabitants were agrarian (contra, e.g., Finkelstein 1996b, who proposes that the inhabitants of central hill-country sites were nomadic in origin). These agriculturalists engaged in mixed farming together with specialized modes of horticultural production. This well-organized community functioned as part of a larger regional economic unit linked together by complementary modes of production and exchange.

43. Only two Late Bronze Age sites were documented in Benjamin, five to six in Ephraim, and two or three in Judah to the south (Finkelstein and Magen 1993, 25–26).

44. None of these sites are considered type-sites in this chapter. Either these excavations were conducted over a half-century ago, are poorly published, reflect the exposure of only a small area of the site, or postdate the twelfth century B.C.E.

45. Ofer (1994, 117–19) concludes that these Iron I settlers originated from heterogeneous groups of local pastoralists and descendants of the local population (contra Finkelstein, who suggests that the Judean hills were settled only during the eleventh century with migrating inhabitants from the north).

46. But see A. Mazar (1990b, 84 n. 12), who observes that in its building techniques the Giloh tower, which is unparalleled at Late Bronze Age sites, resembles the stepped-stone structure excavated in the City of David.

47. A. Mazar (1994b, 90–91) notes two factors that may assist in identifying Israelite sites in the hill country: the nature of the sites and their settlement patterns; and the similarity (or dissimilarity) of the material culture uncovered at sites that have ancient entrenched biblical traditions of being Israelite centers (such as Bethel and Shiloh). On the basis of this comparison, Giloh is identified as a site associated with changing Iron I settlement patterns that form the social boundaries of the ethnogenesis of Israel. As noted by A. Mazar (1994b, 91), the inhabitants of this region might not have identified themselves as "Israel" in this early stage, but they are certainly part of the population groups that provided the nucleus for the eventual rise of an Israelite identity.

48. For an alternative explanation, see Mendenhall (1973, 167–68; 1983, 94–100), who challenged Glueck's interpretations, preferring to attribute the increase in population to peasants fleeing from Cisjordan to Transjordan.

49. See Mittmann 1970; McGovern 1986; 1987; Ibach 1987; Sauer 1986; Boling 1988; MacDonald 1988; Miller 1991; Bienkowski 1992c; LaBianca and Younker 1995; Kamlah 2000. Regarding an updated and revised interpretation of the Middle Bronze Age in eastern Palestine, see Falconer (2001, 285), who argues for a clear "north-south fall-off pattern in Middle Bronze settlement densities, suggesting the possible importance of northerly economic and political ties stemming from the Beth Shan and Jezreel Valleys." For a summary of the Late Bronze Age evidence, see Strange 2001.

50. The transition from the Late Bronze to Iron Ages is characterized as "peaceful" and not marked by major change or upheaval. See McGovern 1987; Ji 1995, 128–30. Regarding the most recent survey work in the Khirbet ez Zeraqon region of Gilead, see Kamlah 2000.

51. Similar findings have been reported for the Jordanian plateau north of Wadi az-Zarqaʿ and for Moab (Boling 1988, 13–28; for discussion, see also Herr 1992; Ji 1995).

52. L. Herr (personal communication) considers Phase 11 at Tell el-ʿUmeiri to be contemporary with the earlier, Stratum II, phase at Mount Ebal.

53. Rather, J. Miller (1989, 11) prefers to characterize settlement patterns as gradually increasing over time from the Middle Bronze Age to the Iron II and suggests that the popu-

lation was largely indigenous in nature. But see Worschech 1990, who suggests that the origins of the Moabites were a result of migration. He argues that sedentary Edomites and nomadic *Shasu* occupied the land of Moab toward the end of the Late Bronze Age. During the Late Bronze–Iron Age transition, an additional nomadic group, the *Shatu,* infiltrated the region and merged with the nomadic *Shasu,* displacing the sedentary Emites.

54. Hart 1992; Knauf 1992; but see Finkelstein 1992a, who proposes that much of the Iron II pottery should be redated to the Iron I; and Bienkowski 1992c with 1992a, b already rebuttal.

55. Based on the still incomplete evidence, recent interpretations of the archaeological evidence in Transjordan have used a "tribal" model to explain the settlement patterns during the final centuries of the second millennium (see LaBianca and Younker 1995; Herr 1998, 258–60).

56. For a discussion of these biblical traditions, see most recently Herr 1999; MacDonald 2000, 101–55.

57. Extensive excavations at Hazor and Dan have uncovered evidence for Late Bronze Age settlements. Following the destruction of these cities sometime during the thirteenth century, Hazor was abandoned for at least a century and only resettled late in the eleventh century (Ben-Tor 1998; 2002; Ben-Ami 2001). Based on the partial publication of the Late Bronze (Stratum VII) and Iron I (Stratum VI) levels at Tel Dan, a similar scenario can be proposed for Tel Dan (Biran 1994a, 105–46; 1994b, 3–6; Ilan 1999, who suggests a complex picture of continuity and change during the thirteenth–eleventh centuries at Dan). Since the Upper Galilee is not part of the central hill country, traditionally considered the heartland of Israelite ethnogenesis, neither site will be discussed in detail in this chapter.

58. See also Herzog (1994, 148), who suggests that groups of different origins gradually settled in the area. Some of them apparently came from the central hill country, while others (including pastoral nomads) arrived from the southern deserts, from the western Negev, and perhaps also from the Judean Desert.

59. See Köhler-Rollefson 1992; van der Steen 1995. Regarding the possible impact of a hypothesized increase in Midianite population at the end of the Late Bronze Age on Edom and Ammon, see Parr 1988. For a summary, see van der Steen 1996, 66–68.

60. Larger settlements are also characteristic in the central Transjordan, as discussed above.

61. See also Finkelstein and Zilberman 1995 for a discussion of this relationship, but see Routledge 2000, 59–60, who disputes this interpretation.

62. Sites that Fritz assigns to this settlement plan include ʿIzbet Ṣarṭah (Stratum III), Tell Esdar, Beer-sheba (Stratum VII), and possibly Arad (Stratum XII). The evidence from these sites is fragmentary, and their reconstruction is largely conjectural, based on unexcavated evidence. In addition, neither of these sites is located in the heartland of the central highland regions, where the most marked settlement shift occurred. Like Finkelstein, Fritz also proposes that the houses are organized into a closed circle or oval with an open area in the middle. He interprets the basic plan as corresponding to the shape of a Bedouin camp, where the tents are grouped around an open area. As mentioned above, this proposal, though attractive, is based on speculative reconstruction. There is little excavated evidence for elliptically shaped sites or sites with a peripheral belt of pillared buildings as they are described in the archaeological literature.

63. Other sites assigned to this settlement type include ʿIzbet Ṣarṭah (Stratum II), Tel Beer-sheba (Stratum VI), and Tel Masos (Stratum II), which are located in peripheral areas.

64. For discussions of the four-room house, see Shiloh 1970; 1973; Braemer 1982; Netzer 1992; D. Clark 1996; Holladay 1992; 1997a; 1997b; Ji 1997; King and Stager 2001, 28–35.

65. See Braemer 1982, 102–5; Ahlström 1984a, 42–48; A. Mazar 1985c, 66–68; 1997c, 252–54; Callaway 1987; Stager 1985a, 17; 1989; Holladay 1997b, 107. This type of house was found in sites in the Shephelah—Tel Batash (A. Mazar 1997c, 58–66, 252–54), and Lachish (Ussishkin

1983, 113, fig. 8)—all dating to the Late Bronze Age. G. Wright (1985, 293–98) has suggested that the antecedents of the Iron Age pillared house go back as far as the Middle Bronze Age.

66. The use and reconstruction of the central space has been a topic of debate. These include interpreting it as an open-air courtyard, as the four-room house at Qasile has been restored (A. Mazar 1999), or as a covered space where the roof could have served as the floor of a second-story open-air courtyard. Netzer (1992, 195–96) prefers the second suggestion.

67. It should be noted that the four-room house is a common feature of Iron Age sites in Jordan, settlements that in the Iron II period cannot be associated with an Israelite ethnos.

68. Bunimovitz and Faust acknowledge M. Weinfield's earlier tentative exploration of this topic; see Netzer 1992, 199 n. 24, who documents a conversation with Weinfield on this topic. This interpretation should be seen as highly speculative, with little supporting primary evidence.

69. For a discussion of agricultural practices, installations, and technologies of the Iron Age, see Hopkins 1985; Borowski 2002.

70. Hopkins (1985, 173–86; LaBianca and Hopkins 1988, 14), on the other hand, claims that terracing developed locally (as early as the Middle Bronze Age) but was not adopted on a wide scale until later in the Iron Age.

71. El-Maqbarah in Wadi el-Farʿah, surveyed by A. Zertal (1996, 398–400), is one of the few cemeteries where evidence of Iron I (rather than transitional Late Bronze II/Iron I) pottery has been found in association with burials. However, since these tombs were disturbed and have not yet been properly excavated, their context is unclear.

72. For an overview of these assemblages, see Finkelstein 1988, 47–53, 56–91, 112–17; A. Mazar, 1992b, 281–296, esp. map 8.3; Dever 2003, 118–25.

73. These typically Late Bronze Age forms and features that are rare in central highland pottery assemblages continue well-known Late Bronze Age shapes and are common elements in the ceramic repertoire of twelfth- and eleventh-century lowland sites in the valleys and coastal plain, such as Keisan (Stratum XII), Megiddo (Strata VIIA–VIA), Tel Qiri (Strata IX–VIII), Dor (Stratum XII), Tel Beth-shemesh (Stratum III), and Gezer (Strata XIII–XI), to name just a few (see pp. 113–36 for a detailed discussion of these vessel types and comparative material). These material-culture boundaries between rural highland village sites and their contemporary lowland settlements to the west are especially remarkable, since many of these sites are within walking distance but appear to have very little interaction or direct contact with each other.

74. This jar makes its debut in modest quantities during the end of the Late Bronze IIB period at several sites along the coast (Nahariya: Yogev 1993, 1088–89; Tel Nami: Artzy 1994, 127–28; Tel Zeror: Ohata 1970, pl. 56; Aphek: Beck and Kochavi 1985, fig. 5:1) and in the Jezreel and Jordan Valleys (Tel Beth-shean: James and McGovern 1993, figs. 23:2, 4; 32:4; Killebrew 2001, fig. 20.1; Megiddo: Esse 1992, n. 47; ʿAfula: M. Dothan 1955, 38–41; Tell es-Saʿidiyeh: Tubb, Dorrell, and Cobbing 1996: Stratum XV: fig. 20), especially at sites along thirteenth and early twelfth century B.C.E. Egyptian-controlled trade routes. Jorgensen (2002, 180–83) documents the appearance of collared pithos in small quantities at Tel ʿEin Ẓippori, located in the Lower Galilee.

75. For synthetic overviews of this jar, its distribution, and typology, see Finkelstein 1988, 275–85; Esse 1991, 99–116; Wengrow 1996, 307–26; Killebrew 2001, 377–98; Raban 2001.

76. See, e.g., Manasseh: Zertal 1991, 35–36; Mount Ebal: Zertal 1986–87, 134–36; Shiloh: Kjaer 1930, 97–104; Buhl and Holm-Nielsen 1969, pls. 15, 16:190, 191, 192; Finkelstein 1988, 220–27; Finkelstein, Bunimovitz, and Lederman 1993, figs. 6.48:1, 2, 4; 6.49:3, 4; Northern Ramat Manasseh (ʿEin Hagit): Wolff 1998, fig. 3; Cohen-Weinberger and Wolff 2001; Bethel: Kelso 1968, pls. 56; 57:1–5; Tell en-Naṣbeh: Wampler 1947, 5, pl. 2:16–23, 26–28; Tell el-Fûl: Sinclair 1960, 16–18, pl. 20:2–17; Khirbet Raddana: Callaway and Cooley 1971, 11; Lederman 1999, 63–67; ʿAi: Callaway 1969, 8–9, fig. 8; 1980, fig. 154; 155:1–13; Giloh: A. Mazar 1981, 27–31, fig. 9, pl. 5A, B; 1990b, fig. 5; Beth-zur: Funk 1968, 44–47, figs. 7; 8:21–29, pls. 21, 22a.

The collared pithos appears in much smaller quantities at Khirbet Rabud (Kochavi 1974, fig. 5:12) and ʿIzbet Ṣarṭah (Finkelstein 1986, 77–84, type 21).

77. For a general overview of the distribution of the collared pithos in Transjordan, see Ibrahim 1978; Ji 1995, 122–26; Wengrow 1996, 315–16. Numerous fortified settlements in the Transjordanian highlands dated to the thirteenth/twelfth–twelfth centuries B.C.E. contain notable quantities of collared pithoi; see, e.g., Herr 2001, who discusses in detail collared pithoi at Tell el-ʿUmeiri. Large pithoi also appear as far south as Edom; see Weippert (1982, figs. 6:9; 8:9) for two pithoi fragments that are not clearly "collared" and Bienkowski (1992a, 167), who dates the pithoi from Buseirah and Tawilan to the seventh century, while Finkelstein (1992a; 1992c, 171) suggests an Iron I date (see Herr 2001, 248, who supports Bienkowski's later dating of the evidence).

78. See, e.g., Dan: Biran 1989, figs. 4.15:8, 4.18:6–8, 4.22, 4.23; 1994a, ills. 92, 95; Hazor: Yadin et al. 1961, pl. CLXVII:1–7, 9–11, CLXVIII: 9–11; Sasa: Bahat 1986, 100: no. 1; Golani and Yogev 1996, 51, fig. 6:4; Stepansky, Segal, and Carmi 1996, 68, fig. 7:2; Tel ʿEin Ẓippori: Jorgensen 2002, 180–83.

79. See, e.g., ʿAfula: M. Dothan 1955, figs. 11:25, 16:4; Megiddo: Loud 1948, pl. 83:4; see Esse 1992 for a summary of the evidence; Tel Qiri: Ben-Tor and Portugali 1987, photos 38–41; Hunt 1987, 200, fig. 36; Taanach: Rast 1978, 9–10, figs. 4:1, 9:1, 10:1, 3, 4.

80. See, e.g., Tell Keisan: Briend and Humbert 1980, pl. 58:1, 2, 2a; Tel Mevorakh: Stern 1978, 68–69, fig. 19:4: Tell Qasile: A. Mazar 1985b, 57–58; Beth-shemesh: Grant and Wright 1938, 129.

81. Kelso (1968, 63) and Rast (1978, 9) divide the collared pithoi at Bethel and Taanach into two main types—tall-necked jars and short-necked jars—with the taller version appearing earlier. Callaway (1969, 8–9) proposes that the length of the folded rim has a chronological significance, concluding that the larger fold of the rim is earlier while the shorter, folded rim is later, unrelated to the length of the neck and vessel. This typology is based on Callaway's confusion regarding the term "collar," which he understands to refer to the folded rim rather than to the ridge at the base of the neck. A different approach is suggested by Finkelstein (1986, 77–78; Finkelstein, Bunimovitz, and Lederman 1993, 159), who distinguishes between the "thick" and "thin" rims and concludes that the thickened rim type seems to be earlier. The great variety of rim and neck forms that appear contemporaneously has been noted by A. Mazar (1981, 28–29) at Giloh and by M. Artzy (personal communication) at Tel Nami. They conclude that it is impossible to develop a chronologically significant typology of collared pithoi based on the evidence from these two sites. Wampler (1947, 4) also notes the great variety of rims and the difficulty of establishing a typological sequence for these jars.

82. The appearance of stamped impressions or incisions on the rims or handles may also be an indication of potters or specific workshops. For a general discussion of these marks, see Ibrahim 1978, 129; Finkelstein 1988, 278–80.

83. This pithos appears at the end of the Late Bronze Age and continues into the early Iron IA. Its rim is reminiscent of rims on pithos CA 26. Form CA 25a appears in noteworthy quantities at the fortified early Iron I site of Tell el-ʿUmeiri (Herr et al. 1991, figs. 5:5, 6, 7, 10, 6:1, 2, 3, 6, 7; Herr 1997, 237–38; see, e.g., figs. 4:14, 4:19:5–8, 4:20:1–3, 5–7), Tel Sasa (Stepansky, Segal, and Carmi 1996, fig. 7:2), and Beth-shean (Killebrew 1999a, ill. III:13).

84. This variation is especially popular in the central hill country (see, e.g., Mount Ebal: Zertal 1986–87, figs 12:1, 13:1, 16:8, 13; Shiloh: Finkelstein, Bunimovitz, and Lederman 1993, figs. 6.48:1, 2, 4, 6.49:3, 4, 6.5.51:1, 4, 6; ʿAi: Callaway 1980, figs. 150:17–28, 154; Bethel: Kelso 1968, pls. 56, 57:1–5; Tell en-Naṣbeh: Wampler 1947, pls. 1:2, 3–11, 2:12–22; Tell el-Fûl: Albright 1924, pl. XXVIII:17–24; Sinclair 1960, pl. 20:10–18; Jerusalem: Steiner 1994, figs. 4–6; Edelstein and Milevski 1994, 19–20, fig. 121–2; Beth-zur: Funk 1968, fig. 7), though it does appear occasionally in the Galilee, Jordan Valley, and the northern coastal plain throughout the Iron I period.

85. Artzy 1994, 137–38; for an overview of the evidence regarding the use of the camel as a beast of burden, see Wapnish 1997.

86. See, e.g., the provenience of pithoi from Tel Dan (Yellin and Gunneweg 1989), Sasa (Cohen-Weinberger and Goren 1996), and Shiloh (Glass et al. 1993).

87. Ethnographic examples of itinerant potters have been described by Asboe 1946, 9–10; Linné 1965; Voyatzoglou 1974; and esp. London 1989a; 1989b, including examples of itinerant potters who produced only pithoi. L. Herr (personal communication) also supports the suggestion that itinerant potters produced hill-country pithoi.

88. See Ibrahim 1978, 120; Finkelstein 1988, 278–80; Zertal 1986–87, 135, 145–47; D. Clark 1997, figs. B.13:1, B.14:1, B.15:1.

89. For a summary of the early scholarly debate regarding the emergence of Israel based on the biblical account and preceding A. Alt's 1925 (for an English translation see Alt 1967) classic masterpiece, see Weippert 1971, 1–4. In the 1970s and 80s, regional surveys and excavations have unearthed large quantities of material culture from the thirteenth–eleventh centuries B.C.E. See, e.g., Frankel 1994, 18–34; Gal 1994, 35–46; Herzog 1994, 122–49; Ofer 1994, 92–121; Kochavi 1985, 54–60; A. Mazar 1982b, 167–78; 1985b, 51–71; 1994b, 70–91; Zertal 1988a; 1994, 47–69; 1998, 238–50. For surveys regarding the problem of ancient Israel's origins, from both textual and archaeological perspectives see e.g. Weippert 1971, 5–62; Finkelstein 1988, 15–23; 295–314; Halpern 1992b, 1120–43; Dever 1995a, 200–13; 1995b, 61–80. For general critiques of the various schools of thought see S. Herrmann 1985; Silberman 1992; Hess 1993, 132–33; 138–139; Frendo 1992; Weinfeld 1993, 99–120; Naʾaman, 1994b, 246–47; Dever 2003, 71–74.

90. For a detailed summary of the evidence for and against the historicity of Joshua's conquest, see Dever 2003, 37–72.

91. Albright's students who adhered to this theory in the past include G. E. Wright 1940, 25–40; 1960, 43–51; Lapp 1967, 283–300. Other scholars who have recently supported the conquest theory include Kaufmann 1953; Bimson and Livingston 1987, 40–53, 66–68; Wood 1990b; and especially Kitchen 1998. For a discussion of the conquest account in the book of Joshua, see Weinfeld 1993, 121–55. For a critique of this theory, see J. Miller 1977; Schoors 1985, 77–92; Finkelstein 1988, 296–302.

92. Alt 1967; Noth 1960; Aharoni 1957a; 1957b; 1976; Kochavi 1985; Zertal 1988b; 1991; 1998; Rainey 1991. For a discussion of the settlement of the Israelite tribes based on the book of Judges, see Weinfeld 1993, 156–82 and bibliography there. For a summary and critique of the peaceful infiltration theory, see Finkelstein 1988, 302–6; Dever 1992b, 552–53. Based on the excavations at Tel Masos, Fritz (1987) modified the peaceful infiltration theory. He sees a nonindigenous desert origin for the Israelites. However, by the thirteenth century B.C.E., preceding their sedentarization, these seminomads had established a "symbiotic" relationship with the Canaanites.

93. Numerous scholars have studied nomadism in its various manifestations. Several models based on economic structures and cultural features have been suggested and have been used by biblical scholars and archaeologists to interpret the demographic, political, and cultural picture at the close of the Late Bronze Age (for a brief review of the issues, see Skjeggestad 1992, 175–76). The different aspects of nomadism include "enclosed" nomadism and questions regarding the nomadic character of early Israel (Malamat 1967; Rowton 1974; 1976; Marx 1977, 343–63; Bar-Yosef and Khazanov 1992; Finkelstein 1995c). See van der Steen 1995 for a discussion of nomadism in the central Jordan Valley. For a recent argument against the nomadic origin of the Israelites (or "Proto-Israelites"), see Dever 1998.

94. Finkelstein (1988, 336–37) points out, however, that desert nomads could not have existed before the domestication of the camel. Evidence indicates that the camel was domesticated only in the late thirteenth century B.C.E., coinciding with the end of the Late Bronze Age (see Wapnish 1997 for a discussion of the camel in the archaeological

evidence). Instead, Finkelstein suggests that the inhabitants of these Iron I villages were originally indigenous Canaanite pastoralists who were forced to settle in small agricultural villages due to the crisis at the end of the Late Bronze Age; see below on the pastoral Canaanite theory.

95. For a thorough discussion of the *ʿapîru,* see M. Greenberg 1955; Mendenhall 1973, 122–41; but see Rainey (1991, 59; 1995b), who argues against their association with the Hebrews. For a general description of the *ʿapîru,* see Lemche 1992.

96. N. Lemche (1985; 1991b) emphasizes the use of comparative anthropological case studies and sociological models. R. B. Coote and K. W. Whitelam (1987) rely mainly on sociological models rejecting the biblical texts as largely unusable. Coote (1991, 42) prefers to call this approach the "political model." For a survey of this approach see Gottwald 1992; 1993; and see Finkelstein 1990a, 677–86 for a review of these two approaches.

97. Gottwald (1979; 1985) suggests four theoretical models within which these inter-Canaanite movements could form a free-agrarian society. These include the peasant rebellion, social revolution, frontier development, and social banditry. For Mendenhall's rejection of Gottwald's Marxist interpretation, see Mendenhall, 1983. Other biblical historians who propose an indigenous Canaanite origin for Israel, though not necessarily a revolutionary model, include, e.g., Chaney 1983; Lemche 1985; Coote 1991; Coote and Whitelam 1987; McGovern 1987. Coote (1991, 46) succinctly sums up his approach as follows: "my understanding of early Israel hinges on six kinds of evidence (scriptures, Merneptah, the archaeology of Palestine, the sea peoples, settlement change in Palestine, and comparative history), three basic issues (discount the Bible, take Israel as a political term, and base the history of early Israel on a generic political history), and three changes of mind (politics more than trade, no more bedouin, and the emergence of Israel and the settlement of the highland are two separate issues)."

98. See Finkelstein 1988, 307–14, for a discussion of this theory and Rainey 1991, 59–60, for a critique of Mendenhall and Gottwald, where he refers to it as the "revolting peasant theory." Although severely criticized by numerous archaeologists, a version of this theory has been supported by Callaway (1985), who also proposes an indigenous, nonseminomadic origin for the settlers of the highlands, suggesting that they migrated from the western lowlands and coastal regions in order to seek refuge from war and violence of the Sea Peoples. Dever (1990, 79) notes the significant continuity in material culture and the lack of evidence for seminomads (but see Dever 1992b, 553–56; 1995a, 200–13, where he suggests some "extra-Palestinian" elements as well as the possibility of pastoralists). Stager (1985b) sees "Israel" mentioned in the Israel (Merneptah) Stela and has identified "Israel" pictorially in Ramesses II's redated battle relief at Karnak with a group of people who closely resemble Canaanites. For a detailed critique of this theory, see Halpern 1983a, 47–106.

99. It should be noted that, although Finkelstein (1988, 28) stresses the indigenous nature of these "hill country people in a process of settling down," he also suggests that "there must be a kernel of historical veracity in the deeply-rooted biblical tradition concerning the origin of Israel in Egypt" and that "certain elements among the settlers may well have come from the outside" (1988, 348). See also Finkelstein and Naʾaman (1994b, 13–15), who stress that "there were groups from other origins as well."

100. Finkelstein 1992b. However, Lemche (1985, 136–47; 1991b, 11–13) points out that, according to anthropological studies, nomadic societies only give up their nomadic way of life when forced to do so by government policy. He suggests that the political conditions at the end of the Late Bronze Age would have encouraged nomadism. Instead of the nomadic model, Lemche supports a gradual development of the twelfth–eleventh century B.C.E. village society out of Late Bronze Age urban society. For a review of this theory, see Frendo 1998; Skjeggestad 1992; Dever 1998. Other scholars, such as Sharon 1994, who stresses the demographic factor, have followed this general model with some modification. Frankel (1994) clearly states that the Iron I population of the western Galilee (the tribes of Asher and

Naphtali) were indigenous people originating from the pastoral nomads or sedentary residents in the lowlands.

101. For a discussion of tribal societies and the coexistence of agricultural and pastoral elements, see Bienkowski and van der Steen 2001 and the references there. See also Rosen 1992, who challenges Finkelstein's notions of the "invisibility" of nomads in the archaeological record.

102. See Roosens 1989; Moore 1994a; 1994b; Whitehead 1996; Geary 2002. Several views regarding the source of ethnogenesis have been proposed. For some, an emerging ethnos can originate from multiple antecedents (Burch et al. 1999); it has also been suggested that this process is inherently based in conflict (Hill 1996).

103. This approach can be classified as a "cladistic," from the Greek *clados,* for "branch." Moore (1994b, 925) defines cladistic theories as those that "emphasize the significance of a historical process by which daughter populations, languages, or cultures are derived from a parent group."

104. This approach may best be defined as "rhizotic," from the Greek *rhiza,* for "root." For a discussion of rhizotic versus cladistic theories, see Moore 1994b.

105. For a discussion of the role of narrative in ethnic identity, or what is termed "narrating ethnogenesis," see Erickson 2003.

106. These types of tribal affiliations and alliances may be reflected in the Song of Deborah (Judg 5). The concept of "tribe," a term that in recent decades has been discredited, is now reappearing in scholarly literature. See, e.g., the articles in Parkinson 2002.

107. See Ahlström 1986; 1991, who tends to give priority to the withdrawal of groups from the lowlands into the highlands but recognizes the need to allow room for the arrival of refugees from Anatolia, Syria, Edom, Ammon, Midian, and Amalek into the highlands, noting that Ezek 16:3, 45–46 indicates a varied ethnic makeup of the hill-country people (Herr, 1998). This cultural complex and the mixed origins of early Israel have been noted and emphasized by a number of scholars, such as LaBianca and Younker (1995) and Herr (1998) in their "tribal" model that emphasizes relationships based on fluid coalitions that "rose, fell, swapped loyalties, and came and went throughout the Iron I" (Herr 1998, 258).

108. For a description of a similar process of Greek ethnogenesis, see J. M. Hall 1995; 2002.

5
The Philistines: Urban Colonists of the Early Iron Age

Modern perceptions of the Philistines as an uncouth and boorish people originate in the negative portrayal of them in the Bible.[1] However, the discovery of richly decorated and cosmopolitan Aegean-style artifacts at urban centers identified as Philistine demonstrates that this biased definition of a Philistine is an undeserved slur (for a history of research, see Dothan and Dothan 1992). This distinctly Aegean-style material culture, dating to the Iron I period at cities located in the southern coastal plain, corresponds closely with Philistine cities and territorial boundaries mentioned in biblical texts (e.g., Josh 13:2–3; fig. 5.1).[2] Armed with this evidence, most scholars postulate a migration from the west Aegean[3] triggered by a collapse of the Mycenaean palace system and the crisis that struck the region during the final decades of the thirteenth and early twelfth centuries B.C.E. (see pp. 37–42 above). I contend that the Philistine phenomenon is the result of a more nuanced and complex cultural interaction between lands surrounding the Aegean Sea and the Levant. Rather than seeing the arrival of peoples bearing an Aegean-style culture as Mycenaean or west Aegean populations fleeing disaster, it is more correct to see the Philistines as representing intentional colonization by enterprising migrating groups in the east. These newcomers were closely connected to an "Aegeanized" and prosperous twelfth-century Cyprus (and perhaps neighboring areas), where continuous contact with the Mycenaean world during the preceding fourteenth and thirteenth centuries B.C.E. resulted in the local adoption and emulation of a popular Aegean koine by the final decades of the Late Bronze Age.

Most scholars have focused on the origins (where) and chronological framework (when) of the Philistines. Less attention has been paid to the reasons (the why and how) for the large-scale settlement of foreign groups bearing an Aegean-style culture on the southern coastal plain of Canaan.[4] What is often lacking in many treatments of the topic is an integration of the Philistine phenomenon within its larger archaeological Late Bronze Age context and an analysis of the conditions that led to the

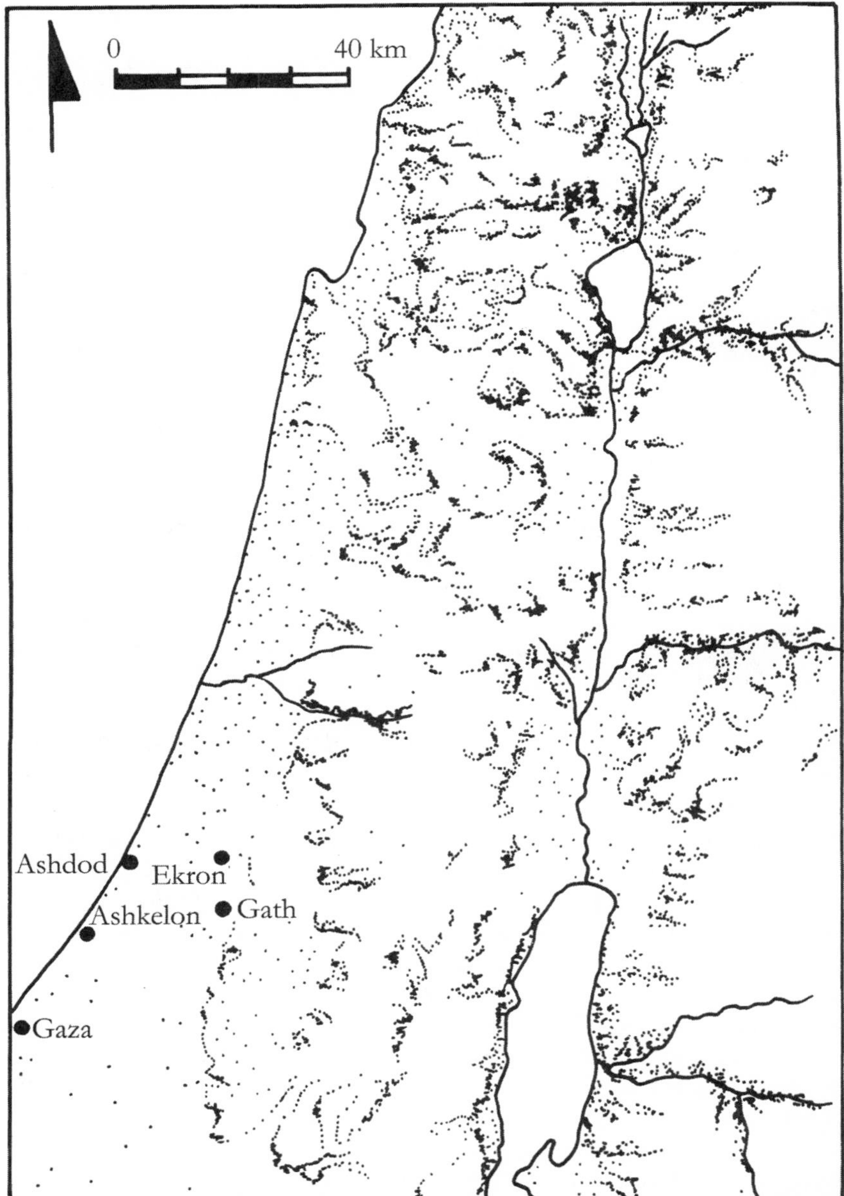

Fig. 5.1. Map of Major Early Philistine Settlements

population displacements and regionalism of the succeeding Iron I period. In the following section I define the terms used in this chapter, summarize the historical and biblical sources, briefly review aspects of early Philistine material culture, and examine in detail ceramic assemblages associated with the initial arrival of the Philistines. Finally, in this case study of cultural diffusion, I address the causes and processes that led to the settlement of the Philistines, which chronologically paralleled the ethnogenesis of early Israel.

Diffusionist versus Indigenist Explanations of Cultural Change

Scholarly interpretations of the Philistines are closely tied to theories of cultural change.[5] Determining the reasons for cultural change over time based on the reading of material culture has proven to be one of the most contentious and challenging aspects of interpreting the archaeological record. Opinions regarding the appearance of Aegean-style material culture associated with the Philistine case study can be assigned to two general approaches: diffusionist (including migrationist)[6] and indigenist (equaling evolutionary or immobilist)[7] interpretations.

Diffusion is the process of transmission by contact that results in the movement of ideas and objects through space and time.[8] The term *stimulus diffusion* refers to the transmission of information, ideas, or elements of material culture and is typically the far more common means transmitting culture. Similar to Irving Rouse's concept of transculturation, stimulus diffusion usually occurs via trade relations or limited small-scale immigration over time, or a combination of the two.[9] The gradual adoption or transculturation of Mycenaean-style material culture and its local production at locations in the east Aegean and Cyprus during the second half of the thirteenth century B.C.E. can best be explained as stimulus diffusion.[10]

Complex diffusion is the transmission of entire complexes of traits and ideas to another culture or region during a relatively short period of time. This less common occurrence of diffusion is usually attributed to large-scale population movement, migration, conquest, displacement or enforced transfer of populations, or colonization.[11] The appearance of an entire complex of Aegean-style material culture in the southern coastal plain of Canaan testifies to a significant migration of peoples bearing an Aegean-style material culture, radically different from indigenous Canaanite culture discussed in chapter 3 above.

Until the 1960s, most archaeologists accepted diffusion as the primary factor in cultural change, especially cultural transmission resulting from migration and invasion. Part of the appeal of migration was no doubt a matter of cultural biases based on modern historical developments, including massive displacements of populations and the Western colonization that characterized much of nineteenth and first half of the twentieth centuries (Rouse 1986, 16–17; Chapman and Hamerow 1997, 3). During the 1960s, corresponding with the rise of New Archaeology, scientific procedures, systems theories, and the use of paradigms to explain cultural change challenged these assumptions.[12] Increasingly processual archaeologists tended to discredit hypotheses of migration and acculturation and to favor theories of local development and transculturation.[13] Anglo-American archaeologists in particular preferred to see indigenist or "immobilist" processes, especially processes that relied on internal evolutionary developments such as social differentiation, population growth, or environmental change, as the major factor in cultural changes.[14]

Migrationism has resurfaced in respected archaeological literature during the past two decades.[15] Postprocessual archaeological theory that emphasizes historical context and ideology is responsible in part for the return to migrationism as an explanation for culture change.[16] Ongoing research in the fields of linguistics, demography, geography, and sociology that successfully documents the cultural impact of migrations also has added credibility to migrationist theories (see Dyen 1956; Adams, Van Gerven, and Levy 1978; Rouse 1986). Of the several possible types of migrationism, the available textual and archaeological evidence points to colonialism as a prime factor responsible for the appearance of the biblical Philistines at sites in Philistia.

Colonialism receives a myriad of definitions and connotations in academic literature.[17] Ancient terms for colonial activities (e.g., Greek *apoikia* or Latin *colonia*) literally refer to residence away from home or the establishment of a settlement elsewhere that may or may not be accompanied by violence and exploitation of indigenous populations (van Dommelen 2002, 121–22). Several recent publications tackle the question of colonialism as manifested in the archaeological record (see Lyons and Papadopoulos 2002b). Following Peter van Dommelen's (1997, 306) definition, colonialism is "the presence of one or more groups of foreign people in a region at some distance from their place of origin (the 'colonizers'), and the existence of asymmetrical socioeconomic relationships of dominance or exploitation between the colonizing groups and the inhabitants of the colonized regions." What distinguishes colonialism from imperialism is the establishment of colonies in a distant land.[18]

Motivation for colonization is usually economic or political and often entails migration. Its impact on indigenous peoples can be expressed physically via material culture as well as cognitively via influence on ideology and social customs (see Lyons and Papadopoulos

2002a). However, colonial activities can be a result of more gradual processes of cultural hegemony that are not always accompanied by large-scale population movements but that can influence cultural styles and norms over the long term.[19] Often this interaction between the colonizing and indigenous peoples develops into a "creolized" society (Jordan and Schrire 2002). This process of the mixing of cultures has also been termed the "Middle Ground," a theoretical approach that explains the resulting hybridization of the local culture or indigenous peoples with an intrusive colonial culture.[20]

Instead of adopting hyper-diffusionist models that attribute the appearance of locally produced Aegean-style material culture in the east to wide-scale population movements of Mycenaean Greeks migrating eastward as a result of the disasters and the collapse of the palace system in the west Aegean, one should recognize that the reality was far more complex, as indicated by more recent excavation results. The material-culture evidence in the eastern Mediterranean during the thirteenth and twelfth centuries B.C.E. hints at several variants of colonialism briefly reviewed above. Aegean-style material culture appearing in the eastern Aegean and Cyprus is a more gradual, longer-term process of interaction between east and west that can be characterized as stimulus diffusion. There is no doubt that economic and cultural connections facilitated by improved communication via the Mediterranean Sea, combined with small-scale and continuous immigration, resulted in the gradual transmission and diffusion to the east of an appealing or profitable Mycenaean or Aegean-style culture. During the final decades of the thirteenth century B.C.E., the local production of Mycenaean IIIB pottery in the east Aegean and Cyprus, which was also exported to the Levant, represented a colonization of the east via long-term immigration and economic relations rather than massive population movements, destructions, and the sudden establishment of new settlements. This interaction between east and west could be violent or peaceful.

In contrast, the archaeological record demonstrates that later twelfth-century Mycenaean IIIC Aegean-style material culture associated with the arrival of the Philistines in the southern coastal plain appeared suddenly and irreversibly changed the cultural character of several sites, which also happen to correspond to the five Pentapolis cities mentioned in the biblical account. However, this phenomenon of complex diffusion should not be interpreted as a result of conquering Mycenaeans fleeing disaster in the west Aegean. Rather, the Philistines were enterprising colonists originating from a prosperous and Aegeanized Cyprus and/or coastal Anatolia who quickly constructed impressive urban centers that dominated the entire region, as is reflected in the biblical account of the early Philistines.

Textual Evidence

Central to any discussion addressing the appearance of the Philistines is the ancient documentation. Although no early Philistine texts or inscriptions have thus far been discovered or conclusively identified,[21] this group's early history is well known from several Egyptian texts and numerous passages in the biblical narrative that describe their encounters with premonarchic Israelites, albeit from a later edited perspective.[22] A careful examination of the primary sources indicates that some of the time-honored assumptions regarding the identity of the Philistines are based on speculative interpretations that are not necessarily supported in the textual evidence.

Egyptian Sources

The name *Peleset*, translated "Philistine," occurs in conjunction with the names of several other groups of peoples referred to in modern scholarship as "Sea Peoples."[23] The Philistines appear in four New Kingdom Egyptian texts. Two are attributed to the reign of Ramesses III (Medinet Habu and the Rhetorical Stela in Chapel C at Deir el-Medineh), one was composed shortly after the death of Ramesses III (Papyrus Harris I), and the fourth (Onomasticon of Amenope) dates to the end of the twelfth or early eleventh century B.C.E. [24]

Medinet Habu

Medinet Habu provides the starting point for most discussions of the biblical Philistines. The text[25] and accompanying reliefs[26] describe battles by land and sea led by Ramesses III during his Year 8 campaign against a coalition of "Sea Peoples," including the Philistines.[27] It should be noted that the Egyptian texts do not specify which groups of Sea Peoples are portrayed in these two major battle scenes. In fact, the warriors with the feathered headdress (fig. 5.2a) are designated in other reliefs relating to Ramesses III's Year 8 campaign as *Denyen* (Epigraphic Survey 1930, pl. 44), *Tjekker* (Epigraphic Survey 1930, pl. 42), or *Peleset* (Epigraphic Survey 1930, pl. 44). According to Ramesses III's typically boastful account, he successfully repelled both the naval and land attacks. The only preserved depiction of a clearly identified *Peleset* chief in the accompanying hieroglyphic text appears on the first court, north side, on one of the bases of the Osirid pillars at Medinet Habu (fig. 5.2b; Epigraphic Survey 1932, pl. 118c; Edgerton and Wilson 1936, 146). It is noteworthy that this captive *Peleset* is bearded and is *not* wearing the trademark "feathered" headdress.

Although most archaeologists and biblical scholars continue to read these texts and depictions literally as historical texts and as an indicator

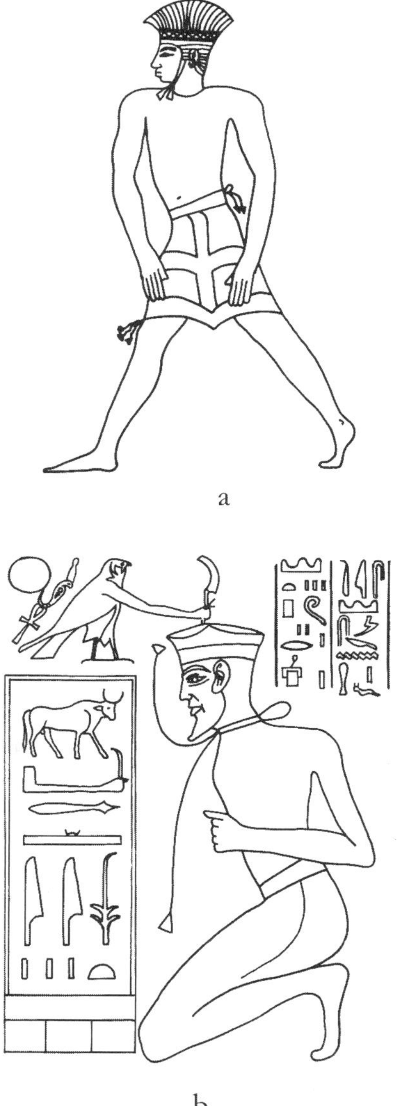

a

b

Fig. 5.2. a: Generic "Sea People"; b: Captured Philistine

of absolute chronology regarding the appearance of the Philistines in Philistia (e.g., T. Dothan 1982, 289; A. Mazar 1990, 307–8; Bietak 1993; Stager 1995, 334–36), most Egyptologists are more cautious in their assessment of their historical value. As Donald Redford (forthcoming) aptly observes, "like other 'historical' texts of the New Kingdom, the Medinet Habu records have many times been culled for their thematic 'units' in order to create a thesaurus of 'propaganda' phrases."[28]

Rhetorical Stela of Ramesses III

A less discussed but no less important text that mentions the *Peleset* is Ramesses III's Rhetorical Stela recovered at Deir el-Medineh. Noteworthy is the appearance of the *Peleset* together with the *Teresh,* who sailed (?) "in the midst of the sea" (Kitchen 1983, 91.11–12; Peden 1994, 64.8). This linking of these two groups, of which the *Teresh* most likely originate from the Anatolian coast, is potentially significant for questions regarding their identity and origins (Sandars 1985, 164–65).

Harris Papyrus I

This document, composed shortly after the death of Ramesses III, supplements the Medinet Habu evidence on the Philistines.[29] Referring to Ramesses III's battle against the Sea Peoples, Harris Papyrus I declares that the *Peleset* were "reduced to ashes" (Breasted 1927, 201; Erichsen 1933, 92.18). No less significant is the description of Egypt's continued involvement in Canaan, indicating that parts of Canaan remained within the sphere of Egyptian control through the reign of Ramesses III (Higginbotham 2000, 56–57). The founding of a temple to Amun at *PaCanaan,* generally identified as Gaza (Gardiner 1920, 204; Redford 1990, 32; but see Higginbotham 2000, 58–59), raises questions about the date of the Philistines' arrival and their establishment of a settlement at Gaza already during the reign of Ramesses III. It should also be noted that only the *Sherden* and the *Weshesh* are mentioned specifically as being brought into captivity to Egypt. Harris Papyrus I adds that Ramesses III settled them in his strongholds, but without any indication of their location. It is speculative to conclude that this text refers to garrisons in Canaan or has any direct bearing on the mode of Philistine settlement on the southern coastal plain.

Onomasticon of Amenope

The term *onomasticon* refers to the cataloguing of things grouped by major themes, including classes, tribes, and types of human beings. The Onomasticon of Amenope, probably dating to the end of the Twentieth Dynasty, is known from at least ten copies or fragmentary versions. This text can be characterized as an instruction or teaching exercise. The Philistines appear in the sequence "Ashkelon, Ashdod, Gaza, Assyria, Shubaru [. . .], *Sherden, Tjekker, Peleset, Khurma* [. . .]."[30] This is the first mention in an Egyptian source of Ashkelon, Ashdod, and Gaza, three of the five Pentapolis cities appearing in the Hebrew Bible, in a listing that implies a connection with the Philistines and possibly other Sea Peoples.[31]

Biblical Accounts

The Philistines or Philistia are mentioned over 250 times in the Bible. Verses alluding to their foreign origins and references to the five cities of the Philistines are the most relevant to our discussion. Taken at face value, the biblical texts can be grouped into four periods of contact connected with Israel's history: the patriarchal period, the premonarchic period of the judges, the period of the Israelite kings, and the Babylonian exile and postexilic periods (Machinist 2000, 54–57). Aspects of the Philistines and their culture appearing in the biblical texts deal with their origins, geographical location, economy, political and military organization, religion, and language.[32] However, the historical value of narrative accounts relating to periods prior to the heyday of the kingdom of Judah during the eighth and seventh centuries B.C.E. needs to be considered with caution.

The Philistines first appear in Gen 10:13–14, where their origins are traced to Egypt (but see Amos 9:7 and Jer 47:4, which state that they originated from Caphtor[33]). Several of the most problematic accounts in the book of Genesis featuring the Philistines are Gen 20–21 and 26, which associate them with the patriarch Abraham. Most scholars see this as a later "update" of the original story directed at a later readership.[34] The Philistines are most frequently mentioned in the Deuteronomistic History, where they are depicted as the archenemies of the Israelites. Joshua 13:2–3 mentions the "five lords" of the Philistines: the Gazite, the Ashdodite, the Ashkelonite, the Gittite, and the Ekronite. During the period of the judges, they are depicted as a serious and recurring threat, culminating in the Philistine defeat of the Israelites on Mount Gilboa and the desecration of the bodies of Saul and his sons (1 Sam 31). Following David's defeat of the Philistine hero Goliath (1 Sam 17) and a brief alliance with the Philistines (1 Sam 27), King David successfully subdued the Philistines (2 Samuel).[35] During most of the period of the divided kingdom, they were only a sporadic threat to the Israelites. In the prophetic texts, the Philistines are associated with soothsayers (Isa 2:6), and their destruction is referred to in Amos 1:8 and Zech 9:6. The close correspondence between the mention of the Philistine Pentapolis cities in the biblical account and the discovery of Iron I archaeological remains at these cities is more than coincidental. It should lend credence to claims that historical kernels predating the rise of the Israelite monarchy and contemporary with the ethnogenesis of ancient Israel are embedded in the redacted texts of the Hebrew Bible.

The Archaeological Evidence

In an attempt to define the essence of the Philistines and the factors leading to their arrival on the southern coastal plain of Canaan, this discussion will focus on the earliest manifestations of Philistine material culture as defined archaeologically and textually.[36] The initial appearance of the Philistines is heralded by a locally produced Aegean-style pottery that is somewhat misleadingly referred to as Mycenaean IIIC:1b (or, as is becoming the preferred term, Mycenaean IIIC Middle[37]), since it is not inclusive of all the Aegean-style ceramic types, such as undecorated fine wares and handled cooking jars. Together with this distinctive pottery, other elements of Aegean-style material culture are found at sites identified in the texts as Philistine. These early levels have been most extensively exposed at Tel Miqne-Ekron and Ashdod (table 1), with indications that this initial phase, as yet unexcavated, also exists at Ashkelon, Gath, and Gaza. Locally produced Mycenaean IIIC:1b pottery (fig. 5.3), or what has also been referred to as monochrome due to its single shade of decoration (Stager 1991, 33–36; 1995, 334), has not been found *in situ* at other sites in the southern coastal plain. The later creolization of Philistine material culture is best represented by the typological development of Mycenaean IIIC:1b assemblages into a pottery decorated with red and black paint, termed bichrome. This evolution of the Aegean-style material culture, associated with the expansion of Philistine influence and the appearance of bichrome pottery at dozens of sites in the southern coastal plain and elsewhere, will not be addressed in this study.[38]

Chronology	**Miqne-Ekron (Field INE)**	**Ashdod (Area G)**	**Pottery**
11th century Iron IB	V	XII–XI	Bichrome pottery
12th/11thcentury Iron IB	VI	XIIIA	Myc. IIIC:1b and Bichrome pottery
12th century Iron IA	VII[39]	XIIIB	Myc. IIIC:1b pottery
13th/12th century Transitional Late Bronze IIB/Iron I	VIII	XIV? (Area H, St. 6?)[40]	Miqne-Ekron: Imported Grey Trojan Wares[41]and wheel-made Cypriot pottery (LCIIC/IIIA?)
13th century Late Bronze IIB	IX	XIV	Imported Myc. IIIB and LCIIC Cypriot pottery

Table 1: Comparative Stratigraphic Chart and Associated Pottery Sequences at Tel Miqne-Ekron and Ashdod.

Fig. 5.3. Mycenaean IIIC:1b Pottery from Tel Miqne-Ekron

Settlement Patterns

The southern coastal plain has been surveyed several times over the past few decades, but few of these surveys have been published. Based on the published and unpublished surveys, Israel Finkelstein (1996c; 2000) attempts to reconstruct settlement patterns during the Late Bronze and Iron I periods. The southern coastal plain and the neighboring Shephelah were two of the most densely settled areas in Canaan during the Late Bronze Age, with a well-developed settlement system comprising several large cities, towns, and numerous villages. Over a period spanning the thirteenth–eleventh centuries B.C.E., Finkelstein traces a decrease in the number of settlements from the Late Bronze II to Iron I periods, the latter typified by the appearance of bichrome Philistine pottery. An additional change was the decline in fortunes of several major Late Bronze Age sites such as Lachish and the increased importance of Tel Miqne-Ekron and Ashdod. Although there was a decrease in the number of Iron I sites, several sites, such as Tel Miqne-Ekron, expanded dramatically in size. Thus, based on Finkelstein's calculations, the built-up area during the Late Bronze and Iron I periods remained constant.

Regrettably, since the survey data reflects longer-term settlement patterns, it is of limited value to the question regarding the initial appearance of the Philistines. The earliest phase of Philistine settlement is associated with the presence of locally produced Mycenaean IIIC:1b pottery in significant quantities that dates to a relatively short period of time. The attempt to understand the settlement process, chronology, and development of Philistine culture requires well-excavated and meticulously recorded *in situ* stratified remains resulting from research-driven excavations. Our quest is complicated by the probable co-existence or overlapping of several different cultural complexes related to Egyptian, indigenous Canaanite, and Philistine presence in the southern coastal plain during the twelfth century B.C.E. Due to ongoing debates regarding chronology and the ceramic typology sequence associated with the Late Bronze–Iron I transition, excavations remain the most reliable barometer of early Iron I settlement patterns in the southern coastal plain.

Excavations at Ashdod[42] and Tel Miqne-Ekron,[43] two of the five Philistine cities mentioned in Josh 13:2–3, have uncovered urban settlements characterized by an Aegean-style culture. These levels have not yet been reached at Ashkelon[44] and Tel eṣ-Ṣafi (biblical Gath),[45] but the recovery of Mycenaean IIIC:1b pottery sherds, though not *in situ,* hints at the existence of early Philistine occupation. Limited probes by W. J. Phythian-Adams (1923, 29) at Gaza uncovered examples of Aegean-style pottery. It is noteworthy that locally produced Mycenaean IIIC:1b pottery has not been recovered in significant amounts from other sites in Canaan, reinforcing the identification of the appearance of locally produced Mycenaean IIIC:1b pottery at the Pentapolis cities with the initial arrival of the biblical Philistines.

At Tel Miqne-Ekron, the salient features of the Aegean-style material culture associated with the appearance of the Philistines include an urban city plan, complete with fortifications. Signs of a destruction characterize the end of the Late Bronze Age at both Tel Miqne-Ekron and Ashdod.[46] The later Iron I Philistine city is marked by an architectural break with the preceding Late Bronze Age settlement and is distinguished by its increased size, urban character, and distinctly Aegean-style culture.

Features of the Early Philistine City

Tel Miqne-Ekron (fig. 5.4) forms the core of this discussion because it offers the most complete and uninterrupted stratigraphic sequence spanning the Late Bronze through Iron Ages. Early Philistine remains heralded by the appearance of Mycenaean IIIC:1b in noteworthy quantities are well documented in Fields I, IV, and X.[47] In this chapter, my discussion focuses on Field INE, the only field where the entire sequence of occupation spanning the Late Bronze and Iron Ages was excavated (figs. 5.5–5.6). I offer a brief overview of the settlement plan and main architectural features, a summary of several features of Philistine material culture that reflect its foreign origins, a discussion of cultic practices and cuisine, and, finally, a detailed description of the pottery assemblage, which serves as a case study of my examination of ethnic identity and social boundaries.

Urban Planning

The Iron I period at Tel Miqne-Ekron evidences a well-fortified city that occupied the entire 50-acre mound. The transition from an approximately 10-acre village or small town confined to the northeast acropolis during the thirteenth–early twelfth centuries (Strata IX–VIII; Gittlin 1992; Killebrew 1996b, 21–27) to a large fortified settlement (Stratum VII) is dramatic and marked in its earliest phases by the appearance of a new city plan together with a distinctly Aegean-style material culture. Stratum VII marks the beginning of the urbanization of Tel Miqne-Ekron and its associated Aegean-style material culture. In the initial phase of Stratum VII, a mudbrick wall 3.25 m in width was constructed (Killebrew 1986, 8–9, 24, 137–38). The earliest phase of this fortification system has been uncovered in Fields I and X, the latter located on the western slope of the tel. Inside the Stratum VII city wall, the eastern slope of the acropolis (Field INE) served as an industrial area, as indicated by the excavation of several pottery kilns used in the production of Mycenaean IIIC:1b pottery (fig. 5.7; Killebrew 1996a).

No signs of the Late Bronze Age occupation were found In Field IV, located in the center of the tel. Instead, the early Philistine remains attributed to Stratum VII were constructed directly on top of the Middle Bronze Age city. Stratum VII includes a single-room structure with two pillar bases and a rectangular hearth and a second rectangular room with a brick-lined silo (fig. 5.8). In the following Iron I strata, these two buildings are combined in Strata VI and V to form a large architectural complex (figs. 5.9–5.10; Dothan and Zukerman 2004, 4). The results from the Tel Miqne-Ekron and Ashdod excavations illustrate that the urban

Fig. 5.4. Aerial View of Tel Miqne-Ekron

character of these two sites was well established already in the twelfth century B.C.E. [48]

Installations and Artifacts

Several architectural features and artifacts make their first appearance in Canaan at early Iron I sites associated with the Philistines. They share an Aegean-inspired origin, but, as will be noted below, the most abundant and closest parallels are found on Cyprus and at several coastal Anatolian sites.

Hearths. Fixed hearth installations make their debut in Canaan during the twelfth century at early Philistine sites. Prior to their appearance here, they are well documented in Asia Minor and the east[49] and west[50] Aegean, Cyprus,[51] and Cilicia[52] during the second millennium B.C.E. (for a general discussion, see Karageorghis 1998; 2000, 266). These hearths are circular, rectangular, square, or "keyhole" in shape (Barako 2001, 14–15; table 2). The classic megaron hearth-room first appears in Asia Minor and Crete.

Fig. 5.5. Aerial View of Field INE, Looking East

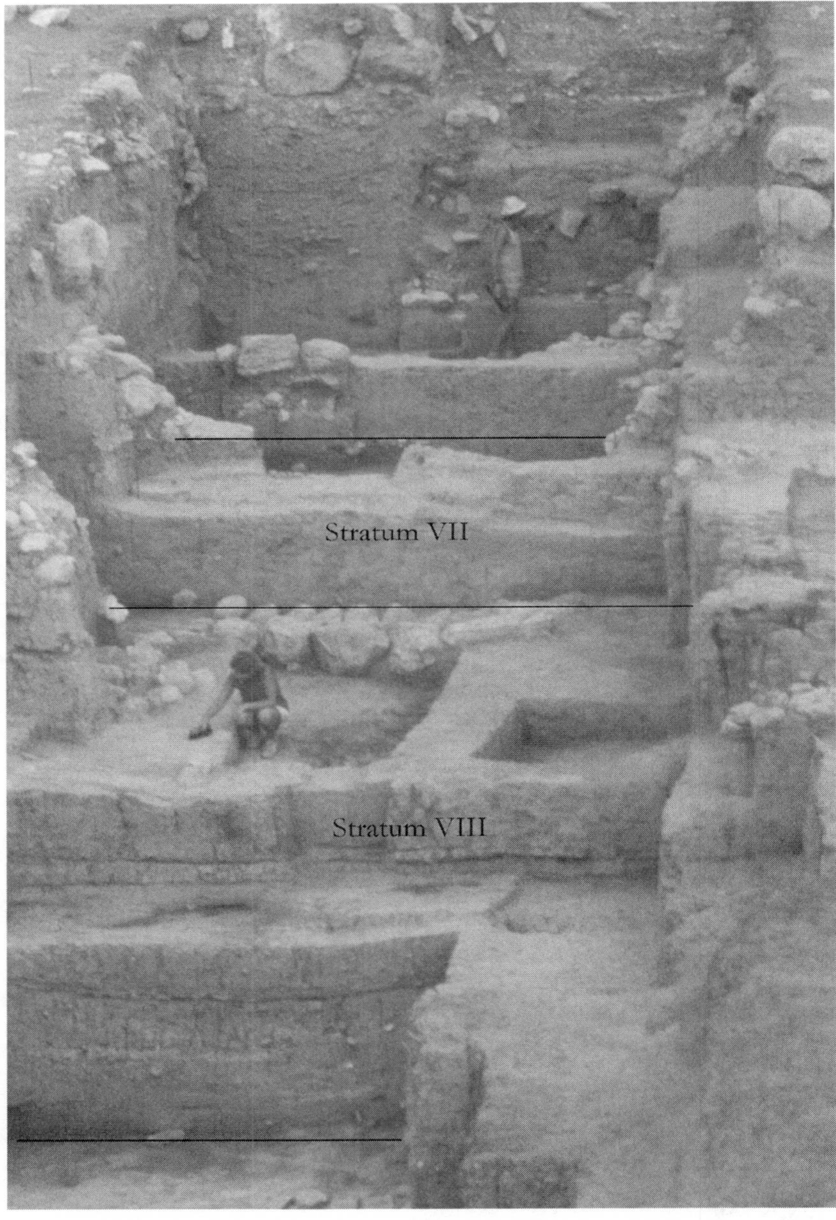

Fig. 5.6. Stratum VIII (End of the Late Bronze Age) and Stratum VII (Early Philistine City), Looking West

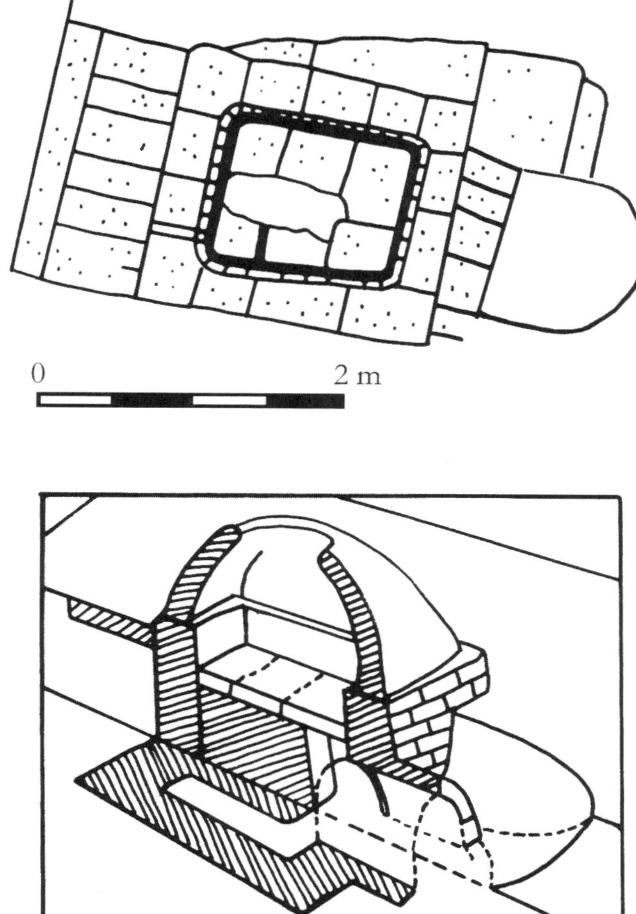

Fig. 5.7. Kiln 4104 Used in the Firing of Mycenaean IIIC:1b Pottery at Tel Miqne-Ekron (Plan and Section through Reconstructed Kiln)

Only later do hearths occur on the Greek mainland, Cyprus, Cilicia, and Philistia. In the Aegean, these hearths are associated with both ceremonial and domestic contexts. George Rethemoitakis (1999, 722) suggests that they fulfilled a multitude of functions, including cooking, social-communal, religious, and industrial. In Late Bronze Age Canaan they are unknown, appearing for the first time during the Iron I at Tel Miqne-Ekron.[53] The earliest hearths at Tel Miqne-Ekron are rectangular in shape (figs. 5.8; 5.11) and appear to be domestic in function. Later hearths are generally circular

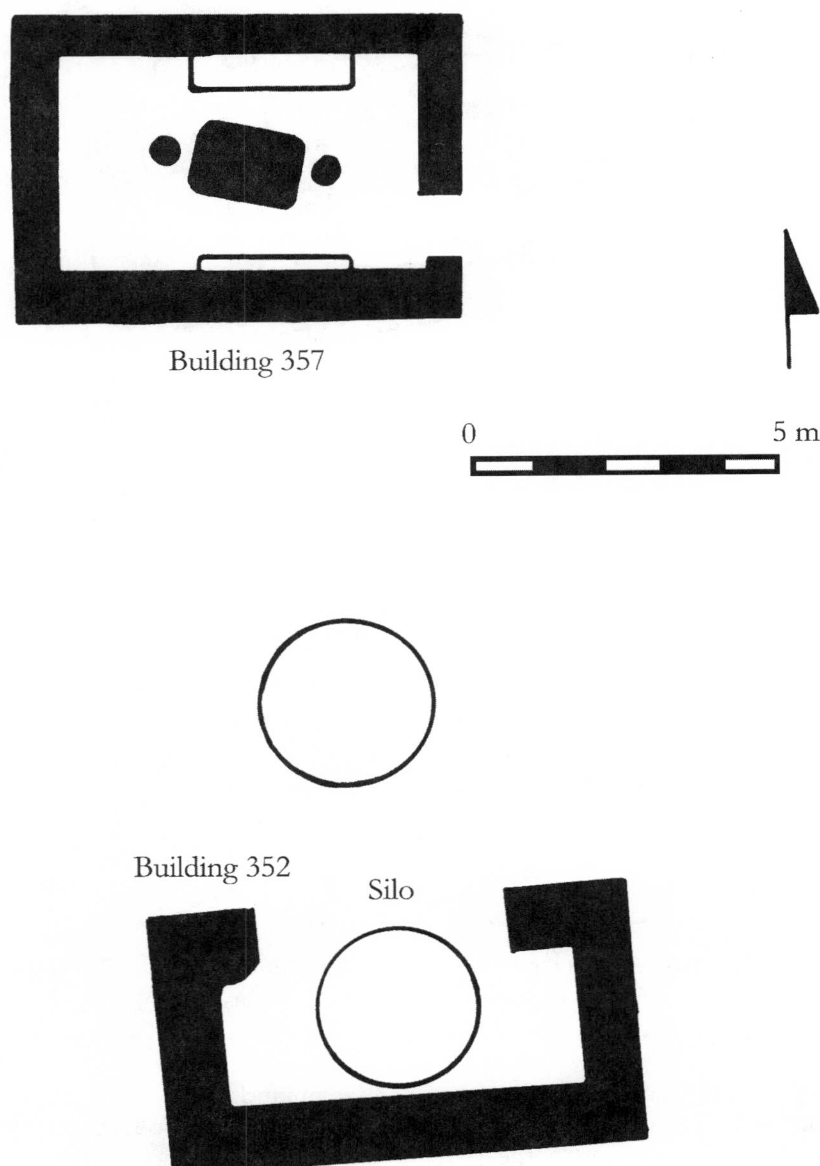

Fig. 5.8. Stratum VII Structures in Field IV at Tel Miqne-Ekron (Note Rectangular Hearth in Room 357)

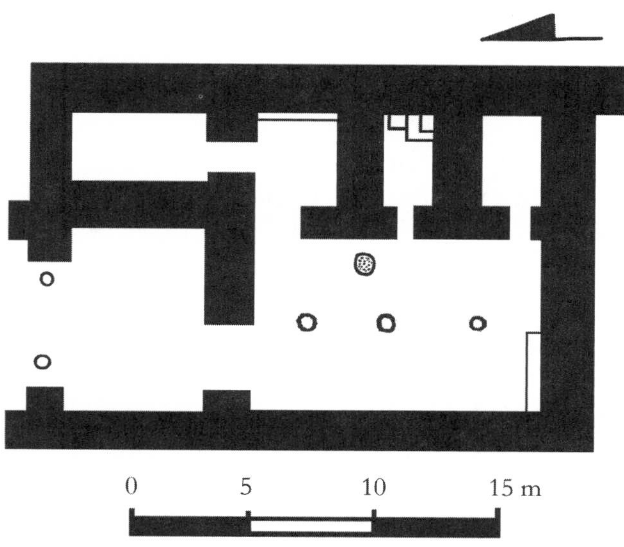

Fig. 5.9. Plan of the Late Iron I Stratum Monumental Building 350 in Field IV at Tel Miqne-Ekron (Note Round Hearth Paved with Pebbles in the Central Room)

Fig. 5.10. Aerial View of Late Iron I Stratum V Monumental Building 350 in Field IV at Tel Miqne-Ekron

in shape (see fig. 5.9). Other hearths have been uncovered in Philistia at Ashkelon (Barako 2001, table 2; Karageorghis 1998, 280), Ashdod (Stratum XIII: M. Dothan 1972, 7), and Tell Qasile (later Iron I: A. Mazar 1986b, 3–6, figs. 2–3; Karageorghis 1998, 279). Although much has been made of the relationship of the Philistine hearths to those found on the Greek mainland (e.g., T. Dothan 2003, 196–201), the best and most numerous parallels to the more modest circular, rectangular, or square domestic hearths typical in Philistia are found on Cyprus.

Bathtubs. Stone and terracotta bathtubs were common during the second millennium in the Aegean and later during the Late Cypriot IIC–III periods on Cyprus (for a detailed discussion, see Karageorghis 2000, 266–74). These bathtubs are generally located near throne rooms, sanctuaries, or bathrooms. In Late Bronze Age Canaan, bathtubs are unknown, making their appearance only during the Iron I at Philistine sites that are associated with Aegean-style material culture (T. Dothan 2003, 202–6 regarding the Philistine evidence), such as Tel Miqne-Ekron (T. Dothan 2003, 204–6), Ashdod (Dothan and Porath 1993, 72, plan 11, pl. 22:2), and Ashkelon (Barako 2001, 15, table 2).

Loomweights. Hundreds of cylinder-shaped unbaked clay reels, usually identified as loomweights, have been recovered from early Philistine levels at Tel Miqne-Ekron (T. Dothan 1995a, 46–47; Bierling 1998, 14, pl. 7b), Ashkelon (Stager 1991, 14–15; 1995, 346; Lass 1994, 32–33), and Ashdod (Dothan and Porath 1993, 64, fig. 24.3–5, pl. 39:4). Identical

Fig. 5.11. Rectangular Hearth from Tel Miqne-Ekron

objects have been found on Cyprus,[54] and there are a few published examples from the Aegean.[55]

Incised Scapulae. Numerous examples of incised bovine scapulae, unknown in Late Bronze Age Canaan, have been recovered from Iron I levels associated with the Philistine settlements at Tel Miqne-Ekron (fig. 5.12; see Gitin and Dothan 1987, 203–4; 1990, 28) and Ashkelon (Barako 2001, 19), as well as from Iron I contexts at Tel Dor.[56] Dozens of incised scapulae are best known from Cyprus, where they have been found in cultic contexts at several Late Cypriot IIIA sites.[57] Although its function remains undetermined, the incised scapula may have been used either for divination (Webb 1985, 324–28)[58] or as part of a musical instrument (Karageorghis 1990a, 159; T. Dothan 1998b, 155; Barako 2001, 18–19). At this point, there is no evidence that scapulomancy was practiced in the Late Bronze Age Mycenaean world.

Female Figurines ("Ashdoda"). The majority of figurines recovered from Iron I levels at Philistine sites are female, suggesting that a goddess played a major role in the cult of Iron I Philistia. The abundance of these female figures contradicts the biblical account that emphasizes the role of a male deity, Dagon, in Philistine religious practices (Machinist 2000, 59–63).[59] The figurines, often identified as a mother goddess, are highly stylized, depicting a woman with a long neck and a small, flattened head in the shape of an inverted cone that resembles a bird head. The nose is pinched, and the eyes and ears are formed out of applied clay pellets. The only complete figurine from an Iron I context is a seated figurine found in Ashdod Stratum XII and nicknamed "Ashdoda." Measuring 17 cm in height, her bichrome decorated body blends into a four-footed flat object

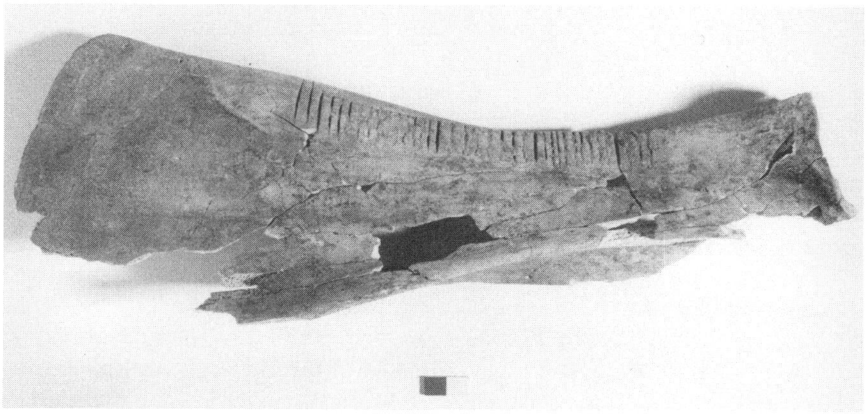

Fig. 5.12. Incised Scapula from Tel Miqne-Ekron

usually interpreted as a throne, couch, or offering table (Hachlili 1971, 129–30; T. Dothan 1982, 234–37; for a recent discussion, see Yasur-Landau 2001). It is noteworthy that none of the published examples originate from the earliest Philistine levels, an observation that has chronological implications.

Numerous scholars have noted the Mycenaean inspiration of Ashdoda,[60] but no less significant possible sources of inspiration originate in Late Cypriot II–III contexts. Already in Late Cypriot II, bird-headed female figurines were fashioned out of Base Ring ware. During the Late Cypriot IIIA, the influence of Mycenaean figurines is evident (Karageorghis 1993; 2001; Yasur-Landau 2001, table 1 for comparisons). Itamar Singer (1989, 26–29, 36–42; 1992b, 432–50), on the other hand, suggests that this deity, who possessed the traits of a mother goddess, was brought by the Philistines from their homeland in Anatolia and should be identified with the mother goddess Kubaba/Kybele (see also Mendenhall 1986, 539–41; Na'aman 1994b, 224–25 and references in n. 17). Based on the comparative material and the lack of exact parallels to Ashdoda, she is best understood as a hybridization of Aegean, Anatolian, and Cypriot styles and influences.[61]

Burials

In the archaeological literature on the material culture of the Philistines, burial in anthropoid clay coffins continues to appear as a mortuary practice used by Philistines.[62] This association is based on the resemblance between the "feathered" Sea Peoples headdress depicted on the Medinet Habu reliefs and the features that appear on several clay anthropoid coffin lids from Tel Beth-shean and Tell el-Farʿah (S).[63] However, no hint of anthropoid coffin burials has been found at any of the Pentapolis cities. In fact, all known anthropoid coffins are found at sites associated with Egyptian outposts in Canaan (see pp. 65–67 above). It is equally unlikely that some of these coffins contained the remains of Philistines or other Sea Peoples who served as mercenaries at Egyptian garrison sites in Canaan. With the exception of a few reported but as yet unpublished intramural infant burials recovered from early Philistine levels at Tel Miqne-Ekron and Ashkelon (oral communication by Seymour Gitin and Lawrence Stager, excavation directors), thus far no burials or cemeteries have been located at any of the Philistine Pentapolis cities nor at sites that can be clearly identified as Philistine. One possible suggestion is that the Philistines practiced cremation, a type of burial practice well known in Anatolia and found at the eleventh-century cemetery at Azor in the southern coastal plain.[64] However, this proposal also remains speculative due to the lack of any evidence regarding mortuary practices in clear early Philistine contexts.

Cuisine

Changes in cuisine mark the transition from the Late Bronze to Iron I levels at Philistine sites, signaled both by the faunal evidence and the appearance of Aegean-style table wares and cooking pots (see below). During the Late Bronze Age, sheep/goat faunal remains typically form the bulk of animal bones recovered from Canaan, with few, if any, pig bones. *Sus* (pig) makes up only 1–3 percent of the faunal material analyzed from Late Bronze Age Tel Miqne-Ekron (Lev-Tov 2000, 82, table 5). With the establishment of urban Iron I twelfth-century settlements at both Tel Miqne-Ekron and Ashkelon, pig bones make up over 15 percent of the assemblage, highlighting an increase in the consumption of pig and cattle at the expense of sheep and goats.[65] This increase in pork consumption has not been observed at contemporary sites in Canaan outside the southern coastal plain.

Recent theoretical work on meat consumption emphasizes ecological and socioeconomic factors as the primary reasons for pig consumption.[66] However, in the Philistine case study, ecological and socioeconomic changes that are usually attributed to pig husbandry are not clearly evident in the archaeological evidence. Rather, cultural practices appear to be the primary cause of the change in subsistence strategies reflected in the decline of sheep and goat in favor of pig and cattle. But caution is advised regarding the use of this data to determine a specific ethnic identity for the Philistines, since pork consumption was widespread in the Bronze Age Aegean,[67] Anatolia,[68] and Europe.[69] In spite of the difficulties in attributing ethnicity to pig consumption, in this case it can be used as indicating a social boundary separating Philistine enclaves from the surrounding indigenous populations. It remains unclear whether the Philistine diet was a reflection of ethnicity or a result of new settlement strategies that formed social and economic regional boundaries. Considered in its broader cultural context, the sudden increase in pork consumption at several sites associated with the Philistines in the southern coastal plain does provide convincing evidence for significant migration of peoples whose origins lay outside of Canaan.

Typology of Philistine Pottery

Aegean-style pottery found in the southern coastal plain of Canaan has long served as the ethnic marker for the Philistines. Initially bichrome pottery formed the focus of archaeological research on the Philistines (T. Dothan 1982, 94–218). However, as more recent excavations have demonstrated, Mycenaean IIIC:1b pottery, the precursor of bichrome pottery, signifies the appearance of the Philistines. Monochrome Mycenaean IIIC:1b pottery differs from indigenous ceramic Canaanite traditions typologically (forms and decorative motifs) and technologically.[70] This discussion includes a description of Aegean-style pottery associated with the earliest Philistine levels. It is followed by a summary of indigenous pottery forms that appear together with the intrusive Aegean-inspired shapes but continue a local Late Bronze Age Canaanite tradition.

Typology of Aegean-Style Pottery. Several detailed discussions of Aegean-style (Mycenaean IIIC:1b pottery and its associated wares) Philistine pottery produced in the southern coastal plain of Canaan have appeared in recent years (Killebrew 2000; Dothan and Zukerman 2004).[71] I focus on the earliest appearance of this pottery, best represented by the well-stratified excavations in Field INE at Tel Miqne-Ekron.[72]

Based primarily on vessel proportion and morphology, the assemblage from Tel Miqne-Ekron can be grouped typologically according to two basic functional categories that probably reflect the primary use of these ceramic vessels: (I) kitchen wares, which include table wares and cooking wares; and (II) containers, which comprise one shape—the stirrup jar—a well-known Aegan-style specialty container. A third category, varia (III), includes Aegean-style shapes that are rare in the Philistine repertoire. The assemblage comprises decorated (Mycenaean IIIC:1b) and undecorated (plain and coarse wares) vessels whose shapes are Aegean- and/or Cypriot-inspired.

Category I—Kitchen Wares: Bowls. The Aegean-style bowls included in this family (AS 1–4) are all semihemispherical to hemispherical in shape, with two horizontal handles, and have no locally produced Canaanite antecedents (Killebrew 2000, 234–39). Bowl AS 1a (fig. 5.13) is a small semihemispherical bowl with two flat horizontal strap handles at the rim or just below it (see also Dothan and Zukerman 2004, 7, Type A). It can be undecorated or decorated on the interior and exterior with simple horizontal bands, occasionally with spirals on the interior of the base. This shape is common in the early Iron I levels at Tel Miqne-Ekron, but it is rare in Canaan. Only one similar example is published from Ashdod (Stratum XIIIb: M. Dothan and Porath 1993, fig. 14:8). This bowl type is most common and best known from Cyprus.[73] Bowl AS 1b, similar in concept to AS 1a, is distinguished from Bowl AS 1a by is slight carination underneath the horizontal handle.[74] Bowl AS 2 (fig. 5.13) is a deeper and rounded version of AS 1, with a more restricted vessel opening and flat horizon strap handles.[75] Bowl AS 3 (fig. 5.13) is a carinated semihemispherical bowl with horizontal handles (see also Dothan and Zukerman 2004, 7–8, Type C). This bowl is well known from early Iron I levels at sites in the southern coastal plain[76] and is popular on Cyprus, the southern coast of Anatolia and coastal Syria, and the Aegean.[77] Bowl AS 4 (figs. 5.13–5.14) is a hemispherical (bell-shaped) bowl with horizontal handles and ring base (Killebrew 2000, 236–39; Dothan and Zukerman 2004, 8–12, Type D). Often termed a skyphos, it is a well-known type in the southern

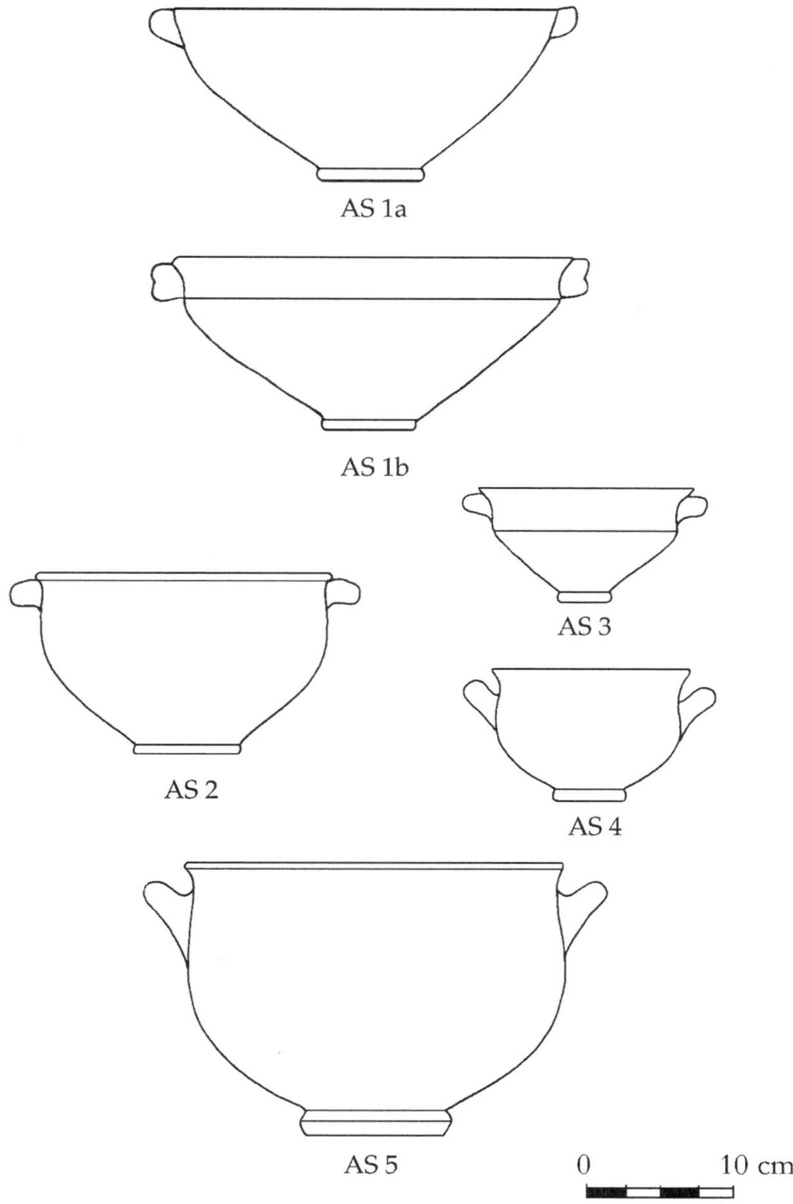

Fig. 5.13. Philistine Pottery Forms AS 1–5

coastal plain,[78] throughout the Aegean,[79] on Cyprus,[80] and at several sites along the eastern Mediterranean coast.[81] The decorative treatment on the bowls from Philistia is quite similar to that on bowls from eastern Cyprus and Cilicia.[82] However, the shape is first known in the Aegean, indicating that Form AS 4 has its antecedents in the Mycenaean world.

Category I—Kitchen Wares: Kraters. The three basic krater forms presented here, AS 5–7, are distinct from the same family of forms known in Canaan during the Late Bronze IIB and Iron IA periods (Killebrew 2000, 239–40). Krater AS 5 (fig. 5.13) is a hemispherical krater. In literature relating to the Philistines, this shape is termed a bell-shaped krater (T. Dothan 1982, 106–15). Krater AS 5 equals the larger version of Furumark's Form 80, or a Deep Rounded Bowl with Horizontal Handles.[83] It is a common shape in the southern coastal plain at sites associated with the Philistines,[84] on Cyprus,[85] and in the Aegean.[86] Krater AS 6 (fig. 5.15), a deep krater-basin with slightly everted rim, is a straight-walled vessel with horizontal handles, thickened rim, and flat base that rises slightly in the center (see also Dothan and Zukerman 2004, 16–21, Form F). The undecorated vessel, often termed a kalathos (Kling 1989b, 145–47, fig. 10c), is found with Mycenaean IIIC:1b and bichrome assemblages at Tel Miqne-Ekron and Ashdod,[87] marking a clear departure from typical Canaanite-style kraters. Its closest parallels originate from Cyprus and differ from similar shapes found on the Greek mainland and west Aegean.[88] Krater AS 7 (fig. 5.15) is a shallow krater tray with a slightly everted, straight-sided vessel profile and high horizontal handle. This form is rare in Philistia but was recovered in Stratum VII, Field INE, at Tel Miqne-Ekron (Killebrew 2000, 12.3:2; see also Dothan and Zukerman 2004, 28, Type L).[89]

Category I—Kitchen Wares: Juglets. Juglet AS 8 (fig. 5.15) is spouted with a globular body profile and a basket handle situated at a right angle to the spout over the opening at the top of the vessel. Examples are known from Tel Miqne-Ekron and Ashdod,[90] Cyprus,[91] and the eastern Aegean, where, it is suggested, this particular shape first developed (Killebrew 2000, 240; Dothan and Zukerman 2004, 24–28, Type J).[92]

Category I—Kitchen Wares: Jugs. Jug AS 9 (fig. 5.15) is characterized by its tall concave neck, often with a trefoil mouth. It is usually decorated with painted linear bands at the rim. Several examples are known from Iron I contexts at Tel Miqne-Ekron and Ashdod.[93] Jugs with and without trefoil mouths appear in the Aegean[94] and Cyprus,[95] but it is noteworthy that jugs with a trefoil spout are an eastern embellishment of a Mycenaean form (Killebrew 2000, 242; see also Dothan and Zukerman 2004, 22, Type H).[96]

Category I—Kitchen Wares: Cooking Pots. The cooking pot evidences a total break with a millennium-long Canaanite tradition (Killebrew 1999b; 2000, 242–43). As noted above, considered together with the faunal

Fig. 5.14. Philistine Pottery Form AS 4

evidence, the new type of cooking vessel is significant since it indicates a change in cuisine. Cooking Jug AS 10 (fig. 5.15) is globular in shape, with a flat base. One or, occasionally, two vertical handles are attached to the rim and shoulder. The rim is usually a simple or slightly thickened everted rim. Form AS 10 first appears in Stratum VII at Tel Miqne-Ekron and is the most popular cooking vessel in the early Iron I levels at Ekron, almost replacing the indigenous cooking pot of the Late Bronze and Iron I periods. It also appears at other sites associated with the Philistines.[97] Both single- and double-handled cooking jugs are well known in Cyprus during the Late Cypriot IIC and IIIA periods.[98] There is no doubt that the inspiration for this general cooking pot shape is the Aegean. However, already in the Late Cypriot IIC this cooking pot was adopted on Cyprus, increasing in popularity during the Late Cypriot IIIA. Since the closest parallels to these cooking pots are found on Cyprus, where they chronologically precede the Philistine examples, it is preferable to see Cyprus and the surrounding region as the direct source for these cooking pots, while recognizing its earlier Aegean origins (contra Dothan and Zukerman 2004, 28–31, Type P, who suggest a direct Aegean source).

Category II—Containers. Specialty container AS 11 (fig. 5.16), or stirrup jar, is a well-known Aegean shape. It is a small jar with two handles that extend from the top of the closed ("false") neck to the shoulder. The

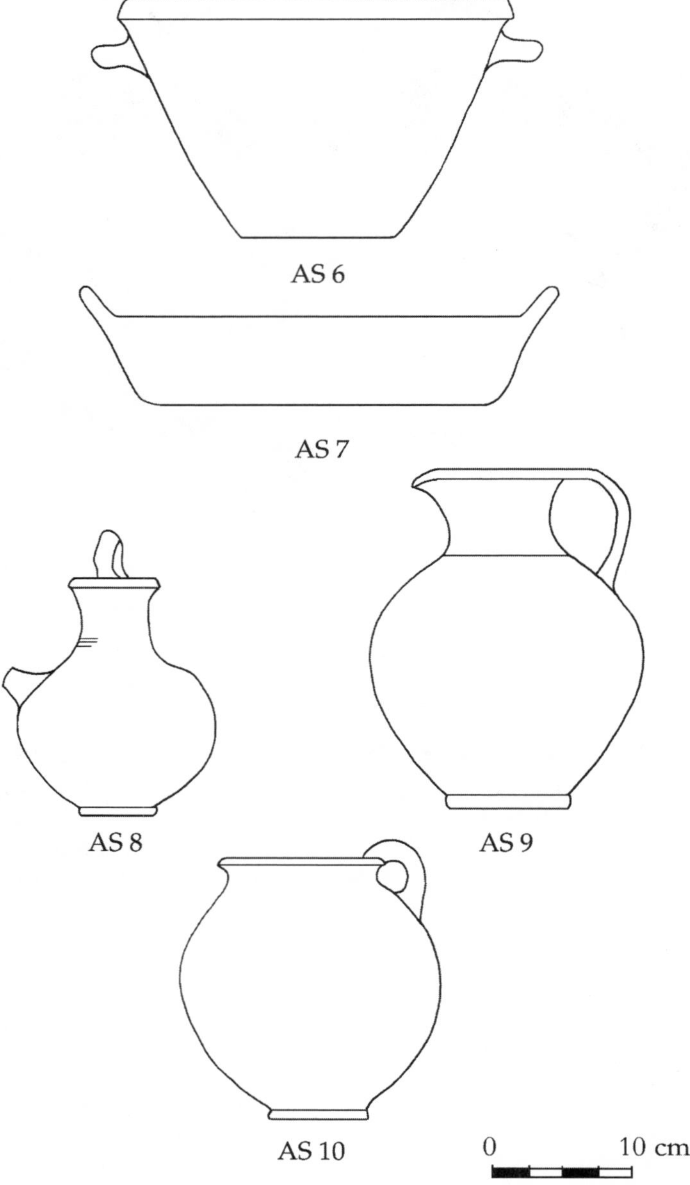

Fig. 5.15. Philistine Pottery Forms AS 6–10

liquid contents of this small jar were poured through a spout located on the shoulder of the vessel. Form AS 11 has a long history in the Aegean and on Cyprus (Kling 1989b, 161–65), already making its appearance in the locally produced Mycenaean IIIC repertoire in Philistia (see Killebrew 2000, fig. 12.3:10; Dothan and Zukerman 2004, 28, Type K) and becoming increasingly popular in the later Iron I bichrome assemblage (T. Dothan 1982, 115–25).

Category III—Varia. Several Aegean-style forms appear in small numbers and are uncommon shapes in the repertoire of Aegean-style pottery in Philistia. These miscellaneous types are assigned to varia (Category III). A rare Aegean-inspired form at Philistine sites is the kylix, designated in this typology as AS 12 (fig. 5.16; Dothan and Zukerman 2004, 22, Type G, fig. 27:2, and see parallels there). It should be noted that the kylix appears on Cyprus already in thirteenth-century LC IIC contexts and continues through the LC IIIB period (Kling 1989b, 141–43). The strainer jug AS 13 makes its first appearance in Philistia in the Iron I period (fig. 5.16; Dothan and Zukerman 2004, 24, Type I, fig. 30:2). This form is known in the Aegean and Cyprus, but recent excavations on Cyprus indicate that the strainer jug first developed there (contra Dothan and Zukerman 2004, 24).[99] Small fragments of what has been identified as a pyxis (Dothan and Zukerman 2004, 28, fig. 3:9) and a bottle (Dothan and Zukerman 2004, 28, fig. 30:10) were also recovered from unstratified contexts at Tel Miqne-Ekron.[100]

Typology of Canaanite-style Pottery. Although Aegean-style pottery forms dominate the earliest Philistine occupation at Tel Miqne-Ekron, especially Stratum VIIA in Field INE, select Late Bronze Age ceramic types appear alongside the Iron I Aegean-inspired assemblages. Several of the shapes are forms known throughout the eastern Mediterranean during the thirteenth century, especially on Cyprus, and can be considered part of an "international" pottery style. The most ubiquitous form is the Canaanite storage jar (see CA 21, pp. 123–25 above). Another international shape known in the eastern Mediterranean during the Late Bronze Age is the flask (see CA 28, pp. 125, 127 above). Two bowls that developed out of the Late Bronze Age Canaanite tradition include the cyma bowl (see CA 7, p. 115 above) and the hemispherical bowl (see CA 8, pp. 115–18 above). Sherds belonging to Canaanite style cooking pots (see CA 18 and 19, p. 119 above) appear in small numbers and could be intrusive. Canaanite-style lamps (see CA 37, p. 132 above), which are also known on Cyprus, also occasionally appear. The types and quantities of Iron I indigenous pottery increase in popularity during the following Strata VI and V and illustrate the process of creolization that was well underway following the first generation of Philistine colonists.

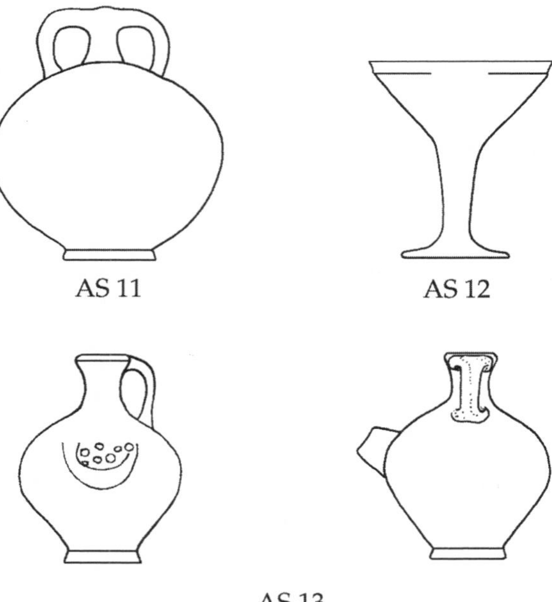

Fig. 5.16. Philistine Pottery Forms AS 11–13

Decorative Motifs. The motifs adorning Mycenaean IIIC:1b pottery represent a new tradition with roots in the Aegean region (for a detailed discussion and parallels, see Dothan and Zukerman 2004, 37–41). Noteworthy in the initial Philistine phase is the paucity of motifs borrowed from the Canaanite decorative tradition (see pp. 132, 136 above). Linear patterns (fig. 5.17a) are a ubiquitous design throughout the early Philistine repertoire of decorated Aegean-style pottery. Common nonlinear motifs include antithetic spirals (fig. 5.17b), stemmed spirals (fig. 5.17c; filled with a net pattern: fig. 5.18c), stemmed tongues (fig. 5.17d), antithetic tongues (figs. 5.14, 5.18a), and scales and zigzags (fig. 5.18d). One unusual decoration that appears occasionally on bowls is a horizontal wavy line comprising interconnected inverted U-shapes (fig. 5.18b; Dothan and Zukerman 2004, 41). More complex decorative compositions are arranged in horizontal registers delineated by vertical bands (triglyphs) and filled by designs that include checkerboards and lozenges (fig. 5.18f). Figurative motifs such as fish (fig. 5.18e) and birds (fig. 5.18f) are less common during the monochrome Mycenaean IIIC:1b phase. These more frequently decorate later bichrome pottery.

All these motifs are originally Aegean inspired, though variations on these themes are widespread throughout the west and east Aegean as well as on Cyprus.

Philistine Pottery Technology. The technology used to produce Aegean-style pottery at Philistine sites also represents a clear break with millennia-long potting practices (for a summary of Late Bronze Age potting techniques, see pp. 136–37 above). These changes are evident in all phases of the pottery production sequence, including clay preparation, formation techniques, and firing temperatures (for a detailed discussion, see Killebrew 1998b, 397–401; 1999a; 1999b). Potters producing the Aegean-style Mycenaean III C:1b pottery sought out a new clay source, preferring a very calcareous local clay comprised of loess and chalk with very little or no temper to fashion their pots. Examination of this ware under the petrographic microscope reveals only small quantities of silty quartz, with no sandy quartz or iron oxide in the clay matrix. Petrographic thin sections and infrared spectrometry of Mycenaean IIIC:1b pottery indicates that large quantities of finely crushed calcite (as much as 30 percent of the paste) were added to the natural clay, creating a distinctly pale off-white or light pink appearance after firing. The Aegean-style cooking jug also differs from its Canaanite predecessors, lacking the generous quantities of shell and limestone temper that characterize Canaanite cooking pot wares. Instead, the Philistine potter added sand-sized quartz, representing the importation of a new technological tradition.

Various formation techniques were used during the Late Bronze II period to manufacture a rich variety of pottery shapes (see Franken and Kalsbeek 1969, 118–32; Magrill and Middleton 1997, 70–71). The Iron I assemblage of delicate Aegean-style pottery was produced solely on the fast wheel. This is observable in the appearance of spiral rhythmic grooves and ridges on the interior of the bases and the preferred orientation of inclusions parallel to the surface. The preference for matt decoration on Philistine pottery contrasts with the lustrous surface treatment of mainland Greek Mycenaean IIIC Middle pottery. Nonlustrous matt decorative motifs also dominate Cypriot Mycenaean IIIC:1b decorated pottery.

Firing is the least predictable stage of pottery production. Initial investigation of Mycenaean IIIC:1b firing temperatures, using infrared spectrometry, stable isotopes of carbon and oxygen, and refiring experiments, indicates a relatively low firing temperature of about 600 degrees Celsius (Nissenbaum and Killebrew 1995).[101] The pottery kilns associated with the production of Aegean-style wares at Tel Miqne-Ekron also represent a previously unknown technological tradition (Killebrew 1996a). The earliest kiln at Tel Miqne-Ekron is an unusual

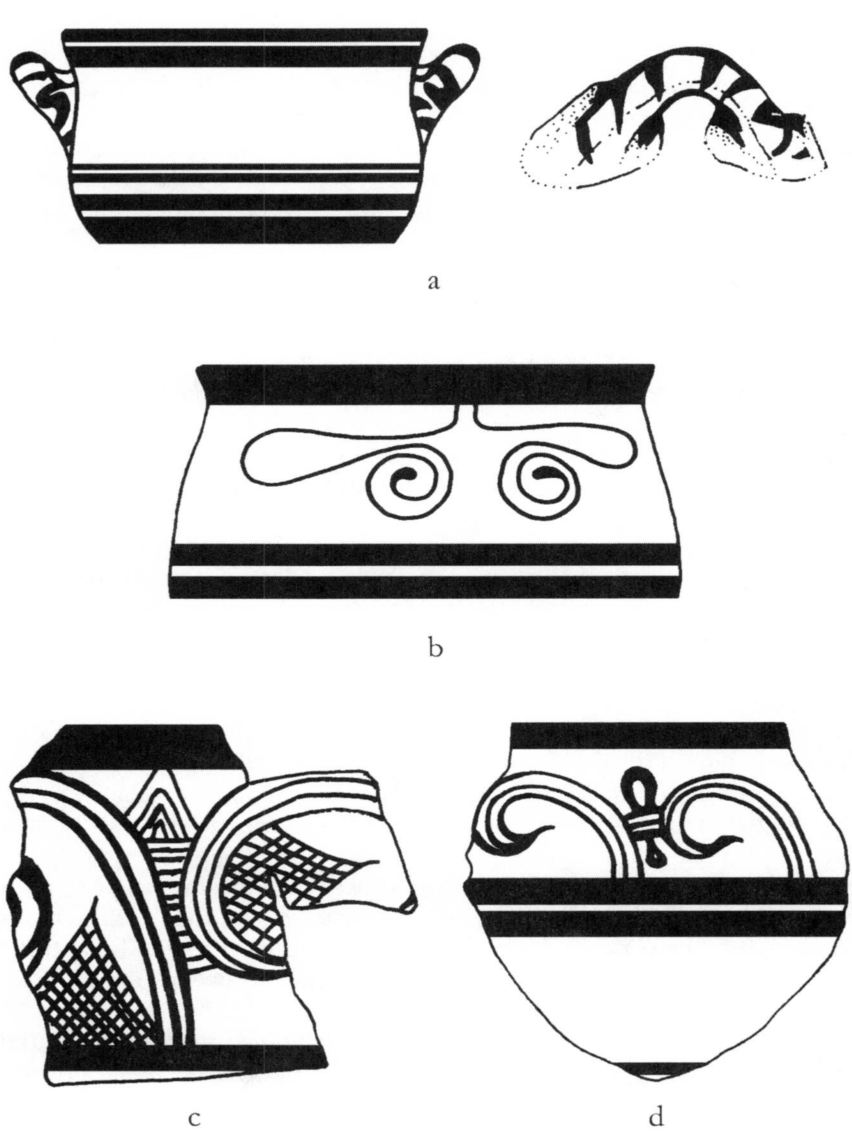

Fig. 5.17. Philistine Pottery Motifs

Fig. 5.18. Philistine Pottery Motifs

square-shaped furnace (fig. 5.7). All the kilns used in the production of early Philistine pottery at Tel Miqne-Ekron lacked vitrification in the interior firing box, confirming a relatively low firing temperature for this pottery.

This examination of Iron I Philistine pottery typology and technology illustrates the dramatic break with previous Late Bronze Age typological and technological traditions. Differences are demonstrated in all aspects of typology (shape and decoration) and in all stages of the pottery-production sequence (selection and preparation of local clays, vessel formation techniques, and firing techniques). Although Mycenaean IIIC:1b pottery on Cyprus and in Philistia continues the traditions that originated in the Aegean, there are subtle differences shared by Aegean-style assemblages on Cyprus and in Philistia. These include the limited repertoire of Aegean-inspired shapes that are shared by both regions, cooking jars that differ from those in the west Aegean, shared decorative motifs, and technology.[102] The ceramic typology and technology associated with the appearance of the Philistines provides overwhelming evidence for a large-scale migration of people to the southern coast of Canaan during the twelfth century B.C.E. , most likely originating from Cyprus and perhaps coastal Anatolia.[103]

Synthesis

Questions related to Philistine origins and chronology have dominated research on the Philistines for the past century. Following a brief review of these theories, I conclude with several observations and suggestions regarding the key issues related to the how and why of Philistine colonization.

Philistine Origins

Scholars have proposed four main theories regarding the location of Philistine origins: (1) Illyria via the Balkans, (2) the western Aegean region, (3) the eastern Aegean region, and (4) the eastern Mediterranean. Gaston Maspero (1896) first suggested a mass migration from Illyria into the southern Balkans region as the initial force that set into motion a series of migrations of Phrygians and Dorians to Asia Minor and the Aegean, resulting in movements of Sea Peoples into the eastern Mediterranean. Based on the philological connection between the name "Philistine" and the name "Pelasgians" of classical sources, later scholars such as G. Bonfante (1946), G. A. Lehmann (1985, 42–49), Fritz Schachermeyr (1984, 162), and Mario Liverani (1988, 632) proposed that the Philistines originated from the Adriatic coast of the Balkans.[104] There is little archaeological evidence to support a direct Illyrian origin for the Philistines, although several proponents of the various Aegean theories postulate that the Philistine tribes are ultimately of Indo-European origin that subsequently continued on to the west Aegean and/or the east Aegean region of western Anatolia.

A west Aegean origin, specifically mainland Greece and Crete, remains the most popular theory, especially among archaeologists working in this region.[105] Proponents of this theory argue for an Aegean homeland for the Philistines based on the similarities evident between the Aegean and Philistine material cultures (e.g., artifacts [especially pottery], cultic practices, and architecture) and the biblical tradition that relates them to Caphtor. What remains unexplained is why and how direct contact was reestablished with the west Aegean after the cessation of mainland Greek imports to the east sometime during the mid to late thirteenth century B.C.E. As indicated by recent pottery provenience studies, by the end of the Late Bronze Age Mycenaean IIIB:2 imports to the Levant originating in the east Aegean and Cyprus dominated, and direct contact between the west Aegean and the Levant had ceased several decades before the appearance of the Philistines.

A third theory traces Philistine origins to the eastern Aegean, including western Anatolia and its off-shore islands. In the past century, western Anatolia had often been proposed for the origins of various groups of Sea Peoples, such as the *Shardana* and *Shekelesh* (Maspero 1896; Hall 1901–2, 181). Asia Minor, specifically Caria, Pamphylia, or Cappadocia, was suggested already in 1914 by R. A. S. Macalister (1914, 22, 25) as the homeland of the Philistines. More recently, Itamar Singer (1988b, 243–44), arguing primarily from linguistic evidence, has proposed western Anatolia as the homeland of the Philistines.[106]

A fourth theory, specifying southeast Anatolia (especially Cilicia) and/or Cyprus in the eastern Mediterranean, has not been clearly distinguished in past literature from the eastern Aegean theory. This theory was embraced by Gerald A. Wainwright (1931a; 1931b; 1939; 1963), who located Caphtor in Asia Minor. Based on linguistic and textual evidence[107]and a comparative analysis of the material culture remains (see above)[108], I propose a variation on this theory and contend that Cyprus and possibly the surrounding regions are most likely the original point of departure of the Philistines. This is not to detract from the obvious fact that the ultimate inspiration of Aegean-style material culture in the east and Philistia lie in the Aegean, albeit removed by several generations.

Philistine Chronology

A second issue of debate is the date of the initial entry of the Philistines and/or Sea Peoples along the southern coastal plain. Currently there are three main schools of thought, which may be designated as "high," middle," and "low" chronologies.[109] The high chronology, or two-wave theory, interprets the appearance of Mycenaean IIIC:1b pottery in Philistia as a result of an earlier, proto-Philistine wave of Sea Peoples who settled along Israel's southern coast before Ramesses III's defeat and expulsion of the Philistines and other Sea Peoples in his eighth year.[110] This would date the appearance of Mycenaean IIIC:1b pottery to roughly 1200 B.C.E., shortly after the reign of Merneptah.

The middle chronology, a view supported by most scholars working in the Levant, dates the appearance of the Philistines in Philistia to the eighth year of Ramesses III, based on the Medinet Habu and Papyrus Harris I texts.[111] Proponents of the middle chronology attribute the appearance of Mycenaean IIIC:1b, the early Philistine pottery, to approximately 1175 B.C.E. and bichrome pottery, which developed out of Mycenaean IIIC:1b pottery, to the mid-twelfth century. As discussed above, there are no objective archaeological grounds to accept Ramesses III's campaign in his eighth year as marking the time that the Philistines appeared in Philistia and constructed their urban centers. A second difficulty is placing the arrival of the Philistines and the establishment of the Pentapolis cities during the reign of Ramesses III, when the Egyptians still maintained a strong presence in the southern coastal plain. Lastly, this theory is becoming more problematic in light of the increasing consensus that Mycenaean IIIC:1b should be equated to Mycenaean IIIC Middle pottery, which is dated to the mid-twelfth century B.C.E., some thirty to forty years later than Ramesses III's eighth year (for a discussion, see Warren and Hankey 1989, 165–69, esp. 168).

The third proposal, or low chronology, maintains that the Philistines, bringing with them their distinctive material culture whose hallmark was Mycenaean IIIC:1b pottery, appeared only after the reign of Ramesses III and the retreat of Egyptian forces from southern Canaan.[112] This would place the appearance of Mycenaean IIIC:1b pottery somewhat later, at roughly 1140 B.C.E., and, as a result, would lower the date of the appearance of bichrome pottery.[113] The low chronology best fits the dating of Mycenaean IIIC Middle at other sites in the eastern Mediterranean and provides a more reasonable dating of bichrome pottery to the eleventh century, based on the Late Bronze II–Iron I stratigraphic sequences at both Tel Miqne-Ekron and Ashdod. At this time, there are no conclusive absolute chronological indicators from Philistine levels at the Pentapolis cities, so the chronological debate remains unresolved.

The How and Why of Philistine Colonization: Concluding Remarks

The closing decades of the Late Bronze Age marked the gradual disintegration of the "age of internationalism," a world system that had connected east and west through much of the fourteenth and thirteenth centuries B.C.E. (see chapters 1 and 3 above). Following the cessation of trade relations and imports from the west Aegean during the final decades of the thirteenth century B.C.E. , economic relations continued between the Levant, Cyprus, and the east Aegean well into the early twelfth century. At several locations on coastal Anatolia and Cyprus, Mycenaean IIIB pottery was being locally manufactured already during the thirteenth century. This gradual adoption and production of Aegean-style material culture in the east Aegean and Cyprus should be attributed to the impact of long-term economic, cultural, and social ties between east and west that flowed in a multidirectional manner. These contacts undoubtedly included small-scale immigration and movements of peoples in both directions, resulting in a gradual diffusion of the style, technology, and ideology of Mycenaean-style culture to the east. In contrast, the later appearance of Aegean-style material culture in the southern coastal plain associated with the Philistines was the consequence of large-scale population movements by prosperous descendants of these "Mycenaeanized" eastern populations who migrated to the southern coastal plain of Canaan. These colonizers of an increasingly unstable Canaan established prosperous colonies sometime during the first half of the twelfth century, coinciding with the decline of Egyptian imperialism in the region.

Regarding the development of Aegean-style Philistine culture, I propose three main phases. (1) The first stage was the initiated by a large-scale migration of peoples who brought with them an Aegean-style culture whose closest parallels are on Cyprus and Cilicia. This included the hallmark of Philistine culture, Aegean-style pottery (Mycenaean IIIC:1b, undecorated Aegean-style plain wares, and cooking wares), as well as numerous other Aegean-inspired material objects and customs. My suggested chronological framework for this event or series of events is Iron IA in the first half of the twelfth century B.C.E. , most likely somewhat late in the reign of Ramesses III (Tel Miqne-Ekron Stratum VII; Ashdod Stratum XIIIb).

(2) Following the first generation of colonists, the Philistines' material culture underwent a process of "creolization," best demonstrated by the development of bichrome Philistine pottery. Later Iron I Philistine pottery increasingly incorporated indigenous features, and the percentages of indigenous Iron I pottery increased. My suggested chronological framework for the beginning of this process is Iron IB, the late twelfth

and eleventh centuries B.C.E. (Tel Miqne-Ekron Strata VI–V; Ashdod Strata XIIIa–XI).

(3) During the Iron II (tenth–seventh centuries B.C.E.), the Philistines completed the process of acculturation with the surrounding indigenous culture (Stone 1995). By the end of the Iron II, the Philistines had lost much of their distinctiveness as expressed in their material culture (see Gitin 1998; 2003; 2004 and bibliography there). My suggested chronological framework for Philistine acculturation spans the tenth to seventh centuries B.C.E. (Tel Miqne-Ekron Strata IV–I; Ashdod Strata X–VI).

The biblical Philistines can best be defined as the descendants and inheritors of the highly sophisticated and cosmopolitan culture of the Late Bronze Age Aegean world. Rather than a diffusion of Aegean-style culture over a large geographical region, as proposed by simplistic hyper-diffusionist theories of invading conquerors or refugees, the spread of this culture is more likely the result of gradual stimulus diffusion that occurred over the course of more than a century of interaction between west and east. Although one cannot discount violent encounters as one means of cultural transmission, the adoption of Mycenaean-style culture in the east was gradual, fueled by the economic world system that characterized the region during the Late Bronze Age. The demise of the Mycenaean palace system and the inevitable instability that ensued undoubtedly encouraged additional dislocation and movements of peoples whose histories are vaguely remembered in the later Homeric epics and the Bible. The legacy of the age of internationalism was prolonged in the east by the large-scale migration of enterprising peoples seeking their fortunes on the coast of southern Canaan. They most likely originated from Cyprus or other archaeologically less explored peripheral areas in the east—regions that survived the upheavals of the late thirteenth century and emerged as winners following the decline and collapse of the Late Bronze Age empires. A biased history of one of these groups, the Philistines, has been preserved in the biblical account in their role as the uncultured archenemies of the Israelites.

Notes to Chapter 5

1. Webster's New Collegiate Dictionary defines a Philistine as "a crass, prosaic often priggish individual guided by material rather than intellectual or artistic values." For a discussion of the history of the negative connotations associated with the Philistines and the incorporation of this word in our modern discourse, see Jobling and Rose 1996.

2. Joshua 13:2–3 specifically mentions Gaza, Ashkelon, Ashdod, Gath, and Ekron as cities ruled by Philistine lords. The term *Pentapolis* is often used to refer to these five cities. At each of these sites, especially Ashdod and Ekron, where large-scale excavations have uncovered twelfth-century levels, Aegean-style material culture has been found in abundance.

3. See T. Dothan 1983; 1989; 1995a, b; 1998b; 2000; 2003; Stager 1991, 36–37; 1995, 337; A. Mazar 1988; Betancourt 2000; Yasur-Landau 2003a; 2003c; see also the discussion below.

For a discussion of the evidence supporting large-scale "seaborne" migration, see Barako 2001; 2003. But see Yasur-Landau 2003a; 2003c, who presents evidence for a land-based migration. Cf. Mendenhall 1986, 541–42, who proposes both a sea and land migration.

4. For recent attempts to address these questions, see Bauer 1998; Bunimovitz 1998; E. S. Sherratt 1998; Barako 2001; Yasur-Landau 2003a; 2003c.

5. Various factors are often cited as responsible for cultural change, including invention (either the discovery of new information or the recombination of preexisting elements), natural internal development or alteration within a culture, diffusion or the spread of information from one culture to another, or the disappearance (extinction) of traits in a culture as a result of societal selection. For a general archaeological introduction to reasons for cultural change, see Renfrew and Bahn 2000, 461–96.

6. See T. Dothan 1982; 1989; 1998b; A. Mazar 1985a; 1988; Stager 1991; 1995; Killebrew 1998a; 2003b; Bunimovitz 1998; Barako 2000; 2001; Yasur-Landau 2003a; 2003c. For an alternative view that supports a more limited migration over a protracted period of time, see Finkelstein 2000.

7. Brug 1985, esp. 201–5; Bunimovitz 1990 (he later revised his views; see 1998); Bauer 1998; Drews 1998; E. S. Sherratt 1998; Vanschoonwinkel 1999. Several of these interpretations are based on out-dated archaeological data. See Hawkes 1987, 203, who first coined the term "immobilist."

8. Rouse (1986, 13–14) suggests three types of diffusion that can lead to culture change: (1) population movement, in which the people of one area expands into another area replacing the latter's population; (2) local development, in which two or more peoples separately evolve through a succession of cultures without losing their own identities but rather influence each other through the process of transculturation; (3) acculturation, in which one people adopts the culture of another people, thereby losing its separate identity.

9. See also Caldwell 1964. Lévi-Strauss (1971, 4, quoted by Rouse 1986, 11–12) divides cultural interaction into two categories: (1) weak interaction that results from trade, intermarriage, religious pilgrimages, and other social activities; and (2) strong interaction, which includes warfare, political control, economic pressure, and other kinds of forcible activities.

10. Ceramic provenience studies have highlighted the complexity of cultural diffusion. See Mommsen, Hertel, and Mountjoy 2001 regarding NAA provenience studies of Mycenaean IIIA2–IIIB pottery recovered from Troy, much of which was locally produced at Troy or along the western Anatolian coast. See Mountjoy 1999b; Becks 2003, 49–51, regarding the archaeological implications and Mountjoy 1997; 1998 for her suggestions regarding a west Aegean–east Aegean "interface." Mountjoy and Mommsen (2001) present the results of NAA studies of Mycenaean pottery recovered from Qantir-Piramesse, whose results indicate that some of the Mycenaean IIIB:2 pottery was produced on Cyprus. This corresponds with evidence from other sites where Cypriot-produced Mycenaean IIIB:2 pottery has been identified, marking what the authors (Mountjoy and Mommsen 2001, 123) note as suggesting that the "supplies of imports from the Argolid had been interrupted" already sometime during the second half of the thirteenth century B.C.E. Regarding the gradual adoption of Mycenaean and Aegean-style pottery in Cyprus, spanning the Late Cypriot IIB and IIIA, see most recently Kling 2000 and bibliography there.

11. See also Tilly 1978, who defines six types of mobility: local, circular, chain, career, colonizing, and forced migrations.

12. Regarding New Archaeology, see Caldwell 1959; Watson, LeBlanc, and Charles 1971; and pp. 3–5 above. One exception to processual archaeology's skepticism of diffusionism as a factor in culture change is Clarke 1968, 411–31. Clarke, who is best known for his work on spatial patterning and social process, accepts the view that invasions can play a major role in the past.

13. For a detailed review and critique of migration as a causal explanation for culture change, see Adams, Van Gerven, and Levy 1978.

14. Several factors are accountable for the rise and fall of the popularity of migration and diffusionist theories in Anglo-American processual archaeology (see e.g. J. G. D. Clark 1966; Adams, Van Gerven, and Levy 1978; Rouse 1986, 17–18; Kristiansen 1989; Renfrew 1987, 123–37). In contrast to Anglo-American intellectual traditions, most of Western European scholarship continued to employ migrations and invasions as explanatory models (an exception to this trend is Denmark and Norway, where processual theory influenced archaeological practice; see Hodder 1991; Chapman 1997, 12–13). German scholarship in particular, dominated by typological and chronological approaches to the past, was largely unaffected by processual trends, and archaeological interpretation remained strongly influenced by migrationist and diffusionist explanations for culture change rather than autochthonous development (Härke 1991; 1998). In the Soviet Union, Marxist philosophy that saw culture and civilization as a result of economic and social factors dominated archaeological thought. Thus, population movements played a small role in the Marxist view of the past and had little to do with the ethnogenesis of peoples. Culture change and ethnic groups were interpreted as largely a result of autochthonous development and intermarriage with other groups (Härke 1998, 23; but see Dolukhanov 1998, 29–30; Klejn 1998, 30–31; Kohl 1998, 31–32, who challenge Hawke's view of Soviet archaeology as dominated by immobilism).

15. Proponents of migrationist theories in archaeology include Anthony 1990; 1992; 1997; Chapman 1997; Chapman and Hamerow 1997. For history of research, see Chapman and Hamerow 1997. For further discussion and specific archaeological case studies, see Rouse 1986; Champion 1990; Megaw and Megaw 1992; Gamble 1993; Chapman 1997; Härke 1998; Yakar 2003.

16. For a critique of postprocessual approaches, see Binford 1982; Bintliff 1991.

17. Colonialism appears in the archaeological literature as both a process and an ideology. In the following section, I refer to colonialism in the archaeological record as a process rather than the impact of modern colonialism on archaeological interpretation. Regarding colonialism and its influence on archaeological practice, see Trigger 1984; Pels 1997 and the bibliography there.

18. For a discussion of these terms, see Said 1993, 9; Dominguez 2002, 65; Lyons and Papodopoulos 2002a, 11–12.

19. For an example of this type of colonialism, see Domínguez 2002. In analyzing the strong Greek influence on Iberian sculpture and language from the sixth to fourth centuries B.C.E. , Dominguez suggests that colonialist agendas were promoted without the presence of substantial numbers of resident colonists. Indigenous elites increased their own prestige and political standing internally through commerce with Phoenician and Greek middlemen. Cooperation with native elites, as illustrated in this case study, has long been a hallmark of colonialism. See also Lyons and Papadopoulos 2002a, 12–13.

20. R. White (1991) first coined this term to describe the interaction between indigenous North Americans and colonizing Europeans during the seventeenth and eighteenth centuries. I. Malkin (2002) has applied this process to Greek and Etruscan colonial encounters during the eighth and seventh centuries B.C.E.

21. Two inscribed seals unearthed at Ashdod in early Philistine levels have tentatively been identified as possible candidates for Philistine script. As noted by Stieglitz (1977, 97), these seals resemble Cypro-Minoan script or Cretan linear syllabaries. The designs on one of the seals are "reminiscent of contemporary Cypriote examples."

22. Regarding the textual evidence relating to the Philistines, see B. Mazar 1971; T. Dothan 1982, 1–24; Brug 1985, 5–50; Katzenstein 1992, 326–28; Noort 1994, 27–112. For a listing of all the primary textual sources relating to the Sea Peoples during the Late Bronze and Iron I periods, including the Philistines, see Adams and Cohen forthcoming. It is beyond the scope of this book to address the rich repertoire of later historical sources mentioning the Philistines. For a detailed treatment of the biblical evidence and Assyrian sources dealing with the later Philistines, see Ehrlich 1996, 105–94.

23. The modern term "Sea Peoples," first used by Maspero (1896), refers to groups of peoples mentioned in the Egyptian texts of Merneptah and Ramesses III as originating from "islands" (see Drews 1993, 57, for a discussion of the term "Sea Peoples"). Earlier in the nineteenth century, de Rougé (1867) posited that the names *Lukka* (Lycia), *Eqwesh* (Achaea), *Tursha* (Trysenia, western Italy), *Shekelesh* (Sicily), and *Sherden* (Sardinia) referred to mercenary bands that originated from these lands in the northern Mediterranean. Maspero took this association one step further, proposing that all the names (including, e.g., *Peleset, Sherden, Tjekker, and Shekelesh*) in the Karnak and Medinet Habu inscriptions referred to ethnica that later were conferred upon lands and islands. The term "Sea Peoples" is somewhat misleading. In fact, the designation "of the sea" appears only in relation to the *Sherden, Shekelesh,* and *Eqwesh* but has somewhat misleadingly been applied to all groups from northern countries who attacked Egypt during the reigns of Merneptah and Ramesses III (Sandars 1985, 157; Redford 1992b, 243 n. 14). From the Egyptian context we can conclude that the groups in question probably lived on the coasts or islands of the Mediterranean (but see Nibbi 1973, who posits an inland west Asian origin for the Sea Peoples). For a comprehensive discussion of the Sea Peoples, see Sandars 1985. See also Artzy 1994, 134; 1997; 1998, who prefers the term "nomads of the sea" as a more accurate model to describe the origins and socioeconomic and political status of the various groups of peoples associated with the Sea Peoples in Egyptian texts.

24. A fifth inscription, referred to as the Pedeset Inscription, appears on a Middle Kingdom statue but dates to the Third Intermediate Period (Steindorff 1939; Singer 1994, 330). Since it is later in date than the early Philistine period, it will not be discussed in this chapter.

25. For an easily accessible translation of the Medinet Habu text relating to the land and sea battle against the Sea Peoples, see Wilson 1969a, 262–63 and full bibliography there. For an analysis of the Medinet Habu inscriptions and their relationship to the Sea Peoples, see Cifola 1988; 1991; Higginbotham 2000, 52–56; O'Connor 2000; Redford 2000, 11–13.

26. See T. Dothan 1982, 5–13, for a discussion and description of the reliefs that depict the land and sea battles against the Sea Peoples. The warriors in feathered headgear should be seen, not as one specific or actual group, but as representing a "generic" Sea People. Recently Sweeney and Yasur-Landau (1999) analyzed the significance of the land battle, particularly the representation of women and children. Regarding the depiction of the Medinet Habu naval battle, see Nelson 1943; Casson 1971, 36–42; Wachsmann 1981; 1982; 1997; 2000 (who, based on the depiction of the Medinet Habu Sea Peoples' ships, argues for a Mycenaean and Central European origin for these peoples); Raban 1988. See also Raban and Stieglitz 1991 for a discussion of Medinet Habu depiction of the Egyptian naval battle against the Philistines. For a discussion of boat depictions dated to the transitional period between the Late Bronze and Iron Ages, approximately contemporary with the Medinet Habu reliefs and often associated with Sea Peoples activities, see Artzy 1987; 1988; 2003; Basch and Artzy 1985.

27. For a more detailed analysis of the specific passages see the following: (1) *Peleset* and *Tjekker* "quiver[ing] in their bodies" (Breasted 1927, §44; Edgerton and Wilson 1936, 30; Epigraphic Survey 1930, pls. 27–28, lines 51–52; Kitchen 1983, 25.5; Peden 1994, 16.51); (2) *Peleset* hiding in their towns in fear of Ramesses III (Breasted 1927, §71; Epigraphic Survey 1930, pl. 29, lines 20–2; Edgerton and Wilson 1936, 35; Kitchen 1983, 28.4); (3) *Peleset, Denyen,* and *Shekelesh* being overthrown by Ramesses III (Breasted 1927, §81; Epigraphic Survey 1930, pl. 44, line 14–15; Edgerton and Wilson 1936, 47; Kitchen 1983, 36.7–8); (4) *Peleset* begging for mercy from Ramesses III (Breasted 1927, §82; Epigraphic Survey 1930, pl. 44, line 24; Edgerton and Wilson 1936, 48; Kitchen 1983, 37.2–3); (5) *Peleset, Tjekker, Shekelesh, Denyen,* and *Weshesh* being named in a confederation against Egypt (Breasted 1927, §64; Epigraphic Survey 1930, pl. 46, line 18; Edgerton and Wilson 1936, 53; Kitchen 1983, 40.3–4; Edel 1985, 225; Peden 1994, 28.18); (6) *Tjekker,* the land of the *Peleset, Denyen, Weshesh,* and *Shekelesh,* being overthrown by Ramesses III (Epigraphic Survey 1932, pl. 107, lines 7–8; Edgerton and

Wilson 1936, 130–31; Kitchen 1983, 73.9–10); (7) countries of the *Peleset* being "slain" by Ramesses III, including depiction of a captive *Peleset* (Epigraphic Survey 1932, pl. 118c; Edgerton and Wilson 1936, 146; Kitchen 1983, 102.8); (8) a captured chief of the *P*[*eleset*] (Breasted 1927, §129; Epigraphic Survey 1970, pl. 600B, line 8; Kitchen 1983, 104.14). The *Peleset* also are referred to in the Medinet Habu Year 5 campaign (Edgerton and Wilson 1936, 30; Kitchen 1983, 25.4–8). Although it relates to the first Libyan war, this inscription was edited *a posteriori*, which may explain why it devotes some lines to the events of Ramesses III's eighth year. See Adams and Cohen forthcoming for a summary of these sources.

28. See Faulkner 1975, 242–44; Lesko 1980. For an analysis of the composition, content, and function of these reliefs and their historical implications, see Cifola 1988; 1991; O'Connor 2000.

29. See also Breasted 1927, §403; Wilson 1969a, 262a; Grandet 1994; Peden 1994, 215.

30. Gardiner 1947, 1:24, 190*–91*, nos. 262–64, 194*–200*, nos. 268–70; see especially no. 270 and pp. 200–205 for a commentary.

31. See Nims 1950 for a favorable review of Gardiner 1947 as the standard translation of these texts.

32. For an overview of the biblical sources relating to the Philistines, see Macalister 1914; T. Dothan 1982, 13–23; Brug 1985, 5–15; Singer 1993; Dothan and Cohn 1994, 62–65; Machinist 2000. For a detailed overview of the biblical accounts relating to the Philistines considered in light of the archaeological evidence, see Bierling 2002.

33. Although most scholars identify Caphtor as Crete, usually associated with the Egyptian toponym *Keftiu*, this identification is far from certain. For a summary of the evidence, see Hess 1992a, 869–70. Regarding other possible translations of the place name Caphtor, see Strange 1980, who situates Caphtor in Cyprus (for a critical review of Strange's identification, see Merrillees 1982). Wainwright (1931a; 1952; 1956) and Vandersleyen (1985) prefer to locate Caphtor and its Egyptian equivalent *Keftiu* with southern Asia Minor or Cilicia. See Strange 1980, 126–38, for a refutation of the Cilician identification. Most recently, see Vandersleyen 2003, who warns "about the fragility of the equivalence *Keftiu*/Crete."

34. For a detailed discussion, see Noort 1994, 52–53; Machinist 2000, 54–55; contra Gordon 1956, 22.

35. For a discussion of David's encounters with the Philistines, see Ehrlich 1996, 26–34; Halpern 2001, esp. 144–59, 320–32.

36. This is by no means a comprehensive discussion of all aspects of Philistine material culture. Rather, the emphasis is on a representative sampling of features associated with the earliest phase of the appearance of the Philistines. Since very little evidence for metalworking has been found thus far in the initial phases of Philistine settlement, I do not address the important issue of metallurgy and the appearance of iron.

37. Locally produced Aegean- and Aegeo-Cypriot style pottery, appearing at the end of the thirteenth and early twelfth centuries B.C.E. in the eastern Mediterranean, is often referred to as Mycenaean IIIC:1b or, in more recent literature, Mycenaean IIIC Middle (see Mountjoy 1986, 155–80; Warren and Hankey 1989, 158–67; Wiener 2003). These two terms describe a class of pottery characterized by Aegean-inspired forms and decorative motifs that was locally produced at numerous manufacturing centers (for Philistia, see Asaro and Perlman 1973; Gunneweg et al. 1986). Its development and typology were first discussed by Furumark (1941a; 1941b; 1944), who saw clear mainland Greek antecedents and cultural influences in the shape and decoration of Mycenaean IIIC pottery. This type appears on mainland Greece following the decline of the Mycenaean palace centers, sometime near the close of the thirteenth century B.C.E. (see Desborough 1964, 3–28; Mountjoy 1986, 134–93; 1999a, 38–51). Significant quantities dating to the twelfth century are found at sites located throughout much of the Aegean, Cyprus, coastal Anatolia, and several cities on the Levantine coast. See Deger-Jalkotzy and Zavadil 2003 for a collection of the most recent detailed discussion of the Late Helladic IIIC period. Although most, if

not all, of the pottery referred to as Mycenaean IIIC:1b should be equated with Mycenaean IIIC Middle elsewhere in the region, I use the term Mycenaean IIIC:1b in this book for the assemblages in Philistia, as has been customary in the literature (see Wiener 2003 for a discussion of attempts to correlate the evidence and terminology from the Aegean, Levant, and Cyprus). What should be noted is that Mycenaean IIIC:1b pottery makes up only a part of the Aegean-style shapes found at Philistine sites that also include Aegean-style cooking pots and undecorated pottery produced out of Mycenaean-style ware. Thus I prefer the term *Aegean-style pottery* for the Philistine assemblage of all pottery—decorated or undecorated, fine or coarse ware—that is Aegean in tradition (see also Killebrew 2000, 234).

38. T. Dothan's 1982 landmark classic on the Philistines focuses mainly on the bichrome phase of Philistine culture. However, following nearly two decades of extensive excavations at Tel Miqne-Ekron, our understanding of the Philistines and their material culture has been transformed.

39. Stratum VII is divided into four subphases: 9d (construction phase), 9c (a pre-Mycenaean IIIC:1b phase represented by one floor), 9b, and 9a (Mycenaean IIIC:1b phases). For the purposes of this book, I do not address the various interpretations of these subphases (see Dothan and Zukerman 2004, table 2, who correlates Stratum VI to the Mycenaean IIIC Middle phase, an attribution with which I do not agree).

40. This stratigraphic interpretation was first suggested by Finkelstein and Singer-Avitz 2001, table 2. Due to the problematic nature of the Ashdod excavations and the final excavation reports, it is difficult to evaluate the stratigraphic sequence at Ashdod. But see Ben-Shlomo 2003, 84–87, and his response to Finkelstein and Singer-Avitz 2001.

41. Regarding the significance of the appearance of Anatolian Grey (Trojan) ware at Tel Miqne-Ekron, see S. H. Allen 1994; Na'aman 2000.

42. Regarding the final field excavation reports, see Dothan and Freedman 1967; M. Dothan 1971; Dothan and Porath 1982; 1993. See Ben-Shlomo 2003 for the most recent discussion of the unpublished stratigraphic evidence.

43. Regarding the field excavation reports presenting the data relevant to the Iron I levels at Tel Miqne-Ekron, see Field INE: Killebrew 1986; 1996b; forthcoming c; Meehl, Dothan, and Gitin forthcoming; Field X: Bierling 1998. A royal dedicatory inscription mentioning the name Ekron discovered during the final season of excavation in 1996 has dispelled any reasonable doubt regarding the identification of Tel Miqne as biblical Ekron (Gitin, Dothan, and Naveh 1997).

44. For a summary of the Iron I at Ashkelon, see Stager 1991, 13–14; 1993, 107. The earliest Iron I levels have not yet been excavated.

45. See Maeir 2001; Maeir and Ehrlich 2001. The earlier Philistine Iron I levels have not yet been excavated. Regarding the identification of Tell eṣ-Ṣafi as biblical Gath, see Bliss and Macalister 1902, 35; Rainey 1975; Singer 1993, 134; Schniedewind 1998, 75.

46. However, due to the differing interpretations of the stratigraphic sequence, the relationship between the destroyed Late Bronze Age settlement and the arrival of the Philistines remains a matter of debate.

47. For the complete field reports, including summary statements, locus descriptions, plans, sections, and pottery assemblages, see Killebrew 1986; 1996b (Field INE); Bierling 1998 (Field X); Meehl, Dothan, and Gitin forthcoming (Field INE).

48. At Ashdod, Areas G and H provide the most significant insights into the earliest Philistine levels. Due to the confused stratigraphy and inconsistencies in the publications, only the most general observations can be made. But the sequence closely parallels the stratigraphic development at Tel Miqne-Ekron briefly outlined here. See T. Dothan 2003; Dothan and Zukerman 2004, 4–7; Ben-Shlomo 2003.

49. Beycesultan (LB II): Macqueen 1986, 83, fig. 56; Miletus (LH IIIA–LH IIIB): Niemeier 1998, 30–31, figs. 8–9, photo 2. It is noteworthy that the earliest documented examples of hearths appear in the eastern Aegean or Asia Minor (see Barako 2001, table 2).

50. Mainland Greece—Mycenae (LH IIIB–IIIC): Wace 1949, 77, fig. 96a; Mylonas 1966, 60–63, figs. 14–16; Taylour 1970, fig. 1; French 1981, 42, fig. 1; Panagia: Shear 1987, figs. 4–5; Pylos (LH IIIB): Blegen and Rawson 1966, 85–87, figs. 22, 66, 73, 404; Tiryns (LH IIIB–IIIC): Mylonas 1966, 47, figs. 12, 51–55; Kilian 1981, 51, 55, figs. 2, 8. For a recent discussion of the Late Helladic evidence on mainland Greece, see Tournavitou 1999. On Crete, hearths are published from Mallia (LM III): Pariente 1993, 789; Driessen 1994, 78; Khania (LM IIIC): Hallager and Tzedakis 1988, 45, fig. 25. On Galatas, hearths appear already during the Middle Minoan period; see Rethemiotakis 1999 for a discussion of Minoan domestic and palatial fixed hearths at Galatas.

51. Alassa (LC IIIA): Hadjisavvas 1994, 108, 113, fig. 2, pl. 15:1; Karageorghis 1998, 279, fig. 3; Maa-*Palaeokastro* (LC IIC–LC IIIA): Karageorghis and Demas 1988, 20, 41, pls. 26:6–7, 30:1–3, plan 7; Enkomi (LC IIIA): Dikaios 1969–71, 106, 112–13, 175–76, 183, 186, pls. 19:4, 20:1, 33:5, 34:1, plans 254, 273–74; Karageorghis 1998, 277, fig. 1; Kition (LC IIIA): Karageorghis and Demas 1985, 64, pls. 42:2, 70:2, plan 1.

52. Tarsus (LB IIA): Goldman 1956, 54, fig. 193, plan 23.

53. Rectangular hearth—Stratum VII: T. Dothan 1992, 96–97; 1998b, 155–56, figs. 7–8; 2003, 197–98, fig. 4; Dothan and Zukerman 2004, fig. 2; circular hearths—Strata VI–V: Dothan 2003, 198.

54. Kition (LC IIIA–Cypro-Geometric I): Karageorghis and Demas 1985, pls. 20:1087, 34:1020, 1024, 57:1020, 1024, 117:5150–56, 195:5149–56, 201:5055a, 5060, 5088, 5102, 5106.

55. Lefkandi (LH IIIC): Popham and Sackett 1968, 13, fig. 16; Troy (Level VIIb2): Blegen Caskey, and Rawson 1958, 208, figs. 256:37–172–73.

56. Stern 1994, 96, fig. 409; 2000, 199, fig. 10.6, who associates them with another group of Sea Peoples, the *Sikila*.

57. See, e.g., Enkomi: Courtois 1971, 277–80, figs. 97, 109–10, 113–14; Kition (LC IIIA and later): Webb 1985 (twelve incised scapulae originating from cultic contexts); Myrtou-Pigadhes (LC IIC–LC IIIA): Taylor 1957, 21, 99–100, pl. V(d). These scapulae are typically found in cultic contexts in Cyprus.

58. Specifically Webb (1985, 324–27) suggests that the scapulae were used for "scapulomancy," which was a common form of oracle-taking in the ancient world.

59. The accounts regarding Dagon (see, e.g., Judg 16:23; 1 Sam 5:1–7; 1 Chr 10:10) and two other deities (Ashtarot and Baʿal-zebub) bear little connection to the Iron I cultic remains associated with the early Philistines, where the main deity appears to be a goddess. The biblical passages most likely reflect later Philistine cultic practices when Dagon was the head of the Philistine pantheon. Neighboring West-Semitic cultures, which had a male god at the head of their pantheons, may have influenced this apparent shift from the primacy of a female deity to a male god.

60. For comparative Mycenaean female figurines, see T. Dothan 1982, 234; A. Mazar 1988, 257–60; Mylonas 1956, 110–21; Yasur-Landau 2001, table 1.

61. See also S. Morris 2001 for a discussion of Late Bronze Aegean east-west interactions and Anatolian contributions to Greek religion.

62. T. Dothan 1982, 252–79; but see Oren 1973, 132–50, who argues for an association with the *Denyen*, another of the Sea Peoples who are also depicted wearing the feathered headdress.

63. T. Dothan 1982, 260–74, and especially 288, where Dothan specifically relates these coffins to the Philistines, whom she concludes served as Egyptian mercenaries. It should be noted that there is no direct textual evidence for this interpretation, nor are Philistines specifically depicted in the Medinet Habu reliefs as wearing "feathered" headdresses. Sites where anthropoid coffins have been found are all well-known Egyptian centers during the Nineteenth and Twentieth Dynasties (see chapter 2 above), with no convincing archaeological evidence for the presence of Philistines, either as settlers or mercenaries.

64. The multiperiod Azor cemetery, whose use spans the Chalcolithic through Iron periods, is the best candidate for a possible Philistine cemetery. Numerous burials with Philistine

bichrome pottery dating to the eleventh century and later were excavated. These include pit burials, jar burials, burials in brick coffins, communal burials, and, most notably, cremation burials that M. Dothan (1993a, 129), the excavator, associates with the "appearance of a new ethnic group." See also Dothan and Dothan 1992, 107–17, for a more detailed discussion.

65. Hesse 1986, 21–22, table 4; Hesse and Wapnish 1997, 148; Barako 2001, 21 n. 17; see also Lev-Tov 2000 for a recent analysis of faunal remains from Tel Miqne-Ekron.

66. Diener and Robkin 1978; Crabtree 1989; Hesse 1990; 1995; Redding 1991; Zeder 1996; 1998; Hesse and Wapnish 1997; 1998; Lev-Tov 2000.

67. The sign for pig appears in Linear B tables from Knossos (Chadwick, Killen, and Olivier 1971, 45–46) and from Pylos (Bennett 1955, 247–48; Chadwick 1973, 205–6).

68. See Hongo 2003, 259, who notes that "in general, faunal assemblages from Anatolia site [*sic*] generally consist of about 50 to 70% sheep and goats, and about 15 to 20% each of cattle and pigs, and 5% or less of wild animals. This basic pattern was established by the Late Neolithic and continued through to the Middle Ages." It should also be noted that recent faunal reports from Anatolia have noted an increase in pig bones from the Late Bronze to Iron Ages (Ikram 2003, 286–89; von den Driesch and Pöllath 2003).

69. Lev-Tov (2000, 221–23) concludes that the Philistines did *not* originate from the Aegean, since "pigs were herded in large numbers and over huge expanse of Bronze Age Europe and elsewhere. There is even less evidence to suggest a link to the Aegean based on the dual cattle-pig dietary regime, given that cattle in that region were uncommon except in the far north (Trantalidou 1990)." Rather, he prefers to follow Hesse and Wapnish's (1998) suggestion that the popularity of swine at Iron I Tel Miqne-Ekron and Ashkelon was more closely related to the pig's suitability for an immigrant population (see also Zeder 1998). Recent discoveries in Greece provide clear evidence for the practice of sacrificing juvenile pigs as burnt offerings at the Late Bronze Age Mycenaean sanctuary of Ayios Konstantinos. See Hamilakis and Konsolaki 2004 regarding a discussion of the evidence and its significance.

70. For the first comprehensive study of Mycenaean IIIC:1b, see Killebrew 2000. See also Dothan and Zukerman 2004 for a second detailed analysis.

71. Typologies of later Iron I bichrome painted pottery, which developed out of the monochrome Mycenaean IIIC:1b wares and are beyond the scope of this book, have been described in depth by T. Dothan (1982, 94–218) and later expanded upon by A. Mazar (1985b).

72. Although abundant quantities of Aegean-style pottery, including substantial amounts of decorated Mycenaean IIIC:1b pottery, have been recovered from Fields III, IV, and X, the earliest Iron I habitation layers with Aegean-style pottery, including ceramic kilns (Killebrew 1996b) that produced these assemblages, are in Field INE. Thus the focus of this discussion will be on the earliest appearance of Aegean-style pottery, so as better to understand the arrival of the new peoples associated with this previously unknown pottery style to Canaan.

73. Form AS 1a, measuring ca. 5–10 cm in depth with a low ring base or disc base, equals A. Furumark's form FS 296, one of the shapes of Form 85. Furumark (1941b, 636; 1992, pls. 161–162, pl. 162:296) described it as belonging to a group he termed Levanto-Mycenaean. It should be noted that Furumark (1944, 235–36) classified this shape as "Decorated Late Cypriote III." Most of Furumark's examples originate from Cyprus, and only a few are from mainland Greece and the Levant. Mountjoy (1986, 133) published two additional examples of FS 296 dating to Late Helladic IIIB2 levels from Tiryns. However, she notes that this type did not become popular until the Late Helladic IIIC period. Several examples of bowl type FS 296, similar to those known from Cyprus, were recovered from a Late Bronze II tomb at Sarepta. See Baramki 1959, nos. 42 (pl. XV:42) and 43 (pl. XV:43), where he terms these bowls Cypro-Mycenaean ware.

On Cyprus, where this bowl was most ubiquitous, the interior design often includes a spiral or set of concentric circles in the interior of the base; occasionally other decorative motifs appear on this type of pottery within the bands on the interior. Locally produced bowls from Cyprus and Philistia are decorated with matte paint, which differentiates them from their imported Aegean counterparts, which are decorated with a glossy paint. Although the popularity of Bowl Form AS 1 in Late Cypriot IIC–IIIB on Cyprus may be due to inspiration from imported Mycenaean ceramics, many features of these bowls are indigenous to the Cypriot ceramic tradition (for a detailed discussion, see Kling 1989b, 131–34; Killebrew 2000, 235, fig. 12.1:1–2).

74. Form AS 1b equals Furumark FS 295 (Furumark 1941b, 636). Following Dothan and Zukerman (2004, 7, Type B), I divide Form AS 1 into two subtypes. Based on similarities in vessel proportions and manufacture, I prefer to see it as a subtype of Form AS 1a.

75. This large semihemispherical to hemispherical bowl is termed FS 294 (Form 85) by Furumark (1941b, 636; 1992, pl. 161:294). This larger bowl, generally with a flat everted rim, is rare on Cyprus and is far less popular than Forms AS 1 and AS 3. Mountjoy (1986, 131–33) notes that FS 294 appears only sporadically on the Greek mainland during the thirteenth century, becoming prevalent only in the twelfth century. See Killebrew 2000, 235, fig. 12:1:3, for a more detailed discussion.

76. Tel Miqne-Ekron (Stratum VII: Killebrew 2000, 235–36, fig. 12.1:4–6); Tell es Safi (Bliss and Macalister 1902, pl. 35:7, 8); Ashdod (Area G, Stratum XIIIb: Dothan and Porath 1993, fig. 14:24–26 [pl. 36:10, 11], 16: 11; Area H: M. Dothan 1971, fig. 74:1).

77. Several Form AS 3 bowls were found in Syria at Ras Ibn Hani (Bounni et al. 1979, fig. 25:3–6). These bowls can be decorated with simple horizontal bands but are often undecorated. Furumark (1992, pl. 162:295) designated this bowl as belonging to Form 85, FS 295. He attributed this bowl type to his Hellado- and Rhodo-Mycenaean group, appearing mainly in Mycenaean IIIC contexts, where it is slightly deeper and more sharply carinated. Kling (1989b, 132, fig. 5b) defined the Cypriot versions as a conical bowl with carinated rim (Late Mycenaean IIIB or Decorated Late Cypriot III), where by the Late Cypriot IIC it had become a very popular form, continuing into the Late Cypriot IIIA periods. Similar bowls are also known from Cilicia (e.g., Tarsus: French 1975, figs. 16, 17). See Killebrew 2000, 235–36, for a detailed discussion.

78. During the Iron I, Bowl Form AS 4 is ubiquitous in the southern coastal plain, where this shape is often referred to as a bell-shaped bowl (e.g., T. Dothan 1982, 98–106; A. Mazar 1985b, 87–90). Early Iron I examples decorated with a monochrome paint are known from Tel Miqne-Ekron (Killebrew 2000, fig. 12.1:8–11; Dothan and Zukerman 2004, figs. 6:12–14, 16–17, 8:1–2, 5, 7–15, 9:1–3, 5–6, 8–9), Ashdod (see, e.g., Stratum XIII: Dothan and Porath 1993, figs. 13:1, 14:9–15, 17–18), Ashkelon (Phythian-Adams 1923, pl. II:7, 12), and Tell eṣ-Ṣafi (Bliss and Macalister 1902, pl. 35:10). It appears at other sites along the northern coast of Canaan, including Akko (M. Dothan 1986, 106, figs. 8.2–8.3, who associates this pottery with the *Sherden,* another group listed among the Sea Peoples). See also examples from Sarepta (Herscher 1975, fig. 52:1–3; Koehl 1985, 199–20, nos. 192–97, figs. 8, 20) and Ras Ibn Hani (Bounni et al. 1978, 281, fig. 28; 1979, 240, fig. 19).

79. The skyphos is a popular shape throughout much of the Aegean during the thirteenth and twelfth centuries B.C.E. It is found mainly in settlements and only rarely in tombs (see Furumark 1941b, 634; French 1966, 222; 1967, 169; 1969b, 74–75, 87; Wardle 1969, 273–75; 1973, 311–18, 334–36; Mountjoy 1976, 87–90; 1985, 181–85, figs. 5.8, 5.16–5.18; 1986, 93, 117–18, 121, 129–31, 134, 149–51, 176–78; for a summary, see Kling 1989b, 106). It is less common in Crete, first appearing at the end of the thirteenth century and probably reflecting influence from Greece (Popham 1965, 328; 1970, 196; Kanta 1980, 258–60; Mook and Coulson 1993, 351; Gesell, Day, and Coulson 1995, 117, fig. 22).

80. AS 4 first appears on Cyprus in the Late Cypriot IIC period, increasing in popularity during the Late Cypriot IIIA period. For a detailed discussion of the numerous parallels from Cyprus, see Killebrew 2000, 236, especially n. 20.

81. See Sherratt and Crouwel 1987, fig. 4:8; Tarsus: Goldman 1956, 220–21, pls. 330, 331, 334, 335; French 1975, figs. 10, 13, 17, 18; Soli: Yağci 2003, figs. 20–24. These recent discoveries from Soli (near Mersin) are remarkable for their similarity in shape and decoration to the Philistine (and Cypriot) examples.

82. Common motifs include linear decorations or more elaborately painted bands at the rim and below the handle, paint at the stumps of handles and on top of the handles, and geometric or occasionally figurative designs in the handle zone.

83. Furumark 1941b, 633; see Killebrew 2000, 239, for a detailed description; Dothan and Zukerman 2004, 12–16, Type E.

84. This form is a common shape at Tel Miqne-Ekron (Stratum VII: Killebrew 2000, figs. 12.1:12–13; 12.2:5) and at other Philistine Pentapolis sites, such as Ashdod (e.g., Stratum XIIIa: Dothan and Porath 1993, figs. 21–22; Stratum XII: Dothan and Porath 1993, figs. 27, 28:1–5, 7, 29:1–3, 5), and Ashkelon (Phythian-Adams 1923, pl. II:10). This form first appears in Mycenaean IIIC:1b (e.g., monochrome) ware but is more common in the later bichrome pottery repertoire. Several examples are also known from Ras Ibn Hani in Syria (Bounni et al. 1979, fig. 25:1–2, 7–8).

85. On Cyprus it first appears in Late Cypriot IIC thirteenth-century contexts at Kition (Floor IV: Karageorghis and Demas 1985, pl. IX:1140), Athienou (Stratum III: Dothan and Ben-Tor 1983, 49, fig. 13:1), and Enkomi (Level IIB: Dikaios 1969–71, 249–50). Kraters dating to the Late Cypriot IIC apparently imitated imported Mycenaean kraters of similar shape. It increases in number and popularity during the Late Cypriot IIIA period and is classified as either Mycenaean IIIC:1b or Decorated Late Cypriot III (see Killebrew 2000, n. 24, for a detailed discussion of Late Cypriot IIIA kraters).

86. Furumark (1941b, 633) distinguishes two variants of this shape: FS 281 (characteristic of Late Helladic IIIB) and 282 (dated to the Late Helladic IIIB–IIIC:1 early). This form is common throughout the Aegean.

87. Tel Miqne-Ekron: Stratum VII: Killebrew 1999a, ills. II:22:25, II:25:17–18, II:26:9, II:28:13; Ashdod: Stratum XIIIb: Dothan and Porath 1993, 58, fig. 24:2; Stratum XI: 88, fig. 41:5.

88. Krater Form AS 6 is related to Furumark's Form 82, FS 291 (deep conical bowl). Furumark (1941b, 635–36) dates FS 291 to the Late Helladic IIIC. This type has concave sides with an angular profile. Only one straight-sided kalathos is catalogued by Furumark. E. S. Sherratt (1981, 231) proposed that the shape developed in early Late Helladic IIIC in the Dodecanese from an earlier form, the conical krater, and spread from there to Cyprus and mainland Greece, mainly during the middle phase of Late Helladic IIIC. Dikaios (1969–71, 267, no. 3845/4) compared this form to kalathoi in the mainland, on Rhodes and at Perati, where Late Helladic IIIC examples are common and appear in several variations. Kling (1989b, 147) concurs with Sherratt's suggestion that the shape was introduced to Cyprus from the eastern Aegean, probably the Dodecanese. The closest examples, similar in general shape and size, are from Cyprus (see, e.g., Enkomi: Level IIIB: Dikaios 1969–71, pl. 120:2 [no. 1734]).

89. Form AS 7 belongs to Furumark's Form 97, FS 322. Examples are known from Asine, Thebes, and Ialysos dating to the Late Helladic IIIB–IIIC (Furumark 1941b, 641). A richly decorated tray was recovered at Phylakopi (Mountjoy 1985, 188, fig. 5.19).

90. Strata VII and VI at Tel Miqne-Ekron (Killebrew 2000, 240), where they are either undecorated or decorated with horizontal bands at the rim, neck, or occasionally the base; Ashdod: Stratum XIIIb: Dothan and Porath 1993, fig. 15:4, 10; Stratum XIIIa: Dothan and Porath 1993, fig. 23:5, 6. This shape continues to appear in later bichrome ware. Juglet AS 8 appears in T. Dothan's (1982, 155–57) typology of Philistine bichrome pottery, and A. Mazar (1985b, 97–98) classifies it as Jug Type 7.

91. Juglet AS 8 is a well-known shape on Cyprus, appearing already at the end of the Late Cypriot IIC (Hadjisavvas 1986, pl. 18:7; 1991, 173) and becoming more prevalent during the Late Cypriot IIIA–IIIB periods. It has been classified under many different terms, such as Gjerstad's (1926, 223) Submycenaean Jug 9, Sjöqvist's (1940, 67, fig. 18) Painted

Submycenaean Jug Type 2, Furumark's (1944, 234–37, fig. 10) Decorated Late Cypriote III Type I, and Åström's (1972, 286–87) White Painted Wheelmade III Type X. For a detailed discussion of the Cypriot evidence, see Kling 1988, 331–32; 1989b, 160, fig. 17c.

92. The origin of this shape has been the subject of debate. Sjöqvist (1940, 74) noted that jugs with a tubular spout and basket handle appear already in the Aegean during the Late Helladic IIIA and suggested a Mycenaean origin for this form (Furumark 1941b, 609, FS 158, 159). Daniel (1942, 292) and T. Dothan (1982, 157) also suggested an Aegean origin for this shape. However, as Furumark (1944, 236–38) noted, the handle placement in line with the spout was more prevalent in the east. See, e.g., Ialysos (Maiuri 1923–24, 142, fig. 63; Jacopi 1930–31, 259, fig. 4); Amorgos (Morricone 1965–66, 252); Chalis (Morricone 1965–66, n. 1); Kos (Morricone 1965–66, 250–51, fig. 276). For a detailed discussion, see E. S. Sherratt 1981, 455–61; Kling 1989b, 160. As has been recently pointed out, the appearance of Form AS 8 in Mycenaean ware is mainly an eastern Aegean phenomenon, in some cases predating the Late Helladic IIIC period. Currently the evidence of an Aegean, probably eastern Aegean, source is most convincing.

93. Tel Miqne-Ekron (Stratum VII): Killebrew 2000, fig. 12:3:5; Ashdod (Stratum XIII): Dothan and Porath 1993, fig. 13:5 (jug without trefoil).

94. See, e.g., Furumark 1941b, 601–2, FS 105, 110. Furumark's (1941b, 603) FS 116, the Levanto-Helladic type, is distinguished by its higher neck.

95. Jugs without trefoil spouts on Cyprus derive from Late Cypriot IIC–IIIA contexts, corresponding to Kling (1989b, 149) fig. 13b. A few fragmentary examples are also known from Tarsus (French 1975, fig. 2). In contrast, jugs with trefoil mouths have a long history in Cyprus and appear in various wares.

96. In the Aegean, jugs with a trefoil spout are regarded as a later feature of middle and later Late Helladic IIIC assemblages (French 1975, fig. 2). It equals Furumark's FS 137 (1941b, 606), which he dated to the Late Helladic IIIC early through Sub-Mycenaean.

97. Ashdod (Stratum XIIIb): Dothan and Porath 1993, fig. 17:4, 5; (Stratum XII): Dothan and Porath 1993, fig. 34:2, 7); Tell ʿEitun: Edelstein and Aurant 1992, figs. 2 (jug on left) and 10:9; Tell Qasile: A. Mazar 1985b, Type CP 3:53, fig. 41:1.

98. Single-handled cooking jug (some with a round base): Hala Sultan Tekke: Öbrink 1979, 23, fig. 111 (F 6171); Åström et al. 1983, figs. 318, 409); Pyla-Kokkinokremos: Karageorghis and Demas 1984, pls. XX:102, XXXVI:102, XX:104, XXXVI:104; classified as Coarse Handmade ware); Maa-Palaeokastro: Karageorghis and Demas 1988, pls. LX:692; CLXXXIII:692; XI:578, CLXXXIII:578; CIX:387, CCXI:387; Athienou: Dothan and Ben-Tor 1983, fig. 50–7–8; Enkomi: Dikaios 1969–71, pl. 106:3; and Kourion: Daniel 1937, pls. II–III, V. See also examples from the southern coast of Anatolia: Tarsus: Goldman 1956, pl. 324:1220–1221.

99. Hadjisavvas 1991, 177–79; see also Kling 2000, 282–86, who notes the eclectic nature of wheel-made painted pottery on Cyprus during end of the Late Cypriot IIC period.

100. Due to the unstratified context and uncertain date of these sherds, these two shapes are not entered into the present typology.

101. The highly calcareous nature of the clay would enable a lower firing temperature for this ware, since $CaCO_3$ begins to break down at 500 degrees Celsius. Most ancient pottery was fired at 700 degrees Celsius or greater. See Killebrew 1999a, 223–29.

102. As has been noted by Catling (Catling and Jones 1986), and E. S. Sherratt (1991) with respect to Mycenaean IIIIC:1b assemblages found on Cyprus, the number of shapes appearing in this typology is select and limited when compared to the rich variety of shapes known from Mycenaean IIIB and IIIC assemblages on mainland Greece. The shapes are largely domestic kitchen wares (with a few exceptions, such as the stirrup jar) used by the producers and consumers of this ware in Philistia and Cyprus.

103. For a recent update regarding the transition between the Late Bronze and Iron Ages in Anatolia, see Fischer et al. 2003, especially Jean 2003 and Yağci 2003 for a discussion of the evidence in Cilicia for Mycenaean IIIC:1b pottery.

104. For a summary of this theory, see Albright 1975b, 512–13; Strobel 1976, 159–65. See also Singer 1988b, 241–42, who notes that Homer in the Odyssey lists the Pelasgians as one of the inhabitants of Crete.

105. These include B. Mazar 1971; Kitchen 1973; T. Dothan 1982, 289–96, 289–96; 1985c, 171; 1995a; 1995b; 1998b; M. Dothan 1979; A. Mazar 1985a; 1988; 1993; Raban and Stieglitz 1991; Stager 1995; Stone 1995; Bunimovitz 1998; Yasur-Landau 2001; 2003a; 2003b; Dothan and Zukerman 2004. Regarding a northern Greek or Dorian origin for the Philistines, see Vogazianos 1994; but see French 1998, 4, who claims that the Philistine origins lie outside of the Aegean. See Margalith 1995 for a recent discussion of the linguistic evidence that he interprets to support an Aegean origin, specifically from the region of Pylos, for the Philistines.

106. The strong Mycenaean influence evident at sites such as Miletus (for a recent overview, see Weickert 1957; 1959–60; Gödecken 1988; Niemeier 1998) adds credence to this theory.

107. Regarding the linguistic evidence, see Barnett 1953; 1975, 364–65, 376–77; Albright 1975b, 513.

108. Concerning the relationship between Cyprus and Philistia, see Karageorghis 1984a. For an up-to-date statement and related bibliography regarding the close connections between Cyprus and the southern coast of Canaan at the close of the Late Bronze and Early Iron I periods, see E. S. Sherratt 1998. She also notes the close similarities between Philistine and Late Cypriot IIIA material culture.

109. For a recent discussion of the various criteria used to determine an absolute date for the appearance of Mycenaean IIIC:1b pottery in Philistia and its implications regarding the dating of the Philistines, see Yasur-Landau 2003b, who leaves the question unresolved.

110. See, e.g., M. Dothan 1971, 20; 1988; 1993b; Iakovides 1979; T. Dothan 1985c, 173; 1989. The first pre-Ramesses III wave of "Proto-Philistines" is associated with the appearance of Mycenaean IIIC Middle pottery along the southern coast of Canaan. According to this theory, the chronologically later bichrome pottery represents the settlement of the Philistines after their defeat by Ramesses III. See also T. Dothan 2000, 156, who proposes four waves of migrating Sea Peoples associated with the appearance of Mycenaean IIIC:1b pottery and the three phases of bichrome pottery. More recently, T. Dothan (2003; Dothan and Zukerman 2004) seems to have retreated from this theory. Most scholars reject the high chronology as having no basis in the archaeological evidence (see, e.g., A. Mazar 1985a).

111. Noth 1958, 36; Albright 1975b, 510–11; de Vaux 1978, 509; B. Mazar 1980, 152; A. Mazar 1985a; 1997a; Singer 1985b; 1992a; Stager 1985b; 1995.

112. Oren 1984, 56; Ussishkin 1985, 223; 1995; for a detailed discussion, see Finkelstein 1995a; 1998a; 2000.

113. See also Finkelstein 1996a for the implications of this low chronology for the redating of Iron II strata in Israel. See A. Mazar 1997b for a rebuttal of the late dating scheme suggested by Finkelstein.

6
Identifying the Egyptians, Canaanites, Philistines, and Early Israel

Biblical narratives of ancient Israel's most bitter enemies—the Egyptians, Canaanites, and Philistines—and Israel's ultimate triumph over its adversaries have served as a source of inspiration for millennia. During the past two centuries these stories have been the focal point for generations of scholars in search of the historical Israel. However, recent studies have cast doubt on the historical reliability of the biblical descriptions, leading some scholars to question of the existence of these peoples, and especially of a biblical Israel. In spite of the recent skepticism (or maybe because of it), the quest to define these peoples in the archaeological record continues.

Like an archaeological tell, the biblical text does not portray any one moment in time or offer a narrative composed by a single author but rather represents a multilayering of stories, events, and ideologies spanning hundreds of years. Building on over a century of archaeological and critical biblical research, this book presents a history of these peoples based on the critical reading of the stratified remains of tells, the propaganda-inspired contemporaneous texts, and the redacted layers of the biblical text. This search draws on the results of multidisciplinary research from the humanities, social sciences, and sciences. I begin with a broader contextualized approach to these groups, where the contemporary texts, the archaeological record, and later biblical accounts serve as the primary data for reconstructing the second-millennium milieu. The fragmentary record is interpreted via historical, literary, processual, and postprocessual approaches to reading the past. Each of these methodologies attempts to reconstruct a different aspect of the past, and all approaches have contributed to our current understanding of these ancient peoples and their changing identities within their ancient and modern contexts.

Key to any interpretation of the past is its larger geographical, cultural, socioeconomic, and historical contexts. As is evident in the preceding chapters, numerous factors must be considered. These include environmental and geographical aspects that often influence, and even determine, human behavior and the course of history over the long term. Broad socioeconomic and political processes can dictate human action over the medium term, while specific historical events, individuals, and ideological developments also sway the course of history. The human experience is both predictable and random, subject to universal paradigms as well as individual actions, ideologies, and unique historical contexts. This book recognizes the complexity of forces that shape human history and behavior but at the same time acknowledges that our interpretations are irrevocably a result of our own cultural context and personal biases. In spite of these difficulties, I contend that it is possible to reconstruct a history, albeit incomplete and fragmentary, of biblical peoples and to identify their material culture, while conceding that this is an ongoing and evolving process that by definition is never complete.

The roots of these biblical peoples lie in the second-millennium world of the eastern Mediterranean. The interconnected world system of the Late Bronze II and its gradual demise spanning the late thirteenth and twelfth centuries B.C.E. encouraged the assertion of local political ambitions long dominated by the imperial interests of the Egyptian and Hittite Empires. The breakdown of this economically based world system triggered an escalation in the movement of peoples and set the stage for the regionally based transformation and restructuring of second-millennium Canaan, the arrival of the Philistines, and the ethnogenesis of early Israel.

Much of biblical scholarship's fascination with Egypt is related to Egypt's role in the exodus saga and the eventual emergence of Israel. Although neither contemporary texts nor archaeology can determine the historicity of the exodus account, an issue much better left as a question of faith, the general historical setting of the narrative and its depiction of Egypt as a brutal slave master is well-suited to Egypt's imperialistic role in Canaan during much of the Late Bronze Age and continuing well into the twelfth century B.C.E. The nature of Egyptian presence in Canaan as an imperial power is reflected in the biblical account, in contemporary texts and inscriptions, and in the archaeological evidence. The impact of Egypt is evident in specific architectural plans, building techniques, and, especially, in the locally produced Egyptian-style utilitarian pottery found at several major Egyptian strongholds in Canaan.

Locally produced Egyptian-style pottery appears only rarely at Canaanite sites that did not serve as Egyptian garrisons or administrative centers. The stability of the Egyptian pottery assemblages in Canaan is probably a result of several factors: (1) most of the Egyptian-style pottery manufactured in Canaan is utilitarian in nature and thus has a tendency to resist change; (2) the potters' craft may have been under Egyptian administrative control; and (3) it is likely that the potters themselves were

Egyptian, sent together with Egyptian envoys and military personnel, rather than indigenous Canaanite potters who learned or imitated Egyptian-style vessels. All these factors point to imperialism as the best model to understand Egyptian interests and activities in Canaan. The lack of internal local stylistic and technological development over time, and the nearly complete absence of creolization or acculturation that typifies the colonialist activities of the Philistines, supplies further support that Egyptian intentions were imperialistic rather than colonialist. The nature of the Egyptian-style culture argues against the suggestion that it was the result of elite emulation and supports the contention that Egyptians were actually stationed in Canaan. With the decline and eventual withdrawal of Egyptian forces, Egyptian-style material culture disappears suddenly at these sites, leaving nary a trace of former Egyptian influence in the region.

The biblical Canaanites were not a cohesive ethnic group bound together by a common ideology or ancestry. Both textual and archaeological evidence indicates that they comprised both indigenous peoples and newcomers from a mixed background whose kinship ties and local allegiances were most likely connected politically and economically to local city-states. Based on extrabiblical sources, we can speak of Canaanites as indigenous inhabitants of mixed ancestry residing in the land referred to as Canaan. Elements of both homogeneity and heterogeneity appear in the material culture. A rich variety of cultic structures and burial customs reflect long-term indigenous traditions as well as the introduction of outside practices. At the same time, homogeneous aspects of their material culture are not indicative of a unified group identity or single ethnicity. Rather, an externally imposed socioeconomic and political structure resulting from Egyptian imperialistic ambitions and the Late Bronze Age world system determined Canaanite social and cultural boundaries. This phenomenon is best exemplified in a relatively homogeneous assemblage of mass-produced pottery manufactured in professional potters' workshops, most likely under the control of local city-state vassal rulers. The formation of regionally based ceramic traditions during the course of the twelfth century B.C.E. illustrates the fragility of this externally imposed and artificial political and economic unity that characterized Late Bronze Age Canaan.

The emergence of Israel was a process of ethnogenesis whose roots lay in Canaan but also included the influx of external groups that I refer to as a "mixed multitude." Although we may never be able to write a definitive history of biblical Israel, it is possible to reconstruct the gradual process leading to Israel's formation based on the biblical, extrabiblical, and archaeological evidence. The emergence of Israel was intimately connected to the breakdown of the eastern Mediterranean world system and may have coincided with longer-term regionally based settlement cycles that typified the Levant over the millennia.

With the gradual decline and disappearance of Egyptian imperialistic control over the Jordan Valley at sites such as Tel Beth-shean and Tell es-Sa'idiyeh, the resulting power vacuum allowed for the redrawing of more regionally based social and cultural boundaries in Canaan and permitted renewed and traditional kinship ties between the highland areas of Transjordan and Cisjordan. This is reflected in the change in settlement patterns from the Late Bronze to Iron I periods, the size and layout of the highland villages, the continuity and discontinuity with Canaanite pottery, and shared elements of the material culture of the highland regions on both sides of the Jordan River. The pottery associated with these small hamlets best illustrates aspects of continuity and discontinuity of the Iron I highland culture. The ceramic assemblage continues the Late Bronze Age tradition but is differentiated by its reduced repertoire of shapes; the predominance of collared-rim pithoi, storage jars in the Canaanite tradition, and cooking pots; and a change in the mode of production from regionally based professional workshops to an itinerant potters' industry.

The emergence of new ideologies eventually proved to be the unifying factor in the formation of Israel. These new external influences may best be reflected in the emergence of an ideology associated with the worship of Yahweh. One can also discern a shift in cultic practices from one that constituted an integral part of the city-state town plan during the Late Bronze Age to a less centrally controlled cult best indicated by the appearance of open-air cultic sites found in association with Iron I highland villages. It is difficult to pinpoint a moment or even a general period when biblical Israel can be identified historically or archaeologically; however, the biblical account of the period of the judges is broadly reflected in the archaeology of twelfth- and eleventh-century Canaan.

The social and cultural boundaries of the early Philistines are the most easily defined borders of the groups discussed in this book. Their distinctive material culture that appears at the five Pentapolis cities in the biblical narrative leaves little doubt that these people were an intrusive group or groups referred to by biblical writers as the Philistines. Taken together with the contemporary New Kingdom Egyptian sources and their eastern Mediterranean context, we can define the early Philistine occupation, surmise with some certainty that their origins were in the eastern Aegean and Cypriot regions, and speculate with regard to their colonialist motivations.

The Philistine case study provides one of the clearest examples of the material expression of colonialism in the archaeological record. The Aegean-style material culture assemblage, which includes urban planning, changes in daily life and cuisine (particularly the introduction of significant pork consumption), and the appearance of the hallmark Mycenaean IIIC:1b decorated pottery and associated Aegean-style utilitarian pots, represents a clear break in tradition from the preceding Canaanite material culture. The production of locally manufactured Mycenaean IIIC wares at multiple locations in the eastern Mediterranean continued the process of decentralization of the palace-controlled production of Mycenaean-style pottery that had begun already in the thirteenth century B.C.E., as illustrated by the gradual diffusion of the production of Mycenaean IIIB:2 pottery in the eastern Aegean and Cyprus. With the collapse of Late Bronze Age imperial or royal economic control, several semiperipheral regions, including Cyprus, prospered during the ensuing twelfth and eleventh centuries B.C.E.

The sudden appearance of Aegean-style material culture at Pentapolis sites along Canaan's southern coastal plain was a result of a significant influx of a culturally distinct group of people from outside Canaan. These people most likely originated from Cyprus or the neighboring regions in the east Aegean and brought with them a well-established pottery style and craftsmen who were well versed in its manufacture, along with colonizers who quickly constructed urban centers based on new city plans and a material culture that was alien to Canaan. In the following generations, Aegean-style pottery underwent a process of creolization and eventually lost is unique character. In this study, the archaeological evidence corresponds to the biblical texts that describe a foreign people, referred to as the Philistines, who settled the southern coastal plain of Canaan sometime in the mid-twelfth century B.C.E.

The combination of the rich thirteenth–eleventh century archaeological record, considered in its textual and biblical contexts, provides a large body of diverse and largely complementary primary data for reconstructing the biblical world. The delineation of social and cultural boundaries and the utilization of sociological and anthropological approaches in the interpretation of the past form the basis for the construction of social, economic, and political processes and relationships that defined the biblical Egyptians, Canaanites, and Philistines and the ethnogenesis of early Israel.

Bibliography

Abd el-Maksoud, Mohamed. 1998. *Tell Heboua (1981–1991): Enquête archéologique sur la Deuxième Période Intermédiare et la Nouvel empire à l'extrémité orietale du Delta.* Paris: Editions Recherche sur les civilizations.

Adams, Matthew J., and Margaret E. Cohen. Forthcoming. The "Sea Peoples" in Primary Sources. In *The Philistines and Other Sea Peoples.* Edited by A. E. Killebrew, G. Lehmann, and M. Artzy. Atlanta: Society of Biblical Literature.

Adams, William Y. 1968. Invasion, Diffusion, Evolution? *Antiquity* 42:194–215.

———. 1977. *Nubia: Corridor to Africa.* Princeton: Princeton University Press.

———. 1984. The First Colonial Empire: Egypt in Nubia, 3200–1200 B.C. *Comparative Studies in Society and History* 26:36–71.

Adams, William Y., Dennis P. Van Gerven, and Richard S. Levy. 1978. The Retreat from Migrationism. *ARA* 7:483–532.

Aharoni, Yohanan. 1957a. Problems of the Israelite Conquest in Light of Archaeological Discoveries. *Antiquity and Survival* 2:131–50.

———. 1957b. *The Settlement of the Israelite Tribes in Upper Galilee* [Hebrew]. Jerusalem: Magnes.

———. 1967. *The Land of the Bible: A Historical Geography.* Translated by A. F. Rainey. London: Burns & Oates.

———. 1975. *Investigations at Lachish: The Sanctuary and the Residency* (Lachish V). Tel Aviv: Tel Aviv University.

———. 1976. Nothing Early and Nothing Late: Rewriting Israel's Conquest. *BA* 39:55–76.

Ahituv, Shmuel. 1978. Economic Factors in the Egyptian Conquest of Canaan. *IEJ* 28:93–105.

———. 1998. The Origins of Israel—The Documentary Evidence. Pages 135–40 in Ahituv and Oren 1998.

Ahituv, Shmuel, and Eliezer D. Oren, eds. 1998. *The Origin of Early Israel—Current Debate: Biblical, Historical and Archaeological Perspectives.* Beer-Sheva 12. Beer-Sheva: Ben-Gurion University of the Negev.

Ahlström, Gösta W. 1984a. The Early Iron Age Settlers at Hirbet el-Mšāš (Tel Māśoś). *ZDPV* 100:35–52.

———. 1984b. Giloh: A Judahite or Canaanite Settlement? *IEJ* 34:170–72.

———. 1986. *Who Were the Israelites?* Winona Lake, Ind.: Eisenbrauns.

———. 1991. The Origin of Israel in Palestine. *SJOT* 5/2:19–34.

———. 1993. *The History of Ancient Palestine from the Paleolithic Period to Alexander's Conquest.* JSOTSup 146. Sheffield: JSOT Press.

Ahlström, Gösta W., and Diana Edelman. 1985. Merneptah's Israel. *JNES* 44:59–61.

Åkerström, Åke. 1975. More Canaanite Jars from Greece. *OpAth* 11:185–92.

Akurgal, Ekrem. 1983. Das Dunkle Zeitalter Kleinasiens. Pages 67–78 in *Griechenland, die Ägäis und die Levante während der "Dark Ages" vom 12. bis zum 9.Jh v. Chr.* Edited by S. Deger-Jalkotzy. Mykenischen Studien 10. Vienna: Österreichischen Akademie der Wissenschaften.

Albright, William F. 1924. *Excavations and Results at Tell el-Fûl (Gibeah of Saul).* AASOR 4. New Haven: Yale University Press.

———. 1932. *The Excavations at Tel Beth Mirsim,* Vol. I: *The Pottery of the First Three Campaigns.* AASOR 12. Cambridge, Mass.: American Schools of Oriental Research.

———. 1935. Archaeology and the Date of the Hebrew Conquest of Palestine. *BASOR* 58:11–18.

———. 1937. Further Light on the History of Israel from Lachish and Megiddo. *BASOR* 68:22–26.

———. 1939. The Israelite Conquest of Canaan in Light of Archaeology. *BASOR* 74:11–23.

———. 1960. *The Archaeology of Palestine.* Harmondsworth, Eng.: Penguin.

———. 1968. *Yahweh and the Gods of Canaan.* London: University of London.

———. 1975a. The Amarna Letters from Palestine. *CAH*[3] 2.2:98–116.

———. 1975b. Syria, the Philistines and Phoenicia. *CAH*[3] 2.2:507–36.

Alcock, Susan E., and John F. Cherry, eds. 2004. *Side-by-Side Survey: Comparative Regional Studies in the Mediterranean World.* Oxford: Oxbow.

Alexander Ralph E., and Robert H. Johnston. 1982. Xeroradiography of Ancient Objects: A New Imaging Modality. Pages 145–54 in *Archaeological Ceramics.* Edited by J. S. Olin and A. D. Franklin. Washington, D.C.: Smithsonian Institution Press.

Alexander, Rani T. 1999. The Emerging World-System and Colonial Yucatan: The Archaeology of Core-Periphery Integration, 1780–1847. Pages 103–24 in Kardulias 1999b.

Algaze, Guillermo. 1993. Expansionary Dynamics of Some Early Pristine States. *American Anthropologist* 95:304–33.

Ålin, Per. 1977. Mycenaean Decline—Some Problems and Thoughts. Pages 31–39 in *Greece and the Eastern Mediterranean in Ancient History and Prehistory Studies Presented to Fritz Schachermeyr on the Occasion of His Eightieth Birthday.* Edited by K. H. Kinzl. Berlin: de Gruyter.

Allen, Mitchell J. 1992. The Mechanisms of Underdevelopment: An Ancient Mesopotamian Example. *Review* 15:453–76.

———. 1997. Contested Peripheries: Philistia in the Neo-Assyrian World-System. Ph.D. diss. University of California, Los Angeles.

Allen, Susan H. 1991. Late Bronze Age Grey Wares in Cyprus. Pages 151–67 in Barlow, Bolger, and Kling 1991.

———. 1994. Trojan Grey Ware at Tel Miqne-Ekron. *BASOR* 293:39–52.

Alt, Albrecht. 1939. Erwägungen über die Landnahme der Israeliten in Palästina. *PJ* 35:8–63.

———. 1967. The Settlement of the Israelite Tribes in Palestine. Pages 172–221 in *Essays on Old Testament History and Religion.* Garden City, N.Y.: Doubleday.

Amberg, C. R., and Jane Hartsook. 1946. Effect of Design Factors on Thermal-Shock Resistence of Cooking Ware. *American Ceramic Society* 25:448–52.

Amiran, Ruth. 1969. *Ancient Pottery of the Holy Land: From Its Beginnings in the Neolithic Period to the End of the Iron Age.* Jerusalem: Massada.

Amitai, Janet, ed. 1985. *Biblical Archaeology Today: Proceedings of the International Congress on Biblical Archaeology Jerusalem, April 1984.* Jerualem: Israel Exploration Society.

Anati, Emmanuel. 1959. Excavations at the Cemetery of Tell Abu Hawam (1952). *ʿAtiqot* 2:89–102.

Andrews, P. B. S. 1955. The Mycenaean Name of the Land of the Achaians. *RHA* 13:1–19

Anthony, David W. 1990. Migration in Archaeology: The Baby and the Bathwater. *American Anthropologist* 92:895–914.

———. 1992. The Bath Refilled: Migration in Archaeology Again. *American Anthropologist* 94:174–76.

———. 1997. Prehistoric Migration as Social Process. Pages 21–32 in *Migrations and Invasions in Archaeological Explanation.* Edited by J. Chapman and H. Hamerow. British Archaeological Reports International Series 664. Oxford: Archaeopress.

Arnold, Dean E. 1985. *Ceramic Theory and Cultural Process.* New Studies in Archaeology. New York: Cambridge University Press.

Arnold, Dorothea, ed. 1981. *Studien zur altägyptischen Keramik.* Deutsches Archäologisches Institut, Abteilung Kairo. Mainz am Rhein: von Zabern.

Arnold, Dorothea, and Janine Bourriau, eds. 1993. *An Introduction to Ancient Egyptian Pottery.* Mainz am Rhein: von Zabern.

Artzy, Michal. 1987. On Boats and Sea Peoples. *BASOR* 299:75–84.

———. 1988. War/Fighting Boats in the Second Millennium BC in the Eastern Mediterranaean. *Report of the Department of Antiquities, Cyprus* 1988:181–86.

———. 1994. Incense, Camels and Collared Rim Jars: Desert Trade Routes and Maritime Outlets in the Second Millennium. *OJA* 13(2):121–47.

———. 1995. Nami: A Second Millennium International Maritime Trading Center in the Mediterranean. Pages 17–40 in *Recent Excavations in Israel: A View to the West.* Edited by S. Gitin. Archaeological Institute of America Colloquia & Conference Papers No. 1. Dubuque, Iowa: Kendall/Hunt.

———. 1997. Nomads of the Sea. Pages 1–16 in *Res Maritimae: Cyprus and the Eastern Mediterranean from Prehistory to Late Antiquity.* Edited by S. Swiny, R. L. Hohlfelder, and H. W. Swiny. Cyprus American Archaeological Research Institute Monograph Series 1. Atlanta: Scholars Press.

———. 1998. Routes, Trade, Boats and "Nomads of the Sea." Pages 439–48 in Gitin, Mazar, and Stern 1998.

———. 2003. Mariners and Their Boats at the End of the Late Bronze and the Beginning of the Iron Age in the Eastern Mediterranean. *TA* 30:232–44.

Artzy, Michal, Isadore Perlman, and Frank Asaro. 1976. Alashiya of the Amarna Letters. *JNES* 35:171–82.

Asaro, Frank, and Isadore Perlman. 1973. Provenience Studies of Mycenaean Pottery Employing Neutron Activation Analysis. Pages 213–24 in *Acts of the International Archaeological Symposium "The Mycenaeans in the Eastern Mediter-*

ranean," Nicosia 27th March—2nd April, 1972. Nicosia: Department of Antiquities, Cyprus.

Asaro, Frank, Isadore Perlman, and Moshe Dothan. 1971. An Introductory Study of Mycenaean IIIC:1b Ware from Tel Ashdod. *Archaeometry* 13:169–75.

Asboe, Walter. 1946. Pottery in Ledakh, Western Tibet. *Man* 46:9–10.

Aspinall, Arnold. 1985. Neutron Activation Analysis in the Study of Ceramics. Pages 9–12 in *The Archaeologist and the Laboratory.* Edited by P. Phillips. CBA Research Report 58. London: Council for British Archaeology.

Assmann, Jan. 1997. *Moses the Egyptian: The Memory of Egypt in Western Monotheism.* Cambridge, Mass.: Harvard University Press.

Aston, David A. 1996. *Egyptian Pottery of the Late New Kingdom and Third Intermediate Period (Twelfth—Seventh Centuries BC): Tentative Footsteps in a Forbidding Terrain.* Studien zur Archäologie und Geschichte Altägyptens 13. Heidelberg: Heidelberger Orientverlag.

———. 1999. *Pottery from the Late New Kingdom to the Early Ptolemaic Period.* Archäologische Veröffentlichungen 95. Mainz am Rhein: von Zabern.

Astour, Michael C. 1965a. New Evidence on the Last Days of Ugarit. *AJA* 69:263–68.

———. 1965b. The Origin of the Terms "Canaan," "Phoenician," and "Purple." *JNES* 24:346–50.

———. 1970. Maʿhadu, the Harbor of Ugarit. *JESHO* 12:113–27.

———. 1972. The Merchant Class of Ugarit. Pages 11–26 in *Gesellschaftsklassen im alten Zweistromland und in den angrenzenden Gebieten: 18. Rencontre assyriologique internationale, Munchen, 29. Juni bis 3. July 1970.* Abhandlungen Bayerische Akademie der Wissenschaften: Philosophisch-Historische Klasse 75. Munich: Bayerischen Akademie der Wissenschaften.

———. 1981. Ugarit and the Great Powers. Pages 3–30 in *Ugarit in Retrospect: Fifty Years of Ugarit and Ugaritic.* Edited by G. D. Young. Winona Lake, Ind.: Eisenbrauns.

Åström, Paul. 1972. *The Swedish Cyprus Expedition, Vol. 4, Part IC: The Late Cypriote Bronze Age: Architecture and Pottery.* Lund: Swedish Cyprus Expedition.

———. 1985. The Sea Peoples in the Light of New Excavations. *Centre d'Etudes chypriotes* 3:3–17.

———. 1987. Die Akropolis von Midea um 1200 v. Chr. Pages 7–10 in *Forschungen zur aegaeischen Vorgeschichte: Das Ende der mykenischen Welt.* Edited by E. Thomas. Cologne: n.p.

———. 1991. Problems of Definition of Local and Imported Fabrics of Late Cypriot "Canaanite" Ware. Pages 67–72 in Barlow, Bolger, and Kling 1991.

Åström, Paul, Elisabeth Åström, Anna Hatziantoniou, Karin Niklasson, and Ulla Öbrink. 1983. *Hala Sultan Tekke 8; Excavations 1971–79.* SIMA 45.8. Goteborg: Åström.

Åström, Paul, and Katie Demakopoulou. 1996. Signs of an Earthquake at Midea? Pages 37–40 in Stiros and Jones 1996.

Åström, Paul, Robert Maddin, James D. Muhly, and Tamara Stech. 1986. Iron Artifacts from Swedish Excavations in Cyprus. *OpAth* 16:27–41.

Axelsson, Lars Eric. 1987. *The Lord Rose Up from Seir: Studies in the History and Traditions of the Negev and Southern Judah.* ConBOT 25. Stockholm: Almqvist & Wiksell.

Bahat, Dan. 1986. The 1975 Excavations at Sasa. Pages 85–105 in *The Western Galilee Antiquities* [Hebrew]. Edited by M. Yedaya. Haifa: Defense Ministry.

Bakir, Abd el-Mohsen. 1970. *Egyptian Epistolography from the Eighteenth to the Twenty-First Dynasty*. Cairo: Institut français d'archéologie orientale.

Balensi, Jacqueline. 1980. Les Fouilles de R. W. Hamilton à Tell Abu Hawam: Niveaux IV et V. Unpublished thesis submitted to the Universitaire de Strasbourg.

Balfet, Hélène. 1965. Ethnographical Observations in North Africa and Archaeological Interpretation. Pages 161–77 in *Ceramics and Man*. Edited by F. R. Matson. Chicago: Aldine.

Bankoff, H. Arthur, Nathan Meyer, and Mark Stefanovich. 1996. Handmade Burnished Ware and the Late Bronze Age of the Balkans. *Journal of Mediterranean Archaeology* 9:193–209.

Bankoff, Arthur H., and Frederick A. Winter. 1984. Northern Intruders in LH IIIC Greece: A View from the North. *Journal of Indo-European Studies* 12:1–30.

Banks, Marcus. 1996. *Ethnicity: Anthropological Constructs*. London: Routledge.

Bar-Yosef, Ofer, and Anatoly Khazanov, eds. 1992. *Pastoralism in the Levant: Archaeological Materials in Anthropological Perspectives*. Monographs in World Prehistory 10; Madison, Wis.: Prehistory Press.

Barako, Tristan J. 2000. The Philistine Settlement as Mercantile Phenomenon? *AJA* 104/3:513–30.

———. 2001. The Seaborne Migration of the Philistines. Ph.D. diss. Harvard University.

———. 2003. One if by Sea ... Two if by Land: How Did the Philistines Get to Canaan? One: By Sea. *BAR* 29/2:26–33, 64, 66.

Baramki, Dimitri C. 1959. A Late Bronze Age Tomb at Sarafand Ancient Sarepta. *Ber* 12:129–42.

Barlow, Jane A., Diane R. Bolger, and Barbara Kling. 1991. *Cypriot Ceramics: Reading the Prehistoric Record*. University Museum Monographs 74. Philadephia: University Museum of Archaeology and Anthropology.

Barnett, Richard D. 1953. Mopsos. *JHS* 73:140–43.

———. 1975. The Sea Peoples. *CAH*[3] 2.2:359–78.

Bartel, Brad. 1985. Comparative Historical Archaeology and Archaeological Theory. Pages 8–37 in Dyson 1985.

———. 1989. Acculturation and Ethnicity in Roman Moesia Superior. Pages 173–85 in Champion 1989.

Barth, Frederik. 1969. Introduction. Pages 7–38 in *Ethnic Groups and Boundaries: The Social Organization of Culture Difference*. Edited by F. Barth. Boston: Little, Brown & Company.

Basch, Lucien, and Michal Artzy. 1985. Ship Graffiti at Kition. Pages 322–44 in Karageorghis and Demas 1985.

Bass, George F. 1963. Mycenaean and Proto-geometric Tombs in the Halicarnassus Peninsula. *AJA* 67:353–61.

———. 1967. *Cape Gelidonya: A Bronze Age Shipwreck*. Philadelphia: American Philosophical Society.

———. 1973. Cape Gelidonya and Bronze Age Maritime Trade. Pages 29–37 in *Orient and Occident: Essays Presented to Cyrus H. Gordon on the Occasion of His*

Sixty-Fifth Birthday. Edited by Harry A. Hoffner. AOAT 22. Kevelaer: Butzon & Bercker.

———. 1986. A Bronze Age Shipwreck at Ulu Burun (Kas) 1984 Campaign. *AJA* 90:269–96.

———. 1987. Oldest Known Shipwreck Reveals Splendors of the Bronze Age. *National Geographic* 172/6:692–733.

———. 1991. Evidence of Trade from Bronze Age Shipwrecks. Pages 69–82 in Gale 1991.

Bass, George F., Cemal Pulak, Dominique Collon, and James Weinstein. 1989. The Bronze Age Shipwreck at Ulu Burun: 1986 Campaign. *AJA* 93:1–12.

Bauer, Alexander A. 1998. Cities of the Sea: Maritime Trade and the Origin of Philistine Settlement in the Early Iron Age Southern Levant. *OJA* 17: 149–67.

Baumgart, Winfried. 1982. *Imperialism: The Idea of Reality of British and French Colonial Expansion 1880–1914*. Oxford: Oxford University Press.

Baumgarten, Jacob J. 1992. Urbanization in the Late Bronze Age. Pages 143–50 in Kempinski and Reich 1992.

Beck, Pirhiya, and Moshe Kochavi, 1985. A Dated Assemblage of Late Thirteenth Century B.C.E. from the Egyptian Residency at Aphek. *TA* 12:29–42.

Beckerath, Jürgen von. 1951. *Tanis und Thebe: Historische Grundlagen der Ramessidenzeit in Ägypten*. ÄF 16. Glückstadt, N.Y.: Augustin.

Becks, Ralf. 2003. Troia VII: The Transition from the Late Bronze to the Early Iron Age. Pages 41–53 in Fischer et al. 2003.

Beit-Arieh, Itzhaq. 1985. Further Burials from the Deir el-Balah Cemetery. *TA* 12:43–53.

Bell, Barbara. 1971. The Dark Ages in Ancient History: I. The First Dark Age in Egypt. *AJA* 75:1–26.

Bell, Daniel. 1975. Ethnicity and Social Change. Pages 141–74 in *Ethnicity: Theory and Experience*. Edited by N. Glazer and D. P. Moynihan. Cambridge, Mass.: Harvard University Press.

Ben-Ami, Doron. 2001. The Iron Age I at Tel Hazor in Light of the Renewed Excavations. *IEJ* 51:148–70.

Ben-Arieh, Sara, and Gershon Edelstein. 1977. *Akko: Tombs Near the Persian Garden*. ʿAtiqot 12 (English series). Jerusalem: The Israel Department of Antiquities and Museums.

Ben-Shlomo, David. 2003. The Iron Age Sequence of Tel Ashdod: A Rejoinder to "Ashdod Revisited" By I. Finkelstein and L. Singer-Avitz. *TA* 30:83–107.

Ben-Tor, Amnon. 1998. The Fall of Canaanite Hazor—The "Who" and "When" Questions. Pages 456–67 in Gitin, Mazar, and Stern 1998.

———. 2002. Hazor—A City State between the Major Powers: A Rejoinder. *SJOT* 16:303–8.

Ben-Tor, Amnon, and Yuval Portugali. 1987. *Tell Qiri, A Village in the Jezreel Valley: Report of the Archaeological Excavations 1975–1977*. Qedem 24. Jerusalem: Institute of Archaeology, Hebrew University of Jerusalem.

Bendor, Shunya. 1996. *The Social Structure of Ancient Israel: The Institution of the Family (Beit ʾAb) from the Settlement to the End of the Monarchy* [Hebrew]. Jerusalem Biblical Studies 7. Jerusalem: Simor.

Bennett, Emmett L. 1955. *The Pylos Tablets: Texts of the Inscriptions Found 1939–1954.* Princeton: Princeton University Press.

Bentley, G. Carter. 1987. Ethnicity and Practice. *Comparative Studies in Society and History* 29:24–55.

Benzi, Mario. 1988. Rhodes in the LH IIIC Period. Pages 253–62 in French and Wardle 1988.

Betancourt, Philip P. 1976. The End of the Greek Bronze Age. *Antiquity* 50:40–47.

———. 2000. The Aegean and the Origin of the Sea Peoples. Pages 297–303 in Oren 2000.

Bienkowski, Piotr. 1989. Prosperity and Decline in LBA Canaan: A Reply to Liebowitz and Knapp. *BASOR* 275:59–63.

———. 1992a. The Beginning of the Iron Age in Edom: A Reply to Finkelstein. *Levant* 24:167–72.

———. 1992b. The Beginning of the Iron Age in Southern Jordan: A Framework. Pages 1–12 in Bienkowski 1992c.

______, ed. 1992c. *Early Edom and Moab: The Beginning of the Iron Age in Southern Jordan.* Sheffield Archaeological Monographs 7. Sheffield: Collins.

Bienkowski, Piotr, and Eveline van der Steen. 2001. Tribes, Trade, and Towns: A New Framework for the Late Iron Age in Southern Jordan and the Negev. *BASOR* 323:21–47.

Bierling, Neal. 1998. *Tel Miqne Ekron: Report on the 1995–1996 Excavations in Field XNW, Areas 77, 78, 79, 89, 90, 91, 101, 102: Iron Age I. Text and Data Base* (Plates, Sections, Plans). Edited by S. Gitin. The Tel Miqne-Ekron Limited Edition Series 7. Jerusalem: Tel Miqne-Ekron Project Office.

———. 2002. *Philistines: Giving Goliath His Due.* Marco Polo Monographs 7. Warren Center, Pa.: Shangri-La.

Bietak, Manfred. 1985. Response to T. Dothan. Pages 216–19 in Amitai 1985.

———. 1993. The Sea Peoples and the End of the Egyptian Administration of Canaan. Pages 292–306 in Biran and Aviram 1993.

Bimson, John J. 1991. Merneptah's Israel and Recent Theories of Israelite Origins. *JSOT* 49:3–29.

Bimson, John J., and David Livingston. 1987. Redating the Exodus. *BAR* 13/5:40–53, 66–68.

Binford, Lewis R. 1962. Archaeology as Anthropology. *AmerAnt* 28:217–25.

———. 1965. Archaeological Systematics and the Study of Cultural Process. *AmerAnt* 31:203–10.

———. 1982. Meaning, Inference and the Material Record. Pages 160–63 in *Ranking, Resources and Exchange.* Edited by C. Renfrew and S. Shennan. Cambridge: Cambridge University Press.

Bintliff, John. 1991. Post-modernism, Rhetoric and Scholasticism at TAG: The Current State of British Archaeological Theory. *Antiquity* 65:274–78.

Biran, Avraham. 1989. The Collared-Rim Jars and Settlement of the Tribe of Dan. Pages 71–96 in Gitin and Dever 1989.

———. 1994a. *Biblical Dan.* Jerusalem: Israel Exploration Society.

———. 1994b. Tel Dan: Biblical Texts and Archaeological Data. Pages 1–17 in *Scripture and Other Artifacts: Essays on the Bible and Archaeology in Honor of*

Philip J. King. Edited by M. D. Coogan, J. C. Exum, and L. E. Stager. Louisville: Westminster John Knox.

Biran, Avraham, and Joseph Aviram, eds. 1993. *Biblical Archaeology Today, 1990: Proceedings of the Second International Congress on Biblical Archaeology*. Jerusalem: Israel Exploration Society.

Biran, Avraham, and Ora Negbi. 1966. The Stratigraphical Sequence at Tel Sippor. *IEJ* 16:160–73.

Bittel, Kurt. 1983. Die archaeologische Situation in Kleinasien um 1200 v. chr. und während der nachfolgenden vier Jahrhunderte. Pages 25–47 in *Griechenland, die Agäis und die Levante während der "Dark Ages" vom 12. bis zum 9.Jh v. Chr.* Edited by S. Deger-Jalkotzy. Mykenischen Studien 10. Vienna: Österreichische Akademie der Wissenschaften.

Blegen, Carl W. 1962. *The Mycenaean Age: The Trojan War, the Dorian Invasion and Other Problems*. Cincinnati: University of Cincinnati Press.

Blegen, Carl W., John L. Caskey, and Marion Rawson. 1953. *Troy: Excavations Conducted by the University of Cincinnati, Vol. 3: The Sixth Settlement*. Princeton: Princeton University Press.

———. 1958. *Troy: Excavations Conducted by the University of Cincinnati, Vol. 4: Settlements VIIa, VIIb and VIII*. Princeton: Princton University Press.

Blegen, Carl W., and Marion Rawson. 1966. *The Palace of Nestor at Pylos in Western Messenia I: The Buildings and Their Contents, Part 1*. Princeton: Princeton University Press.

Bliss, Frederick J., and R. A. Stewart Macalister. 1902. *Excavations in Palestine during the Years 1898–1900*. London: Palestine Exploration Fund.

Bloch-Smith, Elizabeth. 1992a. The Cult of the Dead in Judah: Interpreting the Material Remains. *JBL* 111:213–24.

———. 1992b. *Judahite Burial Practices and Beliefs about the Dead*. JSOTSup 123. JSOT/ASOR Monograph Series 7. Sheffield: Sheffield Academic Press.

———. 2003. Israelite Ethnicity in Iron I: Archaeology Preserves What Is Remembered and What Is Forgotten in Israel's History. *JBL* 122:401–25.

Bloch-Smith, Elizabeth, and Beth Alpert Nakhai. 1999. A Landscape Comes to Life: The Iron I. *NEA* 62:62–92, 101–27.

Bloedow, Edmund F. 1985. Handmade Burnished Ware or Barbarian Pottery and Troy VIIb. *La Parola del Passato* 222:161–99.

Boling, Robert G. 1975. *Judges*. AB 6A. Garden City, N.Y.: Doubleday.

———. 1988. *The Early Biblical Community in Transjordan*. SWBA 6. Sheffield: Almond.

Bonfante, G. 1946. Who Were the Philistines? *AJA* 50:251–62.

Borchardt, Ludwig, and Herbert Ricke 1980. *Die Wohnhäuser in Tell el-Amarna*. WVDOG 91. Berlin: Mann.

Borowski, Oded. 2002. *Agriculture in Iron Age Israel*. Boston: American Schools of Oriental Research. Repr., Winona Lake, Ind.: Eisenbrauns, 1987.

Bounni, Adnan, Élisabeth Lagarce, Jacques Lagarce, and Nassib Saliby. 1978. Rapport préliminaire sur la deuxième campagne de fouilles (1976) à Ibn Hani (Syrie). *Syria* 55:233–301.

———. 1979. Rapport préliminaire sur la troisième campagn de fouilles (1977) à Ibn Hani (Syrie). *Syria* 56:217–91.

Bourriau, Janine. 1985. Technology and Typology of Egyptian Ceramics. Pages 29–42 in vol. 1 of *Ancient Technology and Modern Science.* Edited by W. G. Kingery. Columbus, Ohio: The American Ceramic Society.

———. 1990. Canaanite Jars from New Kingdom Deposits at Memphis, Kom Rabiʿa. *ErIsr* 21:18*–26*.

Bourriau, Janine, and Paul T. Nicholson. 1992. Marl Clay Pottery Fabrics of the New Kingdom from Memphis, Saqqara and Amarna. *JEA* 78:29–91.

Bourriau, Janine, Laurence Smith, and Margaret Serpico. 2001. The Provenance of Canaanite Amphorae Found at Memphis and Amarna in the New Kingdom. Pages 113–46 in *The Social Context of Technological Change: Egypt and the Near East, 1650–1550 B.C.* Edited by A. J. Shortland. Oxford: Oxbow.

Bowlus, Charles R. 1995. Review Article: Ethnogenesis Models and the Age of Migrations: A Critique. *Austrian History Yearbook* 26:147–64.

Braemer, Frank. 1982. *L'Architecture domestique du Levant à l'âge du Fer.* Paris: Éditions Recherche sur les civilizations.

Braudel, Fernand. 1972. *The Mediterranean and the Mediterranean World in the Age of Philip II.* 2 vols. New York: Harper & Row.

———. 1980. History and the Social Sciences: The *Longue Dureé.* Pages 25–54 in Braudel, *On History.* Chicago: University of Chicago Press.

Braun, David P. 1983. Pots as Tools. Pages 107–34 in *Archaeological Hammers and Theories.* Edited by J. A. Moore and A. S. Keene. New York: Academic Press.

Breasted, James H., ed. 1927. *Ancient Records of Egypt: Historical Documents from the Earliest Times to the Persian Conquest, Vol. 4: The Twentieth to the Twenty-Sixth Dynasties.* Chicago: University of Chicago Press.

Briend, Jacques, and Jean-Baptiste Humbert. 1980. *Tell Keisan (1971–1976) une cité phénicienne en Galilée.* Paris: Gabalda.

Bright, John. 1981. *A History of Israel.* 3rd ed. Philadelphia: Westminster.

Brinkman, J. A. 1984. Settlement Surveys and Documentary Evidence: Regional Variation and Secular Trend in Mesopotamian Demography. *JNES* 43:169–80.

Broadhurst, Clive. 1989. An Artistic Interpretation of Sety I's War Reliefs. *JEA* 75:229–34.

———. 1992. Religious Considerations at Qadesh and the Consequences for the Artistic Depiction of the Battle. Pages 77–81 in *Studies in Pharaonic Religion and Society in Honour of J. Gwyn Griffiths.* Edited by A. B. Lloyd. Egyptian Exploration Society, Occasional Papers 8. London: Egyptian Exploration Society.

Bronitsky, Gordon A., and Robert Hamer. 1986. Experiments in Ceramic Technology: The Effects of Various Tempering Materials on Impact and Thermal-Shock Resistance. *AmerAnt* 51:89–101.

Bronitsky, Gordon A., Alan Marks, and Cindy Burleson. 1985. Baptists and Boundaries: Lessons from Baptist Material Culture. Pages 325–40 in *The Archaeology of Frontiers and Boundaries.* Edited by S. W. Green and S. M. Perlman. Orlando: Academic Press.

Bronson, Bennet 1988. The Role of Barbarians in the Fall of States. Pages 196–218 in *The Collapse of Ancient States and Civilizations.* Edited by N. Yoffee and C. L. Cowgill. Tucson: University of Arizona Press.

Brooke, George J., Adrian H. W. Curtis, and John F. Healey, eds. 1994. *Ugarit and the Bible: Proceedings of the International Symposium on Ugarit and the Bible.* Manchester, September 1992. Münster: Ugarit-Verlag.

Broshi, Magen, and Ram Gophna. 1986. Middle Bronze Age II Palestine: Its Settlement and Population. *BASOR* 261:73–90.

Brug, John F. 1985. *A Literary and Archaeological Study of the Philistines.* British Archaeological Reports International Series 265. Oxford: B.A.R.

Brumfiel, Elizabeth M. 1994. Ethnic Groups and Political Development in Ancient Mexico. Pages 89–102 in *Factional Competition and Political Development in the New World.* Edited by E. M. Brumfiel and J. W. Cox. Cambridge: Cambridge University Press.

Brunton, Guy 1930. *Qau and Badari III.* London: British School of Archaeology in Egypt.

Brunton, Guy, and Reginald Engelbach. 1927. *Gurob.* London: British School of Archaeology in Egypt.

Bryan, Betsy M. 1996. Art, Empire, and the End of the Late Bronze. Pages 33–79 in *The Study of the Ancient Near East in the Twenty-First Century: The William Foxwell Albright Centennial.* Edited by J. S. Cooper and G. M. Schwartz. Winona Lake, Ind.: Eisenbrauns.

Bryce, Trevor R. 1989. Ahhiyawans and Mycenaeans—An Anatolia Viewpoint. *OJA* 8:297–311.

Bryson, R. A., H. H. Lamb, and David R. Donley. 1974. Drought and the Decline of Mycenae. *Antiquity* 48:46–50.

Buchignani, Norman. 1982. *Anthropological Approaches to the Study of Ethnicity.* Toronto: The Multicultural History, Society of Toronto.

Buhl, Marie-Louise, and Svend Holm-Nielsen. 1969. *Shiloh: The Danish Excavations at Tall Sailūn, Palestine, in 1926, 1929, 1932 and 1963.* Copenhagen: National Museum of Denmark.

Bunimovitz, Shlomo. 1988–89. An Egyptian "Governor's Residency" at Gezer? Another Suggestion. *TA* 15–16:68–76.

———. 1989. The Land of Israel in the Late Bronze Age: A Case Study of Sociocultural Change in a Complex Society [Hebrew with English abstract]. Ph.D. diss. Tel Aviv University.

———. 1990. Problems in the "Ethnic" Identification of the Philistine Material Cultures. *TA* 17:210–22.

———. 1993. The Study of Complex Societies: The Material Culture of Late Bronze Age Canaan as a Case Study. Pages 443–51 in Biran and Aviram 1993.

———. 1994a. The Problem of Human Resources in Late Bronze Age Palestine and Its Socio-economic Implications. *UF* 26:1–20.

———. 1994b. Socio-political Transformations in the Central Hill Country in the Late Bronze–Iron I Transition. Pages 179–202 in Finkelstein and Naʾaman 1994b.

———. 1995. On the Edge of Empires—Late Bronze Age (1500–1200 BCE). Pages 320–32 in *The Archaeology of Society in the Holy Land.* Edited by T. E. Levy. New York: Facts on File.

———. 1998. Sea Peoples in Cyprus and Israel: A Comparative Study of Immigration Processes. Pages 103–13 in Gitin, Mazar, and Stern 1998.

Bunimovitz, Shlomo, and Avraham Faust. 2003a. Building Identity: The Four-Room House and the Israelite Mind. Pages 411–23 in Dever and Gitin 2003.

———. 2003b. The Four Room House: Embodying Iron Age Israelite Society. *NEA* 66:22–31.

Bunimovitz, Shlomo, and Assaf Yasur-Landau. 1996. Philistine and Israelite Pottery: A Comparative Approach to the Question of Pots and People. *TA* 23:88–101.

Bunimovitz, Shlomo, and Orna Zimhoni. 1990. "Lamp and Bowl" Foundation Deposits from the End of the Late Bronze Age—Beginning of the Iron Age in Eretz-Israel [Hebrew]. *ErIsr* 21:41–55.

Burch, Ernest S., Jr., Eliza Jones, Hannah P. Loon, and Lawrence D. Kaplan. 1999. The Ethnogenesis of the Kuuvaum Kaniagmut. *Ethnohistory* 42/2:291–327.

Burgess, Jonathan S. 2001. *The Tradition of the Trojan War in Homer and the Epic Cycle.* Baltimore: Johns Hopkins University Press.

Butzer, Karl W. 1980. Civilizations: Organisms or Systems? *American Scientist* 68:517–23.

Cahill, Jane M. 2003. Jerusalem at the Time of the United Monarchy: The Archaeological Evidence. Pages 13–80 in Vaughn and Killebrew 2003.

Caldwell, Joseph R. 1959. The New American Archaeology. *Science* 129:303–7.

———. 1964. Interaction Spheres in Prehistory. Pages 133–43 in *Hopewellian Studies.* Edited by J. R. Caldwell and R. L. Hall. Illinois State Museum Scientific Papers 12. Springfield: State of Illinois.

Callaway, Joseph A. 1965. The 1964 Ai (et-Tell) Excavations. *BASOR* 178:13–40.

———. 1969. The 1966 Ai (et-Tell) Excavations. *BASOR* 196:2–16.

———. 1976. Excavating Ai (et-Tell): 1964–1972. *BA* 39:18–39.

———. 1980. *The Early Bronze Age Citadel and Lower City at Ai (et-Tell): A Report of the Joint Archaeological Expedition to Ai (et-Tell), No. 2.* Cambridge, Mass.: American Schools of Oriental Research.

———. 1985. A New Perspective on the Hill Country Settlement of Canaan in Iron Age I. Pages 31–49 in Tubb 1985.

———. 1987. Ai (et-Tell): Problem Site for Biblical Archaeologists. Pages 87–99 in *Archaeology and Biblical Interpretation: Essays in Memory of D. Glenn Rose.* Edited by L. G. Perdue, L. E. Tombs, and G. L. Honson. Atlanta: John Knox.

Callaway, Joseph A. and Robert E. Cooley. 1971. A Salvage Excavtion at Raddana, in Bireh. *BASOR* 201:9–19.

Campbell, Edward F. 1976. Two Amarna Notes: The Shechem City-State and Amarna Administrative Terminology. Pages 39–54 in *Magnalia Dei: The Mighty Acts of God: Essays on the Bible and Archaeology in Memory of G. Ernest Wright.* Edited by F. M. Cross, W. E. Lemke, and P. D. Miller Jr. Garden City, N.Y.: Doubleday.

———. 1991. *Shechem II: Portrait of a Hill Country Vale: The Shechem Regional Survey.* ASOR Reports 2. Atlanta: Scholars Press.

———. 2002. *Shechem III: The Stratigraphy and Architecture of Shechem/Tell Balâtah, Vol. 1: The Text.* Archaeological Reports 6. Boston: American Schools of Oriental Research.

Carpenter, Rhys. 1966. *Discontinuity in Greek Civilization.* Cambridge: Cambridge University Press.

Cashmore, Ellis. 1994. *Dictionary of Race and Ethnic Relations.* 3rd ed. London: Routledge.

Casson, Lionel. 1959. *The Ancient Mariners: Seafarers and Sea Fighters in the Mediterranean in Ancient Times.* New York: Macmillian.

———. 1971. *Ships and Seamanship in the Ancient World.* Princeton: Princeton University Press.

Catling, Hector W. 1961. A New Bronze Sword from Cyprus. *Antiquity* 35:115–22.

———. 1973. The Achaean Settlement of Cyprus. Pages 34–39 in *Acts of the International Archaeological Symposium "The Mycenaeans in the Eastern Mediterranean".* Edited by V. Karageorghis. Nicosia: Department of Antiquities, Cyprus.

———. 1975. Cyprus in the Late Bronze Age. *CAH*[3] 2.2:188–216.

Catling, Hector W., and E. A. Catling. 1981. "Barbarian" Pottery from the Mycenaean Settlement at the Menelaion, Sparta. *ABSA* 76:71–82.

Catling, Hector W., and Richard E. Jones. 1986. Cyprus, 2500–500 B.C.: The Aegean and the Near East, 1550–1050 B.C. Pages 523–625 in Jones, *Greek and Cypriot Pottery: A Review of Scientific Methods.* Athens: British School of Archaeology.

Caubet, Annie. 1992. The Reoccupation of the Syrian Coast after the Destruction of the "Crisis Years." Pages 123–31 in Ward and Joukowsky 1992.

Cavillier, Giacomo. 2001. The Ancient Military Road between Egypt and Palestine Reconsidered: A Reassessment. *Göttinger Miszellen* 185:23–31.

Černý, Jaroslav. 1958. Egyptian Hieratic. Pages 132–33 in Tufnell 1958.

Chadwick, John. 1973. *Documents in Mycenaean Greek.* 2nd ed. Cambridge: Cambridge University Press.

———. 1976. Who Were the Dorians? *La Parola del Passato* 31:103–17.

Chadwick, John, John T. Killen, and Jean Pierre, Olivier. 1971. *The Knossos Tablets: A Transliteration.* 4th ed. Cambridge: Cambridge University Press.

Chambon, Alain. 1984. *Tell el-Fâr'ah I: L'âge du Fer.* Éditions Recherche sur les civilizations 31. Paris: Éditions Recherche sur les civilisations.

Champion, Timothy C. 1989. Introduction. Pages 1–21 in *Centre and Periphery: Comparative Studies in Archaeology.* One World Archaeology 11. Edited by T. C. Champion. London: Unwin Hyman.

———. 1990. Migration Revived. *Journal of Danish Archaeology* 9:214–18.

Chaney, Marvin L. 1983. Ancient Palestinian Peasant Movements and the Formation of Premonarchic Israel. Pages 39–90 in *Palestine in Transition: The Emergence of Ancient Israel.* Edited by D. N. Freedman and D. F. Graf. Sheffield: Almond.

Chapman, John. 1997. The Impact of Modern Invasion and Migrations on Archaeological Explanations. Pages 11–20 in *Migrations and Invasions in Archaeological Explanation.* Edited by J. Chapman and H. Hamerow. British Archaeological Reports International Series 664. Oxford: Archaeopress.

Chapman, John, and Helena Hamerow. 1997. Introduction: On the Move Again—Migrations and Invasions in Archaeological Explanation. Pages 1–10 in *Migrations and Invasions in Archaeological Explanation.* Edited by J. Chapman and H. Hamerow. British Archaeological Reports International Series 664. Oxford: Archaeopress.

Chapman, Malcolm, ed. 1993. *Social and Biological Aspects of Ethnicity.* Oxford: Oxford Univerity Press for the Biological Society.

Chapman, Malcolm, Maryon McDonald, and Elizabeth Tonkin. 1989. Introduction: History and Social Anthropology. Pages 1–21 in *History and Ethnicity.* Edited by E. Tonkin, M. McDonald and M. Chapman. Association of Social Anthropologists of Britain and the Commonwealth Monographs 27. London: Routledge.

Chase-Dunn, Christopher. 1988. Comparing World-Systems: Toward a Semiperipheral Development. *Comparative Civilizations Review* 19:29–66.

Chase-Dunn, Christopher, and Thomas D. Hall. 1993. Comparing World-Systems: Concepts and Working Hypotheses. *Social Forces* 71:851–86.

———, eds. 1991. *Core-Periphery Relations in Precapitalist Worlds.* Boulder, Colo.: Westview.

Childe, V. Gordon. 1942. *What Happened in History.* Harmondsworth, Eng.: Penguin.

———. 1950. *Prehistoric Migrations in Europe.* Instituttet for sammenlignende kulturforskning Serie A: Forelesninger 20. Cambridge, Mass.: Harvard University Press.

Cifola, Barbara. 1988. Ramses III and the Sea Peoples: A Structural Analysis of the Medinet Habu Inscriptions. *Or* 57:275–306.

———. 1991. The Terminology of Ramses III's Historical Records with a Formal Analysis of the War Scenes. *Or* 60:9–57.

———. 1994. The Role of the Sea Peopls at the End of the Late Bronze Age: A Reassessment of Textual and Archaeological Evidence. *Orientis Antiqvi Miscellanea* 1:1–23.

Clamer, Christa. 1976. The Late Bronze Age Alabaster Vessels. M.A. thesis. The Hebrew University of Jerusalem.

———. 1980. A Gold Plaque from Tel Lachish. *TA* 7:152–62.

Clark, Douglas. 1989. Field B: The Western Defense System. Pages 244–57 in *Madaba Plains Project 1: The 1984 Season at Tell el-ʿUmeiri and Vicinity and Subsequent Studies.* Edited by L. T. Geraty, L. G. Herr, Ø. S. LaBianca, and R. W. Younker. Berrien Springs, Mich.: Andrews University/Institute of Archaeology.

———. 1991. Field B: The Western Defense System. Pages 53–73 in *Madaba Plains Project 2: The 1987 Season at Tell el-ʿUmeiri and Vicinity and Subsequent Studies.* Edited by L. T. Geraty, L. G. Herr, Ø. S. LaBianca, and R. W. Younker. Berrien Springs, Mich.: Andrews University/Institute of Archaeology.

———. 1996. Early Iron I Pillared Building at Tall al-ʿUmayri. *BA* 59:241.

———. 1997. Field B: The Western Defense System. Pages 53–98 in *Madaba Plains Project 3: The 1989 Season at Tell el-ʿUmeiri and Vicinity and Subsequent Studies.* Edited by L. G. Herr, L. T. Geraty, Ø. S. LaBianca, and R. W. Younker. Berrien Springs, Mich.: Andrews University Press.

———. 2000. Field B: The Western Defense System. Pages 59–94 in *Madaba Plains Project 4: The 1992 Season at Tell el-ʿUmeiri and Vicinity and Subsequent Studies.* Edited by L. G. Herr, L. T. Geraty, Ø. S. LaBianca, and R. W. Younker. Berrien Stprings, MI: Andrews University Press.

———. 2002. Field B: The Western Defense System. Pages 48–116 in *Madaba Plains Project 5: The 1992 Season at Tall al-ʿUmayri and Vicinity and Subsequent Studies.*

Edited by L. G. Herr, L. T. Geraty, Ø. S. LaBianca, and R. W. Younker. Berrien Stprings, Mich.: Andrews University Press.

———. 2003. Bricks, Sweat and Tears: The Human Investment in Constructing a "Four-room" House. *NEA* 66:34–43.

Clark, J. Grahame D. 1966. The Invasion Hypothesis in British Archaeology. *Antiquity* 40:172–89.

Clarke, David L. 1968. *Analytical Archaeology*. London: Methuen.

Clements, Ronald. 1983. The Isaiah Narrative of 2 Kings 20:12–19 and the Date of the Deuteronomistic History. Pages 209–20 in vol. 3 of *Isaac Leo Seeligman Volume: Essays on the Bible and the Ancient World* [Hebrew]. Edited by A. Rofé and Y. Zakovitch. Jerusalem: Rubinstein.

Cline, Eric H. 1994. *Sailing the Wine-Dark Sea: International Trade and the Late Bronze Age Aegean*. BAR International Series 591. Oxford: B.A.R.

———. 1995. Egyptian and Near Eastern Imports at Late Bronze Age Mycenae. Pages 91–115 in *Egypt, the Aegean and the Levant: Interconnections in the Second Millennium BC*. Edited by W. V. Davies and L. Schofield. London: British Museum Press.

Cohen, Abner. 1974a. Introduction: The Lesson of Ethnicity. Pages ix–xxiv in *Urban Ethnicity*. Edited by A. Cohen. London: Tavistock.

———. 1974b. *Two-Dimensional Man: An Essay on the Anthropology of Power and Symbolism in Complex Society*. Berkeley and Los Angeles: University of California Press.

Cohen, Raymond, and Raymond Westbrook. 2000a. The Amarna System. Pages 1–12 in Cohen and Westbrook 2000c.

———. 2000b. Conclusion: The Beginnings of International Relations. Pages 225–36 in Cohen and Westbrook 2000c.

———, eds. 2000c. *Amarna Diplomacy: The Beginnings of International Relations*. Baltimore: Johns Hopkins University Press.

Cohen, Ronald. 1978. Ethnicity: Problem and Focus in Anthropology. *ARA* 7:379–403.

Cohen-Weinberger, Anat. 1998. Petrographic Analysis of the Egyptian Forms from Stratum VI at Tel Beth-Shean. Pages 406–12 in Gitin, Mazar, and Stern 1998.

Cohen-Weinberger, Anat, and Yuval Goren. 1996. Petrographic Analysis of Iron Age I Pithoi from Tel Sasa. *ʿAtiqot* 28:77–83.

Cohen-Weinberger, Anat, and Sam R. Wolff. 2001. Production Centers of Collared-Rim Pithoi from Sites in the Carmel Coast and Ramat Menashe Regions. Pages 639–57 in Wolff 2001.

Collett, David. 1987. A Contribution to the Study of Migrations in the Archaeological Record: The Ngoni and Kolodo Migrations as a Case Study. Pages 105–16 in *Archaeology as Long-Term History*. Edited by I. Hodder. Cambridge: Cambridge University Press.

Conkey, Margaret W. 1989. The Use of Diversity in Stylistic Analysis. Pages 118–29 in Leonard and Jones 1989.

———. 1990. Experimenting with Style in Archaeology: Some Historical and Theoretical Issues. Pages 5–17 in *The Uses of Style in Archaeology*. Edited by M. W. Conkey and C. A. Hastorf. New Directions in Archaeology. Cambridge: Cambridge University Press.

Connor, Walker. 1984. Eco- or Ethno-nationalism? *Ethnic and Racial Studies* 7:342–59.

Coogan, Michael D. 1987. Of Cults and Cultures: Reflections on the Interpretations of Archaeological Evidence. *PEQ* 119: 1–8.

———. 1990. Archaeology and Biblical Studies: The Book of Joshua. Pages 19–32 in *The Hebrew Bible and Its Interpreters*. Edited by W. H. Propp, B. Halpern, and D. N. Freedman. Biblical and Judaic Studies from the University of California, San Diego 1. Winona Lake, Ind.: Eisenbrauns.

———, ed. and trans. 1978. *Stories from Ancient Canaan*. Philadelphia: Westminster.

Cook, Valerie. 1988. Cyprus and the Outside World during the Transition from the Bronze Age to the Iron Age. *OpAth* 17:13–32.

Cooley, Robert E. 1975. Four Seasons of Excavation at Khirbet Raddana. *Near Eastern Archaeological Society Bulletin* NS 5:5–20.

Cooley, Robert E., and Gary D. Pratico. 1994. Tell Dothan: The Western Cemetery, with Comments on Joseph Free's Excavations, 1953 to 1964. Pages 147–73 in *Preliminary Excavation Reports: Sardis, Bir Umm Fawakhir, Tell el-ᶜUmeiri, The Combined Caesarea Expeditions, and Tell Dothan*. Edited by W. G. Dever. AASOR 52. Boston: American Schools of Oriental Research.

Coote, Robert B. 1990. *Early Israel: A New Horizon*. Minneapolis: Fortress.

———. 1991. Early Israel. *SJOT* 5/2:35–46.

Coote, Robert B., and Keith W. Whitelam. 1987. *The Emergence of Israel in Historical Perspective*. SWBA 5. Sheffield: Almond.

Costin, Cathy L. 1991. Craft Specialization: Issues in Defining, Documenting, and Explaining the Organization of Production. Pages 1–55 in vol. 3 of *Archaeological Method and Theory*. Edited by M. B. Schiffer. Tucson: University of Arizona Press.

Costin, Cathy L., and Melissa B. Hagstrum. 1995. Standardization, Labor Investment, Skill, and the Organization of Ceramic Production in Late Prehispanic Highland Peru. *AmerAnt* 60:619–39.

Coulson, William D. E. 1990. *The Greek Dark Ages: A Review of the Evidence and Suggestions for Future Research*. Athens: Coulson.

Courtois, Jacques-Claude. 1971. Le Sanctuaire du dieu au lingot d'Enkomi-Alasia. Pages 151–362 in *Alasia I*. Edited by C. F. A. Schaeffer. Mission archéologie d'Alasia 4. Paris: Mission archéologie d'Alasia, Collège de France.

Cowgill, George L. 1988. Onward and Upward with Collapse. Pages 244–76 in *The Collapse of Ancient States and Civilizations*. Edited by N. Yoffee and G. L. Cowgill. Tucson: University of Arizona.

———. 1989. The Concept of Diversity of Archaeological Theory. Pages 131–49 in Leonard and Jones 1989.

Crabtree, Pamela J. 1989. Sheep, Horses, Swine and Kine: A Zooarchaeological Perspective on the Anglo-Saxon Settlement of England. *JFA* 16:205–13.

Cribb, Roger. 1991. *Nomads in Archaeology*. Cambridge: Cambridge University Press.

Crielaard, Jan Paul. 1995. Homer, History and Archaeology: Some Remarks on the Date of the Homeric World. Pages 201–288 in *Homeric Questions: Essays in Philology, Ancient History and Archaeology, Including the Papers of a Conference Organized by the Netherlands Institute at Athens (15 May 1993)*. Edited by J. P. Crielaard. Amsterdam: Gieben.

Cross, Frank M. 1973. *Canaanite Myth and Hebrew Epic: Essays in the History of the Religion of Israel.* Cambridge, Mass.: Harvard University Press.

———. 1998. Reuben, The Firstborn of Jacob: Sacral Traditions and Early Israelite History. Pages 53–70 in *From Epic to Canon: History and Literature in Ancient Israel.* Baltimore: Johns Hopkins University Press.

———, ed. 1979. *Symposia Celebrating the Seventy-Fifth Anniversary of the Founding of the American Schools of Oriental Research (1900–1975).* Cambridge, Mass.: American Schools of Oriental Research.

Cross, Frank M., and David Noel Freedman, 1955. The Song of Miriam. *JNES* 14:237–50.

———. 1975. *Studies in Ancient Yahwistic Poetry.* SBLDS 21. Missoula, Mont.: Scholars Press.

Crossland, Ronald A. 1971. Immigrants from the North. *CAH*[3] 1.2:824–76.

Crossland, Ronald A., and Ann Birchall, eds. 1973. *Bronze Age Migrations in the Aegean: Archaeological and Linguistic Problems in Greek Prehistory.* London: Duckworth.

D'Agata, Anna Lucia. 2003. Crete at the Transition from Late Bronze to Iron Age. Pages 21–28 in Fischer et al. 2003.

Dajani, Rafiq W. 1964. Iron Age Tombs from Irbid. *ADAJ* 8–9:99–101.

Daniel, John F. 1937. Two Late Cypriote III Tombs from Kourion. *AJA* 41:56–85.

———. 1942. Review of E. Sjoqvist, *Problems of the Late Cypriot Bronze Age. AJA* 46:286–93.

Daviau, P. M. Michèle. 1993. *Houses and Their Furnishings in Bronze Age Palestine: Domestic Activity Areas and Artefact Distribution in the Middle and Late Bronze Ages.* JSOT/ASOR Monograph Series 8. Sheffield: JSOT Press.

David, Nicholas, and Carol Kramer. 2001. *Ethnoarchaeology in Action.* Cambridge: Cambridge University Press.

Davies, Norman de Garis. 1923. *The Tombs of Two Officials of Tuthmosis The Fourth (Nos. 75 and 90).* Theban Tomb Series, Third Memoir. London: Egypt Exploration Society.

———. 1943. *The Tomb of Rekh-mi-re at Thebes.* New York: Metropolitan Museum of Art.

Davies, Philip R. 1992. *In Search of 'Ancient Israel'.* JSOTSup 148. Sheffield: Sheffield Academic Press.

Davis, Jack L., ed. 1998. *Sandy Pylos: An Archaeological History from Nestor to Navarino.* Austin: University of Texas Press.

Davis, Jack L., Susan E. Alcock, John Bennet, Yannos Lolos, and Cynthia W. Shelmerdine. 1997. The Pylos Regional Archaeological Project, Part I: Overview and the Archaeological Survey. *Hesperia* 66:391–494.

Davis, Thomas W. 2004. *Shifting Sands: The Rise and Fall of Biblical Archaeology.* New York: Oxford University Press.

Day, John. 1994. Ugarit and the Bible: Do They Presume the Same Canaanite Mythology and Religion? Pages 35–52 in Brooke, Curtis, and Healey 1994.

Dearman, J. Andrew. 1992. Settlement Patterns and the Beginning of the Iron Age in Moab. Pages 65–76 in Bienkowski 1992c.

Deetz, James. 1965. *The Dynamics of Stylistic Change in Arikara Ceramics.* Illinois Studies in Anthropology 4. Urbana: University of Illinois Press.

Deger-Jalkotzy, Sigrid. 1983. Das Problem der "Handmade Burnished Ware." Pages 161–68 in *Griechenland, die Ägäis und die Levante während der "Dark Ages" vom 12. bis zum 9.Jh v. Chr.* Edited by Sigrid Deger-Jalkotzy. Mykenischen Studien 10. Vienna: Österreichische Akademie der Wissenschaften.

———. 1998. The Aegean Islands and the Breakdown of the Mycenaean Palaces around 1200 B.C. Pages 105–20 in *Eastern Mediterranean: Cyprus-Dodecanese-Crete Sixteenth–Sixth Cent. B.C. Proceedings of the International Symposium Held at Rethymnon—Crete in May 1997.* Edited by V. Karageorghis and N. Chr. Stampolidis. Athens: University of Crete and the A. G. Leventis Foundation.

Deger-Jalkotzy, Sigrid, and Michaela Zavadil, eds. 2003. *LH IIIC Chronology and Synchronisms: Proceedings of the Inernational Workshop Held at the Austrian Academy of Sciences at Vienna, May 7th and 8th, 2001.* Vienna: Österreichischen Akademie der Wissenschaften.

Denemark, Robert A., Jonathan Friedman, Barry K. Gills, and George Modelski, eds. 2000. *World System History: The Social Science of Long-Term Change.* New York: Routledge.

Desborough, Vincent R. d'A. 1964. *The Last Mycenaeans and Their Successors: An Archaeological Survey c. 1200–c. 1000 BC.* London: Oxford University Press.

———. 1972. *The Greek Dark Ages.* New York: St. Martin's.

Dessel, J. P. 1999. Tell ʿEin Zippori and the Lower Galilee in the Late Bronze and Iron Ages: A Village Perspective. Pages 1–32 in *Galilee through the Centuries: Confluence of Cultures.* Edited by E. M. Meyers. Duke Judaic Studies Series 1. Winona Lake, Ind.: Eisenbrauns.

Dever, William G. 1977. The Patriarchal Traditions. Pages 102–20 in *Israelite and Judaean History.* Edited by J. H. Hayes and J. M. Miller. Philadelphia: Westminster.

———. 1980. New Vistas on the EB IV ("MB I") Horizon in Syria-Palestine. *BASOR* 237:35–64.

———. 1982. Retrospects and Prospects in Biblical and Syro-Palestinian Archeology. *BA* 45:103–7.

———. 1985. Syro-Palestinian and Biblical Archaeology. Pages 31–74 in *The Hebrew Bible and Its Modern Interpreters.* Edited by D. A. Knight and G. M. Tucker. Chico, Calif.: Scholars Press.

———. 1986. *Gezer IV: The 1969–71 Season in Field VI: The "Acropolis."* Annual of the Nelson Glueck School of Biblical Archaeology 4. Jerusalem: Nelson Glueck School of Biblical Archaeology.

———. 1990. The Israelite Settlement in Canaan: New Archaeological Models. Pages 39–84 in *Recent Archaeological Discoveries and Biblical Research.* Seattle: University of Washington Press.

———. 1991. Tel Gezer, 1990. *IEJ* 41: 282–86.

———. 1992a. How to Tell a Canaanite from an Israelite. Pages 27–60 in *The Rise of Early Israel.* Edited by H. Shanks. Washington, D.C.: Biblical Archaeology Society.

———. 1992b. Israel, History of: Archaeology and the Israelite "Conquest." *ABD* 3:545–58.

———. 1992c. The Late Bronze–Early Iron I Horizon in Syria-Palestine: Egyptians, Canaanites, "Sea Peoples," and Proto-Israelites. Pages 99–110 in Ward and Joukowsky 1992.

———. 1993a. Cultural Continuity, Ethnicity in the Archaeological Record and the Question of Israelite Origins. *ErIsr* 24:22*–33*.

———. 1993b. Further Evidence on the Date of the Outer Wall at Gezer. *BASOR* 289:33–54.

———. 1995a. Ceramics, Ethnicity, and the Question of Israel's Origins. *BA* 58:200–13.

———. 1995b. "Will the Real Israel Please Stand Up?" Archaeology and Israelite Historiography: Part I. *BASOR* 298:61–80.

———. 1997. On Listening to the Text—and the Artifacts. Pages 1–23 in *The Echoes of Many Texts: Reflections on Jewish and Christian Traditions: Essays in Honor of Lou H. Silberman.* Edited by W. G. Dever and J. E. Wright. Atlanta: Scholars Press.

———. 1998. Israelite Origins and the "Nomadic Idea": Can Archaeology Separate Fact from Fiction? Pages 220–37 in Gitin, Mazar, and Stern 1998.

———. 2001. *What Did the Biblical Writers Know and When Did They Know It?* Grand Rapids: Eerdmans.

———. 2003. *Who Were the Early Israelites and Where Did They Come From?* Grand Rapids: Eerdmans.

Dever, William G., and Seymour Gitin, eds. *Symbiosis, Symbolism, and the Power of the Past: Canaan, Ancient Israel, and Their Neighbors from the Late Bronze Age through Roman Palaestina: Proceedings of the Centennial Symposium W. F. Albright Institute of Archaeological Research and American Schools of Oriental Research Jerusalem, May 29—May 31, 2000.* Winona Lake, Ind.: Eisenbrauns.

Dever, William G., H. Darrell Lance, and G. Ernest Wright. 1970. *Gezer I: Preliminary Report of the 1964–1966 Seasons.* Jerusalem: Hebrew Union College.

Dever, William G., H. Darrel Lance, R. G. Bullard, D. P. Cole, and J. D Seger. 1974. *Gezer II: Report of the 1967–70 Seasons in Fields I and II.* Edited by W. G. Dever. Jerusalem: Hebrew Union College.

Dickens, Roy S. 1980. Ceramic Diversity as an Indicator of Cultural Dynamics in the Woodland Period. *Tennessee Anthropologist* 5:34–46.

Dickens, Roy S., and James H. Chapman. 1978. Ceramic Patterning and Social Structure at Two Late Historic Upper Creek Sites in Alabama. *AmerAnt* 43:390–98.

Dickinson, Oliver. 1974. Drought and Decline of Mycenae: Some Comments. *Antiquity* 48:228–29.

Diebner, B.-J. 1995. Wann san Deborah ihr Lied? Überlegungen zu zwei der ältesten Texte des TNK (Ri 4 und 5). *Amsterdamse Cahiers voor Exegese en bijbelse Theologie* 14:106–30.

Diener, Paul, and Eugene E. Robkin. 1978. Ecology, Evolution, and the Search for Cultural Origins: The Question of Islamic Pig Prohibition. *CurrAnthr* 19:493–540.

Dietler, Michael. 1989. Greeks, Etruscans, and Thirsty Barbarians: Early Iron Age Interaction in the Rhône Basin of France. Pages 127–141 in *Centre and Periphery:*

Comparative Studies in Archaeology. Edited by T. C. Champion. One World Archaeology 11. London: Unwin Hyman.

Dietler, Michael, and Ingrid Herbich. 1998. *Habitus*, Techniques, Style: An Integrated Approach to the Social Understanding of Material Culture and Boundaries. Pages 232–63 in Stark 1998b.

Dietrich, Walter. 1987. *David, Saul und die Propheten*. BWANT 7.2. Stuttgart: Kohlhammer.

Dikaios, Porphyrios. 1969–71. *Enkomi Excavations 1948–1958*. Mainz am Rhein: von Zabern.

Dolukhanov, Pavel M. 1998. Comments. *CurrAnthr* 39:29–30.

Domínguez, Adolfo J. 2002. Greeks in Iberia: Colonialism without Colonization. Pages 65–95 in Lyons and Papadopoulos 2002.

Dommelen, Peter van. 1997. Colonial Constructs: Colonialism and Archaeology in the Mediterranean. *WorldArch* 28:305–23.

———. 2002. Ambiguous Matters: Colonialism and Local Identities in Punic Sardinia. Pages 121–47 in Lyons and Papadopoulos 2002b.

Doornbos, Martin R. 1972. Some Conceptual Problems Concerning Ethnicity in Integration Analysis. *Civilizations* 22:263–84.

Dossin, Georges. 1973. Une mention de Canaanéens dans une lettre de Mari. *Syria* 50:277–82.

Dothan, Moshe. 1955. Excavations at Afula. *ʿAtiqot* 1(English series):19–70.

———. 1960. Excavations at Tel Mor, 1959 [Hebrew]. *BIES* 24:120–32.

———. 1971. *Ashdod II–III: The Second and Third Seasons of Excavations 1963, 1965, Soundings in 1967*. ʿAtiqot 9–10. Jerusalem: Israel Department of Antiquities and Museums.

———. 1973. The Foundation of Tel Mor and of Ashdod. *IEJ* 23:1–17.

———. 1979. Ashdod at the End of the Late Bronze Age and the Beginning of the Iron Age. Pages 125–34 in Cross 1979.

———. 1986. Šardina at Akko? Pages 105–15 in *Studies in Sardianian Archaeology, Vol. 2: Sardinia in the Mediterranean*. Edited by M. S. Balmuth. Ann Arbor: University of Michigan Press.

———. 1988. The Significance of Some Artisans' Workshops along the Canaanite Coast. Pages 295–303 in Heltzer and Lipiński 1988.

———. 1989. Archaeological Evidence for Movements of the Early "Sea Peoples" in Canaan. Pages 59–70 in Gitin and Dever 1989.

______, 1993a. Azor: Bronze and Iron Age Tombs. *NEAEHL* 1:127–29.

———. 1993b. Ethnicity and Archaeology: Some Observations on the Sea Peoples at Ashdod. Pages 53–55 in Biran and Aviram 1993.

Dothan, Moshe, and David N. Freedman. 1967. *Ashdod I: The First Season of Excavations 1962*. ʿAtiqot 7. Jerusalem: Israel Department of Antiquities and Museums.

Dothan, Moshe, and Yosef Porath. 1982. *Ashdod IV: Excavations of Area M: The Fortifications of the Lower City*. ʿAtiqot 15. Jerusalem: Israel Department of Antiquities and Museums.

———. 1993. *Ashdod V: Excavations of Area G. The Fourth–Sixth Seasons of Excavations 1968–1970*. ʿAtiqot 23. Jerusalem: Israel Antiquities Authority.

Dothan, Trude. 1963. Spinning Bowls. *IEJ* 13:97–112.

———. 1972. Anthropoid Clay Coffins from a Late Bronze Age Cemetery near Deir el-Balah (Preliminary Report). *IEJ* 22:65–72.

———. 1973. Anthropoid Clay Coffins from a Late Bronze Age Cemetery near Deir el-Balah (Preliminary Report II). *IEJ* 23:129–46.

———. 1979. *Excavations at the Cemetery of Deir el-Balah.* Qedem 10. Jerusalem: Hebrew University of Jerusalem.

———. 1981. Deir el-Balah 1979, 1980 (Notes and News). *IEJ* 21:126–31.

———. 1982. *The Philistines and Their Material Culture.* Jerusalem: Israel Exploration Society.

———. 1983. Some Aspects of the Appearance of the Sea Peoples and Philistines in Canaan. Pages 99–117 in *Griechenland, die Ägäis und die Levante während der "Dark Ages" vom 12. bis zum 9.Jh v. Chr.* Edited by S. Deger-Jalkotzy. Mykenischen Studien 10. Vienna: Österreichische Akademie der Wissenschaften.

———. 1985a. Aspects of Egyptian and Philistine Presence in Canaan during the Late Bronze–Early Iron Ages. Pages 55–75 in *The Land of Israel: Cross-Roads of Civilizations.* Edited by E. Lipiński. OLA 19. Leuven: Peeters.

———. 1985b. Deir el-Balah: The Final Campaign. *National Geographic Research* 1/1:32–43.

———. 1985c. The Philistines Reconsidered. Pages 165–76 in Amitai 1985.

———. 1987. The Impact of Egypt on Canaan during the Eighteenth and Nineteenth Dynasties in the Light of Excavations at Deir el-Balah. Pages 121–35 in Rainey 1987.

———. 1989. The Arrival of the Sea Peoples: Cultural Diversity in Early Iron Age Canaan. Pages 1–14 in Gitin and Dever 1989.

———. 1992. Social Dislocation and Cultural Change in the Twelfth Century B.C. Pages 93–98 in Ward and Joukowsky 1992.

———. 1995a. Tel Miqne-Ekron: The Aegean Affinities of the Sea Peoples' (Philistines') Settlement in Canaan in Iron Age I. Pages 41–59 in *Recent Excavations in Israel: A View to the West.* Edited by S. Gitin. Dubuque, Iowa: Kendall/Hunt.

———. 1995b. The "Sea Peoples" and the Philistines of Ancient Palestine. *CANE* 2:1267–79.

———. 1998a. Cultural Crossroads: Deir el-Balah and the Cosmopolitan Culture of the Late Bronze Age. *BAR* 24/5:24–37, 70, 72.

———. 1998b. Initial Philistine Settlement: From Migration to Coexistence. Pages 148–61 in Gitin, Mazar, and Stern 1998.

———. 2000. Reflections on the Initial Phase of Philistine Settlement. Pages 145–58 in Oren 2000.

———. 2003. The Aegean and the Orient: Cultic Interactions. Pages 189–213 in Dever and Gitin 2003.

Dothan, Trude, and Amnon Ben-Tor. 1983. *Excavations at Athienou, Cyprus 1971–1972.* Qedem 16. Jerusalem: Hebrew University of Jerusalem.

Dothan, Trude, and Robert L. Cohn. 1994. The Philistine as Other: Biblical Rhetoric and Archaeological Reality. Pages 61–73 in *The Other in Jewish Thought and History: Constructions of Jewish Culture and Identity.* Edited by L. J. Silberstein and R. L. Cohn. New York: New York University Press.

Dothan, Trude, and Moshe Dothan. 1992. *People of the Sea: The Search for the Philistines.* New York: Macmillan.

Dothan, Trude, and Alexander Zukerman. 2004. A Preliminary Study of the Mycenaean IIIC:1b Pottery Assemblages from Tel Miqne-Ekron and Ashdod. *BASOR* 333:1–54.

Drews, Robert. 1993. *The End of the Bronze Age: Changes in Warfare and the Catastrophe ca. 1200 B.C.* Princeton: Princeton University Press.

———. 1998. Canaanites and Philistines. *JSOT* 81:39–61.

Driesch, Angela von den, and Nadja Pöllath. 2003. Changes from Late Bronze Age in Early Iron Age Animal Husbandry as Reflected in the Faunal Remains from Büyükkaya/Boğazköy-Hattuša. Pages 295–99 in Fischer et al. 2003.

Driessen, Jan. 1994. La Crète mycénienne. *Les Dossiers d'archéologie* 195:66–83.

Druks, Adam. 1966. A "Hittite" Burial near Kefar Yehoshua [Hebrew]. *Yediot Bahaqirat Eretz-Israel Weatiqoteha* (NS) 30:213–20.

Duncan, John G. 1930. *Corpus of Dated Palestinian Pottery.* London: British School of Archaeology and Egypt.

Dunham, Dows, and Jozef M. Janssen. 1960. *Second Cataract Forts, Vol. 1: Semna Kumma, Excavated by G. A. Reisner.* Boston: Museum of Fine Arts.

Dyen, Isidore. 1956. Language Distribution and Migration Theory. *Language* 32:611–26.

Dyson, Stephen, ed. 1985. *Comparative Studies in the Archaeology of Colonialism.* Oxford: British Archaeological Reports.

Earle, Timothy. 1994. Political Domination and Social Evolution. Pages 940–61 in *Companion Encyclopedia of Anthropology.* Edited by T. Ingold. London: Routledge.

Easton, Donald. 1985. Has the Trojan War Been Found? *Antiquity* 59:188–95.

Easton, Donald, J. David Hawkins, Andrew G. Sherratt, and E. Susan Sherratt. 2002. Troy in Recent Perspective. *AnatSt* 52:75–109.

Edel, Elmar. 1985. Der Seevölkerbericht aus dem 8. Jahre Ramses' III. (MH II, pl. 46, 15–18). Übersetqung und Struktur. Pages 232–238 in vol. 1 of *Mélanges Gamal Eddin Mokhtar.* Edited by P. Posener-Kriéger. Cairo: Institut français d'archéologie orientale.

Edelman, Diana. 1988. Tel Masos, Geshur, and David. *JNES* 47:253–58.

———. 1996. Ethnicity and Early Israel. Pages 42–47 in *Ethnicity and the Bible.* Edited by M. G. Brett. Biblical Interpretation Series 19. Leiden: Brill.

Edelstein. Gershon, and Sara Aurant. 1992. The "Philistine" Tomb at Tell ʿEitun. *ʿAtiqot* 21:23–42.

Edelstein, Gershon, and Jonathan Glass. 1973. The Origin of Philistine Pottery Based on Petrographic Analysis [Hebrew, with English summary on p. xvi]. Pages 125–32 in *Excavations and Studies: Essays in Honour of Professor S. Yeivin.* Edited by Y. Aharoni. Tel Aviv: Carta.

Edelstein, Gershon, and Ianir Milevski. 1994. The Rural Settlement of Jerusalem Re-evaluated: Surveys and Excavations in the Raphʿaim Valley and Mevasseret Yerushalayim. *PEQ* 126:2–23.

Eder, Birgitta. 1990. The Dorian Migration—Religious Consequences in the Argolid. Pages 207–11 in *Celebrations of Death and Divinity in the Bronze Age Argolid:*

Proceedings of the Sixth International Symposium at the Swedish Institute at Athens, 11–13 June 1988. Edited by R. Hågg and G. C. Nordquist. Stockholm: Åström.

Edgerton, William, and John Wilson. 1936. *Historical Records of Ramses III: The Texts in Medinet Habu Volumes I and II, Translated with Explanitory Notes.* SAOC 12. Chicago: University of Chicago Press.

Ehrlich, Carl S. 1996. *The Philistines in Transition: A History from ca. 1000–730 B.C.E.* SHCANE 10. Leiden: Brill.

Eitam, David. 1988. The Settlement of the Nomadic Tribes in the Negeb Highlands During the Eleventh Century B.C. Pages 313–40 in Heltzer and Lipiński 1988.

Ekholm-Friedman, Kajsa. 2000. On the Evolution of Global Systems, Part I: The Mesopotamian Heartland. Pages 153–68 in Denemark et al. 2000.

Emberling, Geoff. 1997. Ethnicity in Complex Societies: Archaeological Perspectives. *Journal of Archaeological Research* 5:295–344.

Engelbach, Reginald. 1915. *Riqqeh and Memphis VI.* British School of Archaeology in Egypt and Egyptian Research Account Publications 26. London: Quaritch.

———. *Harageh.* 1923. Publications of the Egyptian Research Account and the British School of Archaeology in Egypt 38. London: British School of Archaeology in Egypt.

Epigraphic Survey. 1930. *Medinet Habu: Field Director, Harold Hayden Nelson, Vol. 1: Earlier Historical Records of Ramses III.* University of Chicago Oriental Institute Publications 8. Chicago: University of Chicago Press.

———. 1932. *Medinet Habu: Field Director, Harold Hayden Nelson, Vol. 2: Later Historical Records of Ramses III.* University of Chicago Oriental Institute Publications 9. Chicago: University of Chicago Press.

———. 1970. *Medinet Habu: Field Director, Harold Hayden Nelson, Vol. 8: The Eastern High Gate.* University of Chicago Oriental Institute Publications 94. Chicago: University of Chicago Press.

Epstein, Claire. 1965. Interpretation of the Megiddo Sacred Area during the Middle Bronze II. *IEJ* 15:204–21.

Erard-Cerceau, Isabelle. 1988. Documents sur l'agriculture mycénienne: Peut-on concilier archéologie et épigraphie? *Minos* NS 23:183–90.

Erichsen, Wolja. 1933. *Papyrus Harris I: Hieroglyphische Transkription.* Bibliotheca Aegyptiaca 5. Brussels: Fondation Égyptologique Reine Élisabeth.

Erickson, Kirstin C. 2003. "They Will Come From the Other Side of the Sea": Prophecy, Ethnogenesis, and Agency in Yaqui Narrative. *Journal of American Folklore* 116:465–82.

Eriksen, Thomas H. 1991. The Cultural Contexts of Ethnic Differences. *Man* NS 26:127–44.

Esse, Douglas L. 1991. The Collared Store Jar—Scholarly Ideology and Ceramic Typology. *SJOT* 5/2:99–116.

———. 1992. The Collared Pithos at Megiddo: Ceramic Distribution and Ethnicity. *JNES* 51:81–103.

Falconer, Steven. 2001. The Middle Bronze Age. Pages 271–89 in *The Archaeology of Jordan.* Edited by B. MacDonald, R. Adams, and P. Bienkowski. Levantine Archaeology 1. Sheffield: Sheffield Academic Press.

Faulkner, Raymond O. 1975. Egypt: From the Inception of the Nineteenth Dynasty to the Death of Ramesses III. *CAH*³ 2.2:217–51.

Faust, Avraham. 2000. The Rural Community in Ancient Israel during the Iron Age II. *BASOR* 317:17–40.

Feathers, James K. 1989. Effects of Temper on Strength of Ceramics: Response to Bronitsky and Hamer. *AmerAnt* 54:579–88.

Feinman, Gary M. 1999. The Changing Structure of Macroregional Mesoamerica: The Classic-Postclassic Transition in the Valley of Oaxaca. Pages 53–62 in Kardulias 1999b.

Finkelstein, Israel. 1984. The Iron Age "Fortresses" of the Negev Highlands: Sedentarization of the Nomads. *TA* 11:189–209.

———. 1986. *ʿIzbet Sartah: An Early Iron Age Site Near Rosh Haʿayin, Israel.* Oxford: British Archaeological Reports.

———. 1988. *The Archaeology of the Israelite Settlement.* Jerusalem: Israel Exploration Society.

———. 1990a. The Emergence of Early Israel: Anthropology, Environment, and Archaeology. *JAOS* 110:677–86.

———. 1990b. Excavations at Khirbet ed-Dawwara: An Iron Age Site Northeast of Jerusalem. *TA* 17:163–208.

———. 1991. The Emergence of Israel in Canaan: Consensus, Mainstream and Dispute. *SJOT* 5/2:47–59.

———. 1992a. Edom in the Iron I. *Levant* 24:159–66.

———. 1992b. Pastoralism in the Highlands of Canaan in the Third and Second Millennia B.C.E. Pages 122–42 in Bar-Yosef and Khazanov 1992.

———. 1992c. Stratigraphy, Pottery and Parallels: A Reply to Bienkowski. *Levant* 24:171–72.

———. 1994a. The Emergence of Israel: A Phase in the Cyclic History of Canaan in the Third and Second Millennia BCE. Pages 150–78 in Finkelstein and Naʾaman 1994b.

———. 1994b. Penelope's Shroud Unravelled: Iron Age Date of Gezer's Outer Wall Established. *TA* 21:271–82.

———. 1995a. The Date of the Settlement of the Philistines in Canaan. *TA* 22:213–39.

———. 1995b. The Great Transformation: The "Conquest" of the Highlands Frontiers and the Rise of the Territorial States. Pages 349–65 in *The Archaeology of Society in the Holy Land.* Edited by T. E. Levy. New York: Facts on File.

———. 1995c. *Living on the Fringe: The Archaeology and History of the Negev, Sinai and Neighbouring Regions in the Bronze and Iron Ages.* Edited by A. B. Knapp. Monographs in Mediterranean Archaeology 6. Sheffield: Sheffield Academic Press.

———. 1996a. The Archaeology of the United Monarchy: An Alternative View. *Levant* 28:177–87.

———. 1996b. Ethnicity and Origin of the Iron I Settlers in the Highlands of Canaan: Can the Real Israel Stand Up? *BA* 59:198–212.

———. 1996c. The Philistine Countryside. *IEJ* 46:225–42.

———. 1996d. The Settlement History of the Transjordan Plateau in Light of Survey Data [Hebrew, with English summary]. *ErIsr* 25:246–51, *97.

———. 1996e. The Territorial-Political System of Canaan in the Late Bronze Age. *UF* 28:221–55.

———. 1997. Pots and People Revised: Ethnic Boundaries in the Iron Age I. Pages 216–37 in Silberman and Small 1997.

———. 1998a. Philistine Chronology: High, Middle or Low? Pages 140–47 in Gitin, Mazar, and Stern 1998.

———. 1998b. The Rise of Early Israel: Archaeology and Long-Term History. Pages 7–39 in Ahituv and Oren 1998.

———. 2000. The Philistine Settlements: When, Where and How Many? Pages 159–80 in Oren 2000.

Finkelstein, Israel, Shlomo Bunimovitz, and Zvi Lederman. 1993. *Shiloh: The Archaeology of a Biblical Site.* Tel Aviv University, Sonia and Marco Nadler Institute of Archaeology, Monograph Series 10. Tel Aviv: Institute of Archaeology of Tel Aviv University.

Finkelstein, Israel, and Zvi Lederman. 1997. *Highlands of Many Cultures: The Southern Samaria Survey: The Sites.* Tel Aviv University, Sonia and Marco Nadler Institute of Archaeology, Monograph Series 14. Tel Aviv: Institute of Archaeology of Tel Aviv University.

Finkelstein, Israel, and Yitzhak Magen, eds. 1993. *Archaeological Survey of the Hill Country of Benjamin.* Jerusalem: Israel Antiquities Authority.

Finkelstein, Israel, and Nadav Naʾaman. 1994a. Introduction: From Nomadism to Monarchy—the State of Research in 1992. Pages 9–17 in Finkelstein and Naʾaman 1994b.

———, eds. 1994b. *From Nomadism to Monarchy: Archaeological and Historical Aspects of Early Israel.* Jerusalem: Israel Exploration Society.

Finkelstein, Israel, and Lily Singer-Avitz. 2001. Ashdod Revisited. *TA* 28:231–59.

Finkelstein, Israel and Yitzhak Zilberman. 1995. Site Planning and Subsistence Economy: Negev Settlements as a Case Study. Pages 213–26 in *The Pitcher Is Broken: Memorial Essays for Gösta W. Ahlström.* Edited by S. W. Holloway and L. K. Handy. JSOTSup 190. Sheffield: Sheffield Academic Press.

Finley, Moses. 1956. *The World of Odysseus.* Rev. ed. London: Chatto & Windus.

———. 1957. Homer and Mycenae: Property and Tenure. *Historia* 6:133–59.

Fischer, Bettina. 2003. Immigration versus Continuity: A View from the Cypriote Sanctuaries. Pages 57–64 in Fischer et al. 2003.

Fischer, Bettina, Hermann Genz, Éric Jean, and Kemalettin Köroğlu, eds. 2003. *Identifying Changes: The Transition from Bronze to Iron Ages in Anatolia and Its Neighbouring Regions: Proceedings of the International Workshop Istanbul, November 8–9, 2002.* Istanbul: Türk Eskiçağ Bilimleri Enstitüsü.

Fischer, Peter M. 1991. Canaanite Pottery from Hala Sultan Tekke: Traditional Clasification and Micro Color Analysis (MCA). Pages 73–80 in Barlow, Bolger, and Kling 1991.

FitzGerald, Gerald M. 1930. *The Four Canaanite Temples of Beth Shean, Part II: The Pottery.* Philadelphia: University of Pennsylvania Museum.

Flannery, Kent V. 1972. The Cultural Evolution of Civilization. *Annual Review of Ecology and Systematics* 3:399–426.

———. 1982. The Golden Marshalltown: A Parable for the Archeology of the 1980s. *American Anthropologist* 84:265–78.

Fleming, Daniel. 1994. "The Storm God of Canaan" at Emar. *UF* 26:127–30.

Frandsen, Paul J. 1979. Egyptian Imperialism. Pages 167–90 in *Power and Propaganda: A Symposium on Ancient Empries.* Edited by M. T. Larsen. Copenhagen: Akademisk Forlag.

Frank, Andre Gunder. 1993. Bronze Age World System Cycles. *CurrAnthr* 34:383–429.

———. 1999. Abuses and Uses of World Systems Theory in Archaeology. Pages 275–96 in Kardulias 1999b.

Frank, Andre Gunder, and Barry K. Gills, eds. 1993. *The World System: Five Hundred Years or Five Thousand?* London: Routledge.

Frankel, Raphael. 1994. Upper Galilee in the Late Bronze–Iron I Transition. Pages 18–34 in Finkelstein and Na᾿aman 1994b.

Frankel, Raphael, Nimrod Getzov, Mordechai Aviam, and Avi Degani. 2001. *Settlement Dynamics and Regional Diversity in Ancient Upper Galilee: Archaeological Survey of Upper Galilee.* IAA Reports 14. Jerusalem: Israel Antiquities Authority.

Franken, Hendricus J. 1964. The Excavations at Deir ʿAlla—1964. *VT* 14:417–22.

———. 1992. *Excavations at Tell Deir ʿAlla: The Late Bronze Age Sanctuary.* Louvain: Peeters.

Franken, Hendricus J., and J. Kalsbeek. 1969. *Excavations at Tell Deir ʿAlla.* Vol. 1. Leiden: Brill.

Frankfort, Henri. 1948. *Kingship and the Gods: A Study of Ancient Near Eastern Religion as the Integration of Society and Nature.* Chicago: University of Chicago Press.

French, Elizabeth. 1966. A Group of Late Helladic IIIB:1 Pottery From Mycenae. *ABSA* 61:216–38.

———. 1967. Pottery from Late Helladic IIIB:1 Destruction Contexts at Mycenae. *ABSA* 62:149–93.

———. 1969a. The First Phase of LH IIIC. *AA* 25:53–75.

———. 1969b. A Group of Late Helladic IIIB:2 Pottery from Mycenae. *ABSA* 64:71–93.

———. 1975. A Reassessment of the Mycenaean Pottery at Tarsus. *AnatSt* 25:53–75.

———. 1981. Cult Places at Mycenae. Pages 41–48 in *Sanctuaries and Cults in the Aegean Bronze Age: Proceedings of the First International Symposium at the Swedish Institute in Athens, 12–13 May, 1980.* Edited by R. Hägg and N. Marinatos. Stockholm: Åström.

———. 1986. Mycenaean Greece and the Mediterranean World in LH III. Pages 277–82 in *Traffici micenei nel Mediterraneo: Problemi storici e documentazzione archeologica atti del Convegno di Palermo 11–12 maggio e 3–6 dicembre 1984.* Edited by M. Marazzi, S. Tusa, and L. Bagnetti. Taranto: Istituto per la storia e l'archeologia della Magna Grecia.

———. 1996. Evidence for an Earthquake at Mycenae. Pages 51–54 in Stiros and Jones 1996.

———. 1998. The Ups and Downs of Mycenae: 1250–1150 BC. Pages 1–5 in Gitin, Mazar, and Stern 1998.

French, Elizabeth, and Paul Åström. 1980. A Collquium on Late Cypriote III Sites. *Report of the Department of Antiquities, Cyprus* 1980:267–69.

French, Elizabeth, and Jeremy Rutter. 1977. The Handmade Burnished Ware of the Late Helladic IIIC Period: Its Modern Historical Context. *AJA* 81:111–20.

French, Elizabeth, and K. A. Wardle, eds. 1988. *Problems in Greek Prehistory: Papers Presented at the Centenary Conference of the British School of Archaeology at Athens, Manchester, April 1986.* Bristol: Britol Classical Press.

Frendo, Anthony J. 1992. Five Recent books on the Emergence of Ancient Israel: Review Article. *PEQ* 124:144–51.

———. 1998. Review of Israel Finkelstein, *The Archaeology of the Israelite Settlement* (Jerusalem, 1988). *Or* 57:410–12.

Frerichs, Ernest S, and Leonard H. Lesko, eds. 1997. *Exodus: The Egyptian Evidence.* Winona Lake, Ind.: Eisenbrauns.

Freu, Jacques. 1988. La tablette RS 86.2230 et la phase finale du royaume d'Ugarit. *Syria* 65:395–98.

Frick, Frank S. 1985. *The Formation of the State in Ancient Israel: A Survey of Models and Theories.* SWBA 4. Sheffield: Almond.

Friedman, Richard E. 1997. *Who Wrote the Bible?* New York: HarperCollins.

Fritz, Volkmar. 1977. Bestimmung und Herkunft des Pfeinlerhauses in Israel. *ZDPV* 93:30–45.

———. 1980. Die Kulturhistorische Bedeutung der früheisenzeitlischen Siedlung auf der Hirbet el-Mšāš und das Problem der Landnahme. *ZDPV* 96:121–35.

———. 1981. The Israelite "Conquest" in the Light of Recent Excavations at Khirbet el-Meshash. *BASOR* 241:61–73.

———. 1983b. Paläste während der Bronze-und Eisenzeit in Palästina. *ZDPV* 99:1–42.

———. 1987. Conquest or Settlement? The Early Iron Age in Palestine. *BA* 50:84–100.

———. 1995. *The City in Ancient Israel.* Sheffield: Sheffield Academic Press.

Fritz, Volkmar, and Aharon Kempinski. 1983. *Ergebnisse der Ausgrabungen auf der Hirbet el-Mšāš (Tel Māśoś) 1972–1975.* Wiesbaden: Harrassowitz.

Funk, Robert W. 1968. The Bronze Age–Iron I Pottery. Pages 35–53 in O. R. Sellers, R. W. Funk. J. L. McKenzie, P. Lapp, and N. Lapp, *The Excavations at Beth Zur.* AASOR 38. Cambridge, Mass.: American Schools of Oriental Research.

Furumark, Arne. 1941a. *The Chronology of Mycenaean Pottery.* Stockholm: Kungl. Vitterhets Historie och Antikvitets Akademien.

———. 1941b. *The Mycenaean Pottery: Analysis and Classification.* Stockholm: Kungl. Vitterhets Historie och Antikvitets Akademien.

———. 1944. The Mycenaean IIIC Pottery and Its Relation to Cypriot Fabrics. *Opuscula Archaeologica* 3:194–265.

———. 1950. The Settlement at Ialysos and Aegean History, c. 1550–1400. *Opuscula Archaeologica* 6:150–271.

———. 1965. The Excavations at Sinda: Some Historical Results. *Opuscula Athieniensia* 6:99–116.

———. 1992. *Mycenaean Pottery III. Plates.* Edited by P. Åström, R. Hägg, and C. Walberg. Skrifter utgivna av Svenska insitutet i Athen, 4o, 20:3. Stockholm: Åström.

Gal, Zvi. 1979. An Early Iron Age Site Near Tel Menorah in the Beth-Shan Valley. *TA* 6:138–45.

———. 1993. Some Aspects of Road-Planning Between Egypt and Canaan. Pages 77–82 in *Studies in the Archaeology and History of Ancient Israel in Honor of Moshe Dothan* [Hebrew]. Edited by M. Heltzer, A. Segal, and D. Kaufman. Haifa: University of Haifa.

———. 1994. Iron I in Lower Galilee and the Margins of the Jezreel Valley. Pages 35–46 in Finkelstein and Na'aman 1994b.

Galaty, Michael L., and William A. Parkinson, eds. 1999. *Rethinking Myceaean Palaces: New Interpretations of an Old Idea.* Cotsen Institute of Archaeology Monograph 41. Los Angeles: Cotsen Institute of Archaeology.

Gale, Noël H. 2001. Archaeology, Science-Based Archaeology and the Mediterranean Bronze Age Metals Trade: A Contribution to the Debate. *EJA* 4:113–30.

______, ed. 1991. *Bronze Age Trade in the Mediterranean: Papers Presented at the Conference Held at Rewley House, Oxford, in December 1989.* SIMA 90. Jonsered: Åström.

Gamble, Clive. 1993. People on the Move: Interpretations of Regional Variation in Paleolithic Europe. Pages 37–55 in *Cultural Transformations and Interactions in Eastern Europe.* Edited by J. Chapman and P. Dolukhanov. Worldwide Archaeology Series 6. Aldershot: Avebury.

Garbini, Giovanni. 1988. *History and Ideology in Ancient Israel.* New York: Crossroad.

Gardiner, Alan H. 1920. The Ancient Military Road Between Egypt and Palestine. *JEA* 6:99–116.

———. 1947. *Ancient Egyptian Onomastica.* 3 vols. Oxford: Oxford University Press.

Garfinkel, Yossi, and Raphael Greenberg. 1997. Area L. Pages 177–294 in *Hazor V: An Account of the Fifth Season of Excavations.* Edited by A. Ben-Tor and R. Bonfil. Jerusalem: Hebrew University of Jerusalem.

Garnsey, Peter D. A., and C. R. Whittaker, eds. 1978. *Imperialism in the Ancient World. Cambridge Classical Studies.* Cambridge: Cambridge University Press.

Garstang, John, and Oliver R. Gurney. 1959. The Geography of the Hittite Empire. London: British Institute of Archaeology at Ankara.

Gates, Marie-Henriette. 1995. Defining Boundaries of a State: The Mycenaeans and Their Anatolian Frontier. Pages 289–97 in *Politeia: Society and State in the Aegean Bronze Age. Proceedings of the 5th International Conference, University of Heidelberg, Archëlogisches Institut 10–13 April 1994.* Edited by W.-D. Niemeier and R. Laffineur. Aegaeum 12. Liège: Université de Liège.

———. Forthcoming. Early Iron Age Newcomers at Kinet Höyük, Eastern Cilicia. In *The Philistines and Other Sea Peoples.* Edited by A. E. Killebrew, G. Lehmann, and M. Artzy. Atlanta: Society of Biblical Literature.

Geary, Patrick J. 2002. *The Myth of Nations: The Medieval Origins of Europe.* Princeton: Princeton University Press.

Geertz, Clifford. 1973. The Integrative Revolution: Primordial Sentiments and Civil Politics in the New States. Pages 255–310 in *The Interpretation of Culture: Selected Essays by Clifford Geertz.* New York: Basic Books.

Genz, Hermann. 1997. Northern Slaves and the Origin of Handmade Burnished Ware: A Comment on Bankoff et al. *JMA* 10:109–11.

Georghiou, Hara. 1979. Relations between Cyprus and the Near East in the Middle and Late Bronze Age. *Levant* 11:84–100.

Gesell, Geraldine C., Leslie P. Day, and William D. E. Coulson. 1995. Excavations at Kavousi, Crete, 1989 and 1990. *Hesperia* 64:67–120.

Geus, Cornelis H. J. de. 1976. *The Tribes of Israel An Investigation into Some of the Presuppositions of Martin Noth's Amphictyony Hypothesis.* SSN 18. Amsterdam: Van Gorcum.

Gibson, John C. L. 1977. *Canaanite Myths and Legends.* Edinburgh: T&T Clark.

Gibson, Shimon. 2001. Agricultural Terraces and Settlement Expansion in the Highlands of Early Iron Age Palestine: Is there Any Correlation Between the Two? Pages 113–46 in A. Mazar 2001.

Giles, Frederick J. 1997. *The Amarna Age: Western Asia.* The Austrian Centre for Egyptology Studies 5. Warminster, Eng.: Aris & Phillips.

Gills, Barry K., and Andre Gunder Frank. 1992. World System Cycles, Crises, and Hegemonial Shifts, 1700 BC to 1700 AD. *Review* 15/4:621–87.

Gilula, Mordechai. 1976. An Inscription in Egyptian Hieratic from Lachish. *TA* 3:107–8.

Gitin, Seymour. 1998. Philistia in Transition: The Tenth Century BCE and Beyond. Pages 162–83 in Gitin, Mazar, and Stern 1998.

———. 2003. Israelite and Philistine Cult and the Archaeological Record in Iron Age II: The "Smoking Gun" Phenomenon. Pages 279–95 in Dever and Gitin 2003.

———. 2004. The Philistines: Neighbors of the Canaanites, Phoenicians and Israelites. Pages 57–84 in *One Hundred Years of American Archaeology in the Middle East: Proceedings of the American Schools of Oriental Research Centennial Celebration, Washington DC, April 2000.* Edited by D. R. Clark and V. H. Matthews. Boston: American Schools of Oriental Research.

Gitin, Seymour, and William G. Dever, eds. 1989. *Recent Excavations in Israel: Studies in Iron Age Archaeology.* AASOR 49. Winona Lake, Ind.: Eisenbrauns.

Gitin, Seymour, and Trude Dothan. 1987. The Rise and Fall of Ekron of the Philistines. *BA* 50:197–205.

———. 1990. Ekron of the Philistines, Part I: How They Lived, Worked and Worshipped for Five Hundred Years. *BAR* 16/1:20–36.

Gitin, Seymour, Trude Dothan, and Joseph Naveh. 1997. A Royal Dedicatory Inscription from Ekron. *IEJ* 47:1–16.

Gitin, Seymour, Amihai Mazar, and Ephraim Stern, eds. 1998. *Mediterranean Peoples in Transition: Thirteenth to Early Tenth Centuries BCE.* Jerusalem: Israel Exploration Society.

Gittlin, Barry M. 1992. The Late Bronze Age "City" at Tel Miqne/Ekron. *ErIsr* 23:50–53.

Giveon, Raphael 1971. *Les Bédouins Shosou des documents égyptiens.* Leiden: Brill.

———. 1975. Two Inscriptions of Ramesses II. *IEJ* 25:247–49.

———. 1978a. *The Impact of Egypt on Canaan: Iconographic and Related Studies.* OBO 20. Fribourg: Universitätsverlag; Göttingen: Vandenhoeck & Ruprecht.

———. 1978b. Two Unique Egyptian Inscriptions from Tel Aphek. *TA* 5:188–191.

———. 1983. An Inscription of Rameses III from Lachish. *TA* 10:176–77.

Giveon, Raphael, and Aharon Kempinski. 1983. The Scarabs. Pages 102–6 in Fritz and Kempinski 1983.

Givon, Shmuel. 1999. The Three-Roomed House from Tel Harassim, Israel. *Levant* 31:173–77.

_____, ed. 1991. *The First Season of Excavation at "Tel Harasim" 1990: Preliminary Report 1.* Tel Aviv: n.p.

———. 1992. *The Second Season of Excavation at "Tel Harasim" 1991: Preliminary Report 2.* Tel Aviv: n.p.

———. 1993. *The Third Season of Excavations at "Tel Harassim" 1992.* Tel Aviv: n.p.

Gjerstad, Einar. 1926. *Studies on Prehistoric Cyprus.* Uppsala: Uppsala Universitets Årsskrift.

———. 1944. The Colonization of Cyprus in Greek Legend. *OpAth* 3:107–23.

Glanzman, William D., and S. J. Fleming. 1986. Xeroradiography: A Key to the Nature of Technological Change in Ancient Ceramic Production. *Nuclear Instruments and Methods in Physics Research* 242:588–95.

———. 1993. Fabrication Methods. Pages 94–102 in James and McGovern 1993.

Glass, Jonathan, Yuval Goren, Shlomo Bunimovitz, and Israel Finkelstein. 1993. Petrographic Analyses of Middle Bronze Age III, Late Bronze Age and Iron Age I Pottery Assemblages. Pages 271–86 in Finkelstein, Bunimovitz, and Lederman 1993.

Glueck, Nelson. 1934. *Explorations in Eastern Palestine, I.* AASOR 14. Philadelphia: American Schools of Oriental Research.

———. 1935. *Explorations in Eastern Palestine, II.* AASOR 15. New Haven: American Schools of Oriental Research.

———. 1939. *Explorations in Eastern Palestine, III.* AASOR 18–19. New Haven: American Schools of Oriental Research.

———. 1971. *The Other Side of the Jordan.* Cambridge, Mass.: American Schools of Oriental Research.

Gmelch, George. 1980. Return Migration. *ARA* 9:135–59.

Gödecken, Karin B. 1988. A Contribution to the Early History of Miletus: The Settlement in Myceanaean Times and Its Connections Overseas. Pages 307–17 in French and Wardle 1988.

Goedicke, Hans. 1985a. The "Battle of Kadesh": A Reassessment. Pages 77–121 in Goedicke 1985b.

———, ed. 1985b. *Perspectives on the Battle of Kadesh.* Baltimore: Halgo.

Golani, Amir, and Ora Yogev. 1996. The 1980 Excavations at Tel Sasa. *ʿAtiqot* 28:41–58.

Goldberg, Paul, Bonnie Gould, Ann Killebrew, and Joseph Yellin. 1986. Comparison of Neutron Activation and Thin-Section Analyses on Late Bronze Age Ceramics from Deir el-Balah. Pages 341–51 in *Proceedings of the 24th International Archaeometry Symposium.* Edited by J. Olin and J. Blackman. Washington D.C.: Smithsonian Institute.

Goldman, Hetty. 1956. *Excavations at Gözlü Kule, Tarsus, Volume II: From the Neolithic through Bronze Age.* Princeton: Princeton University Press.

Goldman, Hetty, ed. 1963. *Excavations at Gözlü Kule, Tarsus Volume III: The Iron Age.* Princeton: Princeton University Press.

Goldwasser, Orly. 1980. An Egyptian Store-Jar from Haruvit [Hebrew]. *Qad* 13:34.

———. 1982. The Lachish Hieratic Bowl Once Again. *TA* 9:137–38.

———. 1984. Hieratic Inscriptions from Tel Seraʿ in Southern Canaan. *TA* 11:77–93.

———. 1991a. A Fragment of an Hieratic Ostracon from Tel Haror [Hebrew]. *Qad* 24:19.

———. 1991b. An Egyptian Scribe from Lachish and the Hieratic Tradition of the Hebrew Kingdom. *TA* 18:248–53.

Goldwasser, Orly, and Stefan Wimmer. 1999. Hieratic Fragments from Tell el Far'ah (South). *BASOR* 313:39–42.

Gonen, Rivka. 1984. Urban Canaan in the Late Bronze Age Period. *BASOR* 253:61–73.

———. 1992. *Burial Patterns and Cultural Diversity in Late Bronze Canaan.* ASOR Dissertation Series 7. Winona Lake, Ind.: Eisenbrauns.

Gooding, D. W. 1982. The Composition of the Book of Judges. *ErIsr* 16:70*–79*.

Gophna, Ram, and Dov Meron. 1970. An Iron Age I Tomb between Ashdod and Ashkelon. *ʿAtiqot* 6 (HS):1–5.

Gophna, Ram, and Juval Portugali. 1988. Settlement and Demographic Processes in Israel's Coastal Plain from the Chalcolithic to the Middle Bronze Age. *BASOR* 269:11–28.

Gordon, Cyrus H. 1956. The Rôle of the Philistines. *Antiquity* 30:22–26.

Gordon, D. H. 1953. Fire and Sword: The Techniques of Destruction. *Antiquity* 27:149–52.

Goren, Yuval. 1987. The Petrography of Pottery Assemblages of the Chalcolithic Period from Southern Israel. M.A. thesis. Hebrew University of Jerusalem.

Goren, Yuval, Shlomo Bunimovitz, Israel Finkelstein, and Nadav Naʾaman. 2003. The Location of Alashiya: New Evidence from Petrographic Investigation of Alashiyan Tablets from El-Amarna and Ugarit. *AJA* 107:233–55.

Goren, Yuval, Eliezer D. Oren, and R. Feinstein. 1995. The Archaeological and Ethnoarchaeological Interpretation of a Ceramological Enigma: Pottery Production in Sinai (Egypt) during the New Kingdom Period. Pages 101–20 in *The Aim of Laboratory Analysis of Ceramics in Archaeology April 7–9 1995 in Lund, Sweden, in Honor of Brigitta Hulthén Ass. Prof. Emer.* Edited by A. Lindahl and O. Stilborg. Kungl. Vittenhets: Historie och Antikvitets Akademien.

Gorny, Ronald L. 1989. Environment, Archaeology and History in Hittite Anatolia. *BA* 52:78–94.

Gottwald, Norman K. 1979. *The Tribes of Yahweh: A Sociology of the Religion of Liberated Israel, 1250–1050.* Maryknoll, N.Y.: Orbis.

———. 1985. The Israelite Settlement as a Social Revolutionary Movement. Pages 34–46 in Amitai 1985.

———. 1992. Ancient Israel: Sociology. *ABD* 6:79–89.

———. 1993. Method and Hypothesis in Reconstructing the Social History of Early Israel. *ErIsr* 24: 77*–82*.

Grabbe, Lester L. 1994. "Canaan": Some Methodological Observations in Relation to Biblical Study. Pages 113–22 in Brooke, Curtis, and Healey 1994.

Grabbe, Lester L., ed. 1997. *Can a "History of Israel" Be Written?* JSOTSup 245. European Seminar in Historical Methdology 1. Sheffield: Sheffield Academic Press.

Grace, Virginia R. 1956. The Canaanite Jar. Pages 80–109 in *The Aegean and the Near East: Studies Presented to Hetty Goldman on the Occasion of Her Seventy-Fifth Birthday.* Edited by S. S. Weinberg. Locust Valley, N.Y.: Augustin.

Grandet, Pierre. 1994. Le Papyrus Harris I (BM 9999). 2 vols. Bibliothèque d'étude. Cairo: Institut Français d'Archéologie Orientale.

Grant, Elihu. 1929. *Beth Shemesh (Palestine), Part IV: Pottery*. Haverford, Pa.: Biblical and Kindred Studies.

Grant, Elihu, and G. Ernest Wright. 1938. *Ain Shems Excavations (Palestine), Part IV: Pottery*. Haverford, Pa.: Haverford College.

Greeley, Andrew M. 1974. *Ethnicity in the United States: A Preliminary Reconnaissance*. New York: Willey.

Green, Stanton W., and Stephen M. Perlman, eds. 1985. *The Archaeology of Frontiers and Boundaries*. Orlando: Academic Press.

Greenberg, Moshe. 1955. *The Hab/piru*. AOS. 39. New Haven: American Oriental Society.

Greenberg, Raphael. 1987. New Light on the Early Iron Age at Tell Beit Mirsim. *BASOR* 265:55–80.

Greenstein, Edward L., and David Marcus. 1976. The Akkadian Inscriptions of Idrimi. *JANESCU* 8:59–96.

Griffith, Francis L. 1890. *The Antiquities of Tell el Yahûdîyeh, and Miscellaneous Work in Lower Egypt during the Years, 1887–1888*. London: Kegan Paul, Trench, Trübner.

Grimal, Nicolas. 1992. *A History of Ancient Egypt*. Oxford: Blackwell.

Groll, Sarah. 1973. A Note on the Hieratic Texts from Tel Seraᶜ. *Qad* 6:56–57.

Gunneweg, Jan, Trude Dothan, Isadore Perlman, and Seymour Gitin. 1986. On the Origin of Pottery from Tel Miqne-Ekron. *BASOR* 264:3–16.

Gurney, Oliver R. 1952. *The Hittites*. London: Penguin.

Gütterbock, Hans G. 1967. The Hittite Conquest of Cyprus Reconsidered. *JNES* 26:73–81.

———. 1983. The Hittites and the Aegean World: Part I. The Ahhiyawa Problem Reconsidered. *AJA* 87:133–38.

———. 1984. Hittites and Akhaeans: A New Look. *Proceedings of the American Philosophical Society* 128:114–22.

———. 1986. Troy in the Hittite Texts? Wilusa, Ahhiyawa, and Hittite History. Pages 33–44 in *Troy and the Trojan War: A Symposium Held at Bryn Mawr College October 1984*. Edited by M. J. Mellink. Bryn Mawr: Bryn Mawr College.

———. 1992. Survival of the Hittite Dynasty. Pages 53–55 in Ward and Joukowsky 1992.

Guy, Philip L. O. 1938. *Megiddo Tombs*. University of Chicago Oriental Institute Publications 33. Chicago: University of Chicago Press.

Guz-Zilberstein, Bracha. 1984. The Pottery of the Late Bronze Age: The Local Pottery. Pages 10–16 in *Excavations at Tel Mevorakh, Part 2: The Bronze Age*. Qedem 18. By E. Stern. Jerusalem: The Institute of Archaeology, Hebrew University of Jerusalem.

Haaland, Gunnar. 1977. Archaeological Classification and Ethnic Groups: A Case Study from Sudanese Nubia. *Norwegian Archaeological Review* 10:1–31.

Hachlili, Rachel. 1971. Figurines and Kernoi. Pages 125–35 in *Ashdod II–III: The Second and Third Seasons of Excavations 1963, 1965, Soundings in 1967*. ᶜAtiqot 9–10. By M. Dothan. Jerusalem: Department of Antiquities and Museums.

Hackett, Jo Ann. 1997. Canaanites. *OEANE*, 408–9.

———. 2001. "There Was No King in Israel": The Era of the Judges. Pages 132–64 in *The Oxford History of the Biblical World*. Edited by M. D. Coogan. New York: Oxford University Press.

Hadjicosti, Maria, 1988. Part 1: "Canaanite" Jars from Maa-Palaeokastro. Pages 340–85 in Karageorghis and Demas 1988.

Hadjisavvas, Sophocles. 1986. Alassa: A New Late Cypriote Site. *Report of the Department of Antiquities, Cyprus* 1986:62–67.

———. 1989. A Late Cypriote Community at Alassa. Pages 32–42 in *Early Society in Cyprus*. Edited by E. J. Peltenburg. Edinburgh: Edinburgh University Press.

———. 1991. LCIIC to LCIIIA without Intruders: The Case of Alassa-*Pano Mandilaris*. Pages 173–79 in Barlow, Bolger, and Kling 1991.

———. 1994. Alassa Archaeological Project 1991–1993. *Report of the Department of Antiquities, Cyprus* 1994:107–14.

Haggis, Donald C. 2001. A Dark Age Settlement System in East Crete, and a Reassessment of the Definition of Refuge Settlements. Pages 41–59 in Karageorghis and Morris 2001.

Haldane, Cheryl. 1992. Direct Evidence for Organic Cargoes in the Late Bronze Age. *WorldArch* 24:348–60.

Hall, H. R. 1901–2. Keftiu and the Peoples of the Sea. *ABSA* 8:157–89.

Hall, Jonathan M. 1995. Approaches to Ethnicity in Early Iron Age Greece. Pages 6–17 in *Time, Tradition and Society in Greek Archaeology: Bridging the "Great Divide."* Edited by N. Spencer. London: Routledge.

———. 1997. *Ethnic Identity in Greek Antiquity*. Cambridge: Cambridge University Press.

———. 2002. *Hellenicity: Between Ethnicity and Culture*. Chicago: University of Chicago Press.

Hall, Thomas D. 2000a. World-Systems Analysis: A Small Sample from a Large University. Pages 3–26 in Hall 200b.

———, ed. 2000b. *A World-Systems Reader: New Perspectives on Gender, Urbanism, Cultures, Indigenous Peoples, and Ecology*. New York: Rowman & Littlefield.

Hallager, Erik, and Yannis Tzedakis. 1988. The Greek-Swedish Excavations at Kastelli, Khania I. The 1989 Excavation, II. The 1990 Excavation. *Athens Annals of Archaeology* 21:15–55.

Halpern, Baruch. 1983a. *The Emergence of Israel in Canaan*. Chico, Calif.: Scholars Press.

———. 1983b. The Resourceful Israelite Historian: The Song of Deborah and Israelite Historiography. *HTR* 76:379–401.

———. 1988. *The First Historians*. San Francisco: Harper & Row.

———. 1992a. The Exodus from Egypt: Myth or Reality. Pages 86–117 in *The Rise of Ancient Israel*. Edited by H. Shanks. Washington, D.C.: Biblical Archaeology Society.

———. 1992b. Settlement of Canaan. *ABD* 5:1120–43.

———. 1993. The Exodus and the Israelite Historians. *ErIsr* 24:89–96.

———. 2001. *David's Secret Demons: Messiah, Murderer, Traitor, King*. Grand Rapids: Eerdmans.

———. 2003. Eyewitness Testimony: Parts of the Exodus Written within Living Memory of the Event. *BAR* 29/5:50–57.

Halsey, Albert H. 1978. Ethnicity: A Primordial Bond? [Review of *Ethnicity: Theory and Experience*, edited by N. Glazer and D. P. Moynihan]. *Ethnic and Racial Studies* 1:124–28.

Hamilakis, Yannis, and Eleni Konsolaki. 2004. Pigs for the Gods: Burnt Animal Sacrifices as Embodied Rituals at a Mycenaean Sanctuary. *OJA* 23:135–51.

Hankey, Vronwy. 1967. Mycenaean Pottery in the Middle East: Notes on the Finds since 1951. *ABSA* 62:107–47.

Hansen, C. K., and J. N. Postgate. 1999. The Bronze to Iron Age Transition at Kilise Tepe. *AnatSt* 49:111–21.

Harding, Anthony F. 1984. *The Mycenaeans and Europe.* London: Academic Press.

Harif, Amos. 1979. Common Architecture Features at Alalakh, Megiddo, and Shechem. *Levant* 11:162–67.

Härke, Heinrich. 1991. All Quiet on the Western Front? Paradigms, Methods, and Approaches in West German Archaeology. Pages 187–222 in *Archaeological Theory in Europe: The Last Three Decades.* Edited by I. Hodder. New York: Routledge.

———. 1998. Archaeologists and Migrations. *Current Anthropology* 39:10–24.

Hart, Stephen. 1992. Iron Age Settlement in the Land of Edom. Pages 93–98 in Bienkowski 1992c.

Hasel, Michael G. 1994. *Israel* in the Merneptah Stela. *BASOR* 296:45–61.

———. 1998. *Domination and Resistance: Egyptian Military Activity in the Southern Levant, ca. 1300–1185 B.C.* Probleme der Ägyptologie 11. Leiden: Brill.

———. 2003. Merneptah's Inscription and Reliefs and the Origin of Israel. Pages 19–44 in Nakhai 2003b.

Hawkes, Christopher. 1987. Archaeologists and Indo-Europeanists: Can They Mate? Hindrances and Hopes. Pages 203–15 in *Proto-Indo-European: The Archaeology of a Linguistic Problem: Studies in Honour of Marija Gimbutas.* Edited by S. N. Skomal and E. C. Polomé. Washington, D.C.: Institute for the Study of Man.

Hawkins, John D. 1990. The New Inscription from the Sudburg of Bogazkoy-Hattusa. *AA* 1990:305–14.

———. 1994. The End of the Bronze Age in Anatolia: New Light from Recent Discoveries. Pages 91–94 in *Anatolian Iron Ages 3: The Proceedings of the Third Anatolian Iron Ages Colloquium held at Van, 6–12 August 1990.* Edited by A. Cilingiroglu and D. H. French. Ankara: British Institute of Archaeology at Ankara.

Hechter, Michael. 1974. The Political Economy of Ethnic Change. *American Journal of Sociology* 79:1151–78.

———. 1986. Theories of Ethnic Relations. Pages 13–24 in *The Primordial Challenge: Ethnicity in the Contemporary World.* Edited by J. F. Stack Jr. Contributions in Political Science 154. New York: Greenwood.

———. 1987. *Principles of Group Solidarity.* California Series on Social Choice and Political Economy. Berkeley and Los Angeles: University of California Press.

Hegmon, Michelle. 1998. Technology, Style, and Social Practices: Archaeological Approaches. Pages 264–79 in Stark 1998b.

Helck, Wolfgang. 1971. *Die Beziehungen Ägyptens zu Vorderasien im 3. und 2. Jahrtausend v. Chr.* 2nd ed. Wiesbaden: Harrassowitz.

———. 1984. *Urkunden der 18. Dynastie, Heft 17: Historisches Inschriften Thutmosis III und Amenophis III.* Berlin: Akademie.

Heltzer, Michael. 1976. *The Rural Community in Ancient Ugarit.* Wiesbaden: Reichert.

———. 1988. The Late Bronze Age Service System and Its Decline. Pages 7–18 in Heltzer and Lipiński 1988.

Heltzer, Michael, and Edward Lipiński, eds. 1988. *Society and Economy in the Eastern Mediterranean (c. 1500–1000 B.C.): Proceedings of the International Symposium Held at the University of Haifa from the 28th of April to the 2nd of May 1985.* OLA 23. Leuven: Peeters.

Hendel, Ronald. 2001. The Exodus in Biblical Memory. *JBL* 120:601–22.

Hennessy, J. Basil. 1966. Excavation of a Late Bronze Age Temple at Amman. *PEQ* 108:155–62.

Herr, Larry G. 1983. *The Amman Airport Excavations, 1976.* AASOR 48. Winona Lake, Ind.: American Schools of Oriental Research.

———. 1992. Shifts in Settlement Patterns of Late Bronze and Iron Age Ammon. Pages 175–77 in Muna Zaghloul et al., *Studies in the History and Archaeology of Jordan IV.* Amman: Department of Antiquities, Amman.

———. 1997. The Pottery. Pages 228–49 in *Madaba Plains Project: The 1989 Season at Tell el-ᶜUmeiri and Vicinity and Subsequent Studies.* Edited by L. G. Herr, L. T. Geraty, Ø. S. LaBianca and R. W. Younker. Berrien Springs, Mich.: Andrews University Press.

———. 1998. Tell el-ᶜUmayri and the Madaba Plains Region during the Late Bronze–Iron I Transition. Pages 252–64 in Gitin, Mazar, and Stern 1998.

———. 1999. Tell al-ᶜUmayri and the Reubenite Hypothesis. *ErIsr* 26:64*–78*.

———. 2001. The History of the Collared Pithos at Tell el-ᶜUmeiri, Jordan. Pages 237–50 in Wolff 2001.

———. 2002. An Overview of the 1994 Season of the Madaba Plains Project at Tall al-ᶜUmayri. Pages 3–22 in *Madaba Plains Project: The 1994 Season at Tall al ᶜUmayri and Subsequent Studies.* Edited by L. G. Herr, D. R. Clark, L. T. Geraty, R. W. Younker, and Ø. S. LaBianca. Berrien Springs, Mich.: Andrews University Press.

Herr, Larry G., Lawrence T. Geraty, Øystein S. LaBianca, and Randall W. Younker. 1991. Madaba Plains Project: The 1989 Excavations at Tell el-ᶜUmeiri and Vicinity. *ADAJ* 35:155–80.

Herr, Larry G., and Muhammad Najjar. 2001. The Iron Age. Pages 323–345 in *The Archaeology of Jordan.* Edited by B. MacDonald, R. Adams, and P. Bienkowski. Levantine Archaeology 1. Sheffield: Sheffield Academic Press.

Herrmann, Christian. 1994. *Ägyptische Amulette aus Palästina/Israel.* OBO 138. Göttingen: Vandenhoeck & Ruprecht.

Herrmann, Siegfried. 1985. Basic Factors of Israelite Settlement in Canaan. Pages 47–53 in Amitai 1985.

Herscher, Ellen. 1975. The Imported Pottery. Pages 85–96 in *Sarepta: A Preliminary Report on the Iron Age.* Edited by J. B. Pritchard. Philadelphia: University Museum, University of Pennsylvania.

Herzog, Zeev. 1983. Enclosed Settlements in the Negeb and the Wilderness of Beer-sheba. *BASOR* 250:41–48.

———. 1984. *Beer Sheba II: The Early Iron Age Settlement.* Tel Aviv: Institute of Archaeology, Tel Aviv University.

———. 1992. Settlement and Fortification Planning in the Iron Age. Pages 231–74 in Kempinski and Reich 1992.

———. 1994. The Beer-Sheba Valley: From Nomadism to Monarchy. Pages 122–49 in Finkelstein and Naʾaman 1994b.

———. 1997. *Archaeology of the City: Urban Planning in Ancient Israel and Its Social Implications.* Sonia and Marco Nadler Institute of Archaeology Monograph Series 13. Tel Aviv: Emery and Claire Yass Archaeology Press.

Hess, Richard S. 1989. Cultural Aspects of Onomastic Distribution in the Amarna Texts. *UF* 21:209–16.

———. 1992a. Caphtor. *ABD* 1:869–70.

———. 1992b. Observations on Some Unpublished Alalakh Texts, Probably from Level IV. *UF* 24:113–15.

———. 1993. Early Israel in Canaan: A Survey of Recent Evidence and Interpretations. *PEQ* 125:123–42.

———. 1998. Occurrences of "Canaan" in Late Bronze Age Archives of the West Semitic World. *IOS* 18:365–72. [*Past Links: Studies in the Languages and Cultures of the Ancient Near East.* Edited by S. Izreʿel, I. Singer and R. Zadok]

Hesse, Brian. 1986. Animal Use at Tel Miqne-Ekron in the Bronze Age and Iron Age. *BASOR* 264:17–28.

———. 1990. Pig Lovers and Pig Haters: Patterns of Palestinian Pork Production. *Journal of Ethnobiology* 10:195–25.

———. 1995. Husbandry, Dietary Taboos and the Bones of the Ancient Near East: Zooarchaeology in the Post-Processual World. Pages 197–232 in *Methods in the Mediterranean: Historical and Archaeological Views on Texts and Archaeology.* Edited by D. Small. Mnemosyne, Bibliotheca Classica Batava Supplement 135. Leiden: Brill.

Hesse, Brian, and Paula Wapnish. 1997. Can Pig Remains be Used for Ethnic Diagnosis in the Ancient Near East? Pages 238–70 in Silberman and Small 1997.

———. 1998. Pig Use and Abuse in the Ancient Levant: Ethnoreligious Boundary-Building with Swine. Pages 123–36 in *Ancestors for the Pigs: Pigs in Prehistory.* Edited by S. M. Nelson. MASCA Research Papers in Science and Archaeology 15. Philadelpia: Museum Applied Science Center for Archaeology, University of Pennsylvania Museum of Archaeology and Anthropology.

Higginbotham, Carolyn R. 1996. Elite Emulation and Egyptian Governance in Ramesside Canaan. *TA* 23:154–69.

———. 1998. The Egyptianizing of Canaan. *BAR* 24/3:36–43, 69.

———. 2000. *Egyptianization and Elite Emulation in Ramesside Palestine: Governance and Accommodation on the Imperial Periphery.* CHANE 2. Leiden: Brill.

Hill, Jonathan D., ed. 1996. *History, Power, and Identity: Ethnogenesis in the Americas, 1492–1992.* Iowa City: University of Iowa Press.

Hodder, Ian. 1979. Economic and Social Stress and Material Culture Patterning. *AmerAnt* 44:446–54.

———. 1981. Society, Economy and Culture: An Ethnographic Case Study amongst the Lozi. Pages 67–95 in *Pattern of the Past: Studies in Honour of David Clarke.* Edited by I. Hodder, G. Isaac, and N. Hammond. Cambridge: Cambridge University Press.

———. 1982. *Symbols in Action*. Cambridge: Cambridge University.
———. 1985. Boundaries as Strategies: An Ethnoarchaeological Study. Pages 141–59 in *The Archaeology of Frontiers and Boundaries*. Edited by S. W. Green and S. M. Perlman. New York: Academic Press.
———. 1986. *Reading the Past: Current Approaches to Interpretation in Archaeology*. Cambridge: Cambridge University Press.
———. 1987a. The Contribution of the Long Term. Pages 1–8 in Hodder 1987b.
———. ed. 1987b. *Archaeology as Long-Term History*. Cambridge: Cambridge University Press.
———. 1991. *Archaeological Theory in Europe: The Last Three Decades*. London: Routledge.
———. 2001. *Archaeological Theory Today*. Malden, Mass.: Blackwell.
Hoffmeier, James K. 1997. *Israel in Egypt: The Evidence for the Authenticity of the Exodus*. New York: Oxford University Press.
———. 2000. The (Israel) Stela of Merneptah. *COS* 2.6:40–41.
———. 2004. Aspects of Egyptian Foreign Policy in the 18th Dynasty in Western Asia and Nubia. Pages 121–41 in *Egypt, Israel, and the Ancient Mediterranean World: Essays in Honor of Donald B. Redford*. Edited by G. N. Knoppers and A. Hirsch. Leiden: Brill.
Hoffmeier, James K., and Mohamed Abd el-Maksoud. 2003. A New Military Site on "The Ways of Horus"—Tell el-Borg 1999–2001: A Preliminary Report. *JEA* 89:169–97.
Hoffner, Harry A., Jr. 1992. The Last Days of Khattusha. Pages 46–52 in Ward and Joukowsky 1992.
Holladay, John S. 1992. House, Israelite. *ABD* 3:308–18.
———. 1997a. Four-Room House. *OEANE* 2:337–42.
———. 1997b. Syro-Palestinian Houses. *OEANE* 3:94–114.
Holloway, R. Ross. 1981. *Italy and the Aegean, 3000–700 B.C.* Louvain-la-Neuve: Institut Superieur d'archeologie et d'histoire de l'art, College Erasme.
Holmes, Yulssus L. 1971. The Location of Alasiya. *JAOS* 91:426–29.
Holthoer, Rostislav. 1977. *New Kingdom Pharaonic Sites: The Pottery*. The Scandinavian Joint Egyptian Expedition to Sudanese Nubia 5/1. Lund: Berlings.
Hongo, Hitomi. 2003. Continuity or Changes: Faunal Remains from Stratum IId at Kaman-Kalehöyük. Pages 257–69 in Fischer et al. 2003.
Hope, Colin A. 1978, *Malkata and the Birket Habu Jar Sealings and Amphorae*. Egyptology Today 2/5. Warminster, Eng.: Aris & Phillips.
Hopkins, David C. 1985. *The Highlands of Canaan*. SWBA 3. Sheffield: Almond.
Hornung, Erik. 1983. Die Israelstele des Merneptah. Pages 224–33 in *Fontes atque Pontes: Eine Festgabe für H. Brunner*. Edited by M. Görg. ÄAT 5. Wiesbaden: Harrassowitz.
Horowitz, David L. 1975. Ethnic Identity. Pages 111–40 in *Ethnicity: Theory and Experience*. Edited by N. Glazer and D. P. Moynihan. Cambridge, Mass.: Harvard University Press.
Horvath, Ronald J. 1972. A Definition of Colonialism. *CurrAnthr* 13:45–56.
Houwink ten Cate, Philo H. J. 1973. Anatolian Evidence for Relations with the West in the Late Bronze Age. Pages 141–58 in Crossland and Birchall 1973.

Hulin, Linda. 1989. Marsa Matruh 1987, Preliminary Ceramic Report. *JARCE* 26:115–26.

Hult, Gunnel. 1983. *Bronze Age Ashlar Masonry in the Eastern Mediterranean: Cyprus, Ugarit, and Neighbouring Regions.* SIMA 66. Göteborg: Åström.

Hunt, Melvin L. 1987. The Tell Qiri Pottery. Pages 139–223 in *Tell Qiri, A Village in the Jezreel Valley: Report of the Archaeological Excavations 1975–1977.* Edited by A. Ben-Tor and Y. Portugali. Qedem 24. Jerusalem: Institute of Archaeology, Hebrew University of Jerusalem.

Iacovou, Maria. 1998. Philistia and Cyprus in the Eleventh Century: From a Similar Prehistory to a Diverse Protohistory. Pages 332–44 in Gitin, Mazar, and Stern 1998.

———. Forthcoming. Aegean-Style Material Culture in Late Cypriote IIIA: Minimal Evidence, Maximal Interpretation. In *The Philistines and Other "Sea Peoples."* Edited by A. E. Killebrew, G. Lehmann, and M. Artzy. Atlanta: Society of Biblical Literature.

Iakovidis, Spyros. 1977. The Present State of Research at the Citadel of Mycenae. *Bulletin of the Institute of Archaeology, London* 14:99–141.

———. 1979. The Chronology of LH IIIC. *AJA* 83:454–62.

Ibach, Robert D. 1987. *Archaeological Survey of the Hesban Region: Catalogue of Sites and Characterization of Periods.* Berrien Springs, Mich.: Andrews University Press.

Ibrahim, Mo'awiyah M. 1978. The Collared-Rim Jar of the Early Iron Age. Pages 117–26 in *Archaeology in the Levant: Essays for Kathleen Kenyon.* Edited by R. Moorey and P. Parr. Warminster: Aris & Phillips.

Ibrahim, Mo'awiyah M., James A. Sauer, and Khair Yassine. 1976. The East Jordan Survey, 1975. *BASOR* 222:41–66.

Ikram, Salima. 2003. A Preliminary Study of Zooarchaeological Changes between the Bronze and Iron Ages at Kinet Höyük. Pages 283–93 in Fischer et al. 2003.

Ilan, David. 1995. The Dawn of Internationalism—The Middle Bronze Age. Pages 297–319 in *The Archaeology of Society in the Holy Land.* Edited by T. E. Levy. New York: Facts on File.

———. 1999. Northeastern Israel in the Iron Age I: Cultural, Socioeconomic and Political Perspectives. Ph.D. diss. Tel Aviv University.

Isaacs, Harold R. 1975. Basic Group Identity: The Idols of the Tribe. Pages 29–52 in *Ethnicity: Theory and Experience.* Edited by N. Glazer and D. P. Moynihan. Cambridge, Mass.: Harvard University Press.

Isserlin, Benekikt S. J. 1983. The Israelite Conquest of Canaan: A Comparative Review of the Arguments Applicable. *PEQ* 115:84–94.

Jacopi, Giulio. 1930–31. Nuovi Scavi nella Necropoli micenea di Ialisso. *Annuario della Scuola italiana de Atene e delle missioni italiani in oriente* 13–14:253–345.

James, Alan. 2000. Egypt and Her Vassals: The Geopolitical Dimension. Pages 112–24 in Cohen and Westbrook 2000c.

James, Frances W. 1966. *The Iron Age at Beth Shean: A Study of Levels VI–IV.* University Museum Monograph 85. Philadelphia: University Museum, University of Pennsylvania.

James, Frances W., and Patrick E. McGovern. 1993. *The Late Bronze Egyptian Garrison at Beth Shean: A Study of Levels VII and VIII.* Vol. 1. University Museum Monograph 85. Philadelphia: University Museum, University of Pennsylvania.

Janko, Richard. 1981. *Homer, Hesiod and the Hymns: Diachronic Development in Epic Diction*. Cambridge: Cambridge University Press.

Jean, Éric. 2003. From Bronze to Iron Ages in Cilicia: The Pottery in Its Stratigraphic Context. Pages 79–91 in Fischer et al. 2003.

Ji, Chang-Ho C., Jr. 1995. Iron Age I in Central and Northern Transjordan: An Interim Summary of the Archaeological Data. *PEQ* 127:122–40.

———. 1997. A Note on the Iron Age Four-Room House in Palestine. *Or* 66:387–413.

Jobling, David, and Catherine Rose. 1996. Reading as a Philistine: The Ancient and Modern History of a Cultural Slur. Pages 381–417 in *Ethnicity and the Bible*. Edited by M. G. Brett. Biblical Interpretation Series 19. Leiden: Brill.

Johnson, Gregory A. 1977. Aspects of Regional Analysis in Archaeology. *ARA* 6: 479–508.

———. 1980. Rank-Size Convexity and System Integration: A View from Archaeology. *Economic Geography* 56:234–47.

———. 1981. Monitoring Complex System Integration and Boundary Phenomena with Settlement Size Data. Pages 144–87 in *Archaeological Approaches to Complexity*. Edited by S. E. van der Leeuw. Amsterdam: Universiteit van Amsterdam.

Johnson, Matthew. 1999. *Archaeological Theory: An Introduction*. Malden, Mass.: Blackwell.

Jones, Andrew. 2002. *Archaeological Theory and Scientific Practice*. New York: Cambridge University Press.

Jones, Delmos J., and Jacquetta Hill-Burnett. 1982. The Political Context of Ethnogenesis: An Australian Example. Pages 214–46 in *Aboriginal Power in Australian Society*. Edited by M. C. Howard. St. Lucia: University of Queensland.

Jones, George T., and Robert D. Leonard. 1989. The Concept of Diversity: An Introduction. Pages 1–3 in Leonard and Jones 1989.

Jones, R. E. 1986. *Greek and Cypriot Pottery: A Review of Scientific Studies*. Fitch Laboratory Occasional Paper 1. Athens: British School at Athens.

Jones, R. E., and Sarah J. Vaughan. 1988. Part 2: A Study of Some "Canaanite" Jar Fragments from Maa-Palaeokastro by Petrographic and Chemical Analysis. Pages 386–95 in Karageorghis and Demas 1988.

Jones, Siân. 1997. *The Archaeology of Ethnicity: Constructing Identities in the Past and Present*. London: Routledge.

Jordan, Stacey, and Carmel Schrire. 2002. Material Cuture and the Roots of Colonial Society at the South African Cape of Good Hope. Pages 241–72 in Lyons and Papadopoulos 2002.

Jorgensen, John S. 1999. Response to J. P. Dessel. Pages 33–37 in *Galilee through the Centuries: Confluence of Cultures*. Edited by E. M. Meyers. Duke Judaic Studies Series 1. Winona Lake, Ind.: Eisenbrauns.

———. 2002. A Typology of the Late Bronze II and Early Iron Age Pottery from Tel 'Ein Zippori, Galilee: Persistence and Change across an Archaeological Horizon. Ph.D. diss. Duke University.

Kallai, Zacharia. 1972. The Land of Benjamin and Mt. Ephraim. Pages 151–93 in *Judaea, Samaria and the Golan*. Edited by M. Kochavi. Jerusalem: Carta.

Kallai, Zacharia, and Hayim Tadmor. 1969. Bit Ninurta = Beth Horon—On the History of the Kingdom of Jerusalem in the Amarna Period [Hebrew]. *ErIsr* 9:138–47.

Kamlah, Jens. 2000. *Der Zeraqon-Survey, 1989–1994: Mit Beiträgen zur Methodik und geschichtlichen Auswertung archäologischer Oberflächenuntersuchungen in Palästina.* Abhandlungen des Deutschen Palästinavereins 27/1. Wiesbaden: Harrassowitz.

Kamp, Kathryn A., and Norman Yoffee. 1980. Ethnicity in Ancient Western Asia during the Early Second Millennium B.C.: Archaeological Assessments and Ethnoarchaeological Prospectives. *BASOR* 237:85–104.

Kanta, Athanasia. 1980. *The Late Minoan III Period in Crete: A Survey of Sites, Pottery and Their Distribution.* SIMA 58. Göteborg: Åström.

———. 2001. Cretan Refuge Settlements: Problems and Historical Implications within the Wider Context of the Eastern Mediterranean Towards the End of the Bronze Age. Pages 13–21 in Karageorghis and Morris 2001.

Kantor, Helene J. 1947. *The Aegean and the Orient in the Second Millennium B.C.* The Archaeological Institute of America Monograph 1. Bloomington, Ind.: Principia Press.

Kaplan, Jacob. 1960. The Excavations at Jaffa (Third Season) [Hebrew]. *BIES* 24:133–35.

———. 1972. The Archaeology and History of Tel Aviv-Jaffa. *BA* 35:66–95.

Kaplan, Jacob, and Haya Ritter-Kaplan. 1993. Jaffa. *NEAEHL* 3:655–59.

Karageorghis,Vassos. 1982. *Cyprus from the Stone Age to the Romans.* London: Thames & Hudson.

———. 1984a. Exploring Philistine Origins on the Island of Cyprus. *BAR* 10/2:16–28.

———. 1984b. New Light on Late Bronze Age Cyprus. Pages 19–22 in *Cyprus at the Close of the Late Bronze Age.* Edited by V. Karageorghis and J. D. Muhly. Nicosia: A. G. Leventis Foundation.

———. 1986. "Barbarian" Ware in Cyprus. Pages 246–64 in *Acts of the International Archaeological Symposium "Cyprus between the Orient and the Occident" Nicosia, 8–14 September 1985.* Nicosia: Zavallis.

———. 1987. Western Cyprus at the Close of the Bronze Age. Pages 115–19 in *Western Cyprus: Connections.* Edited by D. W. Rupp. SIMA 77. Göteborg: Åström.

———. 1990a. Miscellanea from Late Bronze Age Cyprus. *Levant* 22:157–59.

———. 1990b. *Tombs at Palaepaphos. 1. Teratsoudhia 2. Eliomylia.* Nicosia: A. G. Leventis Foundation.

———. 1992a. The Crisis Years: Cyprus. Pages 79–86 in Ward and Joukowsky 1992.

———. 1992b. The Greeks on Cyprus. Pages 137–54 in *Fifty Years of Polish Excavations in Egypt and the Near East: Acts of the Symposium at the Warsaw University 1986.* Warsaw: PAN.

———. 1993. *The Coroplastic Art of Ancient Cyprus II: Late Cyriote II–Cypro-Geometric III.* Nicosia: A. G. Leventis Foundation.

———. 1994. The Prehistory of Ethnogenesis. Pages 1–10 in *Cyprus in the Eleventh Century B.C.: Proceedings of the International Symposium Organized by the*

Archaeological Research Unit of the University of Cyprus and the Anastasios G. Leventis Foundation, Nicosia, 30–31 October 1993. Edited by V. Karageorghis. Nicosia: A. G. Leventis Foundation.

———. 1996. Some Aspects of the Maritime Trade of Cyprus during the Late Bronze Age. Pages 61–70 in *The Development of the Cypriot Economy from the Prehistoric Period to the Present Day.* Edited by V. Karageorghis and D. Michaelides. Nicosia: Department of Antiquities, Cyprus.

———. 1998. Hearths and Bathtubs in Cyprus: A "Sea Peoples" Innovation? Pages 276–82 in Gitin, Mazar, and Stern 1998.

———. 2000. Cultural Innovations in Cyprus Relating to the Sea Peoples. Pages 255–79 in Oren 2000.

———. 2001. The Great Goddess of Cyprus between the Aegeans and the "Eteocypriots." Pages 323–28 in Laffineur and Hägg 2001.

———. 2002. *Early Cyprus: Crossroads of the Mediterranean.* Los Angeles: J. Paul Getty Museum.

Karageorghis, Vassos, and Martha Demas. 1984. *Pyla-Kokkinokremos: A Late Thirteenth Century BC Fortified Settlement in Cyprus.* Nicosia: Department of Antiquities, Cyprus.

———. 1985. *Excavations at Kition V: The Pre-Phoenician Levels: Areas I and II, Part I.* Nicosia: Department of Antiquities, Cyprus.

———. 1988. *Excavations at Maa-Palaeokastro 1979–1986.* Nicosia: Department of Antiquities, Cyprus.

Karageorghis, Vassos, and Vasiliki Kassianidou. 1999. Metalworking and Recycling in Late Bronze Age Cyprus: The Evidence from Kition. *OJA* 18:171–88.

Karageorghis, Vassos, and Christine E. Morris, eds. 2001. *Defensive Settlements of the Aegean and the Eastern Mediterranean after c. 1200 B.C.: Proceedings of an International Workshop Held at Trinity College Dublin, 7th—9th May, 1999.* Nicosia: Anastasios G. Leventis Foundation.

Karantzali, Efi. 2001. *The Mycenaean Cemetery at Pylona on Rhodes.* Biblical Archaeology Review International Series 988. Oxford: Archaeopress.

Kardulias, P. Nick. 1999a. Multiple Levels in the Aegean Bronze Age World-Systems. Pages 179–202 in Kardulias 1999b.

———. ed. 1999b. *World-Systems Theory in Practice: Leadership, Production, and Exchange.* New York: Rowman & Littlefield.

Katzenstein, H. Jacob. 1982. Gaza in Egyptian Texts of the New Kingdom. *JAOS* 102:111–13.

———. 1992. Philistines: History. *ABD* 5:326–28.

Kaufmann, Jecheskel. 1953. *The Biblical Account of the Conquest of Palestine.* Translated by M. Dagut. Jerusalem: Magnes.

Kearney, Michael. 1986. From the Invisible Hand to the Visible Feet: Anthropological Studies of Migration and Development. *ARA* 15:331–61.

Kelley, Allyn J. 1976. *The Pottery of Ancient Egypt: Dynasty I to Roman Times.* Toronto: Royal Ontario Museum.

Kelm, George L., and Amihai Mazar. 1995. *Timnah: A Biblical City in the Sorek Valley.* Winona Lake, Ind.: Eisenbrauns.

Kelso, James L. 1968. *The Excavation of Bethel (1934–1960).* AASOR 39. Cambridge, Mass.: American Schools of Oriental Research.

Kemp, Barry J. 1978. Imperialism and Empire in New Kingdom Egypt. Pages 7–75 in Garnsey and Whittaker 1978.

Kempinksi, Aharon. 1978. Tel Masos. *Expedition* 20/4:29–37.

———. 1983. From Tent to House. Pages 31–34 in Fritz and Kempinski 1983.

———. 1986. Joshua's Altar—An Iron Age I Watchtower. *BAR* 12/1:42.

———. 1992. Middle and Late Bronze Age Fortifications. Pages 127–42 in Kempinski and Reich 1992.

———. 1993. "When History Sleeps, Theology Arises": A Note on Joshua 8:30–35 and the Archaeology of the Settlement Period [Hebrew, with English summary]. *ErIsr* 24:175–83, 237*.

Kempinksi, Aharon, and Ronny Reich, eds. 1992. *The Architecture of Ancient Israel: From the Prehistoric to the Persian Periods.* Jerusalem: Israel Exploration Society.

Kenyon, Kathleen M. 1979. *Archaeology in the Holy Land.* 4th ed.; London: Benn-Norton.

Keswani, Priscilla S. 1993. Models of Local Exchange in Late Bronze Age Cyprus. *BASOR* 292:73–83.

———. 1996. Hierarchies, Heterarchies, and Urbanization Proesses: The View From Bronze Age Cyprus. *JMA* 9:211–50.

Kilian, Klaus. 1980. Zum Ende der mykenischen Epoche in der Argolis. *Jahrbuch des Römisch-Germanischen Zentral-Museums Mainz* 27:166–95.

———. 1981. Zeugnisse Mykenischer Kultausübung in Tiryns. Pages 49–58 in *Sanctuaries and Cults in the Aegean Bronze Age: Proceedings of the First International Symposium at the Swedish Institute in Athens, 12–13 May, 1980.* Edited by R. Hägg and N. Marinatos. Stockholm: Åström.

———. 1988a. Mycenaeans Up to Date: Trends and Changes in Recent Research. Pages 115–52 in French and Wardle 1988.

———. 1988b. The Emergence of *Wanax* Ideology in the Mycenaean Palaces. *OJA* 7:291–302.

———. 1990. La caduta dei palazzo micenei continentali: Aspetti archeologici. Pages 73–116 in *Le Origini dei Greci: Dori e mondo egeo.* Edited by D. Musti. Rome: Laterza.

———. 1996. Earthquakes and Archaeological Context at Thirteenth Century BC Tiryns. Pages 63–68 in Stiros and Jones 1996.

Killebrew, Ann E. 1982. The Pottery Workshop in Ancient Egyptian Reliefs and Paintings. Pages 60–101 in *Papers for Discussion Presented by the Department of Egyptology, the Hebrew University, Jerusalem.* Edited by Sarah Groll. Jerusalem: Hebrew University of Jerusalem.

———. 1986. *Tel Miqne-Ekron: Report of the 1984 Excavations: Field INE/SE.* Edited by S. Gitin. Jerusalem: Albright Institute of Archaeological Research.

———. 1996a. Pottery Kilns from Deir el-Balah and Tel Miqne-Ekron. Pages 135–62 in *Retrieving the Past: Essays on Archaeological Research and Methodology in Honor of Gus W. Van Beek.* Edited by J. D. Seger. Winona Lake, Ind.: Eisenbrauns.

———. 1996b. *Tel Miqne-Ekron: Report of the 1985–1988 Excavations in Field INE: Areas INE.5, INE.6, and INE.7: The Bronze and Iron Ages. Text and Data Base (Plates, Sections, Plans).* Edited by S. Gitin. Jerusalem: Albright Institute of Archaeological Research.

———. 1998a. Aegean and Aegean-Style Material Culture in Canaan during the 14th–12th Centuries BC: Trade, Colonization, Diffusion, or Migration? Pages 159–71 in *The Aegean and the Orient in the Second Millennium: Proceedings of the Fiftieth Anniversary Symposium Cincinnati, 18–20 April 1997.* Edited by E. H. Cline and D. Harris-Cline. Aegaeum 18. Liège: Université de Liège.

———. 1998b. Ceramic Typology and Technology of the Late Bronze II and Iron I Assemblages from Tel Miqne-Ekron: The Transition from Canaanite to Philistine Culture. Pages 379–405 in Gitin, Mazar, and Stern 1998.

———. 1999a. Ceramic Craft and Technology during the Late Bronze and Early Iron Ages: The Relationship between Pottery Technology, Style, and Cultural Diversity. Ph.D. diss. Hebrew University of Jerusalem.

———. 1999b. Late Bronze and Iron I Cooking Pots in Canaan: A Typological, Technological and Functional Study. Pages 83–126 in *Archaeology, History and Culture in Palestine and the Near East: Essays in Memory of Albert E. Glock.* Edited by T. Kapitan. ASOR Books 3. Atlanta: Scholars Press.

———. 2000. Aegean-Style Early Philistine Pottery in Canaan during the Iron I Age: A Stylistic Analysis of Mycenaean IIIC:1b Pottery and Its Associated Wares. Pages 233–53 in Oren 2000.

———. 2001. The Collared Pithos in Context: A Typological, Technological, and Functional Reassessment. Pages 377–98 in Wolff 2001.

———. 2003a. Between Heaven and Earth: Educational Perspectives on the Archaeology and Material Culture of the Bible. Pages 11–30 in *Between Text and Artifact: Integrating Archaeology in Biblical Studies Teaching.* Edited by M. C. Moreland. SBLABS 8. Atlanta: Society of Biblical Literature.

———. 2003b. The Southern Levant during the 13th–12th Centuries BCE: The Archaeology of Social Boundaries. Pages 117–24 in Fischer et al. 2003.

———. 2004. New Kingdom Egyptian-Style and Egyptian Pottery in Canaan: Implications for Egyptian Rule in Canaan during the 19th and Early 20th Dynasties. Pages 309–43 in *Egypt, Israel, and the Ancient Mediterranean World: Essays in Honor of Donald B. Redford.* Edited by G. N. Knoppers and A. Hirsch. Leiden: Brill.

———. Forthcoming a. Cultural Homogenization and Diversity in Canaan during the 13th and 12th Centuries BCE. In *The Transmission and Assimilation of Culture in the Near East Conference Proceedings.* Edited by J. Clark. Council for British Research in the Levant.

———. Forthcoming b. The Emergence of Ancient Israel: The Social Boundaries of a "Mixed Multitude." In *I Will Speak the Riddles of Ancient Times (Abiah chidot minei-kedem—Ps 78:2b): Archaeological and Historical Studies in Honor of Amihai Mazar on the Occasion of His Sixtieth Birthday.* Edited by P. de Miroschedji and A. M. Maeir. Winona Lake, Ind.: Eisenbrauns.

———. Forthcoming c. *Tel Miqne-Ekron: Excavations 1984–1988—Field INE, Areas 2, 3, 4, 8, 9, 36 and 37 (The Sondage); Field INW, Areas 7 and 10; Iron Age I and II.* Edited by S. Gitin. Ekron Limited Edition Series 11. Jerusalem: Tel Miqne-Ekron Project Office.

Killebrew, Ann E., and D. Bruce MacKay. 1994. Pots and Peoples in Canaan during the 13th–12th Centuries B.C.E.: The Ethnic Origin and Identity of

Philistines and Israelites. Paper presented at the ASOR/SBL/AAR Annual Meeting, Chicago, November.

Kimes, T., Colin Haselgrove, and Ian Hodder. 1982. A Method for the Identification of Regional Cultural Boundaries. *JAnthArch* 1:113–31.

King, Philip J. 1983. *American Archaeology in the Mideast: A History of the American Schools of Oriental Research.* Philadelphia: American Schools of Oriental Research.

King, Philip J., and Lawrence E. Stager. 2001. *Life in Biblical Israel.* Louisville: Westminster John Knox.

Kingery, W. David. 1955. Factors Affecting Thermal Stress Resistance of Ceramic Materials. *Journal of the American Ceramic Society* 38:3–15.

Kitchen, Kenneth A. 1966a. *The Ancient Orient and the Old Testament.* Chicago: InterVarsity Press.

———. 1966b. Historical Method and Early Hebrew Tradition. *TynBul* 17:63–97.

———. 1969. Interrelations of Egypt and Syria. Pages 77–95 in *La Siria nel Tardo Bronze.* Edited by M. Liverani. Rome: Centro per le Antichità e la Storia dell'Arte del Vicino Oriente.

———. 1973. The Philistines. Pages 53–78 in *Peoples of Old Testament Times.* Edited by D. J. Wiseman. Oxford: Clarendon.

———. 1975. *Ramesside Inscriptions: Historical and Biographical I.* Oxford: Blackwell.

———. 1979. *Ramesside Inscriptions: Historical and Biographical II.* Oxford: Blackwell.

———. 1982. *Pharaoh Triumphant: The Life and Times of Ramesses II.* Warminster: Aris & Phillips.

———. 1983. *Ramesside Inscriptions: Historical and Biographical V.* Oxford: Blackwell.

———. 1998. Egyptians and Hebrew, from Ra'amses to Jericho. Pages 65–131 in Ahituv and Oren 1998.

———. 2003. The Victories of Merenptah, and the Nature of their Record. *JSOT* 28:259–72.

Kjaer, Hans. 1930. The Excavation of Shiloh 1929. *JPOS* 10:87–174.

Klejn, Leo. 1998. Comments. *CurrAnthr* 39:30–32.

Klengel, Horst. 1974. "Hungerjahre" in Hatti. *AoF* 1:165–74.

———. 1992. *Syria 3000 to 300 B.C.: A Handbook of Political History.* Berlin: Akademie.

Kletter, Raz. 2002. People without Burials? The Lack of Iron I Burials in the Central Highlands of Palestine. *IEJ* 52:28–48.

Kling, Barbara. 1984. Mycenaean IIIC:1b Pottery in Cyprus: Principal Characteristics and Historical Context. Pages 29–38 in *Cyprus at the Close of the Late Bronze Age.* Edited by V. Karageorghis and J. D. Muhly. Nicosia: A. G. Leventis Foundation.

———. 1987. Pottery Classification and Relative Chronology of the LCIIC–LCIIIA Periods. Pages 97–114 in Western Cyprus: *Connections: An Archaeological Symposium Held at Brock University, St. Catharines, Ontario, Canada, March 21–22, 1986.* SIMA 77. Edited by D. Rupp. Göteborg: Åström.

———. 1988. Some Stylistic Remarks on the Pottery of Mycenaean IIIC:1 Style from Maa-Palaeokastro. Pages 317–39 in Karageorghis and Demas 1988.

———. 1989a. Local Cypriot Features in the Ceramics of the Late Cypriot IIIA. Pages 160–70 in *Early Society in Cyprus*. Edited by E. J. Peltenburg. Edinburgh: Edinburgh University Press.

———. 1989b. *Mycenaean IIIC:1b and Related Pottery in Cyprus*. SIMA 87. Göteborg: Åström.

———. 1991. A Terminology for the Matte-Painted, Wheelmade Pottery of Late Cypriot IIC-IIIA. Pages 181–84 in Barlow, Bolger, and Kling 1991.

———. 2000. Mycenaean IIIC:1b and Related Pottery in Cyprus: Comments on the Current State of Research. Pages 281–95 in Oren 2000.

Kloner, Amos. 2001. *Survey of Jerusalem—The Northeastern Sector*. Jerusalem: Israel Antiquities Authority, Archaeological Survey of Israel.

Knapp, A. Bernard. 1983. An Alashian Merchant at Ugarit. *TA* 10:38–45.

———. 1985a. Alashiya, Caphtor/Keftiu and Eastern Mediterranean Trade: Recent Studies in Cypriote Archaeology and History: A Review Article. *JFA* 12:231–50.

———. 1985b. Production and Exchange in the Aegean and Eastern Mediterranean: An Overview. Pages 1–11 in *Prehistoric Production and Exchange: The Aegean and Eastern Mediterranean*. Edited by A. B. Knapp and T. Stech. Los Angeles: Institute of Archaeology, University of California, Los Angeles.

———. 1986. *Copper Production and Divine Protection: Archaeology, Ideology and Social Complexity on Bronze Age Cyprus*. Studies in Mediterranean Archaeology Pocket-Book 42. Göteborg: Åström.

———. 1987. Pots, PIXE, and Data Processing at Pella in Jordan. *BASOR* 266:1–30.

———. 1988a. Copper Production and Eastern Mediterranean Trade: The Rise of Complex Society on Cyprus. Pages 149–69 in *State and Society: The Emergence and Development of Social Hierarchy and Political Centralization*. Edited by J. Gledhill, B. Bender, and M. T. Larsen. London: Unwin Hyman.

———. 1988b. *The History of Ancient Western Asia and Egypt*. Belmont, Calif.: Wadsworth.

———. 1989a. Complexity and Collapse in the North Jordan Valley: Archaeometry and Society in the Middle-Late Bronze Ages. *IEJ* 39:129–49.

———. 1989b. Response: Independence, Imperialism, and the Egyptian Factor. *BASOR* 274:64–67.

———. 1990a. Copper Production and Mediterranean Trade: The View from Cyprus. *OpAth* 18:109–16.

———. 1990b. Cypriote Archaeology: A Review of Recent Symposia. *JAOS* 110:71–78.

———. 1990c. Review of R. S. Merrillees, *Alashia Revisited*. *BO* 47(5/6): cols. 795–800.

———. 1991. Spice, Drugs, Grain and Grog: Organic Goods in Bronze Age Eastern Mediterranean Trade. Pages 21–68 in Gale 1991.

———. 1992a. Archaeology and *Annales:* Time, Space, and Change. Pages 1–21 in Knapp 1992c.

———. 1992b. Independence and Imperialism: Politico-Economic Structures in the Bronze Age Levant. Pages 83–98 in Knapp 1992c.

———. 1993. *Society and Polity at Bronze Age Pella: An Annales Perspective*. JSOT/ASOR Monograph Series 6. Sheffield: Sheffield Academic Press.

———. 1996. Power and Ideology on Prehistoric Cyprus. Pages 9–25 in *Religion and Power in the Ancient Greek World: Proceedings of the Uppsala Symposium 1993*. Edited by P. Hellström and B. Alroth. Acta Universitatis Upsaliensis, Boreas 24. Uppsala: Ubsaliensis S. Academiae.

———. 1997. *The Archaeology of Late Bronze Age Cypriot Society: The Study of Settlement, Survey and Landscape*. Glasgow: University of Glasgow, Department of Archaeology.

———. 2000. Archaeology, Science-Based Archaeology and the Mediterranean Bronze Age Metals Trade. *EJA* 3:31–56.

———. ed. 1992c. *Archaeology, Annales, and Ethnohistory*. Cambridge: Cambridge University Press.

Knauf, Ernst A. 1992. The Cultural Impact of Secondary State Formation: The Cases of the Edomites and Moabites. Pages 47–54 in Bienkowski 1992c.

Knoppers, Gary N. 1993–94. *Two Nations under God: The Deuteronomic History of Solomon and the Dual Monarchies*. 2 vols. HSM 52–53. Atlanta: Scholars Press.

———. 2000. Introduction. Pages 1–19 in Knoppers and McConville 2000.

———. 2001. Intermarriage, Social Complexity, and Ethnic Diversity in the Genealogy of Judah. *JBL* 120:15–30.

Knoppers, Gary N., and J. Gordon McConville, eds. 2000. *Reconsidering Israel and Judah: Recent Studies on the Deuteronomistic History*. Sources for Biblical and Theological Study 8. Edited by G. N. Knoppers and J. Gordon McConville. Winona Lake, Ind.: Eisenbrauns.

Kochavi, Moshe. 1969. Excavations at Tel Esdar [Hebrew]. *ʿAtiqot* 5 (HS):14–48.

———. 1974. Khirbet Rabud = Debir. *TA* 1:2–33.

———. 1985. The Israelite Settlement in Canaan in Light of Archaeological Surveys. Pages 54–60 in Amitai 1985.

———. 1990. *Aphek in Canaan: The Egyptian Governor's Residence and Its Finds*. Jerusalem: Israel Museum.

Koehl, Robert B. 1985. *Sarepta III: The Imported Bronze and Iron Age Wares from Area II, X*. Beyrouth: Université Libanaise.

Kohl, Philip L. 1998. Comments. *Current Anthropology* 39:31–32.

Köhler-Rollefson, Ilse. 1992. A Model for the Development of Nomadic Pastoralism on the Transjordanian Plateau. Pages 11–18 in Bar-Yosef and Khazanov 1992.

Kolska-Horwitz. Liora. 1986–87. Faunal Remains from the Early Iron Age Site on Mount Ebal. *TA* 13–14:173–90.

Košak, Silvin. 1980. The Hittites and the Greeks. *Linguistica* 20:35–48.

———. 1981. Western Neighbours of the Hittites. *ErIsr* 15:12*–16*.

Kowalewski, Stephen A. 1982. The Evolution of Primate Regional Systems. *Comparative Urban Research*. 9:60–78.

———. 1996. Clout, Corn, Copper, Core-Periphery, Culture Area. Pages 27–38 in Peregrine and Feinman 1996.

Kristiansen, Kristian. 1989. Prehistoric Migrations—The Case of the Single Grace and Corded Ware Cultures. *Journal of Danish Archaeology* 8:211–25.

Kuznar, Lawrence A. 1999. The Inca Empire: Detailing the Complexities of Core-Periphery Interactions. Pages 223–41 in Kardulias 1999b.

LaBianca, Øystein S., and David C. Hopkins, eds. 1988. *Early Israelite Agriculture: Reviews of David C. Hopkins' Book: The Highlands of Canaan*. Occasional Papers of the Institute of Archaeology 1. Berrien Springs, Mich.: Andrews University Press.

LaBianca, Øystein S., and Randall W. Younker. 1995. The Kingdoms of Ammon, Moab and Edom: The Archaeology of Society in Late Bronze/Iron Age Transjordan (ca. 1400–500 BCE). Pages 399–415 in *The Archaeology of Society in the Holy Land.* Edited by T. E. Levy. New York: Facts on File.

Laffineur, Robert, and Robin Hägg, eds. 2001. *Potnia: Deities and Religion in the Aegean Bronze Age: Proceedings of the 8th International Aegean Conference/8e Rencontre Egéenne internationale Göteborg, Göteborg University, 12–15 April 2000.* Aegaeum 22. Liège: University de Liège.

Lamberg-Karlovsky, Carl C. 1985. The Longue Durée in the Ancient Near East. Pages 53–72 in *De L'Indus aux Balkans: Recueil a la Mémoire de Jean Deshayes.* Edited by L. Huot, M. Yon, and Y. Calvet. Paris: Éditions Recherches sur les Civilisations.

Lapp, Nancy L., ed. 1978. *The Third Campaign at Tell el-Fûl: The Excavations of 1964.* AASOR 45. Cambridge, Mass.: American Schools of Oriental Research.

Lapp, Paul. 1967. The Conquest of Palestine in Light of Archaeology. *CTM* 38:283–300.

Lass, Egon H. E. 1994. Quantitative Studies in Flotation as Ashkelon, 1986 to 1988. *BASOR* 294:23–38.

Latacz, Joachim. 2001. *Troia: Traum und Wirklichkeit.* Stuttgart: Theiss.

Leclant, Jean. 1971. Fouilles et travaux en Égypte et au Soudan 1969–1970 (G. Kôm Abû Billou). *Or* 40:224–66.

Lederman, Zvi. 1999. An Early Iron Age Village at Khirbet Raddana: The Excavations of Joseph A. Callaway. Ph.D. diss. Harvard University.

Leeuw, Sander E. van der. 1976. *Studies in the Technology of Ancient Pottery.* Amsterdam: University of Amsterdam.

———. 1984. Pottery Manufacture: Some Complications for the Study of Trade. Pages 55–69 in *Pots and Potters: Current Approaches in Ceramic Analysis.* Edited by P. M. Rice. UCLA Instititute of Archaeology Monograph 24. Los Angeles: University of California Press.

Lehmann, G. A. 1970. Der Untergang des hethitischen Grossreiches und die neuen Texte aus Ugarit. *UF* 2:39–73.

———. 1985. *Die mykenisch-frühgriechische Welt und der östliche Mittelmeerraum in der Zeit der 'Seevölker'-Invasionen um 1200 v. Chr.* Opladen: Westdeutscher.

Lehmann, Gunnar. 2001. Phoenicians in Western Galilee: First Results of an Archaeological Survey in the Hinterland of Akko. Pages 65–112 in A. Mazar 2001.

———. 2003. The United Monarchy in the Country-Side: Jerusalem, Judah, and the Shephelah during the Tenth Century B.C.E. Pages 117–162 in Vaughn and Killebrew 2003.

———. Forthcoming. Reconstructing the Social Landscape of Early Israel: Rural Marriage Alliances in the Central Hill-Country. *TA*

Lemche, Niels Peter. 1985. *Early Israel Anthropological and Sociological Studies on the Israelite Society before the Monarchy.* VTSup 37. Leiden: Brill.

———. 1991a. *The Canaanites and Their Land.* JSOTSup 110. Sheffield: Sheffield Academic Press.

———. 1991b. Society, Text and Religion as Key Factors in Understanding the Emergence of Israel in Canaan. *SJOT* 5/2:7–18.

———. 1992. Ḫabiru, Ḫapiru. *ABD* 3:6–10.
———. 1993. City-Dwellers or Administrators Further Light on the Canaanites. Pages 76–89 in *History and Traditions of Early Israel: Studies Presented to Eduard Nielsen May 8th 1993.* Edited by A. Lemaire and B. Otzen. VTSup 50. Leiden: Brill.
———. 1996. Where Should We Look for Canaan? A Reply to Nadav Naʾaman. *UF* 28:767–72.
———. 1998a. Greater Canaan: The Implications of a Correct Reading of EA 151:49–67. *BASOR* 310:19–24.
———. 1998b. *Prelude to Israel's Past: Background and Beginnings of Israelite History and Identity.* Translated by E. F. Maniscalco. Peabody, Mass.: Hendrickson.
Leonard, Albert, Jr. 1994. *Late Bronze Age Aegean Pottery from Syria-Palestine.* SIMA 64. Jonsered: Åström.
———. 1999. "Canaanite Jars" and the Late Bronze Age Aegeo-Levantine Wine Trade. Pages 233–54 in *The Origins and Ancient History of Wine.* Edited by P. E. McGovern, S. J. Fleming, and S. H. Katz. Amsterdam: Gordon & Breach.
Leonard, Robert D., and George T. Jones, eds., 1989. *Quantifying Diversity in Archaeology.* Cambridge: Cambridge University Press.
Lesko, Leonard H. 1980. The Wars of Ramses III. *Serapis* 6:83–86.
———. 1992. Egypt in the 12th Century B.C. Pages 151–56 in Ward and Joukowsky 1992.
Lev-Tov, Justin S. E. 2000. Pigs, Philistines, and the Ancient Animal Economy of Ekron from the Late Bronze Age to the Iron Age II. Ph.D. diss. University of Tennessee, Knoxville.
Lévi-Strauss, Claude. 1967. *Structural Anthropology.* Translated by C. Jacobsson and B. Grundfest Schoepf. Garden City, N.Y.: Doubleday Anchor.
———. 1971. El tiempo del mito. *Plural: Critíca y Literatura* 1:1–4.
Lichtheim, Miriam. 1976. *Ancient Egyptian Literature: A Book of Readings.* Vol. 2: *The New Kingdom.* Berkeley and Los Angeles: University of California Press.
Liebowitz, Harold. 1987. Late Bronze II Ivory Work in Palestine: Evidence of a Cultural Highpoint. *BASOR* 265:3–24.
———. 1989. Response: LB IIB Ivories and the Material Cutlure of the Late Bronze Age. *BASOR* 275:63–64.
Linder, Elisha. 1981. Ugarit: A Canaanite Thalassocracy. Pages 31–42 in *Ugarit in Retrospect: Fifty Years of Ugarit and Ugaritic.* Edited by G. D. Young. Winona Lake, Ind.: Eisenbrauns.
Linné, Sigvald. 1965. The Ethnologist and the American Indian Pottery. Pages 20–42 in *Ceramics and Man.* Edited by F. R. Matson. Viking Fund Publications in Anthropology 41. Chicago: Aldine.
Liverani, Mario. 1968. Variazioni climatiche e fluttuazioni demografiche nella storia siriana. *OrAnt* 7:77–89.
———. 1973. Memorandum on the Approach to Historiographic Texts. *Or* 42:178–94.
———. 1983. Political Lexicon and Political Ideologies in the Amarna Letters. *Ber* 31:41–56.
———. 1987. The Collapse of the Near Eastern Regional Systems at the End of the Bronze Age: The Case of Syria. Pages 66–73 in Rowlands, Larsen, and Kristiansen 1987.

———. 1988. *Antico Oriente: Storia, societáa, economia.* Rome: Laterza.

———. 1994. History as a War Game. *JMA* 7:241–48.

———. 1998. *Tell el-Amarna Tablets.* Brescia: Paidaia.

———. 2000. The Great Powers' Club. Pages 15–27 in Cohen and Westbrook 2000c.

———. 2001. *International Relations in the Ancient Near East, 1600–1100 B.C.* New York: Palgrave.

London, Gloria A. 1989a. A Comparison of Two Contemporaneous Lifestyles of the Late Second Millennium B.C. *BASOR* 273:37–55.

———. 1989b. On Fig Leaves, Itinerant Potters, and Pottery Production Locations in Cyprus. Pages 65–80 in *Cross-Craft and Cross-Cultural Interactions in Ceramics.* Edited by P. E. McGovern, M. D. Notis, and W. D. Kingery. Ceramics and Civilization 4. Westerville, Ohio: American Ceramic Society.

———. 2003. Four-Room Structures at Late Bronze/Iron I Age Hill Country Workstations. Pages 69–84 in Nakhai 2003b.

Loney, Helen L. 2000. Society and Technological Control: A Critical Review of Models of Technological Change in Ceramic Studies. *AmerAnt* 65:646–68.

Long, V. Philips, ed. 1999. *Israel's Past in Present Research: Essays on Ancient Israelite Historiography.* Studies for Biblical and Theological Study 7. Winona Lake, Ind.: Eisenbrauns.

Loprieno, Antonio. 1997. Slaves. Pages 200–12 in *The Egyptians.* Edited by Sergio Donadoni. Translated by Robert Bianchi. Chicago: University of Chicago Press.

Loud, Gordon. 1948. *Megiddo II: Seasons of the 1935–39.* Chicago: University of Chicago Press.

Lucas, Alfred. 1962. *Ancient Egyptian Materials and Industries.* 4th ed.. London: Arnold.

Luce, John V. 1975. *Homer and the Heroic Age.* London: Thames & Hudson.

Lyons, Claire L., and John K. Papadopoulos. 2002a. Archaeology and Colonialism. Pages 1–23 in Lyons and Papadopoulos 2002b.

———, eds. 2002b. *The Archaeology of Colonialism.* Issues and Debates 9. Los Angeles: Getty Research Institute.

Macalister, R. A. Stewart. 1914. *The Philistines: Their History and Civilization.* London: Oxford University Press.

MacDonald, Burton. 2000. *"East of the Jordan": Territories and Sites of the Hebrew Scriptures.* ASOR Books 6. Boston: American Schools of Oriental Research.

MacDonald, Burton, et al. 1988. *The Wadi el Hasa Archaeological Survey 1979–1983: West-Central Jordan.* Waterloo, Ont.: Wilfrid Laurier University Press.

———. 1992. *The Southern Ghors and Northeast ʿArabah Archaeological Survey.* Sheffield: Collis.

Macdonald, Colin F. 1986. Problems of the Twelfth Century BC in the Dodecanese. *ABSA* 81:125–52.

———. 1988. Rhodes during the Twelfth Century B.C. and Its Role in the Aegean. Page 263 in French and Wardle 1988.

Macdonald, Eann, James L. Starkey, and G. Lankester Harding. 1932. *Beth-Pelet II.* Publication of the Egyptian Research Account 52. London: British School of Archaeology in Egypt.

Machinist, Peter. 1994. Outsiders or Insiders: The Biblical View of Emergent Israel and Its Contexts. Pages 35–60 in *The Other in Jewish Thought and History: Constructions of Jewish Culture and Identity*. Edited by L. J. Silberstein and R. L. Cohn. New York: New York University Press.

———. 2000. Biblical Traditions: The Philistines and Israelite History. Pages 53–83 in Oren 2000.

Machlin, Milt. 1990. *Joshua's Altar: The Dig at Mount Ebal*. New York: Morrow.

MacIver, D. Randall, and C. Leonard Woolley, 1911. *Buhen: Eckley B. Coxe Junior Expedition to Nubia, Vol. 7: Text;* Vol. 8: *Plates*. Philadelphia: University Museum, University of Pennsylvania.

Macqueen, James G. 1968. Geography and History in Western Asia Minor in the Second Millennium B.C. *AnatSt* 18:169–85.

———. 1986. *The Hittites and Their Contemporaries in Asia Minor*. Rev. ed. London: Thames & Hudson.

———. 1996. *The Hittites and Their Contemporaries in Asia Minor*. Rev. ed. London: Thames & Hudson.

Maeir, Aren M. 1988–89. Remarks on a Supposed "Egyptian Residency" at Gezer. *TA* 15–16:65–67.

———. 2001. The Philistine Culture in Transition: A Current Perspective Based on the First Season of Excavation at Tell es-Safi/Gath [Hebrew]. Pages 111–29 in *Settlement, Civilization and Culture: Proeceedings of the Conference in Memory of David Alon*. Edited by A. M. Maeir and E. Baruch. Ramat Gan: Bar Ilan University.

Maeir, Aren M., and Carl S. Ehrlich. 2001. Excavating Philistine Gath: Have We Found Goliath's Hometown? *BAR* 27/6:23–31.

Magrill, Pamela, and Andrew Middleton. 1997. A Canaanite Potter's Workshop at Lachish, Israel. Pges 68–74 in: *Pottery in the Making: World Ceramic Traditions*. Edited by I. Freestone and D. Gaimster. London: British Museum.

Maiuri, Amedeo. 1923–24. Jalisos, Scavi della Missione Archaeologica Italiana a Rodi. *Annuario della scuola italiana di Atene e delle missioni italiane in oriente* 6–7:83–341.

Malamat, Abraham. 1967. Aspects of Tribal Societies in Mari and Israel. Pages 129–38 in *La civilisation de Mari*. Edited by J.-R. Kupper. Paris: Les Belles Lettres.

———. 1983. The Proto-History of Israel: A Study in Method. Pages 303–13 in *The Word of the Lord Shall Go Forth: Essays in Honor of David Noel Freedman in Celebration of His Sixtieth Birthday*. Edited by C. Meyers and M. O'Connor. Philadelphia: Eisenbrauns.

———. 1997. The Exodus: Egyptian Analogies. Pages 15–26 in Frerichs and Lesko 1997.

Malkin, Irad. 1998. *The Return of Odysseus*. Berkeley and Los Angeles: University of California Press.

———. 2002. A Colonial Middle Ground: Greek, Etruscan, and Local Elites in the Bay of Naples. Pages 151–81 in Lyons and Papadopoulos 2002b.

Margalith, Othniel. 1990. On the Origin and Antiquity of the Name "Israel." *ZAW* 102:225–37.

———. 1995. Where Did the Philistines Come From? *ZAW* 107:101–9.

Margueron, Jean-Claude. 1995. Le Palais Royal d'Ougarit. Premiers résultants d'une analyse systématique. Pages 183–202 in *Le Pays d'Ougarit autour de 1200 av. J.-C.: Histoire et archéologie: actes du colloque international, Paris, 28 juin-1er juillet 1993*. Edited by M. Yon, M. Sznycer, and P. Bordreuil. Ras Shamra-Ougarit 11. Paris: Editions Recherche sur les civilisations.

———. 2000. A Stroll through the Palace. *NEA* 63:205–7.

Maroukian, Hampik, Kaiti Gaki-Papanastassiou, and Dimitri Papanastassiou. 1996. Geomorphologic-seismotectonic Observations in Relation to the Castastrophes at Mycenae. Pages 189–94 in Stiros and Jones 1996.

Marquet-Krause, Judith. 1949. *Les fouilles de ʿAy (et-Tell) 1933–1935*. Paris: Geuthner.

Marx, Emanuel. 1977. The Tribe as a Unit of Subsistence: Nomadic Pastoralism in the Middle East. *American Anthropologist* 79:343–63.

Maspero, Gaston. 1896. *The Struggle of the Nations*. Edited by A. H. Sayce. Translated by M. L. McClure. New York: Appleton.

Matson, Frederick R. 1989. Shell-Tempered Pottery and the Fort Ancient Potter. Pages 15–31 in: *Pottery Technology: Ideas and Approaches*. Edited by G. Bronitsky. London: Westview Press.

Mattingly, Gerald L. 1992. The Culture-Historical Approach and Moabite Origins. Pages 55–64 in Bienkowski 1992c.

Mayes, Andrew D. H. 1981. *The Story of Israel between Settlement and Exile: A Redactional Study of the Deuteronomic History*. London: SCM.

Mazar, Amihai. 1981. Giloh: An Early Israelite Settlement Site near Jerusalem. *IEJ* 31:1–36.

———. 1982a. The "Bull Site"—An Iron Age I Open Cult Place. *BASOR* 247:25–42.

———. 1982b. Three Israelite Sites in the Hills of Judah and Ephraim. *BA* 45:167–78.

———. 1985a. The Emergence of Philistine Culture. *IEJ* 35:95–107.

———. 1985b. *Excavations at Tell Qasile Part Two the Philistine Sanctuary: Various Finds, the Pottery, Conclusions, Appendices*. Qedem 20. Jerusalem: The Hebrew University of Jerusalem.

———. 1985c. The Israelite Settlement in Canaan in the List of Archaeological Excavations. Pages 61–71 in Amitai 1985.

———. 1986a. A Rare Ceramic Goblet from Tel Qasile. *Yearbook of the Eretz-Israel Museum, TA* (NS) 4:53–55.

———. 1986b. Excavations at Tell Qasile, 1982–1984: Preliminary Report. *IEJ* 36:1–15.

———. 1988. Some Aspects of the "Sea Peoples" Settlement. Pages 251–60 in Heltzer and Lipiński 1988.

———. 1989. Features of Settlement in the Northern Shephelah During the MB and LB in Light of the Excavations at Tel Batash and Gezer [Hebrew]. *ErIsr* 20:58–67.

———. 1990a. *Archaeology of the Land of the Bible: 10,000–586 BCE*. New York: Doubleday.

———. 1990b. Iron Age I and II Tower at Giloh and the Israelite Settlement. *IEJ* 40:77–101.

———. 1992a. The Iron Age I. Pages 281–96 *The Archaeology of Ancient Israel*. Edited by A. Ben-Tor. New Haven: Yale University Press.

———. 1992b. Temples of the Middle and Late Bronze Ages and the Iron Age. Pages 161–87 in Kempinski and Reich 1992.
———. 1993. Beth-Shean: Tel Beth Shean and the Northern Cemetery. *NEAEHL* 1:214–23.
———. 1994a. Four Thousand Years of History at Tel Beth-Shean [Hebrew]. *Qad* 27 (107–108):67–83.
———. 1994b. Jerusalem and Its Vicinity in Iron Age I. Pages 70–91 in Finkelstein and Na'aman 1994b.
———. 1997a. The Excavations at Tel Beth Shean during the Years 1989–94. Pages 144–64 in Silberman and Small 1997.
———. 1997b. Iron Age Chronology: A Reply to I. Finkelstein. *Levant* 29:157–67.
———. 1997c. *Timnah (Tel Batash) I: Stratigraphy and Architecture Text.* Qedem 37. Jerusalem: Hebrew University of Jerusalem.
———. 1999. The Conservation and Management of Mudbrick Buildings at Tell Qasile, Israel. *Conservation and Management of Archaeological Sites* 3:103–8.
———. 2003a. Beth Shean in the Second Millennium B.C.E.: From Canaanite Town to Egyptian Stronghold. Pages 323–40 in *The Synchronisation of Civilization in the Eastern Mediterranean in the Second Millennium B.C. II: Proceedings of the SCIEM 2000—EuroConference, Haindorff, 2nd of May–7th of May 2001.* Vienna.
———. 2003b. Remarks on Biblical Traditions and Archaeological Evidence concerning Early Israel. Pages 85–98 in Dever and Gitin 2003.
———. ed. 2001. *Studies in the Archaeology of the Iron Age in Israel and Jordan.* JSOTSup 331. Sheffield: Sheffield Academic Press
Mazar, Benjamin. 1971. The Philistines and Their Wars with Israel. Pages 164–79 in *Judges.* Edited by B. Mazar. WHJP 3. Tel Aviv: Massada.
———. 1980. *Canaan and Israel* [Hebrew]. Jerusalem: Bialik Institute.
McCown, Chester C. 1947 *Tell en-Nasbeh I: Archaeological and Historical Results.* Berkeley: Institute of Pacific School of Religion; New Haven: American Schools of Oriental Research.
McGovern, Patrick E. 1985. *Late Bronze Palestinian Pendants: Innovation in a Cosmopolitan Age.* JSOT/ASOR Monograph Series 1. Sheffield: JSOT Press.
———. 1986. *The Late Bronze Age and Early Iron Ages of Central Transjordan: The Baqʿah Valley Project, 1977–1981.* Philadelphia: University of Pennsylvania, University Museum.
———. 1987. Central Transjordan in the Late Bronze and Early Iron Age: An Alternative Hypothesis of Socio-Economic Transformation. Pages 267–73 in *Studies in the History and Archaeology of Jordan* 3. Amman: Department of Antiquities.
———. 1989. Cross-Cultural Craft Interaction: The Late Bronze Egyptian Garrison at Beth Shan. Pages 147–95 in *Cross-Craft and Cross-Cultural Interaction in Ceramics.* Edited by P. E. McGovern. Ceramics and Civilizations 4. Westerview, Ohio: American Ceramic Society.
———. 1992. Settlement Patterns of the Late Bronze and Iron Ages in the Greater Amman Area. Pages 179–83 in *Studies in the History and Archaeology of Jordan* 4. Amman: Department of Antiquities, Amman.
McGovern, Patrick E., Garman Harbottle, Joan Huntoon, and Christopher Wnuk. 1993. Ware Composition, Pyrotechnology. and Surface Treatment. Pages 80–94 in F. W. James and P. E. McGovern, *The Late Bronze Egyptian Garrison at*

Beth Shan: A Study of Levels VII and VIII. University Museum Monograph 85. Philadelphia: University Museum, University of Pennsylvania.

McGuire, Randall H. 1982. The Study of Ethnicity in Historical Archaeology. *JAnthArch* 1:159–78.

———. 1996. The Limits of World-Systems Theory for the Study of Prehistory. Pages 51–64 in Peregrine and Feinman 1996.

McKay, James. 1982. An Exploratory Synthesis of Primordial and Mobilization of Approaches to Ethnic Phenomena. *Ethnic and Racial Studies* 5:395–420.

McKenzie, Steven L., and Stephen R. Haynes, eds. 1999. *To Each Its Own Meaning: An Introduction to Biblical Criticisms and Their Application.* Rev. ed. Louisville: Westminster John Knox.

Mee, C. Christopher. 1982. *Rhodes in the Bronze Age: An Archaeological Survey.* Warminster: Aris & Phillips.

———. 1988. A Mycenaean Thalassocracy in the Eastern Aegean. Pages 301–5 in French and Wardle 1988.

———. 1998. Anatolia and the Aegean in the Late Bronze Age. Pages 137–46 in *The Aegean and the Orient in the Second Millennium: Proceedings of the 50th Anniversary Symposium Cincinnati, 18–20 April 1997.* Edited by E. H. Cline and D. Harris-Cline. Aegaeum 18. Liège: Université de Liège.

Meehl, Mark W., Trude Dothan, and Seymour Gitin. Forthcoming. *Tel Miqne-Ekron: Excavations 1995–1995—Field INE East Slope: Late Bronze II-Iron I—The Early Philistine City. Text and Data Base (Plates, Sections, Plans).* Edited by S. Gitin. The Tel Miqne-Ekron Limited Edition Series 8. Jerusalem: Tel Miqne-Ekron Project Office.

Megaw, Vincent, and M. Ruth Megaw. 1992. The Celts: The First Europeans? *Antiquity* 66:254–60.

Mellaart, James. 1968. Anatolian Trade with Europe and Anatolian Geography and Culture Provinces in the Late Bronze Age. *AnatSt* 18:187–202.

———. 1986. Hatti, Arzawa, and Ahhiyawa: A Review of the Present Stalemate in Historical Geographic Studies. Pages 74–84 in *Philia epi eis Georgion E. Mylonan, dia ta 60 ete tou anaskaphikou tou ergou.* Vivlioth eke tes Athenais Archaiologik es Hetaireias 103. Athens: En Athenais Archaiologike Hetaireia.

———. 1993. The Present State of "Hittite Geography." Pages 415–22 in *Aspects of Art and Iconography: Anatolia and Its Neighbours: Studies in Honor of Nimet Özgüc.* Edited by M. J. Mellink, E. Porada, and T. Özgüc. Ankara: Türk Tarih Kurumu Basimevi.

Mellink, Machteld J. 1983. Archaeological Comments on Ahhiyawa-Achaians in Western Anatolia. *AJA* 87:138–41.

———. 1986. Postscript. Pages 93–101 in *Troy and the Trojan War: A Symposium Held at Bryn Mawr College October 1984.* Edited by M. J. Mellink. Bryn Mawr, Pa.: Bryn Mawr College.

Mendenhall, George E. 1962. The Hebrew Conquest of Palestine. *BA* 25:66–87.

———. 1973. *The Tenth Generation: The Origins of the Biblical Tradition.* Baltimore: Johns Hopkins University Press.

———. 1976. "Change and Decay in All Around I See": Conquest, Covenant and the Tenth Generation. *BA* 39:152–57.

———. 1983. Ancient Israel's Hyphenated History. Pages 91–103 in *Palestine in Transition: The Emergence of Ancient Israel.* Edited by D. N. Freedman and D. F. Graf. Sheffield: Almond.

———. 1986. Cultural History and the Philistine Problem. Pages 525–46 in *The Archaeology of Jordan and Other Studies Presented to Siegfried H. Horn.* Edited by L. T. Geraty and L. G. Herr. Berrien Springs, Mich.: Andrews University Press.

Merrillees, Robert S. 1982. J. Strange, *Caphtor/Keftiu. A New Investigation (Leiden, 1980): A Review Article.* Report of the Department of Antiquities, Cyprus 1982:244–53.

———. 1992. The Crisis Years: Cyprus: A Rejoinder. Pages 87–92 in Ward and Joukowsky 1992.

———. 1995. Alashia Revisited Again. *Centre d'Etudes Chypriotes* 23:17–22.

Merrington, Jim. 1994. Liquid Gold of the Pharaohs. *Egyptian Archaeology* 4:10.

Meyer, Eduard. 1928. *Geschichte des Altertums.* Vol. 2, part 1. Berlin: Cotta.

Michalowski, Piotr. 1985. Third Millennium Contacts: Observations on the Relationships between Mari and Ebla. *JAOS* 105:293–302.

Millard, Alan R. 1992. Abraham. *ABD* 1:35–41.

———. 2000. How Reliable Is Exodus? *BAR* 26/4:50–57.

Miller, J. Maxwell. 1977. Archaeology and the Israelite Conquest of Canaan: Some Methodological Observations. *PEQ* 109:87–93.

———. 1989. Moab and the Moabites. Pages 1–40 in *Studies in the Mesha Inscription and Moab.* Edited by J. A. Dearman. Atlanta: Scholars Press.

———. 1992. Early Monarchy in Moab? Pages 77–92 in Bienkowski 1992c.

———. 1999. Reading the Bible Historically: The Historian's Approach. Pages 17–34 in *To Each Its Own Meaning: An Introduction to Biblical Criticisms and Their Application.* Edited by S. L. McKenzie and S. R. Haynes. Rev. ed. Louisville: Westminster John Knox.

———. ed. 1991. *Archaeological Survey of the Kerak Plateau Conducted during 1978–1982 under the Direction of J. Maxwell Miller and Jack M. Pinkerton.* Atlanta: Scholars Press.

Miller, J. Maxwell, and John Hayes. 1986. *A History of Ancient Israel and Judah.* London: SCM.

Miller, Robert D. 2003. A Gazeteer of Iron I Sites in the North-Central Highlands of Israel. Pages 143–218 in *Preliminary Excavation Reports and Other Archaeological Investigations: Tell Qarqur, Iron I Sites in the North-Central Highlands of Palestine.* Edited by N. Lapp. AASOR 56. Boston: American Schools of Oriental Research.

Miller, R. L. 1990. Ds-vessels, Beer Mugs, Cirrhosis and Casting Slag. *Göttinger Miszellen* 115:63–82.

Millett, Martin. 1990. *The Romanization of Britain: An Essay in Archaeological Interpretation.* New York: Cambridge University Press.

Mittmann, Siegfried. 1970. *Beiträge zur Siedlungs- und Territorialgeschichte des nördlichen Ostjordanlandes.* Abhandlungen des Deutschen Palästinaveriens. Wiesbaden: Harrassowitz.

Mommsen, Hans, Dieter Hertel, and Penelope A. Mountjoy. 2001. Neutron Activation Analysis of the Pottery from Troy in the Berlin Schliemann Collection. *AA* 2001:169–211.

Mook, Margaret S., and William D. E. Coulson. 1993. The Late Minoan IIIC Pottery from Kastro at Kavousi. *AJA* 97:351.

Moore, John H. 1994a. Ethnogenetic Theory. *National Geographic Research and Exploration* 10/1:10–23.

———. 1994b. Putting Anthropology Back Together Again: The Ethnogenetic Critique of Cladistic Theory. *American Anthropologist* 96: 925–48.

Moorey, Peter R. S. 1991. *A Century of Biblical Archaeology*. Louisville: Westminster John Knox.

Moran, William L. 1992. *The Amarna Letters*. Baltimore: Johns Hopkins University Press.

———. 1995. Some Reflections on Amarna Politics. Pages 559–72 in *Solving Riddles and Untying Knots: Biblical, Epigraphic, and Semitic Studies in Honor of Jonas C. Greenfield*. Edited by Z. Zevit, S. Gitin, and M. Sokoloff. Winona Lake, Ind.: Eisenbrauns.

Morkot, Robert. 2001. Egypt and Nubia. Pages 227–51 in *Empires: Perspectives from Archaeology and History*. Edited by S. E. Alcock, T. N. D'Altroy, K. D. Morrison, and C. M. Sinopoli. New York: Cambridge University Press.

Morricone, L. 1965–66. Eleona e Langada: Sepolcreti della Tarda Eta de Bronzo a Coo. *Annuario della Scuola italiana di Atene e delle missioni italiani in oriente* 43–44:5–311.

Morris, Ellen Fowles. 2005. *The Architecture of Imperialism: Military Bases and the Evolution of Foreign Policy in Egypt's New Kingdom*. Problem der Ägyptologie 22. Leiden: Brill.

Morris, Ian. 1999. Negotiated Peripherality in Iron Age Greece: Accepting and Resisting the East. Pages 63–84 in Kardulias 1999b.

Morris, Sarah P. 2001. Potnia Aswiya: Anatolian Contributions to Greek Religion. Pages 423–34 in Laffineur and Hägg 2001.

———. 2003. Islands in the Sea: Aegean Polities as Levantine Neighbors. Pages 3–15 in Dever and Gitin 2003.

Mountjoy, Penelope A. 1976. Late Helladic IIIB:1 Pottery Dating the Construction of the South House at Mycenae. *ABSA* 77:77–111.

———. 1985. The Pottery. Pages 151–208 in *The Archaeology of Cult: The Sanctuary at Phylakopi*. Edited by C. Renfrew. London: British School of Archaeology at Athens.

———. 1986. *Mycenaean Deocrated Pottery: A Guide to Identification*. SIMA 73. Göteborg: Åström.

———. 1997. Local Mycenaean Pottery at Troia. *Studia Troica* 7:259–67.

———. 1998. The East Aegean-West Anatolian Interface in the Late Bronze Age: Mycenaeans and the Kingdom of Ahhiyawa. *AnatSt* 48:33–67.

———. 1999a. *Regional Mycenaean Decorated Pottery*. 2 vols. Rahden, Westf.: Leidorf.

———. 1999b. Troia VII Reconsidered. *Studia Troica* 9:295–346.

Mountjoy, Penelope A., and Hans Mommsen. 2001. Mycenaean Pottery from Qantir-Piramesse, Egypt. ABSA 96:123–55.

Muhly, James D. 1972. The Land of *Alashiya:* References to *Alashiya* in the Texts of the Second Millennium BC and the History of Cyprus in the Late Bronze Age. Pages 201–19 in *Acts of the First International Cyprological Congress*. Edited by V. Karageorghis. Nicosia: Department of Antiquities, Cyprus.

———. 1984. The Role of the Sea Peoples in Cyprus during the LC III Period. Pages 39–56 in *Cyprus at the Close of the Late Bronze Age*. Edited by V. Karageorghis and J. D. Muhly. Nicosia: A. G. Leventis Foundation.

———. 1985. The Late Bronze Age in Cyprus: A 25 Year Retrospect. Pages 20–46 in *Archaeology in Cyprus 1960–1985*. Edited by V. Karageorghis. Nicosia: Zavallis.

———. 1989. The Organization of the Copper Industry in Late Bronze Age Cyprus. Pages 298–314 in *Early Society in Cyprus*. Edited by E. J. Peltenburg. Edinburgh: Edinburgh University Press.

———. 1992. The Crisis Years in the Mediterranean World: Transition or Cultural Disintegration? Pages 10–26 in Ward and Joukowsky 1992.

———. 1996. The Significance of Metals in the Late Bronze Age Economy of Cyprus. Pages 45–60 in *The Development of the Cypriot Economy from the Prehistoric Period to the Present Day*. Edited by V. Karageorghis and D. Michaelides. Nicosia: University of Cyprus, Bank of Cyprus.

Muhly, James D., Robert Maddin, Tamara Stech, and E. Özgen. 1985. Iron in Anatolia and the Nature of the Hittite Iron Industry. *AnatSt* 35:67–84.

Murnane, William J. 1990. *The Road to Kadesh: A Historical Interpretation of the Battle Reliefs of King Seti I at Karnak*. 2nd ed. SAOC 42. Chicago: Oriental Institute.

———. 1992. History of Egypt (Dyn. 18–20). *ABD* 2:348–53.

Mylonas, George E. 1956. Seated and Mutiple Mycenaean Figurines in the National Museum of Athens, Greece. Pages 110–21 in *Aegean and the Near East: Studies Presented to Hetty Goldman*. Edited by S. S. Weinberg. New York: Augustin.

———. 1966. *Mycenae and the Mycenaean Age*. Princeton: Princeton University Press.

Na᾽aman, Nadav. 1975. The Political Disposition and Historical Development of Eretz-Israel According to the Amarna Letters [Hebrew with English abstract]. Ph.D. diss. Tel Aviv University.

———. 1981. Economic Aspects of the Egyptian Occupation of Canaan. *IEJ* 31:172–85.

———. 1986. The Canaanite City-States in the Late Bronze Age and the Inheritances of the Israelite Tribes [Hebrew]. *Tarbiz* 55:463–88.

———. 1987. Review of O. Keel and M. Küchler, *Orte und Landschaften der Bibel*. *BASOR* 265:94–95.

———. 1988. Pharaonic Lands in the Jezreel Valley in the Late Bronze Age. Pages 177–85 in Heltzer and Lipiński 1988.

———. 1992. Canaanite Jerusalem and Its Central Hill Country Neighbours in the Second Millennium B.C.E. *UF* 24:275–91.

———. 1994a. The Canaanites and Their Land: A Rejoinder. *UF* 26:397–418.

———. 1994b. The "Conquest of Canaan" in the Book of Joshua and in History. Pages 218–81 in Finkelstein and Na᾽aman 1994b.

———. 1997. The Network of Canaanite Late Bronze Kingdoms and the City of Ashdod. *UF* 29:599–626.

———. 1999. Four Notes on the Size of Late Bronze Age Canaan. *BASOR* 313:31–37.

———. 2000. The Contribution of the Trojan Grey Ware from Lachish and Tel Miqne-Ekron to the Chronology of the Philistine Monochrome Pottery. *BASOR* 317:1–7.

Nagata, Judith A. 1979. *Malaysian Mosaic: Perspectives from a Poly-ethnic Society.* Vancouver: University of British Columbia Press.

Nagel, Georges. 1938. *La Céramique du Nouvel Empire à Deir el Médineh.* L'Institut Français d'archéologie orientale du Caire. Cairo: Institut Français d'archéologie orientale.

Nagel, Joane, and Susan Olzak. 1982. Ethnic Mobilization in New and Old States: An Extension of the Competition Model. *Social Problems* 30:127–43.

Nakhai, Beth Alpert. 1997. Wawiyat, Tell-el. *OEANE* 5:333–34.

———. 2001. *Archaeology and the Religions of Canaan and Israel.* ASOR Books 7. Boston: American Schools of Oriental Research.

———. 2003a. Israel on the Horizon: The Galilee in the Iron I. Pages 131–51 in Nakhai 2003b.

______, ed. 2003b. *The Near East in the Southwest: Essays in Honor of William G. Dever.* AASOR 58. Boston: American Schools of Oriental Research.

Negbi, Ora. 1986. The Climax of Urban Development in Bronze Age Cyprus. *Report of the Department of Antiquities, Cyprus* 1986:97–121.

———. 1991. Were There Sea Peoples in the Central Jordan Valley at the Transition from the Bronze Age to the Iron Age? *TA* 18:205–43.

Negbi, Ora and Moshe Negbi. 1993. Stirrup-Jars Versus Canaanite Jars: Their Contents and Reciprocal Trade. Pages 319–29 in *Proceedings of the International Conference Wace and Blegen: Pottery as Evidence for Trade in the Aegean Bronze Age, 1939–1989 Held at the American School of Classical Studies at Athens, December 2–3, 1989.* Edited by C. Zerner with P. Zerner and J. Winder. Amsterdam: Gieben.

Nelson, Harold H. 1943. The Naval Battle Pictured at Medinet Habu. *JNES* 2:40–45.

Nelson, Richard D. 1981. *The Double Redaction of the Deuteronomistic History.* JSOTSup 18. Sheffield: JSOT Press.

Netzer, Ehud. 1992. Domestic Architecture in the Iron Age. Pages 193–201 in Kempinski and Reich 1992.

Neumann, J., and Simo Parpola. 1987. Climatic Change and the Eleventh-Tenth Century Eclipse of Assyria and Babylon. *JNES* 46:161–82.

Neve, Peter. 1989. Die Ausgrabungen in Bogazkoy-Hattusa 1988. *AA* 1989:271–337.

Nibbi, Alessandra. 1973. The Identification of the "Sea Peoples." Pages 203–5 in Crossland and Birchall 1973.

———. 1989. *Canaan and Canaanite in Ancient Egypt.* Oxford: DE Publications.

Nicholson, Paul T., and Helen L. Patterson. 1992. The Ballas Pottery Project: Ethnoarchaeology in Upper Egypt. Pages 25–47 in *Ceramic Production and Distribution: An Integrated Approach.* Edited by G. J. Bey III and C. A. Pool. Oxford: Westview.

Niemeier, Wolf-Dietrich. 1998. The Mycenaeans in Western Anatolia and the Problem of the Origins of the Sea Peoples. Pages 17–65 in Gitin, Mazar, and Stern 1998.

Nims, Charles F. 1950. Egyptian Catalogues of Things. *JNES* 9:253–62.

Nissenbaum, Arie, and Ann E. Killebrew. 1995. Stable Isotopes of Carbon and Oxygen as a Possible New Tool for Estimating Firing Temperatures of Ancient Pottery. *Israel Journal of Chemistry* 35:131–36.

Noort, Edward. 1994. *Die Seevölker in Palästina.* Palaestina Antiqua 8. Kampen: Kok Pharos.

Noth, Martin. 1958. *The History of Israel.* London: Harper & Row.

———. 1960. Der Beitrag der Archäologie zur Geschichte Israels. Pages 262–82 in *Congress Volume Oxford, 1959.* VTSup 7. Leiden: Brill.

———. 1981. *The Deuteronomistic History.* JSOTSup 15. Sheffield: Sheffield Academic Press.

Nougayrol, Jean. 1968. Textes suméro-accadiens des archives et bibliothéques privées d'Ugarit. Pages 1–446 in J. Nougayrol, E. Larouche, C. Virolleaud, and C. F. A. Shaeffer, *Ugaritica V.* Mission de Ras Shamra 16. Paris: Geuthner.

Novack, Michael. 1972. *The Rise of the Unmeltable Ethnics: Politics and Culture in the Seventies.* New York: Macmillan.

Nowicki, Krysztof. 2000. *Defensive Sites in Crete c. 1200–800 B.C. (LM IIIB/IIIC through Early Geometric).* Aegaeum 21. Liège: Université de Liège.

———. 2001. Sea-Raiders and Refugees: Problems of Defensible Sites in Crete c. 1200 B.C. Pages 23–40 in Karageorghis and Morris 2001.

Nur, Amos, and Eric H. Cline. 2000. Poseidon's Horses: Plate Tectonics and Earthquake Storms in the Late Bronze Age Aegean and Eastern Mediterranean. *JAS* 27:43–63.

———. 2001. What Triggered the Collapse? Earthquake Storms. *Archaeology Odyssey* 4/5:31–36, 62–63.

Öbrink, Ulla. 1979. *Hala Sulta Tekke 6: A Sherd Deposit in Area 22.* SIMA 45:5. Göteborg. Åström.

O'Connor, David. 2000. The Sea Peoples and the Egyptian Sources. Pages 85–102 in Oren 2000.

Ofer, Avi. 1993. *The Highland of Judah during the Biblical Period.* Ph.D. diss. Tel Aviv University.

———. 1994. "All the Hill Country of Judah": From a Settlement Fringe to a Prosperous Monarchy. Pages 92–121 in Finkelstein and Na'aman 1994b.

———. 2001. The Monarchic Period in the Judean Highlands: A Spatial Overiew. Pages 14–37 in A. Mazar 2001.

Ohata, Kiyoshi. 1970. *Tel Zeror III: Report of the Excavation Report of the Third Season 1966.* Tokyo: Society for Near Eastern Studies in Japan.

Okamura, Jonathan Y. 1981. Situational Ethnicity. *Ethnicity and Racial Studies* 4:452–65.

Oren, Eliezer D. 1973. *The Northern Cemetery of Beth Shean.* Leiden: Brill.

———. 1980. Egyptian New Kingdom Sites in Northern Sinai [Hebrew]. *Qad* 13:26–33.

———. 1984. Governors' Residences in Canaan under the New Kingdom: A Case Study of Egyptian Administration. *Journal for the Society for the Study of Egyptian Antiquities* 14:37–56.

———. 1985. Architecture of Egyptian "Governors" Residencies' in Late Bronze Age Palestine [Hebrew]. *ErIsr* 18: 183–99.

———. 1987. The "Ways of Horus" in North Sinai. Pages 69–119 in Rainey 1987.

———. 1992. Palaces and Patrician Houses in the Middle and Late Bronze Ages. Pages 105–20 in Kempinski and Reich 1992.

———. 1993. Haror, Tel. *NEAEHL* 2:580–84.

———, ed. 2000. *The Sea Peoples and Their World: A Reassessment.* University Museum Monograph 108. University Museum Symposium Series 11. Philadelphia: University Museum, University of Pennsylvania.

Oren, Eliezer, and Yosef Shershevsky. 1989. Military Architecture along the "Ways of Horus"—Egyptian Reliefs and Archaeological Evidence [Hebrew]. *ErIsr* 20:8–22.

Ormerod, Henry A. 1967. *Piracy in the Ancient World: An Essay in Mediterranean History.* 1967 Reprint of 1924 publication. Chicago: Argonaut.

Osten, Hans Hemming von der. 1956. *Svenska Syrienexpeditionen, 1952–1953, Vol. 1: Die Grabung von Tell es-Salihiyeh.* Skrifter utgivna av Svenska Institutet i Athen 4. Lund: Gleerup.

Ottoson, Magnus. 1980. *Temples and Cult Places in Palestine.* Uppsala Studies in Ancient Mediterranean and Near Eastern Studies 12. Uppsala: Almqvist & Wiksell.

Owen, David I. 1981. Ugarit, Canaan and Egypt: Some New Epigraphic Evidence from Tel Aphek in Israel. Pages 49–53 in *Ugarit in Retrospect: Fifty Years of Ugarit and Ugaritic.* Edited by G. D. Young. Winona Lake, Ind.: Eisenbrauns.

Palmer, Ruth. 1989. Subsistence Rations at Pylos and Knossos. *Minos* 24:89–124.

Pardee, Dennis. 1997. Review of Ugarit and the Bible: Proceedings of the International Symposium on Ugarit and the Bible, Manchester, September 1992. *JAOS* 117:375–78.

Pardee, Dennis, and Pierre Bordreuil. 1992. Ugarit: Texts and Literature. *ABD* 6:706–21.

Pariente, Anne. 1993. Chronique des fouilles et découvertes archéologiques en Gréce en 1992. *Bulletin de Correspondance Hellénique* 117:757–896.

Parkin, David. 1974. Congregational and Interpersonal Ideologies in Political Ethnicity. Pages 119–57 in *Urban Ethnicity.* Edited by A. Cohen. London: Tavistock.

Parkinson, William A., ed. 2002. *The Archaeology of Tribal Societies.* Archaeological Series 15. Ann Arbor, Mich.: International Monographs in Prehistory.

Parr, Peter J. 1973. The Origin of the Canaanite Jar. Pages 173–81 in *Archaeological Theory and Practice.* Edited by D. E. Strong. London: Seminar Press.

———. 1988. Pottery of the Late Second Millennium B.C. from North West Arabia and Its Historical Implications. Pages 73–89 in *Araby the Blest: Studies in Arabian Archaeology.* Edited by D. T. Potts. Copenhagen: Niehbuhr Institute of Ancient Near Eastern Studies.

Patterson, Orlando. 1975. Context and Choice in Ethnic Allegiance: A Theoretical Framework and Caribbean Case Study. Pages 305–359 in *Ethnicity: Theory and Practice.* Edited by N. Glazer and D. P. Moynihan. Cambridge: Harvard University Press.

Paynter, Robert. 1983. Expanding the Scope of Settlement Analysis. Pages 233–75 in *Archaeological Hammers and Theories.* Edited by J. A. Moore and A. S. Keene. New York: Academic.

———. 1989. The Archaeology of Equality and Inequality. *ARA* 18:369–99.

Peacock, David P. S. 1970. The Scientific Analysis of Ancient Ceramics: A Review. *WorldArch* 1:375–89.

———. 1981. Archaeology, Ethnology and Ceramic Production. Pages 187–94 in *Production and Distribution: A Ceramic Viewpoint.* Edited by H. Howard and E. Morris. British Archaeological Reports International Series 120. Oxford: British Archaeological Reports.

———. 1982. *Pottery in the Roman World: An Ethnoarchaeological Approach.* London: Longman.

Peden, Alexander J. 1994. *Egyptian Historical Inscriptions of the Twentieth Dynasty.* Documenta Mundi Aegyptiaca 3. Jonsered: Åström.

Peet, Thomas E., and C. Leonard Woolley. 1923. *The City of Akhenaten Part I: Excavations of 1921 and 1922 at El-Amarneh.* London: Egypt Exploration Society.

Pels, Peter. 1997. The Anthroplogy of Colonialism: Culture, History, and the Emergence of Western Governmentality. *ARA* 26:163–93.

Peltenburg, Edgar J. 1986. Ramesside Egypt and Cyprus. Pages 149–79 in *Acts of the International Archaeological Symposium: Cyprus between the Orient and the Occident.* Edited by V. Karageorghis. Nicosia: Zavallis.

Perdue, Leo G. 1994. *The Collapse of History: Reconstructing Old Testament Theology.* Minneapolis: Fortress.

Peregrine, Peter N. 1996. Introduction: World-Systems Theory and Archaeology. Pages 1–10 in Peregrine and Feinman 1996.

———. 1999. Legitimation Crises in Prehistoric Worlds. Pages 37–52 in Kardulias 1999b.

———. 2000. Archaeology and World-Systems Theory. Pages 59–68 in Hall 2000b.

Peregrine, Peter N., and Gary M. Feinman, eds. 1996. *Pre-Columbian World Systems.* Monographs in World Archaeology 26. Madison, Wis.: Prehistory Press.

Perlman, Isadore, and Frank Asaro. 1971. Pottery Analysis by Neutron Activation. Pages 182–95 in *Science and Archaeology.* Edited by R. H. Brill. Cambridge: Massachusetts Institute of Technology.

Perlman, Isadore, Frank Asaro, and Trude Dothan. 1973. Provenance of the Deir el-Balah Coffins. *IEJ* 23:147–51

Person, Raymond F., Jr. 2002. *The Deuteronomic School: History, Social Setting, and Literature.* SBLSBL 2. Atlanta: Society of Biblical Literature.

Petrie, W. M. Flinders. 1890. *Kahun, Gurob, and Hawara.* London: Kegan Paul, Trench, Trübner.

———. 1897. *Six Temples at Thebes.* London: Quaritch.

———. 1905. *Ehnasya.* Egypt Exploration Fund Twenty Sixth Memoir. London: Kegan Paul, Trench, Trübner.

———. 1906. *Hyksos and Israelite Cities.* British School of Archaeology and Egyptian Research Account 13. London: British School of Archaeology in Egypt; Quaritch.

———. 1907. *Gizeh and Rifeh.* British School of Archaeology in Egypt and Egyptian Research Account 13. London: British School of Archaeology in Egypt; Quaritch.

———. 1909. *Qurneh.* British School of Archaeology in Egypt Publications 16. London: British School of Archaeology in Egypt.

———. 1930. *Beth-Pelet I.* London: British School of Archaeology in Egypt; Quaritch.

———. 1932. *Ancient Gaza II: Tell el Ajjul.* London: British School of Archaeology in Egypt.

———. 1933. *Ancient Gaza III: Tell el Ajjul*. London: British School of Archaeology in Egypt.

———. 1934. *Ancient Gaza IV: Tell el Ajjul*. London: British School of Archaeology in Egypt.

Petrie, W. M. Flinders, and Guy Brunton. 1924. *Sedment II*. British School of Archaeology in Egypt Publications 35. London: British School of Archaeology in Egypt ; Quaritch.

Petrie, W. M. Flinders, Gerald A. Wainwright, and Ernest MacKay. 1912. *The Labyrinth Gerzeh and Mazghuneh*. London: British School of Archaeology in Egypt.

Pickles, S., and Edgar Peltenburg. 1998. Metallurgy, Society and the Bronze/Iron Transition in the Eastern Mediterranean and the Near East. *Report of the Department of Antiquities, Cyprus* 1998:67–100.

Phythian-Adams, W. J. 1923. Reports on Soundings at Gaza, Etc. *PEQ* 55:11–36.

Plog, Stephen. 1978. Social Interaction and Stylistic Similarity: A Reanalysis. Pages 143–82 in vol. 1 of *Advances in Archaeological Method and Theory*. Edited by M. B. Schiffer. New York: Academic.

———. 1980. *Stylistic Variation in Prehistoric Ceramics Design Analysis in the American Southwest*. Cambridge: Cambridge University Press.

Podzuweit, Christian, 1982. Die mykenische Welt und Troja. Pages 65–88 in *Sudosteuropa zwischen 1600 un 1000 v. Chr.* Edited by B. Hansel. Berlin: Moreland.

Pollard, Helen P. 1994. Ethnicity and Political Control in a Complex Society: The Tarascan State of Prehispanic Mexico. Pages 79–88 in *Factional Competition and Political Development in the New World*. Edited E. M. Brumfiel and J. W. Fox. Cambridge: Cambridge University Press.

Pollock, Susan. 1983. Style and Information: An Analysis of Susiana Ceramics. *JAnthArch* 2:354–90.

Pool, Christopher A. 1992. Integrating Ceramic Production and Distribution. Pages 275–313 in *Ceramic Production and Distribution: An Integrated Approach*. Edited by G. J. Bey III and C. A. Pool. Oxford: Westview.

Popham, Mervyn R. 1965. Some Late Minoan IIIB Pottery from Crete. *ABSA* 60:326–42.

———. 1970. Late Minoan IIIB Pottery from Crete. *ABSA* 65:195–202.

Popham, Mervyn R., and L. H. Sackett, eds. 1968. *Excavations at Lefkandi, Euboea, 1964–1966: A Preliminary Report*. London: Thames & Hudson.

Porat, Naomi. 1989. Composition of Pottery-Application to the Study of the Interrelations between Canaan and Egypt During the Third Millennium B.C. Ph.D. diss. Hebrew University of Jerusalem.

Porter, Bertha, and Rosalind L. B. Moss. 1960. *Topographical Bibliography of Ancient Egyptian Hieroglyphic Texts, Reliefs, and Paintings*. 2nd ed. Oxford: Clarendon.

Portugali, Juval. 1994. Theoretical Speculations on the Transition from Nomadism to Monarchy. Pages 203–17 in Finkelstein and Naʾaman 1994b.

Postgate, John N. 1992. The Land of Assur and the Yoke of Assur. *WorldArch* 23:247–63.

Prag, Kay. 1985. The Imitation of Cypriote Wares in Late Bronze Age Palestine. Pages 154–66 in Tubb 1985.

Pritchard, James B. 1962. *Gibeon, Where the Sun Stood Still: The Discovery of a Biblical City*. Princeton: Princeton University Press.

———. 1963. *The Bronze Age Cemetery at Gibeon*. Philadelphia: University Museum, University of Pennsylvania.

———. 1964. *Winery, Defences and Soundings at Gibeon*. Philadelphia: University Museum, University of Pennsylvania.

———. 1980. *The Cemetery at Tell es-Saᶜidiyeh, Jordan*. University Museum Monograph 41. Philadelphia: University Museum, University of Pennsylvania.

Pulak, Cemal. 1988. The Bronze Age Shipwreck at Ulu Burun: 1985 Campaign. *AJA* 92:1–37.

Raban, Avner. 1980. *The Commercial Jar in the Ancient Near East: Its Evidence for Interconnections amongst the Biblical Lands* [Hebrew, with English summary on pp. 1*–18*]. Jerusalem: Hebrew University of Jerusalem.

———. 1988. The Constructive Maritime Role of the Sea Peoples in the Levant. Pages 261–94 in Heltzer and Lipiński 1988.

______ 2001. Standardized Collared-Rim Pithoi and Short-Lived Settlements. Pages 493–518 in Wolff 2001.

Raban, Avner, and Robert R. Stieglitz. 1991. The Sea Peoples and their Contributions to Civilization. *BAR* 17/6:34–42.

Ragionieri, Rodolfo. 2000. The Amarna Age: An International Society in the Making. Pages 42–53 in Cohen and Westbrook 2000c.

Rainey, Anson F. 1963. A Canaanite at Ugarit. *IEJ* 13:43–45.

———. 1964. Ugarit and the Canaanites Again. *IEJ* 14:101.

———. 1968. Gath-Padalla. *IEJ* 18:1–14.

———. 1973. Amenhotep II's Campaign to Takhsi. *JARCE* 10:71–75.

———. 1975. The Identification of Philistine Gath. *ErIsr* 12:63–75.

———. 1991. Can You Name the Panel with the Israelites? Rainey's Challenge. *BAR* 17/6:56–60, 93.

———. 1992. Who or What Was Israel? Rainey Replies. *BAR* 18/2:73–74.

———. 1995a. Uncritical Criticism. *JAOS* 115:101–4.

———. 1995b. Unruly Elements in Late Bronze Canaanite Society. Pages 481–96 in *Pomegranates and Golden Bells: Studies in Biblical, Jewish and Near Eastern Ritual, Law, and Literature in Honor of Jacob Milgrom*. Edited by D. P. Wright, D. N. Freedman, and A. Hurvitz. Winona Lake, Ind.: Eisenbrauns.

———. 1996. Who Is a Canaanite? A Review of the Textual Evidence. *BASOR* 304:1–16.

———. 2001. Israel in Merenptah's Inscription and Reliefs. *IEJ* 51:57–75.

———. 2003. Amarna and Later: Aspects of Social History. Pages 169–87 in Dever and Gitin 2003.

Rainey, Anson F., ed. 1987. *Egypt, Israel, Sinai: Archaeological and Historical Relationships in the Biblical Period*. Tel Aviv: Tel Aviv University.

Rasmussen, Susan. 1992. Disputed Boundaries: Tuareg Discourse on Class and Ethnicity. *Ethnology* 31:351–65.

Rast, Walter. 1978. *Taanach I: Studies in the Iron Age Pottery*. Cambridge: American Schools of Oriental Research.

Redding, Richard W. 1991. The Role of the Pig in the Subsistence System of Ancient Egypt: A Parable on the Potential of Faunal Data. Pages 21–30 in

Animal Use and Culture Change. Edited by P. J. Crabtree and K. Ryan. Museum Applied Science Center for Archaeology, Supplement to Volume 8. Philadelphia: University Museum, University of Pennsylvania.

Redford, Donald B. 1963. Exodus 1:11. *VT* 13:401–18.

———. 1984. *Akhenaten: The Heretic King*. Princeton: Princeton University Press.

———. 1985. The Relations between Egypt and Isarel from El-Amarna to the Babylonian Conquest. Pages 192–205 in Amitai 1985.

———. 1986. The Ashkelon Relief at Karnak and the Israel Stela. *IEJ* 36:188–200.

———. 1987. An Egyptological Perspective on the Exodus Narrative. Pages 137–61 in Rainey 1987.

———. 1990. *Egypt and Canaan in the New Kingdom*. Edited by S. Ahituv. Beer-Sheva 4. Beer Sheva: Ben-Gurion University of the Negev Press.

———. 1992a. Merenptah. *ABD* 4:700–1.

———. 1992b. *Egypt, Canaan, and Israel in Ancient Times*. Princeton: Princeton University Press.

———. 1997. Observations on the Sojourn of the Bene-Israel. Pages 57–66 in Frerichs and Lesko 1997.

———. 2000. Egypt and Western Asia in the Late New Kingdom: An Overview. Pages 1–20 in Oren 2000.

———. Forthcoming. Observations on the Egyptian Epigraphic and Textual Record and the Classical Origin Stories Bearing upon the So-Called "Sea Peoples." In *The Philistines and Other Sea Peoples*. Edited by A. E. Killebrew, G. Lehmann, and M. Artzy. Atlanta: Society of Biblical Literature.

Redman, Charles L., and J. Emlen Myers. 1981. Interpretation, Classification, and Ceramic Production: A Medieval North African Case Study. Pages 285–307 in *Production and Distribution: A Ceramic Viewpoint*. Edited by H. Howard and E. Morris. British Archaeological Reports International Series 120. Oxford: British Archaeological Reports.

Redmount, Carol A. 1995a. Ethnicity, Pottery, and the Hyksos at Tell El-Maskhuta in the Egyptian Delta. *BA* 58:181–90.

———. 1995b. Pots and Peoples in the Egyptian Delta: Tell El-Maskhuta and the Hyksos. *JMA* 8:61–89.

———. 2001. Bitter Lives: Israel In and Out of Egypt. Pages 58–89 in *The Oxford History of the Biblical World*. Edited by Michael D. Coogan. New York: Oxford University Press.

Rehak, Paul, ed. 1995. *The Role of the Ruler in the Prehistoric Aegean: Proceedings of a Panel Discussion Presented at the Annual Meeting of the Archaeological Institute of America, New Orleans, Louisiana, 28 December 1992*. Liegè: Université de Leigè.

Rendsberg, Gary A. 1992. The Date of the Exodus and the Conquest/Settlement: The Case for the 1100s. *VT* 42:510–27.

Renfrew, Colin. 1975. Trade as Action at a Distance: Questions of Integration and Communication. Pages 12–22 in *Ancient Civilization and Trade*. Edited by J. A. Sabloff and C. C. Lamberg-Karlovsky. Albuquerque: University of New Mexico Press.

———. 1978. Trajectory Discontinuity and Morphogenesis: The Implications of Catastrophe Theory for Archaeology. *AmerAnt* 43:203–22.

———. 1979a. Holistic Behavior and Catastrophe Theory. Pages 419–23 in *Transformations: Mathematical Approaches to Culture Change.* Edited by C. Renfrew and K. L. Cooke. New York: Academic.

———. 1979b. Retrospect and Prospect. Pages 108–19 in *Mycenaean Geography: Proceedings of the Cambridge Colloquium September 1976.* Edited by J. Bintliff. Cambridge: British Association for Mycenaean Studies.

———. 1979c. Systems Collapse as Social Transformation: Catastrophe and Anastrope in Early State Societies. Pages 481–508 in *Transformations: Mathematical Approaches to Culture Changes.* Edited by C. Renfrew and K. L. Cooke. New York: Academic.

———. 1984. Discontinuity and Long Term Change. Pages 358–65 in *Approaches to Social Archaeology.* Cambridge: Harvard University Press.

———. 1987. *Archaeology and Language: The Puzzle of Indo-European Origins.* London: Cape.

Renfrew, Colin, and Paul Bahn. 2000. *Archaeology: Theories, Methods and Practice.* 3rd ed. New York: Thames & Hudson.

Rethemiotakis, George. 1999. The Hearths of the Minoan Palace at Galatas. Pages 721–32 in vol. 3 of *Meletemata: Studies in Aegean Archaeology Presented to Malcolm H. Wiener as He Enters His 65th Year.* Edited by P. P. Betancourt, V. Karageorghis, R. Laffineur and W-D. Niemeier. 3 vols. Aegaeum 20. Liège: Université de Liège.

Reynolds, Vernon. 1980. Sociobiology and the Idea of Primordial Discrimination. *Ethnic and Racial Studies* 3:305–15.

Rice, Prudence. 1981. Evolution of Specialized Pottery Production: A Trial Model. *Current Anthropology* 22:219–27.

———. 1987. *Pottery Analysis.* Chicago: University of Chicago Press.

———. 1989. Ceramic Diversity, Production, and Use. Pages 109–117 in Leonard and Jones 1989.

———. 1991. Specialization, Standardization and Diversity: A Retrospective. Pages 257–79 in *The Ceramic Legacy of Anna O. Shepard.* Edited by R. L. Bishop and F. W. Lange. Denver: University of Colorado Press.

Ricke, Herbert. 1932. *Der Grundriss des Amarna-Wohnhauses.* Leipzig: Hinrichs.

Robertson, David. A. 1972. *Linguistic Evidence in Dating Early Hebrew Poetry.* SBLDS 3. Missoula, Mont.: Scholars Press.

Roosens, Eugeen E. 1989. *Creating Ethnicity: The Process of Ethnogenesis.* Newbury Park, Calif.: Sage.

Rose, Pamela J. 1984. The Pottery Distribution Analysis. Pages 133–53 in Barry J. Kemp, *Amarna Reports I.* London: Egypt Exploration Society.

———. 1986. Pottery from the Main Chapel. Pages 99–117 in Barry J. Kemp, *Amarna Reports III.* London: Egypt Exploration Society.

———. 1987. Pottery from Gate Street 8. Pages 132–43 in Barry J. Kemp, *Amarna Reports IV.* London: Egypt Exploration Society.

———. 1995. Report on the 1987 Excavations House P46.33: The Pottery. Pages 137–45 in Barry J. Kemp, *Amarna Reports VI.* London: Egypt Exploration Society.

Rosen, Steven A. 1992. Nomads in Archaeology: A Response to Finkelstein and Perevolotsky. *BASOR* 287:75–85.

Ross, James F. 1967. Gezer in the Tell el-Amarna Letters. *BA* 30:62–70.

Rothenberg, Benno. 1988. The *Egyptian Mining Temple at Timna: Researches in the Arabah 1959–1984*. Vol. 1. London: Institute for Archaeo-Metallurgical Studies.

Rothschild, Joseph. 1981. *Ethnopolitics: A Conceptual Framework*. New York: Columbia University Press.

Rougé. E. de. 1867. *Extraits d'un mémoire sur les attaques dirigees contre l'Egypte par les peoples de la Méditerranee vers le xxve seicle avant notre ere*. Paris: Didier.

Rouse, Irving. 1986. *Migrations in Prehistory: Inferring Population Movement from Cultural Remains*. New Haven: Yale University Press.

Routledge, Bruce. 2000. Seeing through Walls: Interpreting Iron Age I Architecture at Khirbat al-Mudayna al-ʿAliya. *BASOR* 319: 37–70.

Rowe, Alan. 1930. *The Topography and History of Beth-Shan 1*. Philadelphia: University Museum, University of Pennsylvania.

———. 1940. *The Four Canaanite Temples of Beth-Shan 2/1*. Philadelphia: University Museum, University of Pennsylvania.

Rowlands, Michael, Mogens Larsen, and Kristian Kristiansen, eds. 1987. *Centre and Periphery in the Ancient World*. Cambridge: Cambridge University Press.

Rowton, M. B. 1973a. Auotonomy and Nomadism in Western Asia. *Or* 42:247–58.

———. 1973b. Urban Autonomy in a Nomadic Environment. *JNES* 32:201–15.

———. 1974. Enclosed Nomadism. *JESHO* 17:1–30.

———. 1976. Dimorphic Structure and the Problem of the ʿApiru-Ibrim. *JNES* 35:13–20.

———. 1977. Dimorphic Structure and the Parasocial Element. *JNES* 36:181–98.

Rutter, Jeremy. 1975. Ceramic Evidence for Northern Intruders in Southern Greece at the Beginning of the Late Helladic IIIC Period. *AJA* 79:17–32.

Sabloff, Jeremy A., and C. C. Lamberg-Karlovsky, eds. 1974. *The Rise and Fall of Civilizations: Modern Archaeological Approaches to Ancient Cultures*. Menlo Park, Calif.: Cummings.

Sackett, James R. 1985. Style and Ethnicity in the Kalahari: A Reply to Wiessner. *AmerAnt* 50:154–59.

Said, Edward W. 1993. *Culture and Imperialism*. New York: Vintage.

Sams, G. Kenneth. 1992. Observations on Western Anatolia. Pages 56–60 in Ward and Joukowsky 1992.

Samuel, Delwen. 1994. A New Look at Bread and Beer. *Egyptian Archaeology* 4:9–11.

———. 2000. Brewing and Baking. Pages 537–76 in *Ancient Egyptian Materials and Technology*. Edited by P. T. Nicholson and I. Shaw. Cambridge: Cambridge University Press.

Sandars, Nancy K. 1964. The Last Mycenaeans and the European Late Bronze Age. *Antiquity* 38:258–62.

———. 1985. *The Sea Peoples: Warriors of the Ancient Mediterranean*. London: Thames & Hudson.

Santley, Robert S., Philip J. Arnold, and Christopher A. Pool 1989. The Ceramic Production System at Matacapan, Veracruz, Mexico. *JFA* 16:107–32.

Santley, Robert S., Clare Yarborough, and Barbara A. Hall. 1987. Enclaves, Ethnicity, and the Archaeological Record at Matacapan. Pages 85–100 in *Ethnicity and Culture: Proceedings of the Eighteenth Annual Conference of the Archaeological Association of the University of Calgary.* Edited by R. Auger, M. F. Glass, S. MacEachern, and P. H. McCartney. Calgary, Alb.: University of Calgary.

Sasson, Jack M. 1984. The Earliest Mention of the Name "Canaan." *BA* 47:90.

Sauer, James A. 1986. Transjordan in the Bronze and Iron Ages: A Critique of Glueck's Synthesis. *BASOR* 263:1–26.

Savage, Stephen H., and Steven E. Falconer. 2003. Spatial and Statistical Inference of Late Bronze Age Politics in the Southern Levant. *BASOR* 330:31–45.

Schaar, Kenneth W. 1991. The Architectural Traditions of Building 23A/13 at Tel Beit Mirsim. *SJOT* 5/2:75–98.

Schachermeyr, Fritz. 1980. *Griechenland im Zeitalter derWanderungen vom Ende der mykenischen Ära bis auf die Dorier.* Chr. Vol. 4 of Die ägäische Frühzeit. Mykenische Studien 8. Vienna: Österreichischen Akademie der Wissenschaften.

———. 1982. *Die Levante im Zeitalter der Wanderungen: vom 13. bis zum 11. Jahrhundert v. Chr.* Vol. 5 of Die ägäische Frühzeit. Mykenische Studien 9. Vienna: Österreichische Akademie der Wissenschaften.

———. 1984. *Griechische Frühgeschichte: Ein Versuch, frühe Geschichte wenigstens in Umrissen verständlich zu machen.* Österreichische Akademie der Wissenschaften, Philosophisch-Historische Klasse 425. Vienna: Österreichische Akademie der Wissenschaften.

Schaeffer, Claude F.-A. 1949. *Ugaritica II.* Paris: Geuthner.

———. 1952. *Enkomi-Alasia I.* Paris: Klincksieck.

———. 1968. Commentaires sur les letters et documents trouvés dans les bibliothèques privées d'Ugarit. *Ugaritica V.* Mission de Ras Shamra 16. Paris Geuthner.

Schaeffer, Claude F.-A., Jacques-Claude Courtois, A. H. de Kuscheke, H.-V. Vallois, D. Farembach, R. Charles, Ch. Clairmont, and G.-C. Miles. 1962. *Ugaritica IV.* Mission de Ras Shamra 15. Bibliothèque archéologique et historique 74. Paris: Imprimerie nationale.

Schallin, Ann-Louise. 1993. *Islands under Influence: The Cyclades in the Late Bronze Age and the Nature of Mycenaean Presence.* SIMA 111. Jonsered: Åström.

Scham, Sandra. 2002. The Days of the Judges: When Men and Women Were Animals and Trees Were Kings. *JSOT* 97:37–64.

Schloen, J. David. 1993. Caravans, Kenites, and Casus Belli: Enmity and Alliance in the Song of Deborah. *CBQ* 55:18–38.

———. 2001. *The House of the Father as Fact and Symbol: Patrimonialism in Ugarit and the Ancient Near East.* Studies in the Archaeology and History of the Levant 2. Winona Lake, Ind.: Eisenbrauns.

Schmitz, Philip C. 1992. Canaan (Place). *ABD* 1:82–83.

Schneider, Jane. 1977. Was There a Pre-capitalist World-System? *Peasant Studies* 6:20–29.

Schniedewind, William M. 1996. The Problem with Kings: Recent Study of the Deuteronomistic History. *RelSRev* 22:22–27.

———. 1998. The Geopolitical History of Philistine Gath. *BASOR* 309:69–77.

Schoors, Antoon. 1985. The Israelite Conquest: Textual Evidence in the Archaeological Argument. Pages 77–92 in *The Land of Israel: Cross-Roads of Civilizations.* Edited by E. Lipiński. OLA 19. Leuven: Peeters.

Schortman, Edward M., and Patricia Urban. 1996. Actions at a Distance, Impacts at Home: Prestige Good Theory and a Pre-Columbian Polity in Southeastern Mesoamerica. Pages 97–114 in Peregrine and Feinman 1996.

Schoville, Keith N. 1998. Canaanites and Amorites. Page 157–82 in *Peoples of the Old Testament World.* Edited by A. J. Hoerth, G. L. Mattingly, and E. M. Yamauchi. Grand Rapids: Baker.

Schulman, Alan R. 1976. The Royal Butler Ramessesemperre. *JARCE* 3:51–69.

———. 1988. Catalogue of the Egyptian Finds. Pages 114–47 in *The Egyptian Mining Temple at Timna.* Edited by B. Rothenberg. London: Institute for Archaeo-Metallurgical Studies.

Scott, George M., Jr. 1990. A Resynthesis of the Primordial and Circumstantial Approaches to Ethnic Group Solidarity: Towards an Explanatory Model. *Ethnic and Racial Studies* 13:147–71.

Serpico, Margaret. 1999. New Kingdom Canaanite Amphorae Fragments from Buhen. Pages 267–72 in *Studies on Ancient Egypt in Honour of H. S. Smith.* Edited by A. Leahy and J. Tait. London: Egypt Exploration Society.

Several, Michael W. 1972. Reconsidering the Egyptian Empire in Palestine during the Amarna Period. *PEQ* 104:123–33.

Sharon, Ilan. 1994. Demographic Aspects of the Problem of the Israelite Settlement. Pages 119–34 in *Uncovering Ancient Stones: Essays in Memory of H. Neil Richardson.* Edited by L. M. Hopfe. Winona Lake, Ind.: Eisenbrauns.

Shear, Ione M. 1987. *The Panagia Houses at Mycenae.* University Museum Monographs 68. Philadelphia: University Museum, University of Pennsylvania.

Shelmerdine, Cynthia W. 1985. *The Perfume Industry of Mycenaean Pylos.* Studies in Mediterranean Archaeology Pocket Book 34. Göteborg: Åström.

———. 1997. Review of Aegean Prehistory VI: The Palatial Bronze Age of the Southern and Central Greek Mainland. *AJA* 101:537–85. Reprinted as pages 329–81 in *Aegean Prehistory: A Review.* Edited by T. Cullen. American Journal of Archaeology Supplement 1. Boston: Archaeological Institute of America, 2001.

———. 1998. The Palace and Its Operations. Pages 81–96 in *Sandy Pylos: An Archaeological History from Nestor to Navarino.* Edited by Jack L. Davis. Austin: University of Texas Press.

———. 1999. A Comparative Look at Mycenaean Administration. Pages 555–75 in *Floreant studia Mycenaea: Akten des X. Internationalen Mykenologischen Colloquiums in Salzburg vom 1.–5. Mai 1995.* Edited by S. Deger-Jalkotzy, S. Hiller, and O. Panagl. 2 vols. Vienna: Österreichischen Akademie der Wissenschaften.

———. 2001. The Evolution of Administration at Pylos. Pages 113–28 in *Economy and Politics in the Mycenaean Palace States: Proceedings of a Conference Held on 1–3 July 1999 in the Faculty of Classics, Cambridge.* Edited by S. Voutsaka and J. Killen. Cambridge Philological Society Supplementary Volume 27. Cambridge: Cambridge Philological Society.

Sherratt, Andrew. 1993. What World a Bronze-Age World System Look Like? Relations between Temperate Europe and the Mediterranean in Later Prehistory. *Journal of Euorpean Archaeology* 1/2:1–57.

———. 1994. Core, Periphery and Margin: Perspectives in the Bronze Age. Pages 335–45 in *Development and Decline in the Mediterranean Bronze Age.* Edited by

C. Mathers and S. Stodart. Sheffield Archaeological Monographs 8. Sheffield: Sheffield University Press.

———. 2000. Envisioning Global Change: A Long-Term Perspective. Pages 115–32 in Denemark et al. 2000.

Sherratt, Andrew, and Susan Sherratt. 1991. From Luxuries to Commodities: The Nature of Mediterranean Bronze Age Trading Systems. Pages 351–85 in Gale 1991.

———. 1998. Small Worlds: Interaction and Identity in the Ancient Mediterranean. Pages 329–43 in *The Aegean and the Orient in the Second Millennium: Proceedings of the Fiftieth Anniversary Symposium Cincinnati, 18–20 April 1997.* Edited by E. H. Cline and Diane Harris-Cline. Liège: University of Liège.

Sherratt, E. Susan. 1981. The Pottery of Late Helladic IIIC and Its Significance. Ph.D. diss. Somerville College.

———. 1985. The Development of Late Helladic IIIC. *Bulletin of the Institute of Classical Studies, University of London* 32:161.

———. 1990. "Reading the Texts": Archaeology and the Homeric Question. *Antiquity* 54:807–24.

———. 1991. Cypriot Pottery of Aegean Type in LCII–III: Problems of Classification, Chronology and Interpretations. Pages 185–98 in Barlow, Bolger, and Kling 1991.

———. 1992. Immigration and Archaeology: Some Indirect Reflections. Pages 315–45 in part 2 of *Acta Cypria: Acts of an International Congress on Cypriote Archaeology Held in Göteborg on 22–24 August 1991.* Edited by P. Åströms. Jonsered: Åström.

———. 1994. Commerce, Iron and Ideology: Metallurgical Innovation in the 12th–11th Century Cyprus. Pages 59–107 in *Cyprus in the 11th Century B.C.* Edited by V. Karageorghis. Nicosia: Leventis Foundation; University of Cyprus.

———. 1998. "Sea Peoples" and the Economic Structure of the Late Second Millennium in the Eastern Mediterranean. Pages 292–313 in Gitin, Mazar, and Stern 1998.

———. 2000. Circulation of Metals and the End of the Bronze Age in the Eastern Mediterranean. Pages 82–98 in *Metals Make the World Go Round: Supply and Circulation of Metals in Bronze Age Europe.* Edited by C. Pare. Oxford: Oxbow.

———. 2001. Potemkin Palaces and Route-Based Economies. Pages 214–54 in Voutsaki and Killen 2001.

———. 2003. The Mediterranean Economy: "Globalization" at the End of the Second Millennium B.C.E. Pages 37–62 in Dever and Gitin 2003.

Sherratt, E. Susan, and Joost H. Crouwel. 1987. Mycenaean Pottery from Cilicia in Oxford. *OJA* 6:97–113.

Shipton, Geoffrey M. 1939. *Notes on the Megiddo Pottery of Strata VI–XX.* Chicago: University of Chicago Press.

Shiloh, Yigal. 1970. The Four-Room House: Its Situation and Function in the Israelite City. *IEJ* 20:180–90.

———. 1973. The Four-Room House—The Israelite Type-House? [Hebrew] *ErIsr* 11:277–85.

Shils, Edward. 1957. Primordial, Personal, Sacred and Civil Ties: Some Particular Observations on the Relationships of Sociological Research and Theory. *British Journal of Sociology* 8:130–45.

Shrimpton, G. 1987. Regional Drought and the Decline of Mycenae. *Echos du Monde Classique* 31:137–76.

Silberman, Neil A. 1982. *Digging for God and Country: Exploration, Archeology, and the Secret Struggle for the Holy Land, 1799–1917.* New York: Knopf.

———. 1992. Who Were the Israelites? *Archaeology* 45/2:22–30.

———. 1998. The Sea Peoples, the Victorians, and Us: Modern Social Ideological and Changing Archaeological Interpretations of the Late Bronze Age Collapse. Pages 268–75 in Gitin, Mazar, and Stern 1998.

Silberman, Neil A., and David B. Small, eds. 1997. *The Archaeology of Israel: Constructing the Past, Interpreting the Present.* JSOTSup 239. Sheffield: Sheffield Academic Press.

Sinclair, Lawrence A. 1960. *An Archaeological Study of Gibeah (Tell el-Ful).* AASOR 34–35. New Haven: American Schools of Oriental Resarch.

Singer, Itamar. 1983a. Takuhlinu and Haya: Two Governors in the Ugarit Letter from Tel Aphek. *TA* 10:3–25.

———. 1983b. Western Anatolia in the Thirteenth Century B.C. *AnatSt* 33:205–17.

———. 1985a. The Battle of Nihriya and the End of the Hittite Empire. *ZA* 75:100–23.

———. 1985b. The Beginning of Philistine Settlement in Canaan and the Northern Boundary of Philistia. *TA* 12:109–22.

———. 1986–87. An Egyptian "Governor's Residency" at Gezer? *TA* 13:26–31.

———. 1987. Dating the End of the Hittite Empire. *Hethitica* 8:413–21.

———. 1988a. Merneptah's Campaign to Canaan and the Egyptian Occupation of the Southern Coastal Plain of Palestine in the Ramesside Period. *BASOR* 269:1–10.

———. 1988b. The Origin of the Sea Peoples and their Settlement on the Coast of Canaan. Pages 239–50 in Heltzer and Lipiński 1988.

———. 1988–89. The Political Status of Megiddo VIIA. *TA* 15–16:101–12.

———. 1989. Toward an Identity of Dagon, the God of the Philistines [Hebrew]. *Cathedra* 54:17–42.

———. 1992a. How Did the Philistines Enter Canaan? A Rejoinder. *BAR* 17/6:44–46.

———. 1992b. Towards the Image of Dagon, the God of the Philistines. *Syria* 69: 431–50.

———. 1993. The Political Organization of Philistia in Iron Age I. Pages 132–41 in *Biblical Archaeology Today, 1990: Proceedings of the Second International Congress on Biblical Archaeology. Pre-Congress Symposium: Population, Production and Power. Jerusalem, June 1990. Supplement.* Edited by A. Biran and J. Aviram. Jerusalem: Israel Exploration Society.

———. 1994. Egyptians, Canaanites, and Philistines in the Period of the Emergence of Israel. Pages 282–338 in Finkelstein and Na'aman 1994b.

———. 1999. A Political History of Ugarit. Pages 603–733 in *Handbook of Ugaritic Studies.* Edited by W. G. E. Watson and N. Wyatt. Boston: Brill.

———. 2000. New Evidence on the End of the Hittite Empire. Pages 21–33 in *The Sea Peoples and Their World: A Reassessment.* Edited by E. D. Oren. University

Museum Monograph 108. University Museum Symposium Series 11. Philadelphia: University Museum, University of Pennsylvania.

Sinopoli, Carla M. 1991. *Approaches to Archaeological Ceramics.* New York: Plenum.

Sjöqvist, Erik. 1940. *Problems of the Late Cypriote Bronze Age.* Stockholm: Petter-sons.

Skeat, Theodore C. 1932. *The Dorians in Archaeology.* London: Moring.

Skibo, James M. and Gary M. Feinman, eds. 1999. *Pottery and People: A Dynamic Interaction.* Foundations of Archaeological Inquiry. Salt Lake City: University of Utah.

Skjeggesald, Marit. 1992. Ethnic Groups in Early Iron Age Palestine: Some Remarks on the Use of the Term "Israelite" in Recent Research. *SJOT* 6/2:159–86.

Small, David B. 1990. Handmade Burnished Ware and Prehistoric Aegean Economies: An Argument for Indigenous Appearance. *JMA* 3/1:3–25.

———. 1997. Group Identification and Ethnicity in the Construction of the Early State of Israel: From the Outside Looking In. Pages 271–88 in Silberman and Small 1997.

Smend, Rudolph. 1971. Das Gesetz und die Völker. Ein Betrag zur deuterono-mistischen Redaktionsgeschichte. Pages 494–509 in *Probleme biblischer Theologie: Festschrift Gerhard von Rad.* Edited by H. W. Wolff. Munich: Kaiser.

———. 1981. *Die Enstehung des Alten Testaments.* Stuttgart: Kohlhammer.

———. 2000. The Law and the Nations. A Contribution to Deuteronomistic Tradition History. Pages 95–110 in Knoppers and McConville 2000.

Smith, Anthony D. 1981. *The Ethnic Revival in the Modern World.* Cambridge: Cambridge University Press.

———. 1993. Ethnic Election and Cultural Identity. *Ethnic Studies* 10:9–25.

Smith, Mark S. 2001. *Untold Stories: The Bible and Ugaritic Studies in the Twentieth Century.* Peabody, Mass.: Hendrickson.

Smith, Sidney. 1949. *The Statue of Idri-mi.* Occasional Publications of the British Institute of Archaeology in Ankara 1. London: British Institute of Archaeology at Ankara.

Smith, Stuart T. 2003. *Wretched Kush: Ethnic Identities and Boundaries in Egypt's Nubian Empire.* New York: Routledge.

Snodgrass, Anthony M. 1964. *Early Greek Armour and Weapons: From the Bronze Age to 600 B.C.* Edinburgh: Edinburgh University Press.

———. 1971. *The Dark Age of Greece.* Edinburgh: Edinburgh University Press.

———. 1974. An Historical Homeric Society? *JHS* 94:114–25.

———. 1982. Cyprus and the Beginnings of Iron Technology in the Eastern Mediterranean. Pages 289–95 in *Early Metallurgy in Cyprus, 4000–500 B.C.* Edited by J. D. Muhly, R. Madden, and V. Karageorghis. Nicosia: Zavallis.

———. 1983. The Greek Early Iron Age: A Reappraisal. *Dialogues d'Histoire Ancienne* 9:73–86.

———. 1989. The Coming of the Iron Age in Greece: Europe's Earliest Bronze-Iron Transition. Pages 22–35 in *The Bronze Age-Iron Age Transition in Europe.* British Archaeological Reports International Series 483. Edited by M. L. S. Sorensen and R. Thomas. Oxford: B.A.R.

Soesbergen, Peter G. van. 1981. The Coming of the Dorians. *Kadmos* 20:38–51.

Soggin, J. Alberto. 1993. *An Introduction to the History of Israel and Judah.* Valley Forge, Pa.: Trinity Press International.

Sollors, Werner, ed. 1996. *Theories of Ethncity: A Classical Reader.* New York: New York University Press.

Spalinger, Anthony J. 1979. The Northern Wars of Seti I: An Integrative Study. *JARCE* 16:29–47.

———. 2003. The Battle of Kadesh: The Chariot Frieze at Abydos. *Egypt and the Levant: International Journal for Egyptian Archaeology and Related Disciplines* 13:163–99.

Sparks, Kenton L. 1998. *Ethnicity and Identity in Ancient Israel: Prolegomena to the Study of Ethnic Sentiments and Their Expression in the Hebrew Bible.* Winona Lake, Ind.: Eisenbrauns.

Spencer, A. Jeffrey. 1979. *Brick Architecture in Ancient Egypt.* Warminster: Aris & Phillips.

Spencer, Nigel. 1995. Multi-dimensional Group Definitions in the Landscape of Rural Greece. Pages 28–42 in *Time, Tradition, and Society in Greek Archaeology: Bridging the "Great Divide."* Edited by N. Spencer. Theoretical Archaeology Group. London: Routledge.

Spengler, Oswald. 1926–28. *The Decline of the West.* Translated by C. F. Atkinson. 2 vols. New York: Knopf.

Spieckermann, Hermann. 1982. *Juda unter Assur in der Sargonidzeit.* FRLANT 129. Göttingen: Vandenhoeck & Ruprecht.

Spronk, Klaas. 1986. *Beatific Afterlife in Ancient Israel and in the Ancient Near East.* AOAT 219. Neukirchen-Vluyn: Neukirchener.

Stack, John F., Jr. 1986. Ethnic Mobilization in World Politics: The Primordial Challenge. Pages 1–11 in *The Primordial Challenge: Ethnicity in the Contemporary World.* Edited by J. F. Stack Jr. Contributions in Political Science 154. Westport, Conn.: Greenwood.

Stager, Lawrence. 1985a. The Archaeology of the Family in Ancient Israel. *BASOR* 260:1–35.

———. 1985b. Merenptah, Israel, and Sea Peoples: New Light on an Old Relief. *ErIsr* 18:56*–64*.

———. 1988. Archaeology, Ecology, and Social History: Background Themes to the Song of Deborah. Pages 221–34 in *Congress Volume: Jerusalem, 1986.* Edited by J. A. Emerton. VTSup 40. Leiden: Brill.

———. 1989. The Song of Deborah: Why Some Tribes Answered the Call and Others Did Not. *BAR* 15/1:50–64.

———. 1991. When Canaanites and Philistines Ruled Ashkelon. *BAR* 17/2:24–43.

———. 1993. Ashkelon. *NEAEHL* 1:103–12.

———. 1995. The Impact of the Sea Peoples in Canaan (1185–1050 BCE). Pages 332–48 in *The Archaeology of Society in the Holy Land.* Edited by T. E. Levy. New York: Facts on File.

———. 2001. Forging an Identity: The Emergence of Ancient Israel. Pages 90–131 in *The Oxford History of the Biblical World.* Edited by M. D. Coogan. New York: Oxford University Press.

Stark, Miriam T. 1998a. Technical Choices and Social Boundaries in Material Culture Patterning: An Introduction. Pages 1–11 in Stark 1998b.

———. 2003. Current Issues in Ceramic Ethnoarchaeology. *Journal of Archaeological Research* 11/3:193–242.

———, ed. 1998b. *The Archaeology of Social Boundaries*. Washington, D.C.: Smithsonian Institution Press.

Starkey, James L., and G. Lankester Harding. 1932. *Beth-Pelet II* . Publications of the Egyptian Research Account and British School of Archaeology in Egypt 52. London: British School of Archaeology in Egypt.

Steen, Eveline J. van der 1995. Aspects of Nomadism and Settlement in the Central Jordan Valley. *PEQ* 127:141–58.

———. 1996. The Central East Jordan Valley in the Late Bronze and Early Iron Ages. *BASOR* 302:51–74.

———. 2002. *Tribes and Territories in Transition: The Central East Jordan Valley and Surrounding Regions in the Late Bronze and Early Iron Ages: A Study of Sources*. Groningen: Rijksuniversiteit Groningen.

Stein, Gil J. 1999. Rethinking World-Systems: Power, Distance, and Diasporas in the Dynamics of Interregional Interaction. Pages 153–78 in Kardulias 1999b.

Steindorff, Georg. 1937. *Aniba Vol. II*. Hamburg: Augustin.

———. 1939. The Statuette of an Egyptian Commissioner in Syria. *JEA* 25:30–33.

Steiner, Margreet L. 1994. Redating the Terraces of Jerusalem. *IEJ* 44:13–20.

———. 2001. *Excavations by Kathleen M. Kenyon in Jerusalem 1961–1967, Volume III: The Settlement in the Bronze and Iron Ages*. Copenhagen International Series 9. London: Sheffield Academic Press.

———. 2003. The Evidence from Kenyon's Excavations in Jerusalem: A Response Essay. Pages 347–64 in Vaughn and Killebrew 2003.

Stepansky, Yosef, Dror Segal, and Israel Carmi. 1996. The 1993 Sounding at Tel Sasa: Excavation Report and Radiometric Dating. *ʿAtiqot* 28:63–76.

Stern, Ephraim. 1978. *Excavations at Tel Mevorakh (1973–1976). Part 1: From the Iron Age to the Roman Period*. Qedem 9. Jerusalem: Institute of Archaeology, Hebrew University of Jerusalem.

_____. 1994. *Dor, Ruler of the Sea: Twelve Years of Excavations at the Israelite-Phoenician Harbor Town on the Carmel Coast*. Jerusalem: Israel Exploration Society.

———. 2000. The Settlement of the Sea Peoples in Northern Israel. Pages 197–212 in Oren 2000.

Stiebing, William H. 1980. The End of the Mycenaean Age. *BA* 43:7–21.

———. 1989. *Out of the Desert? Archaeology and the Exodus/Conquest Narratives*. Buffalo, N.Y.: Prometheus.

Stieglitz, Robert R. 1972–75. An Ancient Terra-Cotta Ship from Cyprus. *Sefunim* 4:41–44.

———. 1977. Inscribed Seals from Tell Ashdod: The Philistine Script? *Kadmos* 16:97.

Stiros, Stathis C., and Richard E. Jones, eds. 1996. *Archaeoseismology*. Fitch Laboratory Occasional Paper 7. Athens: Institute of Geology & Mineral Exploration.

Stone, Brian J. 1995. The Philistines and Acculturation: Cultural Change and Ethnic Continuity in the Iron Age. *BASOR* 298:7–32.

Strange, John. 1980. *Caphtor/Keftiu: A New Investigation*. ATDan 14. Leiden: Brill.

———. 1987. The Transition from the Bronze Age to the Iron Age in the Eastern Mediterranean and the Emergence of the Israelite State. *SJOT* 1/1:1–19.

———. 2001. The Late Bronze Age. Pages 291–322 in *The Archaeology of Jordan.* Edited by B. MacDonald, R. Adams, and P. Bienkowski. Levantine Archaeology 1. Sheffield: Sheffield Academic Press.

Strobel, August. 1976. *Der spätbronzezeitliche Seevölkersturm.* BZAW 145. Berlin: de Gruyter.

Sweeney, Deborah. 2004. Section B: The Hieratic Inscriptions. Pages 1601–17 in David Ussishkin, *The Renewed Archaeological Excavations at Lachish (1973-1994) Volume III.* Emery and Claire Yass Publications in Archaeology Monograph Series 22. Tel Aviv: Tel Aviv University.

Sweeney, Deborah, and Asaf Yasur-Landau. 1999. Following the Path of the Sea Persons: The Women in the Medinet Habu Reliefs. *TA* 26:116–45.

Tadmor, Hayim. 1979. The Decline of Empires in Western Asia ca. 1200 BCE. Pages 1–14 in Cross 1979.

Tainter, Joseph A. 1988. *The Collapse of Complex Societies.* New Studies in Archaeology. Cambridge: Cambridge University Press.

Taylor, Joan du Plat. 1957. *Myrtou-Pigadhes: A Late Bronze Age Sanctuary in Cyprus.* Oxford: Department of Antiquities, Ashmolean Museum.

Taylour, William. 1970. New Light on Mycenaean Religion. *Antiquity* 44:270–80.

———. 1981. *Well-Built Mycenae: The Helleno-British Excavations within the Citadel at Mycenae, 1959–1969.* Vol. 1. Warminster, Eng.: Aris & Philips.

———. 1983. *The Mycenaeans.* 2nd ed. New York: Thames & Hudson.

Thomas, Angela P. 1981. *Gurob: A New Kingdom Town.* Vol. 1. Egyptology Today 5. Warminster, Eng.: Aris & Phillips.

Thomas, Patrick M. 1995. Review of Ann-Louise Schallin, *Islands under Influence: The Cyclades in the Late Bronze Age and the Nature of Mycenaean Presence. AJA* 99:156–57.

Thompson, Thomas L. 1974. *The Historicity of the Patriarchal Narratives.* BZAW 133. Berlin: de Gruyter.

———. 1997. Defining History and Ethnicity in the South Levant. Pages 166–187 in *Can a "History of Israel" Be Written?* Edited by L. L. Grabbe. JSOTSup 245. European Seminar in Historical Methdology 1. Sheffield: Sheffield Academic Press.

———. 1999. *The Mythic Past: Biblical Archaeology and the Myth of Israel.* New York: Basic.

———. 2000. *Early History of the Israelite People: From the Written and Archaeological Sources.* Brill's Scholars' List. Leiden: Brill.

Tilly, Charles. 1978. Migration in Modern European History. Pages 48–74 in *Human Migration: Patterns and Policies.* Edited by W. McNeill and R. Adams. Bloomington: Indiana University Press.

Todd, Ian A. 1991. Review of V. Karageorghis and M. Demas, *Excavations at Maa-Palaeokastro, 1979–1986. AJA* 95:547–48.

Tosi, Maurizio. 1984. The Notion of Craft Specialization and Its Representation in the Archaeological Record of Early States in Turanian Basin. Pages 22–52 in *Marxist Perspectives in Archaeology.* Edited by M. Spriggs. Cambridge: Cambridge University Press.

Tournavitou, Iphigenia. 1999. Hearths in Non-Palatial Settlement Contexts. The LBA Period in the Peloponnese. Pages 833–42 in vol. 3 of *Meletemata: Studies in Aegean Archaeology Presented to Malcolm H. Wiener as He Enters His 65th Year.* Edited by P. P. Betancourt, V. Karageorghis, R. Laffineur and W-D. Niemeier. Aegaeum 20. Liège: Université de Liège.

Toynbee, Arnold J. 1933–54. *A Study of History.* Vols. 1–10. Oxford: Oxford University Press.

Trantalidou, C. 1990. Animals and Human Diet in the Prehistoric Aegean. Pages 392–405 in *Thera and the Aegean World III, Volume 2: Earth Sciences: Proceedings of the Third International Congress, Santorini, Greece, 3–9 September 1989.* Edited by D. A. Hardy. London: Thera Foundation.

Trigger, Bruce G. 1977. Comments on Archaeological Classification and Ethnic Groups. *Norwegian Archaeological Review* 10:20–23.

———. 1984. Alterrntive Archaeologies: Nationalist, Colonialist, Imperialist. *Man* NS 19:355–70.

———. 1989. *A History of Archaeological Thought.* Cambridge: Cambridge University Press.

———. 1995. Romanticism, Nationalism and Archaeology. Pages 263–79 in *Nationalism, Politics and the Practice of Archaeology.* Edited by P. L. Kohl and C. Fawcett. London: Routledge.

Tritsch, F. J. 1973. The "Sackers of Cities" and the "Movement of Populations." Pages 233–39 in Crossland and Birchall 1973.

Tropper, Josef. 1994. Is Ugaritic a Canaanite Language? Pages 343–54 in Brooke, Curtis, and Healey 1994.

Tsori, Nehemiah. 1975. The Middle Bronze I and Early Iron I Tombs Near Tel Rehov in the Beth Shean Valley [Hebrew]. *ErIsr* 12:9–17.

Tubb, Jonathan N. 1988a. Tell es-Saᶜidiyeh: Preliminary Report on the First Three Seasons of Renewed Excavations. *Levant* 20:23–88.

———.1988b. The Role of the Sea Peoples in the Bronze Industry of Palestine/Transjordan in the Late Bronze-Early Iron Age Transition. Pages 251–70 in *Bronzeworking Centres of Western Asia c. 1000.538 BC.* Edited by J. E. Curtis. London: Kegan Paul.

———. 1990. Preliminary Report of the Fourth Season of Excavations at Tell es-Saᶜidiyeh in the Jordan Valley. *Levant* 22:21–46.

———. 1995. An Aegean Presence in Egypto-Canaan. Pages 136–45 in *Egypt, the Aegean and the Levant: Interconnections in the Second Millennium B.C.* Edited by W. V. Davies and I. Schofield. London: British Museum Press.

———. 1998. *Canaanites.* Peoples of the Past. London: British Museum Press.

———. 2000. Sea Peoples in the Jordan Valley. Pages 181–96 in Oren 2000.

______, ed. 1985. *Palestine in the Bronze and Iron Ages: Papers in Honour of Olga Tufnell.* London: Institute of Archaeology, University of London.

Tubb, Jonathan N., Peter G. Dorrell, and Felicity J. Cobbing. 1996. Interim Report on the Eighth (1995) Season of Excavations at Tell es-Saᶜidiyeh. *PEQ* 128:16–36.

Tufnell, Olga. 1953. *Lachish III (Tell ed-Duweir): The Iron Age.* New York: Oxford University Press.

———. 1958. *Lachish IV (Tell ed-Duweir): The Bronze Age.* London: Oxford University Press.

Tufnell, Olga, Charles H. Inge, and Lankester Harding. 1940. *Lachish II (Tell ed-Duweir): The Fosse Temple.* London: Oxford University Press.

Turner, Victor W. 1969. Forms of Symbolic Action: Introduction. Pages 3–25 in *Forms of Symbolic Action*. Edited by R. F. Spencer. Proceedings of the 1969 Annual Spring Meeting of the American Ethnological Society. Seattle: University of Washington Press.

Uehlinger, Christoph. 1988. Der Amun-Tempel Ramses' III. in p3-Knʿn, seine südpalästinischen Tempelgüter und der Übergang von der Ägypter- zur Philisterherrschaft: Ein Hinweis auf einige wenig beachtete Skarabäen. *ZDPV* 104:6–25.

Ünal, Ahmet. 1989. On the Writing of Hittite History. *JAOS* 109:283–87.

———. 1991. Two Peoples on Both Sides of the Aegean Sea: Did the Achaeans and the Hittites Know Each Other? *Bulletin of the Middle Eastern Culture Center in Japan* 4:16–44.

Ussishkin, David. 1978. Excavations at Tel Lachish—1973–1977: Preliminary Report. *TA* 5:1–97.

———. 1983. Excavations at Tel Lachish 1978–1983: Second Preliminary Report. *TA* 10:97–175.

———. 1985. Levels VII and VI at Tel Lachish and the End of the Late Bronze Age in Canaan. Pages 213–28 in Tubb 1985.

———. 1995. The Destruction of Megiddo at the End of the Late Bronze Age and Its Historical Significance. *TA* 22:240–67.

Vagnetti, Lucia, and Fluvia Lo Schiavo. 1989. Late Bronze Age Long Distance Trade in the Mediterranean: The Role of the Cypriots. Pages 217–43 in *Early Society in Cyprus*. Edited by E. Peltenburg. Edinburgh: Edinburgh University Press.

Van den Berghe, Pierre L. 1978. Race and Ethnicity: A Sociobiological Perspective. *Ethnic and Racial Studies* 1:401–11.

———. 1987. The Ethnic Phenomenon. New York: Praeger.

Van Seters, John. 1975. *Abraham in History and Tradition*. New Haven: Yale University Press.

———. 1983. In Search of History: *Historiography in the Ancient World and the Origins of Biblical History*. New Haven: Yale University.

———. 1994. *The Life of Moses: The Yahwist as Historian in Exodus–Numbers*. Louisville: Westminster John Knox.

Wijngaarden, Gert Jan van. 2002. *Use and Appreciation of Mycenaean Pottery in the Levant, Cyprus and Italy (ca 1600–1200 BC)*. Amsterdam: Amsterdam University Press.

Vandersleyen, Claude. 1985. Le dossier égyptien des Philistins. Pages 39–53 in *The Land of Israel: Cross-Roads of Civilizations*. Edited by E. Lipiński. OLA 19. Leuven: Peeters.

———. 2003. Keftiu: A Cautionary Note. *OJA* 22:209–12.

Vanschoonwinkel, Jacques. 1999. Between the Aegean and the Levant: The Philistines. Pages 85–107 in *Ancient Greeks West and East*. Edited by G. R. Tsetskhladze. Brill: Leiden.

Vaughan, Sarah J. 1995. Ceramic Petrology and Petrography in the Aegean. *AJA* 99:115–17.

Vaughn, Andrew G., and Ann E. Killebrew, eds. 2003. *Jerusalem in Bible and Archaeology: The First Temple Period*. SBLSymS 18. Atlanta: Society of Biblical Literature.

Vaux, Roland de. 1968. Le Pays de Canaan. *JAOS* 88:23–30.

———. 1978. *The Early History of Israel.* Philadelphia: Westminster.

Vincent, Joan. 1974. The Structuring of Ethnicity. *Human Organization* 33:375–79.

Vogazianos, S. 1994. The Philistine Emergence and Its Possible Bearing on the Appearance and Activities of Aegean Invaders in the East Mediterranean Area at the End of the Mycenaean Period. *Archaeologia Cypria* 3:22–34.

Voutsaki, Sofia, and John Killen, eds. 20001. *Economy and Politics in the Mycenaean Palace States: Proceedings of a Conference Held on 1–3 July 1999 in the Faculty of Classics, Cambridge.* Cambridge Philological Society Supplementary Volume 27. Cambridge: Cambridge Philological Society.

Voyatzoglou, Maria. 1974. The Jar Makers of Thrapsano in Crete. *Expedition* 16:18–24.

Wace, Alan J. B. 1949. *Mycenae: An Archaeological History and Guide.* Princeton: Princeton University Press.

Wachsmann, Shelley. 1981. The Ships of the Sea Peoples. *IJNA* 10:187–220.

———. 1982. The Ships of the Sea Peoples: Additional Notes. *IJNA* 11:297–304.

———. 1997. Were the Sea Peoples Mycenaeans? Evidence of Ship Iconography. Pages 339–56 in *Res Maritimae: Cyprus and the Eastern Mediterranean from Prehistory through the Roman Period.* Edited by S. Swiny, R. L. Hohlfelder, and H. W. Swiny. Cyprus American Archaeological Research Institute Monograph Series 1. Atlanta: Scholars Press.

———. 2000. To the Sea of the Philistines. Pages 103–43 in Oren 2000.

Wainwright, Gerald A. 1931a. Caphtor, Keftiu and Cappadocia. *PEFQS* 63:203–16.

———. 1931b. Keftiu. *JEA* 17:26–43.

———. 1939. Some Sea-Peoples and Others in the Hitttite Archives. *JEA* 25:148–53.

———. 1952. Asiatic Keftiu. *AJA* 56:196–212.

———. 1956. Caphtor-Cappadocia. *VT* 6:199–210.

———. 1959. The Teresh, the Etruscans and Asia Minor. *AnatSt* 9:197–213.

———. 1960. Merneptah's Aid of the Hittites. *JEA* 46:24–28.

———. 1963. A Teucrian at Salamis in Cyprus. *JHS* 83:146–51.

Wainwright, Gerald A., and Thomas Whittemore. 1920. *Balabish.* Egypt Exploration Fund Publications 37. London: Allen & Unwin.

Walberg, Gisela. 1976. Northern Intruders in Mycenaean IIIC? *AJA* 80:186–87.

Waldbaum, Jane. 1978. *From Bronze to Iron: The Transition from Bronze Age to the Iron Age in the Eastern Mediterranean.* SIMA 54. Göteborg: Åström.

Wallerstein, Immanuel. 1974. *The Modern World-System: Capitalist Agriculture and the Origins of European World Economy in the Sixteenth Century.* New York: Academic.

———. 1979. *The Capitalist World-Economy.* Cambridge: Cambridge University Press.

———. 1983. An Agenda for World-Systems Analysis. Pages 299–308 in *Contending Approaches to World Systems Analysis.* Edited by W. R. Thompson. Beverly Hills, Calif.: Sage.

———. 1998. The Rise and Future Demise of World-Systems Analysis. *Review* 21:103–12.

Walløe, Lars. 1999. Was the Disruption of the Mycenaean World Caused by Repeated Epidemics of Bubonic Plague? *OpAth* 24:121–26.

Wampler, Joseph C. 1947. *Tell en-Nasbeh II: The Pottery*. Berkeley: Palestine Institute of Pacific School of Religion and the American Schools of Oriental Research.

Wapnish, Paula. 1997. Camels. *OEANE* 1:407–8.

Warburton, David. 2000. State and Economy in Ancient Egypt. Pages 169–84 in Denemark 2000.

Ward, William A. 1966. The Egyptian Inscriptions of Level VI. Pages 161–79 in F. W. James, *The Iron Age at Beth Shean: A Study of Levels VI—IV*. University Museum Monographs 85. Philadelphia: University Museum, University of Pennsylvania.

———. 1992a. Egyptian Relations with Canaan. *ABD* 2:399–408.

———. 1992b. Shasu. *ABD* 5:1165–67.

Ward, William A., and Martha Sharp Joukowsky, eds. 1992. *The Crisis Years: The Twelfth Century B.C.: From Beyond the Danube to the Tigris*. Dubuque, Iowa: Kendall/Hunt.

Wardle, Kenneth A. 1969. A Group of Late Helladic IIIB:1 Pottery from within the Citadel at Mycenae. *ABSA* 64:261–98.

———. 1973. A Group of Late Helladic IIIB:2 Pottery from within the Citadel at Mycenae: The Causeway Deposit. *ABSA* 68:297–348.

Warren, Peter, and Vronwy Hankey. 1989. *Aegean Bronze Age Chronology*. Bristol: Bristol Classical.

Watrous, L. Vance. 1992. *Kommos III: The Late Bronze Age Pottery*. Princeton: Princeton University Press.

Watson, Patty Jo, Steven LeBlanc, and Charles Redman. 1971. *Explanation in Archaeology: An Explicitly Scientific Approach*. New York: Columbia University Press.

Webb, Jennifer M. 1985. The Incised Scapulae. Pages 317–28 in V. Karageorghis, *Excavations at Kition V: The Pre-Phoenician Levels, Part II*. Nicosia: Department of Antiquities, Cyprus.

Weber, Max. 1978. *Economy and Society: An Outline of Interpretive Sociology*. Edited by G. Rose and C. Wittich. Berkeley and Los Angeles: University of California Press.

Weickert, Carl. 1957. Die Ausgrabung beim Athena-Tempel in Milet 1955. *IstMitt* 7:102–32.

———. 1959–60. Die Ausgrabung beim Athena-Tempel in Milet 1957. *IstMitt* 9–10:1–96.

Weinfeld, Moshe. 1993. *The Promise of the Land: The Inheritance of the Land of Canaan by the Israelites*. Berkeley and Los Angeles: University of California Press.

Weinstein, James M. 1981. *The Egyptian Empire in Palestine: A Reassessment*. *BASOR* 241:1–28.

———. 1992. The Collapse of the Egyptian Empire in the Southern Levant. Pages 142–50 in Ward and Joukowsky 1992.

Weippert, Manfred. 1971. *The Settlement of the Israelite Tribes in Palestine: A Critical Survey of Recent Scholarly Debate*. Naperville, Ill.: Allenson.

———. 1974. Semitische Nomaden des zweiten Jahrtausends: Über die *Š3św* der ägyptischen Quellen. *Bib* 55:265–80, 427–33.

———. 1982. Remarks on the History of Settlement in Southern Jordan during the Early Iron Age. Pages 153–62 in *Studies in the History and Archaeology of Jordan I*. Edited by A. Hadidi. Amman: Department of Antiquities, Amman.

Weiss, B. 1982. The Decline of Late Bronze Age Civilization as a Possible Response to Climatic Change. *Climatic Change* 4:172–98.

Wells, Peter S. 1992. Crisis Years? The Twelfth Century B.C. Pages 31–39 in Ward and Joukowsky 1992.

Wengrow, David. 1996. Egyptian Taskmasters and Heavy Burdens: Highland Exploitation and the Collared-Rim Pithos of the Bronze/Iron Age Levant. *OJA* 15:307–26

Wertime, Theodore A., and James D. Muhly, eds. 1980. *The Coming of the Age of Iron*. New Haven: Yale University Press.

Whallon, Robert. 1968. Investigations of Late Prehistoric Social Organization in New York State. Pages 223–44 in *New Perspectives in Archaeology*. Edited by S. R. and L. R. Binford. Chcago: Aldine.

White, Donald. 2002a. *Marsa Matruh I: The Excavation: The University of Pennsylvania Museum of Archaeology and Anthropology's Excavations on Bate's Island, Marsa Matruh, Egypt 1985–1989*. Philadelphia: Institute for Aegean Prehistory Academic Press.

———. 2002b. *Marsa Matruh II: The Objects: The University of Pennsylvania Museum of Archaeology and Anthropology's Excavations on Bate's Island, Marsa Matruh, Egypt 1985–1989*. Philadelphia: Institute for Aegean Prehistory Academic Press.

White, Richard. 1991. *The Middle Ground: Indians, Empires, and Republics in the Great Lakes Region, 1650–1815*. Cambridge: Cambridge University Press.

Whitehead, Neil L. 1996. Ethnogenesis and Ethnocide in European Occupation of Native Surinam, 1499–1681. Pages 20–35 in *History, Power and Identity: Ethnogenesis in the Americas, 1492–1992*. Edited by Jonathan D. Hill. Iowa City: University of Iowa Press.

Whitehouse, Ruth D., and John B. Wilkins. 1989. Greeks and Natives in South-East Italy: Approaches to the Archaeological Evidence. Pages 102–26 in *Centre and Periphery: Comparative Studies in Archaeology*. Edited by T. C. Champion. One World Archaeology 11. London: Unwin & Hyman.

Whitelam, Keith W. 1989. Israel's Traditions of Origin: Reclaiming the Land. *JSOT* 44:19–42.

———. 1991. Between History and Literature: The Social Production of Israel's Traditions of Origin. *SJOT* 5/2:60–74.

———. 1996. *The Invention of Ancient Israel: The Silencing of Palestinian History*. New York: Routledge.

Whitelaw, Todd. 2001. Reading between the Tablets: Assessing Mycenaean Palatial Involvement in Ceramic Production and Consumption. Pages 51–79 in Voutsaki and Killen 2001.

Whitley, James. 1991. Social Diversity in Dark Age Greece. *ABSA* 86:341–65.

Wiener, Malcolm H. 2003. Introductory Remarks. Pages 245–47 in *LH IIIC Chronology and Synchronisms: Proceedings of the Inernational Workshop Held at the Austrian Academy of Sciences at Vienna, May 7th and 8th, 2001*. Edited by S. Deger-Jalkotzy and M. Zavadil. Vienna: Österreichischen Akademie der Wissenschaften.

Wiessner, Polly. 1983. Style and Social Information in Kalahari San Projectile Points. *AmerAnt* 48:253–76.

———. 1989. Style and Changing Relations between the Individual and Society. Pages 56–63 in *The Meaning of Things*. Edited by I. Hodder. London: Unwin & Hyman.

Wilkinson, David. 2004. The Power Configuration Sequence of the Central World System, 1500–700 B.C. *Journal of World-Systems Research* 10/3:655–720.

Wilson, John A. trans. 1969a. Egyptian Historial Texts. *ANET*, 227–64.

———. 1969b. Egyptian Hymns and Prayers. *ANET*, 365–81.

Wimmer, Stefan. 1990. Egyptian Temples in Canaan and Sinai. Pages 1065–1106 in *Studies in Egyptology Presented to Miriam Lichtheim*. Edited by S. Israelit-Groll. Jerusalem: Magnes.

———. 1998. (No) More Egyptian Temples in Canaan and Sinai. Pages 87–123 in *Jerusalem Studies in Egyptology*. Edited by I. Shirun-Grumach. ÄAT 40. Wiesbaden: Harrassowitz.

Winter, Irene J. 1977. Perspective on the "Local Style" of Hasanlu IVB: A Study in Receiptivity. Pages 371–86 in *Mountains and Lowlands: Essays in the Archaeology of Greater Mesopotamia*. Edited by L. D. Levine and T. C. Young Jr. BMes 7. Malibu, Calif.: Undena.

Wiseman, Donald J. 1953. *The Alalakh Tablets*. Occasional Publications of the British Institute of Archaeology at Ankara 2. London: British School of Archaeology at Ankara.

———. 1954. Supplementary Copies of Alalakh Tables. *JCS* 8:1–30.

Wobst, H. Martin. 1977. Stylistic Behavior and Information Exchange. Pages 317–42 in *For the Director: Research Essays in Honor of James B. Griffin*. Edited by C. E. Cleland. Museum of Anthropology Anthropological Paper 61. Ann Arbor: Museum of Anthropology, University of Michigan.

Wolfram, Herwig. 1990. Einleitung oder Überlegungen zur Origo Gentis. Pages 19–34 in *Typen der Ethnogenese unter besonderer Berücksichtigung der Bayern: Berichte des Symposions der Kommission für Frühmittelalterforschung, 27. bis 30. Oktober, 1986, Stift Zwettl, Niederösterreich*. Vol. 1. Edited by H. Wolfram and W. Pohl. Veröffentlichungen der Kommission für Frühmittelalterforschung 12. Vienna: Verlag der Österreichischen Akademie der Wissenschaften.

Wolff, Samuel R. 1998. An Iron Age I Site at ʿEn Ḥagit (Northern Ramat Menashe). Pages 449–54 in Gitin, Mazar, and Stern 1998.

———, ed. 2001. *Studies in the Archaeology of Israel and Neighboring Lands*. SAOC 59. American Schools of Oriental Research Books 5. Chicago: Oriental Institute of the University of Chicago; Atlanta: American Schools of Oriental Research.

Wood, Bryant G. 1985. Palestinian Pottery of the Late Bronze Age: An Investigation of the Terminal LBII:B Phase. Ph.D. diss. University of Toronto.

———. 1990a. Did the Israelites Conquer Jericho? *BAR* 16/2:44–58.

———. 1990b. *The Sociology of Pottery in Ancient Palestine: The Ceramic Industry and the Diffusion of Ceramic Style in the Bronze and Iron Ages*. JSOTSup 103. Sheffield: JSOT Press.

———. 1991. The Philistines Enter Canaan—Were They Egyptian Lackeys or Invading Conquerors? *BAR* 17/6:44–52, 89–90.

Wood, Michael. 1985. *In Search of the Trojan War*. New York: Facts on File.

Woods, Ann J. 1986. Observation on the Cooking Pot in Antiquity. Pages 157–72 in *Technology and Style*. Edited by W. G. Kingery. Ceramics and Civilization 2. Columbus, Ohio: American Ceramic Society.

Woolley, Leonard. 1955. *Alalakh: An Account of the Excavations at Tell Atchana in the Hatay, 1937–1949*. Reports of the Research Committee of the Society of Antiquaries of London 18. Oxford: University Press for the Society of Antiquaries.

Worschech, Udo F. 1990. *Die Beziehungen Moabs zu Israel und Ägypten in der Eisenzeit: Seidlungsarchäologische und siedlungshistorische Untersuchungen im Kernland Moabs (Ard el-Kerak)*. ÄAT 18. Wiesbaden: Harrassowitz.

Wreszinski, Walter. 1935. *Atlas zur Altägyptischen Kulturgeschichte* 2. Leipzig: Hinrichs.

Wright, George Ernest. 1939. Iron: The Date of Its Introduction into Palestine. *AJA* 43:458–63.

———. 1940. Epic of Conquest. *BA* 3:25–40.

———. 1960. *Biblical Archaeology*. Philadelphia: Westminster.

———. 1965. *Shechem: The Biography of a Biblical City*. New York: McGraw-Hill.

———. 1978. A Characteristic North Israelite House. Pages 149–54 in *Archaeology in the Levant: Essays for Kathleen Kenyon*. Edited by R. Moorey and P. Parr. Warminster: Aris & Phillips.

Wright, George R. H. 1966. The Bronze Age Temple at Amman. *ZAW* 78:351–57.

———. 1971. Pre-Israelite Temples in the Land of Canaan. *PEQ* 103:17–32.

———. 1985. *Ancient Building in South Syria and Palestine*. Leiden: Brill.

———. 2002. *Shechem III: The Stratigraphy and Architecture of Shechem/Tell Balâtah, Vol. 2: The Illustrations*. Archaeological Reports 6. Boston: American Schools of Oriental Research.

Wright, Herbert E., Jr. 1968. Climatic Change in Mycenae Greece. *Antiquity* 42:123–27.

Würthwein, Ernst. 1994. *Studien zum deuteronomistischen Geschichtswerk*. BZAW 227. Berlin: de Gruyter.

Yadin, Yigael. 1972. *Hazor, The Head of all Those Kingdoms*. Schweich Lectures of the British Academy 1970. London: Oxford University Press.

———. 1979. The Transition from a Semi-nomadic to a Sedentary Society in the Twelfth Century B.C.E. Pages 57–68 in Cross 1979.

———. 1982. Is the Biblical Account of the Israelite Conquest of Canaan Historically Reliable? *BAR* 8/2:16–23.

———. 1985. Biblical Archaeology Today: The Archaeological Aspect. Pages 21–27 in Amitai 1985.

Yadin, Yigael, Yohanan Aharoni, Ruth Amiran, Amnon Ben-Tor, Moshe Dothan, Trude Dothan, Immanuel Dunayevsky, Shulamit Geva, and Ephraim Stern. 1989. *Hazor III–IV: An Account of the Third and Fourth Seasons of Excavation, 1957–1958*. Text. Jerusalem: Israel Exploration Society.

Yadin, Yigael, Yohanan Aharoni, Ruth Amiran, Trude Dothan, Moshe Dothan, Immanuel Dunayevsky, and Jean Perrot. 1961. *Hazor III–IV: An Account of the Third and Fourth Seasons of Excavation, 1957–1958*. Plates. Jerusalem: Magnes.

Yadin, Yigael, Yohanan Aharoni, Ruth Amiran, Trude Dothan, Immanuel Dunayevsky, and Jean Perrot. 1958. *Hazor I: An Account of the First Season of Excavations 1955*. Jerusalem: Magnes.

———. 1960. *Hazor II: An Account of the First Season of Excavations 1956*. Jerusalem: Magnes.

Yadin, Yigael, and Shulamit Geva. 1986. *Investigations at Beth Shean: The Early Iron Age Strata*. Qedem 23. Jerusalem: Hebrew University of Jerusalem.

Yağci, Remzi. 2003. The Stratigraphy of Cyprus WS II and Mycenaean Cups in Soli Höyük Excavations. Pages 93–106 in Fischer et al. 2003.

Yakar, Jak. 1976. Hittite Involvement in Western Anatolia. *AnatSt* 26:117–28.

———. 1993. Anatolian Civilization Following the Disintegration of the Hittite Empire: An Archaeological Appraisal. *TA* 20:3–28.

———. 2003. Identifying Migrations in the Archaeological Records of Anatolia. Pages 11–20 in Fischer et al. 2003.

Yancey, William. L., Eugene P. Ericksen, and Richard N. Juliani. 1976. Emergent Ethnicity: A Review and Reformulation. *American Sociological Review* 41:391–402.

Yannai, Eli. 1996. Aspects of the Material Culture of Canaan during the Egyptian Twentieth Dynasty (1200–1130 BCE) [Hebrew]. Ph.D. diss. Tel Aviv University.

———. 2002. A Stratigraphic and Chronological Reappraisal of the "Governor's Residence" at Tell el-Farᶜah (South). Pages 368–76 in *Aharon Kempinski Memorial Volume: Studies in Archaeology and Related Disciplines*. Edited by E. D. Oren and S. Ahituv. Beer-Sheva 15. Beer-Sheva: Ben-Gurion University of the Negev Press.

Yassine, Khair. 1988. The East Jordan Valley Survey, 1976 (Part 2). Pages 189–207 in *Archaeology of Jordan: Essays and Reports*. Edited by K. Yassine. Amman: University of Jordan.

Yasur-Landau, Assaf. 2001. The Mother(s) of All Philistines? Aegean Enthroned Deities of the 12th–11th Century Philistia. Pages 329–43 in Laffineur and Hägg 2001.

———. 2003a. One If by Sea ... Two If by Land: How Did the Philistines Get to Canaan? Two: By Land. *BAR* 29/2:34–39, 66–67.

———. 2003b. The Absolute Chronology of the Late Helladic IIIC Period: A View from the Levant. Pages 235–44 in *LH IIIC Chronology and Synchronisms: Proceedings of the Inernational Workshop Held at the Austrian Academy of Sciences at Vienna, May 7th and 8th, 2001*. Edited by S. Deger-Jalkotzy and M. Zavadil. Vienna: Österreichischen Akademie der Wissenschaften.

———. 2003c. The Many Faces of Colonization: Twelfth Century Aegean Settlements in Cyprus and the Levant. *Mediterranean Archaeology and Archaeometry* 3:45–54.

Yeivin, Shemuel. 1971. The Benjaminite Settlement in the Western Part of Their Territory. *IEJ* 21:141–54.

Yellin, Joseph, Trude Dothan, and Bonnie Gould. 1986. The Provenience of Beerbottles from Deir el-Balah: A Study by Neutron Activation Analysis. *IEJ* 36:68–73.

———. 1990. The Origin of Late Bronze White Burnished Slip Wares from Deir el-Balah. *IEJ* 40:257–61.

Yellin, Joseph, and Jan Gunneweg. 1989. Instrumental Neutron Activation Analysis and the Origin of Iron Age I Collared-Rim Jars and Pithoi from Tel Dan. Pages 133–41 in Gitin and Dever 1989.

Yinger, John Milton. 1981. Toward a Theory of Assimilation and Dissimilation. *Ethnic and Racial Studies* 4:249–64.

Yoffee, Norman. 1988. Orienting Collapse. Pages 1–19 in *The Collapse of Ancient States and Civilizations*. Edited by N. Yoffee and G. L. Cowgill. Tucson: University of Arizona Press.

Yoffee, Normal and George L. Cowgill, eds. 1988. *The Collapse of Ancient States and Civilizations*. Tucson: University of Arizona Press.

Yogev, Ora. 1993. Nahariya. *NEAEHL* 3:1088–89.

Yon, Marguerite. 1992a. The End of the Kingdom of Ugarit. Pages 111–22 in Ward and Joukowsky 1992.

———. 1992b. Ugarit: History and Archaeology. *ABD* 6:695–706.

———. 1992c. Ugarit: The Urban Habitat The Present State of the Archaeological Picture. *BASOR* 286:19–34.

———. 1998. *The Royal City of Ugarit on the Tell of Ras Shamra*. Winona Lake, Ind.: Eisenbrauns.

Yon, Marguerite, Annie Caubet, and J. Mallet. 1982. Ras Shamra-Ougarit 38, 39 et 40e campagnes (1978, 1979 et 1980). *Syria* 59:169–97.

Young, Crawford. 1976. *The Politics of Cultural Pluralism*. Madison: University of Wisconsin Press.

Younker, Randall W. 2003. The Emergence of Ammon: A View of the Rise of Iron Age Polities from the Other Side of the Jordan. Pages 153–76 in Nakhai 2003b.

Yoyotte, Jean. 1962. Un souvenir du "Pharaon" Taousert en Jordaine. *VT* 12:465–69.

Yurco, Frank J. 1978. Merenptah's Palestine Campaign. *Journal for the Society for the Study of Egyptian Anquities* 8:70.

———. 1986. Merenptah's Canaanite Campaign. *JARCE* 23:189–215.

———. 1990. 3200-Year-Old Picture of Israelites Found in Egypt. *BAR* 16:20–38.

———. 1991. Can You Name the Panel with the Israelites? Yurco's Response. *BAR* 17/6:54–61, 92–93.

———. 1997. Merenptah's Canaanite Campaign and Israel's Origins. Pages 27–56 in Frerichs and Lesko 1997.

Zaccagnini, Carlo. 1987. Aspects of Ceremonial Exchange in the Near East during the Late Second Millennium BC. Pages 57–65 in Rowlands, Larsen, and Kristiansen 1987.

———. 1990. The Transition from Bronze to Iron in the Near East and in the Levant: Marginal Notes. *JAOS* 110:493–502.

———. 2000. The Interdependence of the Great Powers. Pages 141–53 in Cohen and Westbrook 2000c.

Zangger, Eberhard. 1994. *Ein neuer Kampf um Troja: Archäologie in der Krise*. Munich: Knaur.

———. 1995. Who Were the Sea Peoples? *Aramco World* 46/3:21–31.

Zeder, Melinda A. 1996. The Role of Pigs in Near Eastern Subsistence: A View from the Southern Levant. Pages 297–312 in *Retrieving the Past: Essays on Archaeological Research and Methodology in Honor of Gus W. Van Beek*. Edited by J. D. Seger. Winona Lake, Ind.: Eisenbrauns.

______, 1998. Pigs and Emergent Complexity in the Ancient Near East. Pages 109–22 in *Ancestors for the Pigs: Pigs in Prehistory*. Edited by S. M. Nelson.

MASCA Research Papers in Science and Archaeology 15. Philadelphia: MASCA, University Museum of Archaeology and Anthropology, University of Pennylvania.

Zemer, Avshalom. 1977. *Storage Jars in Ancient Sea Trade.* Haifa: National Maritime Museum Foundation, Haifa.

Zertal, Adam. 1985. Has Joshua's Altar Been Found on Mt. Ebal? *BAR* 11/1:26–43.

_____. 1986–87. An Early Iron Age Cultic Site on Mount Ebal: Excavation Seasons 1982–1987, Preliminary Report. *TA* 13–14:105–66.

———. 1988a. *The Israelite Settlement in the Hill Country of Manasseh* [Hebrew]. Haifa: University of Haifa.

———. 1988b. The Water Factor during the Israelite Settlement Process in Canaan. Pages 341–52 in Heltzer and Lipiński 1988.

———. 1991. Israel Enters Canaan: Following the Pottery Trail. *BAR* 17/5:30–49, 75.

———. 1992. *The Survey of the Hill-Country of Manasseh I: The Syncline of Shechem* [Hebrew]. Tel Aviv: IDF and the University of Haifa.

———. 1994. "To the Lands of the Perizzites and the Giants": On the Israelite Settlement in the Hill Country of Manasseh. Pages 47–69 in Finkelstein and Na'aman 1994b.

———. 1996. *The Survey of the Hill-Country of Manasseh II: The Eastern Valleys and the Fringes of the Desert* [Hebrew]. Tel Aviv: IDF and the University of Haifa.

———. 1998. The Iron Age I Culture in the Hill-Country of Canaan—A Manassite Perspective. Pages 238–50 in Gitin, Mazar, and Stern 1998.

———. 2001. The Heart of the Monarchy: Patterns of Settlement and Historical Considerations of the Israelite Kingdom of Samaria. Pages 38–64 in A. Mazar 2001.

Zertal, Adam, and Nivi Mirkam. 2000. *The Survey of the Hill-Country of Manasseh III: From Nahal Iron to Nahal Shechem* [Hebrew]. Tel Aviv: IDF and the University of Haifa.

Zevit, Ziony. 2001. *The Religions of Israel: A Synthesis of Parallactic Approaches.* New York: Continuum.

Zwingenberger, Uta. 2001. *Dorfkultur der frühen Eisenzeit in Mittelpalästina.* OBO 180. Fribourg: Universitätsverlag.

Index of Primary Sources

Hebrew Scriptures

Ancient Near Eastern Writings

Greek Writings

Index of Ancient Names and Places

Ancient Names

PN = personal name
RN = royal name
RNf = royal name, feminine
DN = divine name
DNf = divine name, feminine
EN = ethnic name

Geographic Names and Regions

Index of Modern Authorities